Russia by Rail

Athol Yates

Bradt Publications, UK
The Globe Pequot Press Inc, USA

Published in 1996 by Bradt Publications,
41 Nortoft Road, Chalfont St Peter, Bucks SL9 0LA, England
Published in the USA by The Globe Pequot Press Inc, 6 Business Park Road,
PO Box 833, Old Saybrook, Connecticut 06475-0833

British Library Cataloguing in Publication Data
A catalogue record for this book is available from the British Library
ISBN 1 898323 32 1

Library of Congress Cataloging-in-Publication Data
Yates, Athol.
    Russia by rail / Athol Yates.
       p. cm. – (Bradt guides)
    Includes bibliographical references and index,
    ISBN 0-7627-0008-4
    1. Russia (Federation) – Guidebooks. 2. Railroad travel – Russia
    (Federation) – Guidebooks. I. Title. II Series.
    DK510.22.Y38
    914.704'86–dc20   96-17017
                                  CIP

Cover photographs   Ian Button
Front: Cathedral of Our Lady of Kazan, St Petersburg
Back: Preserved 2-6-2 passenger locomotives Su 253-33 and Su 250-74
at Sudislavl
Photographs   Ian Button (IB), Deborah Espinosa (DE),
Marion McNamara (MM)
Maps   *Inside covers:* Steve Munns
Others: Hans van Well (from originals supplied by the author)

Typeset from the author's disc by Wakewing Ltd, High Wycombe HP13 7QA
Printed and bound in Great Britain by the Guernsey Press Co Ltd

CONTENTS

AUTHOR

Athol Yates has had a long fascination with Russian politics, history and language. He has travelled extensively throughout Russia as a student, journalist and rescrcher. He has an engineering degree and graduate diploma in Soviet studies. He studied Russian at Melbourne University, Moscow's Patrice Lumumba University and Hungary's Egar Teachers Institute.

He has written the *Siberian BAM Railway Guide: The Second Trans-Siberian Railway*, and is working on several other books including *Russia by Waterway, The Alternative Guide to Moscow*, and his experiences over eight years of researching the countries of the former Soviet Union, *Russia Off The Rails*.

He is the Asia-Pacific correspondent for the daily Russian railway newspaper *Gudok* (meaning "whistle") and his detailed knowledge of Russian railways has resulted in him being engaged as a consultant in railway infrastructure.

He runs the Russia by Rail world wide web page at http://www.russia-rail. com. and can be contacted at russia-rail@russia-rail.com.

ACKNOWLEDGEMENTS

Special thanks to:
Jacinta Nelligan once again for her editing skill and forbearance.
Ilya Karachevtsev for his months of effort as an excellent guide, researcher and interpreter and Inna Karachevtseva for supporting the boys as they disappeared for months at a time.
Tom and Barbara Yates for their support, interest and advice and, in particular, Tom for his enjoyable company on several research trips.
Tatyana Pozar-Burgar of Darko Photographer, Melbourne, for her great photos.
Elena Lobanov for her editing of the Russian texts.

I am extremely grateful to the following, without whose assistance this book could not have been made:
Alexander P Kornev, Andrew Mich, Bohdan Peter Rekshynskyj, Brent McCunn, Carin Hughes, Carol Paulson, Charles A Ward, David Vivian, Demetris Loizos, Dennis Newkirk, Dimitry Urbanovitch, Dmitry W Moisseev, Dmitry Zinoviev, Doug Keene, Dr Francis W Lim, Dr R Kirchner, George Piszczuk, Georgios Koutepas, Grzegorz Hajduk, Heiko Pleines, Helen Fuge, Hongchan Chun, Ian Button, Ilya Zeldes, Inna Zavodinskaya, James Whitman, Jan-Egil Nyland, Jean Charles Madre, John Sloan, Karjalainen Mika, Karyn R Allen, Lars Gyllenhaal, Lev A Pokrovsky, Margo Ballou, Michael Grossmann, Natalia Gubina, Nicolai N Petro, Peter Kropp, Philip Burgess, Reinhard Kirchner, Rick Snyder, Rick Wilson, Robert Jones, Robert Saldarelli, Robert T Moore, Ron Noyes, Russ Folsom, S A Benedict Hopkins, Steinar Hoibraten, Tanya Yarovaya, Thomas Johanesen, Ursula Doleschal, Valentina and Brian Colyer, Valeri S Fominski, Vladimir Baransky, Yuri Zagvazdin, Zvi Lerman, Andrey Sebrant, Joseph Studholme and Neil Taylor of Regent Holidays.

Introduction

Russia by Rail is a guidebook with a difference. With practical and comprehensive coverage of over 50 major cities and 300 towns and villages of Russia, Belarus and Ukraine, this guide will reveal an enormous number of fascinating places that have previously only been known to specialists on the region.

To help plan an itinerary, the first chapter provides an overview of the three countries and groups a multitude of attractions into interest areas. Even for those on an organised tour, this information will help to identify places to visit in the cities on their itinerary. Then, on arrival, ask the local guide or hotel to organise a personal visit.

The second chapter covers planning for the trip and what to expect when travelling. Thorough preparation will ensure that your trip is safe, meets your budget and is hassle free.

Chapter Three is devoted to practical information of a general nature that will be of use wherever you intend to travel.

Rail is by far the most enjoyable, convenient and safe way of travelling in the countries of the former Soviet Union. Chapter Four details the railways' operations, rail accommodation options and what to expect. For the independent traveller, this chapter also provides invaluable details on where and how to buy tickets.

The bulk of this guide, however, is devoted to the major rail routes through the three countries. Each route contains information both on what you are seeing out of the window and on the places you pass through. Even in the smallest towns, details are provided on local sights and hotels, particularly important for individual travellers who want to be assured of accommodation by booking ahead. To help you navigate around, English transliterations are provided which will enable you to ask for basic directions in Russian.

Coverage of the largest cities, Moscow, Kiev, (Kyiv), Minsk and St Petersburg, is necessarily brief, concentrating on practical information. Details of their attractions are perhaps best found in one of the many existing books on these cities; you will find a list of the best in *Appendix Four*.

All prices in *Russia by Rail* are quoted in US$ rather than inflation-prone local currencies.

And now to innovation. Unlike all other guidebooks, *Russia by Rail* will not go out of date in the foreseeable future, as updates will be continuously available on the internet, at the World Wide Web address of http://www.russia-rail.com. This site also contains travellers' tales. If you do not have access to the internet, your local library probably will and you can always ask the staff to print off the update.

Part One

GENERAL INFORMATION

Chapter One

Background Information

RUSSIAN FEDERATION

The official name of the country is normally shortened to Russia but this disguises the fact that the country is far from homogenous. In fact, Russia is made up of 21 republics, five administrative regions, ten autonomous regions and 49 provinces, containing over 100 nationalities.

Russia is indescribably large, extending north–south from the Arctic to the Black Sea and east–west from the Pacific to the Baltic Sea. Over 80% of Russians live in the western third of their country, centred around Moscow. The eastern parts of Russia and Siberia are mostly vast empty tracts.

The federation of Russian states is far from stable, as illustrated by the Chechnyan Republic's war of independence. The country is ruled by Moscow and, although its power has diminished since the collapse of communism, its tentacles still reach into every corner of the country.

Since independence in 1991, the country has embarked on a programme of democratic and economic reform. The results have been far from successful and the possibility of returning to communist or nationalist rule is never far away.

Although Russia is no longer a closed society, it is still mysterious and alien to most people, a mixture of communist tradition and a predatory capitalism at which even the far right would baulk. Yet, underneath the political ideology is a people of indomitable spirit who have weathered serfdom and Stalinism and are now trying to rebuild their lives.

Russia's rich, colourful but tragic culture and history has been documented, but it is only by travelling around that you can appreciate the true Russia. The country's well-developed rail network provides an excellent way to explore this fabulous country.

Russia facts

Area	17,070,959km²
Capital	Moscow
Population	146 million
Highest point	Mt Elbrus 5,663m
Ethnic mix	83% Russian, 7% Ukrainian, 4% Kazakh, 6% others
Language	The official language is Russian but over 150 languages are spoken

BELARUS

Belarus is a little-known country that is ringed by Poland to the west, Lithuania and Latvia to the north, Russia to the east, and Ukraine to the south. During the post-war Soviet period it was the western province of the Soviet Union, known as the Belorussian Soviet Socialist Republic. Since becoming independent in 1991, it has changed its name to Belarus which means "White Russia". Its capital is Minsk.

With its location between Russia and Europe, Belarus was continually being invaded and carved up by Poland and Russia among others. It was only following World War II that today's Belarusian borders were created.

Belarus is mostly flat; its highest peak, Mt Dzyayzhynskaya, is just 346m. Most of the country is suitable for agriculture and its main crops are grains, flax, potatoes and sugar beets.

In the Soviet era, the country earned half of its income from industry, mostly by importing raw materials and exporting finished goods. However, following the collapse of the Soviet Union and its command economy which ensured raw materials and sales for Belarus, the country's economy collapsed. Today it is improving, but still very sick.

Belarus has an ancient tradition in arts with outstanding church architecture and modern literature. Internationally renowned artists include the poets Maksim Bahdanovich, Alex Harun and Yanka Kupala, fiction writer Maksim Haretsky, and science fiction writer Kondrat Krapiva.

In early 1996, a referendum was held in Belarus to determine if the country should become economically and politically aligned with Russia. The population supported reintegration. For the traveller this decision may result in Russian visas and currency being accepted in Belarus. So if you are going to the country, check with your local Belarusian embassy before organising a Belarusian visa invitation. Tourist facilities are not highly developed, and many of the goods and services taken for granted in other countries are not yet available. Internal travel, especially by air, may be disrupted by fuel shortages and other problems. Train travel is by far the most reliable and is of a good standard. Travelling around Belarus is relatively safe and cheap.

Belarus facts

Area	207,000km^2
Capital	Minsk
Population	10.3 million
Wildlife	European bison, hare, boar, elk, wolf
Ethnic mix	80% Belarusian, 20% Ukrainian and Russian
Language	Official language Belarusian and Russian

UKRAINE

Ukraine lies at the southwest border of the former Soviet Union. It is ringed by Belarus to the north, Russia to the east, the Black Sea to the south, and Moldova, Romania, Hungary, Slovakia and Poland to the west. Its capital is Kiev, now more correctly spelt Kyiv.

The country was not widely called Ukraine until the 19th century, with various states existing in the territory before this, including Kievian Rus (9th–13th centuries), the Galician-Volhynian principality (11th–14th), the Cossack Hetmanate (17th–18th), and the Crimean Khanate (15th–18th).

In Ukraine's north is forest and between it and Kiev is the famous Russian grass steppe. South of Kiev stretches the rich, prairie, black-earth region of Ukraine. At the beginning of the century, Ukraine was known as the "breadbasket of Europe" due to its enormous grain exports.

Ukraine's economic importance is second only to Russia's in the countries of the former Soviet Union. However, since declaring independence in 1991 and shifting its focus from Moscow to Europe, it has suffered enormous economic problems due to its industrial integration with Russia.

Ukraine's culture has its roots in pre-Christian times, and ancient architecture abounds. Its great modern artists include the authors V S Zemlyak and Lesya Ukrainka, and the composers Konstanti Yankevych, Yuli Meytus and brothers Yury and Platon Mayboroda.

Today, Ukraine is a fascinating place to visit. You can travel anywhere without restriction except for the "closed" cities of Sevastopol and Balaklava, and even these can be visited if you go with an organised tour.

Ukraine facts

Area	601,000km^2
Capital	Kyiv
Population	52 million
Highest point	Mt Noverla 2,061m
Wildlife	Wolf, wildcat, wild pig, gopher
Agriculture	Wheat, grains, corn, sugar beet, dairy products
Ethnic mix	75% Ukrainian, 20% Russian, 5% other
Language	Ukrainian

A BRIEF TIMELINE OF RUSSIA, UKRAINE AND BELARUS

This timeline covers present day Russia, Ukraine and Belarus. It is designed not only to place events in their historical context but also to enable travellers to identify places of interest covered in this guide around a particular time period.

Information on each entry can be found under the city, town or station mentioned or in brackets.

482	A settlement at Kiev is founded.
859	Novgorod founded.
862–82	The Viking Prince Rurik is invited by the Novgorod Republic to come and restore order and his descendants rule Russia for the next 700 years.
1147	Moscow founded by Yuri Dolgoruky.
1167	Sacking of Kiev by Andrei Bogolyubsky.
1224	Russia's first encounter with the advance army of Ghenghis Khan which signifies the beginning of the Tatar-Mongol invasion.
1227	Death of Ghenghis Khan.
1252	Moscow becomes an independent principality.
1276–1303	Rule of Danial, First Prince of Moscow.
1325–40	Rule of Ivan Kalita of Moscow.
1352	Black Death visits Novgorod and Moscow.
1359–89	Rule of Dmitri Donskoi.
1382	Moscow taken by Tatar-Mongol Khan Tokhtamysh.
1389–1425	Rule of Vasili I in Moscow, also known as Basil I.
1395	Defeat of Golden Horde by Tamerlane (Astrakhan, Kharabali).
1424–62	Rule of Vasili II the Blind, also known as Basil II.

1448	The Church of Moscow becomes an independent church.
1453	Fall of the Byzantine empire. To symbolise the belief that Russia has become the 'Third Rome', Russia adopts a coat of arms of the double-headed eagle.
1462–1505	Rule of Ivan the Great (Ivan III).
1480	Ivan the Great lifts the Tatar-Mongol yoke, by refusing to pay tribute. The Stand on the Ugra River battle confirms the victory (Kaluga 2).
1505–33	Rule of Vasili III, also known as Basil III.
1533–84	Rule of Ivan the Terrible.
1547	Ivan the Terrible assumes the title tsar which derives from the word *caesar*.
1553–7	Opening of the northern sea route to Russia via Astrakhan by the Englishman, Richard Chancellor.
1556	Conquest of Astrakhan by Ivan the Terrible.
1565–72	Ivan the Terrible's Oprichnina reign of terror which divides the country in two and costs millions of Russian lives (Aleksandrov).
1571–2	Crimean Tatars raid and burn Moscow.
1584–98	Rule of Tsar Feodor Ivanovich. He is the last ruler of the Rurik Dynasty.
1587–98	Boris Godunov acts as Regent.
1598–1605	Rule of Tsar Boris Godunov.
1601–4	Years of famine.
1605–6	Rule of the First False Dmitri.
1608–10	Rule of Second False Dmitri.
1613–45	Rule of Tsar Michael Romanov who becomes the first of the Romanov Dynasty.
1645–76	Rule of Tsar Aleksei.
1654–67	Russian Polish War over Ukraine.
1666	Establishment of postal service in Russia. Church Council deposes Patriarch Nikon.
1667	Poland and Muscovy divide Ukraine between them and Moscow gets Kiev and Smolensk.
1676–82	Rule of Tsar Feodor Alekseevich.
1682–9	Sophia is Regent.
1684	Bogdan Khmelnytsky leads Ukrainian revolt against the Poles.
1689–96	The combined rule of Peter the Great and Ivan V.
1689	The Treaty of Nerchinsk is signed which divides up the present-day Trans-Baikal and Russian far east regions between the Russians and Manchurians.
1696–1725	The rule of Peter the Great.
1703	St Petersburg founded.
1712	St Petersburg becomes capital of Russia.
1721	Peter assumes title of Emperor.
1725–7	Rule of Tsarina Catherine I.
1727–30	Rule of Tsar Peter II.
1730–40	Rule of Tsarina Anna Ivanova.
1740–1	Rule of Tsarina Anna Leopoldovna.
1741–61	Rule of Tsarina Elizabeth I.
1761–2	Rule of Tsar Peter III.
1762–96	Rule of Tsarina Catherine the Great, who acquires Crimea and transforms Russia into a great power.
1768–74	War with Turkey.
1796–1801	Rule of Tsar Paul I.
1801–25	Rule of Tsar Alexander I who acquires Georgia, Azerbaijan, Bessarabia, Finland and Poland.

1812	Napoleon invades Russia. Major battles at Borodino, Vyazma, Semlevo, Gusino, Krasnoe, Maloyaroslavets, Nara, Barysai.
1825–55	Rule of Tsar Nicholas I.
1825	On December 14, Decembrist uprising starts with a group of aristocrats and officers who demand constitutional monarchy and reform of civil society.
1837	First Russian railway connecting St Petersburg and Tsarskoye Selo.
1846	Karl Marx and Friedrich Engels coin the term *communism* in *The Communist Manifesto*.
1853–6	Crimean War.
1855–81	Rule of Tsar Alexander II.
1860	Treaty of Peking.
1867	Russia sells Alaska to the United States.
1881–94	Rule of Tsar Alexander III who acquires land in Central Asia.
1894–1917	Rule of Tsar Nicholas II.
1904–5	War with Japan (Lake Baikal).
1905–7	First Russian revolution starts (Obukhovo).
1914	On July 17, Germany declares war on Russia.
1916	Rasputin is murdered.
1916	Trans-Siberian railway is completed.
1917	On March 2 Tsar Nicholas II abdicates. From March to November the country is run by the Provisional Government. On November 7 1917, the Bolsheviks take control (really on October 25 in the old calendar hence the name the *Great October Revolution*) and establishes Russian Soviet Federal Socialistic Republic. St Petersburg is renamed Petrograd.
1917–20	Russian Civil War and international intervention involves American, Japanese, English and Australian troops (Kandalaksha, Murmansk, Arkhangelsk, Onega, Posolskaya). Military Communism imposed.
1918–22	Soviet Republic is established.
1918	Moscow becomes capital of Russia, Tsar Nicholas II and his family executed in Ekaterinburg in July.
1922	On December 30, the Union of the Soviet Socialistic Republic (USSR) is established.
1924–91	Petrograd is renamed Leningrad.
1924	Lenin dies.
1929–53	Joseph Stalin rules the Soviet Union.
1932–3	Widespread famine in Ukraine kills millions.
1935	On May 15, Russia's first metro is opened in Moscow.
1936–8	Stalin's purges reach their height.
1939	On August 23 the Molotov-Ribbentrop pact is signed which allows for the division of Poland which occurs on September 17.
1939–40	From November 30 to March 12, USSR invades Finland.
1940	August 3–6, USSR annexes Latvia, Lithuania and Estonia. Stalin's rival, Lev Trotsky, is killed with an ice-pick in Mexico on the Soviet dictator's orders.
1941–5	Germany at war with the Soviet Union and this period is known as the Great Patriotic War in the USSR.
1941	On June 22, Germany invades the Soviet Union.
1942	The seven-month Battle of Stalingrad (Volgograd) results in the first major German defeat and is considered the turning point of the war.
1943	During the four-week Battle of Kursk, which was the world's largest ever tank battle, Germany's armoured might was destroyed. The Germans never recovered and the Russians started their long march to Berlin.

1945	On May 9, Germany surrenders. On August 8 the Soviet Union declares war with Japan. On September 2 World War II ends.
1949	First Soviet atomic bomb explodes.
1957–64	Nikita Khrushchev rules the Soviet Union.
1956	In February at the 20th Party Congress, Khrushchev denounces Stalin. Hungary is invaded by the Soviet Union.
1957	On October 4 the world's first satellite is launched.
1961	On April 12, Yuri Gagarin becomes the first person in space.
1964–83	Leonid Brezhnev rules the Soviet Union.
1968	On August 21, the Soviet-dominated countries invade Czechoslovakia.
1979–89	War in Afghanistan.
1980	Summer Olympics in Moscow.
1982–4	Yuri Andropov rules the Soviet Union.
1983	Korean Airlines KAL-007 shot down over Soviet far east.
1984–95	Konstantin Chernenko rules the Soviet Union.
1985–91	Mikhail Gorbachev rules the Soviet Union. *Perestroika* (reconstruction) and *glasnost* (openness) instigated.
1986	On April 26, Chernobyl nuclear power station explodes.
1991	Attempted military coup starts on August 19 (Kubinka), on August 21 coup leaders arrested, on August 23 the Communist Party is banned, on August 24 Ukraine declares independence, and on December 8, the Belovezhskaya agreement is signed by Russia, Ukraine and Belarus which brings the USSR to an end.
1992–6	Boris Yeltsin is president of Russia.
1992	Initial price liberalisation and over the next two months inflation hits 400%.
1993	On April 6, a radioactive waste reprocessing plant blows up at Tomsk-7 contaminating 120 km². In October a parliamentary revolt starts which results in military forces attacking the Parliamentary White House and Ostankino television tower. Ukraine's economic situation dramatically deteriorates.
1994	In July in a striking example of incipient democracy in Ukraine, Leonid Kuchma defeats incumbent president Leonid Kravchuk's bid for a new term in free elections. In November, Russia invades the breakaway Russian republic of Chechnya.
1995	Slow economic progress begins in Ukraine as aid and new policies take effect.
1996	The Belarusian people approve a referendum to bring Belarus politically, economically and militarily closer to Russia. In June Ukraine's Parliament, the Verkhovna Rada, adopted Ukraine's new consititution. Ukraine becomes the first power in history to completely relinquish nuclear arms, of which it had the third largest arsenal. In July, Yeltsin is re-elected as president of the Russian Federation.

Chapter Two

Planning and Preparation

One of the secrets of satisfactory travelling is preparation. Don't leave background reading, travel arrangements and packing to the last minute as you will invariably forget something. This chapter provides the essence of preparing a trip to Russia. Reading it and making a list of what you need to do before departure is highly recommended.

GETTING THERE AND AWAY

Every year there are an increasing number of travel options to Russia, Belarus and Ukraine. Below is a brief overview, but there is additional information under each city heading in *Part Two*.

From most European capitals, and even a few Asian and American ones, there are daily flights to Moscow and Kiev and even a few to Minsk and St Petersburg.

The main western rail gateways to Russia, Belarus and Ukraine are Helsinki, Warsaw, Prague and Budapest. From the east, you can get to Moscow on the Trans-Siberian railway from Vladivostok, and the Trans-Mongolian/Trans-Manchurian railways from Beijing.

The main western water gateways are between St Petersburg and Finland, Norway, Sweden and Germany, and between Ukraine and Turkey.

Getting permission to self-drive is nowadays not difficult but because of the generally poor conditions of roads, difficulty in getting petrol and diesel, and lousy repair services, even seasoned drivers avoid the former Soviet Union. If you do drive, take an old, inconspicuous car such as a 10-year-old Volkswagon, Mercedes, BMW or Opel which decreases the chance of theft. Take an extra fuel tank and lots of spares. A few isolated cases of carjackings of Western-made or foreign-registered cars have been reported in western Ukraine near the Polish border. You will need an international driver's licence. If you have an accident, you cannot move your car until the traffic police arrive. Most petrol in Russia is 76 octane.

Travel options

The three main choices of travelling to Russia, Belarus and Ukraine are group tours, individual travel and student study.

It is impossible to list all the travel agents offering programmes to Russia, Ukraine and Belarus. The ones included below offer unusual programmes, are country specialists or don't distribute their brochures widely as they are mostly small companies. Very few "high street" travel agents have information on trips to this region.

Group tours
There are dozens of travel companies offering group tours ranging from general tours of Moscow and St Petersburg to trekking programmes in Siberia.

For first-time travellers and those who have no Russian language ability, group tours are usually the best choice. The advantages, generally, are travelling with a knowledgeable guide and like-minded people, increased safety, elimination of the need to speak the local language, having all travel arrangements made, and seeing more in less time.

Group tours, normally all-inclusive once you arrive except for alcohol and personal expenses, usually cost between $80 and $140 per person per day. As meals and hotels are expensive when purchased in Moscow, which is inevitably where you will spend most of your time, this is often the cheapest way of visiting the former Soviet Union.

Many travel companies also offer semi-independent programmes which often include pre-booked accommodation, train tickets and transfers. The rest is up to you.

Individual travel
Travelling by yourself is considerably harder in the former Soviet Union than in most countries in the world due to language barriers, visa problems and a lack of tourist facilities. Nevertheless, the biggest advantage of individual travel is flexibility: theoretically you can visit where you want, when you want. Unfortunately, the difficulty in getting rail tickets and a lack of English speakers in rural areas deters most travellers from leaving the largest cities. Another theoretical advantage of individual travel is that it makes your money stretch further. However, in Russia this may not be true, as doing anything by yourself takes much longer.

A good compromise is to get a local travel agent to organise some of your air, train and hotel bookings. There are only a few dozen companies in the former Soviet Union that are experienced in dealing with foreigners as the majority just send locals abroad.

For information on Russian travel agents that can organise services over large areas, see *In-country travel agents*, page 12. Under each city in the route description chapters is a list of local travel agents which can also be contacted.

In the Soviet era, all foreigners were handled by either Intourist (general travel), Sputnik (youth travel) or CCTE (business and government travel). These organisations no longer maintain a cosy monopoly and, while they all still exist, they have been completely reorganised with many of their regional branches being privatised. Today, many of their ex-branches still use their old names but this does not mean that there is a connection between any of them.

Student study
If you have a month or two free, studying a language in the country is the best way to experience the culture. Most programmes consist of study from 09.00–15.00 five days a week, with an organised excursion once a month. Accommodation is in either two- or four-bed dormitory rooms or homestay. It is

advisable to do at least one year of language study in your home country before arriving.

There are both private and government language schools. The advantages of the private schools are that they are more flexible and will help to organise transfers, as opposed to government schools which often have rigid entry requirements and are unwilling to assist in anything but dormitories. However, the biggest advantage of government schools is that they have higher academic standards which are rigidly enforced. Successfully completing a nine month course at a government school will usually give you the qualification to enter a Russian university degree course.

Some of the best language schools are listed below but it is a good idea to check with the Russian department at your local university as they may have a list of others:

Centre of Russian Language and Culture, St Petersburg University, nab Unversitetskaya 7-9, St Petersburg, 199034, tel: (812) 218 9452, fax: (812) 218 1346 or (812) 315 1701. Cost $95 per week for tuition, $30 a week for single room in dormitory or $120–170 a week.

Classic Tours, 148 Curtain Rd, London EC2A 3AR UK, tel: (0171) 613 4441, fax: (0171) 613 4024. Organised language and travel programmes.

Eric Fenster Moscow Study Trips, 7, Av. Jean Moulin, 93100 Montreuil France, tel: & fax: (33 1) 4858 4786, email efenster@igc.apc.org. Month-long trips to explore Russia's political and economic transition. The trips have been organised since 1980 and are open to all adults. No knowledge of Russian is required.

Institute of Youth, Block 6, Office 4, ul Yunosti 5/1, Moscow 111442, tel: (095) 374 7430, fax: (095) 374 7366. Cost: $1,000 a month, including homestay and two meals a day.

KSU Dance & Cultural Programme in Voronezh, 129 Nicholas Hall, Manhattan, KS 66506-2303, tel: (913) 532 6887, fax: (913) 532 7004, email ahavalk@ksuvm.ksu.edu. A month-long study of Russian culture and language through investigating the basic principles of Russian classical ballet and folkloric stage dance. Cost from $2,500 which includes return New York airfare, all local transportation, room and board, tuition, excursions, performances, and two days in Moscow.

Moscow State University's Education Centre, Room 203, 24/35, Building 1, ul Krzhizhanovskovo ul, Moscow 117259, tel: (095) 124 5600, 124 8011, fax: (095) 125 4461.

Novosibirsk State University, Gwendolin Fricker, Foreign Manager, KASSI Language Programme, Novosibirsk State University, tel: (3832) 352 653, fax: (3832) 397 124, email admin@kassi.nsu.nsk.su, http://www.cnit.nsk.su/univer/english/kassi.htm.

Project Harmony, 6 Irasville Common, Waitsfield, VT 05673, USA, tel: (802) 496 4545, fax: (802) 496 4548, email pharmony@igc.apc.org. This is a non-profit-making organisation which arranges exchange programmes that include, but are not limited to, high school students, teachers, police officers, medical personnel, lawyers, farmers, business people, ecologists and performing artists.

Tver Intercontact Group, PO Box 0565, Central Post Office, Tver 170000, Russia (ul Tryokhsvyatskaya), tel: (0822) 425 439 & 425 439, fax: (095) 902 1765, email andrei@ic.tunis.tver.su. Cost: $150 per week.

Visiting Scholars' Programme at Moscow State University. Best contacted through the US Office, 2200 Wilson Boulevard, Suite 102-G, Arlington, VA 22201, USA, tel: (703) 312 8606, fax: (703) 528 1477, email admissions@mgu-usa.org. For academics and post graduate students only.

Adventure travel

Adventure travel was once very popular in Russia but has had a bad press due to shoddy Russian operators, worthless local support and bad food. Consequently, many companies have cut back their programmes. Your best source of information is contained in the book *Trekking in Russia and Central Asia* by Frith Maier, 1993.

Companies still offering adventure trips include:

Bannikov Adventure Expeditions, Vladivostok, tel: (4232) 29 46 26, fax: (4232) 26 45 89, is led by Leonid Bannikov, a member of the Geographic Society for over 25 years. Trips include nature photography, rafting, hiking, cross-country skiing and fishing in the Russian far east.

Exodus, 9 Weir Rd, Balham, London SW12 0LT,UK, tel: (0181) 675 5550, fax: (0181) 673 0779; Suite 5, Level 5, 1 York St, Sydney, Australia, tel: (02) 9251 5430, fax: (02) 9251 5430, offer central Asia and Golden Ring trips.

Explore Worldwide, 1 Frederick St, Aldershot, Hampshire GU11 1LQ UK, tel: (01252) 344 161, fax: (01252) 343170, offer trekking and overland trips.

Inside Russia Sojourns, RR 2 Box 324, Boone NC 28607 USA, tel: (704) 265 4060, run bicycle trips.

Pilgrim Tours, per 1st Kirpichny 17, Moscow 105118, tel: (095) 365 4563, 207 3243, fax: (095) 369 0389, email pilgrimtours@glas.apc.org.

REI Adventures, PO Box 1938, Sumner WA 98380-0880 USA, tel: (206) 891 2631, fax: (206) 395 4744, toll free 800 622 2236 offer trekking, rafting and other adventure programmes.

Russian Nature Tours, PO Box 1627, 2010 Vilnius 10, Lithuania, tel: (370 98) 50 300, fax: (370 27) 40 402, offer wonderful birdwatching tours of Boreal Forests, the Volga delta, eastern Siberia, Russian far east, Kazakhstan and the Baltic. A professional company with a wonderful tour booklet.

Team Gorky Adventure Travel Co, PO Box 93, Nizhni Novgorod, 603137 Russia, tel: 8312 651 999, fax: 8312 691 875, email adv@team-gorky.nnov.ru, http://www.inforis.ru/team-gorky/, organises weekend rafting in the Nizhni Novgorod region, trekking, fishing and white-water rafting in Siberia and bicycling around the Golden Ring.

Travel Russia, korpus 2, per Trubnikovsky 21, Moscow, tel: (095) 290 3439, 290 3088, fax: (095) 291 8783.

Wildlife Foundation, ul Tolstoy 15A, Khabarovsk-49 680049 Russia, tel: (4212) 211 298, fax: (4214) 220 410, email wildlife@wf.khabarovsk.su, offer nature watching and conservation programmes.

In-country travel agents

There are hundreds of in-country travel agents and choosing between companies can be difficult. The following guidelines may help.

Ask for their government-issued international tourist operations licence number. While they may be experts and can organise everything in their own town, how will they, and with whom will they, organise activities in other towns?

Can they issue visa invitations? Can you pay only a deposit and the rest once you arrive? Do they have a hard currency bank account so you can transfer money electronically?

Most important of all, be very explicit about the services you want, and be prepared to suggest a price.

Andrew's Consulting (Russia), Moscow, tel: (095) 126 9413, 232 3601, supply visa invitations.

Baikal Complex (Russia), PO Box 3598, Irkutsk-29, tel: 464 762, 354 417, 432 060, fax: 432 060, 432 322, email youry@baikal.irkutsk.su, offer tickets, visa invitations, and a range of trips such as hiking, skiing and trekking from $44 per day per person for two to four people in a group around Lake Baikal.

BAMTour (Russia), 671717, Severobaikalsk, ul Oktyabrya 16-2, tel: & fax: (30139) 21-560, telex 154215 DWC SU (Att: BAMTour), is the best known company organising tours on the BAM and in the north Lake Baikal region, including seal watching.

Barry Martin Group (Russia), ul Vorontsovskaya 29, Moscow 109044, tel: (095) 271 2609, fax: (095) 271 9242, offer business travel services.

CCTE (Russia), nab Ozerkovskaya 50, Moscow 113532, tel: (095) 235 6277, 235 8222, 235 4426, fax: (095) 230 2784, offer tours, tickets, adventure trips and sport programmes.

East-West Travel (Russia), ul Bolshaya Lubyanka 24/15, Moscow 101000, tel: (095) 924 0629, fax: (095) 925 0460, offer tours, visa services and tickets.

G & R International (Russia), Block 6, Office 4, ul Yunosti 5/1, Moscow 111442, tel: (095) 374 7430, fax: (095) 374 7366, have been operating for four years and run cultural, musical and language programmes as well as organising individual arrangements.

Hostel Holiday (Russia), ul Mikhailova 1, St Petersburg 195009, Russia, (812) 542 7364, fax: (812) 542 7364, email postmaster@hostelling.spb.su, http://www.spb.su/holiday/index.html, can organise tickets from St Petersburg.

IDC-Moscow (Russia), shosse Kashirskoje 88/26-112, 115551 Moscow, fax: (095) 200 2265 (attn IDC), email zarov@host.cis.lead.org, http://www.cis.lead.org/zarov/idc.html, provide visa support, accommodation in Moscow, St Petersburg and Minsk, language courses and railway tickets within Russia and abroad.

Iris Hotels (Russia), Suite 266 MHTK, 59a Beskudnikovski blvd, Moscow 127486, tel: (095) 483 0460, fax: (095) 485 5954, offer accommodation, tickets and tours using their hotel chain across Russia.

Intourist (Russia), ul Mikhovaya 13, Moscow, tel: (095) 292 2260, 292 2365, 292 1278, fax: (095) 292 2034, 292 2547, offer tours and tickets. It is still the largest chain with its network of Intourist affiliates. Most international offices calling themselves Intourist do business with Intourist Moscow.

Marika (Russia), ul Shikhanova 10, Komsomolsk, tel: (42172) 347 63, fax: (42172) 402 69 (att: Marika tel: 347 63) specialise in historical tours in the Russian far east.

Rantek (Russia), Slava Stepashkin, ul Vorovskovo 30/36, Moscow, tel: (095) 290 5464, fax: (095) 230 2938, email slava@slavas.msk.ru, organise customised tours, espccially for historians, sports teams, musical groups. In USA contact John Sloan, 5218 Landgrave Ln, Springfield VA 22151, USA, tel: (703) 321 9072, fax: (703) 321 0927, email johns426@aol.com, http://home.aol.com/johns426.

Russian Tours Travel Agency (Russia), Moscow, tel: (095) 292 2464, 292 2579, fax: 292 2548.

Sindbad Travel (Russia), St Petersburg International Hostel, ul 3rd Sovetskaya 28, St Petersburg, 193036, tel: (812) 327 8384, fax: (812) 329 8019, email sindbad@ryh.spb.su, is a student and youth budget travel agency on the ground floor of the St Petersburg International Hostel. Sindbad Travel provides international and domestic train tickets including the Trans-Siberian, ferry tickets to Finland, Sweden and Germany and visa invitations.

Sputnik (Russia), Hotel Orlyonok, ul Kosygina 15, Moscow 117946, tel: (095) 939 8065, fax: (095) 938 1192, offers tours and tickets. It has a network of offices throughout Russia.

Travellers' Guest House/IRO Travel (Russia), 10th floor, ul Bolshaya Pereyaslavskaya 50, Moscow 129041, tel: (095) 974 1781, 974 1781, 1798, 280 4300, 280 8562, 913 5952, fax: (095) 280 7686, email tgh@glas.apc.org, organise visa invitations, rail bookings and tours through Central Asia.

Tver Intercontact Group (Russia), PO Box 0565, Central Post Office, Tver 170000, Russia (ul Tryokhsvyatskaya), tel: (0822) 425 439 & 425 439, fax: (095) 902 1765, email andrei@ic.tunis.tver.su, organise not only travel programmes but a fascinating culture tour which includes meetings with city officials, business people and journalists. They also organise homestay, visa invitations, tickets and language courses. Their programmes start from $150 a week.

International tour agents
International
Russia-Rail Internet Travel Service, russia-rail@russia-rail.com, http://www.russia-rail.com, can provide visas, organise accommodation and book rail tickets on all railways in the former Soviet Union including the Trans-Siberian, Trans Mongolian, BAM and Moscow–Berlin route. Russia-Rail is run by Athol Yates who wrote this guidebook.

UK
East-West Travel, 15 Kensington High St, London W8 5NP, tel: (0171) 938 3211, fax: (0171) 938 1077, specialise in flight tickets.

Goodwill Holidays, Manor Chambers, The Green, School Lane, Welwyn, Herts AL6 9EB, tel: (01438) 716 421, offer cities tours.

GW Travel, 6 Old Market Place, Altrincham, Cheshire WA14 4NP, England, tel: (0161) 938 9410, fax: (0161) 941 6101, organise rail tours to interesting and unusual destinations with a certain amount of railway interest included as an added attraction. It is not necessary to have any railway interest to enjoy these tours. The tours are on special trains often pulled by steam engines. Typical rail tours include the six-day Capitals of Russia Tour visiting St Petersburg, Pskov, Novgorod and Moscow costing from £1,250; the 33-day Trans-Siberian between Berlin and Vladivostok costing from £7,000; and the 16-day Caucasian and Crimean Express costing from £3,000.

Intourist, 219 Marsh Wall, Isle of Dogs, London E14 9FJ, tel: (0171) 538 8600, fax: (0171) 538 5967, offer a full range of tours and visa services.

Progressive Tours, 12 Porchester Place, London W2 2BS, tel: (0171) 262 1676, fax: (0171) 724 6941, offer tours.

Regent Holidays, 15 John St, Bristol BS1 2HR, tel: (0117) 921 1711, fax: (0117) 925 4866, offer individual travel, flights and trans-Siberian bookings.

Russia Experience Research House, Fraser Road, Perivale, Middx UB6 7AQ, tel: 0181 566 8846, fax: 0181 566 8843.

Travel for the Arts, 117 Regent's Park Rd, London NW1 8UR, tel: (0171) 483 4466, fax: (0171) 586 0639, offer luxury culture tours.

Australia

Baltic & East European Travel, 1st floor, 2 Hindmarsh Square, Adelaide 5000, tel: (08) 232 1228, fax: (08) 244 5528.

Eastern Europe Travel Bureau, Level 5, 75 King St, Sydney, tel: (02) 9262 1144, fax: (02) 9262 4479, organise package tours.

Exodus, Suite 5, Level 5, 1 York St, Sydney, tel: (02) 9251 5430, fax: (02) 9251 5430, offers adventure trips to central Asia and the Golden Ring.

Iris Hotels, PO Box 60, Hurstville NSW 2200, tel: (02) 9580 6466, fax: (02) 9580 7256, organise Trans-Siberian, hotels across Russia, individual travel and motor driving across Russia. Iris Hotels represents the Iris Hotels chain across Russia.

Russian Passport (formerly Red Bear Tours), Suite 11, 401 St Kilda Rd, Melbourne, Victoria, 3004 Australia, tel: (03) 9867 3888, fax: (03) 9867 1055, email bmccunn@werple.mira.net.au, organise Trans-Siberian, visa invitations, group tours, BAM railway tours and individual travel arrangements.

Safeway Travel, 288 Carlisle St, Balaclava, tel: (03) 9534 4866, fax: (03) 9534 4206, offer tours and hotels.

Asia

Intourist Japan, Roppongi Heights 1-16, 4-chome Roppongi, Minato-ku, Tokyo 106, tel: (3) 35 846 618, fax: (3) 35 846 617,

Monkey Business (aka Moonsky Star Ltd), Block E, 4th floor, Flat 6, Chungking Mansions, Nathan Road 36-44, Kowloon, Hong Kong, tel: (852) 2723 1376, fax: (852) 2723 6653, email 100267.2570@compuserve.com; Beijing Commercial Business Complex, No 1 Building, Yu Lin Li, Office 406, 4th floor, You An Men Wai district, 100054 Beijing, P.R. China, tel/fax: (8610) 329 2244 ext 4406, email 100267.2567@compuserve.com, organises Trans-Mongolian, Trans-Manchurian, Turk-Sib and Silk-Route rail tickets. It also offers visas, stopovers in Mongolia and Irkutsk, and budget hotels in Moscow and St Petersburg.

USA and Canada

EuroCruises, 303 West 13th St, New York NY 10014, tel: (212) 691 2099, toll free 800 688 3876, offer cruises to Russian ports and on internal waterways.

General Tours, 139 Main St, Cambridge MA 02142, tel: (617) 621 0977, offer a wide range of packages.

Intourist Canada, 1013 Bloor St, West Toronto, ON M6H 1M1, tel: (416) 537 2165, fax: (416) 537 1627; 1801 McGill College Ave 630, Montreal PQ H3A 2N4, tel: (514) 849 6394, fax: (514) 849 6743.

Intourist USA, 630 Fifth Ave, Suite 868, New York NY 10111, tel: (212) 757 3884, 757 3885, fax: (212) 459 0031.

Pioneer Tours, 203 Allston St, Cambridge MA, tel: (617) 547 1127, specialise in independent travel.

Russian Nature Travel Company, South Acworth NH, tel: (603) 835 6369, toll free 800 304 6369, email s.levin@genie.geis.com, organise nature trips..

Russian Youth Hostels and Tourism (RYHT), 409 N Pacific Coast Hwy, 106/390, Redondo Beach, California 90277, tel: (310) 618 2014 fax: (310) 618 1140, email 71573.2010@compuserve.com, organise visa and travel arrangements with their Russian partner, St Petersburg International Hostel.

Travelling between the Baltic states and Russia, Belarus and Ukraine

A popular way to travel to Russia, Belarus and Ukraine is to fly to one of the Baltic states and then proceed by train.

Although the fiercely independent Baltic states have renounced the vast majority of their ties with the other countries of the former Soviet Union, they have wisely maintained their excellent rail connections. The only differences between the Soviet days and today are that the trains are in better condition, tickets are easier to get, and there are slightly fewer services.

Getting information

The best guide to the Baltic states is Lonely Planet's *Baltic States & Kaliningrad Travel Survival Guide* published in 1994. Other useful guides include Insight's *Baltic States Guide* published in 1993, *Tallinn: A Practical Guide* published by Revalia Publishing, *Tallinn*, and *Visit Lithuania*, published by the Lithuanian Information Institute, Vilnius.

Border crossings

The border crossing checks between the Baltic states, and Russia and Belarus are normally comprehensive. Ensure that your visa is in order and you know how much currency you are carrying so that you can quickly fill in the currency declaration form.

Getting there and away

The main international trains between the three Baltic states and Russia, Ukraine and Belarus are listed below. There are also international trains from Warsaw, Hungary, Berlin and the Czech Republic. As train departure times change frequently, and travel time depends on the train, refer to the *Thomas Cook Rail Guide* or *Russian Passenger Timetable* for the latest information.

International trains are all of a good standard, and the carriages are either *SV*, three-berth *coupé* or four-berth *coupé*. While some trains have a restaurant car attached, it is still advisable to take some food and drink in case your train doesn't.

Remember to take time differences into account when planning your route. The Baltic states are two hours ahead of GMT. This means Helsinki, Sofia, Athens, Bucharest, Kiev and Minsk are in the same time zone as the Baltic states, Moscow and St Petersburg are one hour ahead, and Paris, Prague, Rome, Stockholm, Warsaw, Vienna and Berlin are one hour behind.

International trains

Origin	Dist, km	Entry point	Train no & name	Carr'ge class	No in coupé	Travel time	Day of departure	Destination
Moscow (Leningrad)	964	Narva	34 Tallinna Express	1,2	2, 4	17hr	daily	Tallinn
Moscow (Belorussia)	944	Krasnoe	87	1, 2	2, 4	17hr	Tue, Thur, Sat	Vilnius
Moscow (Rizhski)	922	Zilype	1 Latvijas Ekspresi	1,2	2, 4	16hr	daily	Riga
Tallinn	964	Narva	33 Tallinna Express	1, 2	2, 4	16hr	daily	Moscow (Leningrad)
Vilnius	944	Krasnoe	86	1, 2	2, 4	17hr	Mon, Wed, Fri	Moscow (Belorussia)
Riga	922	Zilype	2 Latvijas Ekspresi	1, 2	2, 4	16hr	daily	Moscow (Rizhski)
St Petersburg (Warsaw)	584	Pskov	37 Baltiya	1, 2	2,4	12hr	daily	Riga
St Petersburg (Warsaw)	368	Narva	17 Admiral Teyets	1,2	2, 4	9hr	daily	Tallinn
St Petersburg (Warsaw)	707	Pskov	25 St Petersburg Express & 191	1, 2	2, 4	13hr	daily	Vilnuis
Riga	584	Pskov	36 Baltiya	1, 2	2, 4	13hr	daily	St Petersburg (Warsaw)
Tallinn	368	Narva	18 Admiral Teyets	1, 2	2, 4	10hr	daily	St Petersburg (Warsaw)
Vilnuis	707	Pskov	26 St Petersburg Express & 190	1, 2	2, 4	13hr	daily	St Petersburg (Warsaw)
Minsk	194	Gudorai	187	1,2	2,4	4hr 30min	daily	Vilnuis
Minsk	542	Gudorai	187	1,2	2,4	11hr	daily	Riga
Minsk	983	Gudorai	187	1,2	2,4	19hr	daily	Tallinn
Riga	542	Gudorai	188	1,2	2,4	11hr	daily	Minsk
Tallinn	983	Gudorai	188	1,2	2,4	19hr	daily	Minsk
Vilnuis	194	Gudorai	188	1,2	2,4	4hr 30min	daily	Minsk
Kiev	1,045	Gudorai	75	1,2	2,4	23hr	daily	Riga
Kiev	798	Gudorai	75	1,2	2,4	17hr	daily	Vilnuis
Riga	1,045	Gudorai	76	1,2	2,4	23hr	daily	Kiev
Vilnuis	798	Gudorai	76	1,2	2,4	17hr	daily	Kiev

NB Vilnius is the capital of Lithuania, Riga is in Latvia and Tallinn is in Estonia.

PLANNING AN ITINERARY

Russia, Belarus and Ukraine cover an enormous area with a wide range of attractions. This section will enable you to identify places worth visiting according to your interests; these places can then form the basis of your itinerary. Further information on each entry can be found under the named city, town or station.

Archaeological

700BC Scythian town (Boiarka), Besovy Sledki Petroglyphs (Belomorsk), Gnezdovo Burial Mounds (Krasny Bor), Krasnoyarsk Burial Ground (Astrakhan), Mezyn (Voronizh), Nanai indigenous people (Kondon), Samosdelskoe Golden Horde city (Astrakhan), Sarai-Batu Golden Horde capital (Kharabali), Shishkino Petroglyphs (Shishkino), Sungir Gully pre-history (Vladimir), Togneda's Tomb (Zaslavl), Turbinski Bronze Age (Perm), Tushino (Planernaya), Zalavruga Petroglyphs (Belomorsk), Zbruch Idol (Volochyske), Zima Petroglyphs (Zima)

Architecture

Constructivist style   Voronezh
Moscow architectural style   Aleksandrov, Sergiev-Posad
Moscow baroque style   Kuntsevo
Stalinist style   Volgograd
Vladimir-Suzdal architectural style   Vladimir, Suzdal, Rostov-Yaroslavski and Pereslavl-Zalesski,
Yaroslavl architectural style   Yaroslavl
Particularly famous buildings and estates   Church of the Intercession on the Nerl River (Bogolyubovo)
14th-century Novgorodian style (Abramtsevo)   Exulted Trinity Monastery of St Sergius (Sergiev-Posad), Talashkino Estate (Smolensk), Lomonosov Estate (Lomonosov), Pushkin Estate (Pushkin), Petrodvorets Estate (Petrodvorets), Gatchina Estate (Gatchina)
Kremlins and castles   Astrakhan, Derazhnia, Kola, Moscow, Mozhaisk, Mukachev, Nizhni Novgorod, Novgorod, Rostov-Yaroslavski, Ryazan, Smolensk, Suzdal, Ternopil, Torzhok, Tula, Vologda, Vyazma, Yaroslavl
Wooden architecture museums   Irkutsk, Kiev, Novgorod, Suzdal, Ulan-Ude, Kizhi Island, Malye Karely in Arkhangelsk, Lviv, Bratsk
Miscellaneous   Model housing (Kuanda), Soviet satellite town (Zelenograd-Kryukovo), Town planning (Glazov), Traditional log huts (Udmurt)

Geological

Geological museums (Chita, Ekaterinburg, Khabarovsk, Ulan-Ude), Black earth (Voronezh), Chara sand dunes (Novaya Chara), Permafrost (Kemen, Petrovski Zavod), Rock rivers (Olekma), Tunnels (Severomuinsk)

Gulags and POW camps

Akikan Gulag Camp remains (Severobaikalsk), Marble Canyon Camp and Verkhni Sakukan Gulag Camp remains (Novaya Chara), German POWs (Volgograd), Japanese POWs (Izvestkovaya, Komsomolsk-na-Amure, Ulan-Ude)

Handicrafts and folk activities

Bell ringing (Rostov-Yaroslavski), carved bone (Kholmogory), clay whistles (Nyandoma), decorative weaving (Krolevets), embroidery (Mstera, Ivanovo and Vladimir), *finift* enamel decoration (Rostov-Yaroslavski), glass (Vyshni Volochek, Leontevo), gold-thread sewing (Torzhok), hand-painted toys (Vyatka, Gorodets), icon painting (Palekh), *matryashka* dolls (Sergiev-Posad), miniature painting (Palekh, Mstera), pottery (Krasnofarforny), *samovars* (Tula)

Indigenous peoples

Buryat (Ulan-Ude), Est (Petrozavodsk), Evenk (Ust-Nyukzha), Izhora (Petrozavodsk), Karel (Petrozavodsk, Belogorsk), Nanai (Bikin, Kondon), Oroch (Bikin), Sami (Lovozero), Tofalar (Nizhneudinsk), Udege (Bikin), Udegeytsy (Khor), Ust-Orda Buryats (Kutulik), Ves (Petrozavodsk)

Military

Military museums   Astrakhan, Borodino (1812), Chita, Khabarovsk, Komsomolsk-na-Amure (open-air military vehicle, military aircraft), Kyakhta (Russian Civil War), Ladozhskoe Ozera (Road of Life), Lviv, Maloyaroslavets (1812), Monino (aircraft), Nizhni Novgorod, Novi Petryvtsi, Ryazan (infantry marines), Orsh, Smolensk, Tula (military weapons), Vladimir, Vladivostok (naval, submarine, border guards), Voronezh, Volgograd, Yaroslavl)

Inter-Continental Ballistic Missile (ICBM) silos and chemical weapons depots
Kansk, Ledinaya, Olovyannaya, Yablonovaya, Maradykovski

Nature reserves and natural wonders
Baikalski Nature Reserve (Tankhoi), Belavezhskaya Pushcha Nature Reserve
(Brest), Bolshe-Khekhzirzkiy Sanctuary (Khor), Botanical Gardens (Khabarovsk),
Bryansk Forest (Bryansk), Byarezinski Beaver Nature Reserve (Bobr), Grafski
Beaver Sanctuary (Grafski), Kandalaksha Nature Reserve (Kandalaksha), Khingan
Nature Reserve (Uril), Kivach Nature Reserve (Petrozavodsk), Kungur Ice Caves
(Kungur), Lake Baikal (Lake Baikal), Lotus flower fields (Volga Delta
[Astrakhan]), Martial Waters Spring Resort (Petrozavodsk), Natural history
museums (Voronezh, Volgograd, Rybnoe, Bryansk-Oplovski), Nizhneudinskiye
Caves and Ukovskiy Waterfall (Nizhneudinsk), Polar-alpine botanical gardens
(Apatity), Pribaikalsk National Park (Port-Baikal), Stolby Nature Sanctuary
(Krasnoyarsk), Taiga (Taiga)

Outdoor sports
Birdwatching   Baraba Steppe (Omsk), Astrakhan
Fishing   Astrakhan
Mountain, volcano and glacier climbing   Novaya Chara, Kuanda
Rafting   Slyudyanka 1, Taksimo
Sailing   Severobaikalsk
Seal watching   Severobaikalsk
Skiing   Daban, Tyya, Kandalaksha
Swimming   Moscow
Trekking   Slyudyanka 1, Daban

Railways
Childrens' railways   Chita, Kiev, Minsk, Svobodny
Funicular railway   Kiev, Vladivostok
Museums   Khabarovsk, Lebyazhe, Mytishchi, Novy Urgal, Omsk, Severobaikalsk,
Shushary, St Petersburg, Svobodny, Tver, Tynda, Volgograd
Preserved locomotives   Erofei-Pavlovich, Lena, Mosselmash, Ulan-Ude,
Vereshchagino, Vologda
Steam engine storage depots   Amazar, Kormilovka, Meget, Sharya, Negarelae

Religious sites
Buddhist Monastery (Gusinoe Ozero), Exulted Trinity Monastery of St Sergius
(Sergiev-Posad), Iversky Monastery (Valdai), Ivolginsk Buddhist Monastery (Ulan-
Ude), Nilova Pustyn Monastery (Ostashkov), Old Believers (Semenov, Uren),
Sectarian religious cult (Zima), Solovetski Monastery (Solovetski), Tibetan
Buddhist Monastery (Ulan-Ude)

Space and aviation
Valeri Chkalov, world famous pilot (Chkalovsk), Yuri Gagarin, first human in
space (Gagarin, Pokrov), Kapustin Yar Cosmodrome (Kapustin Yar), V N
Kubasov, cosmonaut (Vyazniki), Plesetsk Cosmodrome (Plesetskaya), Francis Gay
Powers, American pilot shot down (Ekaterinburg), Space and Aviation Museum
(Brest, Kaluga, Vladimirovka, Vyatka), Space Centre (Zvezdni Gorodok), Space
industry factories (Khimki, Voronezh), Valentina Tereshkova, cosmonaut (Bolshoe
Nikolskoe)

A few itineraries

While the 9,300km Trans-Siberian is one of the world's great rail journeys, there are dozens of other routes in Russia, Ukraine and Belarus that are equally memorable. Below is a list of some of the best routes covered in this book.

Trans-Siberian   Vladivostok to Moscow, 10 days, overnight stops in Khabarovsk, Irkutsk, Novosibirsk and Ekaterinburg.

Trans-Manchurian   Beijing to Moscow (via north China), 10 days, overnight stops in Irkutsk, Novosibirsk and Ekaterinburg.

Trans-Mongolian   Beijing to Moscow (via Mongolia), 12 nights, 3 days in Ulaanbaatar (Mongolia), overnight stops in Irkutsk, Novosibirsk and Ekaterinburg.

Berlin to Moscow   7 days, 2 days in Minsk and overnight in Brest and Smolensk.

Budapest to Moscow   7 days, 3 days in Kiev and overnight in Lviv and Bryansk.

Northwest Russia   St Petersburg to Moscow (via Murmansk and Arkhangelsk), 9 days, overnight in Petrozavodsk, Murmansk, Arkhangelsk and Vologda.

Volga Russia   Moscow to Moscow via Volga region, 6 days, overnight in Voronezh, Volgograd and Astrakhan.

Golden Ring   Moscow to Moscow via the Golden Ring, 7 days, 2 nights in Yaroslavl and Vladimir (day visits to Rostov-Yaroslavl and Suzdal).

VISAS

Visas are the biggest hassle when visiting Russia, Ukraine and Belarus. Visa regulations change regularly and often even the border guards and police do not know the latest law. Therefore, readers are advised to check with their travel agents or the relevant embassies before actually embarking on a trip. Although it may be possible to visit other former CIS countries with a Russian visa, it is best to get a visa for each of the countries you are visiting. It is false economy to think that this is a waste of money – consider the cost of wasted days standing at an embassy in Moscow, Kiev or Minsk. In addition, it is almost always easier and cheaper to get a visa in your own country. Your visa is very important as you will need to show it when staying at a hotel and often when buying a rail ticket.

Many of the overnight trains from St Petersburg or Moscow to the Baltic states and Europe cross the Russian border after midnight. Make sure your visa does not expire a few hours before you cross the border or you may have problems leaving the country.

Children up to 16 years old need their own visa unless they are travelling on their parents' passports, in which case their name has to be included on the visa of the person responsible for them.

It is best to have every city that you intend to visit listed on your visa as some hotels will not let you stay unless you are 'authorised' to be in their city. Take your visa invitation and three photos with you when you travel in case you have to extend your visa or replace it.

The information presented below, especially the duration and price of visas, varies depending on the country of issue, and changes regularly.

Visa invitations

To get a visa to Russia, Belarus and Ukraine, you need either an invitation or some written document that confirms your accommodation details (usually booked accommodation vouchers). Both of these must state your passport details, the duration of your stay and the cities you will visit. When you are requesting an invitation to Russia, ask for it to cover several days on each side of your planned stay, as extending visas is time consuming and expensive. If you are going on a package, then your travel agents will organise everything and you will see none of the paperwork.

Invitations can only be sent by registered companies in these countries and must contain the registered address of the company, the name, passport data and itinerary of those who are invited. If a tourist company invites you, the company must be registered as a tourist company by the Ministry of Foreign Affairs and have a special licence number. That number must be written on the invitation. Local travel companies will usually only issue an invitation for those days that you have paid for as you are their responsibility until you leave their country. However, there are a number of travel companies that are willing just to send you the invitation and leave the rest to you although, as you have to be registered, you must visit the company that issued you the visa and it is best to do this as soon as you arrive. Companies willing to issue visa invitations are listed in *In-country travel agents* on page 12. Normally, faxed invitations are accepted by the consulates.

Russian visas

Visas to Russia are required by virtually all nationalities including Americans, Australians, Britons and Canadians.

The Russian visa is normally a three-leaved document rather than a stamp in your passport. This system is a cold war legacy from when Western countries discriminated against their citizens who had visited the Soviet Union and this would be obvious if there was a stamp in their passport. The visa contains all your passport information, entry and exit dates, the cities that you will visit, and the organisation that invited you.

The Russian embassy requires a completed visa application form, three photos signed on the back, your passport (a photocopy is no longer acceptable), and the invitation or booked accommodation vouchers. Normally, visas will be issued within ten working days.

There are five main types of visa to Russia: transit, tourist, business, private and on-the-spot. Students get a form of business visa.

Transit visa   The transit visa is normally given only to those who are travelling through Russia and are not staying overnight in any city. Most Russian embassies will only issue transit visas for 72 hours, but Russian embassies in China will issue them for up to ten days which will allow you to travel on the Trans-Siberian, stay in Moscow for two days and then leave. Extending a transit visa for up to seven days is possible but a lot of work. To get a transit visa you will normally need to show proof, ie: rail tickets and onward visas, that you will be entering and leaving within 72 hours.

Tourist visa   The tourist visa allows you to stay for up to a year. You can get a double-entry version. To get a tourist visa, you need an invitation.

Business visa   The business visa allows you to stay for up to a year. You can get a double-entry version. To get a business visa you will need to have an invitation from a registered Russian business. It is also possible to get a multi-entry business visa which allows you unlimited entries. This visa is stamped in your passport. To get one requires the inviting Russian company to convince the Consular Division of the Russian Ministry of Foreign Affairs to send a telex to your Russian consulate authorising such a visa.

Private visa This visa is for those who are invited by Russian friends or relatives. Although this sort of visa may seem attractive, it is the worst sort of visa as it can take three months or more to organise. The process involves your Russian friend getting an authorisation known as an *izveshchenia* (извещение) from the OViR office in his home town, and mailing the authorisation to you. You then need to take the authorisation to your Russian embassy which then confirms it with OViR back in Russia. You can only get a private visa for a stay of up to three months, but extensions are common in Russia.

On-the-spot It has been possible to get a business visa for about $200 when you arrive at Moscow's Sheremetevo-2 or St Petersburg's Pulkovo-2 international airports. They are issued by an Intourist office just before passport control. You will need to have a representative of the inviting company waiting for you at the airport, having organised all the paperwork with the Intourist office beforehand. As this system may be stopped and as most airlines will refuse to carry you without a Russian visa, it is best not to rely on it.

AIDS and visas
As of December 1 1995, any foreigner visiting Russia for more than three months will require a doctor's certificate proving that they are not HIV/AIDS positive. This system was introduced as a political gimmick to appeal to anti-West forces in Russian and is "ineffective in terms of public health, discriminatory in terms of human rights, and ludicrous in terms of feasibility", asserted Dr Lola Karimova, a Moscow gynaecologist and the Women's Health Director of Moscow's AESOP Centre. But it's a rule until the Russian government decides that it's too much trouble.

Russian visa costs

Type	Duration	Costs around the world
Single-entry tourist	3 months	£10 (UK), $40* (USA), A$ 60 (Australia), $50 (Beijing)
Double-entry tourist	1 year	$40* (USA), A$80 (Aust), $100 (Beijing)
Single entry business	3 months	£35 (UK), $40* (USA), A$50 (Aust), $100 (Beijing)
Double-entry business	1 year	$40* (USA), A$80 (Aust), $200 (Beijing)
Multi-entry business	1 year	$120 (USA), A$210 (Aust), $300 (Beijing)
Transit visa	72 hours	£10 (UK), $50 (Aust), $80 (Beijing for 10 days)

* the cost of visas in the US is based on the speed of visa processing; the costs are $40 delivered in 7-8 days, $50 in 5-6 days, $60 in 3-4 days, $60 in 2-3 days, $80 next day and $120 in two hours.

Ukrainian visas
Visas to Ukraine are required by virtually all nationalities including Americans, Australians, Britons and Canadians. Ukrainian visas are stamped in the passport.

Ukraine can issue a temporary visa on arrival from Romania, Slovakia, Hungary or Poland at the railway border crossings of Mostyska, Shegini, Uzhhorod, Chop, Porubne, Yalta and Vadul-Siret. Temporary visas will also be issued at Kiev's Borispil, Lviv, Simferopol and Odessa airports. These visas are not issued on the Belarusian or Russian borders with Ukraine. Temporary visas are only valid for three days and staying in Ukraine longer can be difficult. In order to get a tourist visa once you are in the country, you have to go to a local VVTA visa and registration office and present an invitation from a Ukrainian citizen or company.

Thus staying on gets rather expensive (depending on the kind of visa requested, up to $200 for the two visas). In addition, there is the risk that a visa for a longer stay will be denied or that bribes will be demanded for the new visa, since the traveller is in a very unfavourable situation. Ukrainian authorities are rethinking the issuing of visas at the border. A change in the regulations would mean that travellers without a valid visa would no longer be able to enter the country.

Leaving Ukraine for Russia or Belarus can cause a problem. Although the Ukrainian border authorities will take your Ukrainian visa, there are often no Russian border authorities to stamp your Russian visa and give you a customs form. If this happens, you should tell your conductor and get him to organise it.

To get a Ukrainian visa, you need to send your local Ukrainian embassy a completed visa application form, valid passport, three passport size photos and an invitation or booked accommodation vouchers.

Ukrainian visa costs

Type	Duration	Costs around the world
Single entry tourist	3 months	£25 (UK), A$70 (Australia), $60 (Beijing)
Triple-entry tourist	30 days	£10 (UK), $100 (Moscow) $30 (Minsk), $150 (Ukraine), A$70 (Australia), $60 (Beijing)
Transit	3 days	£10 (UK), $15 (Moscow, Minsk), $60 (Ukrainian border), $25 (Beijing)
Private	3 months	£20 (UK), $60 (Beijing)
Business	3 months	£35 (UK), $60 (Beijing)
Multi-entry business		$200 (Beijing)

Belarusian visas

Visas to Belarus are required by virtually all nationalities including Americans, Australians, Britons and Canadians. Visas have to be obtained before arriving in Belarus. As of April 1 1995, visas are no longer issued at Minsk-2 International Airport or at the border crossings of Brest and Grodno.

Russian visas are acceptable for transit through Belarus, for example on the Warsaw–Moscow train. However, if you are travelling from Moscow to Brest, and hoping to buy a cheap suburban rail ticket from Brest to Warsaw, you will only be sold one if you have a Belarusian visa. If you are going from Belarus to Ukraine, your Belarusian (or Russian) visa will be taken as you leave Belarus.

There is no border control on the Belarus-Russian border. This poses a problem if you have entered Belarus on a Belarusian visa as your Russian visa will be unstamped when you enter Russia and you will not get a customs form. You should tell your conductor and get him to organise it.

To get a Belarusian visa, you need a completed visa application form, valid passport and an invitation or booked accommodation vouchers.

Belarus visa costs

Type	Duration	Costs around the world
Single-entry tourist	30 days	$20 (Moscow), $25 (Beijing)
Single-entry private	30 days	$60 (Moscow)
Single-entry business	30 days	$60 (Moscow), $25 (Beijing)
Transit	1 day	$60 (Beijing)
Double-entry tourist		$90 (Beijing)
Double-entry business		$110 (Beijing)
Multi-entry business		$250 (Beijing)

Registration

All visitors to Russia must register with the local police or OViR within 72 hours of arrival. Some Ukrainian and Belarusian consulates also advise travellers to register with the local police or OViR/VVTA but this is not mandatory, only highly recommended. If you are staying at a hotel, this is done automatically by the hotel staff. If you are staying less than 72 hours you do not need to register. The company that issued you the invitation has to register your visa. If you are late in registering you may be fined. If you do not register at all you may be fined at the border and the fine is totally subjective.

When you get registered, you get a stamp on the back of your visa. In the Soviet era, it was important to have registration stamps covering every day to indicate your movements. Nowadays only one stamp is necessary.

OViR and extending visas

To extend your visa, you have to battle with OViR in Russia and Belarus, and VVTA in Ukraine. These are the Ministries of Internal Affairs departments for registering and extending visas for foreigners, and issuing residential permits and passports for locals. They are an annoying remnant of the Soviet big brother.

To extend a visa, you normally have to bring along a letter from the organisation that originally issued your visa, stating the details of the extension. Sometimes an international train ticket is acceptable. In addition you have to show the bank receipt of the extension cost paid into the OViR/VVTA account. This means that you have to pay before you queue up which may mean you waste your money if your application is rejected. As the bank will normally be nowhere near the OViR/VVTA office, and the office is only open for a few hours a day, this process can take two days.

It is essential that you check that your visa can be extended before you pay the money, as some OViR/VVTA offices will not extend some types of visa.

OViR DOESN'T ONLY HASSLE FOREIGNERS

While foreigners often get infuriated over OViR's overbearing rules, spare a thought for the long-suffering Russian citizen. Since 1932, all Soviet citizens have had to have a residence permit, known as a propiska. Without a propiska, you could not get a job, enter university or travel. Technically, the propiska system was abolished by a USSR Constitutional Supervision Committee decision in 1991 but authorities continued to enforce it in nearly all parts of Russia, including Moscow. At the start of 1996, Moscow finally passed laws to remove the system but the authorities still require residents to register. To be able to register, you must satisfy the conditions of having an 18m² living space and, if you own the property, you must pay a one-off tax towards the development of Moscow's infrastructure. This tax is set at 500 times the minimum wage for Russian citizens; foreigners are taxed ten times as heavily as Russians.

CUSTOMS AND BORDER CROSSINGS

Customs forms

When arriving in Belarus, Ukraine and Russia, you must fill in a customs form stating your foreign currency and valuable goods such as cameras and radios. It is better to write down too much rather than too little for, when you leave, customs officials may scrutinise the form closely and compare what you wrote down and what you have now. If you could not have bought the "newly acquired" goods, they will confiscate them, on the basis that they are stolen. This is obviously a scam but an effective one, as you will have limited time to argue before your train or plane departs.

If you arrive by air you may have your goods X-rayed.

To prevent customs officials watching as you count your cash, count it beforehand so you can fill in the form quickly. Occasionally the official may want to see the cash anyway. If you lose the customs form, you are liable to an apparently arbitrary fine which may be 10% of your hard currency cash.

Goods forbidden from being taken out of the country include antique samovars, icons and paintings, gold and silver items made before 1968, military medals, coins and local currency. There is a lot of discretion by the customs official in the definition of antiques so be careful. The only way you can prove that something is new and not an antique is for it to bear the Ministry of Culture's export stamp, so look for this stamp before you buy.

Border crossing procedure

Strict border crossing procedures are maintained between eastern Europe and Belarus, Ukraine and Russia, and between Russia and the Baltic states. However, between the other former republics of the Soviet Union, border crossing is invariably lax or non-existent.

The first step in crossing from eastern Europe into one of the former republics of the Soviet Union is for the border guards to check passports and visas. Your visa will be stamped, one of the three leaves of the visa taken, and a stamp placed on the last page of your passport. In the trains, they will look under your seats and in the luggage area above the corridor for stowaways. As border guards carry guns, be polite.

The next step is for customs forms to be given out and completed. The customs officers may check what you have written, look into your bags and, when they are happy with everything, they will stamp your customs form.

On a train at the eastern European borders with Ukraine and Belarus and between Russia and China, the bogies are changed because the former Soviet Union uses a different railway gauge from the rest of the world. This process involves lifting the carriages individually, and rolling out and replacing the bogies.

BORDER CROSSING TRAVELLER TIP

I think it is very important to have some small and new US$ bills with you when crossing a CIS border on a train. That way you can pay fees, fines or bribes without problems. My experience is that the best thing to do when you have a problem with border guards (because your visa expired a few hours ago or because they do not like something in your luggage) is to ask with an innocent face whether you will have to pay a fine (the Russian word is shtraf). If you call it a bribe you can get into serious trouble, since you can be arrested for an attempt to bribe a state official. But this way you have done nothing wrong and the officer will probably agree happily with your suggestion.

Heiko Pleines, UK, January 1996

The border guard, customs and bogie changing process can take two hours. When leaving the country, the reverse procedure applies.

During the entire border crossing procedure, the toilets are locked and you often cannot leave your carriage. So make sure that you go to the toilet before you get near the border.

EMBASSIES

Russian embassies and consulates

Australia   78 Canberra Ave, Griffith ACT 2603, tel: (06) 295 9033, 295 9474, fax: (06) 295 1847; Consulate, 7-9 Fullerton St, Woollahra NSW 2025, tel: (02) 9327 5065.

Austria   Reisnerstrasse 45-47, A-1030 Vienna, tel: (0222) 712 1229, 712 3233, fax: (0222) 712 3388.

Belarus   vul Staravilenskaya 48, 220002, Minsk, tel: (0172) 345 497, fax: (0172) 503 664.

Belgium   66 Avenue de Fre, B-1180 Brussels, tel: (02) 374 3406, 374 6886, 374 3106, fax: (02) 374 2613, 346 2453; Consulate, Della Faililaan 20, 2020 Antwerpen, tel: (03) 829 1611.

Canada   285 Charlotte St, Ottawa, Ontario K1N 8L5, tel: (613) 235 4341, 235 5376, fax: (613) 236 6342; Consulates, 52 Range Rd, Ottawa, Ontario K1N 8J5, tel: (613) 236 7220, 236 6215, fax: (613) 238 6158; 2355 Avenue du Musée, Montreal, Quebec H3G 2E1, tel: (514) 843 5901, fax: (514) 842 2012.

China   4 Baizhongjie, Beijing 100600, tel: (10) 532 2051, 532 1267; Consulate, 20 Huangpu Lu, Shanghai 20080, tel: (21) 324 2682.

Czech Republic   Podkastany 1, Prague 6, tel: (02) 381 943, 381 940, fax: (02) 373 800.

Denmark   Kristianiagade 5, Dk-2100, Copenhagen, tel: 31 382 370, 31 425 585, fax: 31 423 741.

Estonia   Pikk 19, EE-0001 Tallinn, tel: (22) 443 014, fax: (22) 443 773; Consulate, Vilde 8, EE-2020, Narva, tel/fax: (235) 313 67.

Finland   Suurlahetysto, Tehtaankatu 1B, Fin-00140, Helsinki, tel: (90) 661 449, 661 876, fax: (90) 661 006; Consulate, Vartiovuorenkatu 2, 20700 Turku, tel: (21) 223 6441, (21) 231 9779.

France   40-50 Boulevard Lannes, 75116 Paris, tel: (1) 4504 0550, 4504 7171, fax: (1) 4504 1765; Consulate, 8 Ambroise-Pare, 13008 Marseille, tel: (91) 771 525, fax: (91) 773 454.

Germany   PO Box 200908, Waldstrasse 42, 53177 Bonn, tel: (0228) 312 085, 312 086, fax: (0228) 311 563; Consulates, Unter den Linden 63-65, 10117, Berlin, tel: (030) 229 1420, fax: (030) 229 9397; Am Feenteich 20, 22085, Hamburg, tel: (040) 229 5201, fax: (040) 229 7727; Seidelstrasse 8, 80355 Munich, tel: (089) 592 503, fax: (089) 550 3828.

Hungary   Bajza utea 35, 1062 Budapest V1, tel: (1) 132 0911, 112 1013, fax: (1) 252 5077.

Ireland   186 Orwell Rd, Rathgar, Dublin, (01) 492 3525, 492 2084, fax: (01) 492 3525.

Israel   120 Rehov Hayarkon, Tel Aviv 63573, tel: (3) 522 6744, fax: (3) 522 6713.

Japan   1-1 Azabudai, 2-chome, Minato-ku, Tokyo 106, tel: (3) 3583 5982, fax: (3) 3503 0593; Consulate, Toyonaka-Shi, Nizhimidorigaoka 1-2-2, Osaka-Fu, tel: (6) 848 3452, fax: (6) 848 3453.

Latvia   2 Antonijas Iela, 1397 Riga, tel: (2) 733 2151, fax: (2) 721 2579.

Lithuania   Juozapaviciaus gatve 11, 2000 Vilnius, tel: (22) 351 763, fax: (22) 353 877.

Mongolia Friendship St A-6, Ulaanbaatar, tel: (1) 728 51, 268 36, 275 06.
New Zealand 57 Messines Rd, Karori, Wellington, tel: (04) 476 6113, fax: (04) 476 3846.
Norway Drammensveen 74, 0271 Oslo, tel: 2255 3278, fax: 2255 0070.
Poland ul Belwederska 49, 00-761 Warsaw, tel: (022) 213 453, 219 954, fax: (022) 625 3016.
Slovak Republic Godrova 4, 81106 Bratislava, tel: (7) 313 468, fax: (7) 334 910.
South Africa PO Box 6743, Pretoria 001, Butano Building 316 Brooks St, Menlo Park 0081, tel: (12) 432 731, fax: (12) 432 842.
Ukraine Kiev, vul Kutuzova 8, tel: (044) 294 7936, 294 6701, fax: (044) 292 6631.
UK 13 Kensington Palace Gardens, London W8 4QX, tel: (0171) 229 3628, fax: (0171) 727 8624; Consulate, 58 Melville St, Edinburgh EH3 7HL, tel: (0131) 225 7098, fax: (0131) 225 9587.
USA 2650 Wisconsin Ave, NW, Washington DC 20007, tel: (202) 298 5700, 298 5772, fax: (202) 298 5749; Consulates, 1825 Phelps Place NW, Washington DC 20008, tel: (202) 939 8907, fax: (202) 939 8909; 9 East 91 St, New York, NY 10128, tel: (212) 348 0926, 348 0955, fax: (212) 831 9162; 2790 Green St, San Francisco, CA 94123-6609, tel: (415) 928 6878, fax: (415) 929 0306; 2323 Westin Building, 2001 Sixth Avenue, Seattle, WA 98121-2617, tel: (206) 728 1910, fax: (206) 728 1871, email consul@consul.seanet.com, http://www.seanet.com/RussianPage/RussianPage.html.

Belarusian embassies

Austria Erzherzog K-Strasse 182, 1220 Vienna, tel: (0222) 283 5885, fax: (0222) 283 5886.
Belgium Rue Merlo 8A/9, 1180 Brussels, tel: (02) 332 3884, fax: (02) 332 3885.
China PO 100600, Beijing Chao Yand District, Xin Dong Rd, Ta Yuan Office Building, 2-10-1, tel: (01) 532 6426, fax: (01) 532 6417.
Czech Republic Schweigerowa 2, 16000 Prague 6, tel/fax: (02) 322 039.
Estonia Room 111, 15 Kuramaa, Tallinn, tel/fax: (3722) 632 0070.
France 38 Boulevard Suchet, 75016, Paris, tel: (1) 4050 1066, fax: (1) 4525 6400.
Germany Fritz-Schäffer-Strasse 20, 53113 Bonn, tel: (0228) 265 457, fax: (0228) 265 554; Consulate, Unter den Linden 55-61, 10117 Berlin, tel: (030) 229 2978, fax: (030) 229 2469.
Israel 2 Kaufman St, 68012 Tel Aviv, tel: (03) 510 2236, fax: (03) 510 2235.
Latvia Elizabetes Iela 2, Riga 1010, tel: (22) 732 2550, fax: (22) 732 2891.
Lithuania Klimo gatve 8, Vilnius, tel: (0122) 263 828, fax: (0122) 263 443; consulate, Mutines 4, Vilnius, tel: (0122) 650 871.
Netherlands Piet Heinstraat 3, The Hague, 2518, tel: (070) 363 1566, fax: (070) 364 0555.
Poland ul Atenska 67, 03-978, Warsaw, tel: (02) 617 3212, fax: (02) 617 8441; Consulate, ul Yackova Dolina 50, 80-251, Gdansk, tel: (058) 410 026, fax: (058) 414 026; Consuate, ul Warshiskeho 4, 15-461 Bialystok, tel: 522 875, fax: 521 851.
Russia ul Maroseka 17/6, Moscow 101000, tel: (095) 924 7031 (embassy), (095) 924 7095 (visa), fax: (095) 928 6403.
UK 1 St Stephens Cres, London W2 5QT, tel: (0171) 221 3941, fax: (0171) 221 3946.
Ukraine vul Kutuzova 8, 252011 Kiev, tel: (044) 294 8212, fax: (044) 294 8006.
USA 1619 New Hampshire Ave, N.W., Washington, DC 20009, tel: (202) 986 1604, 986 1606, fax: (202) 986 1805.

Ukrainian embassies

Australia Consulate, 4 Bloom St, Moonee Ponds 3039 Melbourne, tel: (613) 9320 0135, fax: (613) 9326 0139.

Belarus vul Kirova 17, Minsk, tel: (7017) 272 861, 367 101, 367 014, 367 613, fax: (7017) 272 354.

Canada 331 Metcalfe St, Ottawa, Ont K2P 1S3, tel: (613) 230 2961, fax: (613) 230 2400.

Czech Republic 160 00, Prague 6, 20 Charles de Gaulle, tel: (422) 312 0000, 312 1577, fax: (422) 312 4366.

Estonia Endla 8a, Tallin, tel: (3722) 631 1555, fax: (3722) 631 1556.

Finland Tehtaankatu 1B, 00140 Helsinke 1Y, tel: (3580) 308 563, fax: (3580) 680 246.

Germany Waldstrasse, 42, 5300 Bonn 2, tel: (49 228) 318 351, 311 995, 312 139, fax: (49 228) 311 563, 318 351; Unter den Lide 63-65, 10117 Berlin, tel: (49 30) 229 1618, fax: (49 30) 229 1745; Consuluate, Pienzenauerstrasee 15, 8000 Munich 80, tel: (4989) 982 8771, fax: (4989) 982 7141.

Hungary H 1062 Budapest, Ut. Nogzadi, 8, tel: (361) 155 9609, 156 8697, 155 2416, fax: (361) 202 2287, 155 2443.

Israel 12 Stricker St, 62006 Tel Aviv, tel: (9723) 604 0242, 604 0313, 604 0311, 604 0141, fax: (9723) 604 2512.

Italy via Castelgerdo, 50 Roma 00185, tel: (396) 337 809 201, 447 00 174, 447 00 172, fax: (396) 447 00 181.

Latvia 3 Kalpaka Bulv, Riga, tel: (22) 724 3082, fax: (22) 733 2956.

Lithuania Kalvariu 159, Vilnius, tel: (0122) 778 413.

Poland 00580, Warsaw, Aleja Szucha 7, tel: (4822) 293 201, fax: (4822) 296 449.

Russia Moscow, ul Stanislavsky 18, tel: (095) 229 3422, 229 1079, 229 3442, fax: (095) 229 3542.

UK 78 Kensington Park Rd, London W11 2P1, tel: (71) 727 63 12, tel: (71) 792 17 08.

USA 3350 M Street, NW, Washington DC 20007, tel: (202) 333 0606, fax: (202) 333 0817, email 76403.1762@compuserve.com, vmar@aol.com; Consulates, 3350 M Street, NW, Washington DC 20007, tel: (202) 333 7507, 333 7508, 333 7509, fax: (202) 333 7510, 240 East 49th St, New York, NY 10017, tel: (212) 371 5690, fax: (212) 371 5547; 10 East Huron St, Chicago, IL 60611, tel: (312) 642 4388.

WHEN TO GO

The decision about when to go depends on a number of factors, particularly the weather and your interests. For general sightseeing, the best time to visit is from June to August.

Another factor to consider is the availability of fresh food. This is particularly important if you are a vegetarian. Although food is available all year round, the end of summer is the only time when there are plenty of fresh vegetables.

Temperature

Average monthly maximum and minimum temperatures are to be found in the following table.

Place	Elevation	Jan °C		Apr °C		Jul °C		Oct °C	
	m	max	min	max	min	max	min	max	min
Chita	676	–23	–33	5	–6	23	10	4	–7
Irkutsk	476	–15	–25	5	–7	21	10	4	–6
Khabarovsk	50	–19	–25	5	–3	23	17	8	2
Krasnoyarsk	152	–15	–23	2	–5	19	12	2	–4
Omsk	85	–18	–25	4	–6	23	12	4	–3
Ekaterinburg	273	–14	–20	5	–4	21	12	3	–3
Vladivostok	29	–10	–17	7	2	21	15	12	4
Yakutsk	163	–43	–48	–3	–14	22	12	–5	–12
Arkhangelsk	7	–12	–16	2	–5	18	10	2	–1
Astrakhan	14	–5	–9	14	4	29	20	12	4
Vyatka	181	–14	–18	5	–3	22	12	3	–1
St Petersburg	5	–5	–10	7	–1	21	13	7	3
Lviv	298	–1	–5	11	3	24	15	12	6
Minsk	225	–5	–10	8	–1	21	12	8	2
Moscow	154	–6	–12	8	0	23	12	7	2
Volgograd	42	–9	–15	10	2	29	18	11	3

National festivals and holidays

Parades, festivals and holidays occur throughout the year. Large towns are the best places to see big parades such as those held on Defenders of the Motherland Day, and on the Russian Orthodox Christmas, while small towns are often the best places to see small celebrations such as International Women's Day and International Children's Day. Indoor events, such as school performances or photo exhibitions, are normally held in each town's Palace of Culture, while outdoor events, such as parades or concerts, are held along the main street or in the main square. Try to co-ordinate your programme with a celebration as they provide glimpses of a side of Russia rarely seen by outsiders. For the egotistical, visit your sister city on World Sister Cities Day and you will be guaranteed attention.

Public holidays

Jan 1-2	New Year. *Ded Moroz* (Grandfather Frost) and his daughter *Snegurichka* (the snow maiden) give children presents and decorate the *yolka* (Christmas tree). Children normally gather around the yolka and call to *Snegurichka* three times. When she arrives, the fun begins with singing, dancing and games.
Jan 7	Russian/Ukrainian Orthodox Christmas. The orthodox churches use the old Julian calendar which is 13 days behind today's Gregorian calendar.
Jan 13	New Year's Day according to the old Julian calendar.
Feb 15	Defenders of the Motherland Day
1st week in Mar	Maslenitsa Day (Blini Day) when *blini* pancakes are made to celebrate the coming of spring.
Mar 5	Anniversary of the death of Joseph Stalin in 1953
Mar 8	International Women's Day
Mar 25	Old Belarus Independence Day
Apr 7	World Health Day
1st Sun in Apr	Geologists' Day
Apr 22	Lenin Memorial Day (unofficial)
Last Sun in Apr	World Sister Cities' Day
Late Apr/early May	Paskha (Easter)
Week after Easter	Memorial Day where Russians visit cemeteries to remember the dead.

May 1	Holiday of Spring and Labour (formerly May Day or The Working Class People Holiday)
May 9	Great Patriotic War Victory Day
May 28	Border Guard Day
Late May	End of the school year (school concerts and parties are common).
June 1	International Children's Day
June 6	Pushkin's birthday. Poetry readings beside most Puskin monuments.
June 12	Russian Independence Day (post-communist)
Last Sun in Jun	Russian Youth Day
July 20	International Chess Day
2nd Sun in Jul	Fisherman's Day
Last Sun in Jul	Navy Day
1st Sun in Aug	Rail Workers' Day
July 27	Belarus Independence Day
2nd Sun in Aug	Builders' Day
Aug 22	Holiday in honour of the defeat of the 1993 coup
Aug 24	Ukraine independence day
Sept 1 (or next weekday)	Knowledge Day which is the first day of school
3rd Sun in Sept	Forestry Workers Day
Nov 7	Anniversary of the October Revolution (unofficial)
Nov 10	World Youth Day, Militia Day
Nov 17	International Students' Day
Last Sun in Aug	Miners' Day
Nov 19	Rocket and Artillery Forces' Day
Dec 12	Constitution Day, commemorating the promulgation of Russia's 4th constitution
Dec 25	Non-orthodox Christmas Day which is not celebrated widely.

Regional festivals and holidays

Late Feb/early Mar	Goodbye Winter Festival, held at St Petersburg, Petrozavodsk and Murmansk
Last week of Mar	Festival of the North, held in Murmansk and regional towns
Apr/May	St Petersburg Classical Music Spring Festival
May 5–13	Festival of Moscow States
Jun 21–July 11	St Petersburg White Nights Festival
Jun 21–29	St Petersburg Festival of the Arts
Autumn	Moscow International Film Festival (odd years)
Aug 1	Yaroslavl Sunset Music Festival
Aug	Moscow International Marathon
Mid-November	St Petersburg Autumn Jazz Festival
Dec 25–Jan 5	Russian Winter Festival held in most large cities

WHAT TO TAKE

Prepare for your trip well in advance and avoid last minute packing. This will ensure that you enjoy your trip without worrying about buying things you forgot to bring. The following ideas may help in your selection of what to take.

A backpack or soft suitcase is preferable to a hard suitcase as the former are easier to carry on and off trains and buses. If you do take a case, carry two small ones rather than one big one, and bring a two wheeled trolley to move them around. Wheels built into suitcases are of limited use as the stations and pavements are very rough. Carry a small pack for day trips. Do not carry excess luggage; it is expensive on flights and there are no porters at the stations to help you.

A spare set of passport photos should always be carried in case you need another visa. Also take a photocopy of your visa and the first three pages of your passport and keep them separate from your passport and visa.

It is safer to carry money in a money belt than in a pocket. You will also need a guidebook and maps, a pocket dictionary and a diary to record your holiday. A pen and paper are always useful and a good way of carrying them is to buy a pocket sized notebook and staple or glue to its cover a plastic sheath which can hold a pen.

A heavy-duty water bottle which will withstand boiling water from the train's samovar is vital. When cooled, this water becomes your drinking water for the next day. Also useful on the train is a strong plastic cup, a knife, fork and spoon and a can and bottle opener. Much of the food is very bland, so you may like to bring curry powder or other spices. As locals don't normally have milk in their tea, carry a tube of condensed milk if you want white tea. Also good coffee and tea bags are hard to find and it is worth taking your own supply of these. You will probably find it more convenient to carry your own sugar if you use it. Don't forget to carry your own toilet paper.

You should always carry around a pack of good quality unopened biscuits or chocolates, which you can buy locally, as your contribution if you get invited to share a meal.

Bring all the clothes you need and do not rely on buying any when you arrive. On the train you will find it comfortable to wear slip-on sandals.

As the supply of personal items is extremely unpredictable, it is recommended that you take everything you need, for example, baby powder, comb, contact lens solution, contraceptives, ear plugs, hairspray, laundry detergent, lip chaf stick, nail clippers, pocket knife, pocket mirror, sanitary items, sewing kit, shampoo, shaving equipment, soap, sunglasses, sunscreen, tissues, toothpaste. Common western brands of film and camera supplies are readily available, but you may prefer to bring some from home. If you have room, include a 2.5m length of clothesline which has innumerable uses.

You should carry plastic bags as they are not handed out in shops or markets. Resealable containers are also a good idea.

Unless you are staying in the best hotels you will appreciate an electric immersion coil, an alarm clock and a universal sink/bath plug. Don't forget a two-pin electricity adaptor.

A small medical kit should be carried. It should include several syringes, band-aids, antiseptic, headache tablets, antiseptic gauze, anti-ringworm cream, personal medication and insect repellent. Vitamin tablets are a good idea as some nutritional aspects of the diet may be found wanting.

If you play a portable musical instrument, take it along as playing is a good way of making friends.

The best sort of gifts to take are souvenirs from your country such as US flags or kangaroo stick pins, baseball caps, T-shirts, glossy picture books, maps, or travel videos. Pens, calculators and digital watches with your company's logo emblazoned on them are essential if you are travelling on business. The days are gone when locals wanted jeans or trainers (running shoes) as nowadays these can be bought everywhere.

What to leave at home
Always photocopy your valuable documents, such as passport, credit cards and travellers cheques, before you leave home and give the photocopies to someone whom you can notify if you lose your valuables.

What to buy and not to buy
It is prohibited to take antiques, old artworks and medals out of Russia, Ukraine and Belarus. If you are buying new paintings, make sure you get an official receipt stating that the goods can be exported and the year of their production. This also applies to *samovars*.

While many things, such as excellent enamel pots, are cheap in Russia, remember that you have to carry purchases out as mailing goods is very difficult and unreliable.

Clothing
Casual clothes are the norm even when attending high-class cultural art events. See *Temperature* on page 28 to determine what clothing is required. A word of warning for people who have never experienced freezing temperatures: take lined, thick-soled boots, a full-length, padded skiing jacket, thermal underwear, a woollen hat, woollen trousers and thick gloves. Jeans are not warm enough!

HEALTH AND SAFETY
Health
Disease, vaccinations and medical facilities
The health risks of Russia, Belarus and Ukraine include diphtheria, encephalitis, hepatitis A and typhoid.

There is a severe shortage of basic medical supplies, including disposable needles, anaesthetics, vaccines and antibiotics. Elderly travellers and those with existing health problems may be at risk due to inadequate medical facilities. Doctors and hospitals often expect immediate cash payment for health services.

There are no mandatory vaccinations for travelling in Russia, but you should have tetanus and hepatitis innoculations, and take precautions against typhoid and diphtheria. You should check with your local doctor or travellers' medical centre for the latest requirements.

For information about the latest medical recommendations, contact:

UK   Trailfinders, 194 Kensington High St, London, tel: (071) 938 3999 or Thomas Cook, 45 Berkeley St, London, tel: (0171) 408 4157.

Australia   Travellers Medical & Vaccination Centre, Mort St, Canberra, tel: (06) 257 7154.

Thailand   Travellers Medical & Vaccination Centre, 8th floor, Alma Link Building, 25 Soi Chaidlon, Bangkok, tel: (2) 655 1024.

USA   Centre for Disease Control and Prevention, tel: (404) 332 4559.

The most common problem is stomach trouble and the best prevention is to boil all the water that you drink.

If you are going to be in Russia for more than a few weeks, it is advisable to take vitamin tablets as it can be difficult to get a balanced diet most of the year.

At the beginning of spring, in Siberia, some people may suffer nosebleeds and headaches caused by the forest blooming. After a day or so, the problem disappears.

In the Russian far east and Amur region, tic-borne Siberian typhus or Japanese encephalitis can be found. Siberian typhus (also known as North Asian typhus) is a disease similar to Rocky Mountain spotted fever. It is caused by a bacteria (*rickettsia sibirica*) and can be treated with the doxycycline or ciprofloxacin antibiotics. The mosquito-borne Japanese encephalitis is common in rice-growing areas and vaccinations are available in the west.

The standard Russian hospital is considerably less well equipped and supplied than those in the West. However, most doctors are just as competent, so if you land in a hospital for stitches or an X-ray, don't be too concerned. Because of the shortage of medical equipment, hospitals are forced to re-use syringes so it is best to take a few for yourself. Russian hospitals will expect you to pay for your treatment.

In Moscow, St Petersburg, Kiev and Minsk there are a number of Western medical services and your embassy can give you a list of them. Elsewhere you are advised to organise medical evacuation for serious illnesses and it is for this reason that the highest level of medical insurance is absolutely essential in the countries of the former Soviet Union.

In summer in Moscow and parts of Ukraine some beaches close due to cholera outbreaks. Read the English-language *Moscow Times* to find out problem areas in Moscow.

Some 200,000 cases of syphilis were registered in Russia in the first ten months of 1995, according to Yevgenii Belyaev, chairman of the State Committee for the Prevention of Epidemics. He said the figures were unprecedented in Russia and blamed the increase on the easing of travel restrictions, the rise in immigration and a lapse in 'moral standards'. There are a total of 1,033 registered HIV-positive people in the country and more and more cases are being diagnosed among high-school and college students. AIDS support groups believe that the official figures for HIV infection should be multiplied by a factor of ten to get a true picture of the situation in Russia.

Food, water and air quality

The quality of food, water and air in the countries of the former Soviet Union varies widely.

Poor sanitary conditions are the biggest problem with food, particularly in summer. Common sense will decrease your chance of illness, for example not buying food from street vendors or downmarket canteens, washing or peeling fruit, only buying tinned or bottled food, and buying Western products.

Water is a big problem due to Russia's poor water purification systems and the prevalence of the parasite *Giardia lamblia* in places such as St Petersburg. Always boil drinking water, or buy bottled water, soft drink or beer. Be aware that hard spirits can kill you if bought from kiosks. This is because it is not unknown for these kiosks to refill brand-name bottles with a homebrew or industrial alcohol.

Air quality in several Russian, Ukrainian and Belarusian regions is particularly poor and, according to a 1995 World Bank report, improving air quality in just 18 cities in eastern Europe to European Union levels would save 18,000 lives annually. Apparently, industrial pollution kills 30,000 east Europeans annually. Unfortunately, there is little you can do about air pollution except not stay for too long.

LONG-TRIP TRAVELLER TIP

The 50-hour trip from Moscow to the Caucasus via Astrakhan was long and boring. I recommend that travellers take something to read, as the only material sold by people walking through the carriages is in Russian. I also recommend that travellers take plenty of bottled water with them; only beer and a sweet soft drink was sold on the train.

Travellers need to be aware that surprises can happen. In my case, five minutes before leaving Moscow, a family boarded the train with tickets for the beds in my coupé. The conductor evicted me and another person and placed us in another coupé.

The train toilets were disgusting by the time we reached Astrakhan. I recommend that travellers take a small bottle of disinfectant liquid to use on their hands. It was nice to know that when I did eat, my hands were as germ free as possible.

I took toilet paper, not in rolls which tend to take up space, but in small cardboard boxes, similar to those dispensed in a few public toilets. The rectangular shape seems to take less luggage space. I recommend that travellers take a small flannel – it is really refreshing in the heat to give the face and neck a wash.

Andrew Mich, Australia, September 1995

Safety

Safety is a major concern of travellers as the media regularly feature reports of horrific crime in Russia and to a lesser extent in Ukraine and Belarus, although the vast majority of violent crime is targeted at business people, journalists and crime lords.

However, it is undeniable that the level of violence is increasing due to the declining standards of living and rising unemployment. Foreigners are increasingly becoming the target of crime in Moscow and St Petersburg, but the communist legacy of the inviolability of foreigners means that you still are less likely than a local to be a victim.

General safety tips

Being a Westerner you instantly attract attention and envy. For a very small group of Russians, this can mean an opportunity for their quick gain and your quick loss. Common sense is the best safeguard and here are a few rules:

- Minimise the things you carry around.
- Carry money and documents next to your body in a money belt, never in a bag.
- Dress down and blend in with locals.
- Be discreet and don't draw attention to yourself by talking loudly in English or carrying a camera around your neck.
- If you are a woman always say you are married, travel with a male companion or wear a wedding ring.

- Watch where you walk as holes and metal rods coming out of the pavement are common. Don't step on manhole covers as they may give way. In winter be extra careful as heavy falls are common on the slippery ice.
- Be very alert when crossing roads. Traffic has right of way over pedestrians. The centre island between traffic lanes is not safe for pedestrians as vehicles use this as an overtaking lane. It is best to cross at lights or use the underpass.
- Watch out for swarms of gypsy children and vagrants. Never give them anything as they will try to grab your wallet and run. If they start hassling you, scream and Russians will only be too happy to scare them off.
- Always carry the address of your hotel in Russian and its telephone number and that of your embassy.
- If you are going to be in Russia for a while, or are travelling by yourself, contact your embassy when you arrive and tell them your route plan. Get a list of Western medical centres.
- Always self-validate your tram, bus and trolleybus tickets immediately you get on to a vehicle. If it is too crowded, then tap your neighbour's shoulder and gesture to him to pass it on. Ticket checkers prey on foreigners, especially in St Petersburg, and try to intimidate them with on-the-spot 'fines'.
- Airports are the most dangerous places for the unwary. Organise your airport transfer rather than accept a ride from an unmarked taxi. At Moscow's Sheremetovo international airport, there are several companies, such as Intourtrans, that can organise transfers for about $50 when you arrive. One common scam by airport "taxis" is for the drivers to fake an engine failure halfway to the city. The driver will get out and "fix" the problem but ask you to push the car to get it going. When you do, the car starts and drives away.

Money and safety
- Never change money on the street. There are legal change kiosks in most hotels and banks so it is not worth the risk for a 1–2% difference.
- Avoid changing large sums at one time as you many need less than you think.
- While many stores accept credit cards, it is best not to use the service. As credit card fraud in the countries of the former Soviet Union is rampant, always keep your receipts and check your statement immediately you return home.
- Keep your money in a money belt on your body at all times.
- You should also carry a wallet containing a small amount of roubles and hard currency as your normal source of money. As well as enabling you to get to your money quickly, it won't matter too much if the wallet is lost.
- Never display large sums of money. Be especially careful when purchasing souvenirs from street vendors as criminals may be observing how much money you have and where you keep it.
- Keep your bag and camera securely tucked under your arm while shopping.

Railways and safety
There are many stories of crimes on railways. The majority are exaggerations, distortions or complete fabrications. The most outrageous story in recent years has been the so-called "Sleeping Gas Incident" on a Moscow–St Petersburg train. This story involved an entire carriage supposedly being put to sleep by gas and everyone being robbed. After a week of international media coverage, the

Russian journalist who wrote the story admitted that it was fictitious but she still maintained that she did lose her purse when she was asleep!

Despite the ridiculous stories, crime does exist on railways and a few simple precautions will substantially reduce your chances of being a victim. These include: locking the cabin from the inside when you are asleep, by using both the normal door-handle lock and the flick-down lock; putting your bags under the sleeping bench which means that they can't be reached without lifting your bed; dressing down on trains; not displaying cameras; talking softly; and always carrying valuables on your person. The railways are currently installing a new type of lock on *coupé* (cabin) doors in trains which is claimed to be unopenable from the outside. By the end of 1995, they were only fitted on Moscow–St Petersburg trains No 1/2, 3/4 and 5/6.

Some people padlock their bags to the *coupé*'s wall but this is excessive. It is a good idea always to leave someone in the cabin to look after the luggage. If everyone has to leave, ask the conductor to lock your cabin.

Although valuables can be left in a small safe that is located in the chief *provodnik*'s (conductor) cabin, this is not recommended.

If there is a problem, first go to your carriage *provodnik* who will call the head *provodnik*, who in turn will notify the police if it is warranted.

The most common railway crime is luggage theft with 8,215 incidents reported in 1994. In that year there were also 170 murders, 342 assaults resulting in injuries, 114 rapes and 1,017 robberies on the railways. A decade ago, 73% of railway crimes occurred at stations and 23% on trains while today it is 50/50. Most theft occurs when passengers fall asleep at the station after drinking too much vodka, or very rarely, after drinking a drugged drink, or fall asleep in their *coupé* and forget to use the flick-down lock which means that the door can be opened with a railway universal key. (The best protection against this last form is never to leave valuables in your clothes which you hang up near the door.). Card sharks are notorious on a number of trains so never play for money. A common scam which happens to locals but very rarely to foreigners is when someone is waiting for a train. A thief strikes up a conversation and then asks if the passenger minds looking after their bag while they go in search of food. The thief then returns joyfully showing off some bargain and offers to look after the passenger's bag. While the passenger goes shopping, the obvious occurs.

The most dangerous stations in Moscow are Kursk and Kazan, from which trains for central Asia depart, and the most dangerous trains are those destined for central Asia with the worst being the deadly 23/24 Moscow–Dushebe. The safest station is Rizhski from which trains for the Baltic states depart. The safest trains are those for the Baltic states.

Types of police

Regardless of horror stories of corrupt police, the vast majority are honest and trustworthy with foreigners and are your best bet for getting reliable information. The prerequisite of military service to enter the police means that the youngest police officer is 21 and has proven him/herself to be reliable and trustworthy. If you think you are being treated unfairly, you have two options. Firstly, you can stand on your principles, kick up a fuss and demand to see a superior. This will often result in a back down but as they often have time on their side (particularly at airports), it may result in more trouble than it is worth.

Secondly, you can acquiesce and give them what they want which may be nothing more than a bottle of vodka. Remember "natural justice" and "the good guy always wins" is a Hollywood creation.

One of the major reasons for joining the police force is that it is a good, if somewhat dangerous, career with excellent post-career prospects. There are very few female police officers. The police identity card is the standard red vinyl flip-open card carried by all Russians so, unless you read Russian, flashing an identity card means nothing. Police come in many guises, including civilian police, railway police, traffic police and railway property guards, and it is useful to know their areas of responsibility as they are very reluctant, if not prohibited, to work outside them.

It is often hard to distinguish between the types of police as they mostly wear either a military uniform or the civilian police blue uniform, a blue peaked cap with a red band, black T-baton, short range radio and pistol.

Civilian police *(Militsiya)*   These are your average police officers who are responsible for common crime. Most street police teams consist of one plain clothes officer and one in uniform.

Railway police *(Transportnaya militsiya)*   These police wear the normal police uniform but are employed by the Ministry of Railways. There is a railway police officer at every railway station, and they will sometimes travel on trains. If a problem does occur on a train, the chief conductor can radio the next station and the railway police will be ready to storm aboard.

GAI police *(GAI militsiya)*   These police man traffic intersections along major roads. Drivers show them enormous respect as they can levy hefty fines or confiscate your car. When they point their black and white striped baton at your car, you must pull over. The officer will eventually stroll over and demand your driver's licence and passport. They are experts at finding something wrong with your documents or car, but a bribe can get you on your way with the minimum of inconvenience. During the day, they will normally wear a pistol and baton but at night, particularly at the more remote GAI posts, they will carry automatic pistols. This is because evenings are more dangerous and, in the late 1980s, there were a number of cases of posts being overpowered and weapons stolen.

Cossacks *(Kazaky)*   These self-appointed, volunteer paramilitary soldiers should be avoided. The Cossacks were the frontier guards and military shock troops of Tsarist Russia and their descendants feel that, by wearing the old Cossack uniform, consisting of a Russian military uniform with a yellow stripe down the trousers and a yellow hat band around a peaked cap, they are recapturing their true heritage, and are entitled to respect. As most of the Cossacks are louts, the average Russian eyes them warily. An uneasy truce exists between the regular police and the Cossacks. They are not allowed to carry guns but carry truncheons and long whips. Cossacks believe in the three principles of common ownership, military service in support of the state and regional autonomy. These principles made them ideal tools for the tsar in conquering new land and guarding boarders but have little relevance today. Their power base is in the Don region in southern European Russia but you will see them also in Siberia.

NEW RUSSIANS

Since the collapse of the Soviet Union, communism and the state-controlled economy, a new Russian élite has developed, colloquially called "New Russians". These people are at the helm of Russia's predatory capitalism and are renowned for their flashy style and conspicuous consumption. These "New Russians" are mostly old communist power brokers. According to sociologist Olga Kryshtanovska, who presented the results of a survey into the new Russian élite in the newspaper Izvestiya on 10 January 1996, 75% of the new political élite and 61% of the new business élite come from the old Soviet nomenklatura (connected officials). About 38% of businessmen mostly came from the Komsomol (Young Communist Party) and another 38% from economic positions in the Soviet nomenklatura.

According to the Russian Academy of Sciences Sociology Institute, in 1996, the "New Russians" numbered approximately 300,000 in Moscow, 150,000 in St Petersburg, and about 2 million in Russia as a whole. The Institute notes that the reason for material success in Russia contrasts with that of most advanced industrial countries. Traditionally, affluence tends to go hand-in-hand with educational level but in Russia, the better educated a person, the more likely they will earn only a modest salary. The chief determinant of wealth in Russia today, the experts claim, is the position an individual occupied when the Soviet Union collapsed at the end of 1991. Those who were in power then – whether in the Communist Party, in regional government, or in industry – make up the bulk of Russia's contemporary nouveaux riches.

FURTHER INFORMATION ON RUSSIA

The maxim "You get out what you put in" is just as true for travelling as it is for anything else. For this reason, it is advisable to read as widely as possible about Russia, Ukraine and Belarus before travelling. The list of further reading at the back of this book provides a good start.

As the political and economic situation is changing rapidly in the former Soviet Union, the best source of up to date information is the media and information superhighway. When watching the media remember that only bad news sells and that most of the media's coverage of Russia is negative. Typical of this tendency to overexaggerate was the so-called "Food Crisis" in 1991 and the 1994–5 "Crime Wave". Electronic bulletin boards and listservers are excellent sources of information as you can ask questions and get answers from recently returned travellers without delay. See *Appendix Five* for more on these two information sources.

Another source of information is guidebooks on Russia but, unfortunately, most are out of date within two years of being printed. All guidebooks have something to offer, but don't take their word as gospel, particularly on prices.

Chapter Three

Practical Information

TRAVELLING WITHIN RUSSIA, BELARUS AND UKRAINE
Cost

Travellers to Russia, Belarus and Ukraine are often stunned at prices. Some things are ridiculously cheap and others exorbitantly expensive. This is because there are two economies running side by side: the subsidised and government price controlled economy and the free market.

In the Soviet era, the former was dominant and, although the days are gone when the author could buy a plane ticket from Moscow to Lviv (Ukraine) for $2.50, many goods are still very cheap. For example, city maps are often only $0.50.

Today, the last vestiges of the old economy are being taken over by the free market which is rapidly inflating the cost of living and travelling in Russia. This is most readily seen in the price of food. In the early 1990s, a two-course meal at an average restaurant would cost $1 (assuming the place was open) while today a similar meal would cost $20. One of the major reasons for the increase in prices has been the increase in imported food which in 1996 accounted for 58% of Russia's food supply.

The evolving economy has been particularly hard on the Russians, who in 1995 had to deal with inflation of over 300% and a real wage decrease of 12%. In January 1996 the average Russian monthly wage was $115. The average wage for the better paid workers in the energy, ferrous metallurgical and fishing sectors was $225 while in the poorly paid culture, education and agriculture sectors it was $67. The average Ukrainian monthly wage was about $70.

The price of goods and services also depends on their location and in many cases Moscow, St Petersburg and Kiev are considerably more expensive than all other cities. In fact, in 1996 Moscow overtook Tokyo as the most expensive city in the world for business travellers. According to the monitoring agency, EuroCost-Luxembourg, a 24-hour stay in a top-quality hotel in Moscow with meals, telephones and taxis costs an average of $543 compared to $516 in Tokyo. One of the main reasons for Moscow's high cost is the dramatic shortage of four- and five-star hotels. Staying at a standard hotel will lower your costs considerably. If you take out the cost of accommodation, a more accurate picture of the difference of costs due to location is given by the basket of essential consumer goods as defined by the State Statistics Committee. As of January 1996, the national average monthly basket cost $52. In remote Yakutsk it cost $112, in northern Murmansk it cost $66, in Moscow it cost $62 and, cheapest of all, was in Ulyanovsk just north of Moscow where it cost $29.

Below is a guide to the prices in US$ for foreigners for a range of common tourist services as of June 1996.

Item	Moscow	Murmansk	Brest	Kiev	Volgograd
Standard single hotel room	70	30	31	60	26
Two-course meal at restaurant	30	9	5	14	9
Cheap meal at canteen	8	6	3	6	5
Overnight rail ticket	20	18	16	8	15
Metro/bus ride	0.50	0.30	0.20	0.20	0.20
Entry to a large museum	3	0.50	0.30	1	0.50

Below is a guide to the prices for foreigners for rail tickets on *firmenny* trains for journeys that originate in Moscow. (A *firmenny* is a new high-class train.) All prices are in US$ and were accurate in August 1996.

Tickets for destinations outside the former Soviet Union often have to be paid partly in US$. For example, the price for the ticket from Kiev to Budapest is 14.4 million *karbovantsi* plus $25 which is equivalent to $97. For further information on types of train and carriage, see *Chapter Four, page 60*.

CIS trains

Destination	SV	coupé	platskartny
Arkhangelsk	84	42	26
Astrakhan	108	54	34
Brest	84	53	27
Irkutsk	323	161	102
Kiev	62	31	19
Minsk	55	27	18
Novosibirsk	222	134	70
St Petersburg	52	25	16
Vladivostok	583	290	185
Volgograd	87	48	25

International trains

Destination	SV	3-berth coupé	4-berth coupé
Berlin[1]		226	152
Pekin[2]	264		166
Pekin[3]	306		171
Ulaanbaatar[1]	193		122
Ulaanbaatar[4]	232		144
Warsaw[1]	100	66	62
Warsaw[5]	116	72	63

[1]Russian train [2]via Zabaikalsk/Manchuria [3]via Naushki/Mongolia [4]Chinese train [5]Polish train

Ways to save money

There are obvious ways to save money such as travelling with someone so that you can get twin share rooms, and buying food in markets and Russian shops.

Other ways include:

– Paying the local, not the inflated foreigners' price, for museum tickets. Mostly the difference is a few dollars but at places like the Hermitage in St Petersburg or Kizhi Island near Petrozavodsk, the difference can be close to $10. One way to do this is to get a Russian to buy a ticket for you or work out how much the Russians pay and give the exact amount without saying a word. Remember it is fairly easy to spot a foreigner in Russia by their clothes, bags and cameras.

– Paying the railway ticket price for locals and not foreigners. This is risky as you can easily get fined for doing it, especially on the Moscow–St Petersburg line.

– Go on a group tour and get everything for between $80 and $140 a day.

Getting between cities

There are four main ways of travelling within the former Soviet Union: trains, planes, motor vehicles and boats.

Travelling by train in Russia, especially in a first-class (*SV*) overnight train, is both pleasant and convenient. Trains are invariably clean, on time and safe. Although they take longer than flying, they often save accommodation costs and deliver you to the centre of the city. As a general rule, it is best not to spend more than one or two nights on a train as there are rarely any showers. You would be crazy to travel on anything but trains between Moscow and the Baltic states, St Petersburg, Minsk and Kiev. For more information on train travel, see *Chapter Four*.

Internal plane travel in the former Soviet Union is not recommended because of both safety and reliability problems. In the communist era, there was only one national air company, Aeroflot. With the break-up of the Soviet Union, Aeroflot splintered into as many as 500 regional companies which had neither sufficient training and employees nor spare parts. While there were some air crashes, the biggest problem was that most flights never departed due to a lack of fuel and aircraft. Since the mid 1990s, the situation has improved with a rationalisation of air companies and the tightening of safety standards. The number of scheduled flights has now reduced but these are much more likely to depart.

While fuel supplies are still a problem, the greater impediment to flying is the weather. Fog, wind, snowstorms and howling rains can delay planes for several days or more. Getting refunds for cancelled services is extremely difficult. Surprisingly, though, plane tickets can be cheaper than rail tickets over long distances.

It is possible to hire a self-drive car, but, because of the inadequate road signs, bad roads and awful local drivers, it is better to rent a car and driver. You will need an international driver's licence to hire a car. If you do not have one, you can obtain a Russian one in Moscow, after written and practical driving tests, by taking your current licence, payment and a photo to GlavUPDK Spetsavtotsentr, ul Kievskaya 8, tel: 240 2092. A far safer way of travelling on the roads is on a long-distance bus. These leave from long-distance bus stations and serve towns up to six hours away. The buses are usually fairly old and provide an interesting, if uncomfortable, ride.

There are two sorts of passenger vessels which ply Russia's rivers and lakes: hydrofoils and river cruisers. While hydrofoils travel about three times as fast as river cruisers, the latter are a more elegant way of travelling and an excellent way to meet locals. Hydrofoils, commonly known as *raketa*, *kometa* and *meteor*, look quite futuristic with their sleek lines and bubble windows; they only travel during daylight due to the danger of hitting an unseen object.

River cruisers are normally multi-deck ships that can carry several hundred passengers. Those configured as tourist vessels have single-, double- and triple-person rooms, a restaurant, *banya* (Russian sauna), cinema, souvenir kiosk and bar. However, the working ships are more basic with a restaurant, a small number of one- and two-person rooms, and many four- and eight-person rooms. Cruisers stop every few hours at larger towns for up to 30 minutes, allowing time to stretch your legs on land. Tips for travelling on these vessels are the same as for those on trains: take your own food, bring a big book and meet the locals.

Getting around a city

Trams, trolleybuses and buses offer a cheap way of getting around as well as giving a tour of the town. All the routes are circular, so the vehicle will eventually return to where you got on. The big advantage of trams is that you can always follow the tracks to find your way back. To travel on trams, trolleybuses and buses, you need to buy a ticket, normally bought in strips of ten from roadside kiosks or on the vehicle from the driver. You must self-validate your ticket at a validation machine on the inside wall of the vehicle. If you can't reach the machine because of the crush, tap your neighbour's shoulder and he will pass it on. You may be asked by another traveller to pass his ticket on and to refuse is extremely rude. In St Petersburg particularly, ticket inspectors watch out for foreigners who forget to self-validate their tickets and then try to intimidate them into paying an on-the-spot "fine". Public transport normally runs from 06.00 to 01.00.

MAGNETIC METRO CARDS SPEED UP ENTRY BUT SLASH REVENUE

In a move to speed up entry to the metro, a number of metros in Russia have introduced magnetic cards. These cards replace monthly tickets and are given free to metro workers, police and certain classes of pensioners. In the past the free ticket holders passed via the dezhurnaya at the entry turnstiles who checked photo IDs to confirm the name on the free ticket. However, as no-one checks the holders of the magnetic cards, they often loan their tickets to friends and relatives.

A poll in 1995 found that 30% of all St Petersburg metro workers have done this but it was believed that this figure was probably 95% in reality with the other 5% having no friends or relatives. To solve the problem, St Petersburg metro now requires that free magnetic card holders insert the card into the turnstyle, show their documents to the dezhurnaya and, if everything is in order, the card is given back and permission granted to enter the metro. Obviously this defeats the whole purpose of issuing magnetic cards.

Travelling by metro is safe, convenient and even, in some cases, beautiful. Given the increasing traffic congestion, the metro is often the fastest way to travel within the major cities. Metro stations are easily recognised by the big letter "M" on main streets. Tokens may be purchased near the turnstiles. Metros normally operate from 06.00 to 01.00 with peak hours between 07.00 and 10.00, and between 16.00 and 19.00.

Taxis are another option but they are relatively expensive. Remember three rules when dealing with taxis. Firstly, do not get a taxi near a hotel because, if the driver thinks that you are a foreigner, he will insist on an outrageous sum. Secondly, never get in a taxi before you have negotiated a price. Thirdly, never get into a taxi if there is someone else in it, for obvious safety reasons.

There are two sorts of taxis: official taxis which are yellow with a taxi sign on them, and unofficial taxis which are private cars that stop when people put out their hands. While official taxis have distance meters in them, no-one ever uses them as inflation has made them impractical. In Moscow, a taxi ride of 15 minutes should cost about $10 and a 40-minute trip about $40.

WHERE TO STAY

Accommodation choices and standards are slowly improving but are still very poor compared to the rest of Europe. Most hotels have a two-tiered pricing structure with foreigners being charged three to ten times the rate of locals. In most cities, with the notable exceptions of Moscow and St Petersburg, hotel rooms as cheap as $5 are available. The price varies enormously for similar hotels within a city, so consider investigating several before choosing one. It is best to book accommodation in advance. While this does not guarantee you a bed, as hotels rarely reply to confirm or decline your booking, it will increase your chances. Safest is to book through a recognised tour operator (see *Chapter Two*).

In all hotels there will invariably be a forbidding *dezhurnaya* or floor attendant who will supply you with flasks of hot water and sell you tea. She is the guardian of room keys. On the ground floor there is normally a luggage storage room where you pay per item per day. In the basement or backroom will be a representative of OViR who will register your visa.

Only the largest hotels offer official laundry services. Your best bet is to ask the *dezhurnaya* or the receptionist if they know someone who could do it for you. Rather than going to this trouble, most travellers prefer to do it themselves.

In this book hotels are broken into four categories which are based on both facilities and service.

Excellent hotels

These are normally owned by large Western hotel chains such as Radisson and Novotel. While they look glitzy like international hotels everywhere, services still have a touch of Soviet reticence about them. Their restaurants are normally excellent; they have banking facilities, room service and shops; and their staff are motivated. These hotels are mostly found in Moscow, St Petersburg and Kiev. Because of the limited number of four- and five-star hotels in these cities, their prices are between $200 and $400 a night. The hotels of the Iris Hotel chain across Russia also receive an excellent rating although their facilities are not as good as excellent hotels in Moscow. Iris Hotels are owned by the wealthy Russian, Professor Svyatoslav Fedorov, who pioneered conveyor-belt eye microsurgery. One floor in each of his eight, multi-storey, Finnish-built eye clinics has been converted into a hotel. The quality of the food and the motivation of the staff are unusually high. Except for the summer months, the clinics are full of people with eye patches, which takes a bit of getting used to, although for many travellers, staying so close to medical services is very reassuring. There are Iris Hotels in Moscow, St Petersburg, Kaluga, Tambov, Krasnodar, Volgograd, Cheboksary, Orenburg, Ekaterinburg, Novosibirsk, Irkutsk and Khabarovsk. Rooms cost between $50 and $110 per person.

Standard hotels

These are mostly the solid Intourist hotels. They may have all the tourist facilities of restaurants, banks and shops but they are often closed. Their rooms were once nice but lack of maintenance and interest has resulted in a run-down look. In capital cities standard hotel rooms cost from $100 to $200 and in others from $50 to $70.

Basic hotels

It was once impossible for foreigners to stay in "basic" and "very basic" hotels as they were considered to reflect badly on the country. Don't be put off by this description, as basic hotels are invariably clean. They were once for low-level party and government officials, and normally have a restaurant attached, but no shops, banks or room service. The rooms are simple with a TV and fridge; about half will have a bathroom. The best hotel rooms are called *lyuks,* a relative term which just means that it is the best of all the rooms in that one hotel; most hotels have at least one room designated as such. Basic hotel rooms range from $10 to $30.

Very basic hotels

These hotels come in many forms: some are quite good and others dreadful. Very basic hotels, also known as hostels, are often attached to an industrial enterprise or a market so that visiting workers or farmers can stay there. Sometimes foreigners are refused a room because staff think that they create a bad impression for tourists. If you have been refused, be persistent or return later when the reception staff have changed. These hotels will often have neither a restaurant nor a café. Very few rooms will have an attached bathroom and each will have up to four beds. A form of very basic hotel, called a rest room (*komnata otdykha* Комната отдыха), can be found at most stations. You can stay overnight if you have a ticket for a train the next morning. Rooms at very basic hotels cost from $5 to $10.

Other types of accommodation

Other types of accommodation include holiday homes, sanatoriums, homestays and youth hostels.

Holiday homes (*Dom Otdykha* Дом отдыха)   In the Soviet era these were holiday destinations for city dwellers. Like country hotels, they offered meals and some organised activities. Today, the ones that still operate are mostly run down and often do not have even a restaurant. However, some are excellent and remain the holiday choice of the country's élite.

Sanatoriums (*Sanitorti* Санитори)   These are similar to holiday homes with the exception that they have a sauna, therapeutic services and mud or spring pools. You do not have to be sick to stay at one and many locals visit them annually as they believe that this will keep them healthy for another year.

Homestay   A good way to experience Russian life is to stay with a family in homestay. These are still rare but can be organised through a friend or small company. To minimise the clash of cultures, you should remember the following when living with locals:

– Organise a time each day for your meals.

– Be prepared to pay your family for additional services such as organising theatre tickets, sightseeing and taxis. Ask beforehand how much it will cost before agreeing to it and set an upper limit on how much you want to pay.

– Be prepared to supplement the household's food shopping when you visit the markets. Buy fruit or goods that they normally do not have.

– If you don't understand something or know what is expected of you, ask.

Youth hostels   The only places in Russia with youth hostels are Moscow, St Petersburg and Novgorod. These are mainly run by foreigners and dormitory beds cost about $15 a night. Information on these can be obtained from a local business group called the Russian Youth Hostel Association, either in St Petersburg on tel: (812) 329 8018, email ryh@ryh.spb.su; or in the USA on tel: (310) 618 2014.

FOOD AND DRINK

Exotic and tantalising cuisine is definitely not the reason for visiting any country in the former Soviet Union. This is not to say that there are not excellent local recipes, just that you rarely get to taste them.

Travellers on group tours will normally get three meals a day.

Breakfast (*zavtrak*) consists of tea or coffee, eggs, cheese, cold meats or sausage known as *kolbasa*, and bread and butter. Toast is unknown. Most standard hotel restaurants put the food on a Swedish table (smorgasbord) so you can have seconds. If you find this breakfast too heavy, you may have your own breakfast of cornflakes, powdered milk and tea in your room. Fresh milk is hard to obtain, but you can get boiling water from the floor's *dezhurnaya* or bring your own water immersion heater.

Lunch (*obed*) consists of soup, bread and salad as starters and a main course selection of meat, chicken or fish with potatoes and pickled vegetables. The salad is either potatoes, peas and meat doused in mayonnaise, or diced tomato and cucumber with an oil and vinegar dressing.

Dinner (*uzhen*) is similar to lunch with the addition of vodka, champagne and beer.

If you go by yourself to a restaurant, you may initially be delighted by the long menus. Unfortunately, only a few of the choices will be available, and these are normally the ones with prices beside them. Most patrons never look at the menu and just wait for the waiter to tell them what is available. Restaurant staff are very reluctant to make up special meals. Meals will often contain lots of fatty meat, salt and few (if any) spices.

Restaurant food throughout the whole of the former Soviet Union is fairly similar, which is not surprising considering the 70 years of central Moscow control. Regional and national dishes have had a resurgence since the 1980s, but, while visiting these restaurants is worthwhile, you will get a better idea of local dishes by visiting ethnic restaurants in your home country. Asian restaurants are only to be found in Moscow, St Petersburg, Kiev and the Russian far east.

A good three-course meal with alcohol in a Moscow restaurant costs about $40 while in other cities it is about $20.

Home-cooked meals are usually the best of all, particularly if they incorporate native foods such as mushrooms and fish.

Getting quick and palatable snacks is not difficult in Moscow, St Petersburg and Kiev as they have places like Macdonalds, Pizza Hut and hotel coffee shops. In other cities finding snacks can be more difficult and you have to look out for kiosks on the pavement, and cafés and bars.

It is usually worthless to ask locals which restaurants are the best as most have never been to any. A survey in 1993 revealed that just 1% of Muscovites ate out in that year while it is not uncommon to meet a local who has never eaten in a restaurant.

RESTAURANT TIPS
- Many restaurants have dollar prices on their menus, but with very few exceptions all are now required by law to take payment in roubles.
- Tipping is becoming more common in Russia but there is no need to do so automatically. Many restaurants add a service charge of 5–10% to the bill.
- In winter it is normal to leave your coat with an attendant in the cloakroom.
- Always make reservations as some hotel restaurants only cater for groups and booked patrons.
- Don't be in a hurry as meals can take a long time coming.
- Bring a handkerchief with you for wiping dirty silverware and drying your hands after you wash them.

Where to eat
There are three main places to eat in Russia: restaurants, cafés/bars and canteens. The variety, presentation and quality of food is not always wonderful which is why most Russians prefer to eat at home.

In each city the locations of places to eat are included but they are not rated, as their standards vary continuously.

Restaurants (ресторан)   Restaurants are usually attached to every excellent, standard and basic hotel and, as they are used to foreigners with no Russian or Ukrainian language, they are normally the best places to eat. The other common location for a restaurant is the railway station and, while these places will be cheaper, their food quality is often low. Awful classic rock bands usually play in the late evening in restaurants. Locals don't come to restaurants for the food but for the alcohol and the band. It is common practice to be seated at a table already laid out with a spread of cold meat and salad entrées and beer, vodka and champagne. This is particularly common if you have booked a table. It is perfectly acceptable to ask for them to be removed if you do not want them. Restaurants normally open from 11.00 to 23.00 and are closed for a few hours in the late afternoon.

Cafés (кафе) **and bars** (бар)   These places are normally private establishments and have better surroundings but a worst selection of food than canteens. Some specialise in just one selection, such as pilmeni (meat dumpling). Alcohol is invariably available. In some cafés, you have to order from a menu posted at the bar. You pay for the food in advance and wait for it at your table. Cafés and bars normally open from 10.00 till late.

Canteens (столовая)   These are basic eating places for workers. They usually serve three meals a day. If the town is small, this may be the only place where you can buy hot food. The food is normally of average to poor quality, but is cheap and quick. You can get a meal here for as little as $2. Canteens normally open from 08.00 to 19.00.

Buying your own food
Buying your own food and making your own meals is what many travellers do after a few tiring weeks of locating any places to eat with decent food. Nowadays, almost all western foods, from herbal tea to Mars bars, are available everywhere. While this provides a good security net, local food will be cheaper

and shopping for it is an educational experience. Food costs increase outside Moscow due to transport costs, with the most expensive city being Yakutsk where food costs are double those in the capital.

Food that is commonly available all year round in state food shops includes *kolbasa* (salami), cheese, bread, pickled vegetables, preserved fruit, tins of jam, jars of cooked *kasha* (buckwheat), macaroni, rice, milk, butter, cream, dehydrated Chinese noodles, frozen fish, slabs of meat, *salo* (pig fat), eggs, tinned meat, biscuits and dried fruit. Wilted cabbages can be obtained for most of the year while locally grown fresh vegetables only appear in late summer.

Most food stores are open between 08.00 and 17.00, and are closed for an hour between 12.00 and 15.00.

Vegetarians
Being a vegetarian in the former Soviet Union is not easy. Meat is served with every meal and many Russians believe that a vegetarian simply means someone who will not eat solid lumps of red meat. As vegetarians find it difficult to eat a balanced diet, bring some supplies and vitamin pills. The one advantage of being vegetarian is that you will be safe from meat food poisoning, but this is very rare in the rural areas, particularly in winter.

What to drink
Black tea (*chai*) is served with every meal. It usually comes pre-sugared but you can ask for it sugar free. Coffee is rarer and coffee addicts are advised to

---

FOOD TIPS

- Preserved jars of fruit are a great travelling food as you can not only eat the fruit but also drink the juice. For 'wine lovers', you can get preserved grapes in wine.
- A good summer breakfast is a mixture of crushed biscuits, fresh berries and sour cream.
- To stop butter going rancid on long train trips (up to five days), keep it in salt water.
- A great vegetarian food is sea cabbage or morskaya kapusta. This is seaweed cut into thin strips in a little oil. It can be eaten straight out of the tin or as a salad. It is common in shops as the Russians don't particularly like it.
- Chinese noodles are great on trains, particularly those that come in a disposable polystyrene container. The samovar at the end of the carriage provides hot water.
- Take some small resealable plastic containers to prevent butter, eggs, tea, coffee etc from being crushed.
- Take a tube of milk if you like it in your tea or coffee.
- Pack all your food in a large carry bag on the train as this is more convenient than continually opening your backpack.
- While most meat products are safe to eat, it is best not to buy meat products off railway platforms.
- A great travelling food is locally bought dried fruit soaked overnight. Make sure you wash it several times as it is often dirty.
- If you prepare hot food before your train trip and want to carry it on the train, you can always buy cheap, locally produced vacuum flasks.

bring their own supplies. An excellent non-alcoholic drink is *kompot* which is a fruit drink made of berries. Pepsi and other western soft drinks are available almost everywhere.

Common alcoholic drinks are brandy, champagne, beer and vodka. The best brandy (*konyak*) comes from Armenia. Champagne (*shampanskoye*) comes in dry, semi-dry, semi-sweet and sweet forms. Local beer (*pivo*) is excellent but only if it is fresh. It only lasts about seven days before it starts to lose its fizz. The words for fresh beer are *svezhnoe pivo*.

Vodka is the most common drink. Although it comes in an assortment of flavours such as lemon (*limonnaya*), pepper (*persovka*) and ash berry (*ryabinvka*), rarely do locals drink anything but plain vodka. Vodka is drunk neat and in one gulp. Many locals believe that if you make a toast but do not drink it all down in one gulp, then you are not sincere. So, if you propose in your toast something like, "for the well-being of the host" or "to Ukraine", make sure that you drain the glass. If you mix your vodka with juice or water, locals may find it very strange, and call it "a spoilt drink".

To minimise vodka damage, eat butter or fat before you drink as this will line your stomach with a protective layer which will slow the rate of alcohol absorption. Always follow vodka with a water or fruit juice chaser, or something to eat. Of course, don't mix alcoholic drinks.

SHOPPING

In the Soviet era, foreigners shopped only at *beriozka* hard currency stores. Today, you can shop anywhere and everything is paid for in roubles. However, Russia, Ukraine and Belarus are still not shoppers' paradises so when you see something you like, buy it immediately as it may not be there when you return.

It is getting harder to buy things that are distinctively local due to the influx of foreign goods. In the old days it was much easier as everything had Lenin's head embossed on it. Distinctive Russian goods include *matryoshka*, *khokhloma*, lacquer boxes, Vyatka toys and lace. These are described in the glossary. If none of these appeal, you can still find communist goods such as flags, badges, maps and uniforms in front of major Moscow, St Petersburg and Kiev tourist attractions. Attractive books, calendars, maps and postcards are other great mementoes. These are found in book stores and at tourist sites for considerably more.

Most large city department stores (*univermag*) stock the common things you need such as batteries, film and soap. Nowadays, they also carry a large range of western brands.

Shopping the local way

Don't expect Western-style service in shops, as it is unknown to the majority of them. The staff in stores may seem indifferent or even rude but there is no point getting annoyed or upset. At least it makes for great holiday stories when you get home. When you enter a store, watch what the other shoppers are doing and copy them. The procedure can differ a bit, but generally there are four steps to buying goods.

1 Decide exactly what you want to buy.

2 Find out the total price for all the things you want. Get an assistant to write it down for you.

3 Pay the total cost to the cashier and get your receipt. There is often only one cashier and you might have to queue. If the queue is long, then have a friend stand in it while you check out the things you want to buy.

4 Take your receipt back to the counter, show it to the assistant and pick up your goods, which will often have been wrapped while you were paying.

Opening hours

Opening hours vary considerably and below is just a rough guide. It is always risky going to a place at midday as invariably they will be closed for an hour for lunch but this time varies from 12.00 to 15.00. It is best to get a Russian to ring and ask the opening times. It is for this reason that phone numbers of museums have been included in the guide. In Moscow, people like to sleep in a bit more than in other towns and most private shops, trade organisations, universities etc open between 10.00 and 11.00.

- Government offices, Monday–Friday, 09.00(10.00)–17.00(18.00), closed one hour for lunch
- Banks, Monday–Friday, 09.00–17:00, closed 12.00–13.00
- Private currency exchange offices, seven days, 10.00–18.00
- Food shops, Monday–Saturday, 08.00(09.00)–19.00(20.00), closed for lunch 13.00–14.00 in 95% of cases with the remaining 5% closing 14.00–15.00
- General goods stores (univermag), Monday–Friday 09.00(10.00)–20.00(21.00), no lunch hour
- Railway ticket offices, seven days, 07.00–23:00 (most stations), 24 hours (large stations)
- Restaurants, seven days, 11.00–23.00, closed early afternoon
- Canteens, Monday–Saturday, 08.00–19.00
- Cafés and bars, Monday–Saturday, 10.00–late
- Museums, Tuesday–Sunday, 10.00–17.00, closed one hour for lunch. Museum opening times vary considerably and some have their day off on Tuesday, Wednesday or Thursday. All are open at the weekend. The museums normally stop ticket sales 30 minutes before closing time. Museums often display the sign NE RABOTAET (не работает) or NA REMONTE (на ремонте), meaning they are closed for repairs.

COMMUNICATIONS

The communication systems of the former Soviet Union are about the worst in the developed world. Fortunately they are getting better, particularly the internet system.

Post offices and mail

Telephone, telegram and mail services are normally available at the post office. Post offices are divided into two main sections, occasionally located in separate buildings. The first is the postal office from where you send postal items and telegrams; the second is the inter-city and international telephone exchange called the *Peregovorny Punt*. Both sections are difficult to work with.

The postal section of the post office has three main counters: normal for letters and postcards, *banderoli* for books and documents, and *posylki* for other items. The normal section also serves as the poste restante. Unfortunately, the three sections are also occasionally located in different buildings. Be aware that the postal service is very unreliable and items that are valuable often never leave the country. To increase the chance of your mail making it, send everything by registered post. While it is technically possible to mail books and other things, it is not recommended that you do this as it is both very time consuming and frustrating to organise. To export a book you need to pay a tax based on the book's cost. Remember, when you send parcels, don't seal them before going to the post office as they need to be examined.

Airmail letters normally take three weeks to travel from Moscow to anywhere in the West; add a few weeks if you are sending them from other places. If you send material by land and sea mail, allow three to six months for the item to arrive.

Post offices can be very confusing for foreigners as they may have 30 or more counters but only a few have anything to do with mail. The rest are for paying pensions and bills. Your options are to watch for people who are sending letters or say *pismo*, meaning "letter", to the counter staff.

Telephone calls
Telephone calls fall into three categories: local, inter-city and international.

Local calls   These are made in phone boxes on street corners and require a token (*zheton*) which can be bought at post offices and metro station ticket offices.

Inter-city calls   Calls between cities in the former Soviet Union can be made from homes and offices by dialling 8, waiting for the dial tone, then dialling the city code (shown at the start of each city's description in *Part Two*) and the local phone number.

International calls   These can be made from homes and offices by dialling 8, waiting for the dial tone, then dialling 10 and the country code, then the area code and finally the local telephone number. From most hotels you can book international calls but, be warned, the cost of this may be high. An even more expensive, but convenient, way is to buy a phone card and use the special card phones in the upmarket hotels. Calls using these cards can be very expensive and costs of $10 a minute are not unknown. The cheapest, but most difficult, way to make an international call is to go to the telephone section of the post office called *Peregovorny Punt*. Even if you don't want to make a call, you should visit one of these chaotic places to hear tens of locals in individual phone booths yelling to overcome the poor line quality and each other's shouting.

To make a long-distance or international call, you need to fill in a form stating the town, phone number, name of the receiving party, and the length of time you want to talk for. You then pay for the call and wait until your name and telephone booth number are called over the loudspeaker. As soon as you pick up the phone in the booth, your time starts. The operator will tell you over the phone when there are 30 seconds left. If your call can't get through, you get a refund. A typical wait is from 15 minutes to an hour but if you want it to be put through quicker, you can pay a premium for a quick *srochny* call. In some places there are inter-city direct-dial pay phones (*mezhdugorodni avtomat*) which can instantly connect you with other cities in Russia. Tokens for these phones are bought from the cashier. Due to a strange twist of logic, these automatic phones are about twice as expensive as booking a call with the cashier.

If you are making an international call, remember the time zone differences.

Useful numbers

To get assistance by phone, dial the following numbers. If you don't speak Russian, get help from a Russian.

01	Fire
02	Police
03	Ambulance
04	Gas leaks
07/008	Long-distance telephone connections
088	Time
09	Directory assistance

Fax

Faxing to the countries of the former Soviet Union can be very frustrating as the poor quality of their telephone lines frequently results in transmission failure. Fortunately, the phone networks are being upgraded with Western technology which means that faxing to the major Russian, Ukrainian and Belarusian cities is becoming easier.

Telegrams

Telegrams are the easiest way to communicate internationally if there is no fax available. Any post office will send them. They are also relatively cheap. Unlike telexes, which only a few post offices can send, telegrams are sent to the address of the recipient via their country's national post office. They are usually delivered a day or two after they are sent. Telegrams are commonly used within the former Soviet Union to book accommodation and arrange meetings.

Email

Surprising as it might seem, electronic mail is readily available in most Russian cities. Russians have taken to the information superhighway in a big way and most international companies have internet connections as it is the cheapest and quickest way to communicate internationally. There are numerous service providers in Russia which you can connect to and the best way to find their details is to get the file *E-mail and Internet in the NIS and Baltics* at http://www.irex.org/FAQ.htm. If you want to send a one-off email, both the Travellers' Guest House in Moscow and St Petersburg International Hostel offer the service for a small fee.

ENTERTAINMENT

In large cities there is always a range of events: the circus, ballet, opera, classical music, football matches, pop concerts, for example. Tickets to these can be bought at ticket kiosks in most metro stations and pedestrian underpasses. Each kiosk displays in its window the tickets that it has, so buying them is simply a matter of pointing. There is also a large number of museums, exhibitions and cinemas in every city. All foreign films are dubbed into Russian. Cinema listings are displayed on boards around the city. As there will invariably be a concert, parade or performance on one of the official holidays, consult the calendar in *Chapter Two*, *page 29*, so you don't miss it.

Locals entertain themselves by going to the *banya* or *dacha* at the weekends. Outdoor activities include fishing, picnics and berry and mushroom picking. If you get asked go along, as these outings are always interesting.

Local English-language newspapers and magazines are a good source of information on special events and entertainment. These periodicals exist in Moscow, St Petersburg and Kiev. They can be bought at most hotels and in some newspaper kiosks around the cities. For information on these, see *Appendix Four*.

MONEY

All the countries in the former Soviet Union are cash economies. The best cash is the US dollar; other good ones are the British pound and German deutschmark. In the Russian far east, Japanese yen are also accepted.

For a one-month stay on an organised tour, it is worth bringing US$200–500 in cash, with about $100 of smaller notes ($1, 5 and 10).

With a few rare exceptions, such as at Moscow's Sovincentre, automatic teller machines are non-existent.

Customs regulations prohibit sending money through the international mail system and if cash is found in the mail, it will be confiscated.

Credit cards and travellers cheques
Only in the major hotels and restaurants in the largest cities are credit cards accepted. The most widely accepted seems to be Visa. Cash advances against a credit card are readily available in Moscow and St Petersburg for about 3–5% commission but in other cities can be difficult and expensive to organise. As credit card fraud in the countries of the former Soviet Union is rampant, always keep your receipts and check your statement as soon as you arrive home.

Travellers cheques are not widely accepted. Do not depend on these for cash.

Currency exchange
It is technically illegal for Russian organisations to accept US$ as all payments have to be made in roubles. However, in most places something can be arranged with dollars although this is not the case for government services such as train tickets.

Finding an exchange point is never difficult as most large hotels and airports have them. In addition, there are exchange kiosks dotted around large cities and, even in the smallest town, you can always exchange at the local bank. As the rouble is a free floating currency, there is no black market rate any more so, if people on the street offer to exchange, refuse.

Since the collapse of the Soviet Union, each former republic has introduced its own currency.

Russia
Russia's currency is the rouble. A rouble used to be made up of 100 kopeks but, since the massive inflation of the early 1990s, kopeks have been withdrawn and the smallest denominations are now 1, 5, 10, 20, 50 and 100 rouble coins. Notes include 100, 200, 500, 1000, 5000, 10,000, 50,000 and 100,000 roubles. Notes with Lenin's head or the old Soviet Union national emblem on them have been superseded and are not legal tender.

The last few years have seen yearly inflation rates of 500%, but the situation has stabilised, with inflation now down to double figures. The exchange rate in August 1996 was US$1 = 5,136 roubles, £1 = 8,060 roubles.

Belarus
After an initial enormous depreciation, the Belarusian rouble has remained relatively stable since 1994. In August 1996, the exchange rate was US$1 = 15,610 Belarusian roubles, £1 = 24,500 Belarusian roubles.

Ukraine
Following Ukraine's independence, the country introduced a provisional currency known as the *karbovantsi* or "coupon" until the new currency, called a *hryvna*, is introduced. In August 1996, the exchange rate was US$1 = 53,700 karbovanets, £1 = 84,300 karbovanets.

Counterfeit US notes
Counterfeit US currency is a major problem in all countries of the former Soviet Union with claims that up to 40% of all notes are fakes. The scale of the problem was highlighted in January 1996 when the US Treasurer Mary Ellen Withrow claimed that $40 million worth of false bills were in circulation with two-thirds of these circulating outside the USA. New $100 bills were issued in 1996 to make counterfeiting more difficulty but even before they were released several "new" $100 notes had turned up in Russia.

Russian banks and companies will often refuse to accept notes that are more than a few years old and if they do accept them, they will invariably discount the bills several percent. As well as being paranoid about fake currency, many Russians mistakenly believe that the old notes are not legal tender any more. Their belief stems from the Soviet government's practice of replacing old currency with new notes and then outlawing the old currency within a few months.

MISCELLANEOUS
Bribes
Bribes, known as *vzyatka*, are common in the former Soviet Union but unless you are well versed in Russian and the Russian ways, don't ever attempt this. If you are travelling with a Russian let them do it. A better approach for foreigners is to be patient and go through the official channels. If a bribe is expected, let the Russian initiate it. It's appropriate to give a small gift in return for someone's "assistance" in getting a railway ticket, a tour of a closed museum or a reserved room in a "booked-up" hotel.

Electricity
The electricity supply in Russia, Belarus and Ukraine is 220 volt AC, 50Hz and a standard European two-pin plug is used. Adaptors should be purchased before you leave home as they cannot be easily bought in these countries.

Insurance
You should take out medical and travel insurance. A high level of insurance (similar to western Europe) is advisable to allow you to recover the cost of western medical services and international evacuation. This is particularly important if you intend to travel outside the major cities; here it is recommended that you organise evacuation for serious illness as that can be very expensive.

Language

Russian, Belarusian and Ukrainian are all Slavic languages and use the Cyrillic script. While each language is distinct, if you are going to learn any it is best to choose Russian as it was the universal language of the entire former Soviet Union and every citizen has some knowledge of it. At first the Cyrillic alphabet appears complicated but it can be quickly mastered. If you take the time to do this, you will find travelling around much easier and more enjoyable. While some guidebooks recommend taking a basic Russian language guide and reading it on the train, very few people seem to find the time to do so. A much better suggestion is to learn some Russian before you go or take a short course in Moscow before you embark on your Russian trip.

It would also be polite to learn some Belarusian and Ukrainian but don't be surprised if locals don't know their official state language as there is a large population of native Russians in each country. If you do nothing else, refer to *Appendices One, Two* and *Three* at the end of this book.

Photography

In the Soviet period, there was a large list of things that it was forbidden to photograph. The list included military facilities, metros, railway yards, railway stations, tunnels, bridges, airports, power stations and industrial enterprises. Today, most of the restrictions have been lifted but many officials still claim that these subjects should not be photographed. These people may physically stop you from taking the photo or take the film out of your camera. Your best action is to take photos discreetly if you think someone may object or ask them first. In addition, taking photos of subjects that locals perceive as backwards or ugly is frowned upon. Again, it is often best to ask first.

Photography in churches is normally discouraged too and you should never take photos with a flash, as this damages the icons. Having your photo taken standing in front of an icon is considered disrespectful.

TECHNICAL FILM RECOMMENDATIONS FOR RUSSIA

Colour negative film   Without the aid of colour correction filters on your camera lens, 400ASA (preferably Kodak) film works well as it has a higher base fog giving warmth to the cooler colour temperatures in the predominantly overcast conditions of Russia.

Transparencies   Fujicrome 400ASA is good due to its warmth while Ektacrome is too cool. 400ASA is a good film speed for all-round light conditions.

Black and white film   In the flat contrast conditions of Russia, Agfapan 400 achieves high contrast with minimal grain. Print with Agfa products for best results. To get more contrast use a yellow filter.

For the avid photographer willing to experiment with specific underexposure, the contrast may be expanded by complementing the development process. For fog conditions, it is better to overexpose and then increase the development to give a greater range of tonality. In darker conditions, underexposure combined with increased development will give more tonality.

Tatyana Pozar-Burgar of Darko Photography, Australia

Common, Western brands of film can be bought readily everywhere. The larger film retailers include the price of development, but not printing, of the film in their prices.

Physical fitness
A moderate degree of physical fitness is needed in Russia. No special consideration is given to the disabled in the countries of the former Soviet Union.

Time zones
During the Soviet era, there were ten time zones across the country. Today, there are nine zones across Russia, while Ukraine and Belarus are on the same time zone which is one hour behind Moscow. The time on Russian railway and plane timetables is invariably Moscow time regardless of which zone you are in. So, remember to add or subtract the appropriate time difference to work out the train or plane's local arrival and departure times.

Toilets
Finding toilets is always hard. In big towns there is the occasional public toilet but your best bet is any large public building such as a cinema, museum or restaurant. You will normally have to pay a few roubles to enter a public toilet or perhaps the museum entry fee. In small towns there is usually a toilet near the station and that's about all. So the best advice is to go just before you get off the train, and always use a toilet when you find one.

Chapter Four

The Railway Network

RUSSIAN RAILWAYS

Four years after the demise of the Soviet Union, virtually all monolithic state institutions have collapsed, with the exception of the Russian railways. However, even the railways may disintegrate following years of minimal capital investment, high taxes and a $1.5 billion debt due to customers and governments withholding payments. In any normal economy, the Russian railways would have been declared bankrupt but in Russia such an option is unthinkable due to their importance.

Russia's railways are controlled by the Ministry of Railways (MPS) through its 19 divisional railways which manage a total of 87,500 route kilometres. Russian railways occupy the following places in the world railway systems:

- First place for the length of electrified lines
- Second place for the length of operational rail lines, the amount of freight (tons) and the amount of freight distance (tons.km)
- Third place for the amount of passengers and passenger distance (passenger.km)

The MPS owns the vast majority of Russia's passenger rail systems with the notable exceptions of metros, which are each controlled by its city's municipal council, and a number of small rural railways. The mostly narrow-gauge rural railways were often built to take coal, peat or farm produce to market but now offer commuter services. Examples of these just east of Moscow include the railway around Pereslavl-Zalessky owned by the Kupan Co-operative Railway (formerly Kupan Transportation Authority) and the railway between Roshal and Cherusti owned by the Urshel Transportation Authority. The Urshel railway is both narrow and broad gauge. The table on page 58 presents selected characteristics of MPS railways.

An empire within an empire

Russian railways are more than just a transport service, they are an empire in their own right. They control a workforce of 2.15 million, run the nation's largest dedicated telephone network with over a million lines, manage 11 universities and own 402 hospitals. In addition, they have their own farms, and railway manufacturing facilities and own over 90% of all buildings in many towns.

Traditionally, the railways have been the driving force in opening up Russia's vast untouched regions both by building the track and by funding civic and industrial infrastructure. One such project, called the BAM Railway, which was

Russia's most costly civil-engineering project, is about to be reactivated which will again see the MPS controlling the development of an area 3,100km long and several hundred kilometres wide.

The railways' political clout is illustrated by the fact that they are not subordinated to the Ministry of Transport and are represented by the inner cabinet Minister of Railways, Gennadi Fadeev. The power derives from the railways' dominance of the transport sector. In 1994 railways carried a massive 74% of Russian freight (tons.km), excluding pipelines, and 47% of passengers (passengers.km).

Passenger services

There are two main types of MPS trains: suburban electric trains and long-distance (mostly overnight) 10- to 20-carriage trains.

Suburban services are extremely unprofitable, usually achieving just 10–20% cost recovery. Raising ticket prices is politically difficult. This was illustrated by Yeltsin's promise during the last presidential election campaign that if the railways raised ticket prices he would be among the first to lie down on the tracks to protest. Similarly, as a electoral sweetener, in October this year, Prime Minister Chernomyrdin announced that transport prices would be frozen until the end of the year. The MPS solution to this problem is to transfer the control of suburban railways to local governments and let them worry about the problem.

Long-distance services usually achieve 42–70% cost recovery depending on the route, carriage class and train type.

Railway safety

Rail is still the safest transport means in Russia with just 0.096 deaths per billion passenger.km compared with 4.104 for air and 33.269 for motor vehicles in 1994.

However, looking at crime, the railways are perceived as being increasingly risky. In 1994, 71,200 railway crimes, including 170 murders, 342 woundings, 114 rapes and 737 armed robberies, were reported. The most dangerous trains were those heading for central Asia, with the safest being those travelling to the Baltic states. The most common crime was theft when passengers were sleeping. Fortunately, the most widely published crime of putting an entire carriage to sleep with sleeping gas and robbing all the passengers was a hoax dreamt up by a journalist (see *page 35*).

To combat the crime and alleviate travellers' fear, the MPS now employs a 50,000 strong Transport Militia, controlled by the Ministry of Internal Affairs.

Customer service improves despite being ignored

Customer service has always been the least prestigious sector of the railways as it was a seller's market. However, over the last year there has been a marked improvement in railway services which has left Russians saying that Russia is really changing.

The impetus for the change appears to have come from a combination of commercial pressures and from workers afraid of job losses. Manifestations of the client culture on trains include announcements at the beginning and the end of journeys, complimentary bags of toiletries, pre-made beds and individually packed sheets which reduce the chance of getting used sheets. At stations, the change is epitomised by the 1995 renovation of the Moscow station at St Petersburg where a business centre has opened with telephone, fax and photocopy services.

Crisis time coming

The last few years of minimal investment in Russian railways is gradually wearing down the network. To date this has been masked by the using up of surplus rolling stock, increasing speed restrictions and parts cannibalism of locomotives. However, within a few years the Russian government is going to have to make a choice: either accept the high economic costs of a woefully inadequate transport backbone or reinvest massively in the railways.

RUSSIAN RAILWAYS AT A GLANCE

Characteristic	1995 statistic
Operational route distance (km)	87,500
Total length of electrified lines (km)	38,800
Total length of DC line (km)	19,000
Total length of AC lines (km)	19,800
Number of operational electric locomotives	3,729
Number of operational diesel locomotives	2,050
Number of operational freight wagons	396,000
Number of operational passenger carriages	36,179

Steam engines

While working steam engines are virtually extinct in Russia, there are an estimated 1,000 to 5,000 steam engines in storage depots. There are also a handful that are used to pull tourist trains and a few hundred that are used to generate hot water and steam.

Steam engine storage depots

Steam engine storage depots (Базазапаса) contain strategic reserves of locomotives in near working order in case a war erupts. Unlike electric or diesel engines, combustible fuel can always be found to power the steam engines. At the end of the Cold War, over 9,000 locomotives were held in these reserves throughout the USSR, including 300 western engines, some of them German TE 52 class captured at the end of World War II and American Yea class supplied as part of the Lend Lease war effort.

Today, almost every railway administration, of which there are 19 in Russia, five in the Ukraine and one in Belarus, has a steam engine storage depot. These include Roslavl on the Moscow railway, Amazar and Mogzon on the Zabaikalsk railway, Kormilovka on the West Siberian railway, Sharya on the Northern railway, Negarelae on the Belarusian railways, Zlatoust on the South Urals railway, Tikhoretsk on the North Caucasus railway, and Morozovskaya on the Privolzhskaya railway.

Most have about 40 to 100 freight locomotives of the classes L and ER. There are also between four and six World War II vintage armoured trains in working order scattered throughout Russia's storage depots.

The Roslavl steam engine storage depot is typical of most. The depot consists of the repair works at Roslavl 2 station and, about 10km away, the storage depot containing 90 L, P36, Su and TE (German) class locomotives. There were 200 locomotives in 1992; most run on coal but two run on fuel oil. The open-air depot is described as guarded, but invariably no-one is around. The locomotives have had their cranks removed, greased, boxed up and hung near the drive wheels. All moving parts have been coated in a thick grease and windows are boarded up with wood. According to the maintenance staff, it would take only two days for the engines to be ready for operation. Every two years, the engines are brought to the repair works and stripped down, cleaned, tested, painted and re-packed with grease. This process takes one month per train with two to four engines being worked on simultaneously by the 10 to 15 workshop staff. In addition, four people continuously paint and grease the locomotives in the depot. While the last permanent steam locomotive was phased out at Roslavl in 1968, occasionally an engine is recommissioned for shunting and hot-water production such as for a month in 1992 and a week in 1994.

Today, the stock at storage depots is slowly disintegrating as maintenance has virtually stopped now that the army, which used to pay for the depots, is no longer willing or able to pay. In addition, engines are being robbed of souvenirs for Western collectors and sold as scrap to Germany and Korea. A number of Russian enterprises are purchasing complete engines to use them as steam and hot-water generators and a few have been sold to Western countries as museum pieces, for example two German TE class locomotives which were purchased by Switzxerland in the early 1990s.

Steam-powered tourist trains

There are no regular steam-powered tourist trains, but there are a number of private companies that work with the individual Russian railway departments to organise special trips. These engines are normally P36 and Su class.

Steam train generators

The vast majority of operating steam engines in Russia today are used for their steam and hot-water producing abilities. These engines usually have their running gear disconnected and plumbing permanently attached. The most popular type of engines for this purpose are the most powerful freight locomotives, and these can be seen from the railway at Isakogorka near Arkhangelsk and Novy Urgal. The engines are also used in factories such as two American Lend-Lease engines installed in 1994 by the Progress Aerospace Company in Arsenev, 100km northeast of Vladivostok. They were purchased after the local authorities switched off power and heat to the factory because of the unpaid 8 billion roubles utility charge. According to the factory directory, the company could not pay because its customer, the government, had not paid for the Ka-50 and Mi-34 helicopters and An-74 aircraft it had purchased.

To ensure that the stationary steam engines are in good condition, every three weeks the boilers are run up to maximum pressure. Pressure maintenance is checked and samples of the water sent off to laboratories to check for scaling and impurities in the pipes. One of the problems for the factories is finding qualified steam engine drivers. As this skill is not now taught at the railway institutes, the operators are mostly retired drivers.

Steam engines are also run on little used rural railway lines to bring animals from collective farms to market. The hot water is ideal for cleaning out the wagons.

Railway museums

There are dozens of railway museums in Russia but the vast majority are small exhibitions in railway departments, institutes and factories which concentrate on political aspects such as those workers who have received heroic railwaymen awards. The nation's main railway museum is in St Petersburg but this does not have any full size rolling stock. Instead, it has inaccurate models, poor photos and general information. It has no significant archive material as what wasn't destroyed during World War II was, and still is, restricted. The largest open-air museums are at Shushary near St Petersburg and, although not covered in this book, in Tashkent in Uzbekistan. Smaller but interesting museums can be found in Khabarovsk, Lebyazhe, Mytishchi, Novy Urgal, Omsk, Severobaikalsk, Svobodny, Tver, Tynda and Volgograd. For information on all these museums, see under the respective cities.

Children's railways

To encourage young people to develop an interest, and possibly a career, in railways, children's railways were built. These consist of narrow-gauge railways in which teenagers run everything from the ticket booths to track maintenance and from signal boxes to conducting. The only adult is the train engineer.

The first children's railway was opened in 1935 in Tbilisi and in 1990 there were 50 dotted around the former Soviet Union. Each consist of 1.5–5km of 750mm wide track, one or two engines, four or five passenger carriages, a station, teaching facilities, repair shop and laboratory. In 1990, 2 million children and adults took rides on the railways which only operated during school holidays. In that year, over 50,000 children participated in the railway education programme which runs for three years and covers theory, history and safe operations of railways.

Today, children's railways operate in Minsk, Kiev, Chita and Svobodny. There are also children's railways in Rostov-na-Don, Baku, Erevan, Dnepropetrovsk, Khabarovsk, Kharkov, Nizhni Novgorod, Zaprozhe, Khashuri, Yaroslavl and Yuzhno-Sakhalinsk.

TRAIN TRAVEL
Types of train

The major classes of train are fast, passenger, suburban, and *firmenny* trains. There are several other minor classes which are listed in detail in the *Train numbers* section on *page 65*.

Fast trains (*skorye poezdy* скорые поезды) are long-distance express trains stopping only at the largest stations. These trains are typically up to 24 carriages long.

Passenger trains (*passazhirskie poezdy* пассажирские поезды) are also inter-city trains but they stop regularly for locals to get on and off.

Suburban trains (*prigorodnye poezdy* Пригорогные поезды) are normally electric suburban trains like those in the West.

An exciting development is the class of train called *firmenny* (Фирменные поезды). These trains all meet high standards of service, comfort and conditions as defined by government standards. These standards include: the carriages must be less than ten years old or have been factory-reconstructed within the last decade; all bedding must be less than two years old; paintwork must be in good condition; the interior must be well maintained and include flowers in *coupés* and new carpet throughout; passengers must be offered tea in the morning and evening; and the top bunks of *coupés* must be made up. Another requirement for accreditation is that all *provodniks* (conductors) undergo specialist training. All of these conditions make working on *firmenny* trains prestigious and consequently the provodniks are genuinely pleased to help. Their service contrasts markedly with that on most other trains.

All *firmenny* trains have names, such as *Rossiya, Red Arrow* and *Vyatka*, and in timetables have the letter F (Ф) after their number. While most *firmenny* trains have appeared since the early 1990s, they were first introduced in 1931 on the route Moscow–St Petersburg. In the Soviet period, trains that foreigners were permitted to travel on were invariably *firmenny*. However, there is little comparison between the clean but not very pleasant Soviet era *firmenny* and today's *firmenny* trains.

In 1995, there were 82 *firmenny* trains in Russia which accounted for 15% of all trains. The government wants to increase this to 100% by the year 1997. The reason for this is that *firmenny* trains have a cost recovery of 70% compared with 42–48% for fast and passenger trains. To achieve this, the ticket prices of *firmenny* trains are 1.2–1.5 times that of fast trains. For some Russians this is exorbitant and it contributed to a 15% decrease in passengers in 1995 in spite of the fact that in some places there are no alternative trains.

Because *firmenny trains* are commercially orientated and receptive to passenger needs, new routes are always opening; for example, in 1995–6:

- The first of the seven *firmenny* trains known as *Rossiya* which travel the Trans-Siberian has been repainted red, white and blue (like the Russian flag), fitted out with small video players in each compartment of the *SV* carriage, and a mirror installed near the boiler so that the *provodnik* can see what is happening in the corridor from his compartment.

- The Angara *firmenny* train was introduced between Irkutsk and Gidrostroitel (Bratsk) and is fitted with video players in the *SV* carriage.

- The Gilui *firmenny* train was introduced between Tynda and Blagoveshchensk.

- The Vologda Sunrise *firmenny* train was introduced between St Petersburg and Vologda.

- Routes being tested for *firmenny* trains are Cherepovets–Moscow and Vologda–Murmansk.

Types of carriage

There are four types of carriage: *obshchi, platskartny, coupé* and *SV*.

Obshchi (общий) is the lowest class of carriage and it is an old *platskartny* carriage with no bedding. Up to 73 people can be crammed into a carriage and there is no seat numbering. They are normally dirty, stuffy and hell if you have to sleep on them overnight. They are okay to travel on for a few hours but, without any padding, they quickly get uncomfortable. These carriages are normally only attached to passenger trains and used by workmen or fishermen.

Platskartny (платцкартный) are the most common type of carriages in Russia but not the most pleasant to travel in. They are sleeping carriages with two tiers of berths in open compartments on one side of the corridor and a row of berths arranged lengthwise down the other side. These cars accommodate 58 passengers. Mattresses and pillows are supplied. By an ingenious mechanism, the aisle berths can be lifted up and down to make aisle seats and tables. These carriages are noisy, stuffy and lack security. Avoid the berth next to the toilet otherwise the banging door will be next to your head. It is not recommended to travel in *platskartny* unless you sleep well and have no valuables.

Coupé (купейный) carriages are the most common way to travel as they offer privacy, security and comfort at an economical price. A *coupé* carriage consists of several four-bunk enclosed cabins. As you will be sharing the cabin with Russians, there is plenty of opportunity to practice your hand signals or test a phrase book. Most *coupé* carriages have 36 berths while one carriage on every train has only 32 berths. The reason for this is that one of the four-berth *coupés* is occupied by the train's chief *provodnik* who mans the radio, sells tickets and sorts out any problems which the *provodnik* cannot handle.

SV which is short for *spalny vagon* (СВ-спальный вагон) is by far the most comfortable way of travelling. *SV* carriages have two toilets, a *provodnik* compartment and eight two-berth compartments, each containing two beds on the same level. The newest *SV* carriages have seven two-berth compartments, a kitchen and, best of all, a shower. *SV* carriages are also called *myaky* (мягкий) carriages.

Travel in luxury

During Soviet times, very senior party, government, military and railway officials travelled around in luxury saloon railway cars when they didn't want to fly. These cars are rare but every administrative railway has several. These can be hired and attached to regular passenger trains or special tourist trains. Most private rail tours offer these sorts of carriages.

There are two sorts of saloon car. The older style is for one dignitary and staff. It consists of one master bedroom with en-suite bathroom including a bath, two two- or four-berth *coupés,* a kitchen, toilet and large open area at one end of the carriage for meetings. The newer sort is for delegations and contains three two-berth *coupés,* a kitchen, toilet, small study, and large open area in the centre of the carriage. Both saloon styles normally carry a staff of two: a cook and a *provodnik.*

Coupé compartments

The four-berth *coupé* compartments are separated from the corridor by a sliding door which can be locked from the inside. The *provodnik* has a key which can open this lock from the outside. As an additional safety device, there is a flick-down lock high up on the inside of the door which cannot be operated from the outside. Some people go to the trouble of jamming a cork in this lock, ensuring that no-one can open it from the outside, by whatever means.

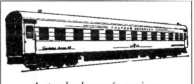

A standard coupé carriage

The two top bunks can be put up during the day to give you more head room. Under the bottom two bunks are luggage spaces which are very secure as they can't be reached unless you get off the bunk. The corridor has a false ceiling which makes space for a luggage shelf accessible from your compartment. At the end of each bed is a reading lamp, and the two- or three-way switch near the door controls the main cabin lights. The loudspeaker volume knob is usually above the window. There is a bottle opener under the table. If the table is in the way, you can fold it up.

Although the bunks are well padded, a mattress and pillow are supplied. You will need to hire a linen set which includes two sheets, a pillow case and small towel. Don't lose any of these as you will have to pay for them. The hire charge is about $1.

In winter, blankets are supplied, but during summer you have to ask for them. As the *provodnik* has only a few which are normally reserved for children, you may have to beg to get one. However, in winter the windows are locked and the heater is turned up high, meaning that you swelter even without a blanket and the cockroaches become more active. To make matters worse, the windows can only be opened with a special key. The only ventilation is a roof vent which can be turned on and off.

There are advantages and disadvantages to sleeping in the upper bunk. While this berth allows you to go to bed when you want and gives you more privacy, it is hotter, difficult to climb up to and much brighter, being closer to the main cabin light.

The worst compartment is the last one, with berth numbers 33–36. This one is closest to the smelly toilet, over the wheels which gives you a rough ride and is closest to the banging corridor door. The compartment with berth numbers 13–16 gives the best ride.

Life in a coupé carriage

Life in the carriage is dominated by the conductor or *provodnik* (проводник). There are normally two *provodniks* on fast and passenger trains. They share a cabin at the end of the carriage. Their job is to ensure the carriage is clean, everyone has tickets and no problems occur. The most zealous *provodniks* will put down a mat in the carriage's entrance so that no-one tramps dirt or snow through their carriage. During summer holidays, the professional *provodniks* are replaced by students who often just wear a track suit with the railways' winged emblem pinned on. At least once a day, all the cabins will be swept and the corridor mopped. If you wonder how the provodnik stops the mop bucket from slopping water around when the train is jolting, the answer is that they put a half full bottle in the bucket which breaks up any waves.

On *firmenny* trains, the *provodnik* will always offer you morning and evening tea in a glass held in a holder called a *podstakannik*. Normally, you pay for the tea as you hand in your sheets at the end of the trip and each cup costs about $0.10.

If you have any problems, such as wanting to move to another berth, go to the *provodnik* and if the matter is not resolved to your satisfaction, go to the chief *provodnik* who is normally located in the centre of the train.

There is a rubbish bin at the end of the corridor in front of the toilet. Unfortunately, environmental awareness has yet to reach most of the *provodniks* as they normally empty the bin by throwing the rubbish out of the train as it is moving.

At the end of the corridor near the *provodnik*'s compartment is a hot-water urn known as a *samovar* (самовар), *kipyatilnik* (кипятильник) which means water heater, or a *titan* (титан) which was the brand name of the first hot-water urns. You can use this water for tea, coffee, soup and dehydrated Chinese noodles. Some *samovars* have a flat top which means that you can warm a meal on them. Most *samovars* are electric, but there are a few coal ones left. A gauge on the side of the *samovar* indicates the temperature. You should use the water only when it is in the red band. Although there is a drinking-water tap near the *samovar,* it is better to pour the *samovar* water into a heavy-duty canteen at night and in the morning it will be cool enough to drink. If the water is not hot in your *samovar* try the next carriage and, if all else fails, go and ask at the restaurant car.

There are no showers on the train and the only washing facility is the basin in the toilet. Water will come out if you push up the lever just behind the spout. Bring your own soap. There is an electric power point near the toilet which is designed for shavers but this often does not work.

The worst aspect of the carriage is the toilet. This is normally unpleasant and most people use it by squatting on its rim rather than sitting on it. Bring your own toilet paper and a reserve roll just in case.

Smoking is forbidden in the carriages with the exception of the connecting ways at the end of each carriage. Interestingly, as well as the overhead light in the connecting way, there is a recessed light covered by a sheet of tin with holes in it. These dimmed lights are designed to let out only a minimal amount of light for blackout conditions and illustrate the Soviet obsession with preparations for war.

In the corridor, there are seats which you can flip down and more power points and loudspeaker knobs. Often the corridor windows are the only ones that can be opened and sitting there in the fresh breeze is extremely enjoyable.

Wear comfortable clothes on the train; a tracksuit and slip-on shoes are ideal. Never sit on someone else's sheets as this is considered dirty and rude. Take earplugs if you can't stand snoring.

About every three hours, the train stops for 10 to 20 minutes while engines are changed, passenger get on and off, the bearings in the bogies are checked, and carriages are added or taken off the train. In winter the provodniks will get off and chip off the ice from the toilet and wash basin outlets. Your fellow passengers will often get off to buy food and beer from hawkers on the station. The best food to buy is traditional Russian "take away" which is a parcel containing a few home-cooked potatoes, pickled cucumbers, brown bread and boiled eggs. These are invariably sold by little old women. Don't wander too far as the train waits for no-one.

Dining cars

Most trains have a restaurant car which normally has just one entrée and a main course. They will often sell alcohol which is curious as it is illegal to drink on a train. If you do drink, keep it discreet as this saves any hassles.

Two-thirds of the dining car contains seats while the remainder is occupied by a kitchen, pantry, scullery and refrigerators. There are 12 four-seat tables together with a table for the supervisor who is also the cashier. Technically, a car's staff consists of seven: two waitresses, a cashier/supervisor, three kitchen staff and another man whose function is difficult to discover. As the car stays with the train for the whole journey, their sleeping berths are in the baggage car. Nowadays, most restaurant cars are staffed by about three people so service is very slow.

There are also some brand-new dining cars which consist of a buffet selling processed food and four *coupé* compartments.

Train numbers

Train numbers are useful for travellers to identify what class and speed of train they are getting. Within each railway administrative area, each train has a unique pair of train numbers. A train with an even number indicates that it is going east or north, while an odd number indicates it is going west or south. For example, the No 1 Trans-Siberian train runs westward (Vladivostok–Moscow) while No 2 Trans-Siberian train runs eastward (Moscow–Vladivostok). The only confusion arises when a train changes direction and in this case, it is given two numbers. For example, train No 21/22 Murmansk–St Petersburg departs Murmansk southward as train No 21 and about 20km before arriving in St Petersburg, it does a loop to the south and arrives into the station from the south (ie: heading northwards). Consequently its number becomes No 22.

Numbers	Class	Comments
1–100	Fast (скорые)	These trains only stop at large cities every few hours where engines are changed and passenger axles checked.
101–150	Fast, summer only (скорые)	These fast trains only run in summer.
151–170	Express (скоростные)	These trains are meant to reach speeds of 141–200km/h. There are only a few of these such as the Moscow–St Petersburg ER-200 train (average speed 130km/h) and Aurora (average speed 108km/h).
171–300	Passenger (пассажирские)	These trains make up the majority in Russia, Belarus and Ukraine trains. They stop regularly at large and medium cities.
301–400	Passenger, summer only (пассажирские)	These passenger trains only run in summer.
401–600	Miscellaneous passenger (пассажирские)	These passenger trains are those that do not fit into other categories, such as irregular and tourist trains.
601–700	Short distance (местные)	These passenger trains do not go more than 150km.
901–948	Mail and luggage (Почтовые и багажные)	These trains carry both mail and luggage and usually have a few *platskartny* (never *coupé*) carriages attached. They usually stop for 10 minutes to several hours at every station and are consequently very slow. Most passengers are workers visiting remote towns.
951–998	Combined freight and passenger (Грузовые/ пассажирские)	These freight trains usually have a few *platskartny* (never *coupé*) carriages attached. They are only used on lines with little traffic such as the Circumbaikal railway. They are slow and unreliable as you never know how much freight has to be dropped off or picked up.
6001–6999	Suburban (Пригорогные)	These trains are usually electric suburban trains, but in non-electrified areas they are diesel multiple-units.

Railway stations

Architecture   There is a marked variation between railway stations depending on their year of construction. The oldest stations of the last century were designed as military quarters and built for defence. By the turn of the century, wooden railway stations were decorated with turrets and other traditional Russian ornaments. In the early 1900s, both the ticket office and waiting room were housed in a single-storey wooden building. Invariably, the station was painted light brown and had ornamentation along the eaves. A picket fence surrounds most platforms. There are very few of these stations left but they can still be seen off the main lines. During the 1930s and 1940s, stations were built in the classic Stalinist style with imposing steps and stairways, tall columns, massive lintels and energy-inefficient high ceilings. The 1970s ushered in an era of ugly, economical, concrete and glass stations.

Services   The larger stations are equipped with a waiting room, restaurant or buffet, a room for mothers and children, ticket windows, baggage rooms, an enquiries office, a bookstall, a first-aid point and a railway police office.

Information   All stations have an information window but only the largest, such as Moscow's Leningrad, Leningrad's Moscow, Brest, Kiev and Minsk station have English speaking Intourist offices and counters.

Local and long-distance train stations   The two types of train normally depart from separate platforms which are near one another. Only at the smallest stations are tickets for both types of train sold in the same hall. In the past, tickets for local trains were sold through ticket machines and they may be again if a token system is developed. Nowadays, you have to go to the ticket window, say your destination and you get a ticket for that particular zone. The ticket is valid for the entire day. It is often hard to find the local train ticket hall in large stations so look for the signs saying *Prigorodny Zal* (Пригородный зал).

Ticket windows   The wide variety of ticket windows are described below in *Buying a ticket*, see *page 71*.

Accommodation   Stations sometimes have an overnight transit (very basic) hotel attached and to stay in them you need to show a ticket for a train departing the next day. The biggest stations often have a carriage which is turned into a hotel (вагон для ночного отдыха пассажиров). They normally open at 20.00 and close at 08.00.

Waiting rooms   Waiting rooms are crowded, stuffy and scented with the odours of pickled cucumber, dried fish, sunflower seeds and water melon. They often have guards at the entrance and you either have to show your ticket or pay to enter.

Left luggage

Every station has a left-luggage office or coin-operated lockers.

The safest is the left-luggage office called a *kamera khranenia* (камера хранения) where you give your luggage to the counter staff and get back an identification tag. As an added security, the staff will often write down your surname and pin it to your luggage. To get the luggage back, you have to give in the tag and state your name. You pay by the day. So if you leave it for two hours, the fee will be the same as for 20 hours. Note down the opening hours of the *kamera khranenia* as a large station may have several which, while operating 24 hours a day, close for breaks at different times.

Coin-operated lockers called *avtomaticheskie kamery khranenia* (автоматические камеры хранения) are more risky but, as there is always a supervisor watching over them, they are not too bad. If your luggage is large, it will probably not fit through the narrow locker doorway which is about 30 x 40cm. You can only leave luggage in the lockers until 23.59 of the next day before it is cleared. The coin-operated lockers operate 24 hours a day but are closed several times a day for breaks of up to 30 minutes. To store luggage, get a token from the supervisor, choose an empty locker within his range of vision, and put in your luggage. On the inside of the door is a set of four combination locks. Select a combination of three numbers and one Cyrillic character. Write the combination and the locker number down immediately. Put in the token and close the door. Twirl around the knobs on the outside of the locker. To get your luggage out, set the combination on the knobs, wait two seconds until you hear the electric lock click back and pull the door handle. Some lockers require you to put in a second token before the electric lock clicks back. If there is a problem in getting things out of the locker, you should call the supervisor. You do not have to bribe the supervisor for help. He will open any locker you ask for, but first you must describe your luggage. The supervisor can open up to three lockers for you at once. If you want more opened because you have forgotten where you put your luggage, the supervisor has to call a militia officer. After finding your things, you have to pay a small fine, fill in a form and show the supervisor your passport. This opening process can take an hour and you may miss your train, so be sure to note down your locker number carefully.

Rail tickets

Booking rail tickets in Russia is easier today than at any time in the past. The basic reason for this is that supply is now greater than demand due to the increase in the cost of tickets. Despite the price rise, overnight rail tickets are still considerably cheaper than in the west, and even hotel rooms in Russia.

When reading this section, please remember that Russian rail travel is continually changing and costs, procedures and regulations may have changed.

To help you buy your own tickets, a Russian–English dictionary of words and phrases used in booking is contained in *Appendix Three*.

Ticket prices

This section discusses the general pricing of tickets while the actual ticket prices are contained in *Chapter Three, page 40*.

In 1996, the cost of tickets is still very low compared to similar journeys in the west but they are rising rapidly. For some routes, notably crossing borders, the rail ticket is rapidly approaching the plane ticket price.

Ticket prices are made up of three components: a booking fee, the class of ticket and the distance to be travelled. The booking fee is about $2. The cheapest class of ticket is *obshchi*, followed by *platskartny, coupé* and *SV* with each class being about 1.5–2 times the cost of the previous class. *Firmenny* tickets are 1.2–1.5 that of *non-firmenny* tickets. The cost per kilometre reduces with distance.

Foreigners have to buy Intourist tickets which are up to 30% more than tickets for residents. However, the railway's long-term policy is for this to decrease. This will be done not by bringing down the cost of Intourist tickets but by raising domestic ones. While most large stations have Intourist ticket windows, some do not which means that you can legally buy locals' tickets. When this happens and you travel using a local's ticket, your *provodnik* may report you to the head *provodnik* and he will demand that you make up the difference in ticket price. You will get an official receipt which you must keep in case a ticket inspector gets on your train. While you may be able to get only locals' tickets from small stations, if you have obtained the locals' ticket dishonestly from a station that sells foreigner tickets, you may have to pay a fine as well as making up the difference. You can try to bribe the *provodnik* and may get away with paying less, but then again, you may pay more than the upgrade price.

Prior to 1993, foreigner tickets had to be paid in hard currency which forced the railways to spend millions in establishing new hard currency accounting procedures, installing safes and issuing hard currency floats to major railway stations across Russia. However, to stop inflation, Yeltsin signed a decree in 1993 which forbade hard currency transactions in Russia. This means that all tickets have to be bought with roubles and all of the effort of the railways was wasted.

Ticket prices also depend on the direction the train travels. This odd situation arises when you cross an administrative boundary between Russia's 19 railways as each has its own tariffs.

Visas and tickets
In the Soviet era, rail tickets would only be sold to foreigners if the destination was written on their visa. Nowadays, this situation occurs only rarely and mostly by rail staff in rural areas who do not know that the law has changed. To avoid the problem, show only your passport and not your visa when you buy a rail ticket.

Return tickets
Technically, it is possible to buy return tickets from every station fitted with the computerised Express-3 booking system. However, it appears that many ticket offices have a policy of refusing to do so. Fortunately, Intourist ticket offices will normally issue return tickets without a problem which is another reason for paying a bit more for an Intourist ticket. There is no price discount for return tickets. The return portion of the trip has to be completed within 30 days of the outward portion.

Multi-train ticket
A little-known service offered by the railways is the *pryamaya platskarta* (прямая платцкарта) meaning "direct reserved ticket booking". This allows you to get a single ticket for a journey between stations which are not served by direct trains. When you order the *pryamaya platskarta* ticket, reservations are made all along the route regardless of the number of times you change trains. At each station where you change trains, you have to go to the stationmaster (*nachalnik stantsii*) who will validate your ticket and give you the number of your berth for the next leg. You have to pay for the *pryanmaya platskarta* but its minimal charge is far better than trying to buy a ticket for each leg. You can't break your journey when you have a *pryanmaya platskarta* ticket.

Student discounts
The official answer on how to get a student discount as a foreigner, is that you need special documents which are determined by special government decree. Unfortunately, very few railway ticket staff know what the decree states and all attempts by the author to locate it have failed. Some stations will not sell student tickets at all as they believe that student discounts were abolished in the early 1990s. Others will give student discounts only to those people who have Russian student discount documents. These are normally student cards issued by a Russian school and tertiary institution. A few foreigners have had luck with their International Student Identity Card (ISIC) cards so it is always worth trying.

Booking tickets in advance
Moscow will issue tickets up to 45 days in advance, large stations and other stations with the computerised Express-3 booking system will issue tickets up to 30 days in advance, and little rural stations may only issue them up to 15 days in advance. It is possible to get tickets further in advance but this requires connections.

Ticket reserve

On every single train, there is always a block of tickets reserved for railway staff, service personnel, government officials, WWII veterans, workers who participated in the Chernobyl clean-up operation and many other groups. Large companies also often have a block booking on particular trains. In remote areas, with only one or two trains a day, this ticket reserve, known as *bron* (бронь), can be up to 30 tickets while on Moscow–St Petersburg trains it is normally only about five. In addition, most large stations on the train route also have ticket reserves. About three hours before the train departs, the surplus berths in the ticket reserve are released. This means that there is always a good chance of getting a ticket at the last minute on "booked up" trains. If you have a good story, such as you are attending a funeral, you may be able to get one of the ticket reserve before they are released to the general public.

What do tickets look like?

There are several types of ticket for long-distance trains but the most common is the long, paper, computer-printed ticket. The ticket contains not only information about the train but also contains your name and any special information such as if it is a child, student or adult ticket. So unless you can understand everything printed on a ticket, don't buy someone else's ticket from them.

Once you get on the train, the conductor tears off a portion of the ticket which prevents it from being used again.

A TYPICAL TICKET EXPLAINED

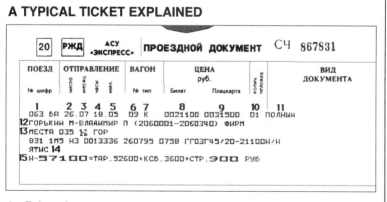

1   Train number
2-5 Departure date, month, hour, minute
6   Carriage number
7   Carriage type (options are Л (L=2 berth *SV*), M (M=4 berth *SV*), K (K=*coupé*), П (P=*platskartny*), O (O=*obshchi*)
8   Price of the upgrade to your carriage type ...
9   ... plus the price of a *platskartna* berth
10 Number of people
11 Type of traveller (options include Полный (*polny*=adult), Детский (*detski*=child), Студенческий (*studencheski*=student), Бесплатный для жд (*besplatny dlya zhd*=free for railway workers)
12 Place of departure and arrival
13 Berth number
14 Name
15 Total price which equals the price as above plus booking and ticketing charges

The conditions are printed on the back of the ticket. These include:
- The ticket is only valid for the particular train printed on it.
- This ticket is invalid if it is used by a foreigner without the folded card of Intourist or other authorised documents.
- The ticket is only valid for two months from the date of purchase.
- The maximum amount of luggage that can be carried on the train is 36kg.
- If the ticket is for trains that originate elsewhere, the berth number is given only after you board the train.

In places where the Express-3 computer booking system is not used, either large, paper tickets or small, thick, cardboard tickets are issued. The large paper tickets have all the classes of berth printed on them and the seller cuts off the options you have not paid for, writes in the destination, train number, compartment number and berth number, and then dates it with a hole punch. Thick cardboard tickets have train number and destination station printed on them. The seller then has just to write in the carriage and berth number and date stamp it. These tickets are normally issued for *platskartny* berths but occasionally for *coupés* as well. Strangely, some stations issue a combination of the two with a cardboard ticket plus a long paper ticket stating the premium for a *platskartny* to *coupé* upgrade. This process negates all the time savings of the pre-printed cardboard tickets.

What happens if you can't get a ticket
There are three main reasons why you might be unable get a ticket. Firstly, you don't have time as the ticket office normally stops selling tickets five minutes before train departure; secondly, because there are no berths; and thirdly, because tickets are only sold a few hours before the train arrives. The third reason applies only to trains that do not originate in your city of departure. This is because no tickets can be sold until the train is approaching your station and the chief *provodnik* has counted up the number of vacant berths and radioed this ahead. This results in a mad scramble to get tickets in the one or two hours before the train arrives.

If you try to jump on a train without a ticket, you will first have to ask the chief *provodnik* if there are any places and if you can buy a ticket on board. If you are allowed on, you will have to pay a fine of $3–10.

If you have tried to get a ticket but are told there are no places at the station, you can wait for the train and ask the chief *provodnik* and any of the carriage *provodniks* if there are spare berths. Sometimes, due to a communication problem, there may be a berth, but more likely they will obtain you one by subterfuge. In the latter case, you will normally pay the *provodniks* the cost of a ticket plus a hefty "assistance" charge. Travelling in this fashion is illegal and the ticket inspectors can have you thrown off the train or arrested.

You could always try to travel free, known as travelling *kak zayzts* meaning "like a rabbit" (как заяц) but the ticket inspectors, *provodniks* and railway police are bound to catch you. You can often pick out *zayzts* passengers on suburban trains as they are the ones pretending to be asleep when the ticket inspectors enter.

Getting off in the middle of a journey
Unknown even by most Russians is the possibility of getting off the train before your destination and using your ticket to reboard a later train. Foreigners and most Russians can do this only once while the disabled and war veterans can

do it twice. While in theory it is simple, in practice it isn't. Firstly, when you get off you have to get the stationmaster to validate your ticket within 30 minutes of arriving. This process is called *prokompostirovat* (прокомпостировать) and involves the ticket being punched with the current time and date. Secondly, you have to rebook a berth for the onward journey which will often only be done by the chief ticket officer. Unless you speak Russian, don't attempt this.

Buying a ticket

Once upon a time, you could book tickets over the phone and they would be delivered to you. Nowadays, only private companies offer such a service, and these only operate in the biggest cities. The Russian railway policy allows only the railways to sell tickets directly, which means that all private companies buy them from the railways and, to make a profit on them, levy a service charge. In most cities you can buy tickets at railway stations and at advance purchase rail ticket offices.

Step 1: Which train?

The first step is to find out which train you want. Check the timetable that will be displayed in the booking hall. It will state the train's number, the time of departure and on which days of the week it travels.

Things to remember:

– The train number indicates which way it is heading. If the number is even it means that it is going to the east or north and if odd, the train is heading west or south.

– The time quoted on timetables is invariably Moscow time. Across a network covering eight time zones (the country is 11 zones), this is the only way the system would work. In rare cases, where timetables are written in local time it will state this at the top of the timetable. The clock in the booking hall is normally set to Moscow time. Some station clocks (eg Khabarovsk) have two hour hands, black for local and red for Moscow time.

– Most trains depart every day, but some run on odd-numbered days (1st, 3rd, 5th etc) and some on even days (2nd, 4th, 6th etc). In addition, a few trains only run in summer or winter.

Step 2: Which window?

There are several sorts of ticket window, known as *kassa,* in the booking hall and it is important to queue at the correct one otherwise you can waste hours. The best practice is to go to the information window and ask if there are any tickets for the train you want to go on, and if there are, which ticket window to use. In addition, ask the price of the ticket. Although there are windows marked "pensioners", "military" and "railway personnel", these are normally irrelevant except in the largest of cities. There is also a ticket for women with children. Before queuing, check the opening hours of the window as each *kassa* has a different closing time. It may be better to queue up at a closed *kassa* which will open in an hour than wait in a long line where the *kassa* might close before you get to the head of the queue. (The reason why one *kassa* is not open all the time is because every ticket seller is responsible for his own tickets and cash, and attributing blame for missing money is too difficult if you have two staff using the same resources.)

A good practice is to leave your bags with your partner so that you can push your way through the queue without worrying about your belongings. If there are three of you, two should queue with one shielding the other from the Russians trying to push in ahead of you. The person guarding the luggage should stack it in a corner near the information window which is the safest place in the hall.

Step 3: Buying the ticket
When you get to the window, tell them the train number, date of departure, class of cabin, and your destination.

Changing your ticket
It is possible to change your ticket at the *kassa* where you bought the ticket but it is best to get it right the first time and avoid the hassle.

If you want to depart on an earlier train, the ticket is simply redated and you pay the booking fee of a few dollars. If you want to depart on a later train, a new ticket is issued and you pay the booking fee.

If you don't want to travel and return your ticket 24 hours ahead of departure, you get a full refund minus the booking fee. It you return it 6–24 hours from departure, you lose 50% of the ticket price if it was a *platskartny* berth or 18% if it was a *coupé*.

If you are late and miss your train by less than three hours, you lose everything if you had a *platskartny* ticket or about 50% if it was a *coupé* ticket. If you arrive at the station more than three hours after the train has left, you will have to fill in some forms which are sent off to the central booking office for a refund decision.

Understanding the ticket selling system
An understanding of the ticket-selling system is useful to maximise the chance of getting a ticket.

Berths 1–36 are sold in each carriage. As the most comfortable ride is in the centre of the carriage, ask what number of berth is being sold to you before you accept it. While most ticket sellers will say either take it or leave it, some will sell you a central berth if you ask them.

As well as the ticket reserve becoming available three hours before the train departs, if your train originates elsewhere, the train's chief provodnik will radio ahead and tell the station's dispatcher the available berths. This will release more tickets about 30 minutes before the train departs.

The time-consuming booking system is a hybrid of computer and manual operations that is slow but effective. The computer system is called Express-3 which connects only 1,000 stations out of Russia's total of 11,000 stations. Of the 1,000 stations, which account for 80% of the nation's reservations, only a few have terminals actually in the *kassas*. The rest must call the Express-3 reservations operator by intercom to book tickets. For the remaining 10,000 stations, reservations are made by calling the closest reservations operator by phone. It is for this reason that some ticket sellers will take several bookings at once and then call them all through together. The Express-3 system will be installed in virtually every ticket office by the year 2000.

The booking staff are unmotivated, which is not surprising due to their conditions, treatment and social standing. During the communist era, government and media attention was always focused on physical production such as number of locomotives built, miles of track laid and tons of freight shipped. Despite the collapse of communism, the service sector is still low in prestige and consequently, most sales people just don't care.

Names on tickets

To get a ticket, you normally have to show your passport. The name on the passport is written down on the ticket. Ticket sellers will often only sell you as many tickets as you have passports. This was introduced to stop speculators from buying tickets and reselling them for a profit when the train is all sold out. In addition, it was used to stop central Asian and Caucusus people from travelling in Russia without Russian documents.

The only way for a ticket to be legally renamed once it is bought is for the ticket selling staff to overstamp the original name with an official stamp and write a new name on it.

TRAVEL TIPS AND FACTS

- The massive increase in the cost of food since the early 1990s has caused a major change in travelling life. In the Soviet era, it was common for everyone in a coupé to share food, even with strangers. This occurs only rarely nowadays.
- The black and white kilometre marking posts beside the railway line are useful. They usually show the distance from a town or junction, and if you are on a main line such as the Trans-Siberian, they show the distance from Moscow. In more remote areas, such as the BAM, they mark the boundaries of administrative regions of the railway and consequently are of limited use.
- If Russians are travelling for long distances and want to protect their suitcases, they will sew them up in white cloth.
- There is an unwritten rule that at bed time, all men leave the compartment so the women can change.
- As travelling can be hot, locals often wear tracksuit trousers and no top. Shorts are another option but are not popular in Russia except with sportsmen and the fashionable hip. You will also occasionally see pyjamas in daytime use, complete with medals.
- Trains going in opposite directions don't stop for the same length of time at the same station. In addition, if the train is late, it will stop for less than its scheduled time. When you get off, always ask the provodnik how long you will wait at the station.
- Locomotives are changed at the end of administrative regions and this normally takes 40 minutes.
- Carry a cloth to clean the windows of your carriage.
- Get up first and go to the toilet before breakfast and well before the end of the trip to beat the rush. Remember, the toilet is locked about 30km (about 30 minutes) from large cities and will not open until you are 30km past.
- If the toilet door is locked you can still wash your utensils at the water tap near the samovar.

OUT OF THE WINDOW

You can gain an understanding of much of Russian, Ukrainian and Belarusian life from the railway carriage window. Below is some of the what you will see.

Multi-storey housing blocks   Most city dwellers live in these bland, Soviet, box-shaped, multi-storey flats. They are often arranged in pentagons as this layout provides a wind-sheltered, snowdrift-free area for children in the centre. Most of the buildings are either five storeys, which is the maximum height before elevators are required, or nine or 14 storeys. On the ground floor of the buildings are often stores.

Russia has the lowest per capita housing allotments in Europe. In 1988 Moscow had an average allocation of 14m2 of living space per person, while in the many rural cities it was just 6.4m2. This may have been tolerable for young, single, short-term workers but it is a major problem for families. The housing shortage still exists today as illustrated by the fact that Russians will only get permanent residency in Moscow if they can prove that they have sole use of 18m^2 of floor space.

Villages   Villages are common throughout the old Soviet Union and are normally made up of single-storey wooden houses with no running water. Romantically they could be described as "rustic", but this camouflages the tough life of the inhabitants. Rural settlements have a variety of historical names in Russian with most carrying connotations of backwardness. The more common names include *selo* meaning "village", *derevnya* meaning "hamlet" or *khutor* meaning "a few dwellings in a forest".

Villages are also found around *kolkhoz* or collective farms. These farms were created by collectivising private farms and are sometimes fancifully known as *agrogorod,* meaning "agricultural towns", and, being relatively recent, have more concrete and brick buildings than older villages.

***Dacha* villages**   On the edges of cities and towns are groups of *dachas* surrounded by small gardens. *Dachas* are owned by high-rise city dwellers who rent their small plot of land from the government for a minimal amount. The owners have to construct their own buildings which normally start out as sheds and gradually get enlarged into little weekend cottages. This is the most common type of *dacha,* rather than the summer holiday homes of the ex-party leaders and today's businessmen which are also referred to as *dachas*. A growing number of people, particularly the unemployed and pensioners, are living permanently in their dachas all year round. Their advantages include more space than apartments and a source of food, while their disadvantages include being a long way from shops and having no running water or electricity. The principal source of heat for cooking is natural gas and tanks are filled every three months by a delivery truck. Large *dacha* gardens can produce the owner's entire year's supply of potatoes, cucumbers, aubergines, strawberries, sunflowers, beans, radishes, cabbages, lettuces, corn, onions and tomatoes.

Garages   In cities, beside the railway line you will often see row upon row of brick single-storey car garages. These are invariably surrounded by wire or steel fences and are guarded round the clock. Garages have only sprung up in the last ten years as, prior to that, few people owned private cars. The garages also double as storage areas for food. Many drivers leave their cars in the garages for the whole winter rather than risk the slippery roads. Sometimes, the garages are built into the side of the railway embankment and from the railway line you can only see the roof hatchway or air vent. Guarded car parks can also often be seen in old stadiums and under road overpasses.

Railway line agriculture and the forest band   Along the railway line is often a 20m wide band of cleared land followed by a 100m wide stretch of forest. Beyond these bands are buildings or fields.

The cleared land is maintained to prevent forest fires from getting close enough to destroy railway sleepers. Locals often use this land for small vegetable plots or as a source of hay. In late summer, you will see the hay cutters out with their scythes. After drying the hay, they stack it into a cone-shaped haystack and lie a branch or sheet of plastic on top to prevent it from losing its shape and letting in water.

The forest band is not maintained to hide anything but for a combination of ecological and health reasons. As toilet effluent discharges straight on to the tracks and people throw rubbish out of the train windows, the forest band reduces contamination into the fields and cities. In addition, in the city it serves as a noise barrier.

Railway yards   Most of the stations have railway yards for exchanging locomotives and filling freight wagons, and the larger ones also have several hectares of repair yards. Strangely, some stations use old steam engines to generate hot water. It is interesting to note that most stations have inefficiently large equipment, such as overhead cranes, rather than more useful forklifts, but this probably reflects Russia's inability to maintain small machines.

For security, the crew of shunting engines often tie their bicycles to the front of their locomotives.

Speciality trains   As the railway is Russia's principal means of transport, it is not surprising that a large number of speciality trains can be seen in railway yards. These include repair, fire, prisoner and postal trains.

Repair trains are self-contained and on 24-hour standby, ready to repair track that has collapsed or to right derailed trains. A large repair train consists of a locomotive with up to 12 carriages which include sleeping quarters for 30 men, a canteen, a crane, a bulldozer, an all-terrain tracked vehicle and a generator. The train also normally has five wagons carrying pre-assembled 25m segments of track. As the priority is to get the line back in operation, the most common repair work is to bulldoze the damaged track off the line and lay the pre-assembled segments in its place.

Fire trains are essential for putting out the frequent fires that are caused by the locomotives, lightning strikes or passengers throwing out cigarettes. The fire trains, which consist of an engine, accommodation carriage, water tanks and a generator to power the hoses, are not designed to put out large forest fires, but simply to protect the railway line and railway structures.

Engine aerials   On top of many houses are nailed head gaskets from large truck engines which serve as excellent TV aerials.

Water wells   Water wells, called *kholodets* (холодец), normally have a peaked roof and water is raised either by turning a crank that winds up a bucket or by pulling down a long pole on a fulcrum which lifts up the bucket. In many rural communities, *kholodets* are the primary source of water.

Hot-water pipes   In every city you will see 1m-diameter pipes above ground. These transport hot water from the city's power or hot-water plants to apartment blocks and factories. Individual hot-water systems in apartments are very rare but are becoming popular because every year for a month over summer, the hot water is turned off. This time is used to repair the pipes. Cold water and sewage are also turned off occasionally but usually only at night.

Prisons   Prisons are easily identified by their razor wire, very high fences and guard towers. They are quite common in Russia as there are over a million inmates in Russian prisons and the number is rising at the rate of 10% a year. Prison overcrowding is a major problem and in the remand prisons alone, 275,000 prisoners are crammed into accommodation designed for only 174,000. According to a 1995 report in the newspaper *Rossiiskie Vesti*, more than a third of remand centres were erected in the 17th–19th centuries and 26 of them are unfit for human habitation.

THE STRANGE RAILWAY GAUGE

The main railway gauge of all countries of the former Soviet Union is 1,524mm (5ft). There is a myth that this gauge was selected to be different from Europe so that foreign rolling stock could not be used on Russian railways, thus hindering any invader.

However, this is wrong for two reasons. Firstly, when an American railway engineer persuaded the tsar in the 1840s to adopt the 5ft gauge, there was no world standard. Secondly, this gauge is wider than the European standard gauge which means that the Russian railways could be regauged by bringing one rail in. Thus European rolling stock could run on Russian railways but, as moving the European rail wider to accommodate the Russian gauge would make the track lopsided, the converse does not apply. In addition, if the Russians were concerned about invaders, they would have lowered the height gauge below Europe's so that foreign rolling stock could not fit under bridges. Incidentally, the Germans hit this problem in the 1880s when they invaded France and consequently, by the turn of the century, all German locomotives had chimneys that could be lowered.

Part Two

ROUTE DESCRIPTIONS

Other Bradt Rail Guides

Australia & New Zealand by Rail
 Colin Taylor

Eastern Europe by Rail
 Rob Dodson

India by Rail
 Royston Ellis

Spain & Portugal by Rail
 Norman Renouf

Sri Lanka by Rail
 Royston Ellis

Switzerland by Rail
 Anthony Lambert

Thailand, Malaysia & Singapore by Rail
 Brian McPhee

USA by Rail
 John Pitt

Available from good bookshops or direct from
Bradt Publications, 41 Nortoft Road,
Chalfont St Peter, Bucks SL9 0LA
Tel/fax: 01494 873478

Bradt

Chapter Five

Moscow and Surrounding Region

MOSCOW   Москва
Population: 9,000,000   Telephone area code: 095

Visiting Moscow is an education. Not only is the city of historical interest but it is also culturally and politically fascinating. It is by far the biggest city in the country and combines the best and worst of Russia. To some travellers Moscow is overwhelming, while others find it compelling.

More than any city in the country, Moscow displays the new post-communist social order. The so-called New Russians, with their expensive cars, affluent attire and bodyguards, frequent the numerous casinos, foreign supermarkets and gaudy restaurants, while ordinary Russians struggle to get by on a paltry salary of $150 a month, hoping to make a few thousand extra roubles selling homegrown produce on the streets, using their cars as taxis or developing schemes to exploit the system.

Architecturally, Moscow is a gem and its buildings can be appreciated both in their own right and as metaphors for past and present Russian life. For example, although the 15th-century, fortified kremlin was designed to keep out rebellious nobles and disgruntled peasants, today its walls contain the country's seat of power and they still insulate the president from the average Russian. Another example is Stalin's eight pompous towering complexes around Moscow. While these are impressive from a distance, close up the poor workmanship and patchwork of continual repairs are revealed, reflecting the superficiality of the success of the Soviet period. A more recent architectural and societal development can be observed in the restoration of Russian Orthodox churches and the participation of priests in blessing everything from the opening of parliament to new breweries. Both business and government actively court the church as a means of gaining legitimacy. So, while visiting the city's highlights, such as the Kremlin, Red Square, the Central Russian Museum, Arbat Street, Tverskaya Street and the metro, is enjoyable, observing and investigating the daily life of Russians may leave a more lasting impression.

This guide concentrates on the little-discussed area of day train trips around the Moscow region. Good general guides to the city are listed in *Appendix Four*.

Moscow is one hour ahead of Helsinki, Sofia, Athens, and Bucharest, two hours ahead of Paris, Prague, Rome, Stockholm, Warsaw, Vienna and Berlin, and three hours ahead of London. St Petersburg and Moscow are in the same time zone. Daylight saving starts on the last Saturday in March and finishes on the last Saturday in September.

Getting there and away

The main international trains to Moscow are listed below. There are also a number of other trains which are not listed that pass through Moscow en route to other major cities. As train departure times change frequently, and travel time depends on the train, refer to the *Thomas Cook Rail Guide* or *Russian Passenger Timetable* for the latest information.

International trains are all of a good standard, and the carriages are either *SV*, three-berth *coupé* or four-berth *coupé*. The majority of trains have a restaurant car attached when they cross the former CIS border or enter Russia, but it is still advisable to take some food and drink in case your train is an exception.

While Moscow is safer than the media coverage would have you believe, it is best to arrive in the morning or early afternoon. Remember to take into account the time difference when planning your route.

International trains

Origin	Dist, km	Entry point	Train no & name	Carr'ge class	No in coupé	Travel time	Day of departure	Destination
Moscow (Leningrad)	1,117	Luzhaika	32 Tolstoy	1, 2	2, 4	15	daily	Helsinki
Moscow (Leningrad)	964	Narva	34 Tallinna Express	1, 2	2, 4	17	daily	Tallinn
Moscow (Belorussia)	944	Krasnoe	87	1, 2	2, 4	17	Tue, Thur, Sat	Vilnius
Moscow (Kiev)		Vadul-Siret	59	1,2	2, 4		Sat, Wed	Istanbul
Moscow (Kiev)	2,110	Chop	15 Tisza Express	1, 2	2, 4	41	daily	Budapest
Moscow (Kiev)	2,164	Ungeny	5 Rumynia Express	1, 2	2, 4	43	Sun, Wed, Fri	Bucharest
Moscow (Kiev)	2,317	Chop	51 Slovkia Express	1, 2	2, 3, 4	42	daily	Bratislava
Moscow (Kiev)	2,363	Chop	9 Pushkin	1, 2	2, 3	46	daily	Belgrade
Moscow (Kiev)	2,550	Vadul-Siret	59 Sofija Express	1, 2	2, 4	53:25	daily	Sofia
Moscow (Kiev)	2,582	Chop	7 Dulka Express	1, 2	2, 3, 4	46	daily	Prague
Moscow (Rizhski)	922	Zilype	1 Latvijas Ekspresi	1, 2	2, 4	16	daily	Riga
Moscow (Smolensk)	1,317	Brest	9 Polonez	1, 2	2, 3	19	daily	Warsaw
Moscow (Smolensk)	1,895	Brest	13 Moskva Express	1, 2	2, 4	34	daily	Berlin
Moscow (Smolensk)	2,969	Brest	15 Ost–West Express	1, 2	2, 3	40	daily	Brussels
Moscow (Smolensk)	2,060	Brest	21	1, 2	2, 3	38	daily	Prague
Moscow (Smolensk)	2,600	Brest	13 Moskva Express	1, 2	2, 3	44	daily	Frankfurt
Moscow (Smolensk)	2,012	Chop	16 Vostok–Zapad Express	1, 2	2, 3	36	Fri, Tue	Vienna
Moscow (Yaroslav)	6,302	Naushki	6	1, 2	2, 4	115	Wed, Thur	Ulaanbaatar
Moscow (Yaroslav)	7,865	Naushki via Mongolia	4	1, 2	2, 4	144	Tue	Beijing
Moscow (Yaroslav)	8,666	Zabaikalsk	20	1, 2	2, 4	176	Fri	Pyongyang
Moscow (Yaroslav)	9,001	Zabaikalsk	20	1, 2	2, 4	159	Fri	Beijing

Moscow (Yaroslav)	10,214	Khasan	2 Rossiya	2	4	202	Tue, Sat	Pyongyang
Beijing	7,865	Naushki via Mongolia	3	1, 2	2, 4	124	Fri	Moscow (Yaroslav)
Beijing	9,001	Zabaikalsk	19	1, 2	2, 4	139	Sat	Moscow (Yaroslav)
Belgrade	2,363	Chop	10 Pushkin	1, 2	2, 3	45	daily	Moscow (Kiev)
Berlin	1,895	Brest	14 Moskva Express	1, 2	2, 4	32	daily	Moscow (Smolensk)
Bratislava	2,317	Chop	52 Slovkia Express	1, 2	2, 3, 4	42	daily	Moscow (Kiev)
Brussels	2,969	Brest	16 Ost–West Express	1, 2	2, 3	42	daily	Moscow (Smolensk)
Bucharest	2,164	Ungeny	6 Pushkin	1, 2	2, 4	46	Thur, Sun, Mon	Moscow (Kiev)
Budapest	2,110	Chop	16 Tisza Express	1, 2	2, 4	40	daily	Moscow (Kiev)
Frankfurt	2,600	Brest	13 Moskva Express	1, 2	2, 3	44	daily	Moscow (Smolensk)
Helsinki	1,117	Luzhaika	31 Tolstoy	1, 2	2, 4	15	daily	Moscow (Leningrad)
Istanbul		Vadul-Siret	60	1, 2	2, 4		Tue, Sat	Moscow (Kiev)
Pyongyang	8,666	Zabaikalsk	19	1, 2	2, 4	176	Sat	Moscow (Yaroslav)
Pyongyang	10,214	Khasan	1 Rossiya	2	4	202	Mon, Wed	Moscow (Yaroslav)
Prague	2,060	Brest	22	1, 2	2, 3	38	daily	Moscow (Smolensk)
Prague	2,582	Chop	8 Dulka Express	1, 2	2, 3, 4	47	daily	Moscow (Kiev)
Riga	922	Zilype	2 Latvijas Ekspresi	1, 2	2, 4	16	daily	Moscow (Rizhski)
Sofia	2,550	Vadul-Siret	60 Sofija Express	1, 2	2, 4	53	daily	Moscow (Kiev)
Tallinn	964	Narva	33 Tallinna Express	1, 2	2, 4	17	daily	Moscow (Leningrad)
Ulaanbaatar	6,302	Naushki	5	1, 2	2, 4	118	Fri, Wed	Moscow (Yaroslav)
Vienna	2,012	Chop	16 Vostok–Zapad Express	1, 2	2, 3	36	Fri, Tue	Moscow (Smolensk)
Vilnius	944	Krasnoe	88	1, 2	2, 4	16	Tue, Thur, Sat	Moscow (Belorussia)
Warsaw	1,317	Brest	10 Polonez	1, 2	2, 3	22	daily	Moscow (Smolensk)

Domestic trains

For information on the domestic trains to Moscow, see the relevant route description chapter.

Moscow stations

There are nine long-distance stations in Moscow and all have metro stations underneath and suburban railway stations beside them. The stations are:

Belorussia station (*Belorusski* Белорусский) pl Tverskaya Sastava 7, tel: 251 6093, 253 4224, 253 4908. Trains arrive and depart for western Europe, Baltic states, eastern Europe, Belorussia and western Russia, including Berlin, Borodino, Brest, Brussels, Gagarin, Kaliningrad, Minsk, Smolensk, Vilnius, Vitebsk and Warsaw. The metro station is Belorusskaya.

Kazan station (*Kazanski* Казанский) pl Komsomolskaya 2, tel: 264 6409, 266 2736, 266 2542. Trains arrive and depart for southern Russia and central Asia including Alma-Ata, Ashkhabad, Bishkek, Kazan, Magnitogorsk, Omsk, Rostov, Samara and Tashkent. The metro station is Komsomolskaya.

Kiev station (*Kievski* Киевский) pl Kievskovo Vokzala, tel: 240 1115, 240 0484, 240 7622. Trains arrive and depart here for the Ukraine, eastern Europe and southwestern Russia including Belgrade, Bratislava, Budapest, Bucharest, Chop, Kiev, Lviv, Odessa and Sofia. The metro station is Kievskaya.

Kursk station (*Kurski* Курский) ul Zemlyani Val 29 (formerly ul Chkalova), tel: 924 9243, 262 8532, 266 5652. Trains arrive and depart here for Armenia, Azerbaijan, the Crimea, Caucasus and southern Russia including Baku, Belgorod, Donetsk, Nizhni Novgorod, Kharkov, Kursk, Perm, Sevastopol, Tbilisi and Tula. The metro station is Kurskaya.

The main entrance of Kazan station

Leningrad station (*Leningradski* Ленинградский) pl Komsomolskaya 3, tel: 262 9143, 262 6038, 262 4281. Trains arrive and depart for Finland, Baltic states, eastern Russia and northern Russia including Helsinki, Murmansk, Novgorod, St Petersburg and Tallinn. The metro station is Komsomolskaya. This is Moscow's largest station and was built at the same time as the identical Moscow Station in St Petersburg.

Paveletski station (*Paveletski* Павелецкий) pl Leninskaya 1, tel: 235 6807 235 3960, 235 4673. Trains arrive and depart here for southern Russia and central Asia including Astrakhan, Donetsk, Lipetsk, Saratov, Tambov, Tashkent, Volgograd and Voronezh. The metro station is Paveletskaya.

Rizhski station (*Rizhski* Рижский) pl Rizhskaya, tel: 971 1588, 281 0118, 266 1176. Trains arrive and depart from here for Baltic states including Riga and Velikie Luki. The metro station is Rizhskaya.

Savelovski station (*Savelovski* Савеловский) pl Butyrskoi Zastavy (formerly pl Savelovskaya), tel: 285 5891, 266 1883, 285 9000. Trains arrive and depart from this small station for western Russia including Rybinsk, St Petersburg (only a handful) and Uglich. The metro station is Savelovskaya.

Yaroslav station (*Yaroslavski* Ярославский) pl Komsomolskaya 5, tel: 921 0817, 266 0301, 266 0595. Trains arrive and depart here for China, Mongolia, Russian far east and the Trans-Siberian including Arkhangelsk, Beijing, Irkutsk, Vyatka, Sergiev Posad (Zagorsk), Ulaanbaatar, Ulan-Ude and Vladivostok. The metro station is Komsomolskaya.

Getting railway tickets and information

There are a number of places around Moscow where foreigners can obtain tickets. These include the railway stations, Transport Agency, Central Railway Booking Agency and resellers. If you can speak Russian, railway information can be obtained on tel: 266 9000 to 266 9009, 927 2105, 262 4202.

Railway stations will only sell tickets for trains that depart from their station. In most of Moscow's railway stations there is an Intourist window selling foreigner tickets on the ground floor of the station. If you are travelling to St Petersburg it is on the second floor of Leningrad station at window No 19. It is hard to find the window as it can only be reached from inside the building, up a set of stairs, and through a waiting room. However, it rarely has a queue and it is worth seeking out. For tickets for Helsinki try window No 35 at Leningrad station.

The easiest place to get tickets to any destination is the Transport Agency known as Transagentsvo. The best one is located opposite the exit of Komsomolskaya metro station on Komsomol Square between Leningrad and Yaroslavl stations. The ticket window for foreigners is on the the second floor in Hall 7, window No 99.

The Central Railway Booking Agency, called *Tsentralnoe Zheleznodorozhnoe Agentstvo*, has four main offices around the city. The offices are open 08.00–19.00, closed 13.00–14.00. All have windows for foreigners and will sell tickets for all destinations. Their details are:

- ul Maly Kharitonevsky 6/11 (formerly ul Griboedova), tel: 262 9605, 262 7935, fax: 921 7934. The closest metros are Turgenevskaya and Krasnaya Vorota
- ul Krasnoprudnaya 1, tel: 266 0004. The closest metro is Komsomolskaya
- pro Leningradskaya 1, tel: 262 3342. The closest metro is Belorusskaya
- ul Mozhayski val 4/6, tel: 240 0505. The closest metro is Kievskaya

There are a number of resellers around Moscow who mark up foreigner tickets a further 5–20%. The easiest place to get tickets is G & R International and IRO Travel as they speak English. Resellers include:

- **Intertrans**, ul Petrovka 15, tel: 927 1181 which is near the Bolshoi Theatre. The closest metro is Kuznetski Most. Open 09.00–20.00 weekdays, 09.00–19.00 weekends, closed for lunch. Rail office on the second floor.
- **IRO Travel**, 10th floor, ul Bolshaya Pereyaslavksaya 50, tel: 971 4059, 280 8562, fax: 280 7686. The closest metro is Prospekt Mira. This office is across the hall from the Travellers Guest House. Open 10.00–18.00.
- **G & R International**, Block 6, Office 4, Institute of Youth, ul Yunosti 5/1, tel: 374 7366, fax: 374 6132. The closest metro is Vykhino. From the front of the station, take bus No 197 or 697 for five or seven stops to the Institute of Youth called Institut Molodyozhi.

For more information on sources of tickets, see *Chapter Four*.

Getting around

The metro is the best way to travel around Moscow as the network is extensive and easy to work out. The metro is based on a spider-web of spokes radiating out from a few central Moscow stations with an outer ring connecting all the spokes.

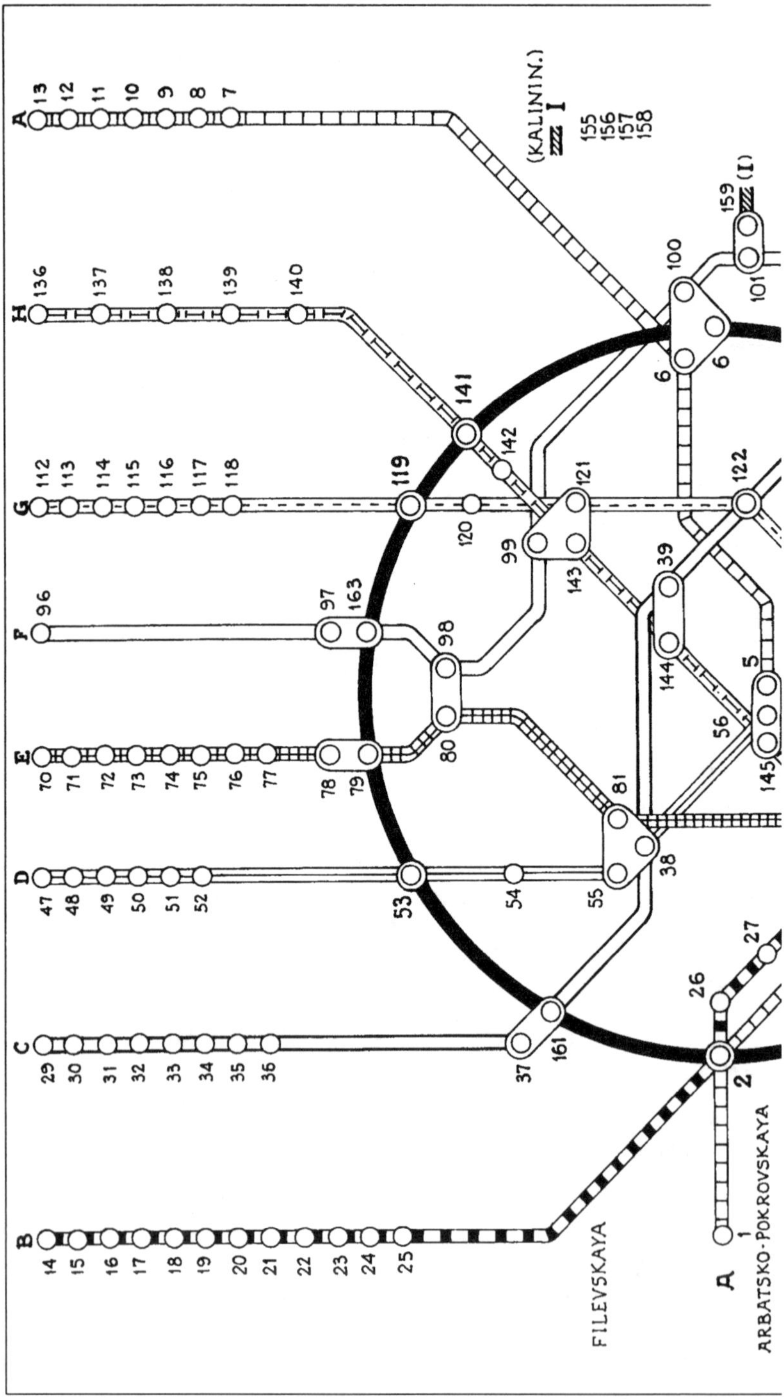
FILEVSKAYA
ARBATSKO-POKROVSKAYA
(KALININ.)
155
156
157
158

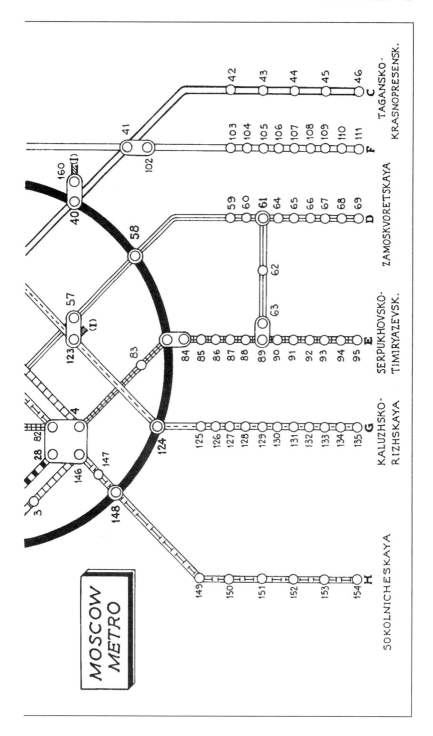

KEY TO MOSCOW METRO Москвое Метро

Metro lines

A	Arbatsko-Pokrovskaya	Арбатско-Покровская
B	Filevskaya	Филевская
C	Tagansko-Krasnopresenskaya	Таганско-Краснопресненская
D	Zamoskvoretskaya	Замоскворецкая
E	Serpukhovsko-Timryazevskaya Line	Серпуховско-Тимирязевская
F	Line under construction	Строяшиеся линии
G	Kaluzhsko-Rizhskaya Line	Калужско-Рижская
H	Sokolnicheskaya	Сокольническая
I	Kalininskaya	Калининская
J	Circular	Кольцевая

Metro stations in alphabetical order

Note: (nb) means not built

51	Aeroport	Аэропорт
127	Akademicheskaya	Академическая
28	Aleksandrovski Sad	Александровский сад
117	Alekseevskaya	Алексеевская
70	Altufevo	Алтуфьево
94	Anino (nb)	Анино
4	Arbatskaya	Арбатская
27	Arbatskaya	Арбатская
158	Aviamotornaya	Авиамоторная
59	Avtozavodskaya	Автозаводская
113	Babushkinskaya	Бабушкинская
22	Bagrationovskaya	Багратионовская
37	Barrikadnaya	Баррикадная
7	Baumanskaya	Бауманская
35	Begovaya	Беговая
53	Belorusskaya	Белорусская
131	Belyaevo	Беляево
71	Bibirevo	Бибирево
146	Biblioteka Lenina	Библиотека им. Ленина
135	Bitsevski Park	Битцевский Парк
111	Borisovo (nb)	Борисово
82	Borovitskaya	Боровицкая
115	Botanicheski Sad	Ботанический сад
110	Brateevo (nb)	Братеево
81	Chekovskaya	Чеховская
137	Cherkizovskaya	Черкизовская
90	Chertanovskaya	Чертановская
143	Chistye prudy	Чистые пруды
100	Chkalovskaya (nb)	Чкаловская
52	Dinamo	Динамо
76	Dmitrovskaya	Дмитровская
162	Dobryninskaya	Добрынинская
67	Domodedovskaya	Домодедовская
97	Dostoevskaya (nb)	Достоевская
103	Dubrovka (nb)	Дубровка
8	Elektrozavodskaya	Электрозаводская
21	Filevski Park	Филевский парк
23	Fili	Фили
149	Frunzenskaya	Фрунзенская
11	Izmailovskaya	Измайловская
10	Izmailovski Park	Измайловский парк
95	Kachalovo (nb)	Качалово
63	Kakhovskaya	Каховская
130	Kaluzhskaya	Калужская
64	Kantemirovskaya	Кантемировская
61	Kashirskaya	Каширская
2	Kievskaya	Киевская
122	Kitai-Gorod	Китай-Город
60	Kolomenskaya	Коломенская
141	Komsomolskaya	Комсомольская
132	Konkovo	Коньково
104	Kozhukhovskaya (nb)	Кожуховская
108	Krasnodonskaya (nb)	Краснодонская
68	Krasnogvardeiskaya	Красногвардейская
161	Krasnoprosnenskaya	Краснопресненская
140	Krasnoselskaya	Красносельская
142	Krasnye vorota	Красные ворота
102	Krestyanskaya Zastava (nb)	Крестьянская Застава
147	Kropotkinskaya	Кропоткинская
17	Krylatskoe	Крылатское
19	Kuntsevskaya	Кунцевская
6	Kurskaya	Курская
24	Kutuzovskaya	Кутузовская
44	Kuzminki	Кузьминки
39	Kuznetski Most	Кузнецкий мост
126	Leninski prospekt	Ленинский проспект
151	Leninskie gory (closed)	Ленинские горы (закрыт)
144	Lubyanka	Лубянка
107	Lyublino (nb)	Люблино
96	Marina Roshcha (nb)	Марьина Роща
109	Marino (nb)	Марьино
160	Marksistskaya	Марксистская
54	Mayakovskaya	Маяковская
112	Medvedkovo	Медведково
78	Mendeleevskaya	Менделеевская
14	Mitino (nb)	Митино
18	Molodezhnaya	Молодежная
86	Nagatinskaya	Нагатинская

87	Nagornaya Нагорная		125	Shabolovskaya Шаболовская
88	Nakhimovski prospekt		13	Shchelkovskaya Щелковская
	Нахимовский проспект		32	Shchukinskaya Щукинская
155	Novogireevo Новогиреево		157	Shosse Entuziastov
57	Novokuznetskaya Новокузнецкая			шоссе Энтузиастов
79	Novoslobodskaya Новослободская		30	Skhodnenskaya Сходненская
129	Novye Chermushki		3	Smolenskaya Смоленская
	Новые Черемушки		26	Smolenskaya Смоленская
145	Okhotny Ryad Охотный ряд		50	Sokol Сокол
124	Oktyabrskaya Октябрьская		139	Sokolniki Сокольники
33	Oktyabrskoe Pole Октябрьское поле		150	Sportivnaya Спортивная
66	Orekhovo Орехово		99	Sretenski bulvar (nb)
72	Otradnoe Отрадное			Сретенский бульвар
148	Park Kultury Парк Культуры		16	Strogino (nb) Строгино
1	Park Pobedy (nb) Парк Победы		25	Studencheskaya Студенческая
58	Paveletskaya Павелецкая		120	Sukharevskaya Сухаревская
105	Pechatniki (nb) Печатники		89	Svestopolskaya Севастопольская
156	Perovo Перово		114	Sviblovo Свиблово
12	Pervomaiskaya Первомайская		40	Taganskaya Таганская
74	Petrovsko-Razumovskaya		56	Teatralnaya Театральная
	Петровско-Разумовская		43	Tekstilshchiki Текстильщики
20	Pionerskaya Пионерская		133	Teply Stan Тёплый Стан
29	Planernaya Планерная		75	Timiryazevskaya Тимирязевская
158	Ploshchad Ilicha площадь Ильичи		123	Tretyakovskaya Третьяковская
5	Ploshchad Revolyutsi		98	Trubnaya (nb) Трубная
	площадь Революции		65	Tsaritsyno Царицыно
163	Ploshchad Suvorova		80	Tsvetnoi bulvar Цветной бульвар
	площадь Суворова		85	Tulskaya Тульская
34	Polezhaevskaya Полежаевская		121	Turgenevskaya Тургеневская
83	Polyanka Полянка		31	Tushinskaya Тушинская
92	Prazhskaya Пражская		55	Tverskaya Тверская
138	Preobrazhenskaya ploshchad		36	ulitsa 1905 улица 1905 года
	Преображенская площадь		136	ulitsa Podbelskogo
128	Profsoyuznaya Профсоюзная			улица Подбельского
41	Proletarskaya Пролетарская		152	Universitet Университет
69	Promzona (nb) Промзона		62	Varshavskaya Варшавская
119	Prospekt Mira Проспект Мира		116	VDNKh ВДНХ
153	Prospekt Verdadskovo		73	Vladykino Владыкино
	Проспект Вернадского		48	Vodny Stadion Водный стадион
38	Pushkinskaya Пушкинская		49	Voikovskaya Войковская
47	Rechnoi Vokzal Речной вокзал		42	Volgogradski prospekt
101	Rimskaya (nb) Римская			Волгоградский проспект
118	Rizhskaya Рижская		15	Volokolamskaya (nb) Волоколамская
93	Rossoshanskaya (nb) Россошанская		106	Volzhskaya (nb) Волжская
45	Ryazanski prospekt		46	Vykhino Выхино
	Рязанский проспект		134	Yasenevo Ясенево
77	Savelovskaya Савеловская		154	Yugo-Zapadnaya Юго-западная
9	Semenovskaya Семеновская		91	Yuzhnaya Южная
84	Serpukhovskaya Серпуховская			

Stations which have changed their names

No.	*New Name*	*Новое название*	*Old name*	*Старое название*
28	Aleksandrovski Sad	Александровский сад	Kalininskaya	Калининская
55	Tverskaya	Тверская	Gorkovskaya	Горьковская
56	Teatralnaya	Театральная	Ploshchad Sverdlova	площадь Свердлова
65	Tsaritsyno	Царицыно	Lenino	Ленино
117	Alekseevskaya	Алексеевская	Shchervakovskaya	Щербаковская
120	Sukharevskaya	Сухаревская	Kolkhoznaya	Колхозная
122	Kitai-Gorod	Китай-Город	Ploshchad Nogina	площадь Ногина
143	Chistye prudy	Чистые пруды	Kirovskaya	Кировская
144	Lubyanka	Лубянка	Dzerzhinskaya	Дзержинская
145	Okhotny Ryad	Охотный ряд	Prospekt Marksa	проспект Маркса

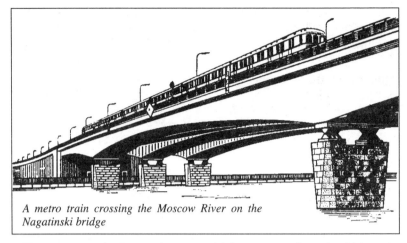

A metro train crossing the Moscow River on the Nagatinski bridge

The metro uses single-use tokens or multiple-use magnetic cards which can be purchased inside the metro station building, near the entry barriers. Once you enter the metro you can travel any distance and change trains as often as you want.

Trains arrive every minute in peak hours and you only have to wait a maximum of five minutes even at midnight. All stations open by 06.00 and close at 01.00. During peak hours, 07.00–10.00 and 15.00–19.00, trains are very crowded. The least crowded parts of trains within the ring are at both ends as the escalators carrying passengers between transfer stations pop up in the middle of the platform. Outside the ring, the reverse is true as the entry points to the platforms are at the stations' ends.

At every station a recorded message announces the next station, warns you not to lean against the doors and, following the wrongly predicted terrorist campaign during the Chechnya war, reminds you not to forget your luggage.

The price of the metro in early 1996 was 1,500 roubles ($0.32). This amount covers only a quarter of the real cost of a trip, according to the Moscow Mayor's Office which is responsible for its finances.

Metro tour

Moscow's gigantic 148 stations and 253km-long metro is not only functional but artistically brilliant. The central stations, with their murals, statues and stained glass, reflect Stalin's preference for grand classical architecture while the outer ring stations with their predominance of concrete and glass reflect the 1960s and 1970s austerity drives.

Some of the most impressive stations are Revolution Square (Ploshchad Revolyutsi) with its 76 bronze statues of professional and military leaders, Komsomolskaya which is the metro's largest station and features traditional Russian architecture and paintings, and Mayakovskaya station which was awarded the Grand Prix at the 1937 World Fair for its brilliant mosaics and columns faced with stainless steel and the rare mineral, radonite.

Over the next few years, new N5 metro carriages from Moscow's Mytishchi railway factory are being phased in. They are significantly quieter, smoother and safer due to automatic fire quenchers and extensive use of fireproof material.

It is interesting to note that while women drive many of Moscow's buses and trams, until recently only men were train drivers. The reason for this is the belief that men handle better the stress of suicidal passengers who jump into the path of the oncoming metro trains.

Moscow Metro Museum

Khamovnicheski val 35, metro Sportivnaya, tel: 222 7309. Open 11.00–18.00 Monday, 09.00–16.00 Tuesday–Friday, closed Saturday and Sunday. This five-hall museum contains maps, working models and documents about the history of Moscow's public transport and metro from the beginning of the 19th century. The museum is part of the Sportivnaya metro station and it is advisable to book a visit.

Where to stay

Below is a listing of the best accommodation in the various categories. It is highly recommended that you pre-book, as arriving without a booking can result in paying more because the staff know you are desperate. However, far worse is that you may be refused a room. This usually occurs because reception staff like to continue the Soviet era tradition of refusing a bed for those who did not pre-book, or because there may simply be no beds, often the case in the hostels in summer.

Very basic

G & R International, Block 6, Office 4, ul Yunosti 5/1, Moscow 111442, tel: 374 7430, fax: 374 7366, has rooms in hostels from $17 a night. The closest metro station is Vykhino which is about 40 minutes out from the centre of Moscow.

Prakash Guest House, ul Profsoyuznaya 83, tel: & fax: 334 2595, runs a hostel with a bed from $10 a night. The closest metro station is Belyaevo.

Travellers Guest House, 10th floor, ul Bolshaya Pereyaslavskaya 50, tel: 971 4059, fax: 280 7686, email tgh@glas.apc.org, runs a hostel with a bed from $15 a night. The closest metro station is Prospekt Mira.

Basic

Hotel Kievskaya, ul Kievskaya 2, tel: 240 1234, $25 twin share/person. The closest metro station is Kievskaya.

Hotel Molodezhnaya, shosse Dmitrovskoe 27, tel: 210 4565, 210 4577, fax: 210 4311, $15 twin share/person. The closest metro station is Timiryazevskaya.

Hotel Sputnik, pro Leninski 38, tel: 938 7106, 938 7096, $25 twin share/person. The closest metro station is Leninski Prospekt.

Hotel Tsentralaya, ul Tverskaya 10, tel: 229 89 57, $25 twin share/ person. The closest metro station is Tverskaya.

Hotel Ural, ul Pokrovka 40, tel: 917 4258, 227 3289, $30 twin share/person. The closest metro station is Krasnye Vorota.

Standard

Hotel Belgrad, ul Smolenskaya 8, tel: 248 1676, fax: 230 2129, $48 twin share/person. The closest metro station is Smolenskaya.

Hotel Budapest, linii Petrovskie 2/18, tel: 921 1060, fax: 921 1266, $60 twin share/person. The closest metro station is Kuznetski Most.

Hotel Intourist, ul Tverskaya 3/5, tel: 956 8400, 203 0125, fax: 956 8450, 203 9475, $75 twin share/person. The closest metro station is Okhoti Ryad.

Hotel Izmaulovo, Block D, tel: 166 4127, fax: 166 7486, $44 twin share/person. This giant hotel is divided into six blocks with Intourist having an office in Block D. The closest metro station is Izmaulovski Park.

Hotel Kosmos, pro Mira 150, tel: 217 0785, fax: 215 8880, $50 twin share/person. The closest metro station is VDNKh.

Hotel Mikof 1, bulvar Beskudnikovski 59A, tel: 483 0460, fax: 485 5954, $45 twin share/person. The place is difficult to get to by public transport so get a taxi. It is about 16km from the kremlin.

Hotel Moscow, Okhotni Ryad 2, tel: 292 1000, fax: 925 0155, $35 twin share/person. The closest metro station is Okhotny Ryad.

Hotel Rossia, ul Varvarka (formerly ul Razina) 6, tel: 298 5400, fax: 298 5541, $35 twin share/person. The closest metro station is Katai-Gorod.

Hotel Ukraina, pro Kutuzovski 2/1, tel: 243 3030, fax: 243 3092, $56 twin share/person. The closest metro station is Kievskaya.

Excellent

Hotel Metropol, Teatralni proezd 1, tel: 927 6000, fax: 927 6010, $190 twin share/person. The closest metro station is Okhoti Ryad.

Hotel Radisson Slavyanskaya, nab Berezhkovsaya 2, tel: 941 8020, fax: 941 8000, 240 6915, $126 twin share/person. The closest metro station is Kievskaya.

Hotel Savoy, ul Rozhdestvenka 3, tel: 929 8500, fax: 230 2186, $175 twin share/person. The closest metro station is Lubyanka.

National Hotel, Okhotny Ryad 14/1, tel: 258 7000, fax: 258 7100, $210 twin share/person. The closest metro station is Okhoti Ryad.

Foreign embassies and consulates in Moscow

Australia per Kropotkinski 13, tel: 956 6070
Austria per Starokonyushenni 1, tel: 201 7317
Belarus ul Maroseka 17/6, tel: 924 7031 (embassy), 924 7095 (visa), fax: 928 6403
Belgium ul Malaya Molchanovka 7, tel: 291 6027
Canada per Starokonyushenni 23, tel: 291 6027
China ul Druzhby 6, tel: 143 1540, 143 1543 (visa)
Czech Republic ul Yuliusa Fuchika 12/14, tel: 251 0540
Denmark per Prechistenski 9, tel: 201 7860
Estonia per Kalashny 8, tel: 290 4655, 290 5013
Finland per Kropotkinski 15/17, tel: 246 4027
France ul Bolshaya Yakimanka 45, tel: 236 0003
Germany ul Mosfilmovskaya 56, tel: 956 1080; consulate, pro Leninsky 94A, tel: 936 2401
Hungary ul Mosfilmovskaya 62, tel: 146 8611
Ireland per Grokholski 5, tel: 288 4101, 230 2763
Israel ul Bolshaya Ordynka 56, tel: 238 2732, 230 6700
Italy per Denezhny 5, tel: 241 1533
Japan per Kalashny 12, tel: 291 8500
Kazakhstan bul Chistoprudny 3A, tel: 208 9852, 927 1836
Latvia ul Chaplygina 3, tel: 925 2707

Lithuania   per Borisoglebski 19, tel: 291 2643
Mongolia   per Borisoglebski 11, tel: 290 6792; consulate, per Spasopeskovski 7, tel: 244 7867
Netherlands   per Kalashny 6, tel: 291 2999
New Zealand   ul Povarskaya 44, tel: 956 3579
Norway   ul Povarskaya 7, tel: 290 3872
Poland   ul Klimashkina 4, tel: 255 0017, 254 3621 (visa)
Slovakia   ul Yuliusa Fuchika 12/14, tel: 251 0540, 251 1070
South Africa   per Bolshoi Strochenovski 22/25, tel: 230 6869
UK   nab Sofiyskaya 14, tel: 956 74 00
Ukraine   ul Stanislavsky 18, tel: 229 3422, 229 1079, 229 3442, fax: 229 3542
USA   bul Novinski 19/23, tel: 252 2451

DAY RAIL TRIPS AROUND MOSCOW
Lenin's Funeral Tour

Despite the collapse of communism, there are still several of Lenin's museums operating in Moscow. An interesting day trip is to visit the two museums associated with his death in 1924.

The first is Lenin's Funeral Train Museum, pl Leninskaya 1, tel: 235 2898, open 10.00–17.00, closed Tuesday. This contains the U127 steam locomotive and carriages which carried Lenin's corpse to Moscow. The locomotive is particularly important to communist mythology as this 1910 engine was one of three rebuilt voluntarily over several Saturdays by railway mechanics on the Ryazano–Ural railway line. This voluntary labour became known as *subbotnik* (from the word *subbota* meaning "Saturday") and such voluntary days became common throughout Russia until the late 1980s. At the 1919 celebration, when the engines re-entered service, the workers voted to give Lenin a locomotive driver's licence of the 14th grade (out of 24 grades) as "they believed that he would be an excellent driver and drive them to a happy future".

To get to the museum, walk to the right after you leave the main entrance of Paveletski station and after 200m you reach a park. Tell the guard at the park's entrance that you are going to the museum, and then walk through the cars parked among the trees to the museum.

The second place on the tour is his death site, Lenin Hills Estate, tel: 548 9309, open 10.00–17.00, closed Tuesday. This park and 18th-century villa was Lenin's favourite retreat after he stayed here during his recovery from the assassination attempt in Moscow on August 31 1918. Today, the building is filled with Lenin memorabilia including touching letters and gifts sent to the dying leader. Lenin died in his bed at 06.50 on January 21 1924 and all the clocks in the building have been stopped at this time.

To get to the estate, which is 37km south of Moscow, take a suburban train from Paveletski station for 45 minutes to Leninskaya station (Ленинская). Then take bus 24 three stops which will bring you to the road that leads to the estate. There is a 500m walk from the stop to the museum. You can also walk from the station which will take you about 35 minutes. To reach the estate by foot, walk for 20 minutes along the road beside the station. This runs at right angles to the railway line and ends at a T-junction. Turn left along this main road and after 700m cross over a stone bridge and another 200m will bring you to a bus stop. The road on the right leads you to the museum.

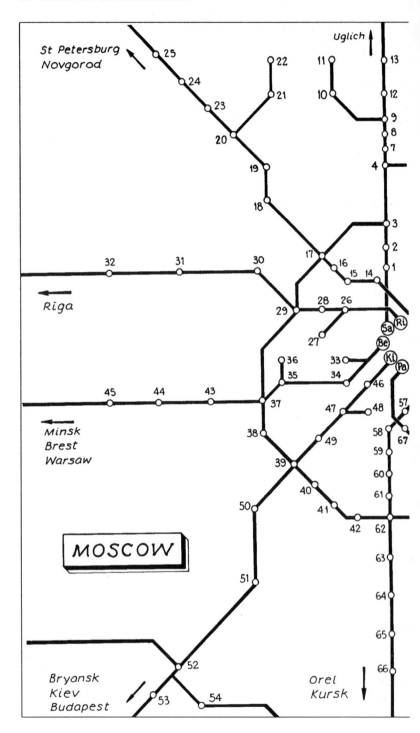

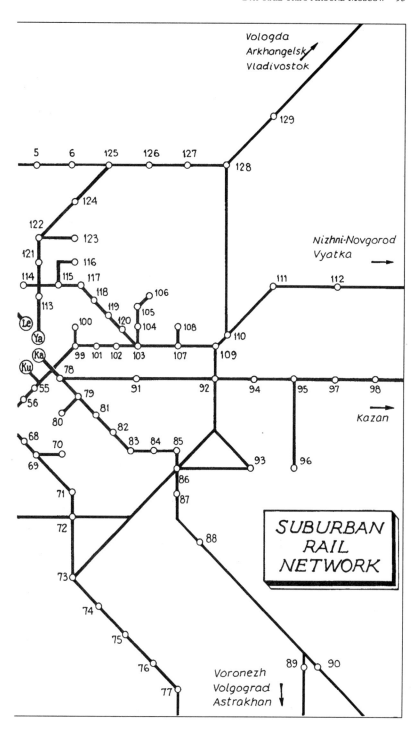

KEY TO MOSCOW SUBURBAN RAIL NETWORK
йригородное железнодорожное сообщение

The table below gives the distance and travelling time on electric suburban trains from Moscow's nine main stations.

Moscow's stations

Initial	Station	станция
Be	Belorussia station	Белорусский вокзал
Ka	Kazan station	Казанский вокзал
Ki	Kiev station	Киевский вокзал
Ku	Kursk station	Курский вокзал
Le	Leningrad station	Ленинграгский вокзал
Pa	Paveletski station	Павелецкий вокзал
Ri	Rizhski station	Рижский вокзал
Sa	Savelovski station	Савеловский вокзал
Ya	Yaroslavski station	Ярославский вокзал

Station	станция	No.	km	Time
47km platform	пл. 47км	82	46	1hr 6min
Aeroport (Vnukovo Airport)	Аэропорт (аэрп. Внуково)	48	33	49min
Akulovo	Акулово	38	73	1hr 30min
Aleksandrov	Александров	128	112	2hr–2hr 15min
Aprelevka	Апрелевка	49	42	54min
Balakirevo	Балакирево	129	130	2hr 20min–2hr 35min
Balashikha	Балашиха	100	27	37min
Barybino	Барыбино	71	57	1hr 10min
Bekasovo	Бекасово	39	89	1hr 50min
Bolshaya Volga	Большая Волга	10	128	2hr 28min
Bolshevo	Болшево	115	25	36min
Borodino	Бородино	44	121	2hr 10min–2hr 20min
Bronnitsy	Бронницы	83	56	1hr 18min
Buryulevo	Бурюлево	67	19	25min
Buzhaninovo	Бужаниново	126	85	1hr 35min–1hr 45min
Bykovo (Bykovo Airport)	Быково (аэро. Быково)	81	33	47min
Chekhov	Чехов	63	75	1hr 30min
Chernetskoe	Чернецкое	42	102	2hr 10min
Cherusti	Черусти	98	156	2hr 45min
Chkalovskaya	Чкаловская	118	38	56min
Dedovsk	Дедовск	28	37	52min
Depo	Депо	56	12	16min
Dmitrov	Дмитров	7	65	1hr 20min
Domodedovo	Домодедово	69	37	40–50min
Domodedovo Airport	Аэропорт Домодедово	70	49	1hr 5min–1hr 10min
Dubna	Дубна	11	131	1hr 56min–2hr 38min
Dzerzhinskaya	Дзержинская	80	31	
Egorevsk-2	Егорьевск-II	93	111	2hr 30min
Elektrogorsk	Электрогорск	108	84	1hr 40min
Elektrostal	Электросталь	104	61	1hr 15min
Fryazevo	Фрязево	103	54	1hr 5min
Fryazino	Фрязино	116	44	1hr 5min
Gagarin	Гагарин	45	180	3hr 10min
Golitsyno	Голицыно	35	44	55min
Golutvin	Голутвин	88	117	1hr 55min–2hr 15min
Gzhel	Гжель	91	57	1hr 13min
Iksha	Икша	3	45	58min
Kaluga-1	Калуга-I	54	188	3hr 20min–3hr 45min
Kaluga-2	Калуга-II	53	182	3hr 15min
Kashira	Кашира	75	115	1hr 50min–2hr
Khimki	Химки	14	19	25min
Klin	Клин	19	90	1hr 35min
Kolontaevo	Колонтаево	120	59	1hr 20min
Konakovo GRES	Конаково ГРЭС	22	141	2hr 5min–2hr 30min
Konakovski Mokh	Конаковский Мох	21	123	2hr 5min
Konobeevo	Конобеево	85	79	1hr 40min
Kostino	Костино	5	91	2hr 10min–2hr 20min
Krasnoarmeisk	Красноармейск	123	61	
Krasny Stroiel	Красный Строитель	58	25	33min
Kresty	Кресты	41	89	2hr
Krivandino	Кривандино	95	135	
Krutoe	Крутое	110	94	1hr 45min
Kryukovo	Крюково	16	39	41–48min
Kubinka-1	Кубинка-I	37	63	1hr 15min

Kupavna	Купавна	102	32	40min
Kurovskaya	Куровская	92	87	1hr 35min–1hr 45min
Lesnoi Gorodok	Лесной городок	47	28	36min
Lobnya	Лобня	1	26	36min
Lugovaya	Луговая	2	31	38min
Lvovskaya	Львовская	61	56	1hr 10min
Lyubertsy-1	Люберцы-I	78	20	31min
Lyublino	Люблино	55	10	15min
Machikhino	Мачихино	40	75	1hr 45min
Maloyaroslavets	Малоярославец	51	121	2hr 5min–2hr 20min
Manikhino-1	Манихино-I	29	55	
Mikhnevo	Михнево	72	74	1hr 15min–1hr 30min
Monino	Монино	119	49	1hr 10min
Mozhaisk	Можайск	43	110	2hr–2hr 10min
Mytishchi	Мытищи	113	18	27min
Nakhobino	Нахабино	26	33	45min
Nara	Нара	50	70	1hr 25min
Noginsk	Ногинск	105	69	1hr 25min
Novoierusalimskaya	Новоиерусалимская	30	59	1hr 15min
Obintsovo	Обинцово	34	24	33min
Orekhovo-Zuevo	Орехово-Зуево	109	89	
Orubevo	Орудьево	8	78	1hr 25min–1hr 45min
Ozherele	Ожерелье	76	124	2hr–2hr 15min
Panki	Панки	79	22	33min
Pavarovo-1	Паварово-I	17	52	
Pavlovskaya Sloboda	Павловская Слобода	27	42	
Pavlovski Posad	Павловский Посад	107	68	
Petushki	Петушки	111	126	2hr 15min
Pirogovo	Пирогово	114	26	42min
Podolsk	Подольск	60	43	53min
Podsolnechnaya	Подсолнечная	18	65	1hr 15min
Post 81	Пост 81км	125	80	
Pushkino	Пушкино	121	30	45min
Rastorguevo	Расторгуево	68	23	32min
Redkino	Редкино	24	133	2hr 15min
Reshetnikovo	Решетниково	20	105	
Reutovo	Реутово	99	15	20min
Rumyantsevo	Румянцево	31	80	1hr 40min
Ryazan-1	Рязан-I	89	197	3hr 35min–3hr 50min
Ryazan-2	Рязан-II	90	198	3hr 35min–3hr 50min
Ryazanovka	Рязановка	96	254	
Savelovo	Савелово	13	130	2hr 25min–2hr 27min
Sergiev Posad	Сергиев Посад	124	70	1hr 20min
Serpukhov	Серпухов	64	99	1hr 50min–2hr
Shatura	Шатура	94	125	2hr 20min
Shchelkovo	Щелково	117	36	50min
Shcherbinka	Щербинка	59	34	43min
Shifernaya	Шиферная	87	93	1hr 50min
Skhodnya	Сходня	15	30	38min
Sofrino	Софрино	122	45	1hr 2min
Solnechnaya	Солнечная	46	16	22min
Stolbovaya	Столбовая	62	64	
Strunino	Струнино	127	104	1hr 55min
Stupino	Ступино	74	99	1hr 40min–1hr 55min
Taldom (Savelovski)	Талдон (Савеловский)	12	111	2hr 12min
Tarusskaya	Тарусская	65	124	2hr 20min
Tikhonova Pustyn	Тухонова Пустынь	52	170	
Tsaritsyno	Царицыно	57	19	26min
Tugolese	Туролесье	97	144	2hr 35min
Tula-1	Тула-I	66	194	3hr 25min–3hr 45min
Tver	Тверь	25	167	2hr 15min–2hr 40min
Usovo	Усово	33	29	45min
Uzunovo	Узуново	77	159	3hr–3hr 10min
Verbilki	Вербилки	9	90	
Vinogradovo	Виноградово	84	71	1hr 35min
Vladimir	Владимир	112	191	3hr 5min–3hr 25min
Volokolamsk	Волоколамск	32	125	2hr 25min
Voskresensk	Воскресенск	86	89	
Yakhroma	Яхрома	4	59	
Zakharovo	Захарово	106	72	1hr 30min
Zavidovo	Завидово	23	119	1hr 53min
Zheleznodorozhnaya	Железнодорожная	101	24	3min2
Zheltikovo	Желтиково	6	102	2hr 25min
Zhilevo	Жилево	73	90	1hr 40min–1hr 55min
Zvenigorod	Звенигород	36	60	1hr 20min

About 200m towards Moscow from Leninskaya station is the now defunct Gerasimovskaya station from where Lenin's funeral train actually departed on January 23 1924. Both Gerasimovskaya station and the Lenin bust on the platform can be seen from the train.

Monino Air Force Museum

About 35km east of Moscow at Monino (Монино) is Russia's largest aeroplane museum, tel: 526 3327 or 584 2180. Over 150 aircraft are on display either in hangars or on an airfield. While most are military, there are a few civilian planes, including the ANT25 which flew over the Polar cap to USA in 1936, and the Tu-144 Soviet concord which never made it into regular service.

As the museum is on an operational airforce base, entry is only possible on a pre-booked organised tour.

To reach Monino, take a suburban train from Yaroslav station. The journey takes 1hr 20min and you can see the main entrance of the airforce base on the right about 500m before the Monino station.

Tula   Тула
Telephone area code: 0872

Tula is a small industrial city famous for its weapons and *samovars*. It is one of Russia's oldest towns, first being mentioned in 1146, and although it was levelled by the Mongols several times, it still played an important part in the military development of Russia. This was because the Imperial small arms factory was founded here in 1712 by Peter the Great and, to this day, it still produces firearms and ammunition. Tula was so important to Russia that both Napoleon and Hitler attempted to take the town but both failed. During the 1941 attempt, the town withstood an intense 45-day bombardment and for the defenders' enormous courage and determination, the town was given the rare title of Hero City of the USSR.

Getting there and away

To get to Tula, catch a train from Kursk station. The suburban train takes 4hr to cover the 193km while a more comfortable and expensive long-distance passenger train takes 3hr 30min.

Where to stay

You can stay at the standard Moscow Hotel, pl Vokzalnaya, tel: 208 952, $23 twin share/person, or the very basic Tula Hotel, pro Lenina 96, tel: 252 312 near the bus station.

You can eat at Restaurant Moscow in the Moscow Hotel, tel: 208 963, or Restaurant Druzhba, pro Lenina 78, tel: 256 407.

What to see

If you have only a few hours, the best place to see is the kremlin. This fortress was built in 1514 and its walls are 3m thick, 13m high and have a total length of 1km. Unlike Moscow, you can explore the entire kremlin as it only contains a Military Weapons Museum in the former Epiphany Cathedral and the Ascension Cathedral. The condition and accessibility of the kremlin makes it one of the best to visit in Russia.

The town's other highlights include the Samovar Museum near the kremlin's entrance, Museum of Regional Studies, ul Sovetskaya 68, tel: 310 319, Art

Gallery, ul Engelsa 144, tel: 254 272, Artists' Exhibition Hall, Zoological Museum and the House-museum of the writer V V Veresaev. Buildings of note include Russia's oldest velodrome, Annunciation Church and the Gorky Drama Theatre built in 1777.

What's in the region

About 14km to the south of Tula is the Yasnaya Polyana Museum Estate, which was the manor house of the famous Russian author, Lev Tolstoi. Tolstoi was born and worked here for much of his life. Half a kilometre away at Stary Zakaz Hill is his grave. Although there is a station called Yasnaya Polyana, the museum estate is about 3km from here and is difficult to reach. The easiest way to get to Yasnaya Polyana Museum Estate is by taxi from Tula.

Getting assistance

Travel agents   Intourist, ul Sovetskaya 52, tel: 272 766, 272 774
Air   Aeroflot, pro Krasnoarmeiski 9, tel: 205 457

Gagarin   Гагарин
Telephone area code: 081 35

If you are interested in Russia's space heroes, Gagarin is the place for you. This small town was named after the world's first man in space, Yuri Gagarin, as he was born nearby. There are six major places of interest in the town. Five of these are together and form the Cosmonaut Museum Complex, ul Gagarina 74, tel: 487 47, open 10.00–18.00, closed Monday. The main attraction here is the Son of Russia Museum, which displays material on Gagarin's life and 1961 space flight including several excellent space models. Morbidly, there is also a small amount of dirt sprinkled with scorched aluminium fragments in one display which is claimed to have been taken in 1968 from Gagarin's fatal plane crash site east of Moscow. Notably absent from the museum is any mention that Gagarin's space flight nearly ended in a fatal disaster. This disaster was only revealed publicly in 1996 with the auction in New York of the private notes of Gagarin's commander, Colonel Yevgeny Karpov. He recorded that the 108-minute flight experienced severe technical problems and nearly ended in the death of Yuri Gagarin.

Next door to this museum is Gagarin's parents' house. This 1970s home displays the parents' bed and the cosmonaut's study when he visited home. Other Gagarin highlights in the immediate area are the School Museum where he studied, his black Volga car encased in glass and a life-like bust. The other Gagarin attraction in the town is the giant Gagarin memorial on the town's main square in front of Hotel Vostok. This monument is recognised as the worst Gagarin memorial in Russia as he looks like a cartoon character in a jumpsuit.

To get to Gagarin, take a train from Belorussia station. Suburban trains take 4hr while passenger trains take as little as 3hr. To find the museum complex, walk 200m from the station towards Moscow and you will reach the town's main road, ul Gagarina, which travels at right angles to the railway line. Turning left down this road, after 800m you will reach the town's main square containing the Gagarin memorial and Hotel Vostok. Keep walking ahead for another 500m and you will pass a bookshop on your right and another 100m will bring you to the museum complex.

Although the town is best known for Gagarin, it has a long history as it was a major trading port in the 18th century. It was called Gzhatsk until 1968, and you can find out about this early period in the Museum of Local Studies, ul Sovetskaya 3, open 10.00–18.00, closed Tuesday.

If you want to know still more about Gagarin's life, you can visit Klushino village, 24km to the north, which is where he was born and where today stands a House-museum of his childhood. The only public transport to Klushino are buses which depart every two hours from Gagarin.

Gagarin's only hotel is the overpriced, basic Hotel Vostok, ul Gagarina 74, tel: 414 65, $36 twin share/person.

Borodino battlefield preserve
Бородинский военно-исторический музей-заповедник

This small village is famous for the massive battle on August 26 1812 between Napoleon's French and Russian armies. The 15-hour battle claimed over 59,000 French and 44,000 Russian lives, and was spread along a 4km front. In 1941, 129 years later, the area witnessed the second battle of Borodino, this time between Hitler's Fascist and the Soviet armies.

The Borodino battlefield has been preserved as a 110km² Field Museum and contains over 40 memorials, trenches and buildings. Highlights include the grey memorial obelisk crowned with a bronze eagle devoted to the 58,000 French deaths and paid for by the French in 1912; the Maslov's fortification; and the grave of the heroic Prince Bagration who was fatally wounded in the battle. Other highlights include the Borodino Museum, tel: 515 46, 510 57, open 10.00–17.00, closed Mondays and the last Friday of the month. The museum, with its cannons lining the entrance way, has several rooms of weapons, maps and paraphernalia from the battle.

To get to Borodino station, take a suburban train from Belorussia station. The 121km journey takes 2hr 20min. To get to the museum, take the road which runs at right angles to the railway line on the side of the station away from Moscow. The road on the side closest to Moscow goes to Borodino village. The distance to the museum from the station is about 4km.

You need the full day to wander around and, although there is a restaurant near the museum, it is more enjoyable to take a picnic lunch and enjoy it in the fields. The best time to visit Borodino is on the first full weekend in September, the official anniversary of the battle. The weekend of festivities culminates on Sunday with an re-enactment of the Borodino Battle with thousands of military enthusiasts dressing up in period costumes. In 1996, this was on the weekend starting September 6.

The Russian military historian, John Sloan, leads tours of the Borodino battlefield on the battle's anniversary in conjunction with Rantek Travel Agency, ul Vorovskovo 30/36, Moscow, tel: (095) 290 5464, fax: (095) 230 2938, email slava@slavas.msk.ru. In USA contact John Sloan, 5218 Landgrave Ln, Springfield VA 22151, USA, tel: (703) 321 9072, fax: (703) 321 0927, email johns426@aol.com, http://home.aol.com/johns426.

Swimming and picnics

Getting out of Moscow in the muggy summer weeks for a swim and picnic can often be a refreshing and informative way to spend a day. There are 22 official *zony otdykha* ("recreational areas") around Moscow with facilities and

This sign occasionally springs up at beaches around Moscow and warns against swimming or fishing because of cholera

swimming places. These are meant to include changing booths, showers, and even umbrella rentals but, with the privatisation of these places, some have maintained or even improved their facilities, while others have collapsed into disrepair. In 1995 12 of the 22 were closed for various reasons, including an outbreak of cholera. Below are three of the best swimming and picnic destinations around Moscow but, before you go, check that they are not closed for health reasons. Of course, you can go to the thousands of unmarked river and lake swimming places around Moscow rivers but it is best to go north, away from Moscow's pollution.

Take your own food and drink as you can't always trust what's for sale.

Serebryanny Bor   Here there is a big, crowded and well-maintained beach and nearby are gay and nude beaches. Entry costs $0.50 and the beach is open 09.00–21.00. To get there, go to Polezhayevskaya metro station, then take trolleybus No 20 which terminates at the beach.

Khimki   This consists of two main beaches around Khimskoye Reservoir; Khimki 1 and Khimki 2. Khimki 1 is awful but easy to get to. Take the metro to Vodny Stadion metro station, and the beach is opposite the station on the west side of pro Leningradski. Walk through the tall yellow gates and go past the tennis courts. You will see the beach on your right. Khimki 2 is far better and costs $1.50 to enter. It operates 09.00–21.00. To get there go to Vodny Stadion metro station, take trolleybus No 2 or 43 north for two stops. Get out at the Imenno Lebeda Theatre, cross over pro Leningradski and walk around the reservoir for 100m which will take you across a bridge. You will see the beach ahead.

Kolomenskoye   This is by far the most attractive place to visit. The Moscow River flows along the eastern boundary of the $4km^2$ Kolomenskoye Royal Estate and the quickest way to get there is through the estate. Take the metro to Kolomenskoye metro station and exit toward Kolomenskoye Museum. It's about a 10-minute walk to the estate and you will enter via the 17th-century Saviour Gate. While you can swim in the estate's ponds, it's much safer in the river. As there are no special sites for swimmers along the banks of the river, stop anywhere you want.

Chapter Six

Kiev and Surrounding Region

KIEV Київ
Population: 2,654,000   Telephone area code: 044

KIEV'S NEW NAME
Traditionally, the spelling Kiev has been used, reflecting the Russian spelling of
the city. Following the independence of Ukraine, the city's name in English has
become Kyiv, reflecting the Ukrainian spelling. However, the traditional spelling
is much more familiar in the West and will be used throughout this guide.

Kiev is the capital of Ukraine and has much to offer the traveller. The city is
considerably older than Moscow; while its official date of foundation is 482AD,
remains of Stone Age settlements dating back to 10000BC have been found in
the area.

In the 9th century, Kiev became the capital of Kievian Rus and its influence
extended into vast areas of present-day Russia. Internal power struggles in the
12th century signalled the beginning of the end and in 1240 the Mongols
completely destroyed Kiev. Over the following centuries, Kiev was rebuilt but it
was always dominated by either Lithuania or Russia despite brief periods of
independence in the mid 1600s and 1918. During the centuries of dominance,
Ukrainian politics, culture and language were all brutally oppressed. Despite
sporadic pushes for Ukrainian independence, it was only with the collapse of
communism within Russia and the disintegration of the Soviet Union that
Ukraine at last gained independence on August 24 1991.

Kiev's centuries of development have resulted in dozens of interesting
churches, historic monuments and architectural achievements such as the
Kievan Cave Monastery, Brotherhood (Bratsky) Monastery and the Golden
Gate, all worth visiting.

For those with special interests, Kiev has many museums with subjects ranging
from the historic treasures of Ukraine to army history; for those interested in the
outdoors there are the Botanical Gardens and the Museum of Folk Architecture.
Rather than discussing these highlights, which are listed in many guidebooks, this
book concentrates on the rarely covered areas of train travel to Kiev and day trips
in the surrounding region. Good guides to the city are listed in *Appendix Four*.

Kiev is in the same time zone as St Petersburg and Moscow. Kiev is one hour
ahead of Helsinki, Sofia, Athens, and Bucharest, two hours ahead of Paris,

Prague, Rome, Stockholm, Warsaw, Vienna and Berlin, and three hours ahead of London. Daylight saving starts on the last Saturday in March and finishes on the last Saturday in September.

A minimum of two days is needed to get an overview of Kiev but three are recommended. Try to coincide your visit with one of Kiev's celebrations. The two best are Kiev Day on the last Sunday of May and Independence Day on August 24. There are also two month-long art festivals in Kiev: Kiev Spring in May and Golden Autumn in August.

Getting there and away
By air
Kiev has several airports, the main one being Boryspil international airport, tel: 296 7609. Buses for Boryspil depart from pro Peremohy. The main domestic airport is Zhulyany airport, tel: 272 1201.

By road
The central bus station is located at pl Moskovska 3, tel: 265 0430. Advance bus tickets can be purchased at blvd Lesya Ukrayinka 14, tel: 225 5015.

By rail
All long-distance trains arrive at Kiev's central railway station, tel: 265 3053. The station is on the western fringes of the city centre at the end of ul Kominterna on pl Vokzalna. Beside the station is the Vokzalna metro station.

International trains
International trains are all of a good standard, and the carriages are either *SV*, three-berth *coupé* or four-berth *coupé*. The majority of trains have a restaurant car attached when they enter Ukraine, but it is still advisable to take some food and drink in case your train is an exception. The main international trains to Kiev are listed below.

Origin	Dist, km	Entry point	Train no & name	Carr'ge class	No in coupé	Travel time	Day of departure	Destination
Kiev	1371	Brest	141	2	4	34hr	daily	Berlin
Berlin	1371	Brest	142	2	4	34hr	daily	Kiev
Brussels	2440	Brest	274	1, 2	2, 3	45hr	Tue	Kiev
Kiev	2440	Brest	273	1, 2	2, 3	45hr	Sun	Brussels
Budapest	1238	Chop	16 Tisza Express	1, 2	2, 3	24hr	twice a week	Kiev
Kiev	1238	Chop	15 Tisza Express	1, 2	2, 3	24hr	twice a week	Budapest
Warsaw	794	Brest	68 Kiev Express	2	4	25hr	daily	Kiev
Kiev	794	Brest	67 Kiev Express	2	4	25hr	daily	Warsaw
Vienna	1515	Chop	52	1, 2	2, 3	27hr	Tue, Thur, Sun	Kiev
Kiev	1515	Chop	51	1, 2	2, 3	27hr	Mon, Wed, Sat	Vienna
Bratislava	1242	Mostiska	44	2	4	24hr	daily	Kiev
Kiev	1242	Mostiska	43	2	4	24hr	daily	Bratislava
Prague	1710	Chop	8 Dulka	1, 2	2, 3	31hr	daily	Kiev
Kiev	1710	Chop	7 Dulka	1, 2	2, 3	31hr	daily	Prague
Sofia	1678	Vadul-Siret	86 Bulgarian Express	2	4	14hr	daily	Kiev
Kiev	1678	Vadul-Siret	85 Bulgarian Express	2	4	14hr	daily	Sofia

Domestic trains

If you are travelling within Ukraine or between Ukraine and Russia, it is best not to travel on the international trains as tickets on these trains are much harder to buy. It is considerably easier to catch domestic trains. The major trains through Kiev are listed below. More detail on the route Moscow–Kiev–Chop can be found in *Chapter Ten*.

Origin	Dist, km	Train no & name	Travel time	Depart	Arrive	Destination
Kiev	485	42	9hr 46min	21.50	07.36	Bryansk (through)
Kiev	872	2	15hr 59min	17.10	09.09	Moscow (Kiev)
Kiev (through)	893	15	17hr 33min	11.55	05.28	Chop (through)
Kiev (through)	627	8	10hr 53min	16.35	03.28	Lviv (through)
Kiev	1,257	188	30hr 46min	22.42	09.28	St Petersburg (Vitebsk)
Bryansk (through)	485	3	7hr 15min	22.50	06.05	Kiev
Chop (through)	893	16	17hr 10min	00.35	17.45	Kiev (through)
Lviv (through)	627	9	11hr 17min	00.34	11.51	Kiev (through)
Moscow (Kiev)	872	1	13hr 36min	19.54	09.30	Kiev
St Petersburg (Vitebsk)	1,257	187	30hr 22min	13.28	19.50	Kiev

Train tickets

Tickets for international trains are best purchased at the Inturyst ticket window No 42 (Intourist Hall) on the second floor of the central station. The ticket windows are open around the clock but closed 02.00–03.00, 07.00–08.00, 14.00–15.00 and 19.00–20.00.

If you want a ticket for a train departing on the same day, you can get it at the central station while advance purchase tickets (ie: for tomorrow or any day up to 30 days in advance) can be purchased at the station or at the ticket office at blvd Shevchenko 38/40 in the lobby of Hotel Expres. This is often very crowded. Another option is the much more expensive Intourist ticket office at vul Hospitalna 12, tel: 224 2559, which is just behind Hotel Kievska. It is open 09.00–18.00, closed 12.00–13.00.

Getting around

Work building Kiev's metro started in 1949 and its first line, consisting of 5.2km, was opened 11 years later. Today, the metro is 43km long, with three lines and a total of 36 stations. Kiev's metro transports about 20% of Kiev urban commuters with a million customers per day.

The system works on tokens which are purchased inside the metro buildings, invariably near the turnstyles. The metro operates 06.00–01.00. Enquiries for lost and found can be made on tel: 226 3809.

Where to stay

Below is a listing of the best accommodation in the various categories. It is highly recommended that you pre-book. Arriving without a booking can result in you paying more or being refused a room.

Basic

Hotel Druzhba, bul Druzhby Narodiv 5, tel: 268 3406, 268 3300, $10 twin share/person. The closest metro station is Lybidska.

Hotel Myr, pro 40th Zhovtnya 70, tel: 268 5383, 264 9651, 264 9646, $18 twin share/person. The closest metro station is Lybidska.

Standard
Hotel Andriyivska, vul Andriyivski 24, $66 twin share/person.

Hotel Bratyslava, vul Malyshka 1, tel: 551 7334, 551 7644, fax: 559 7788, $39 twin share/person. The closest metro station is Darnitsya.

Hotel Dnipro, vul Khreshchatyk 1/2, tel: 229 7193, 229 8179, fax: 229 8213, $80 twin share/person. The closest metro station is Maydan Nezalezhnosti.

Hotel Kievska, vul Hospitalna 12, tel: 227 9555, 220 4044, fax: 220 4568, $100 twin share/person. The closest metro station is Klovska.

Hotel Lybid, pl Tarasa Shevchenka, tel: 274 0063, 224 4261, 224 3206, fax: 224 0578, $48 twin share/person. The closest metro station is Universytet.

Hotel Moskva, vul Intytutska 4, tel: 229 0347, 228 2804, $39 twin share/person. The closest metro station is Maydan Nezalezhnosti.

Hotel Rus, vul Hospitalna 4, tel: 220 5646, 220 4255, fax: 220 4568, $50 twin share/person. The closest metro station is Klovska.

Hotel Salyat, vul Sichnevoho Povstannya 11A, tel: 290 6130, fax: 290 7270, $75 twin share/person. The closest metro station is Dnipro.

Hotel Sport, vul Chervonoarmiyska 55, tel: 220 0327, fax: 220 0257.

Hotel St Petersburg, bul Tarasa Shevchenko 4, tel: 229 7453. The closest metro station is Teatralna.

Hotel Ukraina, bul Tarasa Shevchenko 5, tel: 229 2807, $44 twin share/person. The closest metro station is Teatralna.

Places of railway interest
Funicular railway
A funicular railway was built in 1905 to run up Volodimerska Girka to pl Mikhailovskaya. It starts near Poshtova Ploscha metro station and runs all year round.

Children's railway
On the northwest outskirts of Kiev is a small-gauge 3km-long railway on which a locomotive and six carriages chug around. The railway was opened in 1953. It is run by schoolchildren as part of a railway education programme and consequently, only runs in school holidays. To get to it, go to Shulyavska metro station and take trolleybus No 27 along ul Eleny Teligi. Get off at ul Gonti which is the second stop on the left. The railway is at the end of this road.

Foreign embassies
Austria   vul Lipska 5, Hotel Natsionalny, tel: 291 8848, 291 6068, 291 8840, fax: 291 5468

Australia   vul Malopidvalna 8, tel: 228 7426

Belarus   vul Lutuzova 8, tel: 294 8212, fax: 294 8006

Belgium   vul Kreshchatik 1/2, Hotel Dnipro, tel: 229 7157

Bulgaria   vul Hospitalna 1, tel: 224 5360, 225 5119, 225 2202, fax: 225 4389

Canada   vul Yaroslaviv, 31, tel: 212 0212, 212 2864, fax: 225 1305, 212 2329

China   vul Hospitlna 4, Hotel Rus, tel: 227 8402, 227 8428, 227 8424, 220 1583

Czech Republic   val Yaroslaviv 34, tel: 229 7922, 212 0807

Denmark   vul Hospitalna 4, Hotel Rus, tel: 227 8564, fax: 227 8587

Estonia   vul Kutuzov 8, tel: 296 2886, 294 8514, fax: 295 8176

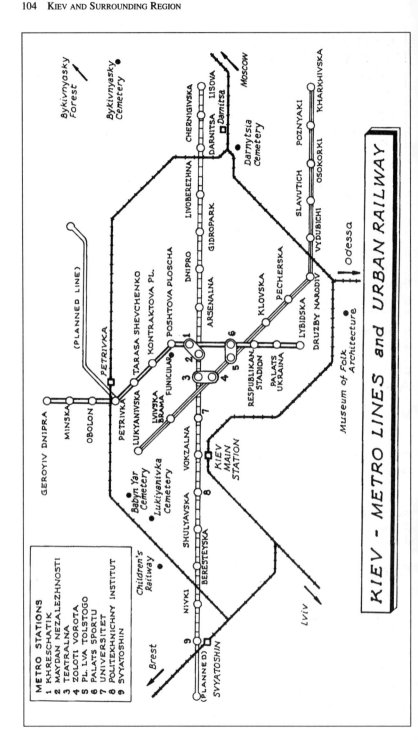

KIEV - METRO LINES and URBAN RAILWAY

KEY TO KIEV METRO
Київського Метро

North–South line

Geroyiv Dnipra	Героїв Дніпра
Minska	Мінська
Obolon	Оболонь
Petrivka	Петрівка
Tarasa Shevchenko	Тараса Шевченка
Kontraktova Ploscha	Контрактова Площа
Poshtova Ploscha	Поштова Площа
Maydan Nezalezhnosti	Майдан Дезалежності
Palats Sportu	Палац Спорту
Respublikanski Stadion	Республіканський Стадіон
Palats Ukraina	Палац Україна
Lybidska	Либідська

Northwest-Southeast

Lukyanivska	Лукянівська
Lvivska Brama	Львівська Брама
Zoloti Vorota	Золоті Ворота
Ploscha Lva Tolstogo	Площа Льва Толстого
Klovska	Кловська
Percherska	Печерська
Druzby Narodiv	Дружби Народів
Vydubichi	Видубичі
Slavutich	Славутич
Osokorki	Осокорки
Poznyaki	Познякі
Kharkivska	Харківська

West-East line

Svyatoshin	Святошин
Nivki	Нивки
Beresteyska	Берестеиська
Shulyavska	Шулявська
Politekhnichny Institut	Політехниічний Інститут
Vokzalna	Вокзальна
Universitet	Університет
Teatralna	Театральна
Khreschatik	Хрещатик
Arsenalna	Арсенальна
Dnipro	Дніпро
Gidropark	Гідропарк
Livoberezhna	Лівобережна
Darnitsa	Дарниця
Chernigivska	Чернігівська
Lisova	Лісова

Finland   vul Hospitalna 4, Hotel Rus, tel: 227 8434, fax: 227 8456

France   vul Reytarsaka 39, tel: 228 8728, 228 7369

Germany   vul Chkalova 84, tel: 216 6794, 216 1477, 216 7854, 216 7498, fax: 216 9233

Hungary   vul Reytarska 33, tel: 212 4004, 212 4039, 225 0298, 212 4134, 212 4104

Italy   vul Lypsky 5, Hotel Natsionalny, tel: 291 8894, 291 8992, 291 8898, fax: 291 8897

Japan   vul Lipskaya 5, Hotel Natsionalnaya, tel: 291 8872, fax: 291 8872

Poland   vul Yaroslaviv 12, tel: (044) 255 5114, 224 6308, 224 8040

Romania   vul Kotsiubynskoho 8, tel: 224 5261, 224 4316, fax: 293 6950

Russia   vul Kutuzova 8, tel: (044) 294 7936, 294 6701, fax: (044) 292 6631

Sweden   vul Lypska 5, Hotel Natsionalny, tel: 291 8848, 291 8969, fax: 291 5468, 291 6233
UK   vul Desiatynna 9, tel: 462 0011, 462 0012, 462 0014, fax: 228 0504, 228 3872
USA   vul Yuriya Kotsiubynskoho 10, tel: 244 7344, 244 7345, 244 7346, 244 7347, 244 7448, 244 7349, 244 7354, fax: 244 7350, 244 7351, telex 131142 CGKIVSU

DAY RAIL TRIPS AROUND KIEV
River trips
An excellent day trip is to take one of the numerous ferries or hydrofoils which ply the Dniepr River. Vessels leave Kiev's main pier at pl Poshtova 3, tel: 416 7372. The closest metro station is Poshtova Ploscha. Vessels travel the river from April to October. Tickets can be purchased one to five days in advance.

Two interesting destinations are Kaniv and Novi Petryvtsi towns.

Kaniv (Канів)   This town is located about 150km downstream of Kiev and contains the grave and two museums of Ukraine's greatest poet, T Shevchenko (1814–61). The combined Grave of T Shevchenko Museum and Preserve is located at Tarasova Hora, tel: (04 736) 223 65, while the T Shevchenko Literary House Museum is located in the town's centre. Kaniv also boasts a Museum of Ukrainian Decorative and Applied Art, ul Lenina 64, tel: 223 91. About 4km south of the town is the 2,000-hectare Kaniv Preserve. This park is littered with architectural, geological and palaeontological monuments and is an interesting place to spend a few hours. The hydrofoil trip to Kaniv takes about three hours one way. Kaniv has a sister city relationship with Sonoma, California.

Novi Petryvtsi (Нові Петрівці)   This was the headquarters of the Soviet's 1st Ukrainian Front during the battle for Kiev in November 1943. The town now has a museum to the battle and it includes pillboxes, other fortifications and a diorama of the Battle of Kiev. Novi Petryvtsi is located 25km north of Kiev and the ferry trip takes 30 minutes one way.

Museum of Folk Architecture
About 12km south of Kiev near Pirogovo village is the Museum of Folk Architecture, tel: 266 2416. The 100-hectare open-air museum contains over 400 old houses, windmills, *banyas* and churches which have been brought from all over Ukraine. Many of the buildings have been furnished with period household goods. The museum operates from May 1 to November 7, closed Wednesday, open 10.00–18.00. During the cold months, you can wander around the museum but all of the buildings are closed.

The best way to get to the museum is on bus No 84 from Lybidska metro station.

Atrocities in Kiev
Since World War II, the sites of German war atrocities around Kiev have been known. However, it has only been since the collapse of communism that the atrocities committed by the Soviets have been revealed.

No other European country suffered as much as Ukraine under Nazi occupation. An estimated 11–14.5 million Ukrainians died, including 600,000 Jews. Kiev's most horrific atrocity site is Babyn Yar. This ravine is the place where the Germans executed over 150,000 people during their 1941–3 occupation of Kiev. Most of those executed were Jewish but large numbers of Soviet prisoners of war, partisans, Ukrainian nationalists, gypsies and anyone regarded as a threat to the Germans were also killed. Today, several Soviet, Ukrainian and Jewish monuments stand in the Babyn Yar Park, near the site of many of the executions. To get to the park, go to Shulyavska metro station and take trolleybus No 27 along ul Eleny Teligi. Get off at the stop called Shevchenkovsky Univermag. Another option is trolleybus No 16 from Maydan Nezhalezhnosti metro station.

The two major sites of Soviet era atrocities in Kiev are: Lukiyanivka Cemetery, just to the south of Babyn Yar at ul Shamrylo 7 (take trolleybus No 16 from Shulyavska metro station); and Bykivnyasky Forest on the Kiev–Chernihiv highway (take a taxi which should cost about $15 for the return trip).

Chapter Seven

Minsk and Surrounding Region

MINSK   Бінск
Population: 1,661,000   Telephone area code: 0172

Minsk is the capital of the Republic of Belarus and is situated on both banks of the Svisloch River. The city was founded over 900 years ago as a trading centre at the crossroads connecting the Black and Baltic Seas and eastern Europe and Russia.

The city suffered enormous destruction during World War II and only two of Minsk's buildings survived totally untouched.

Today, the restored city is surrounded by green parks and is a pleasant contrast to noisy, hectic Moscow.

It is possible to see most of the highlights of Minsk in two days and another day or two visiting places of interest in the region as listed below. There are several festivals of interest during the year, in particular the Belarusian Musical Autumn Arts Festival (November 20–30), the Farewell to Winter Festival (last weekend of February) and the Belarusian Folk Music holiday (June–August).

As numerous guidebooks cover the city of Minsk in detail, this book concentrates on the often ignored regional highlights. Good general guides to the city are listed in Appendix Four.

Getting there and away
By train
Unlike Moscow, Minsk only has one long-distance railway station. It is located in the southeast of Minsk. At the station is the metro station Ploshcha Nezalezhnastsi (formerly Lenin Square). For information on trains in Russian, call tel: 005 or 955 510.

You can get long-distance and international train tickets on the upper floor of the main railway station. A less stressful place to buy them is the Belintourist (formerly Intourist) office at pro Masherava 19, tel: 269 840, fax: 231 143. This office is next door to Hotel Jubileynaya and is open 08.00–20.00. Another ticket office is at pro Skaryny 18, between vul Linina and Kamsamolskaya. It is open 09.00–18.00, closed Sunday. The ticket selling arrangements appear to change regularly so give yourself plenty of time.

International trains
A number of international trains go through Minsk, but it is often hard to get tickets. Below are only those trains which have carriages reserved for passengers to or from Minsk.

Information on through trains can be found in *Chapters Five* and *Eight*.

Origin	Dist, km	Entry point	Train no & name	Carr'ge class	No in coupé	Travel time	Day of departure	Destination
Minsk	1172	Chop	189	2	4	27hr 30min	Mon, Thur	Budapest
Minsk	567	Brest	103	2	4	7hr 30min	daily	Warsaw
Minsk	1139	Brest	13 Moskwa Express	2	4	21hr	daily	Berlin
Minsk	1310	Brest	21	1, 2	2, 3	38hr	daily	Prague
Minsk	2016	Vadul-Siret	195	2	4	17hr 30min	daily	Sofia
Berlin	1139	Brest	14 Moskwa Express	2	4	21hr	daily	Minsk
Budapest	1172	Chop	630	2	4	27hr 30min	Tue, Fri	Minsk
Prague	1310	Brest	22	1, 2	2, 3	38hr	daily	Minsk
Sofia	2016	Vadul-Siret	630	2	4	17hr 30min	daily	Minsk
Warsaw	567	Brest	104	2	4	7hr 30min	daily	Minsk

Domestic trains

If you are travelling within Russia or Belorussia, it is best not to travel on the international trains as tickets are much harder to buy. The major trains through Minsk are listed below. More detail on the route Moscow–Minsk–Brest can be found in *Chapter Nine*.

Origin	Dist, km	Train no & name	Travel time	Depart	Arrive	Destination
Minsk	331	48	5hr 32min	11.48	17.20	Smolensk
Minsk	355	117	5hr 12min	13.01	18.13	Brest
Minsk	750	2	13hr 16min	19.49	09.05	Moscow (Smolensk)
Minsk	750	4	12hr 54min	21.31	10.25	Moscow (Smolensk)
Minsk	863	52	19hr 4min	15.26	10.30	St Petersburg (Vitebsk)
Brest	355	50	5hr 1min	13.00	18.01	Minsk
Moscow (Smolensk)	750	1	10hr 48min	20.17	07.05	Minsk
Moscow (Smolensk)	750	3	11hr 4min	21.37	08.37	Minsk
Smolensk	331	47	3hr 40min	12.57	16.37	Minsk
St Petersburg (Vitebsk)	863	51	16hr 11min	18.45	10.56	Minsk

Getting about

Minsk's metro is small compared to the one in Moscow. It only has two lines, 18 stations and 16.7km of rails. It was opened in 1984 and its 1,000 employees manage the metro's 264,000 passenger journeys per day. The metro operates 06.00–23.30.

Where to stay

Below is a listing of the best standard accommodation in Minsk. As usual, it is highly recommended that you pre-book.

Hotel Belarus, vul Strojevskaya 15, tel: 391 705, 348 252, $30 twin share/person. The closest metro station is Ploshcha Peramohi.

Hotel Druzhba, vul Tolbukhina 3, tel: 662 481, $5 twin share/person. The closest metro station is Park Chaljuskintsau.

Hotel Kastrychnitskaja, vul Enhelsa 13, tel: 293 910, $40 twin share/person. The closest metro station is Kupalawskaja.

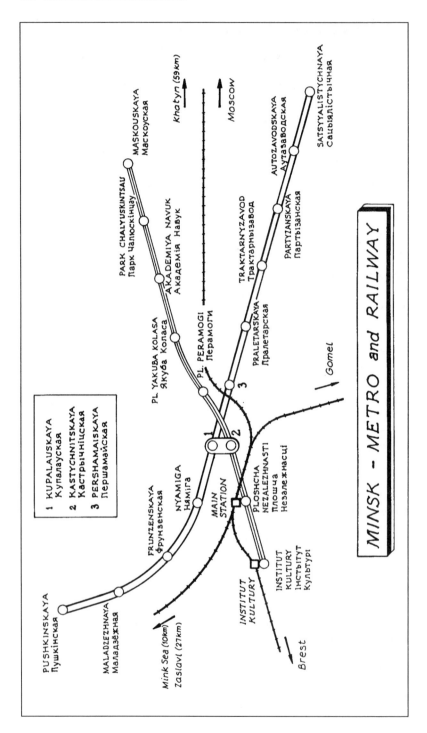

MINSK – METRO and RAILWAY

Hotel Jubileynaya, pra Masherava 19, tel: 269 171, 269 024, $35 twin share/person. The closest metro station is Kupalawskaja.

Hotel Minsk, pra Skaryny 11, tel: 200 132, 200 103, $20 twin share/person. It is near the main railway station.

Hotel Planeta, pra Masherava 31, tel: 267 953, 238 587, $30 twin share/person. The closest metro station is Kupalawskaja.

Hotel Savetskaja, vul Sorsa 5, tel: 253 529, $20 twin share/person. It is about 3km to the southwest of the city centre.

Hotel Svislach, vul Kirava 13, tel: 209 783, 204 211, $15 twin share/person. It is near the main railway station.

Foreign embassies
Czech Republic   Branjavy zavulak 5A, tel: 363 415, fax: 367 435
France   Hotel Belarus, room 1102, tel/fax: 343 4443
Germany   vul Zakharava 26, tel: 332 714, fax: 368 552
Japan   Hotel Kastruchnitskaya, room 303, tel: 274 718, fax: 274 319
Latvia   Hotel Belarus, room 1907, tel: 391 612, fax: 506 784
Lithuania   vul Varvasheni 1/7, tel/fax: 348 788
Poland   vul Rumjantsava 6, tel: 331 114, fax: 364 992
Russia   vul Staravilenskaya 48, tel: 345 497, fax: 503 664, tel/fax: 503 666
UK   vul Zakharava 26, tel: 330 752, fax: 368 552
Ukraine   vul Kirava 17-306, tel: 272 354, fax: 272 861
USA   vul Staravilenskaya 46, tel: 315 000, 347 761, fax: 347 853

DAY RAIL TRIPS AROUND MINSK
Khatyn (Хатынь)
About 59km northeast of Minsk along the Minsk–Vitebsk highway is the Khatyn Memorial Complex. This was formerly the site of Khatyn village which was one of 186 Belarusian villages that were burned down together with its inhabitants. In Khatyn on March 22 1943, 149 villagers were herded into a barn which was set alight. The only survivor was Josef Kaminski and he was found lying beside the body of his son. He became the model for the complex's famous statue of a man carrying the lifeless body of child. The complex is dedicated to all the victims of the German occupation especially those who died in the Nazis' 260 concentration camps and branches. A bell tolls every four minutes to symbolise that every fourth Belarusian died in the war.

As there is no railway nearby, the only way to get there is by bus. Take a direct bus to Khatyn from the long-distance bus station beside the central railway station. Khatyn is actually 5km off the Minsk–Vitebsk highway. If you are fit, you can walk the 5km which means that you can catch any of the many buses that travel along the highway.

Anti-Soviet propaganda claims that Khatyn village was selected as a memorial so that people would confuse it with Katyn village which is where 4,500 Polish officers and soldiers were executed by the Soviet secret police in 1941. Katyn is described in *Chapter Nine, page 141*.

The Minsk Sea
A picturesque artificial lake is just 10km north of Minsk. The shoreline is only 55km long, of which just over 10km is decent beaches. On the western shore is

KALININGRAD

With thanks to Norbert Tempel

The railway between Königsberg and Berlin, the Königliche Ostbahn, was opened in 1857, with the connection through to Russia brought into service in 1860. In 1896, the railway saw the introduction of the "Northern Express", bringing a direct link between Paris and St Petersburg in a journey of just 48 hours.

Since World War II, however, the fortunes of the railway have declined dramatically. The area around the former German port, in the northern part of eastern Prussia (Ostpreussen), was besieged by Russian troops during the war, and finally ceded to Russia in 1945. The city itself was renamed Kaliningrad in 1946 in honour of President Mikhail Kalinin, and the 13,200km² region surrounding it became known as the Kaliningrad Oblast. Shortly after the war, the scenic narrow gauge lines were closed and the trunk lines either closed or altered from standard to broad gauge. However, the Kaliningrad railway still covers a total of 758km, and in 1992 it carried 25 million passengers over a total distance of 1,154 million km, as well as 15.8 million tons of freight.

Although many of the trains to and from Kaliningrad have been withdrawn from service, passengers from Russia can still travel non-stop between here and Moscow. There is also a daily passenger train between Kaliningrad and the Lithuanian capital of Vilnius. Perhaps the best way to approach the city, however, is from the west: at 20.37 each evening, the "Mare Balticum Express" departs from Berlin-Lichtenberg, travelling overnight in style via Szczeczin and Gdansk. In Gdansk, one of the sleeper cars is changed to another train to ride on the newly reopened standard gauge line direct to Kaliningrad's central station, Jushny, crossing the Polish border via Braniewo/Mamonowo. The station at Jushny, or "south station", was built in the 1920s; the original building and roof are still in use.

The more intrepid could also consider the parallel broad gauge line which runs from Kaliningrad to Braniewo, but its reputation as a route for smuggling makes it an unwise choice for Western passengers.

There are a number of direct trains out of Kaliningrad. During the 1970s, the lines from Kaliningrad to Selenogradsk and Swetlogorsk, together with the coastal line between the two places, were electrified, and are now frequently serviced by electric train sets which are over 30 years old. The line to the marine port of Baltisk has also been electrified. Although a closed area, Baltisk is serviced by direct trains and a group permit is available. Other trains run to Bagrationovsk, Zelenogradsk, Svetlogorsk and Sovetsk, and east to the Lithuanian border station of Kibartai via Chernyakhovsk, and Gusev and Nesterov. From Chernyakhovsk, there are trains north to Sovetsk and south to Zheleznodorozhnyy.

Kaliningrad itself has an extended tram network, with ten lines operating throughout the city. Rail buffs may be lucky enough to see some of the standard gauge Class 52 steam locomotives which are stored in the Kaliningrad depot for occasional use drawing tourist trains and heating duties. Around a hundred of these locos were preserved by the Red Army near the border until 1991, but since the end of the Cold War most have been scheduled for the scrap heap.

For further information about the history of the Kaliningrad railways, see Europa-Reiseführer für Eisenbahnfreunde 96-97 and Railways in the Baltic States, both available from LOK Report, PO Box 1280, D-48002, Münster, Germany.

the 14-storey Yunost Hotel, tel: 999 116, but it is much better to make a day trip to the lake from Minsk than to stay in the lakeside hotel. To get to the lake, take a suburban train towards Maladeechna (Маладэечна) and get off at either Zhdanovichi (Ждановичи) or Ratomka (Ратомка). The lake is within 1km of the station. The lake can also be reached by taking bus No 7 from the long-distance bus station or in front of the Jubileynaya Hotel.

Zaslavl architectural reserve

Zaslavl (Заслауе) is one of Belarus's oldest cities and contains a medieval citadel called the fortified Church of the Transfiguration (Spaso-Preobrazhenskaya). The citadel is surrounded by a rectangular rampart and is easily found by its red-roofed, white tower. A Handicrafts Museum is now contained in the fortress, open 09.00–17.00, closed Mondays. Not far away are several interesting archaeological sites. These include the remains of an ancient settlement of the 10th and 11th centuries, Togneda's Tomb (also known as Zamechek) and the Zaslavl Burial Mound. Unfortunately, these sites have been abandoned and there is nothing to see. To get to Zaslavl, take a suburban train towards Maladeechna (Маладэечна) and get off at Belarus (Беларусь) station in the centre of Zaslavl.

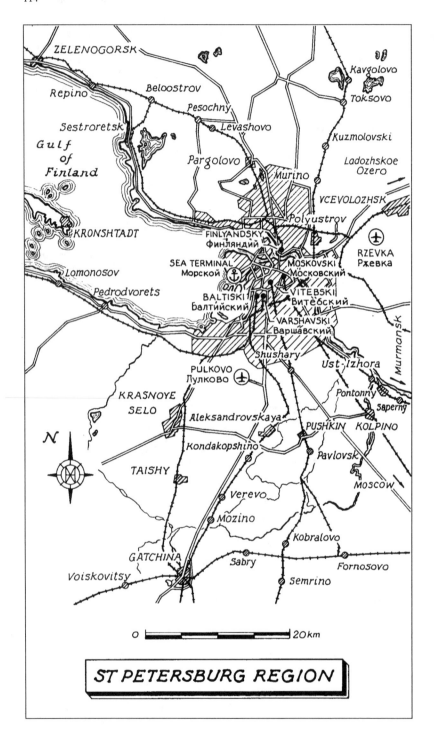

ST PETERSBURG REGION

Chaper Eight

St Petersburg and Surrounding Region

ST PETERSBURG Санкт-Петербург
Population: 4,437,000   Telephone code: 812

St Petersburg is called Russia's gateway to the West and it is the entry point for many visitors. Without doubt, St Petersburg is one of Russia's greatest cities but its architecture, layout and way of life are not typical of the rest of the country.

The differences stem from Tsar Peter I's intention in the early 18th century to build a new modern city, which would incorporate the best of the West and be the driving force for the modernisation of peasant Russia. In 1703, Peter selected the swampy ground near where the Neva River flowed into the Gulf of Finland as the present day site of St Petersburg. A popular misconception is that the city is named after Peter the Great, but in reality Peter named it after his patron saint, Peter, the first of the 12 apostles.

The abundance of water meant that many canals had to be dug and today St Petersburg is spread over 44 islands. For this reason, the city has often been called the second Venice (Venice has 118 islands).

St Petersburg's layout is modelled on Amsterdam, which was the most impressive Western city Peter I visited during his younger years, and the city was designed by the famous Italian architect, Domenico Trezzini. The result is a classically European city with large squares, wide streets, beautiful baroque palaces and gold-encased spires and domes.

The city became the capital of Russia in 1712 and played a central role in the development of the country until 1917, when the country was taken over by communists in what is known as the Great October Socialist Revolution.

The West's hostility towards the communist regime forced Lenin to transfer the seat of power to the more defensible Moscow in 1918. Despite losing political importance, St Petersburg remained a centre for the intelligentsia. This image remains today and is part of the reason most provincial Russians are slightly distrustful of the city's inhabitants.

In 1924, the city was renamed Leningrad in honour of Vladimir Lenin who died that year, but, following the collapse of communism in 1991, the city reverted to its original name of St Petersburg. (From 1917 to 1924 the city was called Petrograd which was the Russification of the German-influenced name of St Petersburg.)

Today, St Petersburg attracts hundreds of thousands of tourists a year and, while the tourist infrastructure is not as good as in the Baltic states, the city is still relatively easy to travel around unaided. Its main attractions include the

Peter and Paul Fortress, Revolution Square, St Isaac's Cathedral, the Hermitage and Nevsky Prospect.

St Petersburg is one hour ahead of Helsinki, Sofia, Athens and Bucharest, two hours ahead of Paris, Prague, Rome, Stockholm, Warsaw, Vienna and Berlin, and three hours ahead of London. St Petersburg and Moscow are in the same time zone. Daylight saving starts on the last Saturday in March and finishes on the last Saturday in September. Once again, this guide will concentrate on the little-discussed areas of day train trips around the St Petersburg region and getting there and away by train. For general guides refer to *Appendix Four.*

Getting there and away
By air
There are daily international flights from Amsterdam, Berlin, Frankfurt, Helsinki, London, Prague, Stockholm and Warsaw, and regular flights from most other European capitals. All international flights land at Pulkovo-2 while domestic flights land at Pulkovo-1. The airports are about 12km to the south of the city. To get from Pulkovo-1 to the city, catch bus No 39 and from Pulkovo-2, catch bus No 13. Buses terminate at Moskovskaya metro which is the third last metro station on the Moskovsko–Petrogradksaya metro line. Buses run every 20 minutes during peak hours.

By train
International trains
International trains are all of a good standard, and the carriages are either *SV*, three-berth *coupé* or four-berth *coupé*. The majority of trains have a restaurant car attached when they enter Belarus or Russia, but it is still advisable to take some food and drink in case your train is an exception.

While St Petersburg is safer than media coverage would have you believe, it is best to arrive in the morning or early afternoon. Remember when planning your route to take account of the time difference.

The main international trains to St Petersburg are as follows.

Origin	Dist, km	Entry point	Train no & name	Carr'ge class	No in coupé	Travel time	Day of departure	Destination
St Petersburg (Warsaw)	1,705	Grodno	26 St Petersburg Express	1, 2	2, 4	32hr	daily	Berlin
St Petersburg (Vitebsk)	2,799	Brest	49	1, 2	2, 3	50hr	Mon, Wed, Sat	Brussels
St Petersburg (Vitebsk)	2,035	Chop	189	2	4	44hr	Mon, Wed, Fri, Sun	Budapest
St Petersburg (Vitebsk)	2,234	Vadul-Siret	53	2	4	28hr	daily	Bucharest
St Petersburg (Vitebsk)	1,133	Grodno	25& 57	1, 2	2, 4	22hr	daily	Warsaw
St Petersburg (Vitebsk)	2,507	Chop	183	2	4	48hr	daily	Prague
St Petersburg Vitebsk)	2,779	Vadul-Siret	53	2	4	30hr	daily	Sofia
St Petersburg (Finland)	443	Luzhaika	33 Repin & 35 Sibelius	1, 2	2,4	8hr	daily	Helsinki
St Petersburg (Warsaw)	584	Pskov	37 Baltiya	1, 2	2, 4	12hr	daily	Riga
St Petersburg (Warsaw)	368	Narva	17 Admiral Teyets	1, 2	2, 4	9hr	daily	Tallinn

St Petersburg (Warsaw)	707	Pskov	25 St Petersburg Express & 191	1, 2	2, 4	13hr	daily	Vilnuis
Berlin	1,705	Grodno	25 St Petersburg Express	1, 2	2, 4	32hr	daily	St Petersburg (Warsaw)
Brussels	2,799	Brest	62	1, 2	2, 3	50hr	Wed, Fri, Mon	St Petersburg (Vitebsk)
Bucharest	2,234	Vadul-Siret	54	2	4	28hr	daily	St Petersburg (Vitebsk)
Budapest	2,035	Chop	54	2	4	44hr	Wed, Fri, Sun, Tue	St Petersburg (Vitebsk)
Helsinki	443	Luzhaika	34 Repin & 36 Sibelius	1, 2	2, 4	8hr	daily	St Petersburg (Finland)
Prague	2,507	Chop	184	2	4	50hr	daily	St Petersburg (Vitebsk)
Riga	584	Pskov	36 Baltiya	1, 2	2, 4	13hr	daily	St Petersburg (Warsaw)
Sofia	2,779	Vadul-Siret	54	2	4	31hr	daily	St Petersburg (Vitebsk)
Tallinn	368	Narva	18 Admiral Teyets	1, 2	2, 4	10hr	daily	St Petersburg (Warsaw)
Vilnuis	707	Pskov	26 St Petersburg Express & 190	1, 2	2, 4	13hr	daily	St Petersburg (Warsaw)
Warsaw	1,133	Grodno	26 & 58	1, 2	2, 4	23hr	daily	St Petersburg (Vitebsk)

Domestic trains

Information on the major routes to and from St Petersburg are listed below or in *Chapters Eleven* (Novgorod, Tver, Moscow) and *Twelve* (Petrozavodsk, Murmansk).

Origin	Dist, km	Train no & name	Travel time	Depart	Arrive	Destination
St Petersburg (Vitebsk)	863	51	16hr 11min	18.45	10.56	Minsk
St Petersburg (Vitebsk)	1,257	53	25hr 25min	22.13	23.38	Kiev
St Petersburg (Vitebsk)	1213	49	20hr	15.20	11.20	Brest
Kiev	1,257	54	30hr 45min	09.08	15.23	St Petersburg (Vitebsk)
Minsk	863	52	19hr 4min	15.26	10.30	St Petersburg (Vitebsk)
Brest	1,213	50	22hr 41min	13.00	11.41	St Petersburg (Vitebsk)
Smolensk	706	216	15hr 48min	17.00	08.48	St Petersburg (Vitebsk)
St Petersburg (Vitebsk)	706	215	15hr 47min	15.59	07.46	Smolensk

St Petersburg stations

There are five long-distance stations in St Petersburg; all have metro stations underneath and suburban railway stations beside them. The stations are:

Baltic station (Балтийский вокзал)   120 Obvodnov Kanal, tel: 168 2972. Trains arrive and depart for St Petersburg's southern environs including Lomonosov and Petrodvorets. Despite the station's name, trains very rarely depart for the Baltic states from here. The metro station is Baltiskaya.

Finland station (Финляндий вокзал)   pl Lenina 6, tel: 168 7685. Trains arrive and depart for Finland and northern Russia including Finland, Repino and Vyborg. The metro station is Ploshchad Lenina. This station was renovated in 1995 and is now the most modern station in St Petersburg. On the station's platform is a glass-encased steam locomotive, the one Lenin worked on as a fireman when he travelled undercover to St Petersburg in August 1917.

Moscow station (Московский вокзал)   pl Vosstaniya 2, tel: 168 0111. Trains arrive and depart for eastern, northeastern and southeastern Russia including Moscow and Novgorod. The metro station is Ploshchad Vosstaniya. This is St Petersburg's largest station and it was built at the same time as the identical Leningrad station in Moscow. St Petersburg's Moscow station contains a business centre and it is possible to make international phone and fax calls from here.

Warsaw station (Варшавский вокзал)   pr Izmailovsky, tel: 168 2972. Trains arrive and depart for the Baltic states, eastern Europe, western Europe and southeastern Russia including Gatchina and Warsaw. The metro station is Baltiskaya.

Vitebsk station (Витебский вокзал)   pr Zagorodny 52, tel: 168 5390. Trains arrive and depart here for Belarus, eastern Europe, Ukraine and southern Russia including Kiev, Minsk, Pavlovsk and Pushkin. The metro station is Pushkinskaya. On the first floor there is a full-size replica of the first train in Russia which ran to Pushkin from here in 1837, and on the second floor are historical pictures about the construction of this railway. There is a foreigners' ticket window here which sells advance purchase tickets.

Getting railway tickets and information

The main Intourist booking office is at nab Kanala Griboyedova 24. The closest metro is Nevski Prospekt. The office works 08.00–20.00 Monday–Saturday and 08.00–16.00 on Sundays. This building sells railway tickets for all long-distance and international train routes but not suburban rail tickets. Foreigners normally purchase tickets at windows 13, 14, or 15 or in the Intourist hall to the left of the entrance. You can try to buy tickets at the relevant station from which your train departs but unless they have an Intourist window, you will probably be told to go to nab Kanala Griboyedova.

There are usually English speakers at nab Kanala Griboyedova who can answer your questions; if you speak Russian you can call railway information on 168 0111 (general), 162 3344 (domestic) and 274 2092 (international).

If you do not want to go to the hassle of buying tickets yourself, you can get them from most hotel service desks (who add on a sizeable commission) or from Sindbad Travel (who add on $5) at the St Petersburg International Hostel, ul 3rd Sovetskaya 28, St Petersburg, 193036, tel: (812) 327 8384, fax: (812) 329 8019, email sindbad@ryh.spb.su.

For more information on sources of tickets, refer to *Chapter Four*.

Getting around

While not as impressive as Moscow's metro, St Petersburg's is still stunning compared to those in London and New York.

The metro uses single-use tokens or multiple-use magnetic cards which can be purchased inside the metro station building, near the entry barriers. A journey costs about $0.10 and once you enter the metro you can travel any distance or change trains as often as you want.

The idea of a metro was first suggested in the beginning of the 19th century but the then tsar, Alexander I, was so unimpressed that he forced the noble who proposed it to sign a statement that he would "not engage in hare-brained schemes in the future, but to exercise his efforts in matters appropriate to his estates". Over the following decades, the idea was dusted off numerous times but always quashed with objections such as "the excavation works would damage building foundations and trade" and "the underground passages running near church buildings would detract from their dignity". Eventually, in January 1941, the project was given the green light but work was terminated six months later when Germany invaded Russia. After the war, work on the metro restarted and in 1955 the first metro line was opened.

The metro incorporates a number of innovative features including stations with no platforms. At these stations, there are simply wide corridors with doors in the wall, and when a train arrives, the doors automatically open. This system prevents passengers from falling on to the track, requires 36% less excavation work than conventional stations, and is a necessary precondition to automating the metro system. Another innovation has been to build the stations on a small hill. This allows the trains to use the decline to accelerate when leaving the station and the incline to decelerate, rather than brake, when approaching the stations. The metro has over 83km of track and 44 stations, and trains run at an average speed of 40km/h. The metro operates 05.35–01.00.

Where to stay
Below is a listing of the best accommodation in the various categories. As mentioned in previous chapters, it is highly recommended that you pre-book.

Very basic
Hostel Holiday, ul Mikhailova 1, St Petersburg 195009, Russia, (812) 542 7364, fax: (812) 542 7364, email postmaster@hostelling.spb.su, offers beds for $12 a night. It is close to Finland station.

St Petersburg International Hostel, ul 3rd Sovetskaya 28, tel: 329 8018, fax: 329 8019, email bookings@ryh.spb.su, offers beds for $15 a night including breakfast. The hostel is near Moscow station.

Summer Hostel, ul Baltiyskaya 26, tel: 252 7563, fax: 252 4019, offers beds for $8 a night. The closest metro station is Narvskaya.

Basic
Hotel Kievskaya, ul Dnepropetrovskaya 49, tel: 166 0456, $15 twin share/person. The closest metro station is Gostiny Dvor.

Hotel Sputnik, pro Morisa Toreza 34, tel: 552 56 32, $20 twin share/person. The closest metro station is Ploshchad Muzhestva.

Standard
Hotel Moskva, Aleksandra Nevskovo 2, tel: 274 3001, $40 twin share/person. The closest metro station is Ploshchad Aleksandra Nevskovo.

Hotel Neptune, nab Obvodnovo Kanala, tel: 315 4854, fax: 164 3749.

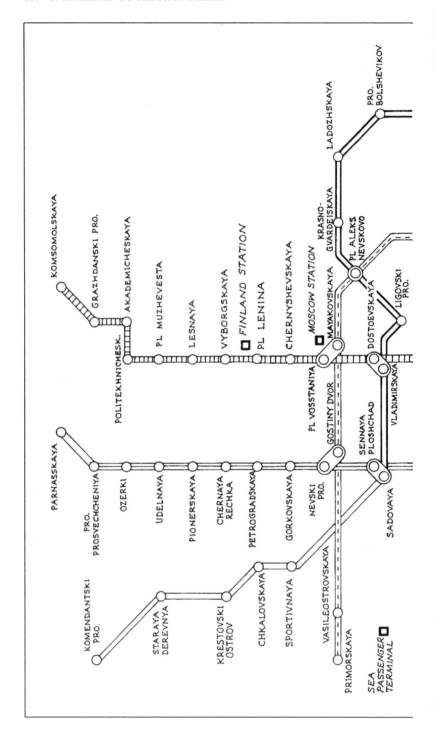

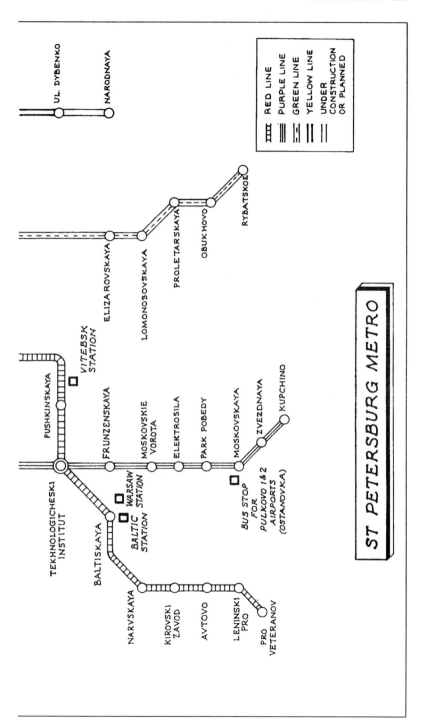

ST PETERSBURG METRO

KEY TO ST PETERSBURG METRO AND RAILWAY STATIONS
Петербургский Метрополитен и вокзалы

Red Line

Prospekt Veteranov	Проспект ветеранов
Leninski Prospekt	Ленинский Проспект
Avoto	Абтобо
Kirovski Zavod	Кировский завод
Narvskaya	Нарвская
Baltiskaya	Балтийская
Tekhnologicheski Institut	Технологический институт
Pushkinskaya	Пушкинская
Dostoevskaya	Достоевская
Pl. Vosstaniya	Пл. Восстания
Chernyshevskaya	Чернышевская
Pl. Lenina	Пл. Ленина
Vyborgskaya	Выборгская
Lesnaya	Лесная
Pl. Muzhestva	Пл. Мужества
Politekhnicheskaya	Политехническая
Akademicheskaya	Академическая
Grazhdanski Prospekt	Гражданский проспект
Komsomolskaya	Комсомольская

Purple Line

Kupchino	Купчино
Zvezdnaya	Звёздная
Moskovskaya	Московская
Park Pobedy	Парк Победы
Elektrosila	Электросила
Moskovskie Vorota	Московские ворота
Frunzenskaya	Фрунзенская
Tekhnologicheski Institut	Технологический институт
Sennaya pl.	Сенная Пл.
Nevski prospekt	Невский проспект
Gorkovskaya	Горьковская
Petrogradskaya	Петроградская
Chernaya Rechka	Чёрная речка
Pionerskaya	Пионерская
Udelnaya	Удельная
Ozerki	Озерки
Prospekt Prosvechcheniya	Проспект Просвещения
Parnasskaya*	Парнасская

Green Line

Rybatskoe	Рыбацкое
Obukhovo	Обухово
Proletarskaya	Пролетарская
Lomonosovskaya	Ломоносовская
Elizarovskaya	Елизаровская
Pl. Aleksandra Nevskovo	Пл. Александра Невского
Mayakovskaya	Маяковская
Gostiny Dvor	Гостиный двор
Vasileostrovskaya	Василеостровская
Primorskaya	Приморская

Yellow Line

Narodnaya*	Народная
Ul. Dybenko	Ул. Дыбенко
Prospekt Bolshevikov	Проспект Большевиков
Ladozhskaya	Ладожская
Krasnogvardeiskaya	Красногвардейская
Pl. Aleksandra Nevskovo	Пл. Александра Невского
Ligovski Prospekt	Лиговский Проспект
Vladimirskaya	Владимирская
Sadovaya	Садовая

Black Line*

Sportivnaya*	Спортивная
Chkalovskaya*	Чкаловская
Krestovski Ostrov*	Крестовский Остров
Staraya Derevnya*	Старая деревня
Komendantski Prospekt*	Комендантский Проспект

Railway stations etc

Finland station (Finlyandsky Voksal)
Финляндий вокзал
Moscow station (Moskovski Voksal)
Московский вокзал
Vitebsk station (Vitebski Voksal)
Витебский вокзал
Warsaw station (Varshavski Voksal)
Варшавский вокзал
Baltic station (Baltiski Voksal)
Балтийский вокзал
Bus stop for Pulkovo 1 & 2 airports (Ostanovka) Автобусная остановка
Sea passenger terminal
Морской вокзал

* = under construction or planned

Hotel Pribaltiyskaya, ul Koroblestroitelei 14, tel: 356 4135, $75 twin share/person. The closest metro station is Primorskaya.

Hotel St Petersburg, nab Vyborgskaya 5/2, tel: 542 9031, $45 twin share/person. The closest metro station is Ploshchad Lenina.

Excellent

Grand Hotel Europe, ul Mikhailovskaya 1/7, tel: 119 6000, fax: 119 6001, $190 twin share/person. The closest metro station is Nevski Prospekt.

Hotel Astoria, ul Bolshaya Morskaya 39, tel: 210 5757, fax: 315 9668, $105 twin share/person. The closest metro station is Nevski Prospekt.

Nevski Palace Hotel, pro Nevski 57, tel: 275 2001, fax: 133 1470, $170 twin share/person. The closest metro station is Nevski Prospekt.

Places of railway interest in St Petersburg

The Central Railway Museum, ul Sadovaya 50, tel: 168 8005, 315 1476, fax: 315 1085, was founded in 1813 which may seem strange as the first conventional railway in Russia, which ran from Pushkin to Pavlovsk in St Petersburg's outskirts, was only built in 1836. However, rather than being simply a repository of historical information, the museum was created to gather worldwide information on a technology that was considered to have strategic importance for Russia. The museum was moved to its current, classically designed building in 1902 and today contains over 40,000 exhibits, many of them over 100 years old. The museum is open 11.00–17.30, closed Friday, Saturday and last Thursday of the month.

The Railway Museum for the October Railway, which controls the line to Moscow and north to Murmansk, is at pro Liteiny 62. There is also the National Railway Bridge Museum on the outskirts of St Petersburg. This museum contains dozens of models of proposed and constructed railway bridges throughout Russia. The museum, at Krasnoe Selo, can only be visited by prior arrangement and the easiest way to do so is through the Central Railway Museum.

Foreign embassies and consulates

Canada pro Malodetskoselski 32, tel: 119 8448, fax: 119 8393
Czech Republic ul Tverskaya 5, tel: 271 0459, 271 6101, fax: 271 4615
Denmark alleya Bolshaya 13, Kameny Ostrov, tel: 234 3755
Estonia ul Bolshaya Monetnaya 14, tel: 233 5548
Finland ul Chaykovskovo 71, tel: 273 7321
France nab Reki Moyki 15, tel: 314 1443
Germany ul Furshtadtskaya 39, tel: 273 5598, 279 3207
Latvia ul Galernaya 69, tel: 315 1774
Netherlands pro Morisa Toreza, tel: 554 4890, 554 4900
Poland ul 5th Sovetskaya 12, tel: 274 4318, 274 4170
UK pl Protetarski Diktatury 5, tel: 119 6036
USA ul Furshtadtskaya 15, 274 8689, 274 8568

DAY RAIL TRIPS AROUND ST PETERSBURG

Petrodvorets Estate   Петродворец

Petrodvorets, meaning Peter's Palace, is the most interesting estate in the St Petersburg region. The construction of the beautiful park, gardens and buildings was ordered by Peter I to commemorate Russia's naval victories in early 1700. Consequently, the theme of the estate is water and it features 144 fountains and four water cascades.

During World War II, 7,363 art objects and 49 statues from the palace were evacuated while 34,214 museum exhibits and 11,700 old books were left for the advancing Germans. Fortunately, much of the "loot" was recaptured during the German's withdrawal to Berlin. Unfortunately, most of the building was destroyed during the 900 days of intense fighting around St Petersburg. All Petrodvorets' buildings have now been rebuilt.

To tour Petrodvorets you need about four hours and, because each museum has a different closing day, you cannot see everything on one visit. Most buildings are open 10.00–20.00. The park's grounds are open during daylight hours. In winter, the fountains are shut down from October to April, and in summer operate 11.00–20.00. You pay separately for each museum. You may well have to pay entry to the grounds unless you arrive before 09.00 which is when the gates' ticket kiosks open.

You can stay in the grounds at the very basic Petrodvorets Sanatorium, ul Avrova 2, costing $8 per person.

To get to Petrodvorets, take the suburban train from Baltic station to Novy Petergof (Новый Петергоф). The 40-minute trip takes you past St Petersburg's main graveyard of suburban trains just outside the Baltic station and over pro Leninski, one of St Petersburg's major roads. About 1km past the Leninski Prospekt station on the left is the pre-fabricated home factory and out in the yard are a number of inspection homes, *banyas* and wooden onion domes. About 5km past the station of Volodarskaya (Володарская) is a practically collapsed metal sign saying "Leningrad" which marks the boundary of the city of St Petersburg. The station of Novy Petergof is of architectural interest as the high arched roof covering the platforms is very like Victoria station in London. From the station, take bus No 350, 351, 352 or 346 and get off at the fifth stop called Park Fontani. This stop is directly in front of the Grand Palace on pro Krasny. Buses run every 15–30 minutes. Although the town of Petrodvorets is small, it contains a military college, a campus of St Petersburg University and one of Russia's most famous clock and watch factories. Strolling back to the station will take about 30 minutes.

A more popular way to get to Petrodvorets is on a 30-minute hydrofoil ride. The hydrofoils depart about every 30 minutes 09.30–19.00 daily during the navigation season which runs from May to September. The trip costs about $4.

Lomonosov Estate   Ломоносов

This large park estate contains a number of 18th- and 19th-century buildings surrounded by ponds and creeks. Peter I and Catherine the Great lived here at various times and in the 1800s Lomonosov was popular with Russian writers, scientists and philosophers. During World War II it formed a small pocket behind German lines and was supplied by ships from St Petersburg. Unlike Petrodvorets, the estate's historic buildings were not destroyed but, while this makes them authentic, they are in worse condition than the rebuilt Petrodvorets.

Although it is only 11km further on from Petrodvorets, Lomonosov is rarely visited by tourists. The museums are open 11.00–18,00, closed Tuesday, the last Monday of the month and in winter. The park's grounds are open during daylight hours. You need about three hours to walk around the park and visit the museums.

To get to Lomonosov, take the suburban train from Baltic station to Oranienbaum station (Ораниенбаум). The 50-minute trip takes you past

Petrodvorets and approaching Oranienbaum you see the Gulf of Finland to your left and pass a memorial signifying the boundary of the defence line protecting the Oranienbaum pocket during World War II. To get to the estate from the station, you exit the platform in the direction you were travelling, pass through the bus stop in front of the station and head towards the Nikolai Ugodnik Church which is 500m away. This white church can't be missed as its coloured domes overlook the town on a hill. The main entrance to Lomonosov Estate is opposite the church.

You can also get to Lomonosov by hydrofoil in the navigational season which runs from May to September. The vessels depart from Tuchkov Bridge on Vasilevski Island every 30 minutes 08.00–18.00.

It is possible to visit both Petrodvorets and Lomonosov in one day.

A monument to Russia's greatest poet, Aleksandr Segeivich Pushkin in the Pushkin Estate

Pushkin Estate   Пушкин

Pushkin Estate is a delightful park complex containing 36 historic buildings including the three-storey Catherine Palace and Pushkin Museum. The estate was the recreational retreat of many tsars and virtually everyone rebuilt the park buildings so various architectural styles are littered throughout the estate.

The palace and museums are open 11.00–18.00, closed Tuesday. The park grounds are open during daylight hours.

To get to Pushkin, take the suburban train from Vitebsk station to Detskoe Selo (Детское Село). The 30-minute trip takes you past the railway museum at Shushary on the left. From the station, take bus No 371 for five minutes and it will drop you off in front of Catherine Palace.

Pavlovsk Estate   Павловск

Four kilometres from the Pushkin Estate is the Pavlovsk Estate which was the official summer residence of the Tsar Paul I in the 1790s. The estate consists of over 600 hectares of landscaped parks, making it one of the world's largest parks. To see the whole park in one day is very difficult, but a tour of the main buildings of the Pavlovsk Grand Palace, Pavilion of the Three Graces and the Mausoleum of Paul I can be completed in an afternoon.

In summer it is possible to hire a boat on the lake, while in winter ice-skating and troika rides are great fun. Concerts are held every Saturday and Sunday in the Grand Palace.

The palace and museums are open 11.00–18.00, closed Friday. The park grounds are open during daylight hours.

To get to Pavlovsk, take the suburban train from Vitebsk station to Pavlovsk (Павловск). The trip takes 35 minutes. From the station take bus 370, 383 or 493 for five minutes and get off at the stop in front of the Grand Palace.

Gatchina Estate   Гатчина

This estate consists of a number of 18th- and 19th-century buildings set amid parklands. The most impressive of these is the Gatchina Palace which is in the style of early classicism with battlements and drawbridge. The park is also attractive with its numerous bridges, terraces and pools.

The palace and associated museum are open 10.00–18.00, closed Monday and last Tuesday of month.

To get to Gatchina, take a suburban train from Warsaw station to Gatchina (Гатчина). The trip takes 1hr 5min. There are several other Gatchina stations nearby such as Gatchina-Varshavskaya but Gatchina is the first and biggest. To get to the estate, walk to the large sign at the bus stop pointing to Gatchina. However, you should ignore this sign as it points down a road parallel with the railway and is the long way around. It is much quicker to walk down the road which is at right angles to the railway line. This 300m road, to the right of the sign, leads you to the front of the Gatchina Palace.

Road of Life Museum   Дорога Жизни

For 900 days during World War II, German troops blockaded St Petersburg and over 750,000 people, 25% of the population, died of hunger and bombing during this time. In the city's darkest hours, the only route of relief was across Lake Lagoda. During summer, patrol boats and barges braved enemy fighters as they raced across the lake, while in winter trucks and troikas carried desperately needed supplies across the ice all the time conscious that it could crack and swallow up their vehicle. The so-called 37km Road of Life operated from September 1941 to March 1943 and on frozen ice it carried over 1.5 million tons of supplies and 450,000 soldiers, while evacuating 1.2 million citizens. St Petersburg's main Road of Life Museum, which contains vehicles, planes, patrol boats and the history of the road, is near Ladozhskoe Ozera station on the shores of Lake Lagoda. The Road of Life Museum is open 11.00–18.00, closed Monday and Tuesday.

To speed up the transportation of goods, the construction of two railway lines across the ice started on November 21 1942. Information on these lines and the work of railwaymen during the war is contained in the Railway Road of Life Museum on the second storey of the Ladozhskoe Ozero station. The museum is open 11.00–18.00, open Saturday, Sunday and Wednesday.

To get to Ladozhskoe Ozero, take the suburban train from Finland station to Ladozhskoe Ozero (Ладожское Озеро). The trip takes 1hr 20min and is quite interesting. About 500m after you leave Finland station you pass Kresty prison on the left which is famous for its death-row prisoners. The inmates' loved ones stand in the street, throwing messages and shouting greetings to the prisoners. Another 500m further on, on the left you pass Sampsoniev Cathedral. After 20 minutes of travelling you reach the station of Rzhevka (Ржевка), the closest station to the regional airport. To the right of the nearby small station of Kovalevo (Ковалево) is one of St Petersburg's cemeteries. There is always a big crowd here selling flowers. Just past Kovalevo station, is the official outskirts of St Petersburg as marked by a decrepit sign stating "Leningrad". There are several large white post markers all along this line highlighting that the railway is part of the Road of Life.

From Ladozhskoe Ozero station walk 200m along the road towards the lake and then another 200m along the road as it follows the lake's shore. You will pass a memorial on the right to those who died during the Road of Life operation before you reach the museum on the left.

Shushary Museum of Railway Technology

This open-air museum has a sizeable collection of preserved steam, electric and diesel locomotives, plus some rolling stock including armoured wagons. A few of the steam locomotives are operational. The museum is open 10.00–17.00, closed Monday and Tuesday. To organise a guided tour, you need to book, tel: 272 4477.

To get to the museum, take a suburban train from either Warsaw or Vitebsk stations to Paravozny Muzei (Музей Паровозов) also known as Post 16km (Пост 16км). The museum is 100m along the track away from St Petersburg.

Lebyazhe Railway Museum Depot

Lebyazhe is an enclosed compound storing the overflow from Shushary Museum of Railway Technology. It contains some of Russia's 50 rarest locomotives and carriages. Of these 26 are steam engines and about four of these are functional. Of special interest are the rare Od and Ok steam locomotives, the SS electric locomotive and Sm-3 electric suburban train set. Even though there is a live-in guard, he will not admit you unless your visit is prearranged. The best way to organise a tour is through the Central Railway Museum in St Petersburg (see *page 123* for details).

To get to Lebyazhe, take the suburban train from Baltic station to Lebyazhe (Лебяжье). The 1hr 20min trip takes you past Petrodvorets, Lomonosov and several well-guarded military storage areas along the coast.

From the station walk 200m along the track away from St Petersburg. Follow the dirt road to the left of a cemetery for 500m until you see a left branch. Go straight along this track for 200m and you will reach the museum's gates.

Repino   Репино

Ilya Repin (1844–1930) was the most famous Russian painter of the Russian realist school. He lived in the village that now bears his name for the last 30 years of his life. Although his house was destroyed during World War II, it has been rebuilt and extended to house a large number of exhibits. It is surrounded by a small park and is known as Penaty Estate. The museum, shosse Primorskoye 144, is open 10.00–17.00, closed Tuesday.

To get to Penaty Estate Museum, take the suburban train from Finland station to Repino station (Репино). The trip takes 35 minutes. Walk the 400m to the coast which is on your left. The road that runs along the coast is shosse Primorskoye. To reach Penaty Estate Museum, walk 2km to the west or catch bus No 312 or 411 for three stops.

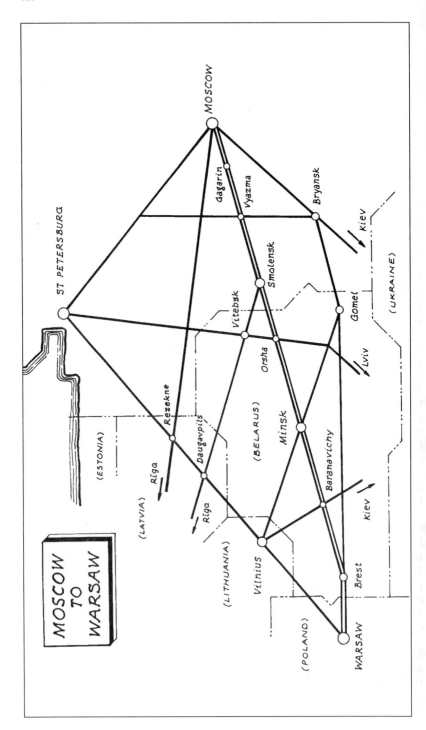

MOSCOW TO WARSAW

Chapter Nine

Moscow–Brest

The 1,097km Moscow–Minsk–Brest railway is the main rail gateway to western Europe via Warsaw and Berlin. Historically, the route was like an arrow aimed at Moscow and dozens of armies have fought, pillaged and destroyed along its length.

Most of the monuments on this route commemorate two major wars, Napoleon's 1812 Russian War and Hitler's 1941–5 Soviet campaign. To appreciate the significance that these wars still have for Belarusians and Russians, it is necessary to understand the magnitude of the death and destruction they caused.

The 1812 war started when Napoleon invaded Russia in June. By September 14 he had reached Moscow but, because of the Russians' scorched earth campaign of destroying all food along the French route, Napoleon's troops were starved out of Moscow in just over a month and departed on October 19. During Napoleon's retreat, the French gratuitously torched most towns and cities. By the time the French forces left Russia in late November, over 250,000 Russian and 450,000 French and Allied soldiers lay dead. In addition, the legacy of destroyed farming equipment, stolen animals and shattered villages was felt for decades by hundreds of thousands of Russian peasants who had lived in the path of the campaign.

An even more devastating war was the Soviet Union's four-year participation in World War II. Until June 1941, the Soviet Union secretly supplied Nazi Germany and it was only when German troops swarmed across the border that Stalin realised the peril Germany posed. Belarus and western Russia fell quickly to the fascists who came within 41km of Moscow before being beaten back. By the time the war was over, nearly 25 million Soviet citizens had been killed. Belarus was particularly badly ravaged by the Germans' policy of slaughtering Jews, gypsies and communists, and of destroying villages as reprisals for partisan attacks. In Belarus, an estimated 2,230,000 citizens died, 209 towns and cities were destroyed and 9,200 villages burnt down. Following the war, the surviving inhabitants not only had to rebuild their lives and property, but also to contend with the Soviet secret police who continued to hunt for collaborators.

Since the collapse of the Soviet Union, other tragedies along the Moscow–Brest route have been discovered, such as mass graves in Minsk filled during the 1930s purges and the 1941 Katyn massacre of Polish prisoners of war by Soviet secret police.

While the scenery along the route is beautiful, it masks enormous human suffering over the last few centuries.

Route highlights

The highlights on this route are the ancient city of Smolensk, the capital of Belarus which is Minsk, and the fortress in the city of Brest. In addition, the town of Yartsevo is of architectural interest. There are also two extensive Belarusian nature reserves which can be reached from Brest and Barysai.

Trains

The Moscow–Minsk–Brest railway is very busy and is mostly serviced by good quality trains. The major segments of the route are:

- 419km Moscow to Smolensk, taking 7hr 40min,
- 331km Smolensk to Minsk, taking 3hr 40min, and
- 355km Minsk to Brest, taking 5 hr.

International trains

The most convenient international distance trains on this route are listed below.

Origin	Dist, km	Entry point	Train no & name	Carr'ge class	No in coupé	Travel time	Day of departure	Destination
Moscow (Smolensk)	1,317	Brest	9 Polonez	1, 2	2, 3	19hr	daily	Warsaw
Moscow (Smolensk)	1,895	Brest	13 Moskva Express	1, 2	2, 4	34hr	daily	Berlin
Moscow (Smolensk)	2,011	Brest	15 Ost-West Express	1, 2	2, 3	35hr	daily	Vienna
Moscow (Smolensk)	2,060	Brest	21	1, 2	2, 3	38hr	daily	Prague
Moscow (Smolensk)	2,600	Brest	9	1, 2	2, 3	48hr	daily	Frankfurt
Moscow (Smolensk)	2,714	Brest	15	1, 2	2, 3	42hr	daily	Brussels
Berlin	1,895	Brest	14 Moskva Express	1, 2	2, 4	32hr	daily	Moscow (Smolensk)
Brussels	2,714	Brest	16	1, 2	2, 3	42hr	daily	Moscow (Smolensk)
Frankfurt	2,600	Brest	132	1, 2	2, 3	48hr	daily	Moscow (Smolensk)
Prague	2,060	Brest	22	1, 2	2, 3	38hr	daily	Moscow (Smolensk)
Vienna	2,011	Brest	16 Ost-West Express	1, 2	2, 3	35hr	daily	Moscow (Smolensk)
Warsaw	1,317	Brest	10 Polonez	1, 2	2, 3	23hr	daily	Moscow (Smolensk)

Domestic trains

If you are travelling within Russia or Belarus, it is best not to travel on the international trains as tickets on these trains are much harder to buy. The most convenient long-distance trains on this route are listed opposite.

ChS7 electric passenger locomotive

Origin	Dist, km	Train no & name	Travel time	Depart	Arrive	Destination
Moscow (Smolensk)	419	104 Smolensk	7hr 15min	00.02	07.17	Smolensk
Moscow (Smolensk)	750	1	10hr 48min	20.17	07.05	Minsk
Moscow (Smolensk)	750	3	11hr 4min	21.37	08.37	Minsk
Moscow (Smolensk)	1,097	27	15hr 17min	14.28	05.45	Brest
Moscow (Smolensk)	1,097	73	15hr 35min	16.43	08.18	Brest
Moscow (Smolensk)	1,097	129	16hr 49min	06.52	23.41	Brest
Brest	1,097	28	17hr 36min	17.10	10.46	Moscow (Smolensk)
Brest	1,097	74	17hr 45min	18.00	11.45	Moscow (Smolensk)
Brest	1,097	130	19hr 46min	08.10	03.56	Moscow (Smolensk)
Minsk	750	2	13hr 16min	19.49	09.05	Moscow (Smolensk)
Minsk	750	4	12hr 54min	21.31	10.25	Moscow (Smolensk)
Smolensk	419	104 Smolensk	7hr 43min	22.38	06.21	Moscow (Smolensk)

ROUTE DESCRIPTION

Moscow   Москва   0km
Trains for Minsk and Warsaw depart from Moscow's Smolensk station, pl Tverskaya Sastava 7, tel: 251 6093, 253 4224, 253 4908. The metro station is Belorusskaya.

Fili   Фили   7km
Just after crossing the Moscow River you reach the inner Moscow suburb of Fili. Early last century, the small village that stood here became known throughout Russia when, in September 1812, Russia's supreme military commander, Field Marshal Kutuzov, called a council of war and decided to abandon Moscow to Napoleon without a fight. The withdrawal was seen as a tactical move as Kutuzov proclaimed "the loss of Moscow does not mean the loss of Russia". The marshal was correct, for within one month, Napoleon's army had deserted Moscow and was retreating westward.

The hut where Kutuzov made the decision was owned by a peasant named Frolov and, although it was burned down in 1868, it was rebuilt and is a museum today.

Kuntsevo   Кунцево   12km
The style of this marvellous, green and white stone station could be called pseudo-kremlin with its decorative fortress walls and battlements.

Tsar Alexei Mikhailovich presented the entire Kuntsevo region to his father-in-law, Kyril Naryshkin, in the mid-1600s. The *boyar* Naryshkin family contributed significantly to the development of Russia and served various tsars until the revolutionary M Naryshkin took part in the democratic riots in the 1860s and for his trouble was exiled to Siberia for eight years.

The Naryshkins patronised an architectural form called Naryshkin baroque, also known as Moscow baroque. Nearby is the Church of the Intercession of the Holy Virgin at Fili, built in 1693, which epitomises this style.

About 1km onwards, the train passes over the Moscow ring road which is the municipal border of Moscow. This is where the toilet is opened.

Odintsovo   Одинцово   25km
About 2km to the left is Vnukovo airport. Vnukovo 1 is the civilian airport for domestic planes, while nearby Vnukovo 2 is the government airport. The secret

metro from near the kremlin pops up here. For more information on this metro, see *Chapter Five, page 83*.

Golitsino   Голицино   45km

One of the future Peter the Great's most staunch allies during the violent struggle for the tsar's throne in 1694 was Peter's adviser and henchman, Prince Boris Golitsyn. As a reward for his service, Peter gave him the Golitsino region. Its most famous resident was Nikolai Przewalski (Nikolai Przhevalsky in Russian) who is known for his exploration of central Asia and for discovering the wild horse that now bears his name.

Kubinka   Кубинка   63 km

This garrison town is home to the Taman Guards Division which drove its tanks to Moscow in support of the 1991 attempted coup. The military base contains one of the two largest tank museums in the world.

Tuchkovo   Тучково   78km
Population: 18,000

This town is named after the brothers Nikolai and Aleksandr Tuchkov. Both were generals and both died on the nearby battlefield of Borodino in 1812. In 1839, the wife of Aleksandr founded the Saviour-Borodino Monastery for Women which is located on the battlefield.

Dorokhovo   Дорохово   86km

This town was also named after a general who distinguished himself at the Battle of Borodino. General Ivan Dorokhov (1762–1815) is noted in Russian history for discovering that Napoleon had fled Moscow and that his troops were heading southwards rather than eastwards which was the way they had come.

Partizanskaya   Партизанская   91km

On the left, just before arriving at the station, you can see a large statue beside the highway. This is of Zoya Kosmodemyanskaya (1923–41) who is one of the most famous partisans of World War II even though she fought for less than a month before being captured in nearby Petrishchevo village. Despite brutal interrogation, this 18-year-old Soviet Joan of Arc did not betray her fellow partisans nor even give her full name. Her execution was held in front of the assembled villagers and, just before she was hung, she proclaimed, "Stalin will come."

Mozhaisk   Можайск   110km

Mozhaisk has had a hard existence, being Moscow's forward bastion guarding the western approaches. This role started in 1541 when Ivan the Terrible ordered that high log walls be thrown up around the town's two monasteries, the Luzhetski Monastery built in 1408 and the Kolochskovo Monastery built in 1413. The fortifications were consolidated in the 1720s when a stone wall ringed the entire town.

In the last two centuries alone, Mozhaisk has been under siege by the Polish in the 17th century, occupied by the French in the 19th century and ransacked by the Germans in 1941–2. Consequently, much of the old part of the town was destroyed and today the town's restored highlights include part of the fortress wall, the walled Luzhetski Monastery and the nearby House-museum of the artist S V Gerasimov (1885–1964). To get to these, walk down the main street, ul Klementevskaya, from the station until you reach the Moscow River. The Luzhetski Monastery and Museum are on your immediate right.

Gerasimov made this town and the surrounding region famous with his series of paintings called Mozhaisk Landscapes, which are on display in the Tretyakov Gallery in Moscow.

Borodino   Бородино   121km
This is the most famous battlefield of Napoleon's 1812 Russian invasion. Over 100,000 Russian and French soldiers were killed or wounded during the 15-hour battle, see *Chapter Five, page 98.*

Drovino   Дровнино   153km
About 3km to the east beside the railway is a small marker signifying the boundary between Moscow and Smolensk *raions.*

Gagarin   Гагарин   180km
Known as Gzhatsk until 1968, this ancient town was renamed after the world's first astronaut, Yuri Gagarin, see *Chapter Five, page 97.*

Vyazma   Вязжьма   243km
A settlement at Vyazma has probably existed since the 9th century as it sits astride the Vyazma River which connects the major trading rivers of the Volga, Oka and Dniepr. The town was fortified in 1630 with the construction of a kremlin with six towers. Unfortunately, the only elements remaining are the 14m-high Spassky Tower and a stretch of the wall.

Due to its strategic location, Vyazma was fought over many times and most of the city's monuments are dedicated to military leaders. These include a monument to the 1812 Vyazma battle between the French and Russians, which cost Napoleon 4,000 dead and a further 3,000 captured, and a monument to Lieutenant General Mikhail Yefremov (1897–1942) who died in the defence of the town against the Germans.

There is a History Museum in the former Bogoroditsy Church, pl Sovetskaya, and a basic hotel at pl Oktyabrya 25. Vyazma station is located on the eastern fringes of the city and there are buses that travel the 2km from the station to the town's centre.

About 32km to the northwest of Vyazma is the town of Khmelita (Хмелита) which contains the Grivoedov Combined Local History Museum and Nature Park. A S Griboyedov (1795–1829) was a reluctant revolutionary whose plays were appropriated by revolutionaries demanding social change. Every year at Khmelita a festival of Griboyedov's work is held. There are regular buses between Vyazma and Khmelita.

Immediately after leaving Vyazma, the train passes over the Vyazma River twice.

Semlevo   Семлево   266km
Although there is a medium-sized settlement around Semlevo station, the real Semlevo town lies 11km to the north of the station.

According to the *Complete Guide to the Soviet Union* by Victor and Jennifer Louis, the nearby Semlevskoye Lake contains the missing treasures pillaged from Moscow by Napoleon's forces but lost during the retreat. This information originally came from the memoirs of Sir Walter Scott who wrote that on November 1 1812, Napoleon felt the danger was too great to continue to transport the loot and ordered that the ancient shields, cannons and the cross from the Ivan the Great belfry should be thrown into the Semlevskoye Lake. It is unlikely that the material will ever be located as 14m of mud has settled on the lake's bottom over the past 150 years.

Izdeshkovo   Издешково   291km

This little village was one of many held for months at a time by partisans during World War II when Germans forces technically occupied the region. Despite repeated violent forays and reprisals in such villages, control of the Soviet countryside eluded the Germans during much of the time they were occupying Russia.

Beside the railway, you will see disused limestone quarries from the last century.

Mitino   Митино   298km

Just after leaving the station, the train passes over the Dniepr River. This 2,200km-long river is second in length only to the Volga in western Russia. The Dniepr River passes through Smolensk and Kiev before flowing into the Black Sea. Large vessels can sail down 1,990km of its length, starting just 28km downstream from Mitino at the port town of Dorogobuzh. The Mitino Bridge is comparatively short as only in the middle reaches of the Dniepr River, where the Dniepr Flood Plain widens to 18km, are long bridges required.

Safonovo   Сафоново   317km

This medium-sized town has only existed for 50 years, following the discovery of coal in the region. This explains why many of the buildings have a grey coating over them.

Yartsevo   Ярцево   371km

Those interested in industrial architecture will find this town fascinating.

Yartsevo was founded in the 1870s when the Khludov family built a cotton mill on the site of a small village. Like most successful merchants, the Khludovs introduced innovations, such as Russia's first steam-powered cotton mill, and developed new markets, such as opening up the Middle Asian market for Russian textiles, all the while ruthlessly exploiting their workers. The unbearable working conditions reached a crisis in September 1880 when the factory's 2,500 workers were told of a 10% wage reduction, new fines and additional deductions from wages. The workers spontaneously went on strike and destroyed much of the factory. Although the military quelled the rioters and 2,000 workers and instigators of the protest were evicted from Yartsevo, the previous wage conditions were restored. However, if the workers believed that life would be better under the "proletariat-led" communism of 1917, they were mistaken. Due to increased work norms, decreases in wages, and management's lack of interest in workers' conditions, seven workers committed suicide in 1927 and 1928 alone.

The Yartsevo cotton factory complex is now the largest cotton mill in the Smolensk region and employs over 9,000 workers. Several of the factory buildings have been preserved and offer a valuable insight into 1870s architecture.

The other building of architectural interest is the 1930s Rossiya Cinema. This building contains both constructivist and neoclassical elements. Beside the cinema is a garden which contains the mass grave of Soviet soldiers killed in nearby World War II battles.

There is a local museum and basic hotel in Yartsevo.

SMOLENSK   Смоленск   419km
Population: 351,600   Telephone area code: 081 00

After the busy, populous cities of Moscow, Minsk and St Petersburg, Smolensk is a refreshing contrast. This small, scenic city is a pleasure to stroll around with its parks, ancient fortress and numerous cafés.

What is most surprising about Smolensk is that it still exists today, despite the city's numerous disasters. The two worst disasters were the 1388 plague and cholera epidemic which left only ten survivors, and the 1812 fire set by Napoleon's retreating troops which left only 500 living inhabitants.

While most of Smolensk can be seen in one day, it is worth spending two days here, and on the second day either having a picnic on the picturesque banks of the Dniepr which divides the town or visiting the historic Talashkino Estate, 18km to the south.

Getting there and away

As Smolensk sits on the major line between Moscow, Minsk and Warsaw, there are numerous trains to travel on. There are a number of international trains on this line but it difficult to get tickets as station staff do not know the number of available berths until these trains arrive. It is far better to buy tickets on trains originating in Smolensk. The best of these trains are:

Origin	Dist, km	Train no & name	Travel time	Depart	Arrive	Destination
Smolensk	331	47	3hr 40min	12.57	16.37	Minsk
Smolensk	419	104 Smolensk	7hr 43min	22.38	06.21	Moscow (Smolensk)
Smolensk	706	216	15hr 48min	17.00	08.48	St Petersburg (Vitebsk)
Minsk	331	48	5hr 32min	11.48	17.20	Smolensk
Moscow (Smolensk)	419	104 Smolensk		00.02	07.17	Smolensk
St Petersburg (Vitebsk)	706	215	15hr 47min	15.59	07.46	Smolensk

Passing through

Most trains stop in Smolensk for at least ten minutes which is long enough to run inside the newly restored station and see the enormous paintings on the walls. These communist and social realist artworks are inspiring even if you hate the style.

If you have 30 minutes, you can easily visit the Church of Sts Peter and Paul, the oldest building in Smolensk, which was built in the 1150s. The church sits at the base of the pedestrian overpass at the end of the station.

Where to stay

There are three standard hotels, the Hotel Tsentralnaya, ul Lenina 2, tel: 336 04, $35 twin share/person, the Hotel Rossiya, ul Dzerzhinskovo 23/2, tel: 339

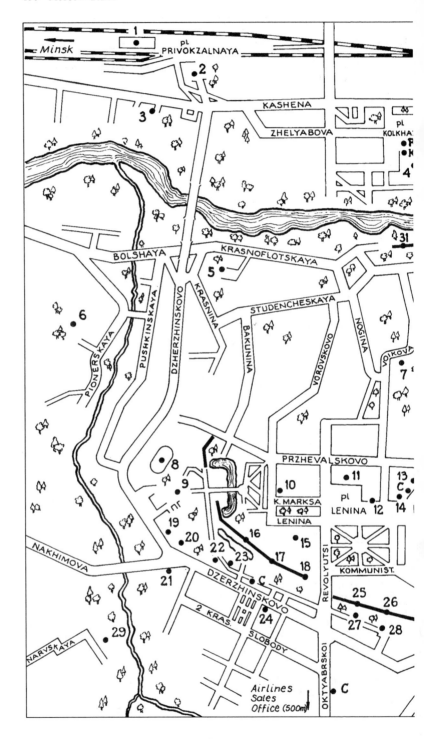

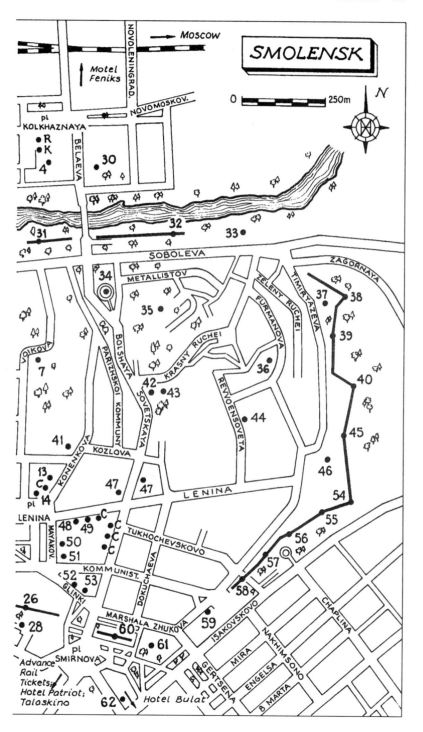

KEY TO SMOLENSK   имоленск

1	Railway station (Vokzal)	Ж-Д вокзал
2	Church of Sts Peter and Paul (Petropavlovskaya)	Петропавловская церковь
3	Bus station (Avtovokzal)	Автовокзал
4	Market (Rynok)	Рынок
5	Church of St John the Divine (Bogoslova)	Иоанна Богословская церковь
6	Church of Michael the Archangel (Mikhaila Arkhangela)	Церковь Михаила Архангела
7	Planetarium (Planetari)	Планетарий
8	Spartak Stadium (Stadion)	Стадион «Спартак»
9	Monument to the Sofia Corps fighting Napoleon	Памятник Софийскому полку воздвигнутый в честь столетия героической обороны Смоленска от французских
10	Smolenskturist	Смоленсктурист
11	City Administration	Город совет
12	Drama Theatre (Teatr)	Драматический театр
13	Smolensk Intourist	Смоленск Интурист
14	Hotel Tsentralnaya (Gostinitsa)	гостиница Центральная
15	Post office (Pochtamt)	Почтамт
16	Kopytenskaya Tower	Копытенская башня
17	Bubleika Tower	Бублейка башня
18	Defence of Smolensk Museum in Gromovaya Tower	Музей «Смоленск-щит России» в Громовой башне
19	Swimming pool (Basein)	Плавательный бассейн
20	Gold Fisherman Swimming pool (Basein)	Плавательный бассейн «Золотая рыбка»
21	Hotel Rossiya (Gostinitsa)	гостиница Россия
22	Molodost Dancing Hall	Танцевальный зал «Молодость»
23	Bust of Pushkin	Бюст Пушкина
24	Puppet Theatre (Teatr)	Театр кукол
25	Donets Tower	Башня Донец
26	World War Two Museum (Muzei)	Музеи «Смоленщина в Великой Отечественной воине»
27	Eternal flame	Вечный огонь
28	Monument to the heroes of the Napoleonic War	Памятник героям Отечественной войны 1812
29	Mass grave of Soviet POWs shot by Germans 1941-1943	Братские могилы советских военнопленных
30	Lower Church of St Nicholas (Nikolskaya)	Нижне-Никольская церковь
31	Water (Vodyanaya) Tower	Водяная башня
32	Arrow (Strelka) Tower	Стрелка башня
33	Kostyrevskaya Tower	Костыревская башня
34	Monument of M I Kutuzov	Памятник кутузову Комплекс
35	Museum and buildings of Cathedral Hill including Museum of Nature (Muzei), Cathedral of the Ascension (Uspenski), Epiphany Gate Church (Bogoyalenski), Church of St John the Baptist (Ioanna Predtechi) and Archbishop's Chambers (Palata)	сооружений «Природа», Успенский собор, Соборного холма (Музеи Богоявленский надвратный собор, церковь Иоанна Предтечи и Архиерейские палаты
36	Church of St Gregory (Geogrievskaya)	Георгиевская церковь
37	Church of the Intercession (Pokrovskaya)	Покровская церковь
38	Veselukha Tower	Башня Веселуха
39	Pozdnyakova Tower	Позднякова башня
40	Orel Tower	Башня Орел
41	Exhibition Hall (Vystavochy zal) in the former Cathedral of the Blessed	Выставочный зал в здании Вознесенского собора
42	Flax Museum (Muzei)	Музей «Смоленский лен»
43	Former Trinity Monastery (Troitski)	Ансамбль бывшего Троицкого монастыря

44	Church of the Saviour (Spasskaya)	Спасская церковь
45	St Avraam Tower	Авраамиевская башня
46	Former St Avraam Monastery	Быв. Авраамиевский монастырь
47	Book shop (Knigi)	Книги
48	History Museum (Muzei)	Музеи «История»
49	Union Palace of Culture (Dom Kultury)	Дом Культуры профсоюзов
50	Konenkov Sculpture Museum (Muzei)	Музей скульптуры Коненкова
51	Palace of Pioneers (Dvorets Pionerov)	Дворец пионеров
52	Philharmonic Hall (Filarmoniya)	Филармония
53	Hotel Smolensk (Gostinitsa)	гостиница Смоленск
54	Zaaltarnaya Tower	Заалтарная башня
55	Voronina Tower	Воронина башня
56	Dolgochevskaya Tower	Долгочевская башня
57	Zimbulka Tower	Башня Зимбулка
58	St Nicholas Tower	Никольская башня
59	House of Officers (Dom Ofitserov)	Дом офицеров
60	Makhovaya Tower	Маховая башня
61	Sheinov Bastion	Шейнов бастион
62	Artist Gallery (Galereya)	Художественная галерея
R	Restaurant (Restoran)	Ресторан
C	Café (Kafé) or Bar (Bar)	Кафе или Бар
K	Canteen (Stolovaya)	Столоваыа

70, $22 twin share/person and the Hotel Smolensk, ul Glinki 11/30, tel: 918 66, $35 twin share/person. Basic hotels are the Hotel Patriot, ul Kirova 22, tel: 349 36 and the Hotel Bulat, ul Rumyantseva 19. The worst, most inconveniently located, but nevertheless well-known hotel is the Motel Feniks, tel: 214 88, $16 double room, which is 3.4km to the north of the city; unless you have no choice, don't go there. The Hotels Rossiya and Tsentralnaya have buffets or restaurants.

Getting around

The station is about 2km from the centre of town. To get to Hotel Rossiya from the station, take trams No 2 or 3 southwards which stop in front of the hotel. To get to the Hotels Tsentralnaya and Smolensk from the station, take tram No 1 to ul Glinka which is near both hotels. Be aware that trams No 2 and 3 depart from in front of the bus station while tram No 1 departs from in front of the railway station. To get to Hotel Patriot from the station, take bus No 2 from in front of the market. This bus goes past the hotel and terminates about 500m further on. To get to the Hotel Bulat from the station, take tram No 1 from in front of the bus station. The tram passes the hotel. To get to the Motel Feniks from the station, take bus No 102 or 137 from the bus station. The trip takes about 40 minutes.

What to see

Among Smolensk's greatest attractions are the restored parts of the Smolensk fortress which was built in the late 1500s. The fortress consisted of 5m thick, 15m high and 5km long walls, which ringed the entire city. This made Smolensk unusual in Russia as the majority of fortresses just protected the city centre, reflecting the rulers' self interest. Today, about 3km of the walls and 17 of the fortress's 38 towers have been restored. Of the towers, you can only enter the Gromovaya Tower. This also contains the Defence of Smolensk Museum, ul Oktyabrskoi Revolyutsi, open 10.00–18.00, closed Monday.

Smolensk's most impressive religious building is the big, green and white, five-domed Cathedral of the Ascension on Cathedral Hill. This is the third church that has stood on this site. The first was destroyed in the early 1600s by the Poles who killed all those who took sanctuary in it; the second was destroyed in 1677 by the Russian Orthodox tsar who despised the Catholic church. The Cathedral of the Ascension took over 30 years to complete and, surprisingly, has survived the town's destructive assaults over the last 200 years. Entering the cavernous building during a service is awe-inspiring. Other buildings on Cathedral Hill include the Epiphany Gate Church, the Church of St John the Baptist and the Archbishop's Chambers. In the former Metropolitan's Chambers is the Museum of Nature, open 10.00–18.00, closed Monday

Strolling around the parks bordering on pl Lenina with its embryonic café culture is pleasant. Dedicated walkers can spend over an hour wandering down the busy shopping strip of ul Bolshaya Sovetskaya. This road is the tram route to the station and goes down the hill, past the Cathedral of the Ascension, through the northern section of the Smolensk fortress wall, across the Dniepr River and ends at the market.

The Flax Museum, ul Bolshaya Sovetskaya 11, open 10.00–18.00, closed Monday, tells the story of the development of the region's textile industry. It is housed in a church of the former Trinity Monastery. The World War II Museum, pl Pamyati Georoev, open 10.00–18.00, closed Monday, is located in a section of the fortress wall and at the back is a large collection of military vehicles.

Other museums in Smolensk include the History Museum, ul Lenina 8, open 10.00–18.00, closed Monday, and the Konenkov Sculpture Museum, ul Mayakovskovo 7, open 10.00–18.00, closed Monday. There are two art galleries: the Exhibition Hall in the former Cathedral of the Blessed, ul Konenkova 9, and the Artist Gallery, ul Tenishevskaya 7.

Getting assistance

Travel agents   The most helpful local travel agency is Smolenskturist, which was based in Hotel Rossiya, but is now located at ul Karla Marksa 14, tel: 324 53 or 327 41, fax: 301 61. Another agency is Smolensk Intourist, ul Konenkova 3, tel: 314 92, fax: 335 08.

Air   Air tickets can be bought at the airlines sales office, ul Oktyabrskoi Revolyutsi 13.

Rail   Tickets can be bought at the railway station or at the advance purchase rail ticket office, pro Gagarina 14/2.

Business centre   Everything for your Company, 2nd floor, ul Lenina 16, tel: 967 01, 963 63, fax: 969 00, email bemy!gela@mastak.msk.su.

What's in the region

About 18km south of Smolensk is a delightful former estate of Princess Maria Tenisheva (1867–1927) called Talashkino (Талашкино), open 10.00–16.00, closed Monday. The estate became an artistic mecca at the turn of the century with workshops for wood carving, musical instrument making, ceramics and embroidery work. One artist, Sergei Malyutin, designed an ornate, blue, wooden shingle house called Teremok (Теремок) which is now a Folk Art Museum containing over 2,000 items. Nearby is a brick church which has a simple exterior but an astonishing interior of exotic murals and mosaics. Many famous painters contributed to the museum including Peter Fabergé of Fabergé egg fame, who guilded the cupola.

Talashkino Estate is part of the Smolensk Art Gallery and it is best to confirm opening hours with them. Bus No 104 travels between Smolensk and Talashkino village. The estate is located 1km from Talashkino at the small settlement of Flenovo (Фленово).

Point of interest

By accident, the Smolensk region provided the West with its first comprehensive insight into the closed Soviet regime. This occurred when over 200,000 pages from Smolensk's archives, covering the period from 1917 to 1938, were captured by the Germans and then fell into American hands at the end of World War II. The captured records provided a detailed understanding of Soviet city and village life, from collective farm communist party cells to street crime and from Stalin's purges to the machinations of the regional parliament.

After being declassified, the material was published in a fascinating book, called *Smolensk Under Soviet Rule* by Merle Fainsod, 1959, which even today is considered the textbook on the early years of Soviet power.

Krasny Bor   Красный бор   428km

After the 1917 revolution with its preference for the colour red, the name of the nearby forest was changed from Chorny (meaning "black") Forest to Krasny (meaning "red") Forest.

On the south side of the railway is one of the world's largest ancient burial grounds. The Gnezdovo burial mounds consist of about 3,000 graves dating from the 10th to 11th centuries. About 850 mounds, some of which are up to 10m high, have been excavated since 1874. Contained in the graves were the cremated remains of the dead, plus a number of household artefacts, decorations, tools, ceramics, weapons and Arab and Byzantine coins. The graves of both noble and lower classes contained mostly Slavs, with a few Scandinavians and Balts. This discovery was instrumental in refuting the popular theory that the foundation of the Russian state resulted from the arrival of Varangians from Scandinavia. According to Soviet historians, this theory was a bourgeois plot to portray ancient Russia as a backward country, incapable of development without foreign influences. The small number of Scandinavians buried with the mostly Russian material found at the Gnezdovo burial mounds proves that the Varangians had no lasting impact, according to those wishing to discredit the theories.

Rakitnaya   Ракитная   434km

Just past the station, the train travels under a railway line which goes to Belarus with the first major stop being Vitebsk which is 138km away.

Katyn   Катынь   452km

About 4km before the station, on the left of the track, is the site of one of the many repulsive atrocities of the Soviet regime. Within 800m of the railway, 4,500 Polish prisoners of war were executed by Soviet secret police in 1941. These Polish troops were part of the 15,000 captured when the Soviet Union and Germany invaded Poland and divided it up between themselves in 1939.

To get to the memorial from Smolensk, take bus No 104 which travels along the highway to Minsk. Get out about 500m past the road overpass and follow a trail starting near the roadside sign pointing to the memorial.

Gusino   Гусино   487km

The region around Gusino and the next station of Krasnoe was the sight of two famous battles of the 1812 war. The first was during Napoleon's advance in August when Russian troops successful slowed the French army and prevented a major rout of the slowly retreating Russians. The second battle was a reverse of the first. Here in November, Napoleon was retreating from Smolensk and he had to sacrifice his best soldiers to minimise the carnage to his fleeing troops. Russian troops killed 6,000 French soldiers and captured another 26,000.

There is a war memorial on the southern outskirts of the town which marks the common grave of 1,029 Red Army soldiers who died here during World War II.

Krasnoe   Красное   487km

About 3km to the west of Krasnoe is the border between Belarus and Russia.

Shukhovtsy   Шухаўцы   497km

This is the first stop in Belarus.

Asinaika   Асінаўка   512km

Following the collapse of the Soviet Union, a border checkpoint between Russia and Belarus was established here. It was torn down in September 1993 following close co-operation agreement between the two countries. The post was established at Asinaika (Osinovka in Russian) and not closer to the border which is 22km away at Shukhovtsy station because Shukhovtsy is small and hard to get to by road.

About 6km to the north of Asinaika is the town Asintorf, meaning "Asin peat bog". This area is famous for its peat which as early as 1917 was dried and used to fuel locomotives at nearby Orsha railway depot.

Orsha   Орша   536km

This ancient Belarusian town spans the Orshitsa River at the point where it flows into the Dniepr. It also sits on a major north–south rail line which carries trains between Kiev and St Petersburg. Like most of Belarus, Orsha was owned at different times by Lithuania, France, Poland and Russia. Its most interesting buildings are the Epiphany Monastery and the Ascension Convent, both of which were known as the Kuteinsky Monasteries after the little Kuteinka River. The Epiphany Monastery was Belarus's most important printing centre in the 17th century.

In the town is a Military Museum which focuses on one of the leaders of the Belarusian partisans, Kanstantsin Zaslonai (1910–42). Before the war, Zaslonai was the chief of the locomotive depot at Orsha. He retreated with the Soviets in the face of the German advance but returned later that year to lead partisan activities. With enormous courage he came into the open and assumed a legal identity in Orsha. Over the next three months he blew up 93 German locomotives. Just before he was to be arrested, he fled into the countryside where he led a partisan unit that continued to target the railway lines. He was killed the next year during a German punitive raid. He received posthumously the Hero of the Soviet Union medal.

For military historians, the town is also interesting as it contains a Katyusha Monument which is dedicated to the first use of the famous Katyusha rocket launchers near Orsha on July 14 1941.

There is a standard hotel in town.

Talachyn   Талачын   579km

The station is 4km from the town of Talachyn. The town's most interesting building is a Roman Catholic church which was built in 1604 and subsequently converted into the Intercession (Pokrovskaya) Russian Orthodox Church. There is also a museum of local studies in Talachyn.

Bobr   Бобр   615km

The town's name translates as "beaver" as the area was once a centre for beaver breeding.

Krupki   Крупкі   629km

The town, which is 5km from the station, was first mentioned in 1686 when Jews here were granted land and tax-free trading rights. Most of the population was Jewish before World War II, but by the end of the war, virtually every Jewish citizen had been exterminated. Nearby is the Rylenki Memorial Complex (Рыленкі) which marks the site of a German concentration camp. Among its victims were 1,500 Jews executed in October 1942. There is a basic hotel in town.

Barysai   Барысаў   669km

The region around the town has been the site of two large massacres in the last two centuries. The first was in November 1812 when the survivors of

---

BEAVERS: MORE VALUABLE THAN SABLE

Beavers are Russia's mightiest rodents. They grow up to 120cm long and weigh up to a massive 20kg. In the wild, beavers have become virtually extinct as their pelts were more valuable than sable, their meat was highly prized, and, most important of all, a gland at the base of the beaver's tail secretes a substance called castoreum which was believed to have magical healing powers. To ensure a supply of beavers for the nobility, beaver farms were established under the control of *bobrovniki,* meaning "beaver people". These woodspeople knew the life and habitat of the beaver, protected their settlements and kept track of their population. According to Russian historians, they also knew the now-lost secret of improving beaver breeding in the wild. *Bobrovniki* were considered such valuable specialists that they were exempt from taxes, military service and even from the obligation to obey local authorities.

Until the discovery in the 1920s of a colony of 19 beavers in the upper reaches of the Byarezinski River, beavers were believed to be extinct in Belarus. The area was quickly made into the large Byarezinski (Berezina in Russian) Nature Reserve and today it has a population of 500 beavers, making it the largest colony in European Russia.

Napoleon's army, who were retreating from Moscow, spent three days building two pontoon bridges across the partially frozen Byarezinski River. Only about 30,000 troops crossed the bridges before they were blown up. Those of the 50,000 stragglers and wounded who did not fall to the sabres of rampaging Cossacks, drowned in the river as they desperately tried to cross or became prisoners of war for the rest of their lives. Only 10,000 Russians died in the actual battle. The battleground is about 15km upstream from Barysai (Borisov in Russian) at Studzenka (Studyonka in Russian) and is today a popular area with treasure hunters who believe that much of the abandoned French loot was buried here.

The second massacre involved the execution by the Germans of the town's entire Jewish population of 8,000 in 1941. Barysai was the pilot project for the extermination of Belarusian Jews, which, when implemented, resulted in only 80 out of the 50,000 southwestern Belarusian Jews surviving World War II.

Zhodino   Жодзіна   687km
Zhodino, a satellite town of Minsk, is famous for its giant trucks which can carry loads of up to 65 tons and are found in mining projects throughout the former communist countries of the world. In the new barter economy within the former Soviet Union, the Zhodino plants are important for getting raw materials for Belarus. For example, in one 1995 deal Belarus trucks and tractors were supplied to Russia's Krasnoyarsk regional government in return for 300,000 tons of grain plus iron ore and railway sleepers, and later that year Belarus exchanged trucks, tractors and 100,000 tons of potatoes with Turkmenistan in return for 2 billion m³ of gas.

There is not much of interest in this town except for the Kupriyanov Monument, dedicated to Anastasia Kupriyanova who lost her five sons in the World War II. One of the sons, Petr, earned the title of Hero of the Soviet Union for saving the lives of his comrades by throwing himself in front of a machine gun.

Smalevichy   Смалявічы   709km
This town is 2km northeast of the railway and its life revolves around peat. The rotted vegetation is used to power the Smalevichy power station and produce oil. It is even the basis of the town's name which is derived from the word *smolokurenie*, meaning "tar extraction".

After about 5km, on the right in the distance is a monument of four giant bayonets protruding from a small hill. This large World War II memorial beside the Minsk–Moscow highway is called Kurgan Slavy meaning "glory hill". It marks the place where troops from different Soviet armies met in a pincer move to cut off the retreat of German forces from the east. In the following battle, over 70,000 Germans were killed and 30,000 captured.

Kalodzishcha   Калодзішч   733km
Just past this station is the border of Minsk municipal area. The toilets on the train are closed here.

Minsk   Мінск   750km
Minsk is the capital of the Republic of Belarus. Although it is an independent country, Belarus is closely tied to Russia and will become even more so in the future, see *Chapter Six*.

The station is to the southwest of the city. After leaving Minsk the train passes the main airport on the right before crossing under the Minsk ring road. This road is 13km from the city centre and defines the city's municipal boundary. The toilet is re-opened past this road.

Koidanava   Коиданава   790km

This town was formerly called Dzerzhinsk, after the region's most famous son, Felix Dzerzhinsky (1877–1926). Dzerzhinsky was a Bolshevik and founder of the hated Soviet secret police called the Cheka, which eventually became the KGB.

Dzerzhinsky was actually born on his family's estate 46km to the northwest of Dzerzhinsk. Near the estate is Ivanets village which now contains the Dzerzhinsky Museum. This two-storey building was opened in 1957 on the 80th anniversary of his birth and it contains a model of his family home which was burned down by the Germans in 1943.

Following the Polish Soviet War of 1919–20, Koidanava became Belarus' most western border town on the railway from Minsk to Warsaw. After World War II, the border was moved 300km to the west.

Nearby is Belarus' highest mountain, the 346m-high Mount Dzerzhinskaya. There is a basic hotel on vul Sovetskaya.

Stoibtsy   Стоўбцы   827km

Just before the town, you cross over the Nieman River which was the former Polish–Belarusian border from 1918 to 1939.

The town's most noticeable building is St Anne's Church, built in 1825, which sits on a small hill in the centre of town. There is a basic hotel in town.

Baranavichy   Баранавічы   895km

Baranavichy is a major railway junction with trains departing in six directions. Before World War II, 50% of the town's population was Jewish, but only a handful lived to see the end of the war as an extermination camp was built here. There is a monument in the town to 3,000 Czech citizens shot by the Nazis in 1942.

The town also boasts a monument to Syargei Grytsavets (1909–39) who was born in nearby Borovtsi village and was a distinguished pilot against the Japanese near Khalkhin-Gol in Mongolia in 1939.

There is a museum at vul Sovetskaya 14 and hotels at vul Komsomolskaya 8 and 28.

About 1km after leaving the town, on the right beside the railway is a monument of a big grey bell with a man beside it. The memorial is on the site of one of the many Belarusian villages that were burnt down by the Germans in World War II.

Baranavichy has a sister city relationship with Binghamton, New York.

Lyasnaya   Лясная   917km

In this village was the German concentration camp, Stalag 337, locally known as the Lesnyanski Death Camp. Today, a monument of a soldier stands on its site, dedicated to the 88,000 people executed by the Germans and their Belarusian henchmen.

Ivatsevichy   Івацэвічы   960km

About 10km to the north is the village of Kossvo which houses an experimental farm run by the Belarusian Academy of Science. The farm investigates farming techniques on reclaimed marsh land.

Bronnaya Gara   Бронная-Гара   980km

Nearby is a large military complex which is responsible for destroying nuclear missiles and excess military equipment left by the Soviet forces. Belarus has committed itself to the destruction of tanks and other armoured vehicles in excess of the ceilings set by the Treaty on Conventional Forces in Europe. This destruction will cost at least $230 million and has been used by the Belarusian government as a bargaining chip in getting foreign loans.

Byaroza   Бяроза   997km

The station is called Byaroza and the surrounding town is known as Byaroza-Kartuskaya (Bereza-Kartuskaya in Russian). In the town, on vul Krasnoarmeiskaya, are the remains of a Catholic monastery which was closed in 1870 to become a large prison. The Germans used it as a concentration camp.

About 5km away is the Osovtsy military airforce base which often stages night firing practice sessions that light up the sky. A helicopter from here shot down a balloon on September 12 1995, during a balloon race from Switzerland, killing two Americans. According to the Belarusian military, the balloon flew over a military base and did not heed warnings to land. Initially the Belarusian president, Alyaksandr Lukashenka, apologised but maintained that much of the blame lay with the balloon competition organisers for failing to inform Belarusian air control services of the possibility of balloons flying over their air space. However, Western outrage at this lie (as they had received permission to fly into Belarus) forced the Belarusian government to allow an international inquiry to investigate the incident in late 1995.

There is a local museum and no doubt the balloon incident will never be included in it.

The basic Hotel Bereza is on Lenina ul.

BREST   Брэст   1,097km
Population: 289,000   Telephone area code: 0162

The town sits on the right bank of the River Mukhovets near where it flows into the Bug River. The Bug marks the border with Poland.

Getting there and away

The most common way of crossing the border into Poland is on a long-distance Russian train. These trains stop at the station and customs officers board the train to check custom declarations. Border guards then check passports and, finally, the train's bogies are changed over to the narrower Polish gauge. After crossing over the Bug River, the train travels 5km to the Polish border town of Terespol (known by the same name in Polish and Russian [Тересполь]) where documentation is checked by Polish border officers.

International trains

There is only one international long-distance train that originates in Brest. The train No 11011/10008 runs between Brest and Warsaw.

It is also possible to travel from Brest to Poland on a Polish electric suburban train. Suburban trains from Brest travel to Terespol, Lukow, Siedlce, Warsaw, Bialystok and Vlodava. The route to Warsaw is: Brest–Terespol (Poland)–Biala Podliaska–Lukow–Siedlce–Warsaw. The route to Bialystok is Brest–Vysoko Litovsk (Belarus)–Cheremha–Hainuvka–Bialystok. The route to Vlodava is Brest–Terespol–Lukow–Lublin–Vlodava. Note that there is a Vlodava in Belarus as well as a Vlodava in Poland. They are on opposite sides of the Bug River which is the border between Poland and Belarus. The train from Brest does not go through Belarusian Vlodava because the bridge between the two Vlodavas was destroyed in World War II and never repaired. Consequently, trains from Brest to Polish Vlodava have to do a 250km hook via Terespol–Lukow-Lublin. All the suburban trains run daily. Suburban trains are the cheapest way to travel between Poland and Belarus. From Brest in 1996, a suburban ticket to Terespol costs $2, to Biala Podliaska $3, to Lukow, Siedlce and Bialystok $5, and to Warsaw $8. These trains are always full of traders taking cheap vodka from Belarus to Poland. These people, known as *spirtovozy* ("spirits-carriers") and *chelnoki* ("shuttles"), make more in one trip than the monthly minimum salary in Belarus which is $9. Consequently, the trains are not the most pleasant to travel on.

At Brest station, the suburban trains depart from the fenced-in platform to the north which can only be reached through customs and passport control in the Intourist Hall. This hall is beside the waiting room on the main platform. Passport formalities take over an hour so get there early.

At the start of this chapter is a list of the major international trains that go through Brest. The ones listed below start or terminate in Brest.

Origin	Dist, km	Entry point	Train no & name	Carr'ge class	No in coupé	Travel time	Day of departure	Destination
Warsaw	314	Brest	10008	2	4	3hr 20min	daily	Brest
Brest	314	Brest	11011	2	4	5hr 15min	daily	Warsaw

Domestic trains

Travelling to the east is difficult on international trains as the railways do not know the number of available berths until the trains arrive. Therefore, it is far better to buy tickets on trains originating in Brest. The best of these trains are:

Origin	Dist, km	Train no & name	Travel time	Depart	Arrive	Destination
Brest	1097	28	17hr 36min	17.10	10.46	Moscow (Smolensk)
Brest	1097	74	17hr 45min	18.00	11.45	Moscow (Smolensk)
Brest	1097	130	19hr 46min	08.10	03.56	Moscow (Smolensk)
Brest	1213	50	22hr 41min	13.00	11.52	St Petersburg (Vitebsk)
Brest	355	50	5hr 1min	13.00	18.01	Minsk
Minsk	355	117	5hr 12min	13.01	18.13	Brest
Moscow (Smolensk)	1097	27	15hr 17min	14.28	05.45	Brest
Moscow (Smolensk)	1097	73	15hr 35min	16.43	08.18	Brest
Moscow (Smolensk)	1097	129	16hr 49min	06.52	23.41	Brest
St Petersburg (Vitebsk)	1213	49	20hr	15.20	11.20	Brest

Where to stay

The closest hotels to the station are the basic Hotel Bug River, vul Lenina 2, tel: 252 083, $31 a double room, and the very basic Hotel Molodezhskaya,

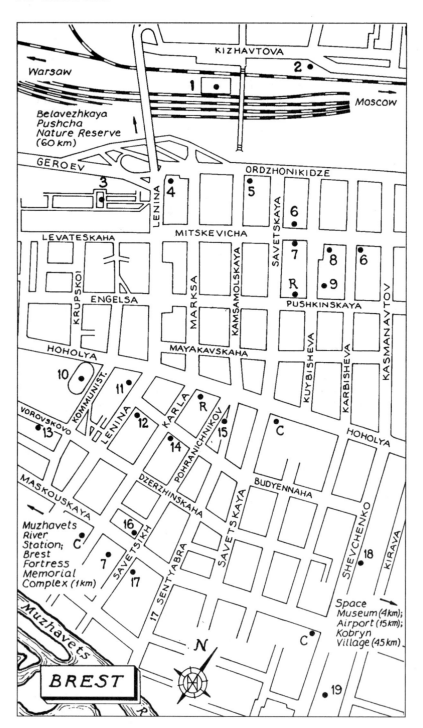

	KEY TO BREST Брэст	
1	Railway station	Чыгуначны вакзал
2	Railway club	Чыгуначны клуб
3	Mass grave	Масавая магіла
4	Hotel Bug River	Гасцініца Буг
5	Hotel Molodezhskaya	Гасцініца Маладзёжская
6	Institute	Інстытут
7	Church	Царква
8	Bus station	Аўтобусны вакзал
9	Market	Рынак
10	Bug stadium	Стадыён «Буг»
11	Drama Theatre	Драматычны тэатр
12	Children's Puppet Theatre	Дзецкі Тэатр Лялек
13	Swimming pool	Басейн
14	Museum of Local Studies	Рэгіянальны Музей
15	Monument in honour of the liberation of Brest from Germans	Помнік у гонар асвабаджэния Брэста ад Немцаў
16	Art gallery	Мастацкая Галерэя
17	Hotel Intourist	Гасцініца Інтурыст
18	Advance purchase railway booking office	Чыгуначны білетныя касы
19	Hotel Belarus	Гасцініца Беларусь
R	Restaurant (Restoran)	Рэстаран
C	Café (Kafe) or Bar (Bar)	Кафэ

also known as Hotel No 1, vul Komsomolskaya 4, tel: 261 076, $12 twin share/ person. The best hotel is the standard Hotel Intourist, vul Moskovskaya 15, tel: 252 083, $56 a double room. Another option is the standard Hotel Belarus, bul Shevchenko 150, tel: 261 161, 252 566, but it is even further away. To get to either from the railway station catch bus No 6 or trolleybus No 2 or 3. All hotels but Hotel Molodezhskaya have restaurants.

What to see

Although the town is pleasant, with a developing café culture and several malls, there is very little to see in Brest except the Brest Fortress Memorial Complex. There is no ancient part of the city as it was moved to its current site when the fortress was built in the middle of the last century.

There is a boring Museum of Local Studies, vul Lenina 34, open 11.00–18.00, closed Monday and last Tuesday of the month, and an Art Gallery, vul Sovetskaya 54. There is a Space Museum inside an Il-18 aircraft at vul Moskovskaya 348/3, which is in the Vostok-2 suburb on the eastern outskirts of town.

The Brest Fortress

As early as the 19th century, Brest's location at the junction of roads to Warsaw, Moscow, Vilnius and Kiev gave it a strategic importance. The town itself was located at the junction of the Bug and Mukhavets Rivers which was the ideal site for a fortress. Consequently, the town's population was forcibly relocated to the present-day city centre before work started on the Brest Fortress in 1833. The powerful circular fortress grew rapidly and occupied nearly 5km^2 spread out over four islands. The whole fortress was ringed by wide canals and 10m-high ramparts. The heart of the fortress was the citadel which was ringed by 1.5m-thick red brick and concrete walls. By the start of World War I, the fortress was so strong that when the Germans invaded, they bypassed it in the hope of starving it out. Following the end of the war and the formation of Poland, the fortress became Polish until 1939. In that year both the Germans and Soviets invaded and divided up Poland. Over the next two years the fortress was modernised and, by the time of the German invasion of the Soviet Union in 1941, the fortress was further protected by dozens of camouflaged sniper's positions, armoured cupolas with anti-tank and anti-aircraft guns, and each island was sub-divided by artificial water courses to further slow down attacking troops.

The remains of the destroyed Brest Fortress have been transformed into a giant museum park, open September–May, 10.00–17.30 weekdays, 09.00–17.30 weekends, May–September, 09.00–17.30 weekdays, 08.00–17.30 weekends. The entrance is from vul Moskovskaya. Bus No 12 runs from in front of the Intourist Hotel to the fortress. A long walkway leads through a giant star sliced out of concrete and speakers blare out battle sounds and martial music. About 500m further on, there is a café on your right. Returning to the main walkway, you pass on your left one of many giant sculptures. This one is of a soldier crawling along the ground. He symbolises the often fatal nightly crawl to the river banks in search of water, following the loss of the defenders' well. Past this monument, you arrive at the main square in the centre of the citadel. This area can hold 25,000 people and is full every military celebration.

On the square is a giant concrete memorial slab with a determined soldier's head emerging from it. Behind it is a semi-destroyed, but now operating, church which was the Garrison Club before the war. To the right of the memorial slab is the museum, open 10.00–18.00, closed Monday and Tuesday. This museum is well done with the rooms decorated to imitate parts of the fortress at various times of the siege. To the left of the slab is the Kholmski Gate which is pitted with shell holes. According to locals, the walls on the right of the gates are not original but have been rebuilt recently including imitation bullet holes. Going through the gate and across the moat takes you to the Brest Archaeological Museum, open 10.00–18.00, closed Monday and Tuesday. The museum is actually a pavilion covering a giant hole in the ground which contains a re-created village that was here centuries ago. The White Palace was where the negotiations of 1918 Treaty of Brest-Litovsk occurred which ended Russia's involvement against Germany in World War I.

There have been numerous Soviet propaganda books written on the fortress, the best being *His Name Was Not Listed* by Boris Vassilyev and published by Progress Press.

Getting assistance

Travel agents   Intourist is at the Hotel Intourist, vul Moskovskaya 15, tel: 250 510 or 252 968. Brest-turist offers a large range of travel programmes, bul Shevchenko 6, tel: 590 12, 590 39.

Air   The air ticket sales office is at vul Naberezhnaya 2 and the railway station.

Rail   International rail tickets can be bought at the railway station and the advance purchase railway booking office is at bul Shevchenko 120.

Information and business   The non-profit Independent Information & Resource Center organises electronic mail services, business and cultural contacts, and advice. Contact Valeri S. Fominski, blvd Kosmonavtov 48, tel: 232 123, 234 229, 222 123, email Valeri@ssw.belpak.brest.by. The centre funds the

Regional Educational and Medical Information Network Development and seeks donations for its work.

What's in the region

About 45km to the east is the village of Kobryn (Кобрын). This ancient settlement was given to Russia's greatest military leader, General Suvorov, in 1795 by Catherine II. The village now houses the Suvorov Military History Museum at vul Suvorova 16. There are suburban trains to Kobrun. In Kobrun is the basic Hotel Belarus.

About 60km to the northeast is Belavezhskaya Pushcha Nature Reserve. This is one of the world's oldest animal and plant sanctuaries and covers 130,000 hectares, 75,000 hectares of which are in Belarus. The reserve contains tarpans (wild horses), red deer, roe deer and wild boar but its highlight is the European bison. In 1921, only 26 of these hairy animals existed in the world but a breeding programme has resulted in over 80 living on the reserve today. There is a museum and a basic hotel here. To visit the reserve it is best to organise a tour at the reception desk of Hotel Intourist, tel: 250 510 or 252 968.

Point of interest

Like the rest of the Soviet Union, the soldiers of Brest never expected the German invasion on June 22 1941. Consequently, soldiers and families were simply waiting for their trains at Brest station when the German war machine unleased its fury in the early hours of the morning. The station was quickly surrounded and heavy shelling forced the defenders into the station's cellars. For the next ten days they withstood attack by flamethrower and gas. However, they were finally dislodged when raw sewage was pumped into the cellars. Only about 25 defenders fought their way out of the German encirclement, leaving over 80 dead comrades.

As very little of the original station, built in 1866, survived the attack, it was completely rebuilt by 1956 into the Stalinist edifice you see today.

Terespol   1,102km

After crossing over the River Bug which delineates the Polish border, you arrive at the first stop in Poland. Here, your passport and visa will be checked. It is no longer possible to get transit visas at the border so if you do not have a Russian or Belarusian visa, you will be thrown off the train.

Warsaw   1,317km

For information on Warsaw, see *Eastern Europe by Rail* by Rob Dodson, published by Bradt Publications.

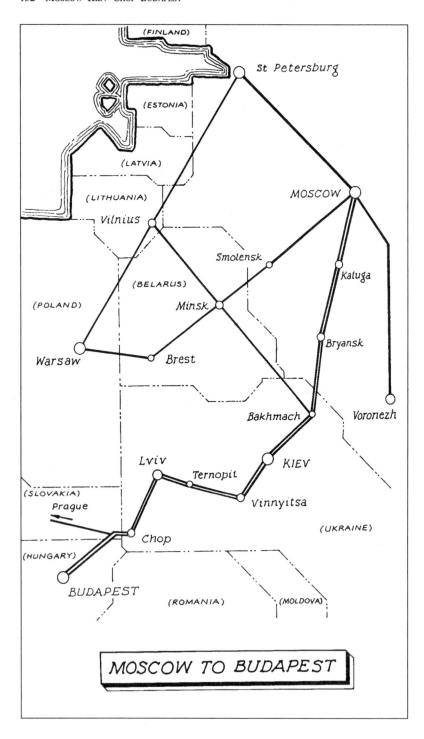

MOSCOW TO BUDAPEST

Chapter Ten

Moscow–Kiev–Chop–Budapest

While Ukraine has only been an independent country since August 24 1991, the country has had a distinct culture with its own language for centuries.

Unfortunately, few visitors to the former Soviet Union have had the opportunity to experience the true Ukrainian national culture as that imposed by Russians/Soviets dominated for decades. Nowadays, Ukrainian culture has come out of hibernation and this, coupled with the removal of Soviet era travel restrictions, has made travelling around the little-known Ukraine enjoyable, educational and cheap.

Of all of the former countries of the Soviet Union, Ukraine has taken the process of derussification (removing the traces of Russia) the furthest. Some of the more noticeable changes have been the virtual elimination of Russian language from public signs, and the change of the capital from "Kiev" (the English transliteration of the Russian spelling) to "Kyiv" (the English transliteration of the Ukrainian spelling). However, the most important change has been the practice of referring to the country as "Ukraine" rather than "The Ukraine". Deleting the word "The" will save you a tirade of abuse from nationalists who believe that to refer to the country as "The Ukraine" means that you have fallen victim to a Russian/Soviet semantic ruse which conveys the idea that Ukraine was merely a region of Russia, such as "The Black Earth Region" or "The Caucasus".

Trains from Poland, Slovakia, Hungary and Rumania travel on the Moscow–Kiev–Chop railway which makes this route a convenient way of travelling between eastern Europe and Russia.

Route highlights

The 1,242km rail journey through Ukraine carries you over the Carpathian Mountains in the east, via the Galician city of Lviv, through the Soviet era reconstructed city of Ternopil and quaint Vinnytsya, to the nation's capital of Kiev, before entering the Bryansk Forests in Russia.

To discover what Ukraine has to offer, it is worth spending two days each in Lviv and Kiev and preferably a day each in Ternopil and Vinnytsya. There are a number of other fascinating places to stop en route, such as the Carpathian resort town of Skole or historic Nizhin.

Within Russia there are several interesting places to visit including the industrial town of Bryansk, Maloyaroslavets and Kuluga.

Although the climate is warmer than European Russia, it is still best to travel through Ukraine in late spring, summer or early autumn. The best time for festivals is May. This is the month of the Kiev Day celebration (held on the last Sunday in May), the Kiev Spring Festival and the Lviv National Virtuosos Festival.

The whole of Ukraine is in the same time zone as Moscow, St Petersburg and Belarus. Kiev is one hour ahead of Helsinki, Sofia, Athens, and Bucharest, two hours ahead of Paris, Prague, Rome, Stockholm, Warsaw, Vienna and Berlin, and three hours ahead of London. Daylight saving starts on the last Saturday in March and finishes on the last Saturday in September.

Trains
The Moscow–Kiev–Chop railway is very busy and is mostly serviced by good quality trains. The major segments of the route are:

- 873km Moscow to Kiev, taking 13hr 30 min
- 627km Kiev to Lviv, taking 11hr 17 min
- 266km Lviv to Chop, taking 5hr 30 min

Trains on this line head for Romania, Slovakia, the Czech Republic and Hungary with carriages joining other trains which go as far as Venice.

International trains
The most convenient international distance trains on this route are listed below.

Origin	Dist, km	Entry point	Train no & name	Carr'ge class	No in coupé	Travel time	Day of departure	Destination
Moscow (Kiev)		Chop	15	1, 2	2, 3		Wed, Sun	Venice
Moscow (Kiev)	2,110	Chop	15 Tisza Express	1, 2	2, 4	40hr 50min	daily	Budapest
Moscow (Kiev)	2,317	Chop	51 Slovakia	1, 2	2, 3, 4	42hr 21min	daily	Bratislava
Moscow (Kiev)	2,363	Chop	9	1, 2	2, 3	46hr 17min	daily	Belgrade
Moscow (Kiev)	2,582	Chop	7	1, 2	2, 3, 4	46hr 27min	daily	Prague
Belgrade	2,363	Chop	10	1, 2	2, 3	44hr 31min	daily	Moscow (Kiev)
Bratislava	2,317	Chop	52 Slovakia	1, 2	2, 3, 4	42hr 27min	daily	Moscow (Kiev)
Budapest	2,110	Chop	16 Tisza Express	1, 2	2, 4	40hr 1min	daily	Moscow (Kiev)
Prague	2,582	Chop	8	1, 2	2, 3, 4	46hr 31min	daily	Moscow (Kiev)
Venice		Chop	16	1, 2	2, 3		Fri, Tues	Moscow (Kiev)

Domestic trains
If you are travelling within Russia or Ukraine, it is best not to travel on the international trains as tickets are much harder to buy. The most convenient long-distance trains on this route are listed below.

Origin	Dist, km	Train no & name	Travel time	Depart	Arrive	Destination
Moscow (Kiev)	389	99	6hr 44min	23.01	05.45	Bryansk
Moscow (Kiev)	872	1	13hr 36min	19.54	09.30	Kiev
Moscow (Kiev)	1,499	73	27hr 16min	09.24	12.40	Lviv
Bryansk	389	100	6hr 44min	23.52	06.37	Moscow (Kiev)
Kiev	872	2	15hr 59min	17.10	09.09	Moscow (Kiev)
Lviv	1,499	74	29hr 11min	00.06	05.37	Moscow (Kiev)

MOSCOW
Above: *Fountains, Exhibition of Economic Achievements (VDNKh)* (IB)
Below: *Kremlin and cathedral from the Moskva River* (IB)

MARKET VENDORS
Above: *Potato vendors at Khabarovsk's central market* (DE)
Below: *Tomatoes and peppers for sale at the green market in Uzhgorod, Ukraine* (MM)

Rebuilt church at the Museum of Wooden Architecture, Irkutsk (IB)

ULAANBAATAR
Above: *Schoolchildren* (IB)
Below: *Ganden Monastery* (IB)

ROUTE DESCRIPTION

Moscow   Москва   0km
The station is located at pl Kievskovo Vokzala, tel: 240 1115, 240 0484, 240 7622. The closest metro station is Kievskaya.

Solnechnaya   Солнечная   16km
This station is just outside the ring road around metropolitan Moscow and the toilet door opens here.

Lesnoi Gorodok   Лесной Городок   24km
On the left is a 5km branch line to the Vnukovo airport.

Aprelevka   Апрелевка   42km
This town has the largest record-producing plant in Russia, producing 60% of the country's plastic discs.

About 1km after leaving the station, the train crosses over the Desna River and directly on the right is the famous three-colour, five-domed Cathedral of St Demidov. The four-sided classical church has four wings which are symmetrically laid out.

Nara   Нара   70km
Nara serves the ancient town of Naro-Fominsk (Нара-Фоминск) which is spread over both banks of the Nara River. Naro-Fominsk was formed from two villages, Fominskoe and Malaya Nara. Its most famous visitor was Napoleon, who stayed overnight in the church during his army's retreat from Moscow in 1812.

Some of the most famous paintings depicting the 1812 war were painted by V V Vereshchagin who visited Naro-Fominsk many times to produce the paintings' preliminary sketches. His paintings are on display at both the Historical Museum in Moscow and at Maloyaroslavets 1812 Military Museum.

Since the 1840s, paper, cloth and fabric factories have sprung up in Naro-Fominsk. The town boasted the first factory in Russia to produce cloth from *kapron* and *lavsan*, the Soviet equivalents of rayon and dacron.

Today, Naro-Fominsk is home to the élite 199th Airborne Regiment which took part in the Bosnian peacekeeping operation. The town's only other attractions are the scenic Nara River and the local museum. There is a basic hotel in town.

Balabanovo   Балабаново   96km
Balabanovo is an odd mix of ugly 1970s and 1980s Soviet buildings and single-storey wooden peasant buildings on the outskirts. There are very few old buildings in the centre of the town because the Germans torched it during the war.

The town has two interesting factories: one produces platinum needles for acupuncture, and the other, with the wonderful name of the Gigant Experimental Match Factory, produces matches for polar explorers, hunters and special anniversaries.

Obninskoe   Обнинское   106km
Once strictly closed to foreigners, this city is the site of the world's first atomic power station. Built in 1954, the 5MW power station provided operational data

for the Soviet's first generation of stations. Several related research institutes are based in the city and these investigate medical radiology and nuclear physics. In October 1995, Russia's first comprehensive system for monitoring uranium and plutonium stocks was built around the Obninskoe nuclear storage facility which holds seven tons of fissionable materials.

The city has a museum of local studies with information about the atomic power station.

Obninskoe has a sister city relationship with Tennessee.

Maloyaroslavets   Малоярославец   121km
Telephone area code: 08431
Maloyaroslavets was founded in the 14th century and served as a fortress protecting Moscow from the raids of both the Crimean Tatars and Lithuanians in the 15th and 16th centuries.

However, the most important event in the town occurred on October 12 1812 when a desperate battle took place between the French and Russian armies. Although the Battle of Maloyaroslavets claimed just 5,000 French and 3,000 Russians lives, it succeeded in blocking Napoleon's southern escape route and was a major Russian strategic victory.

Even today, the battle plays a prominent role in the town as there are 43 monuments to it in the nearby region with the largest being a memorial of French cannon balls and guns in the centre of town. There is also a chapel and the (Assumption) Uspenski Church built in honour of the battle. Information on the battle can be found in the Maloyaroslavets 1812 Military Museum which is a ten-minute walk from the station and is at ul Moskovskaya 13, tel: 42 711.

Another interesting site in town is the functioning Nikolski Chernoostrovski Monastery. This monastery was burnt down during the communist era but is slowly being rebuilt.

There are numerous suburban trains from Moscow to Maloyaroslavets and the trip takes nearly 2hr 30min. Only a few long-distance trains stop here and these take just over 2hr.

Tikhonova Pustyn   Тихонова Пустынь   170km
The branch line from here to the east takes you to the regional centre of Kaluga after 18km. To get there, you can either change trains here or catch a bus from Kaluga 2 station which is 12km further on.

KALUGA   Калуга   188km
Population: 346,800   Telephone area code: 084 22
At the start of the 19th century, Kaluga was as big as Kiev, its size being due to its strategic position on the Oka River, a major trading route. However, the shallowing of the river and new railways directly connecting the agricultural areas with Moscow resulted in a rapid decline in Kaluga's importance by the end of the last century.

Today, Kaluga is a major industrial centre with several plants producing components for the car industry.

Getting there and away
There are direct suburban trains from Moscow and the trip takes just over 4hr. All long-distance trains stop at nearby Kaluga 2 station where buses ply

between the station and Kaluga itself. The trip by long-distance train from Moscow to Kaluga 2 takes just over 3hr.

Where to stay
Accommodation is available at the Hotel Kaluga, ul Kirova 1, tel: 49 740, $68 twin share/room, Hotel Oka, pl Lenina, tel: 772 20, $50 twin share/person, and Hotel Priokskaya, ul Suvorova 132, tel: 427 33, $25 twin share/person. The best accommodation is the excellent Hotel Iris, ul Vishnevskovo 1, tel: 736 55, 925 32. The hotel is about 1km to the west of the city centre.

What to see
Among the architectural landmarks are the Korobovs' Chamber (1697), a number of stone houses from the 18th century, the Protection of the Blessed Virgin Mary Church on the Moat (1687) and the early 19th-century Meshkovs' house which is now the state bank.

There are two museums, located at ul Korolieva 2, that are devoted to the locally born aeroplane and space scientist, K E Tsiolkovski. One is in his childhood house and the other encompasses his contribution to the study of cosmonautics. In addition, there is a museum of local studies and an art gallery.

Getting help
Travel agents   Intourist, ul Lenina 81, tel: 78 763, 76 454; The Bureau for Travel and Excursions, ul Engelsa 14, tel: 78 142.
Air   Aeroflot, ul Lenina 35, tel: 23 345.

Kaluga 2   Калуга 2   182km
Long-distance trains from Moscow to Kiev stop here as it is the closest station to the city of Kaluga. There are regular buses between Kaluga 2 and Kaluga.

Just after leaving Kaluga 2, the train crosses over the Ugra River at the point where it flows into the Oka which is on the left of the railway. This river junction is the site of the famous battle called the "Stand on the Ugra River". The battle resulted from Tsar Ivan III's decision in 1476 to cease paying the annual tribute to the Golden Horde, the strongest of the Tatar-Mongol khanates which grew from the breaking up of Ghengis Khan's empire. At that time, there was nothing the Tatar-Mongol khan could do about the rebellion as his troops were busy fighting in the Crimea. However, in 1480 the khan decided to snuff out the revolt and his army marched north until it reached the banks of the Ugra River. For the next four days, his army tried repeatedly to storm across the river but was continuously repulsed by the Russians on the north bank. For the next few days, the two forces faced each other across the water biding their time. The khan was waiting for the never-to-arrive reinforcements from his ally, the king of Poland-Lithuania, while Tsar Ivan III's forces grew stronger as regiments controlled by his brothers arrived. Seeing that he was outnumbered, the khan's forces turned and fled south, ending centuries of Tatar-Mongol domination of Russia.

Sukhinichi Glavnye   Сухиничи Главные   261km
In the first half of the 18th century, a few huts in the area coalesced to form several small villages and then, at the start of the 19th century, these villages merged to create a government commune called Sukhinichi. The commune

inhabitants worked as guides and porters, carrying locally produced goods through mountain passes to nearby rivers from where the products sailed down to ports on the Volga River, before being transported to far away Riga and St Petersburg. During winter, villagers made between 6,000 and 10,000 trips a year.

Unlike Kaluga, when the railways arrived in the late 1800s, Sukhinichi's importance increased as it became a major rail junction with railways heading in six directions. As well as being a major freight centre, the town today has a factory producing valves which are still used in Russian radios, televisions and amplifiers.

BRYANSK   Брянск   387km
Population: 460,000   Telephone area code: 0832

Bryansk is one of the oldest towns of central Russia and excavations have revealed its origins in the year 985. Bryansk arose as a fortress on the right bank of the Desna River, near the junction of the Osetr and the Trubesh Rivers, on the orders of Vladimir, Grand Duke of Kiev. The city was originally called Bryn then Debriansk which is from the word *dyebry* meaning "thick, impenetrable forest". It stood at an important strategic position on the trade route between Moscow and Ukraine and served as a stronghold defending the borders of Moscow state from assaults by the Tatars, Poles and Lithuanians.

During the reign of Peter the Great a larger fortress and a shipyard were built here. The ships were used in the 1737–9 Turkish Campaign. In 1783 an arsenal was constructed here, which cast siege and field artillery pieces, on orders of Catherine the Great. The importance of this factory is reflected in the city's coat of arms which includes a cannon and cannon balls.

During World War II, Bryansk was occupied by the Germans for nearly two years and during this time 90% of the city's buildings were destroyed. The region was a hive of partisan activity and over 80,000 of the region's inhabitants died in fighting and German retaliation. It is for this reason that Bryansk is called the City of Partisan Glory and it is littered with monuments to partisans.

Bryansk's military significance declined as its industrial importance rose in the 19th century. Today, the city is a heavy-engineering centre with its most famous factory being the Bryansk machine works. The works produce Russia's TEM-2 shunting diesel locomotives, five-car, silver-coloured refrigerated rail wagon sets for hauling perishable goods, and diesel engines for ships.

Getting there and away
Bryansk is only seven hours from Moscow and there are two night trains which start in Bryansk for Moscow. They leave within an hour of each other and are listed in the table below. A more pleasant way of travelling is to catch an early morning day train from Moscow, stop at midday in Maloyaroslavets before proceeding to Bryansk in the early evening.

There are no trains that originate in Bryansk and terminate in Kiev. Therefore you have to catch one of the many through trains from Moscow to Kiev. This 485km trip takes about eight hours.

The city's major railway station is called Bryansk-Orlovski and trains stop here for 20 minutes. Trains stop at the minor station of Bryansk-Lgovski for only one minute.

There are daily regular flights from Bryansk to Moscow and Kiev, and it is expected that international flights will start arriving once the airport's upgrade is completed.

The most convenient long-distance trains on this route are listed below.

Origin	Dist, km	Train no & name	Travel time	Depart	Arrive	Destination
Bryansk	389	100	6hr 45min	23.52	06.37	Moscow (Kiev)
Moscow (Kiev)	389	99	6hr 44min	23.01	05.45	Bryansk
Bryansk (through)	485	3	7hr 15min	22.50	06.05	Kiev
Kiev	485	42	8hr 46min	21.50	07.36	Bryansk (through)

Where to stay
The best hotels are the standard Hotel Bryansk (formerly Hotel Rossia), pro Lenina 100, tel: 466 844, $15 twin share per person; standard Turist Hotel, ul Duki 62a, tel: 747 711, 747 492, $30 twin share per person; and Hotel Desna, pl Lenina, tel: 740 135, $12 twin share per person. Other options include Hotel Chernigov (former Tsentralnaya), tel: 743 206, and the very basic Hotel DOSAAF, pro Lenina, tel: 460 871. Hotel Bryansk and Hotel Desna have buffets.

Getting around
The Desna River divides the city into four districts: Sovetsky, Beshitsky, Fokinsky and Volodarsky. All of them are linked by bridges over the river. The nucleus of the city is Pokrovskaya (Protection of the Blessed Virgin Mary) Hill which is on the steep right (south) bank of the Desna River. The city's main railway station is called Bryansk-Orlovski and it is located on the left (north) bank of the river.

To get to the centre of town from Bryansk-Orlovski station, take trolleybus No 1 which goes to pl Partizan or No 2 which goes to the Quay stop before turning into bul Gagarina and ending at the square, pl Lenina.

What to see
The city's major attractions are the Museum of Local History, pl Partizana, tel: 410 390; the Museum of Culture, ul Oktyabrskaya 86, tel: 747 053, 741 503; the Museum of Decorative Fine Arts, ul Emlyutina 39, tel: 471 503; and the Fine Arts Museum, bul Gagarina 19. These museums are open 10.00–17:00, closed Monday. An interesting museum is the Bryansk Forest Museum which is situated in the city's A K Tolstoi Park which also contains carved wooden sculptures. The museum focuses on the 100,000-hectare Bryansk Forest to the north of the city which you passed through just before arriving. The forest consists mainly of pine, fir and broad-leaved trees and has been studied intensely since the creation in 1906 of a training and experimental forestry station. During World War II, the forest hid over 60,000 partisans who tied down tens of thousands of German troops and destroyed vital supply lines. Specialist museums include the Bryansk Machine Works' Engineering Museum.

The large church on pl Revolyutsi was designed by Rastrelli who also built the famous Peter and Paul Cathedral in St Petersburg.

Historically important but not much to look at is Peter the Great's Custom House at ul Karla Marksa 3. Peter stayed here once and now the building houses a children's musical school.

On the southern outskirts of the city is the Svenk Monastery. It was built in 1288 by Tsar Roman and between the 17th and 20th centuries it was the site of one of

Russia's largest annual fairs. To get to the Svensk Monastery from the centre of town take trolleybus No 1 or 4, or bus No 119 and get off at the Telecenter stop.

Getting assistance
Travel agents Council for Tourism and Excursions, ul Pionerskaya 33, tel 465 451.
Air Aeroflot, pro Lenina 57, tel 748 430, 748 482.
Bus The long-distance bus station, ul Peresveta 1.
Rail Tickets can be bought at the railway station and at the advance booking office, pro Lenina 57.

Zernovo   Зерново   519km
The town surrounding the station is called Seredina-Buda (Середина-Буда) and is the Russian border town closest to Ukraine's border.

Druzhba   Дружба   539km
The name of this town, the first major stop in Ukraine, used to be Khutir Mykolayivski or "Michail's khutir". The term *khutir* was used in the times of the Russian Empire to denote a rural settlement built on privately owned land. The land may have been owned by a wealthy landowner or simply occupied by one peasant's family. During the Soviet period of collectivisation in the late 1920s and 1930s, *khutirs* were abolished and single households were moved to collective farms, their land confiscated by the commune. In 1962, the town's name was changed to Druzhba, meaning "friendship".

You are now in the centre of sugar beet country.

Voronizh   Вороніж   585km
About 35km from the station is the village of Mezyn, the site of the oldest settlement in Ukraine. Over 2,500 years ago, during the late Palaeolithic Age, a village arose and disappeared here. Since 1908, when the remains were discovered, over 4,000 flint utensils, agricultural tools and sculptures made of mammoth tusks have been uncovered. Today, the Mezyn Museum stands on the site of the excavation which is called the Mezyn Stoyanka.

Krolevets   Кролевець   611km
Sitting on the picturesque Svidnya River, Krolevets is an attractive ancient city. It was founded in 1601 under Bogdan Khmelnytsky, the future leader of independent Ukraine, as a military camp for a company of the Nizhin Regiment. This regiment is named after Nizhin town, 135km away.

Krolevets became a major trading town and its lasting legacy is the decorative weaving of embroidered cloths (*rushnyky*), skirts, kerchiefs and bedspreads.

As well as sugar beet and maize, hemp is common here. Hemp, also known as marijuana, is used for paper and cloth production and, despite Western anti-drug hysteria, commercial hemp poses no danger as its drug potency is far lower than cough syrup.

The only place to stay is the basic Zhovten Hotel, vul Franko 7.

Altynivka   Алтинівка   626km
About 26km to the north of the station is the village of Korop (Короп). The revolutionary M Kybalchych (1853–81) was born here and there is a museum to

his life, M Kybalchych Memorial Museum, Provulok Kybalchycha 18, tel: (046 56) 217 07. Kybalchych was a member of the revolutionary organisation Zemlya i Volya and was sentenced to death for his involvement in a plot to assassinate the Russian Tsar Alexander II.

There are two other interesting buildings in Korop: the fortified Church of St Elias' (Illinska), built from 1750 to 1760 with walls 2m thick, and the Church of the Ascension (Voznesenska) built in 1764.

Konotop   Конотоп   651km

Konotop was originally founded by the Polish state in 1640 as a fortress and became an important railway junction in the 19th century. Today, the town boasts a large locomotive and wagon repair plant, while the largest factory is the Chervonyi heavy-engineering plant. With the downturn of the Ukrainian economy, this plant has laid off thousands of workers and now operates only part of the year.

Information on local factories and the history of the town, another base of the Nizhin regiment, is on display in the local museum.

Bakhmach   Бахмач   676km

This town sits on another important railway junction but there is nothing to see except for the dried vegetable and chemical machinery factories.

Kruty   Круты   726km

Around the station on January 29 1918 raged a brutal battle which, during the Soviet era, was claimed as a victory for the communist forces, and nowadays is viewed as a symbol of patriotic self-sacrifice for the independence movement of Ukraine. The battle was fought between 4,000 Bolsheviks under the command of Muraviyov and just 600 Ukrainians who tried to stop the communists advancing along the railway line to Kiev. Over half the Ukrainians were killed and, while most were buried locally, 14 were entombed ceremonially near Askold's Grave in Kiev. Every year on the anniversary, a requiem mass is held at the memorial cross in Kruty village.

Nizhin   Ніжин   746km
Telephone area code: 04631

First mentioned in 1147, Nizhin has since belonged to Poland, Russia, and Germany at various times. In 1625, the town was fortified and in 1631, 1637 and 1638 the inhabitants took part in uprisings against the Polish occupiers. These revolts were brutally suppressed and around the town's main square, pl Hohol, and along the roads leading to it, gallows and stakes were erected on which the rebels were executed. From 1648 to 1782, the city was the headquarters of the Nizhin regiment, a military unit and administrative territory.

Nizhin is now the cultural centre of the region and boasts one of the first institutes of higher learning in the former Soviet Union devoted to humanities. Its most famous student was the Russian writer Nikolai Gogol (1809–52) who graduated in 1828. The institute is now known as the N V Gogol Nizhin Pedagogical Institute. Today, Nizhin has over 20 churches and other architectural monuments, an art gallery and the basic Hotel Nizhin, vul Batyuka 1. In addition, it has the Gogol Memorial Museum, a Rare Books Museum and a Museum of Local Studies at vul Batyuk 14, tel: 231 28.

Very few long-distance trains stop here and those that do are slow trains. However, there are several suburban trains from Kiev to Nizhin; the journey takes just over three hours. The station is about 3km north of the town centre and bus No 3 travels between the two.

Nosivka   Носівка   768km

The town has a large sugar refinery which processes the beets from the surrounding region. Once the sugar is extracted from the beets, the pulp is sold to nearby farms as animal feed.

Brovary   Бровари   842km

The town's name is derived from *brovaren,* meaning "brewing". However, today Brovary is now more famous for its refrigerators and non-standard municipal equipment. It was founded in 1628 and in 1918 was the site of a large-scale battle between the Bolsheviks and the Ukrainian National Republic forces.

Darnitsa   Дарниця   858km

Just past the station on the left is the site of a Nazi concentration camp used during the occupation of Kiev from 1941 to 1943. Here, and at nearby Syrets camp, over 100,000 Soviet prisoners of war died.

About 2km past the station, the train crosses over the Dniepr River. On the western bank on the left is the Ukrainian Botanical Gardens set in a 180-hectare park which also includes the Vydubychi Monastery.

Kiev   Київ   872km

Kiev is the capital of the Republic of Ukraine. For information on this city, see *Chapter Six.*

After leaving the station, the train passes the regional Nyvky airport.

Boiarka   Боярка   894km

This town is beautifully located among pine forests and is the site of a tuberculosis sanatorium.

During the 7th to 3rd centuries BC, a fortified Scythian town was built here, and some of its earthworks can still be seen today. The Scythians were originally from the north Black Sea area and their occupation contributed significantly to Ukraine's development of crafts, farming and military affairs. The local museum contains displays of burial weapons and grave goods.

Vasylkiv   Васылкив   908km

This town produces *majolica* pottery which is an Italian pottery coated with enamel and decorated in rich colours. The ancient town was founded during the second half of the 10th century. At the beginning of the 14th century it was conquered by the Grand Principality of Lithuania, before joining Russia in 1686.

During 1918–9, Ukrainian nationalists and Bolsheviks occupied the town several times each.

The two buildings of interest in the town are the Cathedral of Sts Anthony and Theodosius on vul Karla Marksa built in the late 1750s in typical Ukrainian baroque style and the Church of St Nicholas (Mykolayivska) built in 1792 which combines both classical and baroque styles and is located on vul Shevchenko.

Fastiv   Фастів   936km

This town sits at an important railway junction and was the centre of partisan activity during World War II. Consequently, the town's population was victim to numerous German reprisals. The town contains the Church of the Protection of the Blessed Virgin Mary (Pokrovska Church), a masterpiece of Ukrainian wooden architecture, which was built from 1779 to 1781. Another interesting building is the beautiful Roman Catholic stone church (1903–11) in the centre of the town. The town also has a museum of local studies.

The northwest branch line runs to Zhytomyr (Житомир) where red, pink and white granite and labradorite are mined. It was from here that stone was taken for Moscow's Lenin Mausoleum and several of the Russian capital's metro stations.

Kozhanka   Кожанка   955km

The town is 3km from the station and its only attraction is the wooden Church of the Protection of the Blessed Virgin Mary (Pokrovska) built in 1761. While there is a church of the same name in nearby Fastiv, the architecture is radically different.

Koziatyn   Козятин   1,031km

This town is on a railway junction and took an enormous beating during the early years of the communist revolution. The first battle around Kazatin started in late 1918 when Ukrainian insurgent forces clashed with the German Army. Then in February 1919 the pro-independence Ukrainian Sich Rifleman Corps battled with the Red Army, and finally in summer of that year, the Ukrainian Galician Army fought the Bolsheviks.

VINNYTSYA   Вінниця   1,099km
Population: 379,000   Telephone area code: 0432

This attractive 600-year-old city is spread over both sides of the Pivdennyi Buh River (Yuzhny Bug River in Russian) and is well worth visiting. The town is well known not only for its historical buildings but also for its tragic history under Soviet and German rule. Forty thousand locals were killed during the German occupation but worse crimes were committed by the infamous Soviet secret police during the great Stalin purges between 1937 and 1938. The execution of 9,439 Ukrainians buried in 66 mass graves was only revealed in 1943 when the occupying Germans needed anti-communist propaganda after the tide of World War II had turned against them.

The first mass grave to be discovered is 2km from the centre of town at vul Pidlisna 1, and two other major grave sites are at the Orthodox Cemetery and in the City Park.

Both Hitler and Goering stayed in Vinnytsya in June 1942 and just to the north near Kolo-Mikhailovka village are the remains of one of Hitler's heavily protected bunker complexes.

Getting there and away
By air   The airport is in nearby Havryshivka village.
By train   All long-distance trains stop here. It is 3hr 30min to Kiev, 5hr to Ternopil and 7hr to Lviv.

Where to stay

The best hotel is the Hotel Vinnytsya, shosse Khmelnytske 69, tel: 326 540, $10 twin share/person; and the Hotel Zhovtnevy, vul Pyrohov 2, tel: 326 540. Other hotels are the Hotel Podillya, vul Pushkina 4, tel: 326 878, $31 a double room; Hotel Ukrayina, vul Kozytsky 36, tel: 321 771, $15 a double room; Hotel Pivdennyi Buh, pl Zhovtneva, tel: 323 876, $30 a double room, and Hotel Druzhba, vul Trydtsyatyrichcha Peremohy 21, tel: 683 93.

Getting around

The railway station is located in the east of the town. Trolleybus No 5 and trams Nos 1, 4 and 6 travel through the centre of town along vul Kotsiubynskoho which becomes shosse Khmelnytske.

What to see

Most of the town's highlights are around the town's central street, the 2.5km-long shosse Khmelnytske (formerly ul Lenina). These include the Dominican Monastery, shosse Khmelnytske 23. Built in 1634, this was originally a wooden structure and part of a defensive fortification. In 1760 it was rebuilt into a Roman Catholic brick church. Preserved defence fortifications include the church, nearby caves and a defence tower. Next to it, at shosse Khmelnytske 19, is the Museum of Local Studies, tel: 322 671, open 10.00–18.00, closed Monday, and beside it, at shosse Khmelnytske 17, are the ruins of the Muri Jesuit Monastery. At vul Pershotravneva is a Military Museum, open 09.00–17.00, closed Monday, which focuses on the Afghanistan War (1979–89).

Other places of interest in the town include the House-museum of the Ukrainian writer and friend of Gorky, Mikhail Kostyubinsky (1864–1913) at vul Bevzy 17, tel: 352 687, open 10.00–18.00, closed Wednesday, and the Museum of Decorative and Applied Art in the Church of St Nicholas (Mykolayivska) built in 1746 at vul Mayakovsky 6, open 10.00–17.00, closed Monday. There is also a museum to the surgeon M Pyrohov (1810–81) called the M Pyrohov Villa Museum, vul Pyrohov 157, tel: 366 937. There are also memorials at several sites to the Vinnytsya Massacre including one in the City Park. The park also has a Summer Theatre and Rayduha Cinema and Concert Hall.

Regular hydrofoils ply along the Pivdennyi Buh River and provide a pleasant day trip.

Getting help

Travel agents Inturyst is located in the Hotel Zhovtnevy, vul Pyrohov 2, tel: 356 181. Other options are Sputnyk, shosse Khmelnytske 87, tel: 324 739, and Vinnitsaturist, vul Pushkina 4, tel: 325 959, fax:: 324 063, telex 119117 TURUX, teletype 119225 TUR.
Air International Connecting Flight Agency, pl Gagarina, tel: 256 60; the airport in Havryshivka village, tel: 322 808.
Rail The railway station, pl Heroyiv Stalinhrada, tel: 372 943.

What's in the region

On a branch line 22km to the east is the village of Voronovitsa. This contains the house of Alexsander Fedorovich Mozhaski, Russia's answer to the American aircraft builders, the Wright Brothers. Mozhaski (1825–90) worked in the Russian Navy building fortresses among other projects until he became interested in flight in 1856. It took him 20 years to develop a working model and on November 3 1881, Mozhaski received Russia's first patent on a flying device. In 1881, he started building an aircraft with two 20hp and 10hp steam engines. Although there are no documents to indicate whether the plane was a success, it is believed that the full-scale plane did not fly. His house still exists and is now a school.

Hitler's Wehrwolf war bunker
Prepared with the assistance of military historian Russ Folsom
About 12km north of Vinnytsya and 2km east of Strizhavka village are the remains of one of Hitler's 13 World War II bunker complexes scattered around his conquered empire. Hitler himself christened it Wehrwolf though many histories mistakenly spell it as Werwolf. Hitler stayed here between July 16 and November 1 1942 and between February 17 and March 13 1943.

The massive complex consisted of about 200 buildings surrounded by a barbed-wire perimeter fence 1,500m long and 300m wide. Just inside this was a 50m-wide belt sown with thousands of mines. Inside this were three security zones and in the middle was the Wehrwolf HQ compound. The compound was made of 19 rough-hewn logs cabins and two reinforced concrete underground bunkers dug down to a depth of 10–12m. The largest bunker was in the centre of the compound and was for the use of all personnel. The other bunker, attached to the conference quarters, was for Hitler's personal use. The compound also had a swimming pool, cinema, casino, tea house and a barber.

Vinnitsaturist Travel Company, vul Pushkina 4, 286000 Vinnytsya Ukraine, tel: (0432) 325 959, fax: (0432) 324 063, telex: 119117 TURUX, teletype: 119225 TUR, organise tours of the bunker from Vinnytsya. The cost of transport is $60 and a guide is $5 per hour.

Zhmerynka   Жмеринка   1,140km
This town is a Ukrainian sin city as its major employers are a tobacco plant, a winery and distillery.

Derazhnia   Деражня   1,188km
About 25km to the north is Medzhybizh (Меджибіж) village which contains a castle that is an important monument to military engineering. Construction of the fortress started in the 14th century and major renovations were made to it in the 16th and 19th centuries, each reflecting the changing role of castles. It is possible to wander around the fortress and information on it is contained in the local museum, vul Zhovtneva, tel: 971 30.

KHMELNYTSKY   Хмельницький   1,240km
Population: 260,000   Telephone area code: 038 22
This city was first mentioned in 1493 as a signal post to warn neighbouring regions of advancing enemies. It was destroyed twice by the Crimean Tatars, in 1512 and 1593.

This town was called Poskuriv until 1954 when it was renamed after Bogdan Khmelnytsky on the 300th anniversary of the union of Russia and the Ukraine. Khmelnytsky led and won the Ukrainian War of Liberation from 1648 to 1654.

Khmelnytsky has a sister city relationship with Modesto, California.

Getting there and away
All long-distance trains stop here. It is 7hr to Kiev, 2hr to Ternopil and 4hr 30min to Lviv.

Where to stay
The accommodation choices are Hotel Eneyida, vul Teatralna 8, tel: 912 42, $9 a double room, Hotel Zhovtnevy, vul Proskurivska 44, tel: 646 69, Hotel Podillya, vul Shevchenko 34, tel: 610 83, and Hotel Tsentralny, vul Gagarina 5, tel: 647 23, $8 a double room.

Getting around
The airport can be reached on bus No 17 from the centre of the city.

What to see
Strange as it might seem, the most interesting place in town in the 19th century was the railway station, according to Russian writer, Alexei Kuprin, who was an officer in the town's 46th Dniepr Infantry Regiment. He wrote, "The railway station was the only place where people could go to enjoy themselves. They would even go there for a game of cards. The ladies went to wait for the passenger train to come in as a diversion in the tedious existence of provincial life."

Fortunately, there is slightly more to see nowadays. Attractions include the 19th-century Church of the Protection of the Blessed Virgin Mary (Pokrovskaya) at vul Kamianetska 72, the Regional Ethnography Museum at vul Podilska 12, tel: 650 65, the Regional Art Museum, vul Proskurivska 47, tel: 647 61, and the Vereysky Art Memorial Museum at vul Chervonoarmiyska 5, tel: 685 59, open 10.00–17.00, closed Wednesday. This last museum is devoted to the artist Georgi Vereisky (1886–1962) who was born in the city.

Getting help
Travel agents   Inturyst-Khmelnytsky is located in the Podillya Hotel, tel: 693 67; the Travel and Excursion Agency, vul Proskurivska 15, tel: 663 62.
Air   Airport, tel: 646 35.
Rail   The railway station, vul Shevchenko 85, tel: 651 11.

Volochyske   Волочиськ   1,284km
The town is on the Zbruch River. During the last century this was the border between the Russian and Austrian empires and, until 1939, the border between Ukraine and Poland. Following the annexation of Poland by both Germany and the Soviet Union, the Ukrainian border was pushed 240km west to today's present location.

TERNOPIL   Тернопіль   1,358km
Population: 190,000   Telephone area code: 035 22
Although this industrial city, with its mostly post-war buildings, looks new it dates back to the early 1500s. The reason for this misconception is that during World War II, 85% of the buildings were levelled in 45 days of fighting to liberate the city.

Ternopil has a sister city relationship with Yonkers, New York.

Over the centuries, the city's population was victimised by various regimes with the worst in recent history being the German extermination of Ternopil's Jews. For more information on this, see *Point of interest, below.*

Getting there and away
All long-distance trains stop here. It is 9hr to Kiev, 2hr to Khmelnytsky and 2hr 30 min to Lviv.

Where to stay
The accommodation choice consists of the basic Ukrayina Hotel, blvd Shevshenko 23, tel: 246 47, the standard Ternopil Hotel, vul Zamkova 14, tel: 242 63, 330 20, 242 68, $20 a double room, the standard Halychnya Hotel, vul Zaozerna 3, tel: 361 16, 353 94, $20 a double room, and the basic Chayka Hotel, vul Naberezhna 65-a, tel: 291 84.

What to see
There are a few remaining restored buildings in Ternopil and the most interesting are the late 16th-century Christ of the Nativity (Rizdva Khrystovoho) Church built in the Podilian architecture style, the 18th-century Roman Catholic Church of the Dominican and the late 16th-century Elevation of the Holy Cross (Vozdvyzhenska) Church constructed in the style of a fortress. The town once had a castle built in 1540 but it did not save it from being destroyed over the next hundred years by the Turks and Tatar-Mongol hordes. The remains of the 4.5m thick fortress walls, moats and a defence tower can still be seen today.

The town's museum has been moved out of the Roman Catholic Church of the Dominican, vul Medova 3, and is now in a new building on vul Zatserkovna, tel: 244 77, open 10.00–18.00, closed Monday. The Art Museum is also worth visiting, vul Krushelnytska 1-a, tel: 280 72.

Getting help
Travel agents   Inturyst-Ternopil, Stary Rynok 2, tel: 506 65; Ternopil Travel and Excursion Agency, vul Teatralna 4, tel: 281 05.
Air   The airport is located on Pidvolochyske Shosse, tel: 413 22; Ukrainian Airlines, tel: 236 47.
Rail   Train ticket information can be found on tel: 210 63.

Point of interest
Before World War II, Ternopil had a large Jewish population. This swelled by thousands as Polish Jews fled to Ukraine when the advancing Germans invaded Poland. The Soviet forces who annexed this part of old Poland were suspicious of Jews and many were forced to accept Soviet passports which stipulated that they were not allowed to live in large cities like Ternopil. While this meant deportation to the east, the Soviet regime was preferable to the Nazi one.

The German's whirlwind invasion of the Soviet Union started on June 22 1941 and just 12 days later they had captured Ternopil with its population of 18,000 Jews. Many nationalistic Ukrainians welcomed the arrival of the Germans with their promise of an independent Ukraine and were only too pleased to implement the German's Final Solution policy on the Jews, who were irrationally blamed for the years of Soviet oppression.

Abraham Ochs described what occurred on the third day of German occupation of Ternopil in the chapter "The Dark Clouds", in his book *Alliance for Murder: The Nazi-Ukrainian Nationalist Partnership in Genocide*. Suffice it to say that when the Soviet forces liberated the city in 1944, only 139 Jews remained alive out of the pre-war population of 18,000. To put the extermination of Ternopil in perspective, during the years of German occupation, a total of 23,000 civilians, Jews and Soviet partisans were executed and 42,000 deported from the city and surrounding region.

Zboriv   Зборів   1,400km

The town is famous for the nearby Battle of Zboriv in 1649 which, while not significant in itself, was an important step towards Ukrainian independence. Although the battle was inconclusive, it resulted in the Treaty of Zboriv which gave Ukraine semi-independence. The lack of a conclusive victory resulted in the war resuming in 1651.

Today, the town's only attraction is a baroque church of the late 18th century and a monument to Bogdan Khmelnytsky.

Zolochiv   Золочів   1,422km

The town was first mentioned in the chronicles in 1442 and today there are three buildings of note. They are the Church of St Nicholas's (Myolayivska) built in the 16th century, the Galician renaissance Church of the Resurrection (Voskresenska) built in the 1620s, and the 16th-century castle on Kupyna Hill which was built in an Italian renaissance style.

LVIV   Львів   1,499km
Population: 800,000   Telephone area code: 0322

Lviv is well worth visiting with its architecture, atmosphere and 700 years of history. Most appealing are the older parts of the city which are a maze of cobbled streets, dotted with restored ancient buildings and numerous pleasant parks.

Lviv was founded in 1256 by Prince Danylo Romanovych of Galicia. Initially, a border post and trading centre, it quickly became a polyglot city with Ukrainian, Russian, Polish, German, Italian, Greek, Serbian and Moldavian traders. This large ethnic diversity can be seen today in the wide range of churches of various faiths.

Lviv was also a successful stronghold as it survived a protracted siege of the Golden Horde, withstood an expansion of Teutonic knights and the Vatican, and survived a devastating Swedish artillery bombardment and resultant fire which unfortunately destroyed many ancient buildings and museum collections.

In 1387, the city was captured by the Polish, then in 1772 it was annexed into the Austro-Hungarian Empire. In 1918, it was again recaptured by Poland and only after the 1939 division of Poland between Germany and the Soviet Union did the city become part of Ukraine. Following the Soviet annexation, mass arrests of Ukrainian activists followed and in the last days of June 1941, when the Germans were approaching Lviv, the Soviet secret police executed hundreds of Ukrainian prisoners at their Lontsky and Zamarstynivsky prisons.

The German occupation and Soviet reprisals following the town's recapture in 1944 destroyed a generation of Ukrainian nationalists and it was only in the 1960s that a notable dissident movement developed in Lviv. The activities of these dissidents, and those in the 1980s, had a significant impact on the eventual collapse of communism and the Soviet Union.

A good time to visit Lviv is in May when the city hosts the Festival of National Virtuosos.

Getting there and away

Lviv is easy to get to as it is the region's capital and transport hub. The main station is called Lviv-Glavni which over the next few years is undergoing a renovation as part of a European Bank of Reconstruction US$120 million scheme to upgrade Lviv's stations and the 84km railway line to Poland via Mostiska and Medika. A four-star hotel is being built as part of the Lviv-Glavni station.

International trains

There are no international trains with Lviv as their origin or destination; you have to travel on one of the through trains. The most convenient international trains on this route are listed below.

Origin	Dist, km	Entry point	Train no & name	Carr'ge class	No in coupé	Travel time	Day of departure	Destination
Moscow (Kiev)		Chop	15	1, 2	2, 3		Wed, Sun	Venice
Moscow (Kiev)	2110	Chop	15 Tisza Express	1, 2	2, 4	40hr 50min	daily	Budapest
Moscow (Kiev)	2317	Chop	51 Slovakia	1, 2	2, 3, 4	42hr 21min	daily	Bratislava
Moscow (Kiev)	2363	Chop	9	1, 2	2, 3	46hr 17min	daily	Belgrade
Moscow (Kiev)	2582	Chop	7	1, 2	2, 3, 4	46hr 27min	daily	Prague
Belgrade	2363	Chop	10	1, 2	2, 3	44hr 31min	daily	Moscow (Kiev)
Bratislava	2317	Chop	52 Slovakia	1, 2	2, 3, 4	42hr 27min	daily	Moscow (Kiev)
Budapest	2110	Chop	16 Tisza Express	1, 2	2, 4	40hr 01min	daily	Moscow (Kiev)
Prague	2582	Chop	8	1, 2	2, 3, 4	46hr 31min	daily	Moscow (Kiev)
Venice		Chop	16	1, 2	2, 3		Fri, Tues	Moscow (Kiev)

Domestic trains

The most convenient long-distance trains on this route are listed below.

Origin	Dist, km	Train no & name	Travel time	Depart	Arrive	Destination
Lviv	1499	74	29hr 11min	00.06	05.37	Moscow (Kiev)
Lviv (through)	266	15	5hr 34min	23.54	05.28	Chop (through)
Lviv (through)	627	9	11hr 17min	00.34	11.51	Kiev (through)
Chop (through)	266	16	5hr 39min	12.00	17.39	Lviv (through)
Kiev (through)	627	8	10hr 53min	16.35	03.28	Lviv (through)
Moscow (Kiev)	1499	73	27hr 16min	09.24	12.40	Lviv

Where to stay

There are numerous places to stay in Lviv. In descending order of pleasantness are: excellent Hotel Grand, pro Svobody 13, tel: 769 060, $50 twin share/person; standard Hotel Dnestr, vul Matetji 6, tel: 720 783, $31 twin share/person; standard Hotel Inturyst (also known as Hotel Zhorzh), pl Mitskevycha 1, tel:

725 952, fax: 742 192, $34 twin share/person; standard Hotel Lviv, vul 700-letia Lviva 7, tel: 792 270, $10 twin share/person; standard Hotel Turist, vul Konovalets 103, tel: 352 391, 351 065, $5 twin share/person; standard Hotel Sputnyk, vul Knyahynya Olha 116, tel: 652 421, 652 429, $10 twin share/person; basic Hotel Ukrayina, pl Mitskevycha 3, tel: 726 646; basic Hotel Rossiya, vul Klepariyska 30; basic Hotel Pershotravnevaya, pro Svobody 21, tel: 742 060; standard Hotel Kiev, vul 1-ovo Travna 15, tel: 742 105; Hotel Arena, val Horodotska 83; Hotel Narodnaya, val Kostiushka 1; Hotel Kolkhoznaya, pl Vossoedineniya 14; Hotel Dniepr, ul pro Svobody 45; and standard Hotel Ulyanovsk, vul Marchenka 6, tel: 728 512.

All hotels are in the centre with the exception of Hotel Turist which is 3km south of the city's centre (to get to it take tram No 2 from vul Russkaya), Hotel Rossiya to the north, and Hotel Ulyanovsk which is just southeast of the centre.

Getting around
From the railway station, trolleybuses Nos 1, 6 and 9, and buses Nos 2 and 18 depart. From the bus station, trolleybuses Nos 3 and 5, and bus No 18 depart.

The airport is 7km west of the city and can be reached on trolleybus No 9.

What to see
The most interesting sights are Lviv's streets with their mix of architectural styles, exterior stone carvings and monuments. The largest variety is seen along vul Russka and vul Armyanska.

Churches of note include the 13th-century St Nicholas Church even though it has lost its original appearance, the Gothic-style Latin Catholic Church, the Boim Chapel (named after a family of Hungarian merchants) and the Armenian Cathedral. In addition, there are numerous buildings built in the Empire, classicist and art nouveau styles.

The best place to start any tour of Lviv is the old market square (pl Rynok). This square was important during the 14th to 19th centuries but in the last two centuries trade has moved elsewhere. Over the last few years, the wide plaza has attracted cafés and now is becoming a pleasant spot to have a snack. Ringed around the square are numerous interesting buildings. These include the three buildings of the Lviv History Museum, at pl Rynok, 4, 6 and 24, tel: 720 671, which cover the history of western Ukraine. At pl Rynok 10 is a part of the Museum of Ethnology and Art. These and most other Lviv museums are open 10.00–18.00, closed Wednesday.

The Square of Adam Mitskevich, Lviv

There are several museums devoted to famous inhabitants of Lviv. These include the E Kulchytski Artist Museum (he lived here 1938–67) at vul Mitskevycha 7; the A K Novakovski Artist Museum (he lived here 1913–35), vul Mitskevycha 11; tel: 729 408, the Ivan Franko History Museum, ul Bogdana Khmelnitskovo; and the Ivan Franko Literary Museum (he lived here 1902–16) at vul Ivana Franko 152, tel: 764 417. Others include the I Trush Memorial Art Museum, vul Trush 28, tel: 353 413; the L Levytsky Museum, vul Ustyanovych 10, tel: 724 878; the Rusalka

Dnistrova Museum, vul Kopernyk 42, tel: 724 796; and the Krushelnytska Literary Museum, vul Chernyshevsky 23, tel: 729 296.

Other museums include the Icon Museum (formerly the Lenin Museum) at pr Svobody 20, the Lviv Literary Museum (formerly a museum of Y A Galan who lived here 1944–9) at vul Hvardiyska 18, tel: 351 033; the Museum of Photography at vul Gonty, the Pharmacy Museum at Drukarska 2, tel: 720 041; and the Museum of Old Weapons at vul Pidvalna 5, tel: 721 901, which was formerly the city arsenal building. The Museum of Ukrainian Art has two locations, vul Drahomanova 42, tel: 728 063 and pr Svobody 20, tel: 742 280. There is also the Lviv Art Gallery at vul Stetanyka 3, tel: 744 047; the Lviv University Museum at vul Universitetskaya 1; the Natural History Museum, ul Teatralnaya 18; the Military Museum, ul Stryiska; the Religious History Museum at pl Stavropihiyska 1, tel: 720 032; and the Museum of Regional Ethnography and Artistic Crafts, pr Svobody 15, tel: 727 01.

There is also the Museum of National Architecture and Life, Chernecha Hora 1, tel: 718 017, open 11.00–18.00, closed Monday. Composed of wooden buildings of past centuries this is set in the large beautiful Chernechna Gora Park on the eastern outskirts of the city. There are over 100 wooden buildings dotted around the 65-hectare open-air museum. They have been transported from other regions to this museum. To see them all takes almost five hours but a two-hour visit is usually enough for most visitors. Unfortunately, there is no direct public transport to get to the museum, which is 3km from the centre of Lviv, so it is best to get a taxi. However, if you have the time, catch tram No 2 or 7 or bus No 7 or 10 and get off at Nizhinskaya stop. Nizhinskaya is the name of the street which leads to the museum. The walk to the museum is about 600m.

Getting help

Travel agents There are numerous travel agents in Lviv. The biggest is Lvivturyst, vul Stryiska 12, tel: 725 052. The company has a number of tourist resorts including the Pearl of the Sub-Carpathians in Drohobych city, vul Turskavetska 83, the Carpathian Springs in Rozluch village and the Arnica Tourist Complex in Dubyna village. Other travel agents are Truskavets Travel Agency, vul Shevchenko 2, tel: 513 84, and Sputnyk, vul Ohiyenko 18, tel: 729 503.

Air The airport can be called on tel: 692 112; and Ukrainian Airline, pl Peremohy 5, tel: 727 558, 727 818.

Bus The bus station is 3km to the south of the city at vul Stryiska 271, tel: 632 473; to get to it catch trolleybus No 3 or 5 or bus No 18.

Rail The railway station is on pl Vokzalna, tel: 748 2068. Tickets can also be bought in the lobby of Hotel Intourist at the ticket office, open 09.00–18.00, closed Sunday, for a small additional charge.

Mykolaiv Миколаїв 1,549km

The town is 3km from the station and was famous as the training ground for the pro-independence Ukrainian Sich Riflemen in 1917.

Stryi Стрий 1,574km

Although this town was first mentioned in 1396, most of its buildings date from the late 19th century following a catastrophic fire in 1886. The town sits on the left bank of the Stryi River, which is a tributary of the Dniepr, and has the region's largest theatre and concert hall.

Stryi was one of the first centres of the Ukrainian women's movement and the first women's rally was held here in 1891 with the first edition of the women's almanac, *Our Fate*, published here in 1893.

The town has a local museum, vul Dzerzhinsky 15.

Lyubentsy   Любенцы   1,591km

The town's name is derived from *lubi*, meaning "footwear". In the last century birch tree bark shoes were made here. Its most famous citizen was the school teacher and song writer Roman Savitski.

Skole   Сколе   1,612km

Approaching Skole the train starts its ascent of the Carpathian foothills. Skole is situated in a picturesque section of the forested Carpathian Mountains on the banks of the Opir River.

The area is notable for its family feuds. In 1015, the area was fought over by two Kievan princes who were brothers, and in the 16th century, the town was in a tug of war between two noble Polish families. The name of the area is believed to have derived from the battle between the two brothers where one commanded his troops to "gore them all". The word "gored" translates into Ukrainian as skole.

Skole is a popular destination for travellers, skiers and campers. Its most notable inhabitant was Baron Groedel who so dominated the region that he even issued his own money. His manor house is now a museum. Another interesting building is the 17th-century tripartite wooden Church of St Paraskeva which contains a unique baroque iconostasis. The church was a museum until 1991, but now is again a practising church.

Slavske   Славське   1,638km

About 3km before arriving at the station, on the right, is the area's highest peak. Called Mount Magura, it stands 1,362m high. Slavsko, sitting at the confluence of the Opir and Slavskaya Rivers, is a popular holiday destination although it is less well known than Skole.

Volovets   Воловець   1,669km

This town is another Carpathian Mountain tourist destination with its well-known Plai tourist base. The town also includes a folk art gallery and not far away is a the wooden Protection (Pokrovska) Church and a compression station for the Urengi–Uzhhorod gas pipeline.

Svaliava   Свалява   1,697km

The town once had salt mines and its name comes from the Slavic word for salt. Today, it is renowned for the 100 mineral water springs in the region which have been popular since the 13th century. Three bottling plants in the city produce over 85 million bottles of mineral water a year.

The attractive town sits on the Latorytsya River in the wooded Carpathians and its most interesting buildings are the St Nicholas Church built in 1759, and the late 20th-century Lumbermen's Palace which now houses the local museum. There is another museum near the post office and the only hotel is the Carpati Hotel, vul Oktyabrskaya 4. Another interesting sight is the wooden Church of St Michael (Mykhaylivska) built in 1588 in nearby Bystry village.

THE CARPATHIAN MOUNTAINS

The Carpathian Mountains are a range of young mountains that rise up to 1.4km above the nearby plains and stretch in a 1,500km arch from Bratislava to the Danube River.

At one time all the Carpathians were covered with forests and topped with meadows and rock fields. Nowadays, most of the foothills have been converted to farming lands, but much of the actual mountains retain their original cover.

The lowest forest belt grows up to 600m and consists of deciduous and mixed forests of mostly oak, maple and pine. From 600m to 1,100m are mountain forests of beech and coniferous trees with an undergrowth of raspberries and willows. Above the forest belt are highland pastures of meadows and subalpine areas of rhododendron and dwarf juniper.

The fauna is fairly uniform throughout all belts and common species include red deer, wolf, forest marten, mole and squirrel. Unfortunately, the brown bear and wildcat have almost entirely disappeared.

About 11km to the west is the Solnechnoye Zakarpatiye sanatorium which uses the healing benefits of the water to treat liver diseases.

Kolchino   Колчіно   1,718km

The town is dominated by a castle built at the end of the 14th century and used as a prison by Germans in World War II.

Mukacheve   Мукачеве   1,724km
Telephone area code: 03131

The centrepiece of this ancient town is Mukacheve Castle which sits on a hill above the town. Although the fortress was built at the end of the 14th century, archaeological remains date from the Stone Age. The castle is now being restored and today houses a museum, open 09.00–17.00, closed Monday.

On the right bank of the Latoritsa River, which cuts through the town, is the Church and Monastery of St Nicholas (Mykolayivska), vul Pivnichna 2, which today houses an order of nuns. Another interesting building is the Bily Budynok (White Building) Manor House, vul Myru 28. This building belonged to Count Shenbons and was originally built in the 15th century and rebuilt in the mid 1700s in a baroque style.

The accommodation choices are the Zirka Hotel, pl Myra 20, tel: 20 08, or Hotel Latorika, vul Dykhovycha 93, tel: 23 201, $20 a double room. Both hotels have restaurants.

Most long-distance trains stop here and the time to Chop is one hour. There are also suburban trains between Mukacheve and Chop.

CHOP   Чоп   1,765km
Population: 12,000   Telephone area code: 031 37

Chop is the border crossing for trains to and from both Hungary and Slovakia.

The first stop in Hungary is the small station of Zahony (Záhony in Hungarian and Захонь in Russian) which is 4km from Chop, while the first major Hungarian town is Kisvarda. The border is delineated by the River Tysa.

The first stop in Slovakia is the major city of Kralovsky Chlmec (Královský Chlmec in Slovakian and Чьерна-над-тисоу in Russian) which is 6km from Chop.

The border crossing procedure involves a customs check, a passport and visa inspection and finally changing the bogies of the passenger carriages so that they can travel on Hungary's and Slovakia's narrower-gauge railways.

Chop's attractive Stalinist era, yellow railway station sits on pl Lenina and on the west side of the square is the Ukrayina Hotel, vul Privokzalnaya 4. There are numerous war monuments in the town as Chop was the site of a month-long battle between Soviet and German forces in 1944

Getting there and away
International trains
There are no international trains with Chop as their origin or destination; you have to travel on one of the through trains. The most convenient international trains on this route are listed below.

Origin	Dist, km	Entry point	Train no & name	Carr'ge class	No in coupé	Travel time	Day of departure	Destination
Moscow (Kiev)		Chop	15	1, 2	2, 3		Wed, Sun	Venice
Moscow (Kiev)	2110	Chop	15 Tisza Express	1, 2	2, 4	40hr 50min	daily	Budapest
Moscow (Kiev)	2317	Chop	51 Slovakia	1, 2	2, 3, 4	42hr 21min	daily	Bratislava
Moscow (Kiev)	2363	Chop	9	1, 2	2, 3	46hr 17min	daily	Belgrade
Moscow (Kiev)	2582	Chop	7	1, 2	2, 3, 4	46hr 27min	daily	Prague
Belgrade	2363	Chop	10	1, 2	2, 3	44hr 31min	daily	Moscow (Kiev)
Bratislava	2317	Chop	52 Slovakia	1, 2	2, 3, 4	42hr 27min	daily	Moscow (Kiev)
Budapest	2110	Chop	16 Tisza Express	1, 2	2, 4	40hr 01min	daily	Moscow (Kiev)
Prague	2582	Chop	8	1, 2	2, 3, 4	46hr 31min	daily	Moscow (Kiev)
Venice		Chop	16	1, 2	2, 3		Fri, Tues	Moscow (Kiev)

Domestic trains
The most convenient long-distance trains on this route are listed below.

Origin	Dist, km	Train no & name	Travel time	Depart	Arrive	Destination
Chop (through)		16	17hr 10min	00.35	17.45	Kiev (through)
Chop (through)	266	16	7hr 39min	12.00	17.39	Lviv (through)
Kiev (through)		15	17hr 33min	11.55	05.28	Chop (through)
Lviv (through)	266	15	5hr 34min	23.54	05.28	Chop (through)

Visa
If you are arriving in Ukraine and do not have an Ukrainian visa, you will be issued a three-day temporary visa in Chop. Be warned that getting this converted into a standard visa in Ukraine is difficult and expensive.

Zahony   Záhony   1,769km
After crossing over the River Tysa which delineates the Hungarian border, you arrive at the first stop in Hungary. Here your passport and visa will be checked.

Budapest   Budapest   2,110km
For information on Budapest, see *Eastern Europe by Rail* by Rob Dodson, published by Bradt Publications.

Chapter Eleven

Moscow–St Petersburg

The 650km line between Moscow and St Petersburg is Russia's busiest and most prestigious railway. Consequently, high standards are maintained, both in terms of carriage conditions and service. When the line was opened in 1851, the average travel time was 25 hours. Today, most of the overnight trains take eight hours with the weekly, high-speed ER-200 train taking just five hours. This compares to over ten hours if you travel by car on the shosse Petersburgskoe (St Petersburg Highway).

The most scenic time of the year on this route is between April and October and in particular during autumn when the leaves turn. There is not much to see during winter as it is only light from 10.00 to 16.00, so it is better to travel at night at that time of year.

Route highlights

The major highlights on the trip are historic Klin, the picturesque Ivankovskoe Reservoir near Zavidovo, the ancient city of Tver, the famous gold-thread sewing town of Torzhok, Venice-like Vyshni Volochek, the huge canyon near Torbino, quaint Chudovo and fabulous Novgorod.

A five-night travel programme is recommended: three nights in Tver, including day trips to Torzhok, Vyshni Volochek and Kalyazin; and two nights in Novgorod, including a day trip to Chudovo. Both Klin and the Ivankovskoe Reservoir are best visited on a day trip from Moscow.

Trains

There are over 20 departures every day in both directions on the Moscow–St Petersburg route. Most travellers prefer an overnight journey as it saves accommodation costs and maximises daytime sightseeing. The best straight-through daytime train is the high speed ER-200 which makes the journey only once a week. If you only want to go as far as Tver from Moscow or Tosno from St Petersburg you can catch a cheap suburban train. The longest route between Moscow and St Petersburg is via Kalyazin and Uglich. This 775km trip, which takes a massive 23 hours, is not covered in this chapter. Trains on this tortuous loop depart from Moscow's Savelovski station.

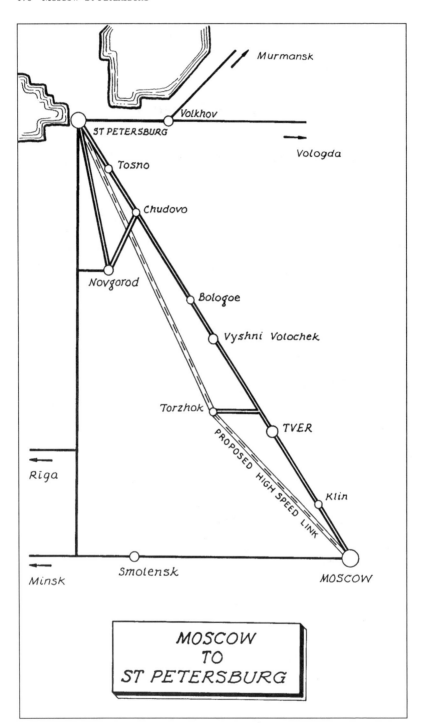

Murmansk

Volkhov

ST PETERSBURG

Vologda

Tosno

Chudovo

Novgorod

Bologoe

Vyshni Volochek

Torzhok

TVER

Riga

PROPOSED HIGH SPEED LINK

Klin

Minsk

Smolensk

MOSCOW

MOSCOW
TO
ST PETERSBURG

Origin	Dist, km	Train no & name	Travel time	Depart	Arrive	Destination
Moscow (Leningrad)	650	2 Red Arrow	8hr 30min	23.55	08.25	St Petersburg (Moscow)
Moscow (Leningrad)	650	4	8hr 30min	23.59	08.29	St Petersburg (Moscow)
Moscow (Leningrad)	650	6 Inturist	7hr 25min	23.10	07.35	St Petersburg (Moscow)
St Petersburg (Moscow)	650	1 Red Arrow	8hr 30min	23.55	08.25	Moscow (Leningrad)
St Petersburg (Moscow)	650	3	8hr 29min	23.59	08.30	Moscow (Leningrad)
St Petersburg (Moscow)	650	5 Inturist	7hr 10min	23.33	07.43	Moscow (Leningrad)
Moscow (Leningrad)	650	8 Neva	7hr 25min	22.15	06.40	St Petersburg (Moscow)
Moscow (Leningrad)	650	14 Avrora	8hr 30min	20.35	05.05	St Petersburg (Moscow)
St Petersburg (Moscow)	650	7 Neva	8hr 25min	22.45	07.10	Moscow (Leningrad)
St Petersburg (Moscow)	650	19	9hr 23min	21.55	06.18	Moscow (Leningrad)
Moscow (Leningrad)	650	158 ER-200	4hr 59min	12.21 (Fridays only)	17.20	St Petersburg (Moscow)
St Petersburg (Moscow)	650	157 ER-200	4hr 59min	12.15 (Thursdays only)	17.14	Moscow (Leningrad)
Moscow (Leningrad)	650	134	8hr 55min	09.38	18.33	St Petersburg (Moscow)
St Petersburg (Moscow)	650	135	10hr 39min	10.55	21.34	Moscow (Leningrad)
Moscow (Leningrad)	167	24	2hr 4min	12.27	14.31	Tver
Tver	167	23	2hr 57min	19.18	22.15	Moscow (Leningrad)
Moscow (Leningrad)	606	41	8hr 24min	22.16	06.40	Novgorod
Novgorod	606	42	8hr 3min	21.55	05.58	Moscow (Leningrad)
Novgorod	666		3hr	07.05	11.05	St Petersburg (Moscow)
St Petersburg (Moscow)	666	161	2hr 40min	06.55	09.35	Novgorod
St Petersburg (Moscow)	483	23	3hr 11min	13.05	19.16	Tver
Tver	483	24	6hr 8min	14.32	20.40	St Petersburg (Moscow)

High-speed trains

By international standards, Russia's high-speed train is fairly slow. The ER-200 fast train, which only runs between Moscow and St Petersburg, averages just 130km/h for the entire trip with bursts of speed up to 180km/h. This is despite the train having a technical cruising speed of 200km/h (hence its name, the ER-200). This is because the ER-200 is really only a showpiece, as well as being unreliable and extremely unprofitable. For this reason the train does the 5hr trip only once a week. From Moscow, No 158 departs every Friday at 12.21 and from St Petersburg No 157 departs every Thursday at 12.15.

The ten-carriage train has only lounge seats which are often fully booked. This is despite the fact that the cost of the ticket is twice that of an overnight *coupé* ticket on other trains. There are two features of this train that make it popular with Russians. Firstly, there is a trolley service selling newspapers and drinks, and secondly, there is a buffet car which also shows videos.

In 1993, work started on a new high-speed railway between Moscow and St Petersburg which will slash the travelling time to just 2hr 25min. The $3.2 billion railway will not be completed until 2001 as the work involves designing a new train, laying 654.3km of new track and building 200 major bridges.

This railway is Russia's largest civil-engineering project since the collapse of the centralised communist system, so completion delays and cost overruns are expected. Already track clearing has been slower than expected as the line is going through land untouched since the end of World War II and unexploded bombs and mines are continually being found. In addition, environmentalists have promised protest activity unless the track through the Valdai Nature Reserve is constructed in an environmentally sensitive manner.

The high-speed train, called the *Sokol*, meaning "falcon", will carry 800 passengers in 12 cars and, by 2005, it is expected that there will be 30 trains a day in each direction, travelling at an average speed of 260km/h.

Despite the appearance of the *Sokol*, overnight trains will still operate on the current track. This is because the *Sokol* will not be used overnight as few passengers would want to depart and arrive in the middle of the night.

Getting tickets
For information on getting tickets, see *Chapters Five* and *Eight*.

ROUTE DESCRIPTION

Moscow   Москва   0km
Trains for St Petersburg all depart from Leningrad station, pl Komsomol 3, tel: 262 9143, 262 6038, 262 4281, with the exception of a handful that go the tortuous route via Uglich. Leningrad station is the oldest in Moscow, and its mid-1850s late, classical period architecture is typical of many buildings in St Petersburg. The metro station is pl Komsomolskaya.

Rizhskiya   Рижская   2km
Rizhskiya is another of Moscow's major long-distance stations. Trains depart from here for Riga and Velikie Luki. Nearby is the large Rizhski market, Moscow's most violent bazaar.

Ostankino   Останкино   4km
Just before this stop on the right is the Ostankinskoe cemetery. Further in the distance you can see the Ostankino television centre (*Ostankinskaya televizionnaya bashnya*, Останкинская телевизионная башня). When it was built in 1978, the 640m tower was the largest in the world. Without doubt, it is a great engineering achievement as it can withstand an earthquake that can sway the tower's top by 14m, yet its foundations are only 4.5m deep. In the communist era, a giant red flag flew from the tower but today the Russian flag appears only on holidays and, of course, on June 3, International TV Tower Day.

After leaving Ostankino, you will see Moscow's main botanical gardens about 800m away on the right.

Mosselmash   Моссельмаш   14km
The station is named after the nearby enormous industrial plant, the agricultural machine building complex. About five minutes past the station on the right is a preserved Shch-1 locomotive, Russia's first main-line diesel engine, which was built in 1924.

Khovrino Ховрино 15km

Three kilometres past this station, the train travels over Moscow's outer ring road. This 109km-long road rings Moscow at a radius of 18km and used to mark the boundary of the City of Moscow. In the 1980s, the sprawling suburban satellites burst out past the ring road and on this side of the city the boundary now extends another 11km towards St Petersburg.

Levoberenaya Левобережная 18km

Two minutes past this station, the train crosses over the wide Moscow Canal which connects the Moscow and Volga Rivers. Built between 1932 and 1937, the canal is 129km long, 85.5m wide and 5.5m deep and allows ships to travel between the Arctic, White, Black, Azov and Caspian Seas. The canal is also the chief source of water for Moscow and consequently the train's toilets are opened only after you pass over the canal.

Khimki Химки 19km

The station gets its name from the little Khimka River which is now submerged under the Moscow Canal. Four kilometres after the station, the railway crosses over the 719km-long shosse Petersburgskoe (St Petersburg Highway).

One of Khimki's biggest factory is Energomash, a giant space engine manufacturer. The plant builds RD-170 engines, now used on the first stage of the Russian Zenith space booster. The plant's engines are so well thought of that a joint venture with the US company Pratt & Whitney was formed in 1995 to develop a liquid-fuelling rocket engine which they hope will be chosen to modernise the American Atlas booster rocket.

Planernaya Планерная 24km

The station's name derives from the word *planyer* which means "glider", as glider training was taught at the nearby Tushino military aerodrome. There is a large public airshow held here on Aviation Day.

Tushino is an ancient town first founded in 1380. From 1608 to 1610, the town was the fort of the Second False Dmitri who attempted to become the Tsar of Moscow Principality by pretending to be Tsar Dmitri Ivanovich, who was killed in an uprising in 1606. Strangely, Tsar Dmitri Ivanovich is known as the First False Dmitri as he himself was believed to be an impostor, pretending to be the missing son of Ivan the Terrible. The Tushino fort was completely destroyed by retreating Polish mercenaries who served the Second False Dmitri and is still being excavated as it is a valuable source of archaeological remains.

Skhodnya Сходня 30km

Just before reaching the station, the train passes over the Skhodnaya River which was a major trading route centuries ago. Boats would travel up as far as Skhodnaya village, be dragged over 1km and launched into the nearby Klasma River which eventually flowed into the Volga.

Firsanovka Фирсановка 33km

Nearby is the Serednikovo Estate which was owned by a friend of the poet Mikhail Lermontov who spent every summer here between 1829 and 1832. Today the 18th-century Serednikovo Manor House is a museum and sanatorium.

Kryukovo   Крюково   39km

The station is surrounded by the Soviet era model satellite town of Zelenograd. Rather than a suburb, a satellite is a small self-contained city with its own factories, housing complex and energy infrastructure. Zelenograd sprang up in 1960–3, and its "factory buildings are constructed so that they organically blend in with the general plan of the city", according to the *Great Soviet Encyclopedia*. Before the town was built, the area was the site of a fierce battle in November and December 1941 and, at just 41km from Moscow, was the closest the Germans got to the city. There are several monuments to the battle and it was from a local mass soldiers' grave that the remains of an unknown soldier were exhumed and transferred in 1966 to Moscow's Tomb of the Unknown Soldier in front of the kremlin wall.

Radishchevo   Радищево   47km

The station was named after the writer, Aleksandr Nikolaevich Radishchev (1749–1802). His most famous book was *A Journey from Petersburg to Moscow* which describes an imaginary trip along the dirt road and his encounters with various people who speak out against Russian autocracy, serfdom and censorship.

Podsolnechnaya   Подсолнечная   65km
Telephone area code: 096 26

Surrounding the station is the industrial town of Solnechnogorsk (Солнечногорск). To the right of the line is the artificial Senezhskoye Lake which was part of the first Moscow–Volga Channel. Although the canal was abandoned in 1850, only 25 years after construction started, the massive civil-engineering work was not wasted as the lake has become one of Moscow's most popular holiday spots. Consequently, the town's population swells significantly in summer and suburban trains are always packed at the weekends.

Frolovskoe   Фроловское   81km

The Russian composer Peter Tchaikovsky lived here from 1888 to 1891. While his house has been destroyed, there is a monument to show where it was and a nearby village bears his name.

Klin   Клин   90km
Telephone area code: 098 24

This town attracts thousands of tourists a year on day trips from Moscow. The main attraction is the large, 200,000 item Tchaikovsky Museum, ul Chaykovskovo 48, tel: 539 81, 212 03, 10:00-18:00, closed Wednesday, Thursday and the last Monday of the month, which was opened over 100 years ago. The composer lived in and around Klin from 1885 to 1893. His Klin house has been turned into a museum and remains virtually as he left it, when he went to St Petersburg for the first performance of his Sixth Symphony. It was during this trip that he died, allegedly of cholera. However, Klin researchers have recently revealed that it appears that Tchaikovsky was blackmailed into taking poison to prevent his liaison with the nephew of a St Petersburg noble being made public. The visitors' book contains famous names including the Belgian Queen Elizabeth and President Nixon. At one end of the museum is a concert hall which is used twice a year, on the composer's birthday of May 7 and his Name Day of November 6 which also coincides with the anniversary of the Sixth Symphony. Beside the museum is Tchaikovsky's house.

Another Klin museum, on ul Gaidara, open 10.00–18.00, is dedicated to the Soviet writer, A P Gaidar, who lived in the town between 1938 and 1941. His most famous story was called *Timur and His Team* which was about his teenage son, Timur, and his young communist friends as they worked towards building socialism. Interestingly, Timur was the father of Yegor Gaidar, the Minister of Economics and Finance of Russia 1991–2 and First Deputy Prime Minister 1993–4, the man who implemented many of the economic reforms that directly contributed to the collapse of Russia.

Klin also has a Museum of Local Studies on ul Gagarina, about 500m to the north of the railway station, and a number of interesting buildings including the Ascension (Uspenski) Church, ul Papivina 15, the Church of the Resurrection (Voskresenskaya), pl Sovetskaya, and the Trading Row, ul Liteinaya.

The basic Klin Hotel is at ul Lenina 37, tel: 253 13.

Reshetnikovo   Решетниково   105km

Just past the station on the right is a 36km northern branch line to the town of Konakovo (Конаково). The two attractions of this town are the Konakovo hydro-electric station and the Kuznetsov china factory. The factory, founded in 1809, is recognised internationally for its artistic work and distinctive souvenirs. This town is named after P P Konakovo, a pottery artist and revolutionary who died in the 1905 revolution.

Zavidovo   Завидово   119km

The town around this station is Novozavidovski (meaning New Zavidovo). About 6km away is Old Zavidovo, also known as Zavidovo, and you will see this settlement on the right as you approach Novozavidovski. Before the railway was built, Zavidovo was a post station on the Moscow–St Petersburg road where horses were changed. Today, New Zavidovo is infamous as the playground for Moscow's élite as many have *dachas* on the banks of the nearby Ivankovskoe Reservoir. These *dachas* are in areas where armed guards man roadblocks to prevent "undesirables" from entering.

There is nothing to see in New Zavidovo, but there is a House-museum of the poet S D Drozzhin (1848–1930) in Old Zavidovo.

After leaving Zavidovo station, the train travels on a 4km bridge over the Ivankovskoe Reservoir, also known as the Moscow Sea (Moskovskoe More). This reservoir was created in 1940 by damming the Volga River for hydro-electric power. While those living in the area moved to high ground, the buildings of several towns could not be saved. The largest submerged town was Kalyazin and today the only sign of it is a 35m ornate spire of the Cathedral of St Nicholas protruding defiantly above the water. The spire can be seen by visiting the Kalyazin Dam which is reached by hydrofoil from Tver.

Redkino   Редкино   133km

Eight kilometres to the right of the railway lies Radchenko (Радченко) village, named after the founder of the Soviet peat industry, Ivan Radchenko (1874–1942). Peat is a valuable fuel which the Russians use to fire electric power stations and hot-water generating plants. Peat is also used for fertiliser, insulation and to produce industrial alcohol. In Radchenko, there is an experimental peat station which has been at the forefront of research for the last century. There is a museum dedicated to peat in Radchenko.

TVER   Тверь   167km
Population: 460,000   Telephone area code: 08222

This small city is well worth visiting. It is not only interesting in itself but it is also a good base from which to explore the region. The city was named Kalinin from 1931 to 1991 after Soviet President Mikhail Kalinin (1875–1946) who was born here. After the collapse of communism the city's name reverted to Tver.

Tver developed from a trading post on the left bank of the Volga River at its confluence with the Tvertsa and Tmaka Rivers. In 1240, Grand Prince Yaroslav Vsevolodovich of Vladimir built a wooden kremlin on the right bank and soon Tver grew into a large fortified town surrounded by a moat. While the kremlin has disappeared under the Khimik sports stadium, part of the moat can still be seen in the City Park. In 1246, Tver became an independent principality under Yaroslav, brother of one of Russia's greatest heroes, Aleksandr Nevsky.

The town quickly grew into an important regional centre and at various times even challenged the power of Novgorod and Moscow. While a huge fire in 1763 destroyed much of the city, it also allowed civic authorities to instigate a massive redevelopment. The result is one of the finest examples of European architecture of the 18th and 19th centuries. Most stunning are the granite-lined waterfront with its rows of mansions, and the area around Post Square and Fountain Square which contains the City Council Chambers (1770–80), the House of the Nobility (1766–70) and a school (1786).

Getting there and away

Tver can be reached on both suburban and long-distance trains. From Moscow, suburban trains run hourly and the trip takes about 2hr 40min, while to the west, suburban trains start in Bologoe and pass through Vyshni Volochek before terminating in Tver. The main long-distance trains passing through Tver are listed below. For information on buses and trains to Torzhok and Vyshni Volochek, see under these towns later in this chapter.

Origin	Dist, km	Train no & name	Travel time	Depart	Arrive	Destination
Moscow (Leningrad)	167	24	2hr 4min	12.27	14.31	Tver
Tver	167	23	2hr 57min	19.18	22.15	Moscow (Leningrad)
St Petersburg (Moscow)	483	23	3hr 11min	13.05	19.16	Tver
Tver	483	24	6hr 8min	14.32	20.40	St Petersburg (Moscow)

Where to stay

There are a large number of hotels and hostels in Tver, and homestay can also be organised.

Centrally located in the centre of the old part of Tver is the standard Hotel Tsentralnaya, ul Novotorzhskaya 33/8, tel: 38 157, $22 double room with bathroom. It has a restaurant. Directly in front of the railway station is the standard Hotel Turist, ul Kominterna 47/102, tel: 36 178, $35 double room with bathroom. It has a restaurant and cafés on several floors.

The basic Hotel Volga, ul Zhelyabova 1, tel: 38 100, $18 double room with bathroom has a restaurant. About 8km from the centre of the city is the basic Tver Motel, shosse Petersburgskoe 130, tel: 556 96, 596 96. To get there take bus No 7 which runs along ul Sovetskaya, pro Tverskoi, nab Nikitina and shosse Petersburgskoe past the motel. You can also catch trams No 3, 4, 5, 7 and 10 to its terminus on shosse Petersburgskoe which is about 2km east of the motel. From the terminus you can catch bus No 7, 109 or 134.

Other hotels include the standard Hotel Seliger, ul Sovetskaya 52; Hotel Tvertsa, nab Afanasia Nikitina 90/2, tel: 11 663; basic Hotel Yunost, pro Komsomolski 10, tel: 55 692; and basic Hotel Zaya, ul Trekhsvyatskaya.

The best hotel is the excellent Hotel Berezovaya Roshcha, shosse Petersburgskoe, tel: 92 632, which was built for a secluded meeting between Khrushchev and Castro. The typically ugly, 1960s-style hotel is surrounded by a beautiful forest on the eastern outskirts of Tver. The hotel today is the haunt of officials and mafia overlords which means that the unconnected will find it difficult to get a room.

Getting around

Trams No 5, 6 and 11 travel from the station along pro Chaikovskovo and Tverskoi before crossing the Tverski Bridge. The airport is located 10km to the north of the city. Bus No 111 travels between the railway station and the airport while bus No 101 travels between the river station and the airport.

What to see

A visit to Tver is not complete without walking down Trekhsvyatskaya Street pedestrian mall. While not as large as Arbat Street in Moscow, Tver's mall is just as enjoyable.

Tver is littered with museums. The Museum of Local Studies and Picture Gallery with paintings by Repin, Surikov, and Aivazovski are located in the Journey Palace, pl Revolutsi 3, open 11.00–18.00, closed Monday and Tuesday.

The Museum of Old Tver, ul Gorkovo 31/3, open 11.00–17.00, closed Monday and Tuesday, is located in an 18th-century merchant's house and displays the everyday life of past generations. Its exhibits include *samovars,* paintings and traditional hats, called *soroka,* meaning "magpie", which were worn by women to hide their hair after marriage. The museum is actually in a side street, just off ul Gorkovo.

The House-museum of Saltykov-Schedrin, ul Saltykov-Schedrin 11/37, open 11.00–18:00, closed Monday and Tuesday, is dedicated to the satirical writer Mikhail Saltykov-Schedrin (1826–89) who became Tver's vice-governor in 1860.

For railway buffs, Tver's Railway Carriage Manufacturing Plant Museum is a must. It displays photos, models and memorabilia from the carriage plant next door which now produces virtually all of Russia's passenger carriages. The museum, tel: 559 210, open 10.00–16.00, closed weekends, is beside the Tver railway carriage manufacturing plant which is behind the Metal Workers Palace of Culture at 39 shosse Peterburgskoe. It can be reached by trams No 3, 4, 5, 7 and 10 and is the second to last stop.

There are several theatres in Tver, the most famous and biggest being the puppet theatre, Kukol. Unfortunately, the theatre troupe is so popular that it travels for most of the year so only rarely do locals see their own theatre.

The Church of the White Trinity has daily services.

Getting assistance

Travel agents There are two excellent travel agencies in Tver. The first is Tver Intercontact Group which organises not only travel programmes but a fascinating culture tour which includes meetings with city officials, business people and journalists. They also organise homestay, tickets and language courses. Their programmes start from $150 a week. Tver Intercontact Group, PO Box 0565, Central Post Office, Tver 170000, Russia (ul Tryokhsvyatskaya), tel: 425 439 & 425 439, fax: 902 1765, email andrei@ic.tunis.tver.su. The second is the Meridian Tourist Agency, ul Uritskovo 16, tel: 256 06 & 391 47, fax: 35020, teletype 171254 KRUIZ.

Air Aeroflot, pl Kaposhvara.

Rail Tickets can be purchased at the railway station and at the advance purchase rail ticket office, pro Pobedy 3.

What's in the region

As well as being an attractive centrepiece to Tver, the Volga River offers an enjoyable way of visiting a number of nearby highlights. The most popular is Orsha Monastery which can be reached by sailing 20km down the Volga. A tour of the functioning monastery and its religious community is fascinating. The Tver Intercontact Group, mentioned above, organises these trips in conjunction with the Tver Yacht Club.

Other interesting river destinations include Konakovo, described under *Reshetnikovo,* and Radchenko, described under *Redkino, see page 181.*

It is also possible to travel on regular passenger hydrofoils to any town on the timetable and to return to Tver by a later vessel or by bus. Despite Tver's gigantic river station and the three-storey passenger ships that are often tied up in front of it, the only vessels for locals are two regular hydrofoils. The passenger ships just stay in Tver for a few days as part of an organised tour from St Petersburg to Moscow, and tickets for these vessels can only be purchased in these cities. The first hydrofoil travels 35km up the Volga River to Morkino village and the route is via the airport and *dacha* village. Hydrofoils depart at 07.00 and 17.00, and arrive back at 09.45 and 19.45. The 2hr 40min trip costs $0.50. The second hydrofoil travels 210km down the Volga River to Kalyazin, passing through the lock near Dubna and near the submerged Cathedral of St Nicholas. There is only one 4hr 40min trip daily departing at 06.45 and returning at 20.00. A one-way ticket costs $1.80.

Other day trips in the region include those to the old Russian town of Ostashkov (see *Bologoe, page 188*), Torzhok and Vyshni Volochek (see *pages 185 and 186* respectively).

Point of interest

For centuries, the Volga River was the main trading route connecting northwest Europe with Russia and central Asia. However, since the advent of road and rail, its importance has declined to the situation of today when there is only one major river caravan a year. Every summer, this caravan, comprising various state and private traders, sails down the river, stopping off at various villages and cities where the traders set up a bazaar. The caravan normally arrives in Tver in June and sets up camp in the park around the river station.

Proletarka   Пролетарка   172km
One kilometre past the station, the train crosses over the 200m-wide Volga River.

Doroshikha   Дорошиха   174km
Just past this station, the railway passes under Gorbati (meaning "hunchback") Bridge which carries the shosse Petersburgskoe (St Petersburg Highway). This unusually low bridge, built in the late 1840s, has the macabre reputation of killing dozens of roof riders, particularly during the Civil War period when the irregular trains were always overcrowded.

Kulitskaya   Кулицкая   194km
About 12km south of the station is the little village of Mednaya (Медная) where, in the surrounding forests in 1941, 6,000 captured Polish officers and soldiers were executed by the Soviet secret police. There are no monuments yet to the victims, see *Chapter Nine, page 141.*

Likhoslavl   Лихославль   209km
There is a 33km branch line from here to the ancient town of Torzhok (Торжок).

TORZHOK   Торжок
Population: 55,000   Telephone area code: 082 51
Torzhok is famous for its annual Pushkin Festival and traditional handicrafts made with gold sewing thread.

The town was first mentioned in 1139 and was sacked over 30 times in tug-of-war battles between the rival Tver and Novgorod principalities.

Although it appears to be a sleepy town, Torzhok actually has dynamic manufacturing industries. These include the fire truck and equipment factory, the partly Spanish-owned ink plant that used to produce 90% of the USSR's printers' ink, the mothballed military plant MARC, and the specialist railway plant which used to build wagons for launching missiles and satellites but now makes more useful suburban trains.

Torzhok's prime position on one of the busiest river trading routes guaranteed that the town would continue to be rebuilt. Today, a number of buildings from various eras can be seen including the ancient stone and brick kremlin, the 17th-century Church of the Ascension, the 1812 Cathedral of the Saviour and Transfiguration, and the late-19th-century Fireman's Hotel. A plaque on the former hotel notes that Pushkin stayed here and quotes his letter to a friend that recommends the rissoles.

Getting there and away
By bus   Buses travel to Tver every hour, making this the best form of transport.
By train   There is one train from Moscow and three suburban trains from Tver each day.

Where to stay
The only working hotel in town is the basic Tvertsa Hotel, nab Tveretskaya 26, tel: 521 41.

What to see
To honour the poet who visited Torzhok many times, the town organises a Pushkin Festival on the first Saturday in June. The events are hosted on a stage

on the Tvertsa River surrounded by models of the heroes of Pushkin, and include poetry readings, performances of the local folk group called Lenok, and displays of local handicrafts. The Pushkin Museum, ul Stepan Razin 71, tel: 520 60, open 11.00–17.30, closed Monday and Tuesday, organises the event.

Torzhok is also famous for its gold-thread needlework. This ancient craft developed from gold and silver embroidery on Moroccan leather which was popular in Russia several centuries ago. In 1928, the country's only school for teaching gold-thread sewing was established. The workers mostly produce work for sale, but they still do commissions such as the costumes used in the Russian films, *Anna Karenina* and *War and Peace*. An extensive collection of gold-thread work is displayed in the Museum of Local Studies, pl Ananin 8, tel: 518 43, open 11.00–19.00, closed Monday and Tuesday.

What's in the region
North of Torzhok are a number of interesting sights that can be reached on bus No 119 which departs from the main bus station beside the Pushkin Museum. The first stop is the Wooden Architecture Museum in Vasilevo (Василево) village, 7km from Torzhok at bus stop Sanatari (Санатарный). Another 1km further on, the bus reaches Mitino (Митино) village which has a bizarre 19th-century stone pyramid allegedly built as a cool room for potatoes or alternatively as a New Age "temple of power concentration". Eight kilometres from Torzhok the bus reaches Prutnya (Прутня) village which contains the grave of Pushkin's long-time lover, A P Kern.

Lokottsy   Локотцы   216km
For the next 43km the line is particularly smooth and a fence encloses the railway on both sides because this stretch is used for high-speed testing; animals wandering on to the track could cause devastating accidents. The latest speed record was set in October 1993 with a modified TEP80 experimental diesel-electric locomotive which touched 271km/h.

Lyubinka   Любинка   260km
For the next 4km on the right of the railway line is a peat bog farm. The trenches which you see are dug through the bog to drain off over 85% of the peat's water. A harvester then travels through the bog cutting off the top 25mm of peat. The cut peat lies on top of the bog and after two days of being sun dried, it is collected and the next 25mm is cut. This is repeated about 28 times before the autumn rain makes harvesting impossible.

VYSHNI VOLOCHEK   Вышний Волочек   286km
Population: 64,300   Telephone area code: 082 33
This attractive town is a miniature St Petersburg with 30 bridges, 32km of canals and granite embankments. From 947, the site of the town was the point where ships were hauled out of the Tvertsa River, dragged 9km across land on logs and launched into the Tsna River, thus enabling ships to travel from the Baltic to the Caspian Sea. The town's name relates directly to this activity as *volochek* means "to drag".

In 1703, Peter I commissioned Russia's first artificial waterway linking the two rivers in order to improve the speed of transport. Although 20,000 serfs worked and died building a series of canals and locks, the result was totally inadequate for the size of the ships. So, in 1719, Peter ordered the network to be rebuilt by the Russian M I Serdjukov who in 1722 built the 1280m-long Tsninski Canal connecting the two rivers. According to Russian historians, he also invented the rather obvious idea of damming water from the spring thaw to provide an artificial lake which is then used to feed the locks.

Vyshni Volochek's importance collapsed after the construction of the Moscow–St Petersburg railway and, by 1900, all commercial river traffic through the town ceased. Nowadays, the low bridges over the Tsninski Canal prevent anything but small boats from passing between the rivers. However, it is possible to travel between the rivers via the 5km-long Novo–Tveretski Canal, 10km to the south of the town. This canal was dug in 1943 to form part of the Great Volga Water System and is one of many water sources used to generate power while raising and regulating the Volga's water flow.

Getting there and away
Vyshni Volochek is only 130km (1hr 30min on the train) from Tver so it is best to make a day trip to the town rather than an overnight stay. There are over a dozen daytime trains that travel between Vyshni Volochek and Tver. There are also hourly buses to Tver.

Where to stay
The only place to stay in town is the basic Berezka Hotel at the corner of pro Lenina and ul Kirova.

Getting around
To get from Vyshni Volochek station to the centre of town, take trolleybus No 1, 2 or 12 from in front of the station. The buses travel down the town's main street of pro Lenina. The Berezka Hotel and central post office are located on the corners of pro Lenina and ul Kirova, which is the first major road the bus crosses from the station. About 500m to the left along ul Kirova is the inter-city telephone office while 1.5km to the right is the long-distance bus station. The trolleybuses terminate at the old Trading Row and local bus station, which is also close to the museum and Krasni Mai shop. The canals are located straight ahead down pro Lenina and to the right along ul Ostashkova which will also take you to the Cathedral of St Michael.

The long-distance bus station is about 1km out of town and buses travel between the stations every 30 minutes.

What to see
As well as the canals, there are a number of buildings in town worth seeing. These include the slowly renovated 19th-century Trading Row which was the trading centre in the 1800s, the turn-of-the-century pseudo-Doric Cathedral of St Michael and the two-storey stone house where Peter I stayed when he travelled between Moscow and St Petersburg. There is also a Museum of Local Studies at pro Sovetov 5, tel: 11 546, and nearby on the corner of pro Lenina and pro Sovetov is a shop selling artistic and functional glasswork from the nearby Krasni Mai glass factory. For more information on this factory, see *Leontevo, page 188*.

Two other interesting sights in town are the radioactivity meter in front of the post office which does not instil confidence in the nuclear power plants at

Udomlya 40km to the north (hopefully the meter shows 15 microRads/hour or below), and a monument to the local Oleg Imarionovits Matveev (1917–45) who followed the Soviet kamikaze tradition of crashing his damaged plane into a German tank.

Leontevo Леонтьево 294km

About 6km from Leontevo is the village of Krasnomaiski which is famous for its Krasni Mai ("Red May") glassworks. The factory was founded in 1859, and its greatest achievement was crafting the giant ruby glass stars on top of the spires in the Moscow kremlin in 1945. Today, they make a range of artistic and practical glassware which can be bought from the shop in Vyshni Volochek, only 7km away by road. The factory has a large museum, tel: 456 77, 454 94, open 09.00–17.00, closed weekends, which is worth visiting and a tour of the plant can also be organised. The best way to get to Krasnomaiski from Vyshni Volochek is by bus No 3 which departs every 30 minutes from both the long-distance and local bus stations.

Akademicheskaya Академическая 305km

This town was an artistic centre in the last century when such famous artists as Ilya Repin lived there.

Bologoe Бологое 331km
Population: 35,000   Telephone area code: 082 38

Despite Bologoe being a railway junction with three branch lines, the town is quite small and the branch lines have little traffic. Bologoe, like nearby Chudovo, has an island station with the station buildings wedged between the east and west platforms. In Russia, island layouts are reserved for only the largest stations as the necessary overpass or underpass adds greatly to the initial and continuing costs, while expansion of platforms is very difficult. These stations were built in the late 1800s but the estimated traffic flows never came about, and railway engineers admitted that both Bologoe and Chudovo stations were a very costly mistake.

The town celebrated its 500th anniversary in 1995, but the only building older than 50 years is the water tower near the station. The rest were destroyed during World War II.

This area has numerous lakes and is a popular holiday and camping destination. Beside the station, there is a memorial to the railway workers who died in World War II.

There is a basic hotel on the third floor of Bologoe station and rooms cost $5–15 a night.

Sixty kilometres along the northeast branch line, is Udomlya (Удомля). This sleepy town had a population of 11,000 in 1976 but this grew to 32,000 in the early 1990s following the start of construction of a three-reactor, nuclear power station. The plants have been plagued by controversy as many engineers believe that the nearby water resources will only support two reactors and the third will raise the nearby rivers' water temperature considerably, destroying the ecosystem.

The two other branch lines have more interest for travellers.

The east line passes through Valdai (Валдай) which is 50km away. The 19,700-inhabitant town is a popular holiday retreat as it rests on the banks of the picturesque Valdai Lake and nearby is the Valdai Nature Reserve. The town is famous for its handicrafts, including coach bells and artistic embroidery, and the 17th-century Cathedral of Iversky Monastery, which is on Ryabinovom Island in the centre of the lake. Valdai's excellent hotel is one of the best bargains in Russia. It was a popular place with the Soviet era élite with its excellent rooms, swimming pool, billiard rooms and detached two-bedroom cottages. It costs only $15 twin share/person for a standard room or $28 twin share/person for a luxury suite.

The south branch line passes through Ostashkov (Осташков) which is 100km away and is another major holiday destination. The town sits on the bank of Seliger Lake, considered to be one of the most beautiful places in the region. The lake consists of numerous interconnected lakes and cruise ships regularly ply the waters. A short boat trip will take you to the town's oldest monastery, Nilova Pustyn. The monastery was a traditional place of pilgrimage for Orthodox believers, beginning in the 18th century.

Berezaika   Березайка   345km
The train passes over the Berezaika River which is where the town got its name.

Torbino   Торбино   434km
Just past Torbino, the line makes a 12km loop to the north. If you look at a map of the Moscow–St Petersburg railway, it is fairly straight with just this one bump. This resulted in a popular story that the bump came about when the repressive Tsar Nicholas I drew a straight line between the two cities with a ruler to indicate the route and, not noticing his thumb, he drew around it. Being fearful of questioning the tsar, the engineers dutifully built it as he drew it. However, the truth is that there is a deep, narrow canyon near Torbino which only appears on the most detailed topographical maps. Consequently, rather than building a massive bridge, the tsar's engineers chose to cross the canyon 5km to the north where only a 50m-high bridge was needed. The view from the bridge is spectacular.

Mstinski Most   Мстинский мост   461km
There is another large bridge over the Mstinski River just before the station.

CHUDOVO   Чудово   532km
Population: 18,000   Telephone area code: 816 65
This is a main railway junction with a 75km branch line to the south terminating at Novgorod and a north branch line to Murmansk. The town gets its name from the Chud tribe who inhabited the area centuries ago. Today, Chudovo is famous for its match factory which now provides 10% of Russia's supply.

The factory, which can be seen to the right just after Chudovo station, was formerly called the Flag of the Proletariat and is now intriguingly named Sun Enterprise of High Culture. As can be imagined, the town is a mecca for matchbox collectors and is awash with a wonderful array of regular and anniversary boxes.

What to see
The main attraction of the town is the House-museum of the famous Russian poet N A Nekrasov (1821–77) who lived here every summer from 1871 to 1876.

The museum, at ul Kosinova 1, tel: 54 267, is open 10.00–18.00, closed Tuesday.

There is also a Museum of Local Studies in the Palace of Culture which is located in the centre of town. Nearby is the basic Zvanka Hotel, ul Parainenskaya 3, tel: 54 600, $17 twin share/person.

To get to the museums and hotel cross the pedestrian bridge over the tracks and walk towards the bus stop. This stop is on the corner of the main street which runs at right angles to the railway line.

On the left of the station is a memorial to the railway workers who died during World War II and slightly further away is the now active Sofia Mother of God Church.

What's in the region

About 2km away in the village of Syabrentsy, which is on shosse Petersburgskoe (St Petersburg Highway), is the House-museum of the democratic writer G I Uspenski (1834–1902) who lived there from 1881 to 1892. The museum is open 10.00–18.00, closed Tuesday, tel: 55 433.

An interesting half-day trip is to the village of Krasnofarforny (Краснофафорный), meaning "red pottery", which obviously takes its name from the main factory, the Kuznetsov red pottery works. This factory was founded in 1876 and produces some of Russia's most famous artistic crockery. While the works have an interesting museum, a tour of the decrepit 700-worker factory is much more informative. The factory and museum operate only about half the week so it is essential to book a tour through the chief artist, V A Biryukov, tel: 648 (work), 714 (home). The cheapest way to get to Krasnofarforny is on a local bus from Chudovo. The 20-minute, 13km trip is interesting as you pass the Energomash factory which produced heavy electrical engineering equipment, with its workers' apartment blocks beside it. Luckily for the workers, when Energomash sacked most of them in the early 1990s, many found employment across the road at the new Cadbury chocolate factory which started operation in late 1996.

If you are based in Novgorod, it is possible to visit both Chudovo and Krasnofarforny in one day.

NOVGOROD Новгород
Population: 250,000   Telephone area code: 816 00

Once Novgorod was the largest city in Russia, but today it is a quiet, distinctively Russian backwater. Many travellers consider it to be Russia's nicest city as it is large enough to have a variety of attractions, yet small enough to be able to walk around. It has little motor traffic and is well laid out so it's hard to get lost.

The town was founded in 859 and was simply known as "new city" or *novgorod*. The trading city was based around the mouth of the Volkhov River as it flows into the Ilmen Lake.

The Novgorod Principality was often at war with Tver, and later Moscow, and while it was spared by the Mongols, Ivan the Terrible comprehensively sacked it by putting 60,000 inhabitants to the sword. The city was never the same again and its importance as a trading centre was finally destroyed when St Petersburg was founded and the Moscow–St Petersburg road and railway were constructed, both of which bypassed Novgorod.

Getting there and away

Novgorod is located 74km south of Bologoe which is on the Moscow–St Petersburg railway. Trains to Bologoe take 1hr 39min. There are regular buses to a large range of destinations including St Petersburg, Moscow, Bologoe, Chudovo, Vyshni Volochek and Tver. The major trains to and from Novgorod are listed below.

Origin	Dist, km	Train no & name	Travel time	Depart	Arrive	Destination
Moscow (Leningrad)	606	41	8hr 24min	22.16	06.40	Novgorod
Novgorod	606	42	8hr 3min	21.55	05.58	Moscow (Leningrad)
Novgorod (Moscow)	190	666	3hr	07.05	11.05	St Petersburg
St Petersburg (Moscow)	190	161	2hr 40min	06.55	09.35	Novgorod

Passing through

The railway station in Novgorod is extremely attractive following its completed renovation in May 1996.

Where to stay

The city's best hotel is the excellent Beresta Palace Hotel, ul Studencheskaya, tel: 347 07, which was established by the Marco Polo luxury hotel chain. The chain no longer runs the hotel but, as its staff was trained by them, it still has excellent services and facilities including tennis courts, pool and health club. A double room is $130–160 depending on the season.

The next best hotel is the excellent Hotel Intourist, ul Dmitrievskaya (ul Velikaya) 16, tel: 730 87, 942 61, 746 44, fax: 741 57, email root@intour.nov.su, $27.5 twin share/person including breakfast. Before the collapse of the Soviet Union, the Intourist Hotel commissioned an Indian company to expand it significantly. About 50% of the project was completed by 1995 but, as the money has run out, it may never be finished.

Very conveniently located is the standard Hotel Volkhov, ul Nekrasova 24, tel: 924 98, 759 39, $15 twin share/person. The hotel has a restaurant. Next door is the very basic Hotel AZOT, ul Nekrasova 24, $7 twin share/person (all rooms shared facilities). Also reasonable but on the opposite side of the river are the standard Hotel Rossiya, nab Aleksandr Nevskovo 19/1, tel: 341 85, 360 86, $12 twin share/person. The hotel has a restaurant. Basic hotel options are the Hotel Sadko, pro Gagarin 16, tel: 753 66, $15 twin share/person and Hotel Ilmen, ul Bolshevikov 1, tel: 780 74. At the bottom of the range are the very basic Hotel Kruz, ul Russkaya, tel: 771 74, $4 twin share/person, and Hotel Rynok, ul Zhelyabova, tel: 773 55, $4 twin share/person.

A youth hostel has opened in the Institute of Advanced Studies dormitory, ul Lushinskaya 27A, tel: 714 58 or 720 33. It has single, double and triple rooms. A double room costs $28. Rooms at the youth hostel can be booked through St Petersburg International Hostel.

Getting around

Standing in front of the station, looking past the statue of Karl Marx's head down pro Karla Marksa, you see the local bus stop on the right while on the left is the long-distance bus station. To get to Hotels Sadko and Volkhov, walk down pro Karl Marx for 20 minutes. If you want to go by public transport, take bus No 4,

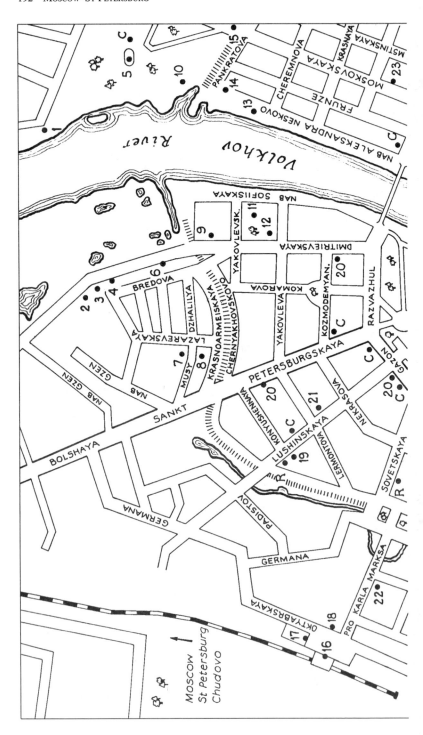

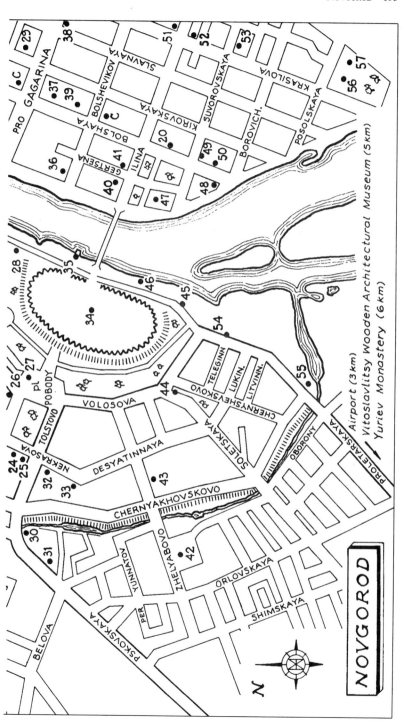

KEY TO NOVGOROD   Новгород

1	Hotel Beresta Palace (*Gostinitsa*)	гостиница «Береста Паласе»
2	Church of Simeon Bogopriimets	церковь Симеона Богоприимца
3	Cathedral and Church of Intercession Monastery	собор и церковь Покрова Зверина
4	Church of St Nicholas the White	церковь Николы Белого
5	Elektron Stadium (*Stadion*)	Стадион «Электрон»
6	Church of Saints Peter and Paul	церковь Петра и Павла
7	Church of the Trinity (*Troitsy*) of Spirits Monastery	церковь Троицы
8	Cathedral of Holy Spirit Monastery	Собор Духова монастыря
9	Hotel Inturist (*Gostinitsa*)	гостиница Интурист
10	Church of John the Divine	церковь Иоанна Богослова
11	Drama Theatre (*Teatr*)	Драматический театр
12	Casino	Казино
13	Aleksandr Nevski monument	Памятник Александру Невскому
14	Church of Saints Boris and Gleb	церковь Бориса и Глеба
15	Polytechnic (*Institut*)	Политехнический институт
16	Railway station (*Vokzal*)	Ж-Д вокзал
17	Bus station (*Avtovokzal*)	Автовокзал
18	Aeroflot	Аэрофлот
19	Youth hostel (*Gostinitsa*) at the Institute of Advanced Studies (*Institut*)	гостиница ПУУ в Институте усовершенствования учителей
20	Book shop (*Knigi*)	Книги
21	Church of Fedor Statilat	церковь Федора Стратилата
22	Advance purchase rail ticket office	Предварительная ж-д касса
23	Church of Nikita Muchenik	церковь Никиты Мученика
24	Hotel AZOT (*Gostinitsa*)	гостиница АЗОТ
25	Hotel Volkhov (*Gostinitsa*)	гостиница Волхов
26	Telephone office (*Peregovorny punkt*)	Переговорный пункт
27	Lenin monument	Памятник Ленина
28	Playing area of *gorodki* game	Парк «Городки»
29	Church of Fedor Statilat in Ruche	церковь Федора Стратилата на Ручье
30	Palace of Culture (*Dvorets*)	Дворец культуры
31	Agricultural Institute (*Institut*)	Сельскохозяйственный институт
32	Bus stop to Vitoslavlitsy Museum	Остановка за музей «Витославлицы»
33	Church of the 12 Apostles	церковь Двенадцати Апостолов
34	Kremlin	Кремль
35	Kremlin river pier (*Prichal Kremlya*)	Причал Кремля
36	Hotel Ilmen (*Gostinitsa*)	гостиница Ильмень
37	Church of Kliment	церковь Климента
38	Hotel Sadko (*Gostinitsa*)	гостиница Садко
39	Church of Dmitri Solunski	церковь Дмитрия Солунского
40	Vasilev's Palace of Culture (*Dvorets*)	Дом культуры им. Васильева
41	Post office (*Pochtamt*)	Почтамт
42	Market (*Rynok*)	Рынок
43	Hotel Rynok (*Gostinitsa*)	гостиница Рынок
44	Vlasiya Church	церковь Власия
45	Freedom from Fascist Germany monument	Монумент Победы в честь освобождения
46	Beach (*Plyazh*)	Пляж
47	Yaroslav's court	Ярославово дворище
48	Hotel Rossiya (*Gostinitsa*)	гостиница Россия
49	Church of the Archangel Michael	церковь Микаила Архангела
50	Church of Annunciation on the Market	церковь Влаговещения на Торгу
51	Church of the Saviour and Transfiguration on Ilin	церковь Спаса Преображения на Ильине
52	Apparition of the Virgin Monastery (*Znamenski*)	Знаменской монастырь
53	Church of Apostle Phillip	церковь Филиппа Апостола
54	Church of the Trinity (*Troitsy*)	церковь Троицы
55	Church in Bronnits village	церковь в Бронницах
56	Church of Ilya Prorok	церковь Ильи Пророка
57	Church of Saints Peter and Paul	церковь Петра и Павла на Славне
R	Restaurant (*Restoran*)	Ресторан
C	Café (*Kafé*) or Bar (*Bar*)	Кафе или Бар

6, 19 or 20 to pl Pobeda. There are no buses to the Hotel Intourist, but buses No 4, 6 and 19 stop at bus stop Univermag which is a 10-minute walk from the hotel. Near Hotel Rossiya is the terminus for buses No 2, 12,13, 16 and 17.

What to see

The city's highlights are mostly to be found in the kremlin. First built in 864, the walled fortress contains the Museum of History and Art, open 10.00–18.00, closed Tuesday and the last Thursday of the month; the Cathedral of St Sophia, open 10.00–18.00. closed Wednesday and last Monday of the month, which is one of the oldest buildings in Russia, having been completed in 1050; and the Monument to 1,000 Years of Russian Existence. This 1862 monument is like a wedding cake symbolising the Russian state. On top are figures of Mother Russia and the Orthodox Church, in the middle layer are heroes of Russia and on the bottom layer are minor nobles. Ironically, a parody of this structure, with the church and tsar on top, grovelling nobles, warmongering generals and fat businessmen in the middle, and peasants and workers being crushed under the weight of the top two layers, was extensively used in communist propaganda. There is an icon and church paraphernalia exhibition in the Granovitaya Chamber. Tickets and tour times for this exhibition can be obtained from the Museum of History and Art. Within the kremlin, there is also a large theatre which often has excellent performances, an eternal flame to those who died in World War II and lots of churches. Entrance to the kremlin is free but you have to pay for the Museum of History and Art, and the Granovitaya Chamber.

The kremlin sits on the banks of the Volkhov River which can be crossed by a footbridge in front of the south entrance of the fortress. To the right of the bridge is a beach and, to the left, the pier which is the river station. This area is always crowded in summer. Near the river station at the side of the kremlin is a playing area for the game of *gorodki*. This strange game involves throwing wood and metal staffs at wooden blocks which are arranged in various patterns. The aim of the game is to knock the blocks out of the game square and this gets harder as the blocks are laid out in wider patterns.

The gates to the kremlin are usually locked at nightfall unless there is a concert.

On the other side of the river are more parks and historic buildings.

The Yuriev Monastery

What's in the region

Since the collapse of communism, the river ferry has run infrequently. If it does operate, it departs from in front of the kremlin, 100m upstream of the footbridge. Intourist organises river cruises to Ilmen Lake which take an hour and cost $5/person for groups of ten.

On the western outskirts of the town is the Vitoslavlitsy Wooden Architectural Museum. The open-air museum contains about ten buildings including the 17th-century Ascension (Uspenski) Church brought from Kuritskaya village on the shores of Lake Ilmen. To get to the museum, take bus No 7 from the railway station or pl Pobedy, which runs past the airport, and get off at bus stop Vitoslavlitsy (Витославлицы). The trip takes about 25 minutes and buses run hourly. In summer, the museum is open 10.00–18.00, closed Wednesday, while in winter it is only open for the few daylight hours.

About 800m back along the road in the direction from which you came is the Yuriev Monastery. This walled complex, which includes two cathedrals and one church, dates from the 9th century and is an important example of Russian architecture of that time. The monastery is situated in a picturesque spot on the banks of the Volkhov River and there is a pier here where local ferries from Novgorod stop. The monastery is currently being restored but is still open to the public from 10.00–17.00, closed Tuesday. Bus No 7 goes past it.

From Novgorod, it is possible to make a day trip to the nearby towns of Chudovo and Krasnofarforny in one day. These are described under *Chudovo, page 189*.

Torfyanoe   Торфяное   547km
Shosse Petersburgskoe (St Petersburg Highway) again joins the railway and runs parallel on the left.

Lyuban   Любань   567km
From the middle of the 19th century, the town became a holiday destination for residents of St Petersburg. At the station there is a monument to Pavel P Melnikov (1804–80) who was responsible for planning the Moscow–St Petersburg railway, and is buried in the town.

Ushaki   Ушаки   586km
Ten kilometres south of Ushaki is the historic Marino Manor House Estate. The estate is located near the village of Andrianovo, which can be reached by regular bus from Ushaki.

Tosno   Тосно   597km
Telephone area code: 812 61
Despite the town's existence since 1500, Tosno today looks like a typical Soviet town of squat five-storey accommodation blocks. This is because nearly 70% of all buildings were destroyed during the two-year German occupation in World War II. About 18km to the southwest is the village of Lisino-Korpus, which was a hunting and nature resort for rich residents of St Petersburg in the 18th century. The estate is now a museum and regular buses travel between Tosno and Lisino-Korpus.

Just past Tosno is Tosno-2 station which was built to service the Tosno railway carriage repair complex.

Sablino   Саблино   609km
The town surrounding the station is Ulyanovka (Ульяновка), named after Lenin's mother who lived here with her daughter. There is a plaque on their house.

Kolpino   Колпино   625km
Kolpino is St Petersburg's largest satellite industrial town. It was decreed into existence by Peter I in 1722 following the discovery of nearby iron ore deposits. Since then the town's biggest enterprise, the massive Izhorski factory, has been

manufacturing earth-moving machines, steel and, because of its discreet distance from the prying eyes of tourist/spies in St Petersburg, military equipment. During the 1917 October Revolution the factory workers played a pivotal role by giving 17 armoured cars to Lenin's supporters; during the Russian Civil War, it built armoured trains that were used to great effect by Trotsky. Because of its military importance, German forces desperately attempted to take Kolpino during the 900-day siege of St Petersburg in World War II. Although the front line passed through parts of the town, the Izhorski factory was not taken. There are many monuments in the region to the heroic defence of the town which saw 1,856 out of the town's 2,183 houses destroyed. Today, the Izhorski factory produces an enormous range of electrical engineering products including nuclear power plant equipment. The factory's office and brick wall are classified as heritage buildings.

Beyond Kolpino, at the 631km mark, 19km out from St Petersburg, there is a monument beside the railway commemorating the start of the construction of the Moscow–St Petersburg high-speed railway on July 1993.

Obukhovo   Обухово   639km
Just before reaching the station, there is a branchline which goes to Murmansk. Just after the station, the railway is flanked by two cemeteries. On the left is the Jewish Cemetery and on the right is the Cemetery in Honour of the Victims of January 9. The latter contains many of the 1,000 peaceful protesters gunned down by Tsarist troops on January 9 1905 when they attempted to present a petition for greater freedom at the Winter Palace. Bloody Sunday, as it became known, marked the beginning of the failed First Russian Revolution.

The train now passes through one of St Petersburg's main freight yards.

St Petersburg   Санкт-Петербург   650km
The train arrives at Moscow station, pl Vosstaniya 2, tel: 168 0111. The nearby metro station is pl Vosstaniya. This is St Petersburg's largest station, which was built at the same time as the identical Leningrad station in Moscow.

The Wooden Architectural Museum at Vitoslavlitsy

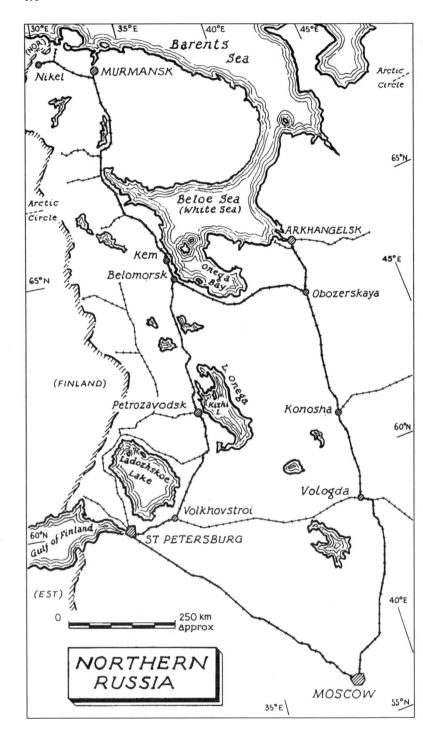

NORTHERN
RUSSIA

Chapter Twelve

Northern Russian Routes

Northern European Russia encompasses an area the size of western Europe but with only a few million inhabitants. Only by travelling by train do you get an understanding of the sheer size of this desolate land.

For travellers with a specific interest, such as indigenous cultures, history or fishing, this region is particularly fascinating. But even for general travellers, an eight-day tour of this region is well worthwhile.

Without doubt, the best time of the year to visit northern Russia is in mid-summer when the temperature in Murmansk peaks at 20°C. While it is also pleasant to go in spring and autumn, you need to keep in mind that hydrofoils to Kizhi run from May 25 to October 15, boats to Solovetski Archipelago run from June to September and that the midnight sun in Murmansk is visible from May 17 to July 27. Going in winter is miserable and dull as the sun never appears and temperatures are rarely above –20°C.

There are several ways of exploring this region. The possibilities are: to make direct return trips from Moscow to Arkhangelsk or St Petersburg to Murmansk; to travel in a loop of St Petersburg, Murmansk, Arkhangelsk and Moscow; or to go one way by rail and fly back. More information is given below under each route's *Travel suggestions*.

ST PETERSBURG–MURMANSK
Route highlights
The highlights of a trip to Murmansk are relaxing Petrozavodsk with the nearby Kizhi Island Wooden Architecture Museum, Solovetski Archipelago which contains one of the world's largest monasteries and, of course, Murmansk itself.

Travel suggestions
A good way of exploring the region is to take a day train from St Petersburg to Petrozavodsk and stay in the town for two days. This will give you time to take a day trip to the famous Wooden Museum on Kizhi Island. Depart from Petrozavodsk on an overnight train to Belomorsk or Kem. During your stay in one of these towns you will be able to visit Solovetski Archipelago and the petroglyphs around Belomorsk. To complete the final leg of the journey to Murmansk, take an overnight train from Belomorsk or Kem. From Murmansk, there are direct trains to Moscow, Vologda or Arkhangelsk.

Trains

The most convenient long-distance trains on this route are listed below.

Origin	Dist, km	Train no & name	Travel time	Depart	Arrive	Destination
St Petersburg (Moscow)	401	658	9hr 25min	21.50	07.15	Petrozavodsk
Petrozavodsk	379	56	8hr 10min	23.06	07.16	Belomorsk
Belomorsk	85	22	55min	9.15	10.10	Kem
Kem	610	16	12hr 27min	0.52	13.19	Murmansk
Petrozavodsk	401	55	7hr 25min	23.00	06.25	St Petersburg (Moscow)
Belomorsk	379	21	7hr 34min	22.00	05.34	Petrozavodsk
Kem	85	15	1hr 11min	7.18	08.29	Belomorsk
Murmansk	610	15	11hr 30min	19.24	06.54	Kem
Petrozavodsk	1,044	16	21hr 18min	16.01	13.19	Murmansk
Murmansk	1,044	15	21hr 6min	19.24	16.30	Petrozavodsk
Petrozavodsk	920	17	15hr 8min	19.25	10.33	Moscow (Leningrad)
Moscow (Leningrad)	920	18	16hr 3min	18.22	10.25	Petrozavodsk
Moscow (Leningrad)	1,964	16	36hr 11min	00.30	13.19	Murmansk
Murmansk	1,964	15	36hr 33min	19.24	08.57	Moscow (Leningrad)

Route description

St Petersburg   Санкт Петербург   0km

The train departs for Murmansk and Arkhangelsk from St Petersburg's Moscow station, pl Vosstaniya 2, tel: 168 0111.

Obukhovo   Обухово   11km

Just before the station, the railway is flanked by two cemeteries. On the left is the Jewish Cemetery and on the right is the Cemetery in Honour of the Victims of January 9. The latter cemetery contains many of the 1,000 peaceful protesters gunned down by Tsarist troops on January 9 1905 when they attempted to present a petition for greater freedom at the Winter Palace. Bloody Sunday, as it became known, marked the beginning of the failed First Russian Revolution.

Just past the station, the Murmansk train leaves the St Petersburg–Moscow line for the north.

Izhory   Ижоры   20km

Nearby at Ust-Izhora, which sits on the Neva River, the young Novgorod Prince Aleksandr routed Swedish invaders in a major battle in 1240. In honour of victory, he took the surname of Neva. The main street of St Petersburg is named after Aleksandr Nevsky who was reburied in the city.

Pella   Пелла   36km

The station gets its name from the nearby Pella Palace which was one of Tsarina Catherine II's favourite retreats. Unfortunately, it was destroyed by the Germans during their World War II occupation.

Mga   Мга   49km

This station sits on a major railway junction with lines to St Petersburg, Volkhov, Gatchina and Kaliazin. During World War II, German forces captured Mga on August 31 1941, thereby cutting off the last railroad linking St Petersburg with the centre of Russia. Thousands of Soviet soldiers died in this disastrous battle and several of the leaders of the Soviet forces were promptly executed for incompetence. Mga was eventually liberated on January 21 1944, thus breaking the 900-day siege of St Petersburg.

Voibokalo   Войбокало   92km

At the station is a memorial of a Zis-5 truck on a plinth. The monument honours the drivers who drove supplies to besieged St Petersburg along unmarked tracks while braving German aircraft and artillery attacks.

Volkhovstroi 1   Волховстрой 1   121km

The town, known as Volkhov (Волхов) rather than Volkhovstroi since 1940, contains a showpiece of the early years of Soviet power: the Lenin Volkhov hydro-electric power plant.

The train passes over the walls of the dam which, with its nine vaulted arches on the dam's facade, is hailed as a seminal influence in world industrial architecture. In front of the station is a bronze memorial to the dam's engineer, G O Graftio. More information on him and the town can be found in the Museum of Local History. Also near the station is the Eu708-89 steam train which hauled the first relief train into St Petersburg in 1944, breaking the city's 900-day blockade.

Murmanskie Vorota   Мурманские Ворота   123km

This quaintly named station means "The Gates of Murmansk".

Lungachi   Лунгачи   150km

There is a short branch line to the village of Syasstroi (Сясьстой), a port on the Syas River.

Yugi   Юги   167km

For the next 70km, the M18 St Petersburg–Murmansk highway can be seen on the left of the railway.

Oyat-Volkhovstroi   Оять-Волховстрой   199km

On the left is a large nature reserve called Nizhnesvirsk Zapovednik.

Lodeinoe Pole   Лодейное Поле   242km

Lodeinoe Pole, meaning "icy field", sits on the left bank of the Svir River. The town, formerly known as Mokrishvitsa, was founded by Peter the Great as a ship-building yard and port due to its strategic position on the Volga–Baltic waterway. The shipyard was closed in 1830, after building more than 400 vessels, but the population did not decrease as it was also a place of exile.

From 1941 to 1945, the city withstood 1,005 days of attacks from German forces trying to cut off the supply route to St Petersburg. For more information on this route, visit the Museum of Local History or see *Road of Life Museum* in *Chapter Eight, page 126.*

Immediately after leaving the station, the railway passes over the top of the Nizhnesvirski hydro-electric station as the train heads due north.

Podporozhe   Подпорожье   279km

The station is 4km from the town of Podporozhe which can be seen after you leave the station. Within a kilometre of the station, the train travels across a dam wall which contains the Upper Svir hydro-electric station.

Tokari   Токари   315km

You have now crossed from Leningrad Oblast into the Republic of Karelia. There is a marker at the crossing point.

Onezhski   Онежский   393km

On the left is the 2,000-inhabitant, strangely named Chicken Factory village (Птицефабрика).

PETROZAVODSK   Петрозаводск   401km
Population: 279,000   Telephone area code: 814 00

Petrozavodsk (meaning "Factory Town of Peter the Great") is the capital of the Republic of Karelia and one of the nicest places to visit in northern Russia.

The centre of this prosperous town is pleasantly laid out, the 1940-style buildings are excellently maintained, the shops are well stocked, there are numerous restaurants, and the attractive lake embankment is full of strolling families.

Although the town was founded in 1703 as a cannon factory by Peter the Great, virtually all the town's buildings were built after World War II. From October 2 1941 to June 28 1944 Finnish troops occupied the city and in their final eviction the town was destroyed. Those who rebuilt Petrozavodsk should feel proud of their work.

Today, the town is a major shipping, rail and road centre, and there are over 50 industrial plants in the city including steel works, tool makers, military factories and Russia's largest log-carrying tractor manufacturing plant. These plants are located in Petrozavodsk's suburbs which extend 25km along the coast of Lake Onega, and do not affect the harmony of the central part of the city.

Getting there and away

By air   There are flights with Finnair from Helsinki and Joensuu, Finland.

By bus   There is an overnight bus to St Petersburg which departs at 22.00 and arrives at 07.45. The bus runs on Monday, Friday, Saturday and Sunday, and returns at the same time the next day.

By train   There are five trains a day from St Petersburg to Petrozavodsk. Four travel the 401km direct route which this chapter covers, while one travels the 551km westerly route via Matkaselkya near the Finnish border which takes 16hr 20min. There are two trains daily to Moscow and three to Murmansk.

The most convenient long-distance trains on this route are listed below.

Origin	Dist, km	Train no & name	Travel time	Depart	Arrive	Destination
St Petersburg (Moscow)	401	658	9hr 25min	21.50	07.15	Petrozavodsk
Petrozavodsk	379	56	8hr 10min	23.06	07.16	Belomorsk
Petrozavodsk	401	55	7hr 25min	23.00	06.25	St Petersburg (Moscow)
Belomorsk	379	21	7hr 34min	22.00	05.34	Petrozavodsk
Petrozavodsk	1,044	16	21hr 18min	16.01	13.19	Murmansk
Murmansk	1,044	15	21hr 6min	19.24	16.30	Petrozavodsk
Petrozavodsk	920	17	15hr 8min	19.25	10.33	Moscow (Leningrad)
Moscow (Leningrad)	920	18	16hr 3min	18.22	10.25	Petrozavodsk

Where to stay

The best hotel in the city is the standard Karelian Government Hotel, ul Sverdlova 10, tel: 756 61. It was the Communist Party hotel and has been renovated by the Finns and is now very good. Double rooms cost $52. It has English-speaking staff and a restaurant. The next best option is the standard Hotel Kareliya, ul Gyullinga 2, tel: 523 06, 588 97, $18 twin share/person. It has a good restaurant. The cheaper, centrally located, standard Hotel Severnaya, pro Lenina 21, tel: 763 54, costs $18 twin share/person. Hotel Severnaya contains the Intourist office and a restaurant. The Finns have recently renovated the river station hotel called Hotel Fregat, Onezhskaya nab, tel: 780 41, 617 70. It is now a standard hotel and costs $27 twin share/person. It is also possible to get very basic accommodation at the railway station Komnata Otdykha, tel: 942 67, at the basic Hotel Vitrazhi, ul Promyshlennaya 9, tel: 597 38, on the outskirts of town, and at the basic Hotel Pietari, shosse Shuyskaya 16, tel: 453 97, $14 twin share/person.

What to see

Strolling around the granite-lined embankment is very pleasant, with its modern art, large parks and piers full of hydrofoils, fishing boats and large tourist ships. The Museum of Local Studies has several halls devoted to the Karel, Est, Izhora and Ves indigenous peoples and early books, pl Lenina 1, tel: 727 91, open 10:00-19:00, closed Friday. A branch of the museum is also at pro Uritskaya 32, tel: 513 28. The Museum of Karelian Decorative Arts has two sites. Its major building is at pro Karla Marksa 8, tel: 737 13, open 10.00–19.00, closed Monday, and a minor two-storey building on pl Lenina, open 10.00–19.00, closed Friday.

The Palace of School Children, ul Krasnaya 8, is worth visiting for its weird architecture. Swimmers can visit the beach on the Lososinka River which meanders through the city 500m to the south of the river station. On each side of the river is a 400m-wide green belt which is very popular in summer.

Near pl Lenina there is a mass grave of soldiers and the Tomb of the Unknown Soldier with its eternal flame is a constant reminder of World War II.

Water cruising

Being a major port, Petrozavodsk offers a variety of trips on local lakes, rivers and canals. There are several hydrofoils a day to Vytegra (Вытерга) which is 142km away, Tipinitsy (Типиничы) 98km, Kuzaranga (Кузаранга) 128km, Tolvuya (Толвуя) 165km and Sennaya Guba (Сенная губа) 59km. Tickets for these are sold at the river station. There are organised cruises from Petrozavodsk, such as the four-day trip to Kizhi, Vytegra and Vollen on Lake Onega and Svir River. Information on these can be obtained from the river station or by contacting one of two companies:

- Belomorsko-Onezhskoe Parokhodstvo (White Sea and Onezhski Lake Ship Company), ul Rigachina 7, fax: 577 17, satellite fax: 00873 140 202
- Karelia (a Finland based company), tel: (Finland): +358 73 163 326, fax: 00 873 140 4202

What's in the region
Kizhi Island Outdoor Wooden Architecture Museum

The highlight of the region is the world-famous Kizhi Island which is 66km from Petrozavodsk. It contains 15 wooden buildings that were typical of those in Karelia in the 13th to 20th centuries. While most of the buildings are original, none was built on its present spot. All the buildings were transported here from various nearby locations as this is the only way they can be preserved, according to Russian curators. About 3km to the north of the main exposition is a village which contains several of these buildings with locals still living in them.

The highlight of Kizhi Island is the 22-cupola Cathedral of the Transfiguration (Preobrazhenskaya) built in 1714, as famous for Russians as St Basil's Cathedral on Red Square in Moscow. Unfortunately, it has been closed for years as work to stabilise its deterioration continues. Two other highlights are the ninedomed Church of the Intercession (Pokrovs-kaya) with its nine cupolas and a fabulous four-tiered iconostasis.

There are also several buildings displaying the life of middle-class landowners including a windmill and the obligatory *banya*.

The 22-cupola Cathedral of the Transfiguration

The museum is open 09.00–19.00 from May 25 to October 15 and 11.00–14.00 the rest of the year. Entry is $2.50 for locals but a whopping $14 for foreigners, so practise imitating a Russian. Tickets are bought at the booth about 500km from the pier on the wooden walkway towards the museum. While there are food kiosks and *shashlik* stands at the pier, and the occasional working floating restaurant nearby, it is best to bring your own lunch.

You need at least two hours to wander around the main museum area, and most of the day to get to the other end of the island.

To get the 66km to the museum, take a hydrofoil. The tickets are purchased on the ground floor of the river station. There are about ten hydrofoils a day in peak season and it takes 75 minutes to reach the island. The return trip costs $5.70 and if you want to return on a specific hydrofoil you need to state this when you buy your ticket. Otherwise you have to wait until the booked passengers jump on and then, if there is room, you are let on. A great photo opportunity of the museum occurs just as you arrive and depart from the island's pier. The hydrofoil runs from May 25 to October 15. Once the lake freezes over in January, it is possible to ski, drive or fly in an AN-2 plane to the island.

Martial Waters Spring Resort

The most interesting part of Martial Waters Spring Resort is its history, but if you have nothing to do for a day, it's worth a visit all the same. The resort dates from the early 1700s when Peter the Great returned from his European discovery tour deeply embarrassed that Russia lacked any health-giving mineral water springs. At that time, mineral springs were popular in Europe and were constantly visited by the élite. Peter's scouts scoured the countryside and the only one of reasonable size to be found was in a rugged area 50km north of Petrozavodsk. Despite visiting it four times, Peter never made the spring popular and, as soon as he died, it was abandoned. Today, the resort consists of a basic 250-bed hotel, a museum and four mineral springs, 7–14.5m deep, which together produce a total of 330,000 litres/day. There is usually no problem in getting a bed if you want to stay overnight, but a day trip is long enough to see everything. To visit the resort, either organise a trip with Intourist, hire a taxi for the day or take one of three daily buses which terminate at Spasskaya Guba (Спасская губа). About 5km before reaching Spasskaya Guba, the bus passes Martial Waters Spring Resort. The bus trip takes 1 hr 45min and to make a day trip, catch the bus that departs at 06.15 and returns to Petrozavodsk at 20.35.

Kivach Nature Reserve
The other regional sight is the 10,000-hectare Kivach (Кивач) Nature Reserve. Its claim to fame is that it has Europe's second biggest waterfall on a plain, as distinct from mountains, with a water drop of 10.7m. It is about 70km from Petrozavodsk. If you want to visit Kivach just for a day, you can take the once-a-week bus, stay a few hours and then catch it on the return journey, or take an Intourist tour. Not recommended.

Tomitsy   Томицы   408km
A branch line heads off to the left which is the slow route to St Petersburg via Matkaselkya (551km, taking 16hr 20min) and to Kostomuksha in the north on the Finnish border (531km, taking 14hr 32min). Trains run once a day to these destinations.

Kondopoga   Кондопога   453km
Telephone area code: 814 51
This town owes its existence to a massive newspaper-making factory which, until the collapse of communism, produced one-third of the nation's newsprint. Another major employer is a quarry which produces over 30 different coloured and patterned granites and marbles. The quarry was founded in the 18th century and many of St Petersburg's great buildings, including the St Isaac's and Kazan Cathedrals, used stone from here.

Despite this industrial presence, the area is a popular tourist destination. Particularly popular is the 42m-high, wooden Church of the Ascension (Uspenskaya) (1774) on the shores of the Kondopoga Bay of Lake Onega.

Medvezhya Gora   Медвежья Гора   556km
This town was founded to build and service the St Petersburg–Murmansk railway line in 1916. It was also a major centre in the construction of the Belomorsk Canal, which starts just 15km to the southeast in the village of Povenets. There is nothing to see in the town except the museum of local studies.

Segezha   Сегежа   671km
This industrial town depends on the railways and a large paper and pulp factory, founded in 1936. There is a museum but most of it concerns the paper factory.

Nadvoitsy   Надвойцы   681km
On the left is lock 10 on the Belomorsk Canal.

Shavan   Шавань   698km
On the left is lock 11 on the Belomorsk Canal.

Kochkoma   Кочкома   710km
A 120km branch line is being built here going east to link up with Ledmozero town where there is already a railway to the Finnish border. The branch line has already reached Vacha (Вача) which is a distance of 40km.

Letni   Летний   743km
On the opposite side of the Belomorsk Canal is the abandoned village called 74th Kvartel which was the 74th concentration camp for construction of the canal.

BELOMORSK   Беломорск   780km
Population: 19,000   Telephone area code: 814 37
This town is infamous for two things: the vile-smelling Belomorsk Canal cigarettes and the Belomorsk Canal that claimed the lives of tens of thousands of forced labourers in the 1930s. Less well known but far more interesting are the petroglyphs. The town is also the junction of the railway to the east leading to Arkhangelsk and Moscow.

The town is spread over three islands connected by bridges. The station is probably the worst on the St Petersburg–Murmansk line considering the town's size, and the fact that people change trains here. The station consists of two wooden 1940s era shacks on the opposite side of the railway from the city. The shack on the platform is a small waiting room and by crossing a road, you reach the ticket office and another small waiting room. It is planned to build a new station and transfer the railway freight yard from Kem to here but problems of money and regional politics have stymied the project. Near the ticket office is a bus stop which is mostly for regional buses; if you want to get to the town you have to walk.

There is no real centre of town as most buildings are scattered along the 3km-long main street. This street becomes the road between the railway shacks, so getting to town involves walking along it towards St Petersburg. After 600m, the road crosses the railway line and after 1km you reach a bus stop which is where most buses start and end. Another 1km will bring you to the town's only hotel, the basic Gandvik Hotel (meaning "Viking's hand"), ul Pervomaiskaya 18, tel: 225 69, $16 twin share/person.

In the basement of the hotel is the Museum of Local Studies, ul Pervomaiskaya 18, tel: 226 05. It was moved to this temporary site following a fire in the original building, and consequently is rarely open. The museum is very active in organising excursions and can organise trips to the Belomorsk Canal and petroglyphs.

Getting there and away
The most convenient trains on this route are listed below. Information on eastbound trains from Belomorsk to Arkhangelsk/Vologda are contained in the Obozerskaya–Belomorsk section, see *page 224*.

Origin	Dist, km	Train no & name	Travel time	Depart	Arrive	Destination
Kem	85	15	1hr 11min	07.18	08.29	Belomorsk
Petrozavodsk	379	56	8hr 10min	23.06	07.16	Belomorsk
Belomorsk	85	22	55min	09.15	10.10	Kem
Belomorsk	379	21	7hr 34min	22.00	05.34	Petrozavodsk

What's in the region
Belomorsk Canal

Of all the concentration camp projects of the Stalin era, the 277km-long Belomorsk Canal is the most infamous. (The canal is often translated as the Baltic–White Sea Canal or the Belomorsko–Baltiski Canal.) The massive project involved digging 37km of canal between numerous lakes and rivers and building 19 locks, 15 dams, 49 dykes and 12 floodgates. Stalin ordered the canal to be built in just 20 months starting in September 1931. The deadline was achieved but at the expense of the lives of frozen, beaten and malnourished prisoners. Solzhenitsyn in his book, *The Gulag Archipelago*, claimed that 100,000 labours died in the canal's construction.

This canal was one of the most important construction projects of the first Soviet five-year plan (1929–32) as it enabled ships to travel from the seas of European Russia to the Arctic Ocean, thus reducing the trip from St Petersburg to Arkhangelsk by 4,000km as it was no longer necessary to sail around the Scandinavian peninsula. At one time, hundreds of ships and barges travelled along the canal each month but today, one a day is lucky.

The penultimate lock, lock 18, is the easiest to get to from Belomorsk. Take bus No 5 from the main bus stop and after 15 minutes, it terminates at the lock. While there are guard posts and signs to say that entry is only possible with a special pass, no-one ever checks now. However, it is still not advisable to photograph the lock. Knowing the canal's history results in most visitors feeling let down by the ordinariness of the canal.

BELOMORSK CANAL CIGARETTES
On the scale of one to ten, Belomorsk Canal cigarettes score a zero. In Russian, these foul cancer sticks, which smell like stale socks even before they're smoked, are called papirosi. As papirosi lack filters and use the worst tobacco, their only appeal is their price. Belomorsk papirosi cost just $0.13 a packet compared to $2 for Camel. However, despite their cheapness, the market for papirosi is rapidly contracting as Russian smokers flock to the more expensive, filter-tipped cigarettes.

Petroglyphs
The shores of the Belomore Sea are littered with neolithic and Bronze Age rock drawings, known as petroglyphs, and the two sets that are easiest to reach are around Belomorsk. The closest set is called Besovy Sledki (Бесовы следки) and consists of a number of petroglyphs enclosed in a pavilion. To get there, take bus No 1 which terminates at Zolotets (Золотец) village. From Belomorsk, the bus crosses over the railway line to Arkhangelsk, passes an anti-aircraft military base, goes through Vygostrov (Выгостров) village, passes Besovy Sledki pavilion, and drives over a hydro-electric dam before arriving in Zolotets. You can either walk back 1km from Zolotets or walk

800m onwards from Vygostrov to reach the pavilion. The pavilion has haphazard opening times and, as it is under the control of Belomorsk's museum, it is best to ask there before you go. Bus No 1 runs every 40 minutes and the trip to Vygostrov takes 15 minutes.

A better set of petroglyphs is the 1,200 drawings on the banks of the dried-up Zalavruga (Залавруга) River. These depict individual figures and animals, as well as complete scenes of elk and white whale hunting. The most famous of the 3,500-year-old drawings is the 2m long "devil's footprint". Although the Zalavruga petroglyphs are only 2km from Zolotets, they are difficult to find and it is best to organise a visit through the museum.

Solovetski Archipelago

It is possible to travel from Belomorsk to the Solovetski Archipelago, see *Kem, below*. Every Saturday and Sunday in summer, the boat called the *Belomore* makes the return trip. The boat trip costs $11, while a one-day guided tour of Solovetski costs $18. The boat departs from the port which can be reached on bus No 4, getting off at the stop Naplavnoi Most. The company Akva-Tur Service manages the boat, tel: 412 20, 412 93, 226 05 or 230 72.

Myagreka   Мягрека   823km

Just before reaching Kem, you cross over the Kem River. About 20km upstream is the three-unit Podduzhemski hydro-electric station which is praised in a three-storey Soviet era billboard on the side of a housing block in Kem beside the Kem Tourist Hotel.

KEM   Кемь   835km
Population: 22,000   Telephone area code: 814 58 (345 81)

Even on a warm day, Kem feels cold. The grey, badly kept buildings all huddle beside giant boulders and treeless mounds protecting themselves against wild winds from the Belomore Sea. The town sits at the mouth of the Kem River and, although it has been in existence since the 15th century, it was only with the construction of a railway in 1916, that the town's population grew. The importance of the railway is demonstrated by the town's only public hall, the Railway Workers' Palace of Culture.

The town has only two places of medium interest, but is a launching place for a gem of Russia, Solovetski Archipelago.

Within Kem, it is worth visiting the Museum of Local Studies, ul Vitsyna 12, tel: 225 71, open 09.00–17.30, closed Monday and Tuesday, with its collection of indigenous Karelian art and political prisoner memorabilia. Opposite the museum is the wooden Cathedral of the Ascension (Uspenski) (1711–17) with an eight-sided tent roof on the main cathedral and two side chapels with tent-shaped roofs. In the cathedral's five-tiered iconostasis, dating from the end of the 18th century, are icons painted in the 17th-century Novgorodian style.

To get to the museum and cathedral take bus No 3 from the station to its terminus beside the cathedral. The bus route takes you through the centre of town, along the foreshore and past a small port. The main port is 10km downstream and, while there is a railway line there, it is only for freight. To get to the main port, in Podvore village, take bus No 1 from the railway station.

Getting there and away
The most convenient trains on this route are listed below.

Origin	Dist, km	Train no & name	Travel time	Depart	Arrive	Destination
Kem	85	15	1hr 11min	07.18	08.29	Belomorsk
Murmansk	610	15	11hr 30min	19.24	06.54	Kem
Belomorsk	85	22	55min	09.15	10.10	Kem
Kem	610	16	12hr 27min	0.52	13.19	Murmansk

Where to stay
The only hotel and restaurant in town is the basic 80-bed Kem Tourist Hotel run by the very friendly director, G Volokhova. Its address is ul Energetikov 22, tel: 203 85, $7 twin share/person. Soviet era literature refers to a hotel at ul Energetikov 12 but this is now closed.

Solovetski Archipelago
Fifty kilometres to the east of Kem is one of northern Russia's great undiscovered treasures, Solovetski Archipelago. The archipelago consists of six main islands and tens of smaller ones in the middle of the White Sea just 150km south of the Polar Circle. It is the site of the Spaso-Preobrazhensky (meaning "Redeemer and Transfiguration") Monastery, one of the world's largest monasteries. Its significance is probably only comparable with Grecian Aphon or one of the great English abbeys. The archipelago, with its total land area of only 300km^2 and 564 lakes, contains over 170 architectural monuments and is listed by UNESCO.

The islands' isolation and beauty made them a sacred place for ancient people as indicated by the large ceremonial rock circles which can still be seen today.

While the monastery and other churches are open every day, the museum works 08.00–18.00 Wednesday, Saturday and Sunday, 10.00–18.00 Tuesday, Thursday and Friday, closed Monday.

As there is a very basic hotel on the island, you can stay there in moderate comfort for up to three days without getting bored. As there are tours to the island from Arkhangelsk and Belomorsk, you may be able to catch a boat there.

The best months to visit Solovetski are July and August when it is about 15°C. It is only possible to visit the island from June to September because after that the lake freezes. Unfortunately, the ice is not stable and skiing to Solovetski is very dangerous.

Getting to the island requires planning but is worth the effort. You can go by boat from Arkhangelsk or Kem, or by plane from Arkhangelsk. From Kem, you have to join a group of Russians from the Turbaza Kem who charter a boat for a day. These groups of 15 to 20 people usually go once a week, starting at 08.00 and returning at 21.00. The $44 day trip includes transport from the hotel to the port, return boat trip which takes 2hr 30min one way, and a six-hour tour of the Solovetski Monastery and region. For details, call the Turbaza Kem on tel: 203 85. From Arkhangelsk, there is a weekly passenger boat taking 14 hours and costing $14 one way. For information on the boat, go to the river station or contact the service desk at Pur-Navolok Hotel, nab Severnoi Dviny 88, tel/fax: 436 509. Flights between Arkhangelsk and Solovetski run three times a week and cost $25 one way.

Loukhi   Лоухи   1,000km

There is a 84km branch line to the settlement at Sofporog (Софпорог) to the west. The town's miserable highlights are a museum and a fox fur farm.

Polyarny Krug   Полярный Круг   1,055km

This little station sits on the Arctic Circle and there is a small monument to mark the exact location of the circle.

Zhemchuzhaya   Жемчужая   1,129km

This station derives its name from *zhemchug,* meaning "pearls" in Russian. The nearby Belomore Sea grows some of the world's best pearls due to its year round low temperature and low saltiness. Like gold-mining regions, the northern banks of the Belomore Sea, where most of the pearls are grown, are closed areas and only those with a special pass can enter.

Ruchi-Karelskie   Ручьи-Карельские   1,140km

There is a 97km branch line to Alakurtti (Алакуртти) and eventually this line will be extended to join the Finnish rail terminus at Salla.

Kandalaksha   Кандалакша   1,168km

Kandalaksha has existed since the 11th century when it was a stop on the post road to fortified Kola, near Murmansk. Its small size and strategic importance led to it being sacked and burnt down by the Swedish in 1590 and by the British in 1855. It again saw fighting between 1918 and 1920 when British and American soldiers fought here to stop the advance of the communists towards Murmansk. These incidents make the museum worth a visit.

Today, it is the centre of a major sporting area and the yearly highlight is a 70km cross-country skiing marathon. Two kilometres from town is a ski resort with a chair lift, and the large, standard Spolokhi tourist hotel. Nearby is the Kandalaksha Reserve, which includes islands and small areas of the continental coast of Kandalaksha Bay in the Belomore Sea, as well as parts of the Murmansk coast in the Barents Sea. The reserve protects the nesting area of seabirds, particularly the eider.

Near the station is the steam engine SO17-2874 built in 1948.

Pinozero   Пинозеро   1,189km

There is an 117km branch line to the iron-ore mining centre Kovdor (Ковдор) in the east. Consequently, freight cars are often backed up at Pinozero.

Polyarnye Zori   Полярные Зори   1,196km
Telephone area code: 815 55

About 15km to the west of Polyarny Zori on the shores of Lake Imandra is the only nuclear power plant in the Murmansk region. While the location of the Kola nuclear power plant may seem strange – being in the middle of nowhere – it is in fact located in the centre of a 240km diameter ring of the industrial cities of Monchegorsk, Kirovsk, Apatity and Kandalaksha. You can organise a tour of the plant with several days' notice by calling Petr Danilov, Public Affairs Manager, tel: 681 40, 639 10.

Beside the station is the Museum of the Polar Partisan, open 10.00–17.00, closed Wednesday and Thursday. The town's only hotel is Hotel Nevsky Berega, ul Lomomosov 1, tel: 641 51, $30 double room. It has a restaurant.

Apatity Апатиты 1,260km

The town is named after the mineral, apatite, which is used to make mineral fertilisers. You can see parts of a 2km apatite open-cut mine on the left of the railway. The town's massive Apatity chemical and fertiliser plant employs 15,000 workers.

Apatity contains the large Kola Science Centre which consists of ten research institutes, the Kola Regional Seismological Centre, a publishing house, enormous scientific library, a network of observatories and monitoring stations, two research vessels, and a design office to build experimental equipment. In 1995 the Nordic Study Centre was opened on the campus of the Kola Science Centre. Its main activities include publishing environmental information, combined research and ecological tourism and organising international projects such as student exchanges, seminars and expeditions. For information on its programmes, contact Alexander A Baklanov, Ekonord Centre, Box 220, Kola Science Centre, ul Znovieva 14-65, 184200 Apatity, Murmansk Region, tel: (81555) 377 62, fax: 7970 153 07, or tel:/fax: (4778) 914 118, email soceco@glas.apc.org.

There is a 23km branch line to the east which terminates at the mining town of Kirovsk-Murmansk (Кировск-Мурманский). This town boasts the world's most northerly polar-alpine botanical gardens on nearby Mount Budyavrchor and the Iukspor meteorological station which studies avalanches. It also has a House-museum of Sergei Kirov, who directed the development of apatite deposits in 1929, before becoming the Mayor of St Petersburg. Near the town is the Khibiny Mountain Range, popular with skiers as it has the region's best downhill skiing resort in northeast Russia. Accommodation is available at the large, basic Khibiny Hotel.

From Kirovsk-Murmansk there is a freight railway line that runs for about 50km along the Khibiny Mountain Range, terminating in the mining town of Revda (Ревда). The Apatity City Administration, pl Lenina 1, tel: (81533) 305 76, 306 01, 315 04, 348 30, fax: 327 59, is attempting to organise tourist trains along this remote route.

Nefelinovye Peski Нефелиновые Пески 1,285km

Even in the middle of summer, you will see snow on the Khibiny Mountain Range to the right.

Olengorsk Оленгорск 1,333km

The town is focused around a copper and nickel ore dressing plant, and the maintenance of a 31km branch line to Monchegorsk (Мончегорск). This 68,200-inhabitant city is far more interesting than Olengorsk because it was created to be a model city in the late 1930s when the ore deposits were discovered.

The town's cultural life is well catered for with the Metalist Palace of Culture, a Museum of Coloured Glass and a Museum of Local Studies. The town has the large basic Hotel Laplandiya, pro Metallurgov 32, tel: 245 26, $10 twin share/person which is often full of sportsmen who visit the nearby Lapland Nature Reserve, and the standard Hotel Sever, pro Metallurgov 4, tel: 226 55.

Don't be too inquisitive around Olengorsk because you may be arrested as a spy: nearby is one of Russia six 300m-long early warning Hen radar stations which track inbound nuclear missiles.

About 87km to the east of here is the small town of Lovozero. This town of only 1,500 residents is mainly inhabited by the reindeer-herding Sami indigenous people who were relocated from all around the Kola region to this town in the 1960s. The town's greatest attraction is the Museum of Sami Culture. While the restaurant/hotel is technically closed, accommodation can still be organised there. Ask the staff at the museum about this or get one of the Murmansk travel agents to organise it. The town also boasts one of the best bakeries outside Murmansk. To get there you can either catch one of several daily buses from Olengorsk or a once-a-day bus from Murmansk. The trip from Murmansk takes about four hours.

Kola   Кола   1,435km

About 2km before you reach Kola station, on the right you can see the small town of Kola. This ancient town is steeped in history, being first mentioned in 1264. Its trading importance grew and, by 1550, it became a fortified town. Its defences were strong and successfully withstood Swedish attacks in 1589 and 1591. Its isolation made it ideal as a place of exile and its population was fortified with prisoners from the mid-16th century until 1804. The remains of its historic past are restricted to a small museum and the crumbling fortress walls and moat which enclose the well-preserved Cathedral of the Annunciation. The church houses a small museum, open 10.00–17.00, closed Monday.

As Kola is just 12km south of Murmansk, it can be reached easily by local train or on bus No 106 for a half day excursion. Neither train nor bus goes into Kola so you have to walk for about 15 minutes.

After leaving Kola, the train follows the eastern shore of the fjord-like Kola Gulf. This waterway is 57km long, 7km wide at its entrance, narrowing to 1km in the south near the town of Kola. In the north, the gulf's sides drop quickly to 200–300m while in the south a gradual drop has created a few beaches crowded with rusting hulks. The majority are excess World War II freighters. As Murmansk does not have large ship-cutting equipment or a furnace to melt the scrap metal, the ships simply accumulate. In 1996, the Barents Council decided to make the construction of a ship-scrapping yard in Belokamennaya Bay one of their 14 priority projects. However, due to Russia's cash shortage, it is unlikely that the yard will be built in the next few years.

MURMANSK   Мурманск   1,445km
Population: 468,000   Telephone area code: 815 00

Murmansk has an exotic reputation. It is the largest city in the Arctic Circle, it bathes under midnight sun from May 17 to July 27, and is in perpetual darkness for 52 days of the year as part of its nine-month-long winter. It is also the location of Russia's greatest naval fleet and a place where both English and American soldiers died.

However, Murmansk is a bit of a disappointment. It looks just like any other drab Soviet city, the only difference being its constant wind.

Founded on September 21 1916 with the name of Romanov-on-Murman, the city is relatively new. The Russian name hid the fact that the site was selected by the British as a base to supply material for the Russian's war effort in World War I. Its greatest appeal was that it sits on the Kola Gulf which never freezes due to a branch of the Gulf Stream.

The small city was completely destroyed in World War II although it was never occupied. A well-thought-out plan was produced for post-war reconstruction and the result can be seen in the three-tiered structure of the city as it climbs up the nearby hill. On the lowest level is the industrial zone and port, the centre level contains the station and central shopping district, while the third level consists of high-rise apartment blocks.

Following the war, the city was closed as it became home to the Red Banner Northern Fleet which at its height contained hundreds of warships. Murmansk opened its doors to foreigners in the early 1990s and, although today authorities are still not overly receptive to individual travellers exploring the 20km-long city unescorted, they are getting used to it.

Getting there and away
By air   In summer there are regular international flights to Oslo, and Tromsø/Kirkenes (Norway) by Braathens Air Transport, SAS and Finnair. As many oil workers depart here for rigs in Russia's desolate north, it may be possible to hitch a lift to somewhere very unusual.

By boat   It is possible to go the 810km to Arkhangelsk by boat but there are only two or three passenger boats a month in the sailing season. In addition, foreigners need to organise permission with the security authorities as the boat travels along militarily sensitive stretches of the coastline. Information can be had from the sea passenger terminal, poezd Portovy 25.

By bus   There are daily bus services from Murmansk to Ivalo (800 Finnish marks one way) in Finnish Lapland and one to Kirkenes in northern Norway. Both of these towns are a long way from railway lines – Rovaniemi and Narvik respectively.

By rail   There are three daily trains to St Petersburg, and two to Moscow via Petrozavodsk. There is one daily train to Vologda which travels along the Belomorsk–Obozerskaya line with a carriage which separates for Arkhangelsk. For information on this train see *Obozerskaya–Belomorsk, page 224*. There is also a train to Nikel/Pechenga, see *Point of interest, page 216*.

The most convenient long-distance trains on this route are listed below.

Origin	Dist, km	Train no & name	Travel time	Depart	Arrive	Destination
St Petersburg (Moscow)	401	658	9hr 25min	21.50	07.15	Petrozavodsk
Kem	610	16	12hr 27min	00.52	13.19	Murmansk
Murmansk	610	15	11hr 30min	19.24	06.54	Kem
Petrozavodsk	1,044	16	21hr 18min	16.01	13.19	Murmansk
Murmansk	1,044	15	21hr 6min	19.24	16.30	Petrozavodsk
Moscow (Leningrad)	1,964	16	36hr 11min	00.30	13.19	Murmansk
Murmansk	1,964	15	36hr 33min	19.24	08.57	Moscow (Leningrad)

Where to stay
The best hotel in town is the excellent Hotel Ogni Murmanskaya, ul Furmanova 11, tel: 598 778, fax: in Finland (3589) 4929 2459. The hotel is Russian run but up to the best Western standards and facilities. A double room costs $120. The hotel is near the 69th Parallel Hotel and to get to it, take trolleybus No 3 which runs down pro Lenina to its terminus on ul Radishcheva. Walk back the way the bus came for 200m and you reach ul Furmanova. If you are booking a room at Hotel Ogni Murmanskaya, it is best to get them to meet you at the station.

The worst value hotel is the standard Hotel Arktika, pro Lenina 82, tel: 557 411, $45 single, $55 twin share/person. Opposite it is the standard Hotel Meridian, ul Vorovskovo 5/23, tel: 557 876, $21 twin share/person.

A good choice is the standard Hotel Polyarnye Zori, ul Knipovicha 17, tel: 552 470, $37 single, $16 twin share/person. The price of accommodation includes breakfast. Nearby is basic Hotel Moryak, pro Knipozicha 23, tel: 555 527, $13 single, $15 twin share/person, while on the outskirts of town is the standard Hotel 69th Parallel, pro Lyzhnyi 14, tel: 565 645, $25 double room. While the first three hotels can be reached by walking from the station, the best way to get to the 69th Parallel Hotel is on trolleybuses No 1 or 6 from the centre heading south. The standard Hotel Administration, ul Sofi Perovski 3, tel: 559 237, charges $80 a double room. All the above hotels have restaurants.

There are two other basic hotels in the city but in early 1996 foreigners were not allowed to stay in them. This restriction may be lifted in the future. They are Hotel Shakhter, ul Pushkinskaya 10 and Hotel Kolos, ul Baumana 38.

What to see

There is really not a great deal to see in Murmansk except for monuments and museums. The best of the monuments is the Giant Watcher who symbolises eternal vigilance. The area is called the Valley of Glory and it includes an eternal flame and several other World War II monuments. The Watcher, nicknamed Alyosha, can be seen from the station as it overlooks it and the harbour. To get to it catch trolleybus No 3 or 4 to the north and get off at the first stop on top of the hill.

Murmansk is richly endowed with museums. It has one of Russia's largest regional museums with three floors of exhibits at pro Lenina 90, tel: 520 379, open 11.00–18.00, closed Friday. The Art Museum, ul Kominterna 13, tel: 572 834, is open 11.00–18.00, closed Monday. The Polar Institute's Museum of

---

RUSSIA'S FISHING CAPITAL

Murmansk is home to the Russian Far North Fishing Fleet, one of the country's major suppliers of tinned and frozen fish. In the past, the vast majority of the fish were caught by huge floating fish factory ships but nowadays, more is being caught by the economical, medium sized fishing vessels.

These 1,000 ton ships spend two weeks at sea where they can catch up to 200 tons. Following the fish can take them in a radius bounded by Spitsburger, Novaya Zemlya and the Barents Sea, and can find them battling mild 5–8m waves in the Barents Sea or horrendous 30m waves in the Arctic Sea.

Sailors who fall overboard have a 15-minute life expectancy in the 0°C water but, as most are lost at night and in storms, being found is rare. It is cold comfort to know that falling overboard does not usually attract a punishment as the water is sufficient penalty, but your superior will be reprimanded and imprisoned if a severe safety breach has occurred.

The problem of leaking nuclear waste dumped into the Barents Sea by the Soviet Navy is taken seriously and all fishing vessels are fitted with radioactivity detectors. Officially, there are no areas closed for this reason but fishing vessels are prohibited from entering breeding areas and military zones around Murmansk's numerous naval bases.

Marine Life and Oceanography at ul Knipovicha 6 is theoretically open 10.00–17.00, closed Saturday and Sunday, but you may have to book to get in. The Museum of the Polar Olympics is at ul Knipovicha 23a. To the north of the city in the suburb of Rosta (Роста) is the Museum of the North Fleet, ul Tortseva 1, tel: 332 578, open 09.00–17.00, closed Tuesday and Wednesday. This is an excellent military museum and well worth visiting. To get there, catch bus No 3 from the station and get off at the fourth street (ul Tortseva) after crossing the railway line. Turn left down ul Tortseva and the museum is 100m on the left. In the southern suburb of Nagornoe (Нагорное) is the boring Museum of Fire Fighting at ul Shevchenko 32.

There are rumoured to be the graves of British and American interventionist troops at the cemetery on Berkhne-Postinskoe opposite Srednee Lake. However, it is so overgrown that it is impossible to find graves that are more than 20 years old.

Getting assistance

Travel agents   Intourist offers trips around the city, boat trips on the Kola Gulf and visits to fish processing factories. Each three-hour trip costs $55 for three people. Intourist is located in both Hotel Polyarnye Zori, tel: 554 385, 554 372, and 69th Parallel Hotel.

Bus   The main bus station is on the north side of the railway station, ul Kominterna 16.

Rail   The railway ticket office is separated with tickets for trains departing that day only being sold in the north side of the station while tickets for future departures are sold over the road opposite the station in the main ticket office.

Diplomatic representation   Norwegian consulate, ul Sofi Petrovskoi 5, tel: 510 037 (also honarary Swedish Consulate); Finnish consulate, ul Karla Marksa 25A, tel: 543 275.

What's in the region

Murmansk's second best military monument is a large memorial complex at Cape Abram (Абрам-мыс) village. The complex, dedicated to the 1st Anti Aircraft Corps who defended the harbour during 97 German air raids, incorporates the old gun positions, aircraft, radar and missiles. Abram Cape is directly opposite the centre of Murmansk on the opposite side of the Kola Gulf. To get there you either have to drive around via Kola or take a water taxi from the river station. Tours of the complex are organised by the Veterans Association who can be contacted on tel: 555 778, 15.00–17.00 weekdays.

Since the film Red October with Sean Connery, the Polyarny submarine pens, 45km north of Murmansk, have been made famous. While it is impossible to visit the military town of Polyarny (Полярный), much of the North Fleet and the fleet's headquarters can be seen at Severomorsk (Североморск), 31km north of Murmansk. Severomorsk, which has a population of 67,000, was known as Vaenga (Ваенга) until 1951, and this is the current name of the railway station. The town has been completely rebuilt after a massive explosion in 1984 at the fleet's principle munitions depot. The explosion was so large that, initially, Western intelligence agencies suspected a nuclear detonation.

While Severomorsk is theoretically closed, no-one checks documents on the hourly buses from the bus station beside the Murmansk railway station. Severomorsk can also be reached by train but the service is irregular. If you arrive by boat you will go past the naval port and see dozens of Mikes, Yankees and 300-metre Typhoons – all classes of submarine.

The major attractions of the city are the World War II K-21 Submarine Museum and Safonova Military Aircraft Museum. It is necessary to organise a visit to see these, so contact Intourist.

Point of interest
For those not satisfied with reaching Murmansk, it is possible to go even further north by train. Just south of Murmansk, at Kola, there is a 196km branch line to the northwest, terminating at Pechenga. Just before reaching Pechenga, the line again branches to Nikel, very close to both the Norwegian and Finnish borders.

Pechenga (Печенга) was founded in 1533 with the construction of Pechenga Monastery. The ownership of the town and region oscillated between Russia and Finland due to the region's massive copper and nickel deposits. Pechenga railway station is 9km from the town, which sits on the junction of the Pechenga River and Pechenga Harbour. The railway actually goes on a further dozen kilometres or so to the town of Liinnahamari (Лиинахамари) although this stop is not marked on railway maps nor in timetables. The reason for this is that there is a large naval base there. There are plans to build a large commercial oil and gas port which will eventually open this region to foreigners.

The town of Nikel (Никель) is located near Lake Buets-Iarvi and, as can be guessed from its name, nickel ore processing is the town's main industry. Nikel is a few kilometres from the Norwegian border and the nearest large Norwegian town is Kirkenes (population 8,000) about 50km away. From Kirkenes you can get a regular bus down the Norwegian coast to the city of Fauske. This is the northern end of the railway which runs to Oslo. You can also catch the Hurtigruta Ferry which runs from Kirkenes to Bergen. From Kirkenes you can catch a local bus to the Norwegian town of Neiden, 5km from the Finnish border. From the border there are daily long-distance buses to Finland's capital, Helsinki. To get from Neiden to the Finnish border, you can catch a taxi. A taxi from Kirkenes to the Finnish border is about 450 Norwegian kroner or, if you book a taxi from Finland to pick you up, it is cheaper, costing about 260 Finnish marks. For a Finnish taxi, call Mr Esa Tarkiainen on (358) 697 672 551.

Providing you have a valid visa and passport, there will be no problems crossing the Russian–Norwegian border.

To get to Nikel, you can catch a daily train from Murmansk. This trip takes 8hr 27min, giving the train an average speed of just 23km/h. Fortunately, this railway is destined to be upgraded following an 1996 agreement by the Barents Council which made it one of their 14 priority infrastructure projects in Russia.

About 46km east of Nikel, at the rail junction of Luostari (Луостари), the train breaks up, with some carriages heading 14km south to Pechenga and the rest travelling onwards to Nikel. From this point onwards, armed guards in watch towers are a common sight as this border zone is militarily sensitive with its radar and anti-aircraft defences. To avoid any problems, ensure that you have either or both Pechenga and Nikel written on your visa.

As you approach the area, you will also notice that the trees are sick and the rivers are dead due to the industrial pollution.

There are four buses a week to both Pechenga and Nikel from Murmansk and they take 2hr 30min and 4hr respectively.

MOSCOW–ARKHANGELSK
Route highlights
In the first eight hours of travel you pass a number of towns worth exploring including the ancient Aleksandrov, Yaroslavl and Vologda. However, from Vologda to Arkhangelsk there is very little to see as the railway was cut through forests in a straight line rather than through the region's towns which are mostly on the Severnaya Dvinya and Vaga Rivers.

Travel suggestions
A good way of exploring the region is to take an overnight train from Moscow to Vologda, explore Vologda during the day, and then take an overnight train to Arkhangelsk (or vice versa).

Trains
The most convenient long-distance trains on this route are listed below.

Origin	Dist, km	Train no & name	Travel time	Depart	Arrive	Destination
Moscow (Yaroslav)	495	148 Vologda	9hr 5min	22.45	07.40	Vologda
Vologda	495	147 Vologda	9hr 15min	21.35	05.50	Moscow (Yaroslav)
Vologda	639	16	12hr 30min	20.40	09.10	Arkhangelsk
Arkhangelsk	639	15	12hr 35min	19.10	07.45	Vologda
Arkhangelsk	1,134	15	21hr 20min	19.10	16.30	Moscow (Yaroslav)
Moscow (Yaroslav)	1,134	16	21hr	12.10	09.10	Arkhangelsk

Route description

Moscow   Москва   0km
Trains for Vologda and Arkhangelsk depart from Yaroslav station, pl Komsomolskaya 5, tel: 921 0817, 266 0301, 266 0595. The metro station is Komsomolskaya.

The first 357km of the route from Moscow to Yaroslavl, through **Sergiev-Posad**, **Aleksandrov** and **Rostov-Yaroslavski**, is covered in *Chapter Thirteen, pages 230–50*. The *Passing through* section under each of these cities discusses sights you will see from the train's window.

Danilov   Данилов   357km
This town is at a junction with railways to the north and to the east. Trains for the Trans-Siberian turn right from here.

The town was first mentioned in the late 1500s when it was called Danilov's *sloboda* or Danilov's "tax-free settlement". Such settlements were a common way of attracting workers and artisans until the tax reforms of the 17th century.

The town contains the Kazan God of Mother Cathedral which was consecrated in 1918. In this early stage of the communist state, Lenin was forced for expediency to tolerate such practices but once power was consolidated, churches were rapidly closed.

Gryazovets   Грязовец   449km
This town is the butter capital of the region and even includes a butter churn in the town's coat of arms. Today, the factories have disappeared but the town is still famous for its low-fat milk powder. Visit the local museum to see an amazing range of milk separators, butter churns and butter pats. The museum also has a collection of the local traditional handicraft of wooden plates and Vologda-stitched crocheted items, although a better range is seen in Vologda.

VOLOGDA   Вологда   495km
Population: 290,000   Telephone area code: 844 2
While this town was built over 1,000 years, it only takes half a day to see it unless you are interested in churches. It is an attractive town sitting on the banks of the Vologda River, but it is spread over a large area, making getting around difficult. The town was first mentioned in 1147 but it was only when a trading agreement with England was signed in 1555 for goods to be shipped north to Arkhangelsk via Vologda that the town flourished.

As well as being a staging post, Vologda developed its own local industry and one successful export which is still popular today is Vologda lace which is now produced to make bedspreads, curtains and napkins.

From the 1800s, political exiles were sent here, the most famous being Lenin's mother, who stayed here from 1913 to 1914.

Getting there and away
Getting to Vologda is easy. There are over ten daily trains from Moscow as the station is at a major rail junction. As well as the trains listed below, there is one daily train to Murmansk, taking 38hr 20min, and two daily trains to St Petersburg taking 14hr.

The most convenient long-distance trains on this route are listed below.

Origin	Dist, km	Train no & name	Travel time	Depart	Arrive	Destination
Moscow (Yaroslavski)	495	148 Vologda	9hr 5min	22.45	07.40	Vologda
Vologda	495	147 Vologda	9hr 15min	21.35	05.50	Moscow (Yaroslavski)
Vologda	639	16	12hr 30min	20.40	09.10	Arkhangelsk
Arkhangelsk	639	15	12hr 35min	19.10	07.45	Vologda

Where to stay
The best hotel is the excellent Hotel Oktyabr, ul Oktyabrskaya 25, tel: 201 45, $13 twin share/person. This hotel is only a few years old and replaces the now closed Hotel Oktyabr at ul Karla Marksa. Take Trolleybus No 1 from in front of the railway station. The standard Hotel Sputnik, ul Puteiskaya 14a, tel: 227 52, $24 twin share/person, and standard Hotel Vologda, ul Mira 92, tel: 230 79, $15 twin share/person, are both a five-minute walk from the station. Close to the old part of town is the standard Hotel Zolotoi Yakor (formerly Hotel Severnaya), pro Sovetski 6, tel: 214 54, $14 twin share/person. The remotest hotel is the basic Hotel Sport, ul Mayakovskovo 26, tel: 507 61. There are restaurants in all the hotels.

Getting around
The old part of Vologda is located about 2km from the station around the Vologda River. To get to this part, take bus No 1 from in front of the railway

station (or No 4 from the main street to the Arkhangelsk side of the station) to its terminus at the Vologda River.

What to see

The town is littered with old buildings and the best is the well-preserved kremlin which today houses the Museum of Local Studies, ul S Orlova 15, tel: 222 83, open 10.00–17.00, closed Monday. At the front of the kremlin is the operating Cathedral of St Sofia.

Another interesting building is the House-museum of Peter the Great, pro Sovetski 7. There is an artists' Exhibition Hall at ul M I Ulyanovoi 37. There are also a number of monuments to heroes of Vologda, including the cosmonaut P I Belyaev, aircraft designer S V Ilyushin, and the poet K N Batyushkov.

If you are interested in railways, there is an SO-class steam engine on a plinth near the locomotive depot. To get there simply go over the footbridge over the rail yard and you will see it on the right.

Vologda's City Day celebrations are held on the last Sunday in June.

Getting assistance

Travel agents   Vologda Tours & Excursions, pl Kremlovskaya 8, tel: 225 93, 243 89.
Air   Aeroflot, ul Gertsena 45.
Bus   Bus tickets can be bought at the bus station in front of the railway station or at the bus ticket office, ul Gorkovo 86.
Rail   Tickets can be bought at the station and at the advance purchase rail ticket office, ul Gertsena 45.

What's in the region

Two kilometres to the northeast of Vologda is the Prilutski-Saviour Monastery. Work started on the monastery in 1371 and it is dominated by the cubic Cathedral of the Saviour with its five domes and four pillars. It is surrounded by a steep two-tier gallery on three sides and a four-tier belfry on the other. If you don't have time to visit the monastery, you get an excellent photo opportunity of it on the left as you go over the Vologda River. If you are looking out of the wrong side of the train, all you will see is the airport.

To get to the Prilutski-Saviour Monastery, you can go by either bus or train. Bus No 3 departs from in front of Vologda railway station and passes through pl Vozdrozhdeniya before going past the monastery. Bus No 103 from the railway station also passes by the monastery. A local train departs from Vologda railway station northwards and the stop about 1km after the monastery is Rybkino (Рыбкино).

Kharovskaya   Харовская   584km

One of the town's wood-working factories specialises in making musical instrument components, primarily for pianos and accordions. There is information about this factory and the glass factory founded in 1903 in the museum of local studies.

Ertsevo   Ерцево   684km

During the Soviet era, Ertsevo was infamous for its nearby harsh P-233 prison camp complex. Not a nice place to visit.

Konosha   Коноша   707km

There is a major branch line from this town to the northeast which leads to the remote, inhospitable but resource-rich regions around Kotlas, Vorkuta and Syktyvkar. Much of the 1,500km of rail line to these cities was built by *gulag* labourers in the 1930s to 1950s.

Nyandoma   Няндома   793km

About 80km to the east from Nyandoma on R2 highway is the ancient town of Kargopol (Каргополь), famous for its clay toy whistles. Archaeological excavations have discovered duck-shaped whistles that are over 5,000 years old. Local craftspeople still produce the toys today, and while you can visit the 13,000-inhabitant town to see their work on one of the regular buses from Nyandoma, excellent examples are on display in most museums in the region and also in Moscow and St Petersburg.

Puksa   Пукса   906km

From here there is a 22km branch line to the west, terminating at Navolok (Наволок) station. The surrounding town is called Oksovski (Оксовский) and its main industry is a pulp mill.

Plesetskaya   Плесецкая   918km

Plesetsk (Плесецк) is Russia's most active cosmodrome and at one time was the world's busiest spaceport. The Plesetsk Complex is spread over 100km and includes four major complexes and nine launching pads. Most of the cosmodrome's launches are military so the area is well protected by surface-to-air missile installations and patrolling guards.

Unfortunately, nothing of the spaceport can be seen from the station. However, it is possible to glimpse the space city of Mirny (Мирный) which is 1km to the right of the railway, just after leaving Plesetskaya station. There is a branch line from Plesetsk to the city and another 60km of freight railway in the area to the various space complexes and pads.

Obozerskaya   Обозеррская   1,001km

The branch line to Murmansk starts from here. If you are on the Arkhangelsk–Murmansk train carriage, you will wait directly in front of the station for the train for the rest of your journey. As the small village's most interesting place is the lime factory, let's hope your wait isn't too long.

Kholmogorskaya   Холмогорская   1,047km

This town is named after the ancient and interesting town of Kholmogory, over 70km to the northeast. There are no roads from this little railway siding so go to Arkhangelsk if you want to get to Kholmogory.

Isakogorka   Исакогорка   1,120km

This station is the main rail yard for Arkhangelsk. Just past the station on the right are several operating steam engines which are used to provide steam and hot water for the rail workshops.

Many passengers get off at Isakogorka to change trains for nearby Severodvinsk (Северодвинск). This 249,000-inhabitant city, which is 49km away, was called Molotovsk from 1938 to 1957 after the disgraced Soviet

Foreign Minister who signed the 1939 Ribbentrop-Molotov Pact, dividing up Poland with the Nazis. Today, Severodvinsk is a ship-building centre and naval port which contains many decommissioned nuclear submarines.

Visitors to Severodvinsk are advised not to sit on the toilet for too long due to potential radioactive exposure. In 1990, an unknown quantity of liquid radioactive waste from the Zvezdochka shipyard was dumped into the Severodvinsk sewer system. The radiation level at the sewage processing plant surged to about 200 times the normal background level and is now 5–10 times the level. As a result of the incident, waste from the processing plant can no longer be used as fertiliser.

Severodvinsk is a closed city and you risk arrest if you arrive without its name written on your visa.

Bakaritsa   Бакарица   1,124km
After this station the train passes over the Severnaya Dvina River on a 800m bridge which offers a fabulous view of the downstream Severnaya Dvina river delta, port and beach. Swimming at this beach is not advisable as the upstream paper mill is notorious for its "accidentally" concentrated chlorine waste discharges, a practice that is made even worse by their failure to inform residents of the emissions.

ARKHANGELSK   Архангельск   1,134km
Population: 416,000   Telephone area code: 818 22
The city was founded in 1584 near the mouth of the Severnaya Dvina River as it flows into the Belomore Sea. In 1613 its name was changed from Novokholmogory to Arkhangelsk after the nearby Monastery of the Archangel Michael which was founded in the 12th century. When Peter the Great became tsar in 1682, Arkhangelsk was Russia's only outlet to the sea. In an effort to develop sea links he ordered the construction of a fort and building of wharves. Trade slowly developed until, by the late 1700s, Arkhangelsk was Russia's largest lumber port.

During World War II, Arkhangelsk was a major sea port both for receiving Lend Lease supplies from the allies and as a base for the North Sea Fleet. Consequently, it was targeted by the Germans and from August to September 1942, over 21,000 fire bombs were dropped, which burnt the mostly wooden city down.

Today, Arkhangelsk is a major port and the city is spread out over a number of islands in the Severnaya Dvina delta. Arkhangelsk is blocked by ice for up to 190 days per year but with the use of icebreakers, its port stays operational for most of the year.

Getting there and away
By boat   It is possible to travel the 810km from Murmansk by boat but there are only two or three passenger boats a month in the sailing season. In addition, foreigners need to organise permission with the security authorities as the boat travels along militarily sensitive stretches of the coast.
By train   There are two daily trains to Moscow, one daily train to St Petersburg via Vologda taking 28hr 25min, and one carriage to Murmansk taking 38hr 30min. For information on the carriage between Arkhangelsk and Murmansk, see *Obozerskaya–Belomorsk, page 224*. While you are waiting in the railway

building, check the digital radiation meter – if it shows 15 microRads/hour or below, it's safe.

The most convenient long-distance trains on this route are listed below.

Origin	Dist, km	Train no & name	Travel time	Depart	Arrive	Destination
Vologda	639	16	12hr 30min	20.40	09.10	Arkhangelsk
Arkhangelsk	639	15	12hr 35min	19.10	07.45	Vologda
Arkhangelsk	1,134	15	21hr 20min	19.10	16.30	Moscow (Yaroslav)
Moscow (Yaroslav)	1,134	16	21hr	12.10	09.10	Arkhangelsk

Where to stay

There are three hotels in Arkhangelsk. Within walking distance of the station is the basic Hotel Belomorskaya, ul Timme 3, tel: 462 667, $27 twin share/person. Near the embankment is the better, but not by much, standard Hotel Dvina, pro Troitski 52, tel: 268 502, 495 502, $25 twin share/person. To get to the Hotel Dvina take trolleybus No 2 or 4 to the embankment and it is then a five-minute walk. The third option is the excellent Hotel Pur-Navolok, nab Severnoi Dviny 88, tel: 430 126, 432 389, tel:/fax: 436 509, but is very expensive at $120 twin share/person. All hotels have restaurants or buffets.

Getting around

It is not easy getting around Arkhangelsk as the main part of the city, which runs from the railway station down the main street of ul Voskresenaya to the river embankment, is over 3km long. Trolleybuses Nos 2 and 4 travel this route. Most of the interesting sights are near the embankment end of the city.

What to see

There are a number of architectural highlights to the town including the former Arcade (1668–84) at nab Severnoi Dviny 86, Solovetskoe Gate (18th century) at nab Severnoi Dviny 77, and Trinity Church (1745) at ul Komsomolskaya 1.

There are two monuments to British and American combatants: one as enemies and one as friends. The enemy monument consists of a British World War I tank left behind when the Interventionist' forces evacuated Arkhangelsk in 1919. This well-maintained tank now sits in the Children's Park on the corner of nab Severnoi Dviny and ul Voskresenskaya. The friendly monument consists of an obelisk in the Kuznechevskoe Cemetery of Allied sailors and soldiers who died in the World War II naval operations to supply the Soviet Union with Lend Lease war material. Next to the well-maintained Allied graves are the graves of Russian soldiers who died in Afghanistan and Chechnya. The Kuznechevskoe Cemetery is on the corner of ul Gaidara and pro Ovodny Kanal.

Unlike many local museums, Arkhangelsk's Museum of Local Studies, pl Lenina 2, open 10.00–18,00, closed Friday, has updated its displays

A poster advertising an exhibition at the Museum of Local Studies

since the collapse of communism. Consequently, you can learn more about the real Russia and Soviet Union than visiting a dozen other museums. Highlights of Arkhangelsk's museum are memorabilia of residents who died fighting in Afghanistan displayed in coffins, a display of ridiculous communist propaganda, and information on the winter deaths of 4,000 out of 6,000 children who were exiled to the area with their parents during the early 1930s. The Museum of Graphic Art next door, pl Lenina 2, open 10.00–17.00, closed Wednesday, is comparatively boring with its two storeys of icons and carved bone artwork. However, the kiosk in the foyer sells a large range of calendars, badges, postcards and books for collectors.

On the river embankment is the Museum of Northern Navigation, nab Severnoi Dviny 80. Opposite it on a pier is the old Finnish built Zapad sailing ship which has an exhibition of World War II convoys and defence of the port in its belly.

There is also an artists' Exhibition Hall, pro Sovetskikh Kosmonavtov 178.

Like all cities, Arkhangelsk has a number of monuments. A particularly interesting one is Russia's first monument to the great Russian genius, Mikhail Lomonosov. Interestingly, the monument was dedicated to his poetry, not his scientific achievements which are more famous.

If you are in Arkhangelsk on the last Sunday in June, you will see the Day of the City celebrations.

What's in the region
About 28km from Arkhangelsk on the right bank of the Severnaya Dvina River is the Malye Karely (Малые Карелы) Open-air Wooden Architecture Museum, open 10.00–17.00, closed Tuesday. This picturesque 140-hectare museum contains more than a hundred wooden buildings from the 17th to 20th centuries which were brought here from all over the region. To get there, you can take a bus No 104 or 111 which terminate at Malye Karely. The trip takes 40 minutes.

There is a 212km branch line from Arkhangelsk to the east to Karpogory (Карпогоры) but there's nothing there to see.

There are boats and planes to Solovetski from here. Details of these are described under *Kem, page 208.*

About 75km south of Arkhangelsk is the village of Lomonosovo (Ломоносово), the birthplace of Russia's greatest scientist M V Lomonosov. His father's house is now a museum devoted to the scientist's early life. Confusingly, the village was called Mishaninskaya prior to Lomonosovo and before the 19th century it was known as Denisovka.

Nearby is the town of Kholmogory (Холмогоры) which sits on the banks of the Severnaya Dvina River. This town was founded in the 14th century as a trading town between Novgorod and the north but, following the contract between the tsar and the English Muscovy Trading Company in 1555, the town blossomed.

Kholmogory is famous for its carved bone handicrafts (see *Point of interest below*) and cattle pedigree stock farm. Kholmogory dairy cattle were developed in the 18th and 19th centuries by cross-breeding local cattle with Holstein-Friesians. The animals are usually white with black markings and acclimatise readily. They have been introduced to many northern and northeastern regions of European Russia and Siberia.

Point of interest

Kholmogory carved bone is a type of traditional Russian bone carving made primarily from walrus tusks and ordinary animal bone but also from sperm whale teeth and mammoth tusks. The techniques were developed in the 18th century and used to produce combs, snuff boxes, decorative boxes, furniture faced with bone, plates and goblets. After suffering a decline in the second half of the 19th century, the craft of Kholmogory carved bone was revived with the founding, in 1930, of a technical school and, in 1932, the M I Lomonosov factory for artistic bone carving. Today, the local artisans produce a range of objects including decorative boxes, cigarette cases, letter openers, pendants and earrings. Examples of these can be seen in the Museums of Local Studies in both Kholmogory and Arkhangelsk.

OBOZERSKAYA–BELOMORSK
(connecting Arkhangelsk with Murmansk)

The Obozerskaya–Belomorsk railway was built secretly just before the Soviet Union's entry into World War II and resulted in a strategic mistake on the part of the German Forces High Command. Until the railway was built, the only rail link with Murmansk was from St Petersburg. Cutting this link was essential to any siege of Murmansk and the easiest point to do so for the invading Germans and Finns was around Petrozavodsk. This action tied up tens of thousands of German and Finnish soldiers and had no effect on Murmansk. Expecting Murmansk to starve into submission, the Germans saw no need for costly frontal attacks; however, soldiers in Murmansk used this time to consolidate their defences. By the time the Germans realised their mistake, taking Murmansk was no longer militarily possible.

The 353km Obozerskaya–Belomorsk railway is best undertaken at night as there is very little to see. The single-track line runs close to the southern end of Onega Bay in the Belomore Sea. In the last few decades, the major industry was logging but nowadays there is very little high-quality timber left. Tragically, what remains is the residue of appalling logging practices.

Most apparent are the piles of abandoned, rusting logging machinery at most of the stations. However, far worse are the dead lakes and streams which have been fouled by logging waste being dumped into them for years. The thousands of tons of rotting vegetation release pollutants into the water which slowly destroy the delicate ecosystem. Consequently, the area is deprived of fish which would be a valuable source of food. This has contributed directly to an exodus of locals. The area is notable for its lack of habitation and even the biggest towns have a population of only a few hundred.

Travel suggestions

The train timetabling on this railway is very odd. The only long-distance train on this route is between Murmansk and Vologda. Interestingly, this train is a historical legacy of World War II when the majority of trains carrying Lend Lease war material from Murmansk stopped at Vologda goods yards where the wagons were split up and joined trains for their final destination. This means locals who live on the Obozerskaya–Belomorsk line are in one of the very few places where there are no direct trains to Moscow.

While no trains travel the line starting or terminating in Arkhangelsk, a single Arkhangelsk *platskatny* carriage is coupled or uncoupled to the

Obozerskaya–Belomorsk train at Obozerskaya station. This means that you can travel in one carriage between Arkhangelsk and Murmansk. However, the condition of the *platskatny* carriage makes this trip unpleasant so a better option is to buy a *coupé* ticket between Murmansk and Obozerskaya, and buy a *platskatny* ticket at Obozerskaya for the final 134km trip to Arkhangelsk. The only problem with this plan is that if the train is late to Obozerskaya, you have to rush. While you can reverse the order for going from Arkhangelsk, it is risky trying to get a *coupé* ticket at Obozerskaya. Good luck.

The trains on the Obozerskaya–Belomorsk line are all very slow with the fastest averaging just 35km/h.

There are several trains which travel on parts of the Obozerskaya–Belomorsk line. These trains travel between Kem/Belomorsk and Malenga, Maloshuika and Emtsa, Konosha and Onega, and Vonguda to Onega.

Trains
The only long-distance trains on this route are listed below.

Origin	Dist. km	Train no & name	Travel time	Depart	Arrive	Destination
Murmansk	664	173	16hr 13min	15.32	07.45	Belomorsk
Belomorsk	353	173	10hr 30min	08.00	18.30	Obozerskaya
Obozerskaya	505	173	11hr 15min	18.40	05.55	Vologda
Obozerskaya	134	34	3hr 33min	19.00	22.33	Arkhangelsk
Belomorsk	664	174	17hr 3min	12.50	05.53	Murmansk
Obozerskaya	353	174	10hr 10min	02.10	12.20	Belomorsk
Vologda	505	174	11hr 48min	13.55	01.43	Obozerskaya
Arkhangelsk	134	15	2hr 48min	19.10	21.58	Obozerskaya

Route description
Obozerskaya   Обозерская   0km
As the station is small, the Arkhangelsk–Murmansk carriage waits directly in front of the station to join the train along the Obozerskaya–Belomorsk line.

Vonguda   Вонгуда   168km
There is a 43km branch line to Onega (Онега) in the north. This ancient town sits on the Onega River, 7km upstream from where it flows into the Belomore Sea. The 26,100-inhabitant logging town has a museum, as both American and English soldiers fought in the area between 1919 and 1920. There are three trains a day between Vonguda and Onega and one a day to Konosha (Коноша) which is near Vologda.

Just after leaving Vonguda, the train passes over the Onega River. The large bridge is guarded by soldiers, which is probably a hangover from World War II. On the banks of the river, are thousands of washed up logs, indicative of the logging companies' attitude to waste and pollution.

Maloshuika   Малошуйка   230km
For some strange reason this minute settlement is the terminus of a local train to Emtsa (Емца) which is just south of Obozerskaya.

Malenga   Маленга   225km
This town once also had a logging and timber collective. Most families disappeared with the collective although there is still a train that terminates here from Kem on the St Petersburg–Murmansk railway.

Nyukhcha   Нюхча   237km
This little village of 350 inhabitants sits on the Nyukhcha River and was where Peter the Great dragged his warships across land to another river during his war with Sweden. This enabled him to travel from the Belomore to the Baltic Sea and surprise the Swedish, with devastating results.

Sumski Posad   Сумский Посад   296km
This is the most easterly station to be electrified and so the locomotives will be replaced and a diesel engine will pull the train from here to Arkhangelsk or Vologda. From here to Belomorsk, the Belomore Sea is often visible on the right.

Virma   Вирма   307km
This little village has a number of inhabited wooden buildings from the 17th and 18th centuries, including the Church of Sts Peter and Paul.

Belomorsk   Беломорск   353km
The station sits on the St Petersburg–Murmansk line and you change here for trains to or from St Petersburg. There is also a daily short-distance train through here between Kem and Malenga on the Belomorsk–Obozerskaya line. See *page 206* for more information on this town.

The wooden house of the rich landowner, Oshevnev,
on Kizhi Island

Chapter Thirteen

The Golden Ring

To the northeast of Moscow are a number of ancient towns and cities which formed the birthplace of the mighty Russian state. This region is known as Russia's Golden Ring as it brought Moscow its great wealth.

Most of the Golden Ring towns were founded in the 11th century and rapidly grew into political, religious and commercial centres following the transfer to Vladimir in 1169 of the capital of Kievian Rus, the first feudal state in eastern Europe. After the decimation of Russia following the Tatar-Mongol invasion in 1236, the Golden Ring cities slowly regained their strength and again became important centres of power. Meanwhile, Moscow's power had grown even faster because it had acted as the Tatar-Mongol's tax collector and, in 1318, its prince was granted the title of Grand Prince by the invaders, symbolising the transfer of regional power from Vladimir to Moscow. Gradually, Moscow annexed the Golden Ring principalities and used their economic and military power to expand its domination. By the end of the 1500s, Moscow had become a large powerful state.

While several of the Golden Ring cities continued to have commercial importance due to their location on major trading routes, the golden era of these cities was over. Fortunately, however, many of the Golden Ring's architectural, religious and cultural treasures have been preserved.

Town layout

The typical Golden Ring town of the 11th to 18th centuries consisted of a kremlin, a *posad* and a *sloboda*.

The kremlin, or "fortress", usually occupied an elevated position and was originally ringed by earth embankments topped with wooden walls. Watch towers were positioned strategically along the wall's length. Over time, the earth and wooden walls were replaced by stone and brick. Inside the kremlin were the prince's residence, religious buildings and administrative complexes.

Outside the kremlin was the undefended *posad* which was the merchants' and artisans' quarters. The *posad* was owned by the prince and the inhabitants had to pay tax.

Next to the *posad* was usually the *sloboda* which was a tax-exempt settlement. *Sloboda* were often established to attract a new workforce.

Most of the buildings of the *posad* and *sloboda* were wooden until the 17th century and consequently only a few have survived the ravages of time. The ones that still exist have invariably been moved to a museum of wooden architecture and the best of these in the Golden Ring is located in Suzdal.

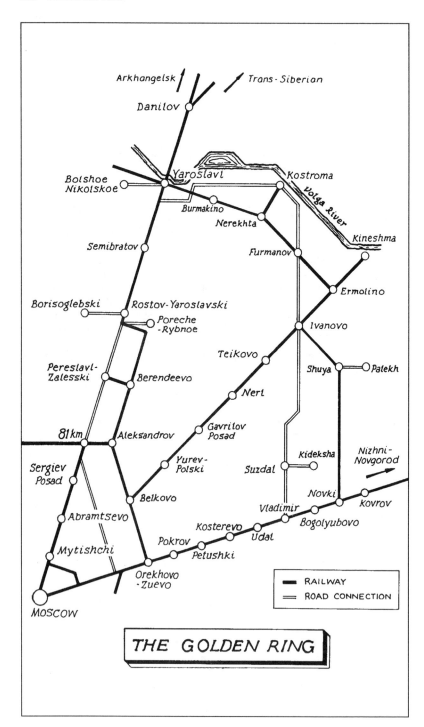

Power in the Golden Ring

During the years of glory of the Golden Ring, power in each region, called a principality, was vested in a feudal prince. The head of several principalities was the Grand Prince whose title from 1547 became tsar, meaning "caesar".

Route highlights

The most famous Golden Ring highlights are the cities of Vladimir, Suzdal, Palekh, Sergiev-Posad, Rostov-Yaroslavski and Yaroslavl. Less well known, but equally interesting, are Abramtsevo, Aleksandrov, Pereslavl-Zalesski and Ivanovo. Before deciding on your itinerary, read through all the attractions in this chapter, including the unknown towns between the major attractions, as you may find something particularly interesting.

In addition, there are several other minor Golden Ring towns that are worth visiting which are covered in *Chapter Eighteen*. These are Kovrov *(page 424)*, Mstera *(page 425)*, Vyazniki *(page 425)* and Gorokhovets *(page 426)*.

Architecture

After the transfer of the capital of Kievian Rus to Vladimir in 1169, the Kiev architectural style of gigantic, elaborately decorated churches was replaced with more modest buildings. In addition, interior decoration of mosaics of smalt (glass made from fusing cobalt oxide and silica) was replaced with fresco painting on wet plaster and majolica tiles. This became known as the Vladimir-Suzdal architectural style.

Following the rise to power of Moscow in the 14th century, the Moscow architectural style evolved which was renowned for its elaborate iconostases and frescoes.

By the beginning of the 15th century, external decoration using glazed tiles had became common and this style was known as Yaroslavl architecture.

From the start of the 18th century, Peter the Great encouraged the adoption of European traditions and Moscow baroque became the vogue but, by the middle of the 18th century, classicism had become the dominant style.

While buildings from each of these architectural periods can be seen in most cities, the best examples of the Vladimir-Suzdal architectural style can be seen in Vladimir, Suzdal, Rostov-Yaroslavski and Pereslavl-Zalesski, of Moscow architectural style in Aleksandrov and Sergiev-Posad, and Yaroslavl architecture style in Yaroslavl.

Crafts

The towns and cities of the Golden Ring were the cradle of many traditional Russian crafts and examples of these crafts can be found in craft museums and bought in workshops. In particular, watch out for icon and miniature paintings in Palekh and Mstera, embroidery in Mstera, Ivanovo and Vladimir, *finift* enamel decoration in Rostov-Yaroslavski and *matryashka* dolls in Sergiev-Posad.

Travel suggestions

If you do not have time for a comprehensive tour of the Golden Ring, you can make day forays from Moscow. Good day trips are to Abramtsevo, Sergiev-Posad and Vladimir. A much better option is a two-day trip to Sergiev-Posad and Aleksandrov, or to Vladimir and Bogolyubovo.

Unless you have a particular interest in the Golden Ring, a good itinerary is the four-day trip Moscow–Sergiev-Posad–Rostov-Yaroslavski–Yaroslavl or the three-day trip Moscow–Vladimir–Suzdal–Bogolyubovo.

For the most comprehensive tour of the Golden Ring you can follow the route descriptions below. If you stop a day in each of the major places of interest, you will need about 15 days.

Trains

The entire Golden Ring can be travelled on suburban trains which is the cheapest way of travelling and the easiest to organise as getting tickets is never a problem. The timetable for suburban trains varies considerably depending on the time of the year.

It is possible to travel on long-distance trains for most of the Golden Ring route. While this is the most comfortable way of travelling, it is also much more expensive. It can often be difficult getting tickets for such short distances, especially on long-distance trains departing from Moscow.

Details of both suburban and long-distance trains on each route are provided below.

MOSCOW–YAROSLAVL
via Abramtsevo, Sergiev-Posad, Aleksandrov, Pereslavl-Zalesski and Rostov-Yaroslavski

Buses   To get to Pereslavl-Zalesski you need to get a bus as the railway is only for freight trains. Buses run from Pereslavl-Zalesski to Moscow, Sergiev-Posad, Rostov-Yaroslavski and Vladimir.

Suburban trains   Both suburban and long-distance trains on this route depart from Yaroslav station. From Moscow, suburban trains go as far as Aleksandrov passing through Abramtsevo and Sergiev-Posad. The trip to Abramtsevo takes 1hr 10min, to Sergiev-Posad it takes 1hr 30min and to Aleksandrov it takes 2hr 10min. From Aleksandrov, suburban trains go as far as Yaroslavl passing through Rostov-Yaroslavski. The trip to Rostov-Yaroslavski takes 2hr 10min and to Yaroslavl takes 3hr 20min.

Long-distance trains   From Moscow, long-distance trains travel to Yaroslavl which is on the main Trans-Siberian railway. Most trains stop only at Aleksandrov and Yaroslavl. The trip on the fastest train to Aleksandrov takes 1hr 51min, to Rostov-Yaroslavski takes 4hr 10min and to Yaroslavl takes 4hr 40min.

Moscow   Москва   0km

The train for Yaroslavl departs from Yaroslav station, pl Komsomolskaya 5, tel: 921 0817, 266 0301, 266 0595. The metro station is Komsomolskaya.

Losinoostrovskaya   Лосиноостровская   10km

About 1km before reaching Losinoostrovskaya station, the train crosses over the M8 Yaroslavlskoe shosse. This highway runs roughly parallel with the railway for the next 250km until Yaroslavl.

Los   Лось   13km

Just after this station, the train crosses over the Moscow ring road. This road marks the city's metropolitan border and after this, the toilet doors are opened.

Mytishchi   Мытищи   18km

Mytishchi is famous for its railway carriage factory, monument factory and shooting range.

The railway carriage factory, Metrovagonmash, manufactures all of the Soviet Union's metro cars and is building the new N5 metro carriages that can be seen currently in Moscow's metro. Although there is a museum at the factory, the arrogant general manager Yuri Goulko will only let you in if you are a potential customer. The Metro Museum in Moscow is the best place to view the development of Russian metro systems, see *Chapter Five, page 89.*

The Mytishchinsky monument factory has produced many of the country's greatest Lenin sculptures, war memorials and artistic sculptures. Its achievements which can be seen in Moscow include the giant Lenin in front of Oktyabrskaya metro station, Moscow's founder Yuri Dolgoruky on horseback on Tver Square (pl Tverskaya), and the Karl Marx across from the Bolshoi Theatre. Today, the Mytishchinsky monument factory is a shadow of its former self and now, ironically, it produces art banned in the Soviet era such as religious statues, memorials to Stalin's purges and busts of mafia heads.

The Dynamo shooting range was used during the Moscow Olympic games for both pistol and skeet shooting. The complex consists of a 50m shooting range with 90 targets, a 25m range with 16 targets, three moving targets and four skeet ranges.

Just after Mytishchi is a branch line on the right which leads to Russia's manned spaceflight centre 5km away. This is known as Zvezdni Gorodok, meaning "Star City". This city of about 20,000 people is a smaller version of the US Johnson Space Center in Houston and is responsible for controlling all manned spacecraft and space station activities. It is also the main training ground for cosmonauts and contains Soyuz, Prognoz, and Salyut rocket simulators. Its official name is the Gagarin Training Centre. Other interesting places to visit include the Star City Museum, the Space Station Simulators Hall where mock-ups of all MIR space station modules are kept, the Neutral Buoyancy Simulator which is a big water tank with a mock-up of the MIR station on the tank's bottom, and the main centrifuge with 18m arm to imitate g-forces during takeoff. The area is also home to several military space research institutes so be discreet when taking photos.

The station that services Zvezdni Gorodok is Podlinki (Подлинки) and the town encompassing the area is called Kaliningrad (Калинград).

Zvezdni Gorodok has a sister city relationship with Nassau Bay, Texas.

If you want to organise a visit to the Gagarin Training Center, contact Anton Nemchimov at the Youth Space Academy at Baumann Technical Institute in Moscow, tel: (095) 263 6994, fax: (095) 262 6511 (Mark it BOX 4462 FOR YOUTH SPACE CENTER), email: ipjakk@redline.ru, http://www.seds. org/ysc/. Another option is Piotr Klimuk, Head of the Cosmonaut Training Centre in Zvezdni Gorodok, fax: (095) 526-2612.

Pushkino   Пушкино   30km

This town was founded in 1499 as a resting place for clergy on the road between Moscow and the monastery town of Sergiev-Posad. With the arrival of the railway in 1862, the place became a popular summer holiday destination for Moscow's élite. From 1890 to 1910, Pushkino became known as Russia's summer arts capital with its renowned summer theatre. While the theatre has gone, the five-cupola Nikolskaya Church built in the 1690s remains. This church was built on the order of Patriarch Adrian and is decorated with polished bricks.

Pravda   Правда   36km

To the left of Pravda station, which translates to mean "truth", is the village of Zavety Ilicha (Заветы Ильича). This name, which figuratively means "the Commandments of Ilich Vladimir Lenin", was a popular name, not only for dozens of Soviet towns, but also for collective farms, metro stations and ships.

The phrase *Zavety Ilicha* was frequently evoked in political speeches to command authority but it often carried no specific meaning. For, unlike the Christian god who left his/her Ten Commandants written down, Lenin never wrote down a definitive set of commandments. Consequently, every Soviet leader interpreted Lenin's writings in the way that most suited him and, by then shrouding their orders in the cloak of *Zavety Ilicha*, they were ensured unquestioning obedience.

Abramtsevo   Абрамцево   57km

This rural retreat spread over a dozen hectares was one of the most important centres of Russian culture in the second half of the 19th century. Today, the Abramtsevo Estate is a museum consisting of a number of buildings set in a picturesque park on the banks of the Vorya River. As Abramtsevo has no communist significance, it remains a popular place for Russians.

The estate was originally known as Obromkovo Pustosh when the current wooden house was built in the 1770s. The estate was bought in 1843 by the Slavophile writer Sergei Aksakov and became the regular haunt of eminent Russian writers and actors including N V Gogol and I S Turgenev. In the spring of 1870, the estate was purchased by the railway tycoon and art connoisseur, Savva Mamontov (1841–1918). It was then turned into an artistic colony for artists who shared a belief in the greatness of Russian native art and architecture but were concerned that it faced extinction by rapid industrialisation. This was ironic considering the estate's patron.

To put words into practice, many of the visiting artists wrote, painted, designed and constructed buildings at Abramtsevo. The most famous building is the Church of Spas Nerukotvornyi, built in the 14th-century Novgorodian style by the renowned architect Victor Vasnetsov. Work started on this church in September 1881 and the interior iconostasis was painted by Repin and Vasili Polenov. The church was consecrated the following year but closed after the 1917 revolution. Other artistic buildings include the Teremok bath house and the wooden Hut on Chicken Legs designed by Viktor Vasnetsov. The design of this hut was based on a traditional Russian fairy tale of the wicked Baba Yaga witch who lived in a walking hut and travelled in a mortar and pestle.

Several workshops were built on the estate, including a carpentry shop making carved furniture and souvenirs constructed in 1885 and a pottery shop built in 1889. Numerous great painters worked at the Abramtsevo Estate and it features in many paintings of that period such as Nesterov's *The Young Sergei*, which can be seen in the Tretyakov Gallery.

The estate's main building is the grey two-storey manor house which was originally built in the 1770s and remodelled in a classical style in the 1870s. This is now a museum, tel: (54) 324 70, open 10.00–17.00, closed Monday and Tuesday.

To get to Abramtsevo from Moscow, take a suburban train from Yaroslavl station destined for either Sergiev-Posad (Сергиев Посад) or Aleksandrov (Александров), both of which are to the north of Abramtsevo. Get off at Abramtsevo station. This trip takes about 1hr 10min.

The walk from the station to Abramtsevo takes 15 minutes. From the station, cross the tracks toward the big wooden "Abramtsevo" sign and after a few metres you meet a gravel road. Follow this for a short distance until you meet a paved road. Turn left down and as the road curves left it follows a pond which is an outer boundary of the Abramtsevo Estate. The road then curves right, crosses the water and goes uphill. You can either continue walking on the road or take the trail off to the left. The road passes the entrance of Abramtsevo while the trail leads you to a café, from where you can see the estate's entrance on the other side of the road.

Khotkovo   Хотьково   59km

Khotkovo has a well-preserved old part on the high bank of the Pazha River which flows through the centre of the town. The most impressive building here is the large Intercession of Khotkovo (Pokrovski Khotkova) Monastery which was founded in 1308 and was the rationale for Khotkovo's existence. Most of the original buildings in the monastery have been replaced by ones built after the 18th century. The second most interesting building is the classical Intercession (Pokrovski) Cathedral. It was built from 1811 to 1816 and is decorated with four Corinthian columns and crowned with a massive round rotunda and four cupolas. Buried inside this cathedral are the parents of Saint Sergius of Radonezh, Russia's patron saint and founder of the Trinity Monastery of St Sergius at Sergiev-Posad.

Other interesting buildings include the three-span, baroque, 1850s North Gate Church which leads to the Church of the Nativity of John the Baptist built in combined baroque and classical styles, the southern Water Gates built in 1833, and the big cathedral built in the Russian-Byzantium style from 1898 to 1904.

The train crosses over the Pazha River just before it reaches Khotkovo station and you can see several of these buildings on the left.

SERGIEV-POSAD   Сергиев Посад   70km
Population: 110,000

Sergiev-Posad is the most popular tourist attraction in the Golden Ring and a must even for those who are "all churched out". The city contains Russia's religious capital: the Exulted Trinity Monastery of St Sergius (Troitse-Sergiyeva Lavra). Entering the white-walled, 600-year-old monastery is like taking a step back into medieval Russia with long bearded monks, dressed in traditional black robes and wearing tall *klobuki* hats, wandering around, and continuous chanting emanating from lamp-lit, incense-filled churches.

Many of the churches are open for services. You can enter those holding services but you may be turned away if you are wearing shorts or have bare shoulders. Photography is normally frowned upon and you should never take photos with a flash, as this damages the icons, nor have your photo taken standing in front of an icon, which is considered disrespectful.

The monastery was founded in 1340 by Sergius of Radonezh (1321–91) who later became the patron saint of Russia. Between 1540 and 1550, the monastery was ringed with a massive stone wall and 12 defensive towers.

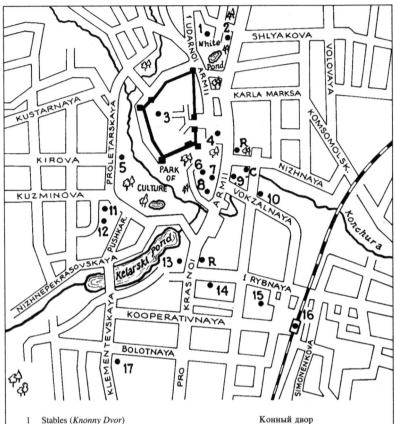

1	Stables (*Knonny Dvor*)	Конный двор
2	Hotel Druzhba	гостиница Дружба
3	Exulted Trinity Monastery of St Sergius (*Troitse-Sergieva Lavra*)	Троице-Сергиева Лавра
4	Krasnogorskaya Chapel	Красногорская часовня
5	Former Hospital of the Trinity Monastery of St Sergei	Больница-Богадельня Троице-Сергиевой лавры
6	St Paraskeva Pyatnitsa (*Pyatnitskaya*) Church	Пятницкая церковь
7	Presentation of the Mother of God (*Vvedenskaya*) Church	Введенская церковь
8	World War II memorial	Памятник 1941-1945гг
9	Chapel over St Paraskeva Pyatnitsa's (*Chasovnya Pyatnitskovo*) Well	Часовня Пятницкого колодца
10	Lookout	Смотровая площадка
11	Kazan (*Kazanskaya*) Church	Казанская церковь
12	Elijah the Prophet's (*Ilinskaya*) Church	Ильинская церковь
13	Toy Museum (*Muzei Igrushki*)	Музей игрушки
14	Ascension (*Voznesenskaya*) Church	Вознесенская церковь
15	Bus station (*Avtovokzal*)	Автовокзал
16	Railway station (*Vokzal*)	Ж-Д Вокзал
17	Dormition (*Uspenskaya*) Church	Успенская церковь
R	Restaurant (*Restoran*)	Ресторан
C	Café (*Kafé*) or Bar (*Bar*)	Кафе или Бар

SERGIEV-POSAD

Besides its military function, the monastery was a great centre of learning. It became famous for its *sergievski* style hand-copied books adorned with gold and vermillion letters. Several of these books are on display in the monastery's museum.

The monastery was once the richest in the country, owning over 20,000 peasant households in 1700, and by 1764 it had grown to encompass nearly 100 separate estates, containing 106,000 peasants.

During the 18th century the monastery's spiritual power grew considerably. In 1744, it was elevated to a *lavra* monastery which meant that it was a "most exulted" monastery. In 1749 a theological college was opened at Sergiev-Posad and in 1814 an ecclesiastical academy was created.

Two years after the communists came to power, the monastery was closed down and it was only opened in 1946 after Stalin met his side of a pact with the Orthodox Church for their support during World War II.

From 1930 to 1991, the town was called Zagorsk (Загорск) after Vladimir Zagorsk, the secretary of the Moscow Council of the Communist Party who was blown to bits by an anarchist's bomb in 1919.

Where to stay
Hotel Druzhba, also known as Hotel Zagorsk, is located on pl Sovetskaya. Rooms cost $34 twin share/person, and the hotel has a restaurant.

Exulted Trinity Monastery of St Sergius
The Exulted Trinity Monastery of St Sergius is spread over six hectares and ringed by a white-washed, 1km long wall which is up to 15m thick. Originally, there were only 12 defensive towers but one was later demolished and the two most westerly ones, the Cellarer's and Beer Towers, were added later. None of the towers has been preserved in its original form. The brown brick Duck Tower is interesting as it has a metal duck on its spire which was put there for the young Peter the Great to use for archery practice.

The monastery is open 10.00–18.00 daily and entry is free unless you want to take photos.

Approaching the monastery
About 200m from the monastery on the road to Moscow are two churches about 10m apart. Both the Church of St Pareskeva Pyatnitsa and the Church of the Presentation of the Mother of God were built in 1547, the year Ivan the Terrible was crowned tsar. Near the churches is the World War II memorial and on the opposite side of the road is the attractive Pyatnitsa Well Chapel.

You enter the monastery via the Red Gate which leads to the Holy Gates, above which is the Church of St John the Baptist. The roof of the gateway is covered by frescoes depicting the life of St Sergius.

Inside the monastery
The sky blue and gold-starred, five-cupola Assumption Cathedral is the heart of the monastery. It was consecrated in 1585 in honour of Ivan the Terrible's victory over the Mongols near Astrakhan and Kazan and was the church in which many of the tsars were baptised. Outside the western door of the cathedral is the tomb of Tsar Boris Godunov, his wife and two of their children. Tsar Godunov ruled from 1598 to 1605 and is the only tsar buried outside Moscow or St Petersburg.

RUSSIAN ORTHODOX ICONOSTASIS

The iconostasis, a wooden frame supporting rows of icons, developed in Russia from a low altar screen. Though the size and number of rows varies from church to church, most iconostases extend the full width of the church and consist of at least four rows of icons, arranged in a particular order.

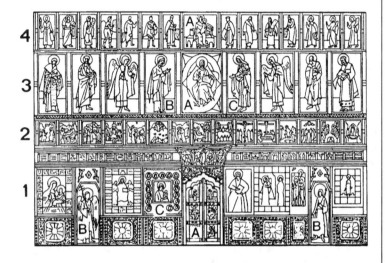

1 The lowest row is the Veneration Tier, those icons which can be reached by the worshippers. In the centre is the Tsar Door (1A) , which leads to the altar. It is often decorated with six panels representing the four Evangelists and the Annunciation. The Eucharist is sometimes portrayed above the central door. To the left is always a large icon of the Virgin and Child (1C). To the right, either Christ or the Saint to whom the church is dedicated. The two side doors in the iconostasis often depict the archangels Michael and Gabriel (1B).

2 The next tier of smaller, square icons, usually depicts Church Holy Days. The number of icons varies, but from left to right usually includes the Annunciation, Nativity, Presentation at the Temple, Baptism, Transfiguration, Entry into Jerusalem, Last Supper, Crucifixion, Descent from the Cross, and Ascension.

3 The Deesis Tier is the main row of icons. In the centre is Christ enthroned (3A), with the Virgin on the left (3B), and John the Baptist on the right (3C), flanked by archangels and saints. The figures are depicted standing, and are usually life-size or larger.

4 The Prophet's Row has an icon of the Virgin and Child in the centre (4A). The prophets are depicted holding scrolls. Large cathedral iconostases sometimes have two tiers of prophets.

The Chapel over the Well was built over a sacred spring which is claimed to have appeared during the Polish siege of 1608. Chapels like this one, and the Pyatnitsa Well Chapel outside the monastery, are often visited by pilgrims who use them to fill drinking bottles with holy water.

Work started on the five-tiered, 93m-high bell tower, the monastery's tallest building, in 1740 and wasn't finished until 30 years later. The turquoise and white baroque tower once held 40 bells.

The large, 73m-long refectory building was built from 1686 to 1693 and served as a dining hall for pilgrims. You can't miss this red, blue, green and yellow chequered building with its carved columns and sculptured frieze incorporating scallop shells.

Outside the refectory is the squat Church of St Sergius crowned with a single golden dome.

The Church of the Descent of the Holy Spirit was built in 1476. Its bell tower was the monastery's highest building and consequently it served as a watch tower. The blue-domed and gold-banded church contains the grave of the first Bishop of Russian Alaska.

The Trinity Cathedral is the most sacred place in the monastery as it is on the site of the original wooden church built by St Sergius. It contains St Sergius' corpse in a dull silver sarcophagus donated by Ivan the Terrible. Memorial services for St Sergius are held all year round here and you can witness them from 10.00–17.00. It was built in 1422 in honour of St Sergius' canonisation and contains 42 icons by Andrei Rublev, Russia's most famous icon painter. The cathedral has several chapels including the Chapel of St Nikon dating from 1548.

The Church of Our Lady of Smolensk resembles a rotunda decorated in baroque style. It was built to house the icon of the same name in 1745.

The white, tent-roofed Church of Sts Zosimus and Savvaty adjoins the red brick and yellow and white sandstone building which was the town's hospital in the 17th century.

The Tsar's Palace was built at the end of the 17th century to be the residence of the visiting Tsar Alexei and his entourage of over 500 people. The building now houses a theological college and ecclesiastical academy.

THE METROPOLITAN

The title of Metropolitan was originally used by the head the Russian Orthodox Church. However, following the creation of the Office of Patriarchate in the 16th century, the title of Metropolitan became an honorific conferred on the most important archbishops.

Following the transfer of Russia's ecclesiastical centre from Kiev to the Golden Ring city of Vladimir at the beginning of the 14th century, the Metropolitan of the Orthodox Church took up residence in Vladimir. However, in 1326 Moscow enticed the Metropolitan to the city where it remained until the Office of Patriarchate was created in 1589. To reflect the power of the archbishops of Rostov-Yaroslavski, Novgorod, Kazan and Krutitsy (a town near Moscow), which were the country's four largest and most powerful dioceses, these archbishops were conferred with the title of Metropolitan.

Over time the seats of the Metropolitans moved, such as from Rostov-Yaroslavski to Yaroslavl in the 17th century, and by the end of the Tsarist period the only Russian Metropolitan dioceses were in Moscow, St Petersburg and Kiev.

The obelisk was built in 1792 and its bas reliefs show the history of the monastery.

It is possible to climb up the Pilgrim Gate Tower and walk along part of the wall.

Monastery museums

There are three museums, within the monastery complex, all open 10.00–17.00, closed Mondays, tel: 41 358, and you have to buy separate tickets from the kiosk at the north end of the Art Museum. The Old Art Museum is located in the vestry and contains one of Russia's richest collections of religious art as well as gifts of portraits, china, glass, furniture, jewellery and handicrafts presented to the monastery. The Art Museum, which has specific opening times on the ticket, is located in the former residence of the Metropolitan and contains mostly Russian handicrafts from the 14th century to the present. The History Museum is contained in the former hospital.

What else to see in the town

Sergiev-Posad has always been associated with carved wooden toys as St Sergius used to make and distribute them to children. The city now boasts Russia's only Toy Museum, pr Krasnoi Armii 136, open 10.00–17.00, closed Monday.

Matryashka dolls feature prominently in the collection although they were only invented about 100 years ago. Locally produced *matryashkas* are distinctive as they are painted with gouache and covered with varnish.

Aleksandrov   Александров   112km

This little-known town was, for nearly two decades in the 14th century, the real capital of Russia. From 1564 to 1581, Ivan the Terrible lived here and directly ruled the half of the country which he called *oprichnini* while abandoning the other half to the authority of *boyars* ("nobles") and monasteries.

A good place to start your tour of Aleksandrov is the History Museum. It contains a large collection of icons from the 15th to 17th centuries, fine art from the 16th to 18th centuries, and information on Russia's first printing works founded in Aleksandrov in 1578 by Andronik Timofeev Nevezhi, a pupil of Russia's first printer, Ivan Fedorov.

The city's most notable building is the monumental brick Trinity (Troitski) Cathedral built in 1513 in the style of early Moscow architecture. It has two brass doors pillaged from other churches by Ivan the Terrible during his sacking of Novgorod and Tver, and above each entrance are richly carved stone portals. Another notable building is the tent-roofed Intercession (Pokrovskaya) Church of the 16th century which has interior frescoes. This church was Ivan the Terrible's court chapel and after his death a refectory was added. Next to his chapel is the Crucifixion (Raspiatskaya) Bell Tower and residential quarters built in the 1560s to which Maria Alekseevna, the half-sister of Peter the Great, was banished from 1698 to 1707 for suspected plotting against the tsar. Peter the Great's daughter, Elizabeth, was also forced to live here for nine years before becoming tsarina.

The Assumption (Uspenski) Monastery, also called the Aleksandrov kremlin, is ringed by 3m-high walls and fortified towers and was built in the 17th century. The five-cupola Assumption Church dates from the 16th century. In the monastery grounds is the grave of Maria Alekseevna.

Aleksandrov is most famous today for a TV factory which produces the popular Rekord brand.

"A STINKING DOG LIVING IN DRUNKENNESS, ADULTERY, MURDER AND BRIGANDAGE"*

Ivan the Terrible has a justifiably infamous reputation even among Russian rulers known for their callousness and brutality. Also called Ivan IV (1530–84), Tsar Ivan the Terrible was relatively stable emotionally until the death of his beloved wife Anastasia in 1560. His paranoid mind decided that she was killed by boyars and he became focused on destroying them and their wealthy cohorts, the monasteries. He embarked on his assault by executing selected boyars, generals and government members and by dividing Russia into two parts: the zemshchina and oprichnina. The zemshchina continued to be governed by the existing boyar and church authorities while the oprichnina (from the word oprich meaning "apart") became Ivan's private domain. The oprichnina was policed by oprichniki who were mostly low-class thugs, mercenaries and foreign adventurers who murdered, pillaged and destroyed at their pleasure. They were dressed in black uniforms, rode black chargers and carried a dog's head and a broom at their saddle to symbolise their readiness to bite the enemies of the tsar and to sweep treason off Russian soil.

The centre of the oprichnina was Aleksandrov's Trinity Fortress Monastery and from here Ivan commanded the oprichnina reign of terror from 1565 to 1572, which claimed millions of Russian lives. The building was a medieval fortress rather than a pious monastery. The complex of dungeons, churches, barracks and warehouses was surrounded by a 1.4km-long wall dotted with eight massive towers and serviced by over 100,000 serfs. Surrounding this was a deep moat, a palisade of sharpened stakes driven into the ground and barricades on all approaches to the fortress.

* Ivan the Terrible describing himself in a self-flagellating letter to the abbot of the Monastery of St Cyril in the late 1500s.

Berendeevo   Берендеево   145km

There is a 21km branch line to the west from here which terminates at Pereslavl-Zalesski.

PERESLAVL-ZALESSKI   Переславль-Залесский
Population: 43,000   Telephone area code: 085 235

This town, sitting on the southeastern shore of Lake Pleshcheevo, has had a glorious history, reaching its zenith in the 17th century when it was one of Russia's 16 greatest towns. Its wealth can be judged by the fact that there were over 50 monasteries scattered around the town. It is renowned throughout Russia as the birthplace of Aleksandr Nevsky and Russia's navy.

The prince of Novgorod, Aleksandr Nevsky (1220–63), became one of Russia's greatest heroes when he defeated Swedish invaders in 1240 near present day St Petersburg. This victory so impressed the Tatar-Mongol khan, who ruled most of Russia at that time, that he gave Nevsky the title of Grand Prince of Vladimir which was then the capital of Russia.

The birth of the Russian navy resulted from the young Peter the Great's fascination with ships and navigation. After finding an old English yacht near Moscow in 1688, Peter started building and sailing boats before moving to Lake Pleshcheevo which offered more room to sail. Over the next few years, Peter built up a fleet of over 100 boats and yachts, and even organised a parade in 1692 for numerous Moscow nobles and foreign ambassadors. Peter's interest in sailing vessels remained with him for his entire life and launched Russia as a world naval power.

Officially, Pereslavl-Zalesski was founded in 1152 by Yuri Dolgoruky who had founded Moscow just five years before. However, ancient indigenous peoples had colonised the region centuries before and the most obvious trace of their habitation is an enormous blue stone on the lake's southeast shoreline. The stone clearly had great religious significance.

The site for the town was chosen because it overlooked a major river trading route while guarding the eastern approach to the Vladimir-Suzdal Principality. Dolgoruky named the town after Pereslavl near Kiev and and it was called this until the 15th century when the word *zalesski,* meaning "beyond the forests", was added to its name.

Unfortunately for the inhabitants, Dolgoruky's kremlin did not withstand the first Tatar-Mongol attack in 1238. Despite being destroyed several more times by the Tatar-Mongols, Pereslavl-Zalesski became a major trading centre over the following two centuries thanks to the development of the Moscow–Arkhangelsk river trading route.

The best day to be in Pereslavl-Zalesski is May 2 as this is a holiday in honour of the town.

Getting there and away
By bus　The only public transport to the city is bus. There are four daily buses between Moscow's Shchyolkovski bus station and Pereslavl-Zalesski, and the journey takes 2hr 30min. There are about three buses a day to Sergiev-Posad which take 1hr 10min, and about five to Rostov-Yaroslavski which take 1hr 30min. There are also dozens of buses a day which start in Moscow and run through Pereslavl-Zalesski on their way to Borisoglebsk, Gavrilov, Yam, Yaroslavl, Vologda, Kostroma, Rybinsk, Tutaev and Komsomolsk. It is possible to catch one of these and get off in Pereslavl-Zalesski.

By train　You cannot get to Pereslavl-Zalesski by railway as its main line station is only for freight. The narrow-gauge railway only serves local villages and collective farms.

Where to stay
The standard Hotel Pereslavl is located at ul Rostovskaya 27, tel: 217 87, 215 59, $60 for a single room, $50 for a double room. There are two restaurants in the building with one upstairs and the other on the ground floor.

Getting around
The town is compact enough to walk around. The freight railway station is to the northeast of the town. The north–south road through the centre of town is the bumpy M8 Moscow–Arkhangelsk highway. Bus No 1 travels along the M8 between the Slavich photography factory (just to the north of the city) and Selkhoztekhnika (to the south of the city) so catch this bus to get to Goritsky Monastery and Fedorovski Monastery. Bus No 2 travels between the Slavich photography factory and Lake Pleshcheevo.

See *Kupan Narrow Gauge Railway, page 241* for information on using the narrow-gauge railway.

What to see in the centre

It is a pleasant walk from the freight railway station to the Pereslavl Hotel which takes you past Temerin's House built in the late 18th century, Russia's first photographic factory built in 1931, the Church of St Simeon built in 1771 in a western baroque style and the Trading Row of the early 1800s. Across ul Rostovskaya is the 18th-century Intercession Church, ul Plescheyevskaya 11. This was the town's only active church during the late communist era. Continue onwards and cross over the Trubezh River and walk along the picturesque river banks until you come to Forty Saints Church sitting on the shores of the lake in what was known as the Fishermen's Settlement (Rybnaya Sloboda). The Forty Saints Church, built in 1775, has a steep tent roof and five domes.

The kremlin and Transfiguration Cathedral

The barely visible, 2.5km-long, earthen kremlin walls are the only remnants of the actual fortress which was completed in 1157. However, the Transfiguration of the Saviour Cathedral, dating from the same time, is considered the gem of Pereslavl-Zalesski. It shares, with a church in Suzdal, the honour of being the oldest standing building in northeastern Russia. The first stone of this simple, cubic, single-domed, white limestone church was laid by Yuri Dolgoruky himself and several local princes are buried in it.

Near the statue of Aleksandr Nevsky is the Church of Aleksandr Nevsky built in 1746 on what was called the Village on the Hill (Nagornaya Sloboda).

The tent-roofed, octagonal-framed Church of St Peter the Metropolitan, ul Sadovaya 5, was built from both stone and brick in 1585, based on traditional wooden cabin churches of northern Russia. A new two-tier bell tower was added to the church's south side in the 1800s and the whole complex was restored in 1889 and again in 1957.

KUPAN NARROW GAUGE RAILWAY
by Dmitry Zinoviev

One of the attractions of Pereslavl-Zalesski is the 100km-long, 750mm-wide narrow-gauge railway network that runs around Pleshcheevo Lake. It was originally built to cart harvested peat moss but when the Moscow railway authorities decided to close the unprofitable network, the local farm communes and industrial enterprises formed the Kupan Transport Authority and took it over. Originally, the network included the stretch from Pereslavl-Zalesski to the main line railway connecting Rostov-Yaroslavski to Moscow but this stretch was upgraded in 1976 to a broad-gauge railway (1,520mm). Then, in the late 1980s, the narrow-gauge railway connecting the railway station at the bus station with the Pereslavl-Zalesski freight station was abandoned. Its rails can still be seen imbedded in the M8 highway. Since the Kupan Transport Authority took over the network, the line between Veksa and Beklemishevo has been closed. This line may be reopened if tourism picks up. The railway's only depot is at Kupan, and the network is often visited by rail enthusiasts due to its unusual narrow-gauge locomotive and carriages.

The railway is the most interesting way to get to the Botik Museum near Veslevo village. The train departs from behind Pereslavl-Zalesski's bus station at 09.00, 13.00, 16.30 and departs from Veslevo to Pereslavl-Zalesski at about 12.30, 16.00 and 20.30.

The five-domed, baroque Church of St Vladimir was built in 1745 to take over from the Transfiguration Cathedral which had become too small.

What to see on the southern outskirts
Goritsky Monastery

The white-walled Goritsky Monastery dates from 1337 although its original wooden buildings have been replaced by brick ones constructed at least three centuries later. The monastery sits on a small hill and, while there are two decorative brick gates through the 800m-long fortified walls, only the one near the tank memorial operates. This is called the Holy Gate and above its large archway passage is the Church of St Nicholas. The monastery's most interesting building is the seven-domed Assumption Cathedral built in 1757 which has a traditional Russian exterior design but a western baroque interior and iconostasis. The monastery also includes the All-Saints Church, a bell tower and a refectory which has been turned into a History and Art Museum, open 10.00–17.00, closed Tuesday. The museum has a large icon collection, furniture display and numerous paintings by the locally born painter Dmitry Kardovsky (1866–1943). Particularly interesting are the beautifully carved Tsar Gates from the Church of the Presentation; Rastrelli's plaster mask of Peter the Great taken from the living tsar in 1719; and Falconet's original model for the Bronze Horseman statue in St Petersburg. At the front of the monastery is a monument to Yuri Dolgoruky and a T-34 tank of World War II vintage.

Fedorovski Monastery

The Fedorovski Monastery is 6.5km from the centre of town. It was founded in 1551 and the main building is the Cathedral of St Theodore Stralites which was built in 1557 to commemorate the birth of Ivan the Terrible's son, Fedor. Other buildings are the Presentation of the Mother of God Church built in 1710, the Kazan Hospital Church built in 1714, and the bell tower built in 1705.

St Danil Monastery

The St Danil Monastery is 5km from the centre of town. It was founded in 1508 by the monk Danil and its main church is the single-domed Trinity Cathedral which was built in honour of the newly born Ivan the Terrible by his father, Vasily III. The other buildings in the monastery include the All Saints' Church built in 1687, a two-storey refectory built in 1695, the two-storey Glory of Our Lady Church and a large, tent-roofed bell tower built in 1698. The bell from this tower is now in the Moscow kremlin's Ivan the Great Bell Tower. During World War II, the monastery was a German prisoner-of-war camp.

What to see on the northern outskirts

About 3km to the north of the city along the M8 highway is the fortress St Nikita Monastery. It was founded by the monk Nikita in 1170. His bones now lie in the crypt of the Cathedral of St Nikita which was commissioned by Ivan the Terrible in 1561. The complex includes the Annunciation Church with its huge 17th-century refectory and bell tower built in 1668, and the Archangel Gabriel Gate Church which sits over the monastery's entrance.

What to see on the western outskirts

About 3km from Pereslavl-Zalesski is the Botik Museum near Veslevo village. This museum displays a range of nautical gear and one of Peter's sailboats, the *Fortuna*. The only other boat in existence from Peter's flotilla is on display in St Petersburg's Naval Museum. Although Peter passed an egotistical law in 1722 that required care be taken of his Pereslavl-Zalesski fleet due to its historical importance, almost every vessel was lost in a fire later that century. It was only in 1803 that a new museum, open 10.00–17.00, closed Monday, opened on the former estate of Botik. The estate includes a wooden palace, dance hall, several of Peters' naval guns, two large anchors, a monument to Peter the Great and a pink and white triumphal arch built in 1852.

To get to the museum, catch the narrow-gauge railway or take a local bus from the bus station towards Nagorye, Yuryevo or Kubrinsk. The buses run more frequently than trains.

Getting assistance

Travel agents   There is a travel service in the Hotel Pereslavl.

Petrovsk   Петровск   200km

About 15km after passing through Petrovsk, you will see Lake Nero on the right. Rostov-Yaroslavski sits on the western shore of this lake.

ROSTOV-YAROSLAVSKI   Ростов-Ярославский   224km
Population: 37,000   Telephone area code: 085 36

This is one of the most pleasant Golden Ring cities to visit as it is small but packed with interesting places and set along the scenic shoreline of Lake Nero.

The city records its foundation year as 862, when the first reference was found to it in the Russian chronicles. However, archaeological excavations have found that Rostov-Yaroslavski was the site of non-Slavic villages centuries before. The earliest known settlers were from the Meria tribe of Finno-Ugric descent and, although they have long since disappeared, traces of their language can still be heard today in the names of local villages, rivers and even Lake Nero itself.

Although it is not obvious to visitors, Rostov-Yaroslavski played a major role in the formation of Russia and at one time was as big as the mighty capitals of Kiev and Novgorod.

The Slavic history of the city, which is named after Prince Rosta, really took off in the late 10th and early 11th centuries when Grand Prince Yaroslav the Wise, and then his brother Boris, ruled Rostov-Yaroslavski. These brothers were the sons of Vladimir Monomakh who brought Christianity to Russia. As an indication of its rapid growth into a major trading centre, during the reign of Yuri Dolgoruky, who founded Moscow in 1147, Rostov received the honourable and rare title of *veliki* meaning "great". Rostov-Veliki soon became an independent principality but, after the death of its ruler Vsevolod in 1212, his four sons couldn't agree on power sharing so they broke up the principality.

After being rebuilt from the Tatar-Mongol sacking, Rostov-Veliki continued to have political importance for two more centuries until the local prince sold the remainder of his hereditary domain to Moscow's Grand Prince Ivan III in 1474. The city remained an important ecclesiastical centre as it was the religious capital of northern Russia and home to a Metropolitan. However, in the 17th century the Metropolitan was moved to the larger city of Yaroslavl and with it went the last remnants of Rostov's greatness. No longer called Rostov the Great, the city became known as Rostov-Yaroslavski, meaning Rostov near Yaroslavl as distinct from Rostov on the Don River.

Much of Russia's dreadful coffee comes from here as there is a factory for roasting chicory roots which are substituted for, or added to, coffee beans.

Passing through
Approaching the city, you will see Lake Ozero on the right and at certain points, by sticking your head out the window, you can see the golden domes of the Rostov kremlin ahead.

About five minutes before you reach the station of Rostov-Yaroslavski, you cross the Ishna River. On the right, about 500m downstream where the river flows into Lake Nero, is the St Jacob Monastery which guarded the city's southern approach centuries ago.

About three minutes after leaving the station, you can see on the right the St Avraamy Monastery on the shores of Lake Nero. This monastery guarded the northern approach to the city.

Where to stay
One of the most appealing places to stay in all of Russia is in the kremlin. The former servants quarters have been turned into a basic hotel run by the International Tourist Centre, tel: 318 54. The rooms cost $22 twin share/person. There is a café in the same building. Other places to stay are the standard Hotel Intourist, ul Engelsa 115, tel: 659 066; basic Hotel Rostov, ul Svedlova 64, tel: 391 818; and basic Hotel Moskovskaya, ul Engelsa 62, tel: 388 700.

Getting around
To get from the railway station to the kremlin and the main bus station, take bus No 6. To get from the main bus station to the St Jacob Monastery, take bus No 1 or 2 and to the St Avraamy Monastery, take bus No 1.

The Rostov kremlin
The white-walled Rostov kremlin is one of the most photogenic in the country. It is spread over two hectares, has six churches and is ringed by 11 towers.

The kremlin dates from 1162 when the first stone was laid by Prince Andrei Bogolyubsky, son of Yuri Dolgoruky. However, all traces of the original buildings disappeared in the 17th century when it was rebuilt. This reconstructed kremlin, which is what you see today, is actually an imitation fortress despite its mighty 12m-high and 2m-thick walls and towers, which seemingly bristle with battlements and loop-holes through which the defenders could fire arrows. In reality, it is just a lavish fence for a rich castle as all the elements of real fortifications are missing. For example, the towers have no loop-holes low enough or angled sufficiently for the defenders to fire directly downward; almost all the walls have windows in them through which attackers could swarm; and the wall loop-holes are more decorative than functional. The architect of this false fortress kremlin was the ambitious 17th-century Metropolitan Ion Sisoyevich who wanted a residence to reflect his importance.

While Ion's private kremlin, which is also called the Rostov Metropolitan, may have been relatively defenceless, strong earth wall ramparts ringed the kremlin. These walls were built in 1631 and their remnants can still be seen today. After the 17th century, when the Metropolitan was moved to nearby Yaroslavl, the kremlin became derelict. By the beginning of the 19th century, it had become such an eyesore that it was offered for sale for only 28,000 roubles. Luckily for posterity, no-one took up the offer. It was only in the 1870s that restoration work started and today most of the buildings have been restored to their 16th- and 17th-century condition.

The Rostov kremlin, which is made up of 20 million 8kg bricks, has the peculiar feature for the 17th century of having all the structures connected on their second floor by walkways and terraces with the exception of the Assumption Cathedral. Thus, once you are on the kremlin's walls, it is possible to enter every building.

The kremlin is divided by walls into three parts: the northern part containing the main church, called the Assumption Cathedral, the large central part with its five churches and numerous buildings, and the southern part consisting of the Metropolitan's orchard. There are four gates, with two leading from the outside to the central part, one from the outside to the orchard, and one between the central and northern part.

The kremlin grounds are always open as the gate on the eastern wall is never locked. The museums are normally open 10.00–17.00, closed Wednesday.

The northern part of the kremlin

The Assumption Cathedral is a 16th-century, 60m-high, five-domed building with white stone friezes decorating the outside. Since 1071, there have been several cathedrals on this site and the copper lion handles on the inside of the massive main doors on the west side come from a church built on the site in the 12th century. The cathedral contains the tomb of the canonised Bishop Leontius who was martyred by Rostov's pagans in 1071 during his Christianity drive. The Metropolitan Ion is also buried here. The six-tiered iconostasis dates back to the first half of the 18th century.

The bell tower contains superb examples of 17th-century Russian bells with the largest weighing 32 tons. There are 13 bells in all and they can be heard up to 20km away. The four-domed bell-tower is 32m long, 17m high and has four arched openings. It was completed in 1687 to resemble the Moscow kremlin's Ivan the Great Bell Tower so that Metropolitan Ion could look out of his window and be reminded of his aspirations to win the patriarchy in Moscow. Major peals of the bell tower in the Rostov kremlin can be heard at 13.00 on Saturday and Sunday with minor ones at other times.

The central part of the kremlin

This is the kremlin's largest section and contains five churches. Notice that the religious area of each church occupies only the second floor as the ground floor was left for animal husbandry, storage and accommodation.

The kremlin's main entrance is on its western side through the St John the Divine Gateway Church built in 1683 which has a richly decorated facade. The ticket office is in this building.

There is another entrance in the eastern wall. The entrance to the kremlin's northern section from the central part is through the Resurrection of Christ Gate

Church built in 1670. This church has an iconostasis made of stone instead of the traditional wood.

The Transfiguration of the Saviour above the Cellars Church is one of the gems of the kremlin as it was the private church of the Metropolitan. It is quite austere from the outside but its interior is lavish. This church is the tallest in the kremlin and has a single dome.

The White Chamber is connected to the Transfiguration of the Saviour above the Cellars Church and was designed as a sumptuous dining hall. It was at one time the biggest such structure in Russia with its broad vaults supported by a single pylon. The White Chamber now houses a museum of local Rostov crafts.

The Church of Virgin Hodegetria was erected 20 years after the death of Metropolitan Ion and has a chequered exterior with a Moscow baroque interior. It now contains an exhibition on church trinkets.

The Prince's Chambers, built in the 16th century, is the oldest kremlin building. It is a claustrophobic building with small dark passages, narrow doors and slits of windows filled with slivers of mica which is an opaque mineral that was used before glass was invented. This building is a good place to get an impression of the life of 16th-century Russian nobility.

The Metropolitan's House is also known as Samuil's House or the Cross-Vaulted Chamber. Its lower floor was built in the 16th century, its second floor added during Metropolitan Ion's lifetime and finally, in the 18th century, the third storey was added by Metropolitan Samuil. Today, it is a museum, open 10.00–17.00, closed Wednesday. and has a large collection of *samovars,* stone carvings, wooden sculptures, 14th- and 15th-century doors from local churches and several shrouds of Christ.

The Red Chamber is a spacious two-storey structure built as a residence for visiting tsars and their large retinues. It was constructed in 1680 and is now the hostel of the International Youth Tourism Centre and its rooms contain three to five beds.

The Church of St Gregory the Theologian is not in very good condition.

What else to see

In front of the eastern entrance of the kremlin is the Saviour on the Market Place Church, per Sovetskaya. It was built in the late 1600s and is now a library. It is also called the Ruzhnaya Church. Beside the church is the Arcade built in the 1830s and on the opposite side of the street is the Traders' Row.

The neoclassical St Nicholas in the Field Church on ul Gogola was built in 1813 and was one of two main churches in Rostov that conducted services during the communist era. It has a golden iconostasis with *finift* enamel decorations and icons from the 15th to 19th centuries.

The single-domed refectory Church of the Tolg Virgin, also known as the Church of St John the Kind, on ul Dekabristov, was built in 1761 along with its bell tower. It was the other church allowed to operate under communism.

The single-domed Church of St Isidore the Blessed, ul Karla Marksa, dates from the 16th century and was originally called Ascension Church. It was erected in 1566 on the order of Ivan the Terrible and this is recorded on a stone slab on the church's west wall. In 1770 a side-chapel was added to the western wall and it was dedicated to St Isidore the Blessed.

The Church of the Virgin Birth, pl Sovetskaya, built in 1678, is all that remains of the Nativity Monastery.

In front of the kremlin's main gate on the western side, ul Kamenny Most, is the Metropolitan's Horse Stables, a building which was one of the greatest architectural discoveries in Rostov over the last few decades. It was planned to demolish this nondescript two-storey building as it blocked the view of the kremlin's main gate and the Church of St Gregory the Theologian as you travel up the road from Moscow. However, after the plaster was knocked off the walls, it was discovered that the building was more than 300 years old. Further research revealed that this building was part of the Metropolitan's transportation complex which included large stables, rooms for saddles, sledges, carriages, horse tack, offices, haylofts and larders, and quarters for grooms, coachmen and watchmen. These complexes were essential for any large household in 16th- and 17th-century Russia and the one in Rostov is one of only a few that have survived.

There used to be a Loom Museum and the shop Russky Len (Russian Flax) at ul Slavyanskaya but these are also closed.

It is possible to hire rowing boats at the river station. Local ferries run from here but there are no hydrofoils from Rostov to Moscow as the river is too shallow.

Getting assistance
Travel agents Intourist, Rostov Kremlin, tel: 312 44; Travel Service, ul Okruzhnaya 64, tel: 319 47.
Air Aeroflot, ul Karla Marksa 17, tel: 317 43.

What to see on the city's outskirts and in the region
St Avraamy Monastery
Guarding the northern approach to Rostov-Yaroslavski is the fortress St Avraamy Monastery on ul Zhelyabovskovo. It was built in the 11th century, making it one of the oldest existing monasteries in Russia. It sits on the site of the ancient, pagan Veles Temple dedicated to the god of cattle.

All of the monastery's original wooden buildings have disappeared and there are only three left of those built in the 16th century. These are the Presentation of the Virgin Church built in 1650, in which the father of Metropolitan Ion is buried; the Gateway Church of St Nicholas which was built in 1655 but retains little of its original form due to numerous reconstructions; and the Epiphany Cathedral. This five-domed cathedral, built from 1552 to 1554, is probably the oldest building in Rostov-Yaroslavski. It was erected on the orders of Ivan the Terrible in honour of his defeat of the Kazan Khanate in 1552 and the role that the St Avraamy Monastery played in this victory.

To get to St Avraamy Monastery, take bus No 1 from the main bus station.

St Jacob Monastery
Guarding the southern approach to Rostov-Yaroslavski is the fortress St Jacob Monastery on ul Dobrolyubovo. It was founded in the 14th century and commands a much more prominent position than the St Avraamy Monastery, for it can be seen from miles around. Its most important buildings are the St Jacob Church built in 1725; the five-domed Church of the Immaculate Conception built in 1686 with a number of internal frescoes which are considered some of the country's best late 17th-century monumental painting; and the St Dmitry

Church built in 1794 with a massive dome and a variety of decor. The monastery also has a three-tier bell tower built in 1780.

Outside the monastery is the two-column, five-domed Saviour on the Sand Church. Built in 1603, this is the only surviving building of the Saviour Monastery (also known as the Princesses' Monastery) which was founded in the 1200s but merged with the St Jacob Monastery in 1764. The Saviour Monastery was built by Princess Maria, whose husband was killed by invading Tatar-Mongols in the 14th century. It specialised in recording details of life over the centuries and, by the 17th century, it contained one of the biggest libraries in Russia.

To get to the St Jacob Monastery, take bus No 1 or 2 from the main bus station.

St John the Baptist Upon Ishnya River Church
About 3km from the centre of Rostov-Yaroslavski, near the village of Borogslovo (Богослово), is the wooden St John the Baptist Upon Ishnya River (Ion Bogoslava na reke Ishna) Church built in 1689. It is a rare example of a 17th-century wooden building that has remained on its original site; most have been moved to wooden architectural museums.

According to legend, this church was floated down the Ishna River fully assembled as it appeared virtually overnight. Surprisingly, this is quite close to the truth as it was typical for the frames and structural elements of buildings to be cut and assembled in the forest and floated down the river. In the case of this church, it is quite feasible that it took only three days for most of it to be erected. You can wander through the church looking at various exhibitions about rural and religious life over the previous centuries and take particular note of the excellent condition of the actual building which is over 300 years old. The church is closed Wednesday.

There is no public transport that runs past the church but you can get there by catching a bus to Ishna village and walking from there.

Borisoglebski Monastery
About 20km to the west of Rostov-Yaroslavski in the village of Borisoglebski (Борисоглебский) is the Borisoglebski Monastery, open 10.00–17.00, closed Tuesday, named after Russia's first two saints, Boris and Gleb.

The monastery was built in the 14th century and substantially fortified in the 16th century to protect Rostov-Yaroslavski from Polish invaders. It sits on the Ustye River and has ten buildings dating from the 16th and 17th centuries, ringed by a 1.5km-long wall studded with 13 mighty towers and two gates. The monastery is of architectural interest as several of its most successful stone building innovations can be seen in those of the Rostov kremlin which was built over a century latter.

Work started on the sprawling Sts Boris and Gleb (Borisa I Gleba) Cathedral in 1522 and its single dome was replaced with a tent roof in the 17th century, then a figured cupola was added in the 18th century and various annexes were built haphazardly over the years.

Next to it is the Annunciation (Blagovezhchenskaya) Church and refectory built from 1524 to 1526.

To the north of the Annunciation Church is the 16th-century Residence of the Father Superior. Its most interesting feature is the wide band of ornamental brickwork that runs the length of the walls.

The two gateway churches are flanked by towers. The first, the Gateway Church of St Sergius, was built in 1545 and is now a museum. From the museum, you can get on to the monastery wall. The second, the Gateway Church of Purification, was built in 1680.

To get to the monastery, catch a bus for Borisoglebski village or Uglich and get off in Borisoglebski. The trip takes 30 minutes.

Poreche-Rybnoe

About 18km to the southeast of Rostov-Yaroslavski is the ancient town of Poreche-Rybnoe (Поречье-Рыбное) which contains a number of preserved buildings. These include the five-domed Sts Peter and Paul (Petra I Pavla) Church built in 1767 to which a tent-shaped bell tower was added at the end of the 18th century; the single-domed Nikita Muchenik Church in 1799; and the striking circular bell tower built from 1772 to 1779. Towards the town's historical centre are stone buildings of the 18th and 19th centuries. Regular buses run between Rostov-Yaroslavski and Poreche-Rybnoe with the trip taking 30 minutes.

Points of interest

The Golden Ring is littered with disused churches and monasteries, many of which are slowly being restored. Most people assume that all the abandoned buildings were boarded up by anti-religious communists, but the truth is that dozens were simply abandoned before the 1917 revolution.

Examples of this are the Goritsky Monastery in Pereslavl-Zalesski and the kremlin in Rostov, both of which were deserted in the 18th century. The former was abandoned in 1788 when Catherine the Great dissolved the diocese for which the Goritsky Monastery was the centre. The latter, which was an ecclesiastical centre, was abandoned when the religious centre in Rostov was moved to Yaroslavl.

Finift enamel art

Rostov-Yaroslavski's most famous handicraft is *finift* multi-coloured enamel work. This craft originated in Byzantium, as can be seen from its name which derives from the Greek *fingitis* meaning "colourful and shiny". *Finift* was used to decorate icons, sacred utensils and gospel covers, as well as in portraits of people. The enamel's greatest advantages are that it cannot be damaged by water and does not fade with time.

The process to make the enamel is extremely complex and involves oxidising various metals to produce different colours. The metals are mixed with various chemicals and fired three times at temperatures as high as 1,000°C. The enamels are then painted with fusible colours and fired several more times.

Finift has been produced in Rostov-Yaroslavski since the 12th century and is still being produced today in the Rostov *finift* factory which has been working since the 18th century. Although there is no factory shop in the city, there is one in nearby Yaroslavl. There are no regular tours of the Rostov *finift* factory but if you talk to the director on tel: 352 29, you may be able to organise something.

Bell ringing

From the 17th century, Rostov-Yaroslavski became the centre of bell ringing in Russia, taking over from the pullers of Moscow and Novgorod. Bell ringing has been a part of Russian life since the 10th century and peals were used to celebrate victorious battles, welcome troops returning from battles, announce holidays and provide directions for lost travellers. A special alarm bell was a feature of every large Russian town and it was only rung to call the inhabitants to arms or to attend a disaster. It was a common practice for the alarm bell of a conquered town to be carried off or sent into exile. This occurred when the bell from defeated Novgorod was sent to Aleksandrov by Ivan III while the bell from the Golden Ring city of Uglich was exiled to Siberia by the Tsar Boris Godunov for what he considered was traitorous action by the town.

Many famous composers, such as Glinka and Moussorgsky, used bells in their music. The famous French composer Hector Berlioz visited Rostov just to hear the bells.

YAROSLAVL Ярославль 282km
Population: 637,000 Telephone area code: 0852

For centuries, travellers have been drawn to Yaroslavl to see its famous architecture. Not only does it include buildings from three periods of Old Russian architecture, but it is also the home of the Yaroslavl architectural style. In many ways, Yaroslavl's buildings surpass those of Moscow as they have not suffered as much from the ravages of war, rapid industrialisation or city reconstruction.

The first two periods of Russian architecture are described at the beginning of this chapter. Yaroslavl architecture arose in the second half of the 16th century and is epitomised by tall and pointed tent roofs, free-standing bell towers, large airy churches with side chapels, use of external glazed tiles, and the employment of large interior frescoes and mosaics. Yaroslavl has many buildings in this style as its evolution coincided with a massive reconstruction drive following the great fire in 1658. The wooden buildings that did survive were finished off over the summers of the following two years when fires again raced through the city. The Yaroslavl architectural style arose here because the city had developed a rich merchant class which commissioned churches to its own taste. As this style also appealed to hereditary nobles and peasants, it became widespread throughout Russia, much to the chagrin of the conservative clergy.

The city's architectural styles, coupled with the small hills through the central part of the city and the tree-lined streets and squares, make Yaroslavl one of the most beautiful cities in Russia.

A particularly good time to visit the city is from August 1 which is the start of the Yaroslavl Sunset Music Festival.

History

Yaroslavl is the Volga River's oldest city as it was founded in 1010 by Grand Prince Yaroslav the Wise (978–1054). However, a sizeable pagan settlement had existed here before this date, although Yaroslav the Wise destroyed much of it when he stormed the village in 998.

Yaroslavl's location on the Volga River, which was a major trading route, enabled it to grow into a large settlement. In 1213, it became an independent principality but was destroyed in 1238 by the Tatar-Mongol invasion. It was quickly rebuilt and, after being incorporated into the Moscow Principality in 1463, its industrial, political and military capabilities were used by Moscow to increase its power.

With the expansion of the Volga River in the 16th and 17th centuries to allow trade from the far north seaport of Arkhangelsk to the Middle East in the south, Yaroslavl grew to become the country's second most populous city after Moscow and the third largest trading city after Moscow and Kazan. Until the opening of the Moscow–Volga River Canal in 1937, giving Moscow direct access to the Volga, Yaroslavl was Moscow's main port.

Today, the city is an industrial engineering centre with machine-building, plastics and oil-refining industries.

Passing through

About five minutes after entering Yaroslavl's outskirts, you pass the suburban station of Kotorosl (Которосль) and on the left you can see the Church of Sts Peter and Paul with a 58m bell tower beside it. The church was built in 1736 by a wealthy textile factory owner in honour of Peter the Great who was a valuable customer. The church is constructed in the popular St Petersburg baroque style and, as a last sycophantic gesture, he designed it to look like the Cathedral of Sts Peter and Paul in St Petersburg.

A minute or so later you cross over the Kotorosl River giving you a good view of several landmarks. On the right of the train, on the southern river bank just before the road bridge, is the 15-domed Church of St John the Baptist. On the left of the train, also on the southern bank, is the Church of St Nicholas by the Water Mills.

From the square in front of the station, you can see the Church of the Vladimir Mother of God built in 1678.

About five minutes after leaving the station, the train changes direction from the north to the east and crosses over the mighty Volga River. The river is about 1km wide at this point. On the right side of the river you will see the main road bridge across the river and quays on both side of the river.

Where to stay

The options consist of the standard Hotel Yubileynaya, nab Kotoroslennaya 11A, tel: 224 159, $21 twin share/person; the standard, very noisy Hotel Yaroslavl, ul Ushinskovo 40 with an entrance also at ul 2 Svobody, tel: 221 275, $42 twin share/person; the standard Hotel Kotorosl, ul Bolshaya Oktyabrskaya 87, tel: 212 415, $27 twin share/person; and the basic Hotel Volga, ul Kirova 10, tel: 229 131, formerly known as the Bristol Hotel, $13 twin share/person. Beside one another are the basic Hotel Vest, ul Respublikanskaya 79, $12 twin share/person; and the standard Hotel Yuta, ul Respublikanskaya 79, tel: 218 793, $24 twin share/person. All the hotels have restaurants.

Getting around

There are two stations carrying the name of the Yaroslavl. The main station is Yaroslavl-Glavny (meaning "Yaroslavl-main") on the north side of the Kotorosl River; Yaroslavl-Moskovski (meaning "Yaroslavl-Moscow") is on the south side of the river. All trains to Yaroslavl go through Yaroslavl-Glavny while only those trains travelling along the east and west line (such as from Ivanovo and St Petersburg) go through Yaroslavl-Moskovski. To prevent problems, always catch the train from Yaroslavl-Glavny.

To get from the station to pl Volkova, where Hotel Yaroslavl is located, catch trolleybus No 1. To get from the station to Hotel Kotorosl, take tram No 3 which goes past it. The airport is to the north of the city with its closest railway station being Molot (Мотол) which is on the railway to St Petersburg. To get to the airport, take bus No 140 from pl Sovetskaya.

What to see
Transfiguration of Our Saviour Monastery

This attractive white monastery, at pl Podbelskovo 25, is well worth visiting as its architecture is interesting and it contains four museums.

The monastery was founded in the 12th century but the oldest building to be seen today dates from 1516 when the wooden walls were replaced by stone and brick. The monastery became a major centre of learning, was the site of the first school in northern Russia, and had a large library which was famous throughout the country. Following new fortifications built in the 16th century, the monastery was considered so strong that a part of the tsar's treasury was stored here and protected by a military garrison.

In 1787, the garrison was abolished when the monastery was closed and converted into a residence for the local archbishop.

The monastery is open daily but the museums are closed on Monday.

The Transfiguration of Our Saviour Cathedral occupies central place in the monastery. This three-domed cathedral was built in 1516 after the original building was destroyed in a fire in 1501. The interior frescoes created in the 1560s are particularly interesting. In the 17th century a covered porch was added to the cathedral's exterior. A number of Yaroslavl princes are buried here. The church is currently being renovated.

The Church of Yaroslavl's Miracle Workers was built from 1827 to 1831 in the late classical style, and is now used as a cinema and lecture hall.

The refectory was built in the first half of the 16th century and the exterior of the two-storey building is quite simple. The second floor is impressive as a single mighty pillar supports the vaults, creating a large, open area for the monks' meals. This area now contains a History Museum of the Yaroslavl region, tel: 220 272, open 10.00–17.00, closed Monday.

The Nativity Church, also known as the Refectory Church, is now a Natural History Museum, open 10.00–17.00, closed Monday.

The Archbishop's Chambers were built in the 17th century.

The pillar-shaped bell tower is a combination of a church, museum and viewing platform. It was built in the 16th century and the pseudo-gothic top added in 1808. On the tower's ground level is the Virgin of the Caves Church which has its iconostasis painted directly on to the stone wall. This area now houses an exhibition of Russian and European bells from the 16th to the 19th centuries. If you climb the tower to the viewing platform at the top, you are rewarded with a panoramic view of the city. Directly above you is the monastery's main bell which was cast in 1738. The bell tower's clock was installed in 1624 after it was brought from the Saviour (Spassky) Tower in the Moscow kremlin.

The Monks' Cell Block consists of four buildings and was built at the end of the 17th century. It now contains a large Museum of Old Russia, open 10.00–17.00, closed Monday, which includes icons, handicrafts, weapons, armour and books.

The Holy Gates were built in 1516 and renovated in the 17th century so they would be particularly attractive. Later, another entrance, a gateway church and a tall watch-tower with a pointed roof were added to the Holy Gates.

The monastery's 3m-thick and 818m-long walls are interesting as they display two different styles. The northern walls have remained more or less untouched since they were built in 1516 and easily withstood Polish attacks during their 24-day siege in 1609. The southern walls, however, were lowered and remodelled at the turn of the 18th century so that visitors approaching the city from Moscow could obtain a better view of the monastery's buildings. The towers on each side also reflect this difference. The northern Uglich and Virgin Towers, both of which were built in the middle of the 17th century, are squat and heavily fortified while St Michael's and the Epiphany Towers, which were added in 1803, are small, round and purely decorative.

Entry to the grounds is free but you will have to pay for each of the museums.

Around the Transfiguration of Our Saviour Monastery

This area is rich in churches and other historic buildings.

Directly opposite the monastery on the Moscow Highway is the Epiphany Church, pl Podbelskovo 25a. The five-domed church was completed in 1693 and paid for by the merchant Aleksei Zubchaninov. It has nine large windows which make the interior extraordinarily light. It is an excellent example of the Yaroslavl style of architecture with its glazed tiles and festive decorations. It is now a museum, open 10.00–17.00, closed Tuesday, May 1 to September 30.

The Theological Consistorium, pl Podbelskovo, is the place where the Ecclesiastical Council met. It was built in 1815 and its columned front makes an impression as you approach it from the direction of Moscow.

The Church of St Demetrius of Thessalonica, ul Bolshaya Oktyabrskaya 41, was built from 1671 to 1673 using bricks left over from the reconstruction of the monastery in the 1660s.

The Church of Metropolitan Peter, nab Kotoroslnaya, was built in 1657 and is a small refectory church.

The House of Ivanov, ul Chaikovskovo 4, is a typical two-storey residence of a well-to-do town dweller built at the end of the 17th century. The ground floor was used for storage and the upper floor contains the sleeping and living rooms.

The two-storey neoclassical Seminary, ul Respublikanskaya 108, was built in 1818.

The five-domed Church of St Nicholas on the Waters, ul Chaikovskovo 1, was built from 1665 to 1672 and has marvellous glazed bands around the alter windows.

The Church of the Tikhvin Virgin is a small church designed for winter worship as it can be heated. It has extensive glazed tile work on its exterior.

The bell tower of St Nicholas the Martyr, ul Saltykova-Shchedrina 30, was built in 1693 and is all that remains of that long-gone church.

The Volga River embankment

A stroll down the landscaped, high, right bank of the Volga River from the river station to the Metropolitan's Chambers is an enjoyable way of exploring this area.

The river station, at the end of ul Pervomaiskaya, has two parts: one for long-distance hydrofoils and, slightly downstream, another for local passenger ferries.

From the river station you pass a park at the beginning of the street, ul Pervomaiskaya, which contains a monument to the great Russian writer, Nikolai

Nekrasov (1821–77). He lived and worked 15km away in the town of Karabikha and his residence there is now a museum. For information on this, see *The Estate of Nikolai Nekrasov, page 256.*

The Nativity Church, ul Kedrova 1, was built over nine years starting in 1635 and paid for by the rich Nazaryev merchant family. This tent-roofed church is famous as it was the first church to use glazed tiles for external decoration. This practice was soon adopted everywhere and led to the development of the Yaroslavl architectural style. In the mid-17th century a bell tower was added and the church was reconstructed in the 19th century.

The small, classical-style Provincial Governor's Rotunda-Pavilion on the riverbank was built in 1840.

The St Nicholas-Nadeyina Church, per Narodny 2a, is so called because it was funded by the wealthy merchant, Nadey Sveshnikov. It was erected from 1620 to 1622, although its baroque iconostasis was carved in 1751. The Annunciation Chapel to the side of the church was built for Nadey's private use so that he could pray in the company of only his closest friends. It has an interesting iconostasis which is framed in ornamental lead. The church is now a museum and is open 10.00–17.00, closed Sunday and Monday, May 1 to September 30.

The small Art Museum is housed in the former governor's residence and contains artwork from the 18th century and onwards. It is located at nab Volzhskaya 23 and is open 10.00–17.00, closed Friday.

There are three interesting buildings around one city block which are worth looking at. The House of Matveev, pl Sovetskaya 12-14, has two wings built in the 18th and 19th centuries, and a central four-column portico; the House of Vakhrameev, pl Chelyuskintsev 12/4, was built in 1780; and the Physicians Society House, nab Volzhskaya 15, with its neoclassical facade, was built in the 18th and 19th centuries.

The Volga Tower, also known as the Arsenal Tower, sits on the river bank at nab Volzhskaya 7. It is one of two towers that remain from the former Yaroslavl kremlin. The tower was finished in 1668 and is now a naval club.

The Church of the Patriarch Tikhon, nab Volzhskaya 5, was built from 1825 to 1832 and sits on the site of the city's first church, built by Yaroslav the Wise nearly 1,000 years ago.

The Metropolitan's Chamber, nab Volzhskaya 1, was built in the 1680s for the Metropolitan of the nearby city of Rostov-Yaroslavski. The two-storey building is now one of the country's richest Museums of Old Russian Art, open 10.00–17.00, closed Friday. While Yaroslavl's most revered icon, *The Sign of the Virgin*, painted about 1218, now sits in Moscow's Tretyakov Gallery, the museum contains a number of other notable icons.

The centre of Yaroslavl

The centre of the city is defined as Soviet Square (pl Sovetskaya) because all major roads lead off it. On the east side of the square is the Church of St Elijah the Prophet and on the north side are government offices built in 1780.

The Church of St Elijah the Prophet is a large, imposing structure and its construction was paid for by one of the richest and most influential Russian merchant dynasties, the Shripins. The northeastern chapel was erected in honour of the family's protectors, Saints Gury, Samon and Aviv. The southeastern chapel is the Chapel of the Deposition of the Robe. It also has a 36m bell tower.

A highlight of the church, which was completed in 1650, is its frescoes, painted in 1680 and still in excellent condition. The church also contains prayer benches carved for the Tsar Aleksei, who was the father of Peter the Great, and Patriarch Nikon, who lost his job as the Russian Orthodox Patriarch due to his unpopular reforms of the church. The prayer benches were moved here in 1930 from the Church of St Nicholas on the Water. The church is now a museum and is open 10.00–18.00, closed Wednesday, May 1 to September 30

Near the church is an obelisk commemorating the defeat of a 16-day revolt of White Guard forces by the communists in July 1918.

In the Chelyuskintsev Gardens is a World War II memorial and eternal flame.

The Traders' Arcade, ul Pervomaiskaya 10, was built from 1814 to 1818. The area near the arcade is still a busy shopping area.

The Vlasyevskaya Tower, also known as the Sign (Znamenskaya) Tower, ul Pervomaiskaya 21, is the second of the two towers that remain from Yaroslavl's original kremlin.

The Volkov Drama Theatre, pl Volkova, was built in 1911 and is named after Fedor Volkov (1729–63) who established the Russian national theatre in the 1750s. He was the first to stage *Hamlet* in Russia.

Other places of entertainment are the Planetarium, ul Trefoleva 20, the Circus, ul Svobody, the Children's and Puppet Theatres, ul Svobody, and the Philharmonic Theatre, ul Komitetskaya 13.

The little-known Military Museum, ul Uglichskaya 44a, tel: 230 056, is interesting.

Although the Rostov *finift* enamel factory is based in the nearby city of Rostov-Yaroslavski, the factory shop is here at ul Kirova 13, next to the Hotel Volga. It has a great range of *finift* enamel gifts.

Log Town

Log Town (Rubleny Gorod) was the name of the wooden settlement which grew up around the town's original kremlin. Like the kremlin, Log Town was totally burned down in 1658. The kremlin was never rebuilt as the better fortified Transfiguration of our Saviour Monastery guarded the town's southern approach well. Today, there are only three interesting buildings in this area.

The plain white-washed Church of St Nicholas in Log Town, nab Kotoroslnaya 8, was built in 1695 and has five elegant domes and a slender bell tower with a pointed tent roof. The Church of the Saviour in the Town, ul Pochtovaya 3, was built in 1672 in the centre of Log Town's market place. In 1693, frescoes were painted telling the history of Christianity in Russia. The red brick Church of Archangel Michael, nab Kotoroslnaya 14, was built in 1658 and its frescoes date from the 1730s.

Korovnitskaya Sloboda historic district

Korovnitskaya Sloboda, which means "cattle breeding settlement on the outskirts of town", sits on the right bank of the Kotorosl River as it flows into the Volga.

The historic district's focal point is the Church of St John Chrysostom, nab Portovaya 2, which was built from 1649 to 1654. It has four domes and two tent-shaped side chapels which make it appealingly symmetrical. As it was built at the height of the decorative arts in Yaroslavl, its ornamentation is very elaborate.

The Church of Vladimir Mother of God is very similar in style but significantly smaller than the Church of St John Chrysostom, as it is was designed to be heated so that it could be used in winter. The Church of Vladimir Mother of God was built in 1669.

Connecting the two churches is a wall and in its centre are the Holy Gates which were built in the Moscow baroque style at the turn of the 17th century.

The most obvious building in the historic area is the pointed 37m high bell tower which carries the nickname of the Candle of Yaroslavl. It was erected in 1680.

Tolchkovski historic district

This district was once famous for its leather work. There are three churches of interest here.

The 15-domed Church of St John the Baptist, nab Kotoroslnaya 69, which can be seen from the railway as you cross over the Kotorosl River, is considered the architectural pinnacle of Yaroslavl. From a distance it looks as if it is trimmed in lace and carved of wood but this deception is created by carved and patterned bricks. It was built from 1671 to 1687 and consists of the two side chapels of Sts Gury and Varsonofy on either side of the main part of the church. The chapels are very unusual as they are nearly as tall as the church and, instead of having the traditional tent roofs, are each crowned with five domes. The central church also has five domes. The church's interior is a mass of frescoes, allegedly more than in any other Russian church. The church also has an impressive six-tiered carved wooden iconostasis. At the back is a 45m bell tower built in about 1700. The church is now a museum, open 10.00–18.00, closed Tuesday.

The Church of St Theodore, ul Yaroslavskovo 74, has five shingled domes and its construction was funded by local parishioners. It was built in 1687 and its frescoes were painted in 1715. Beside this church is the Church of St Nicholas Pensky which was built in 1691.

Other places of interest on the south riverbank

The Church of St Nicholas by the Water Mills, ul Stackek 60, is a basic church finished in 1672 with its frescoes completed in 1707.

The Church of Sts Peter and Paul and the 58m bell tower beside it are both described in *Passing through, page 251*.

The House of Korytov, ul Zelentsovskaya 7, was built in the 17th century and is one of the few secular buildings remaining in the region.

The Church of St Pareskeva Pyatnitsa on the Hill of Sorrows is a single-domed church, built in 1692, on the site of a bloody uprising by locals who failed to overthrow the occupying Tatar-Mongols in 1257.

Getting help

Travel agents   Intourist is in the Yubileynaya Hotel, office 230A, nab Kotoroslennaya 11A, tel: 221 613, fax: 229 306.

Air   Aeroflot, ul Svobody 20, tel: 222 420.

What's in the region
The Estate of Nikolai Nekrasov

About 15km south of Yaroslavl on the Moscow Highway is the former estate of the poet Nikolai Nekrasov near the town of Karabikha (Карабиха).

Nikolai Nekrasov (1821–77) was a great Russian poet who believed in traditional Russian values which endeared him to the Russian and the Soviet governments. He lived here from 1861 to 1875. Today, the estate consists of a large central building which contains a museum and is surrounded by landscaped gardens.

In front of the building, near the car park, is the grave of Nekrasov's brother who bought the estate from Nikolai and then rented it back to the cash-strapped Nekrasov. To the side of the building is the landscaped English Park leading down to the Kotorosl River 500m away.

The museum is open 10.00–17.30, closed Monday. Every July the estate hosts the annual National Nekrasov Poetry Festival.

Tereshkova Cosmos Museum in Bolshoe Nikolskoe village

About 27km to the northwest of Yaroslavl in the village of Bolshoe Nikolskoe (Большое Никольское) is the Cosmos Museum of Valentina Tereshkova. Tereshkova became the world's first woman cosmonaut when on June 16 1963 she orbited the earth 48 times during her 70 hours in space. She was born nearby and lived in Bolshoe Nikolskoe until moving with her family to Yaroslavl in 1945. The museum has an exhibition on her life, a copy of her space capsule and displays on the achievements of the Soviet space programme. The museum is open 10.00–17.30, closed Monday.

Tolgsky Monastery

About 14km to the north of Yaroslavl near the town of Tolgobol (Толгоболь), at the junction of the Tolga and Volga Rivers, is the Tolgsky Monastery. This monastery is famous for its miracle-working icon called *Our Lady of Tolga* which is now in the Metropolitan's Chamber Art Museum in Yaroslavl.

The monastery's interesting buildings include the massive five-domed Presentation of the Mother of God Cathedral (1681–83), the winter Raising of the Cross Church (17th century), the summer Church of the Saviour, the Gate Church of St Nicholas (1672) and the bell tower (1683–5). The monastery is now run by nuns.

The best way to get there is to take a regular boat from the river station. The trip takes 35 minutes.

YAROSLAVL–NOVKI
via Furmanov, Ivanovo and Shuya (Palekh)

Suburban trains　From Yaroslavl, suburban trains go as far as Ivanovo passing through Furmanov. The trip to Furmanov takes 3hr and to Ivanovo takes 3hr 40min. From Ivanovo, suburban trains go as far as Novki passing through Shuya. The trip to Shuya takes 50min and to Novki takes 2hr 30min.

Long-distance trains　From Yaroslavl, long-distance trains travel through Novki on their way to Nizhni Novgorod. All trains on this route are slow passenger trains which stop at virtually every station. The trip to Furmanov takes 2hr 51min, to Ivanovo takes 3hr 16min, to Shuya takes 4hr 30min and to Novki takes 5hr 25min.

Yaroslavl　Ярославль　0km
See *page 250.*

Nerekhta   Нерехта   50km

This small town dates back to 1214 and slowly developed into a major fabric manufacturing centre. So closely woven into the fabric of the town's history are textiles that the building of the first linen factory, built in 1761, has been classified as an architectural monument.

Although a big fire in 1838 destroyed most of the town, several other interesting buildings remain, including the Church of our Lady of Vladimir (Vladimirskaya) built in the 1670s, the Church of St Nicholas (Nikolskaya) built from 1710 to 1725 and the Monastery of the Trinity and St Simeon (Troitskoe-Simonova) dating from the 18th century.

Furmanov   Фурманов   98km

This town was originally called Sereda before it was renamed after the communist writer Dmitry Andreevich Furmanov (1891–1926) who was born here. There is a museum here dedicated to his life and works. The only other places worth seeing are the Art Gallery and the Textile Workers' Palace of Culture built in the 1930s constructivist style. The palace is now known as the Druzhba Cinema.

IVANOVO   Иваново   137km
Population: 480,000   Telephone area code: 0932

Unlike most of the other cities in the Golden Ring, Ivanovo has no religious significance although it was of both industrial and political importance. For this reason most people avoid the city but, if you are visiting nearby Palekh, it is worth spending half a day in Ivanovo.

Although a settlement on the site of present day Ivanovo predated 1561, this is taken as the city's foundation as it is the first recorded mention of the city's existence. In that year, Ivan the Terrible gave the town as a dowry to his new parents-in-law. Ivanovo took off in 1710 when Peter the Great ordered weaving mills and printing factories to be built here. Within a few years, the city became known as the Russian Manchester and was famous for its calico and chintz, which is a printed cotton. Today, the city and surrounding textile mills produce about 25% of the nation's fabric.

The city has an airport 10km on the southeastern outskirts of the city.

Where to stay

The most popular place for foreigners is the standard Hotel Tourist, ul Naberezhnaya 9, tel: 376 519, $40 for a twin share room. Other hotels are Hotel Intourist, ul Ermaka 20, tel: 376 519; Hotel Sovetskaya, pr Lenina 64, tel: 372 547; Hotel Ivanovo, ul Karla Marksa 46, tel: 374 024; and Hotel Tsentralnaya, ul Engelsa 1, tel: 228 122.

What to see

The Museum of Local Studies, ul Baturina 6/40, open 11.00–18.00, closed Monday, has a number of displays focusing on textiles and printing.

The Art Museum, pro Lenina 33, open 11.00–18.00, closed Tuesday, is based on the antique collection of Dmitry Burylin, a local millionaire factory owner.

The former office of the great communist revolutionary Mikhail Frunze has been turned into a museum, ul Rabfakovskaya 6. Frunze (1885–1925) worked here both before and after the 1917 communist revolution.

Ivanovo was the location of Russia's first Workers' Soviet (council) during the first Russian revolution in 1905. A red brick museum, Sadovaya St, open 11.00–18.00, closed Monday, has been built next to the building that housed the short-lived Soviet.

On the north side of the railway line, on ul Svobody, is an impressive memorial complex of sculptures and an eternal flame called Krasnaya Talka. This area was just fields in 1905 when over 15,000 workers gathered here late in the 72-day strike, demanding better pay, conditions and political control. The protest was broken up by brutal Cossacks and dozens died.

The large white Transfiguration Cathedral, ul Kolotilova 39, was built in 1892 and currently holds services.

The wooden Ascension Church, ul Frunze 7, was built in the 17th century and moved here in 1904 from a shrinking village in the region.

The red brick, five-domed Presentation of the Virgin Church, at the corner of the streets ul Spartak and Engelsa, now houses the city's archives.

Ivanovo entertainment venues include the Big Drama Theatre, ul Engelsa 58, the Musical Comedy Theatre, ul Krasnoi Armii 8/2, the Puppet Theatre, ul Kiznetsova 59, the Circus, pro Lenina, and the Planetarium in Stepanov Park, ul Ermaka.

The House of Grachov, ul Kolotilova 43, is a mansion built by a rich serf who bought his freedom in 1793. The house is now a meeting hall.

Getting assistance
Travel agents Intourist, pr Engelsa 1/25, tel: 323 292; Bureau of Travel and Excursions, ul Ermaka 20, tel: 320 651; Sputnik, ul Stepanova 14, tel: 326 048.
Air Aeroflot, pr Stroitelei 24, tel: 261 623.
Bus Bus station, tel: 234 154.

Shuya   Шуя   165km
This textile town is dominated by the 106m-high bell tower built in 1810 when it was a rich trading city famous for its sheepskins, sleighs and wagons. The town's places of interest include the Museum of Local Studies, pl Lenina, and a museum, ul Torgovaya 11, to the communist revolutionary M V Frunze who worked here in 1905–6.

The station buildings at Shuya are the oldest in northern Russia and celebrated their 100th anniversary in 1996. The original station was built in 1868 when the town was a booming industrial centre but it was burnt down 25 years later. The reason why the station looks so good after a century is because it was renovated in time for its anniversary celebrations.

Palekh   Палех
For centuries this town was one of Russia's most famous icon-painting centres until the communist revolutionaries banned its work in 1917. However, rather than wasting the artists' talents and simultaneously to dispel the notion that the Soviet regime was formed of philistines, a new form of art was created a few years later called the *palekh* miniatures. This is a genre of Russian folk miniature painting where scenes of contemporary life, literature, fairy tales and folk songs, are painted on to little papier-mâché boxes, cigarette cases and powder compacts. The precisely drawn figures and landscapes, and abundant gilding are normally painted on using tempera and often cover the entire surface of the lid.

Today, over 200 craftspeople work in the Palekh Art Studio and an exhibition of one of the town's greatest exponents, Ivan Golivko (1886–1937), can be found in a museum in his former house on ul Bakanova.

The Museum of Palekh Art, ul Bakanova 50, tel: 220 54, 210 54, closed on Monday, is well worth visiting, both for its extensive collection of *palekh* work and also for the building itself. The museum is housed in the green and white former Elevation of the Holy Cross (Krestovozdvizhenski) Cathedral which has inspiring frescoes on the ceiling and a baroque-style golden iconostasis carved and painted by local artists.

There is a very basic hotel in Palekh.

There is no railway to Palekh so you need to catch a bus. Buses run from Shuya station 31km away, from Ivanovo bus station 62km away, and from Vladimir bus station.

Novki   Новки   224km

This large town sits on the line Moscow–Vladimir–Nizhni Novgorod. It is the terminus for suburban trains from Ivanovo. There are suburban trains from Novki to Vladimir and the journey takes 52 minutes. There are also suburban trains in the direction of Nizhni Novgorod which go as far as Vyzaniki.

IVANOVO–BELKOVO
via Yurev-Polski

This route has only a few trains each day.

Suburban trains   From Ivanovo, suburban trains go as far as Belkovo passing through Yurev-Polski. (An occasional train goes an extra 18km to Aleksandrov.) The trip to Yurev-Polski takes 2hr 19min and to Belkovo takes 4hr.

Long-distance trains   From Ivanovo, long-distance trains travel to Belkovo on their way to Moscow. The trip on the fastest train to Yurev-Polski takes 2hr 3min, to Belkovo takes 3hr 5min and to Aleksandrov takes 3hr 17min.

Ivanovo   Иваново   0km
See *page 258.*

Nerl   Нерль   62km
This small, textile town is named after the Nerl River which is 4km past the town.

Gavrilov Posad   Гаврилов Посад   82km
The town was founded in the 16th century by Ivan the Terrible as a royal staging post. Its greatest asset is the horse stud for the Vladimir breed of draft horses.

Yurev-Polski   Юрьев-Польский   117km
This town was founded in 1152 by Yuri Dolgoruky who also founded Moscow. Translated, the town means "Yuri standing in the field". From a distance, the town is hard to see as it is sits in a hollow. However, this camouflage didn't save it from being destroyed by the Tatar-Mongols in 1238, 1382 and 1408, nor by the Polish-Lithuanian mercenaries in 1612.

All that remains of the original kremlin are the earth walls. Near these fortifications are the town's most noticeable building, the Cathedral of St George (Georgievski). This example of the Vladimir-Suzdal school of

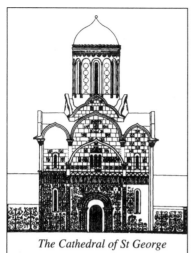

The Cathedral of St George

architecture was built between 1230 and 1234 but collapsed in the 1460s. Since then it has been rebuilt several times. The cathedral looks squat and sprawling with its massive dome on low walls and three adjoining porches. The stone-carved facade is very interesting as it includes mostly Christian motifs interspersed with pagan figures.

In the northeast part of the town is the fortified Archangel Michael (Mikhailo-Arkhangelski) Monastery which is ringed by a wall with three towers. Although the monastery was founded in the 13th century, most of it dates from four centuries later. These include a 17th-century bell tower topped with a tent-shaped superstructure; a cathedral with five cupolas built in 1792; the Apparition of the Virgin (Znamenskaya) Refectory Church built in 1652; and the Divine (Bogoslovskaya) Church built in 1670. This last church sits above the Holy Gates which were built in 1653 and restored in 1963.

The centre of the town is pleasant to stroll through with numerous stone and wooden buildings of the 19th and 20th centuries.

Belkovo   Бельково   189km
This small railway town is at the junction of the railways Aleksandrov–Orekhovo-Zuevo and Belkovo–Ivanovo.

ALEKSANDROV–OREKHOVO-ZUEVO
via Belkovo

Suburban trains From Aleksandrov, suburban trains go as far as Orekhovo-Zuevo, passing through Belkovo. The trip to Belkovo takes 10min and to Orekhovo-Zuevo takes 1hr 55min.
Long-distance trains From Aleksandrov, long-distance trains travel to Orekhovo-Zuevo on their way to Vladimir and Nizhni Novgorod. No train stops at Belkovo and only a few stop at Orekhovo-Zuevo. The trip on the fastest train to Orekhovo-Zuevo takes 1hr 35min and to Vladimir takes 3hr 40min.

Aleksandrov   Александров   0km
This city sits on the main railway line Moscow–Aleksandrov–Yaroslavl. See *page 238*.

Belkovo   Бельково   19km
See above.

Orekhovo-Zuevo   Орехово-Зуево   79km
The city sits at the railway junctions of the Moscow–Vladimir and Orekhovo-Zuevo–Aleksandrov lines. See *page 262*.

MOSCOW–NOVKI
via Orekhovo-Zuevo, Vladimir (Suzdal) and Bogolyubovo

Both suburban and long-distance trains on this route depart from Kursk station. In the recent past, long-distance trains also departed from Yaroslav station.
Suburban trains   From Moscow, suburban trains go as far as Vladimir, passing through Orekhovo-Zuevo. The trip to Orekhovo-Zuevo takes 1hr 28min and to Vladimir takes 3hr 30min. From Vladimir, suburban trains go through Bogolyubovo and Novki on their way to Vyazniki. The trip to Bogolyubovo takes 14min and to Novki takes 53min.
Long-distance trains   From Moscow, long-distance trains travel through Vladimir on their way to Nizhni Novgorod and Vyatka on the Trans-Siberian railway. Most trains stop only at Vladimir and not at Orekhovo-Zuevo, Bogolyubovo or Novki. The trip on the fastest train to Vladimir takes 3hr 25min.

Moscow   Москва   0km
Trains for Vladimir leave from Kursk station, ul Zemlyani Val 29, tel: 924 9243, 262 8532, 266 5652. The closest metro station is Kurskaya.

Pavlovski-Posad   Павловский-Посад   68km
This ancient town is a centre of textile manufacturing. This is reflected in the museum of local studies which has an enormous collection of handkerchiefs and head scarves.

Orekhovo-Zuevo   Орехово-Зуево   90km
The city sits on the Klyazma River at the railway junctions of the Moscow–Vladimir and Orekhovo-Zuevo–Aleksandrov lines.

The town was formed in the mid-19th century as a result of the merger of large textile factories in the settlements of Zuevo, Nikolskoe, Orekhovo and Dubrovka. By the late 1800s, Orekhovo-Zuevo had grown to 17 factories and 30,500 workers. The town became famous for the Morozov strike of 1885 which was the largest protest in Russia up to that time. The town received its current name in 1917 and today is a major textile production centre.

Pokrov   Покров   106km
Near Pokrov is the village of Novoselovo (Новосёлово). This was where the world's first astronaut, Yuri Gagarin, died in a plane crash in 1968. Another plane crossed his path when he was flying close to the ground and the resulting turbulence destabilised him, slamming his plane into the ground.

Petushki   Петушки   126km
Nearby is Russia's main zoo for animals used in films. Consequently, the area around Petushki features in many Russian films involving bears, horses and other animals. The only other industry in town comes from the spool and bobbin factories.

The town sits on the left bank of the Klyazma River. It has basic accommodation in the Hotel Rossiyanka, ul Mayakovskovo 19, tel: 241 53, $16 twin share/person.

Kosterevo   Костерево   135km

Not far away lived the famous Russian painter, Levitan. His house has been moved to Kosterevo and is now a museum.

Undol   Ундол   161km

The station is named Undol after the famous Russian bibliographer, V M Undolski, who was born here. The town around the station is known as Lakinsk (Лакинск) after the revolutionary M I Lakin who was killed here in 1905.

While the town is known for these two men and the great Russian general A V Suvorov who lived here, it is most famous for its beer. The Lakinsk brewery was built using Czechoslovakian technology and it uses a Czechoslovakian recipe. When you are in Vladimir, ask for this beer.

VLADIMIR   Владимир   191km
Population: 356,000   Telephone area code: 092 22

Vladimir is a convenient, cheap and interesting place to visit, either as part of a extensive tour of the Golden Ring or just on a day trip from Moscow.

To see all of Vladimir and the nearby sites of Suzdal, Bogolyubovo and the Church of the Intercession on the Nerl River, you need to spend at least two nights here. Tour Vladimir on the first day and a half, visit Bogolyubovo and the Church of the Intercession on the Nerl River in the afternoon of the second day and then make a day return trip to Suzdal on the third.

History

Although Vladimir was officially founded in the year 1108, from about 500BC there was a village, whose inhabitants planted crops and raised animals, on the site of the present-day city.

During the great migration of Slavs from the disintegrating Kievian Rus empire at the end of the 10th and beginning of the 11th centuries, the Vladimir region was settled and the previous inhabitants evicted.

In 1108, Grand Prince Vladimir Monomakh of Kiev founded the Vladimir fortress to protect his eastern lands. The city is named after him. Vladimir's grandson, Andrei Bogolyubsky, stormed Kiev in 1157, pillaged its wealth and took its master craftsmen with him to build a new capital in Vladimir. In a conciliatory gesture to the inhabitants of Kiev, who felt that he had abandoned them, he left Kiev under the protection of a holy icon. After a few years, he transferred the icon to Vladimir, where it became known as *Our Lady of Vladimir*.

Over the next seven years, Andrei oversaw the creation of a new city which included numerous impressive buildings such as the Ascension Cathedral and Golden Gates. By the time he was murdered in 1174 by disenchanted *boyars* from Suzdal, he had achieved his dream of building a grander city than Kiev and developing a powerful state centred around Vladimir.

Unfortunately, Andrei's successor and brother, Vsevolod III, did not have the strength to maintain the integrity of the Vladimir Principality and soon the territory was divided up amongst family members.

Despite its defeat by the Tatar-Mongols in 1238, the city remained the political centre of northeastern Russia and the religious centre of the whole

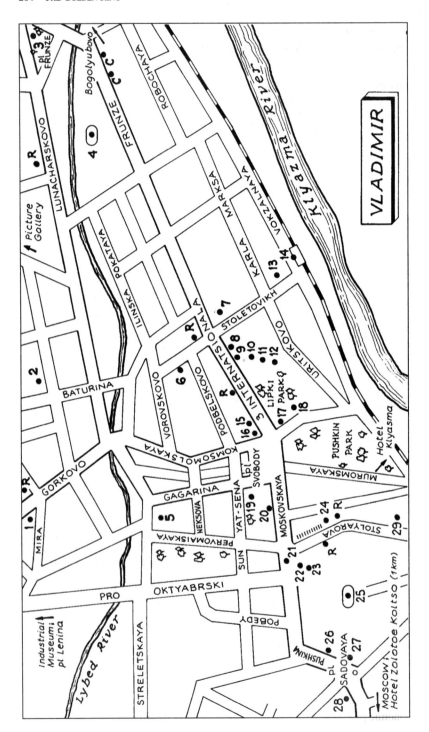

KEY TO VLADIMIR   Владимир

1	Central Soviet Building	Центральный Совет
2	Market (*Rynok*)	рынок
3	Frunze Monument	Памятник Фрунзе
4	Stadium Stroitel (*Stadion*)	Стадион «Строитель»
5	Ascension (*Uspenski*) Cathedral at the Princess's (*Knyaginina*) Monastery	Успенский собор Княгинина монастыря
6	House Museum of the Brothers Stoletov (*Muzei*)	Дом-музей братьев Столетовых
7	Hotel Vladimir	гостиница Владимир
8	Nativity (*Rozhdestvenovo*) Monastery	Рождественский монастырь
9	History Museum (*Muzei*)	Исторический музей
10	Planetarium (*Planetari*)	Планетарий
11	Cathedral of St Demetrius (*Dmitrievski*) of Salonica	Дмитриевский собор
12	Former Provincial Government Building	Здание бывших губернских присутственных
13	Bus station (*Avtovokzal*)	Автовокзал
14	Railway station (*Vokzal*)	Ж-Д Вокзал
15	House of Officers (*Ofitserov*)	Дом офицеров
16	Bank	Банк
17	Monument to the 850 Anniversary of Vladimir	Монумент в честь 850-летия Владимира
18	Ascension (*Uspenski*) Cathedral	Успенский собор
19	Puppet (*Kukol*) Theatre	Театр кукол
20	Traders' Row (*Torgovye ryady*)	Торговые ряды
21	Golden Gates (*Zolotye vorota*) and Military Exposition	Золотые Ворота и Военно-историческая экспозиция
22	Crystal, Lacquered & Embroidery Museum (*Muzei*)	Музей хрустале, лаковой миниатюры и вышивки
23	Drama (*Dramaticheski*) Theatre	Драматический театр
24	Old Vladimir Museum (*Muzei*)	Музей «Старый Владимир»
25	Stadium Torpedo (*Stadion*)	Стадион «Торпедо»
26	Clocks and Time Museum (*Muzei*)	Музей «Часы и время»
27	Taneev Concert (*Kontsertny*) Hall	Концертный зал им Танеева
28	Hotel Zarya (*Gostinitsa*)	гостиница Заря
29	Church of St Nicholas on the Waters (*Nikoly Mokrovo*) in Galei	Церковь Николы Мокрого
R	Restaurant (*Restoran*)	Ресторан
C	Café (*Kafe*) or Bar (*Bar*)	Кафе или Бар

country as the See of the Metropolitan of All Rus was relocated from Kiev to Vladimir in 1300.

However, in 1320 the religious power of Vladimir disappeared with the transfer of the Metropolitan See to Moscow by Metropolitan Peter. Vladimir's brief period of glory ended in 1392 when the city and its region were absorbed into the Moscow Principality, and to reinforce its new found insignificance, in 1395 the holy *Our Lady of Vladimir* icon was carted off to Moscow.

Vladimir rapidly became a backwater and by 1668, the city's inhabitants numbered just 990.

While the city slowly grew from this low point, it played no role in the revolutionary turmoil at the turn of the 20th century. During the early years of communism, Moscow's central planners decided that Vladimir should become an industrial centre and consequently the large Vladimir tractor factory, the Avtopribor automotive parts engineering plant and another 48 major factories were built. While most still exist, their output is minimal due to the country's economic problems.

Passing through

All long-distance trains through Vladimir stop here for about 15 minutes. This is enough time to run to the Moscow end of the platform and have a look through the dirty windows of the blue building. This 1920s building is the railway bogie repair shop and you will immediately appreciate the arduous working conditions of most Russian factories.

On the eastern outskirts of Vladimir you pass through the city's industrial zone. On the right is the city's hot-water plant and on the left is the Synthetic Resin Research Institute, the Avtopribor automotive instrument manufacturing plant and the Vladimir chemical works.

Slightly further on is the famous Sungir Gully archaeological site. Over 25,000 years ago warriors were buried here. The only examples in the world of spears made of mammoth tusks were found here and these are on display in Vladimir's History Museum.

Where to stay

The closest hotel to the station is the basic Hotel Vladimir, ul 3rd Internatsionala 74, tel: 230 41, 273 49, $12 twin share/person. It has a restaurant. From the station, you can reach the hotel more quickly on foot than you can by catching trolleybus No 5 which does a big loop from the station before passing the hotel.

The standard Hotel Zarya, ul Pushkina 36, tel: 252 19, 914 41, $37 twin share/person, can be reached on trolleybus No 5 which stops directly in front of it. Foreigners are housed in the new wing of the hotel but only up to the seventh floor. This is because higher floors give an excellent view of the nearby military base. It has a restaurant.

The standard Hotel Klyazma, shosse Sudogorodskoye 15, tel: 242 37, 223 10, 244 83, $29 twin share/person, is set in a picturesque area about 2km from the centre of the city. To get to it take trolleybus No 5 to pl Svobody, then cross the road and go down the stairs to the underpass. From here catch trolleybus No 6 which passes the hotel just before it terminates. It also has a restaurant.

Another option is Hotel Zolotoe Koltso, ul Chaikovskaya 27, tel: 48 807, 48 819, $44 twin share/person. It has a restaurant. The hotel is on the corner of ul Chaikovskaya and ul Balakireva. To get to it, take trolleybus No 10 from the railway station or trolleybus No 8 from pl Svobody. Get off at the stop Gostinitsa Zolotoe Koltso.

Getting around

The long-distance bus station and the railway station are opposite one another.

Trolleybus No 5 starts at the railway station and travels east then north until it reaches pl Frunze at the eastern end of the main street. From here, the trolleybus runs westward along the main street. Bus No 14 also travels along the main road but does not go to the station.

To get to the market, the Art Gallery, the Industrial Museum and pl Lenina, take trolleybus No 7 from pl Svobody.

What to see

Almost everything of interest in Vladimir lies along the main road which has five names. From the west it is known as pro Lenina, then ul Pushkina, then ul Moskovskaya, then ul 3rd Internatsionala and finally ul Frunze.

The Golden Gates

The entire city of Vladimir was once ringed by several kilometres of earth ramparts topped with oak walls, making the Vladimir fortress an unusual design. Traditionally, a city kremlin consisted of a small, heavily fortified citadel with an unprotected settlement beyond its walls. By building a defensive wall around the entire city in the 1150s, Vladimir's population swelled quickly as settlers arrived seeking security.

Today, the only remnants of Vladimir's great defences are the Golden Gates and nearby earth embankments.

In 1158, Prince Bogolyubsky built the Golden Gates which were modelled on the Golden Gates of Kiev which in turn were based on the Golden Gates of Constantinople. This symbolised the transfer of power from the capital of the Second Roman Empire to Kiev and finally to Vladimir. To illustrate further the city's majesty, the gate's thick, oak outer doors were covered with sheets of gilded copper. On top of the gate was the golden-domed Gate Church of the Deposition of the Robe.

In those days, the gates were more modest as it was only in 1785, when the earth walls were removed, that the two round ornamental towers on each side were added. The removal was necessary as they could no longer deal with the main road's increased traffic, and the gates became the centre of a roundabout. The ornamental towers served as buttresses to stop the gates from collapsing sideways.

Today, the gate church has become a Military Exposition, ul 3rd Internatsionala and ul Moskovskaya, tel: 225 59, open 10.00–17.00, closed Monday and Tuesday, whose central focus is a large diorama of the storming of Vladimir by the Tatar-Mongols in 1238. The diorama has a light show and English-language audio track which will be switched on if you ask the attendants. To get to the Military Exposition, walk up the narrow, 60-step internal staircase. The entrance is at the base of the gate's left side as you face it from the front.

At the base of the gate's right side is a time capsule buried in 1983 on the city's 875th anniversary. It is to be opened in 2108 and will probably surprise its readers by its greetings to those living in a "communist paradise".

On the top of the white-washed Golden Gates you will see a copy of the Byzantine *Our Lady of Vladimir* icon (as distinct from Andrei Rublev's *Vladimir Mother of God* icon). The original Byzantine icon used to be hung here but is now in Moscow.

Remnants of Vladimir's earth walls can be seen beside the Golden Gates along val Kozlov (meaning "goat embankment") which runs to the Exhibition of Old Vladimir.

Ascension Cathedral

The city is justifiably proud of this church. It was built by Prince Andrei Bogolyubsky in 1160 to rival Kiev's St Sophia Cathedral in the former capital of Kievian Rus. It was dedicated to the Ascension (elevation of the Virgin Mary after her death) for two reasons in order to symbolise Vladimir's succession over Kiev. Firstly, the Ascension was the chief festival of St Sophia's Cathedral. Secondly, just as the Ascension reunited at Mary's deathbed the 12 apostles who had scattered all over the earth, Andrei's Ascension Cathedral was to bring the princes of the fragmented Kievian Rus back together.

The cathedral was the tallest building in all of Russia at that time and, following a fire in 1185, was enlarged to hold a massive 4,000-member congregation. All the rulers from Andrei Bogolyubsky to Ivan III (the Great) were crowned here and it served as the burial vault for numerous Russian notables including Andrei Bogolyubsky, Vsevolod III and the great medieval Russian writer, Serapion of Vladimir.

The Ascension Cathedral was so famous that it was used as the model for the Ascension Cathedral in Moscow's kremlin which was built at the end of the 15th century.

One of most interesting aspects of the cathedral is the 25m-high iconostasis containing 100 icons. It once included famous icons by the artist Andrei Rublev but these are now held in Moscow's Tretyakov Gallery and St Petersburg's Russian Museum. However, Rublev's work can still be seen in the form of frescoes done in 1408.

The Ascension Cathedral, ul 3rd Internatsionala 56, is a practising church and it may be hard to get in without waiting or being properly attired. Tourists are normally only admitted from 13.30 to 16.30.

Outside the cathedral is the winter Church of St George which could be heated. It was built in 1862. Next to it is the three-storey bell tower with a gilded spire built in 1810 after the old tent-roofed bell tower was destroyed by lightning.

Cathedral of St Demetrius of Salonica

While the unusual, single-domed, square Cathedral of St Demetrius of Salonica, ul 3rd Internatsionala 60, is nowhere near as impressively large as the Ascension Cathedral, it is still extremely interesting. It was built from 1194 to 1197 as Vsevolod III's court church, as his palace once stood nearby. It is built from white limestone blocks and has over 1,300 bas relief carvings on its outside walls. These carvings show a range of people, events, animals and plants.

The cathedral is now managed by the nearby History Museum which may open it up if asked.

What else to see

The Clocks and Time Museum, ul Pushkina 1, contains dozens of intricate and clever clocks. The museum building was once the Church of Archangel Michael. It was closed in early 1996 and no-one knows when it will be reopened.

In front of the Golden Gates is the Museum of Crystal, Lacquer Miniatures and Embroidery, ul Moskovskaya 2, tel: 248 72. The two-storey, red brick museum building was formerly the Old Believers' Trinity Church, built in 1913.

Just to the south of the Golden Gates is the Exhibition of Old Vladimir, val Kozlov, tel: 254 41, open 10.00–17.00, closed Monday, housed in the red brick, four-storey, 19th-century, former water tower. The top floor is an enclosed observation deck which offers panoramic views of the city.

Behind the Lenin monument, unveiled on July 5 1925, on pl Svobody is the old state bank building, Gosbank, which can be identified by the large advertising sign of БАНКЪ on its roof.

On the west side of pl Svobody is the pseudo-Russian-style City Duma building, erected in 1907. It was the Palace of Weddings and is now the Palace of Culture.

The House of Officers, ul 3rd Internatsionala 33, formerly the Noblemen's Assembly Club, was built in 1826 and has a portico with six pairs of Ionic columns. This building played an interesting role in the campaign against religion during the 1970s and 1980s. Every time a major religious service was held in the Ascension Cathedral opposite, such as at Easter, loud speakers in the House of Officers blared out Western rock music to attract members of the congregation to the free disco. This tactic was particularly effective with young people as at that time Western rock music was rarely heard. For the local Soviet leadership, the decision to use decadent Western music to destroy insidious religion must have been full of anguish.

The monument to the 850th anniversary of Vladimir was unveiled in 1958. This obelisk symbolises the communist theory that people are the makers of history and is expressed by the three bronze figures of an architect, a soldier and a worker.

The Traders' Row Arcade was built from 1787 to 1792 and is slowly being renovated into a retailing district.

The three-storey stucco, Provincial Administrative Offices, ul 3rd Internatsionala 62, was built from 1785 to 1790 and is famous as the site of a number of trials of factory strikers late last century.

The Vladimir Museum of History, ul 3rd Internatsionala 43, tel: 224 84, 22 515, open 10.00–16.30, closed Monday, contains archaeological finds, coins, weapons and rare books. Its most interesting exhibits are the white stone sarcophagus of Aleksandr Nevsky and the *Vladimir Mother of God* icon which is attributed to Andrei Rublev.

The Nativity Monastery, ul 3rd Internatsionala 33, was built from 1191 to 1196, and was the city's most important religious monastery until the end of the 16th century. The great Russian hero, Aleksandr Nevsky, was buried here in 1262 until Peter the Great had him disinterred and reburied in St Petersburg in 1724. His sarcophagus can be seen in the nearby Museum of History.

Nestled against the monastery's side wall is the Planetarium which is open weekdays and Sunday. The building was formerly the Church of St Nicholas-Kremlevskaya built in 1761.

The Frunze monument honours the communist revolutionary Mikhail Frunze who carried out revolutionary work in Vladimir, Ivanovo and Shuya. About 300m away from the monument is the still-operating, maximum-security Vladimir prison in which Frunze was imprisoned in 1907 for revolutionary activities. According to communist propaganda, Frunze was the only inmate ever to escape from it. Near the monument once stood the Silver Gates which marked the boundary of Old Vladimir. The walls around this part of the city followed the Lybed River which now flows under the road through large pipes.

The wooden House-museum of the Stoletov Brothers, ul Stoletovykh 3, tel: 231 26, is dedicated to Nikolai Stoletov (1833–1912), who was a general and hero of the Shipka Pass Battle during the Russian-Turkish War of 1877–8, and Aleksandr Stoletov (1839–96), who was a well-known scholar and physicist.

The Princess's Convent is the site of the third oldest building in Vladimir, and the first building built after the Tatar-Mongol sacking of Vladimir. The monastery was founded in 1220 by Maria Shvarnovna who was the wife of Grand Prince Vsevolod III. She was buried in the Assumption Cathedral as were many of the female side of the Grand Prince's family. The cathedral was destroyed a few decades later and rebuilt in the 15th century. The cathedral now hosts the Museum of Religion, pos Vorovskovo 70, tel: 263 73, is open 11.00–17.00, closed Tuesday, which was known in the Soviet times as the Orthodoxy and Atheism Museum.

The Picture Gallery is in the 850 Anniversary of Vladimir Park and has a good collection of 18th-century portraits.

The Industrial Goods Exhibition, pro Oktyabrski 47, tel: 388 54, contains products produced by the region's 400 enterprises and is being turned into a showroom.

There is a Museum of Precise Engineering Products at the Tochmash factory, ul Severnaya 2a, tel: 731 08. One of their products is high-precision clocks and the company claims to have built the ones shown on Russian TV news every evening.

The white Church of St Nicholas in the Wet in Galei was built in 1732 to 1735 and is a basic refectory church with a tent-shaped bell-tower.

Getting assistance
Travel agents   Intourist, ul 3rd Internatsionala 74, tel: 242 62, 275 14; Bureau for Travel and Excursions, ul Kremlevskaya 5A, tel: 264 14, fax: 224 28.
Air   Aeroflot, pr Lenina 7, tel: 437 16, 247 36.

What's in the region
The three places of interest around Vladimir are Suzdal, Bogolyubovo and the Church of the Intercession on the Nerl River, all of which are covered in the next few pages.

Bogolyubovo   Боголюбово   202km
This ancient town was the site of the royal palace of Prince Andrei Bogolyubsky who developed Vladimir into the capital of Rus following his destruction of Kiev in 1157. He chose this site rather than nearby Vladimir because Bogolyubovo sat at a strategic position on the junction of the Klyazma River which goes through Vladimir and the Nerl River which goes through the rival city of Suzdal.

A recreation of the Bogolyubovo Palace as it was in 1165

The Bogolyubovo town and fortress quickly became the real power centre of Vladimir but, following Andrei's murder here in 1174, the whole lot was turned over to the Bogolyubovo Monastery. Andrei's assassins were powerful *boyars* from Suzdal who wounded him in his bed chamber before stabbing him to death on a staircase.

Today, there is only one tower and a covered archway which date from Andrei's time. The rest dates from the 19th century after several buildings collapsed following shaky renovations in 1722. The main buildings still standing are the Holy Gates, the bell tower built in 1841, the two-storey monks' cell building from the early 19th century and the huge five-domed Bogolyubovo Cathedral of the Icon of the Mother of God built in 1866. The cathedral is slowly being renovated and is open for services.

To get to Bogolyubovo, take a suburban train from Vladimir. There are 13 suburban trains a day to Bogolyubovo and the trip takes 14 minutes. The station is about 400m from the walled Bogolyubovo Monastery which can be easily seen from through trains.

You can also catch one of the more numerous buses from Vladimir's central bus station, opposite the railway station, to Bogolyubovo.

The Church of the Intercession on the Nerl River

About 1.5m to the east of Bogolyubovo is one of Russia's most famous churches outside Moscow and St Petersburg. The white stone, single-green-domed Church of the Intercession of the Nerl River sits in the middle of a field right at the junction of the Nerl and Klyazma Rivers.

The church was built in a single summer in 1165 on the orders of Andrei Bogolyubsky for several symbolic reasons. Firstly, the church sits on the river that flows into the major trading waterway, the Volga, and whenever ambassadors visited they saw this marvellous church that seemed to arise from nowhere. Secondly, to show Vladimir's succession over Byzantium and Kiev, the church was consecrated to the Intercession of the Virgin and Andrei created a holiday on this day without asking permission from the patriarch of Byzantium or Kiev. Thirdly, and possibly just legend, the church was built in memory of his son who died at a victorious battle against the Volga Bulgars.

The church is open during summer from 10.00–16.00, closed Monday. Even if it is closed it is still worth visiting because it is the outside of the church which is particularly interesting. It is best visited in summer, because every thaw, flood waters surround the church's small hill, cutting it off from the path.

About five minutes after leaving Bogolyubovo on the train, the church can be seen on the right. There are no roads to the church so you have to walk about 1.5km from Bogolyubovo. The quickest way to get there is from the Bogolyubovo railway station. Walk directly across the tracks going away from the station and follow any of the paths through the forest belt which is about 100m wide. All the paths lead to an open field and slightly to your left, you will see the church about 1km in the distance. There is a unmarked path across the field to the church and walking there takes about 15 minutes.

Novki   Новки   240km

This large town sits on the junction of two railways lines: the Moscow–Vladimir–Novki–Nizhni Novgorod railway and Novki–Shuya–Ivanovo railway. See *Yaroslavl–Novki, page 257*.

SUZDAL   Суздаль
Population: 12,100   Telephone area code: 09231

This town must hold the record for the most number of churches per capita. Incredibly, at one time there was a church for every 12 people. Other claims to fame include having 15 monasteries, the most in any Russian city except for Moscow, and over 100 major architectural monuments in just 8km².

Although most of the religious buildings have not survived, there are still over 40 in Suzdal. The reason why there were so many churches is because in medieval times, every street in every town had a small, invariably wooden, church. Suzdal's shrinking population maintained this tradition which was forgotten elsewhere, but took it a step further by replacing the wooden churches with durable stone ones when they collapsed.

Two other factors ensured that the town was preserved as if stuck in a time warp. Firstly, in 1788 a town plan was adopted which stated that only two-storey stone houses could be built in the city. This forced the poor to the edge of the town, reducing the need for land. Consequently, older buildings remained standing, whereas in other cities they were continually being replaced. Secondly, in 1862 the railway from Moscow to Nizhni Novgorod bypassed Suzdal by 30km which reduced the town to a backwater till the present day. In the last days of communism, over 800,000 visitors a year were attracted to this magnificently preserved town but nowadays it would be lucky to attract one tenth of that.

History
Suzdal's first recorded mention was when its townsfolk were put to the sword in 1024 by the local prince because of a peasant rebellion led by pagan priests. By the end of that century, the first major fortification had been built in the town and in 1152, Prince Yuri Dolgoruky transferred the seat of power of his principality here. The town quickly grew and within a few years had a larger population than London at that time.

Despite Dolgoruky's son, Andrei Bogolyubsky, moving the capital to nearby Vladimir, Suzdal still grew until, in 1238, it was devastated by the Tatar-Mongols. The town tried to rebuild itself as a trading and political centre but its dreams were shattered after another rebellion was put down by Moscow in the mid-15th century. While most of the population moved away, Suzdal still remained a strong religious centre and at its height, had seven churches and cathedrals in the kremlin, 14 within the city ramparts and 27 more scattered around the town's various monasteries.

In 1573, the town had just 400 households, and disasters over the next few centuries ensured that the number never rose much. Between 1608 and 1610, the town was raided several times by Polish and Lithuanian forces; in 1634 it was devastated by Crimean Tatars; in 1644 most of its wooden buildings were burnt down; in 1654 the plague wiped out nearly 50% of the population; and finally in a huge fire in 1719 virtually every wooden building in its centre was destroyed.

Today the town main's industry is tourism.

Getting there and away
Suzdal is not on any railway but it is easy to get to by bus from Vladimir which is 35km away. Buses leave every hour from Vladimir's central bus station which is opposite the railway station. You can also catch one of ten daily buses to Ivanovo which is 78km to the north of Suzdal.

Suzdal's long-distance bus station is about 1km east of the centre of the town and local bus No 3 runs from the bus station through the town to the Main Tourist Complex.

Where to stay

Most visitors stay at the large sprawling Main Tourist Complex on the northwestern outskirts of the town. This complex was built in 1976 with beds for 430 people. It is spread out along a bend in the River Kamenka and is just 350m from the nearest monastery. By road it is about 1.5km from Suzdal's main street but, by a footbridge over the river, it is only about 500m away. The complex includes a concert hall, cinema, sauna and swimming pool. The rooms cost $40 twin share/person. The hotel is at ul Korovniki, tel: 215 30, fax: 206 66. Next to the complex is a motel which has 100 rooms, and costs $50 twin share/person. There is a restaurant and canteen here.

There are 30 rooms in wooden cabins at the Intercession Convent, tel: 208 89, 209 08. A double room costs $82. These may close as the convent has been handed back to the church. There is a restaurant here in the refectory church.

The best place to stay is Likhoninsky Dom, ul Slobodskaya 34, tel: (09231) 219 01, 204 44, which provides bed and breakfast, $30 per person. The building is a renovated 17th-century house. It only has a few rooms so booking is advisable.

The worst accommodation is the very basic but cheap Hotel Rizopolozhenskaya in the Monastery of the Deposition, tel: 214 08, double rooms cost $8.00.

Getting around

Virtually everything to see in Suzdal is within walking distance of the centre of town with the exception of Yuri Dolgoruky's Royal Estate in Kideksha village.

What to see
Kremlin

The Suzdal kremlin started out as an 11th-century fortress ringed by 1.4km of earth embankments topped with log walls and towers. The fortifications were maintained until the 18th century but nowadays the only remnants of them are the small earth walls dotted around the city. Today, there are three interesting buildings within the kremlin.

The enormous Cathedral of the Birth of the Mother of God is the most striking building with its five blue onion domes dotted with golden stars. The cathedral was built in two years, starting in 1222, and the upper tier was rebuilt in 1530 after it collapsed in 1445.

The octagonal, tent-roofed bell tower was built in 1635 and was the tallest building at that time. It was once fitted with bells that chimed, not only on the hour but on the minute.

Attached to the bell tower by a gallery is the Archbishop's Chambers, built from the 15th to 18th centuries. A staircase leads up to the first floor where the Cross Chamber, open 10.00–17.00, closed Tuesday, is located. This was the Archbishop's ceremonial reception area and is a great feat of engineering as the chamber is over 305m^2 but does not have any supporting central pillars. The Suzdal History and Art Museum, open 10.00–17.00, closed Tuesday, is also located in this building. On the ground floor of the chamber is the Refectory Restaurant.

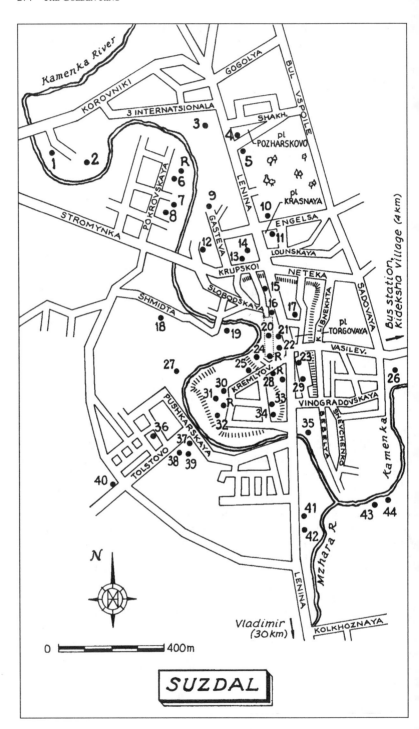

SUZDAL

KEY TO SUZDAL   Суздаль

1	MTK Motel	Мотель
2	Main Tourist Hotel (*MTK*)	Главный туристский комплекс
3	Monastery of the Savior and St Euthimius (*Evfimievski*) and five museums (*Muzei*)	Спасо-Евфимиевский монастырь и 5 музеея
4	Our Lady of Smolensk (*Smolenskaya*) Church	Смоленская церковь
5	Posad House of the 18th century	Посадский дом
6	Intercession (*Pokrovski*) Monastery	Покровский монастырь
7	Church of Sts Peter and Paul (*Petropavlovskaya*)	Петропавловская церковь
8	Church of St Nicholas (*Nikolskaya*)	Никольская церковь
9	St Alexander Nevsky (*Aleksandrovski*) Monastery	Александровский монастырь
10	Bank	Банк
11	Post office (*pochtamt*)	почтамт
12	Likhoninsky Dom	Лихонинский Дом
13	Hotel Rizopolozhenskaya (*Gostinitsa*)	гостиница Ризоположенская
14	Monastery of the Deposition of the Robe (*Rizopolozhenski*)	Ризоположенский монастырь
15	Churches of St Lazarus and St Antipius (*Lazarevskaya i Antipevskaya*)	Церкви Лазаре и Антипия
16	Holy Cross Church (*Krestovskaya*)	Крестовская церковь
17	Churches of Emperor Constantine (*Tsarekonstantinovskaya*) and Virgin of All Sorrows (*Skorbyachshenskaya*)	Цареконстантиновская и Скорбященская церкви
18	Church of the Virgin of Tikhvin (*Tikhvinskaya*)	Тихвинская церковь
19	Churches of Epiphany (*Bogoyavlenskaya*) and Nativity (*Rozhdestvenskaya*)	Богоявленская и Рождественская церкви
20	Trading arcade (*Gostiny dvor*)	Гостиный двор
21	Kazan Church	Казанская церковь
22	Resurrection (*Voskresenskaya*) Church and museum (*Muzei*)	Воскресенская церковь и музей
23	Market (*Rynok*)	Рынок
24	Churches of the Entry into Jerusalem (*Vkhodoierusalimskaya*) and St Paraskeva Pyatnitsa (*Paraskeva Pyatnitskaya*)	Входоиерусалимская и Параскева Пятницкая церкви
25	Ascension (*Uspenskaya*) Church	Успенская церковь
26	Monastery of St Basil (*Vasilevski*)	Васильевский монастырь
27	Church of Elijah the Prophet (*Ilinskaya*)	Ильинская церковь
28	Church of St John the Baptist (*Ioanna Predtechi*)	Церковь Иоанна Предтечи
29	Hotel Sokol	гостиница Сокол
30	Cathedral of the Birth of the Mother of God (*Rozhdestva*)	Собор Рождества Богородицы
31	Archbishop's (*Arkhiereiskie*) Chambers and History Museum (*Muzei*)	Архиерейские палаты и Историко-художественный музей
32	Church of St Nicholas (*Nikoly*) from village of Glotovo	Церковь Николы из села Глотово
33	Church of St Nikolas (*Nikolskaya*)	Никольская церковь
34	Nativity (*Khristorozhdestbenskaya*) Church	Христорождестбенская церковь
35	Church of Sts Kosma and Damian (*Kosmodemyanskaya*)	Козьмодемьянская церковь
36	Church of Sts Boris and Gleb (*Borisoglevskaya*)	Борисоглебская церковь
37	Church of the Transfiguration (*Preobrazhenskaya*)	Преображенская церковь
38	Resurrection (*Voskresenskaya*) Church	Воскресенская церковь
39	Museum of Wooden Architecture and Peasant Life of the 18th to the start of the 20th century (*Muzei*)	Музеи деревянного зодчества и крестьянского быта 18-начала 20вв
40	Ivanovskoe village church	Церковь в Ивановское
41	Church of the Deposition of the Robe (*Rizopolozhenskaya*)	Ризоположенская церковь
42	Church of the Sign (*Znamenskaya*)	Знаменская церковь
43	Church of St Michael the Archangel (*Mikhailo-Arkhangelovo*)	Церковь Михайло-Архангелого
44	Church of Flora and Laura	Церковь Флора и Лавра
R	Restaurant (*Restoran*)	Ресторан

In the southeastern part of the kremlin is the Church of St Nicholas which was built from 1720 to 1739. It is considered one of Suzdal's finest 18th-century buildings.

In the southwest of the kremlin is another Church of St Nicholas, also built in the 18th century. This one is made of wood and was transported here from the nearby village of Glotovo. This is a typical village church of the period.

Near the kremlin
The Church of the Entry into Jerusalem was built in 1707 and stands on the moat of the kremlin. It is a very simple church with a single dome.

Nearby is the Church of St Paraskeva Pyatnitsa, built in 1772, with a dome in the shape of a flower pot.

Trading Square
On one side of the Trading Square (pl Torgovaya) is the town's trading arcade, built at the turn of the 19th century. It now contains tourist shops and at its southern end is the Gostiny Dvor Restaurant. There was once a second line of arcades facing the Kamenka River, but this was pulled down.

In front of the arcade is the smooth walled Church of the Resurrection which houses an exhibition of peasant wood carving from the 17th to 19th centuries. Nearby are the small Church of Our Lady of Kazan built in 1739 and the Church of Emperor Constantine built in 1707. There is a small park on the square dedicated to those who lost their lives during World War II. From Suzdal, 912 locals went off to war and only 446 returned.

The Museum of Wooden Architecture and nearby
To preserve the few remaining wooden buildings left in the Vladimir region, a Museum of Wooden Architecture, open 09.30–16.30, closed Tuesday, was created in 1960 near the kremlin. A large range of buildings has been moved here, including churches, peasant houses, windmills, barns, granaries and a foot-powered treadmill.

There are several notable buildings. The Church of the Transfiguration was built in 1756 at one of the most ancient Suzdal monasteries, called St Demetrius, in the village of Kozlyatevo. It has an interesting interior and iconostasis. The Church of Resurrection, built in 1776 in the village of Potakino, was built boat-wise as the sanctuary, main body and porch all lie in a straight line. The peasant house, with the date 1862 carved on its front, came from the village of Kamenevo and was built for two families. A number of the buildings are fitted out with period clothes, hand looms, kitchen utensils and agricultural equipment.

You can visit the buildings all year round but the interiors of most are only open from May 1 to September 30.

Nearby is the Church of Sts Boris and Gleb, dating from the 18th century. This church is the only one in Suzdal to contain baroque features.

Convent of the Intercession
The convent provides a rare insight into the patriarchal nature of traditional Russian society which saw women as little more than breeding animals.

The convent was euphemistically known as a place for high-spirited women but in reality it was a place of banishment for infertile wives, victims of dynastic squabbles and women who broke any of the harsh customs of medieval Russian society.

It was first used as a place of exile in 1525 by Moscow's Grand Prince Vasily whose wife Solomonia Saburova bore him no heirs. At that time divorce was unknown so Vasily had to bribe the clergy in Byzantium to get an exemption. Solomonia achieved her revenge by outliving her ex-husband and his second wife. She is buried in the crypt of the Intercession Cathedral.

Other famous women discarded by their husbands and sent to the convent were Praskovya Solovaya, the second wife of Ivan the Great; Anna Vasilchikova, Ivan the Terrible's fourth wife; and Evdokya Lopukhina, Peter the Great's first wife.

The three-domed Gateway Church of the Annunciation sits above the Holy Gates. The Holy Gates have two arches: one for carriages and the other for pedestrians.

The three-domed Cathedral of the Intercession was completed in 1518 and its crypt contains the tombs of a number of famous women. The cathedral never had any wall paintings which must have made this black-tiled-floor building very depressing.

The two-storey Refectory Church of the Conception of St Anna was built in 1551 on the orders of Ivan the Great. Experts believe that this unusually decorated building was designed by a Pole.

In the convent's southwestern corner, by the convent wall, is the 17th-century Administrative Office which now houses the Museum of the Convent's History, open 10.00–17.00, closed Tuesday. The museum contains an exhibition of linen embroidery from the 19th and early 20th centuries and a display of the furnished cells of a nun and the novice who attended her.

Wooden cabins have been built in the convent which makes it a much more interesting place to stay than the large Main Tourist Complex. Most of the rooms have private facilities.

Near the convent is the large, five-domed Church of Sts Peter and Paul, built in 1694. A small side chapel was added in honour of Peter the Great's son, Aleksei, by Evdokia Lopukhina, the wife of Peter the Great. Lopukhina had been banished here and Aleksei had been murdered on Peter's orders. Beside the church is the single-domed winter Church of St Nicholas.

Monastery of the Saviour and St Euthimius and nearby

This strongly fortified monastery was founded in the middle of the 14th century and protected Suzdal's northern approaches. However, it was only in 1664 that the fortifications which can be seen today were built. These fortifications consist of a 1.2km-long stone wall reinforced with 12 towers. The monastery is now home to five museums which are open 10.00–17.00, closed Monday.

To get into the monastery, you pass through the 22m-high entrance tower gate followed by the Gate Church of the Annunciation. This church contains an exhibition of the locally born hero, Prince Dmitry Pozharsky, who teamed up with Kuzma Minin, a village elder in Nizhni Novgorod, and raised a volunteer army which liberated Moscow from the Polish-Lithuanian forces in August 1612. Just outside the entrance to the museum is a bust of Pozharsky. His grave is located on the eastern wall of the monastery's Cathedral of the Transfiguration of the Saviour.

The main building of the monastery is the large, five-domed, cubic Cathedral of the Transfiguration of the Saviour, completed in 1594. In a side chapel is the grave of the first father superior, Euthimius, who founded the monastery in 1352 and was canonised in 1507.

Adjoining the tent-roofed Church of the Assumption, built in 1525, is the two-storey Father Superior chambers. The upper storey contains the Museum of Six Centuries of Books.

The combined Church of St Nicholas and two-storey infirmary was built in 1669 and the rooms of the infirmary contain a museum called The Golden Treasury. On display are more than 500 works of Russian decorative arts from the 13th to 20th centuries.

Near the infirmary is a long, single-storey building which was the monastery prison. The prison consists of solitary confinement cells, normal cells and exercise yards. It was used until 1905 for those who had committed crimes against the faith. Today, the building contains the Convicts of the Monastery Prison Museum.

The long Monks' Cell building now contains the Folk Art Museum of Russian Amateurs. Its exhibits include many weird and wonderful things from carved bone boxes to pictures made of coloured rice.

To the east of the monastery is a pair of winter and summer churches. The large summer Church of Our Lady of Smolensk, completed in 1707, is a spacious building topped with four domes. The church is now a museum and is open 10.00–17.00, closed Monday. The small, heated winter Church of St Simeon was built in 1749.

To the south of the monastery is Suzdal's only example of late 17th-century secular architecture. This building, the *posad* ("artisan quarter") house, was formerly the home of the owner of a bakery and tavern, and is now fitted out with 150 household articles of a typical middle-class family in the second half of the 18th century.

Monastery of the Deposition of the Robe

Founded in 1207, this is Suzdal's oldest monastery. However, all the buildings have disappeared except for the Holy Gates and Cathedral of the Deposition of the Robe with its bell tower.

The asymmetrical, double-arched Holy Gates were built in 1688 and are capped by two octagonal tent roofs topped with tiny onion domes.

The Cathedral of the Deposition of the Robe was erected in the first half of the 16th century and has a plain facade. Next to it is the 72m-high bell tower which can be seen from everywhere in the town. It is believed that it was erected in honour of Napoleon's defeat during the 1812 Russian War. There is an observation deck on its upper floor.

There is an unappealing hotel here.

Convent of St Aleksandr Nevsky

This convent was believed to have been founded by the Russian hero Aleksandr Nevsky in 1240 for the wives of noblemen killed in the Tatar-Mongol invasion. The convent was closed down in 1764. Nothing remains of its original structures, but it does contains two interesting buildings from the turn of the 18th century.

The Holy Gates are the only remnants of the convent's walls. The gates are cube-shaped with a single archway surmounted by two small towers.

The white Church of the Ascension was built in 1694 and funded by Peter the Great's mother, Natalia Naryshkina. Attached to its northern side is a small chapel which served as a heated winter church.

Today, this convent serves as a research and education centre on restoration techniques.

Kideksha

About 4km to the east of Suzdal in the village of Kideksha (Кидекша) is the 12th-century former royal estate of Yuri Dolgoruky who founded Moscow and made Suzdal the capital of his principality. The estate was built in the 12th century and included a wooden fortress with a watch tower and a white stone church. All of these have gone except for the church which has been renovated beyond recognition.

Today, the estate consists of the charming Church of Sts Boris and Gleb, the Church of St Stephen and the Holy Gates, surrounded by a low stone fence. The Church of Sts Boris and Gleb, built in 1152, is one of the two oldest buildings in northeast Russia; the other is the cathedral in the Golden Ring city of Pereslavl-Zalesski. The single-domed, almost square church was restored in the 17th century and it was then that the present tent roof replaced a helmet-shaded dome and a new vault was added. Inside the church are fragments of 12th-century frescoes. The church is now a museum and is open 10.00–17.00, closed Tuesday.

The small Church of Stephen was built in 1780 and served as the heated winter church.

To get to Kideksha, you can either walk or catch a bus from Suzdal's long-distance bus station towards Kameshkovo (Камешково).

The Church on the Nerl River at Bogolyubovo
as it was originally

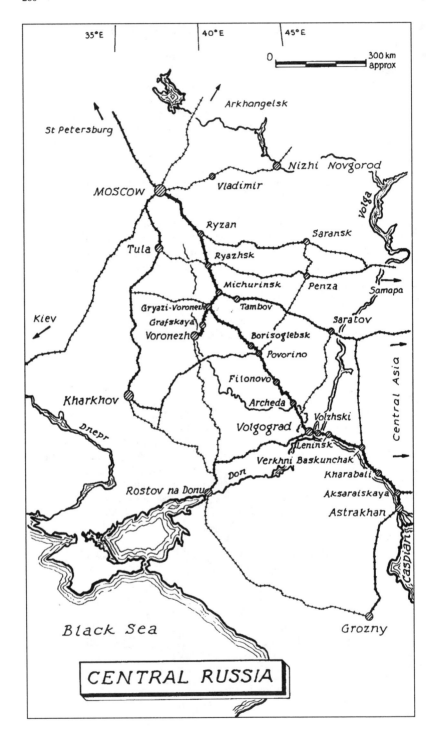

CENTRAL RUSSIA

Chapter Fourteen

Moscow–Voronezh–Volgograd–Astrakhan

This chapter is designed for travellers covering the route Moscow–Voronezh–Volgograd–Astrakhan. Trains that go directly from Moscow to Astrakhan take a different route through Tambov and Saratov, which is not covered in this book.

Route highlights

The three cities of Voronezh, Volgograd and Astrakhan are the most interesting on this route with Volgograd the best of all. The only other place worth visiting is Ryazan which is best reached by a two day trip from Moscow. The reason for this is that the journey onwards to Voronezh is too short for an overnight trip.

Travel suggestions

This Moscow–Voronezh–Volgograd–Astrakhan route was selected because travel between each city is a good overnight journey, which saves accommodation costs and minimises wasted time.

From Astrakhan, there are two travel options back to Moscow besides the train. You can fly back on one of three daily flights (in 1996, the ticket cost one way was $106), or you can catch one of the weekly Volga River cruise ships (in 1996 the ticket cost $151). About 80km north of Astrakhan at Aksaraiskaya, you can also catch a train to Kazakhstan or Uzbekistan but this is not recommended, see *Aksaraiskaya, page 300*.

Trains

The most convenient long-distance trains on this route are listed below.

Origin	Dist, km	Train no & name	Travel time	Depart	Arrive	Destination
Astrakhan	1,532	5	30hr 20min	22.25	04.45	Moscow (Paveletski)
Astrakhan	448	38/37	7hr 35min	18.45	04.20	Volgograd
Moscow (Paveletski)	1,076	2	21hr 12min	14.10	11.22	Volgograd
Moscow (Paveletski)	1,532	6	29hr 45min	13.15	19.00	Astrakhan
Moscow (Paveletski)	636	26	12hr 57min	20.10	09.07	Voronezh
Volgograd	1,076	1	21hr 48min	12.55	10.43	Moscow (Paveletski)
Volgograd	448	37/38	9hr 35min	10.20	19.55	Astrakhan
Volgograd	660	223/4	18hr 25min	14.10	08.35	Voronezh
Voronezh	636	25	12hr 28min	19.29	07.57	Moscow (Paveletski)
Voronezh	660	224/3	19hr 30min	15.10	10.40	Volgograd

Route description
Moscow Москва 0km
The train departs from Paveletski station, pl Leninskaya 1, tel: 235 6807 235 3960, 235 4673. The metro station is Paveletskaya.

Within 2km of the station, the train passes close to the Moscow River on the left. It then crosses over the Warsaw Highway twice before reaching Moscow's outer ring road. After crossing over this road, the toilets are opened.

About 37km from the ring road, the train passes the Domodedovo airport on the left which is one of Moscow's four domestic airports.

A further 80km on, the train reaches the town of Stupino (Ступино) and at its southern outskirts it crosses over the wide photogenic Oka River.

Before reaching Ryazan, the train passes through Rybnoe (Рыбное). This town of 18,500 is most famous for Russia's only horse-breeding scientific research institute and the bee-keeping scientific research institute. There is a bee-keeping museum in the town and nearby is the birthplace and museum of the great Russian poet S A Esenin. The museum is often visited on a half day trip from Ryazan.

RYAZAN 2 Рязань 2 198km
Population: 528,000 Telephone area code: 0912
Ryazan is an ancient city but you wouldn't know it from the train. This is because the city's old part is near Ryazan 1 station and the train bypasses this as it goes to the town's new centre around Ryazan 2 station.

Ryazan started out as a fortress and parts of the preserved kremlin date from 1095. However, it was only in the 12th century that Ryazan became a town, when the residents of Old Ryazan, which was 50km to the southeast, fled here after their city was torched by the Tatar-Mongols.

Where to stay
Hotels choices are the Hotel Lovich, pl Dimitrova 4, tel: 726 920, and Hotel Priokskaya, ul Kalyaeva 13E, tel: 771 257.

What to see
The eight-building kremlin contains several cathedrals and the Bishop's Chamber Museum. Other places of interest in Ryazan include the Infantry Marines Museum, the Art Gallery, the Regional Art Museum, ul Svoboda 57, tel: 779 500, and the House-museum of I P Pavlov, the scientist of Pavlov's dog fame.

Getting assistance
Travel agents Sputnik Travel, ul Lenina 35, tel: 773 925.
Air Aeroflot, ul Dzerzhinskovo 69, tel: 764 110.

Michurinsk Мичуринск 408km
This town is named after Russia's famous geneticist, Ivan Vladimirovich Michurin (1855–1935), who indirectly led to the Soviet Union's backwardness in genetics for decades. Michurin worked here from 1872 and, despite now being in disgrace, the town's genetics laboratory, which is one of the country's largest, remains named after him.

The town, originally called Kozlov, was founded in 1635 on the orders of Tsar Mikhail Romanov as a site for a fortress to stop attacks from the southern Tatars.

FOREIGN BOURGEOIS BIOLOGY

From the 1940s to the 1960s, the Soviet Union was decades behind the West's understanding of plant biology and this can by indirectly linked to Russia's famous geneticist, Ivan Vladimirovich Michurin (1855–1935).

Michurin was an amateur plant breeder who, through skilful cross-breeding, created a number of varieties of fruit trees suitable for the climate of central Russia. He based his approach on theories of inheriting acquired characteristics which totally rejected the Mendelian chromosome theory of heredity. (Mendelian theory states that you can't inherit acquired characteristics. For example, if you cut off a rat's tail, its offspring will still be born with tails, regardless of the number of rat generations you mutilate. While this theory has been accepted for nearly a century, in the last few years researchers have proven that some acquired characteristics can be inherited.) This radical approach became known as Michurinist biology and was perverted by the ruthless communist geneticist, Trofim Denisovich Lysenko, who maintained that inheritable changes could be brought about in plants by environmental influences such as subjecting wheat to extremes of temperature and by grafting. Lysenko (1898–1976) claimed that his beliefs were supported by communist theory and condemned all those who supported "foreign bourgeois biology". Dozens of Soviet biologists were purged and executed in the 1940s for their support of the chromosome theory and Lysenko became Stalin's biological science dictator. In 1948, all textbooks and courses were changed to reflect Lysenko's views and the now-dead Michurin was elevated to become a Stalinest cult figure. Lysenko's monopoly over plant biology as director of the prestigious Institute of Genetics stifled all developments in genetics in the Soviet Union until 1965 when Lysenko himself was purged.

A shipyard was built 12km away in 1659 and the vessels produced here were essential for Peter the Great's great naval battles of 1695 and 1696.

The sights in Michurinsk are limited to a House-museum of Michurin and the Manor House-museum of the artist Aleksandr Mikhailovich Gerasimov. Gerasimov (1881–1961) was born here and is famous for his portrait, landscape and historical paintings and some of these are on display in the town's exhibition hall and in Moscow's Tretyakov Art Gallery.

From the train you will see a large pipeline a metre in diameter which runs through the town. This massive 7,200km-long pipeline carts crude oil from central Russian oil-fields to eastern European refineries and even has its own name. It is called the Trans-European Friendship (*druzhba* in Russian) pipeline.

Gryazi-Voronezh   Грязи-Воронеж   472km

This is a major rail junction where trains take different branch lines to Voronezh, Volgograd and Lipetsk. As the train stops here for a few minutes, you can quickly have a look at the memorial plaque on the platform which commemorates a speech given to workers at this very spot by the future Soviet President Mikhail Kalinin in 1920.

The only other sights here are a History Museum and a Katusha rocket-launching truck dedicated to the Rocket Troops of World War II. About 10km northwest of Gryazi on the way to Lipetsk is the Gryazinski Botanical Reserve on the shores of the Matyrskoe Water Catchment Basin.

There is a basic hotel in town.

Usman Усмань 572km

This small town is full of communist history, albeit minor history.

There is a preserved house with a balcony from which N N Ispolatov, the first head of the Usman Soviet (meaning "council"), proclaimed Soviet power on November 10 1917. There is also a plaque on the house where the future Soviet President Mikhail Kalinin gave an address in 1919, and another plaque on the house where Marxist posters were illegally printed in 1905–6. More information about these events can be found in the museum of local studies.

Within 5km of Usman you enter the Voronezh Nature Reserve.

Grafskaya Графская 595km

The town around the station is known as Krasnolesny (Краснолесный) and it sits at the centre of the Voronezh Nature Reserve. This reserve has protected 54 species of mammals, 208 species of birds, 39 species of fish and more than 6,000 species of insects since 1932.

About 4km to the east of here is the Grafski Beaver Sanctuary which was the world's first beaver breeding farm. More information on the sanctuary and how to get there is listed in Voronezh below.

Volya Воля 609km

This stop consists of just one small building and a very rare, guarded bike bay on the left. The wire-enclosed park contains the bicycles of dozens of locals who ride between the station and the *dacha* village of Orlovo (Орлово) 4km away. Such a communal solution to a transport problem is extremely rare in Russia.

The section from here to Voronezh contains a number of popular swimming spots and local summer trains are always crowded.

Otrozhka Отрожка 628km

This town is Voronezh's main railway depot. There are dozens of defunct steam, diesel and electric trains waiting to be scrapped here. You can see them on the left as you approach the station. The line to the atomic power station at Novovorenzh branches off from here.

VORONEZH Воронеж 636km
Population: 902,000   Telephone area code: 0732

While Voronezh is considered an old Russian city, human settlement in the region pre-dates the Slavic settlers by a millennium. Archaeological excavations at the nearby villages of Kosenki and Borchevo on the Don River date the first human settlements as from the palaeolithic period, while other sites contain material dating back to the Bronze Age. Artefacts from these periods and from the ancient Slavs and Scythians can be found in the History Museum.

The city's official founding date is 1586 which was when Tsar Fedor Ivanovich gave the order to build the Voronezh fortress as part of a chain of defences called the Belgorod Line. This line stretched across the Don Steppes and was designed to stop the Crimean Tatars. The city is strategically located on the Voronezh River near where it flows into the Don which in turn flows 800km down to the Black Sea. It was in Voronezh that Peter the Great decided to build Russia's first large naval fleet in order to attack the Turkish fortress of Azov at the mouth of the Don.

Although Voronezh took a battering during the Russian Civil War when it was occupied several times by both sides, it was in World War II that the city was most damaged. The city sat on the front line for nearly 200 days as the Germans tried unsuccessfully to cross the Don. During the bloody battle, over 92% of the city's buildings were reduced to rubble.

After the war, the buildings were rebuilt in their original style so, while many of the city centre's constructivist-style buildings look like they were built in the 1930s, in reality they are 1950s recreations.

Today, the city is most famous for its heavy industry which stretches for 16km along the eastern bank of the Voronezh Sea. The city's highest profile industry is aviation and here most Soviet spacecraft, the Soviet TU-144 Concorde, and engines for the Soviet Buran space shuttle are built.

The city is well known to many English students as up to a hundred a year studied Russian here in the last few years of the Soviet Union.

Getting there and away
The most convenient long-distance trains on this route are listed below.

Origin	Dist, km	Train no & name	Travel time	Depart	Arrive	Destination
Moscow (Paveletski)	636	25	12hr 57min	20:10	9:07	Voronezh
Volgograd	660	223/4	18hr 25min	14:10	8:35	Voronezh
Voronezh	636	25/6	12hr 28min	19:29	7:57	Moscow (Paveletski)
Voronezh	660	224/3	19hr 30min	15:10	10:40	Volgograd

Passing through
When you are approaching Voronezh from Moscow, about 5km from the station your train crosses over the Voronezh Sea and on the left you can see the city. About 500m further, on the righthand side of the track, is a World War II memorial.

Where to stay
The best hotels are the standard Hotel Brno, ul Plekhanovskaya 9, tel: 509 247, $26 double room; the standard Hotel Don, ul Plekhanovskaya 8, tel: 555 315, $37 double room; and the standard Hotel Rossiya, ul Teatralnaya 23, tel: 555 898, $22 double room. These all have restaurants. The other hotels are the basic Hotel Tsentralnaya (formerly Bristol), pr Revolutsi 43, tel: 550 418; the basic Hotel Mayak, ul Kukolkina 3, tel: 571 323; and the basic Hotel Luch, ul Koltsovskaya 45, tel: 574 358. Hotel Voronezh, pl Lenina 8, tel: 550 752, was closed in 1995 but may reopen once demand for rooms increases.

Getting around
Voronezh sits on both banks of the Voronezh Sea which flows into the Don River a few kilometres to the south. The central part of the city, which contains the railway station and the old section of the city, is on the right bank while the industrial area and new suburbs are on the left. There are three road bridges connecting both banks. The northern bridge, called Severny, is a two-storey bridge, the upper level being for trams.

In front of the railway station is Cheryakhovsky Square complete with a giant monument to General Ivan Cheryakhovsky. This winner of the Hero of the Soviet Union award was the army commander during the World War II fight for Voronezh.

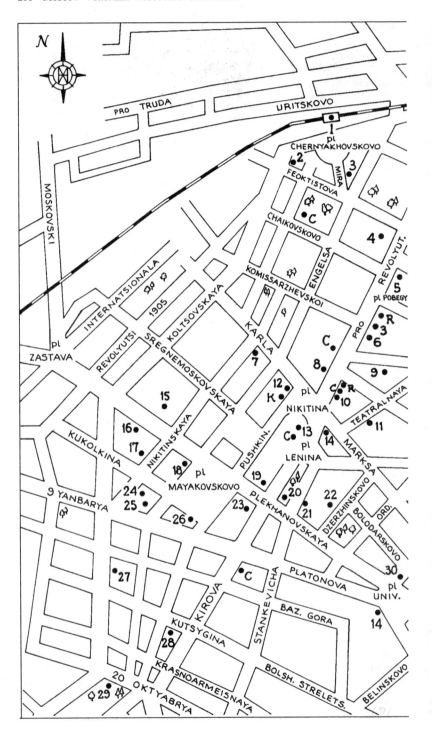

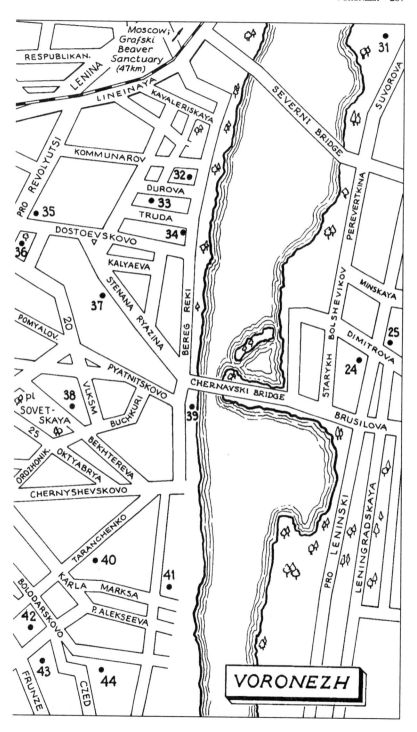

KEY TO VORONEZH (Воронеж)

1	Railway station (*Vokzal*)	Ж-Д вокзал
2	Medical Institute (*Institut*)	Медицинский институт
3	Book store (*Dom Knigi*)	Дом Книги
4	Art Museum (*Muzei*)	Художественный музей
5	Memorial Complex 1941-1945	Мемориальный комплекс 1941-1945
6	Post office (*Pochtamt*)	Почтамт
7	House Museum of Nikitin (*Muzei*)	Дом музей Никитин
8	Puppet Theatre (*Teatr*)	Театр кукол
9	Drama Theatre (*Teatr*)	Театр драмы
10	Hotel Tsentralnaya	гостиница Центральная
11	Hotel Rossiya (*Gostinitsa*)	гостиница Россия
12	Olga Travel Company	Ольга
13	Philharmonic Theatre (*Teatr*)	Филармония
14	Intourist	Интурист
15	Museums of Architects (*Muzei*)	Музей архитекторов
16	Museum of Local Studies (*Muzei*)	Краеведческий музей
17	Hotel Mayak (*Gostinitsa*)	гостиница Маяк
18	Hotel Brno (*Gostinitsa*)	гостиница Брно
19	Hotel Voronezh (closed)	гостиница Воронеж
20	Unmarked German military cemetery	Немецкое кладбище
21	Aeroflot	Аэрофлот
22	Youth Theatre (*Teatr*)	Театр юного зрителя
23	State Opera and Ballet Theatre (*Teatr*)	Театр оперы и балета
24	Market (*Rynok*)	Рынок
25	Bus station (*Vokzal*)	Автовокзал
26	Hotel Don (*Gostinitsa*)	гостиница Дон
27	Hotel Luch (*Gostinitsa*)	гостиница Луч
28	Art gallery	Выставочный зал
29	Circus (*Tsirk*)	Цирк
30	Koltsov Literature Museum (*Muzei*)	Музей Кольцова
31	Church of Kazan (*Kazanskaya*)	Казанская церковь
32	House Museum of Durov (*Muzei*)	Дом музей Дуров
33	Church of the Presentation of the Virgin (*Vvedenskaya*)	Введенская церковь
34	Monastery of St Akatov	Акатов Монастырь
35	Technical Institute (*Institut*)	Технологический институт
36	Peter the Great monument	памятник Петру 1
37	Arsenal Military Museum (*Muzei*)	Музей Арсенал 1941-1945
38	Cathedral of the Intercession (*Pokrovski*)	Покровский собор
39	River station (*Vokzal*)	Речной вокзал
40	Church of St Nicholas (*Nikolskaya*)	Никольская церковь
41	Admiralty (*Admiralteiskaya*) Church	Адмиралтейская церковь
42	University Zoological & Geological Museum (*Muzei*)	Музей университета
43	Church of the Saviour (*Spasskaya*) and Koltsevo Drama Theatre (*Teatr*)	Спасская церковь Театр драмы Кольцова
44	Church of Elijah (*Ilinskaya*)	Ильинская церковь
R	Restaurant (*Restoran*)	Ресторан
C	Café (*Kafe*) or Bar (*Bar*)	Кафе или Бар
K	Canteen (*Stolovaya*)	Столоваыа

The airport is 15km to the north of the city and to get to it from the station catch bus No 120. From the station, trolleybus 1 goes through the centre of the city along pr Revolyutsi, pl Lenina and ul Kirova. This trolleybus passes near all hotels except for Mayak and Luch. But even these are only a ten-minute walk from pl Lenina.

What to see

Voronezh is a pleasant place to stroll around as the buildings are constructed in various styles from the last two centuries. Even knowing that what you are seeing are forgeries built in the 1950s doesn't take away any of the enjoyment.

The main museums are the Art Museum, pr Revolutsi 18, tel: 552 843, open 10.00–17.00, closed Monday; the Museum of Local Studies, ul Plekhanovskaya 29, open 11.00–19.00 on Tuesday, Wednesday and Friday, and 10.00–18.00 on Thursday, Saturday and Sunday; and the Arsenal Military Museum, ul Stepana Razina 43, open 11.00–19.00 on Tuesday, Wednesday and Friday, and 10.00–18.00 on Thursday, Saturday and Sunday.

The strangest museum is the House-museum of Durov, ul Durova 2. Anatoly Durov (1865–1916) was a famous Russian circus clown and founder of a circus dynasty. Other museums immortalising locals are the House-museum of Nikitin, ul Nikitinskaya 19, open 10.00–18.00, closed Wednesday, and the Koltsov Literature Museum, ul Plekhanovskaya 3. Ivan Nikitin (1824–61) was a popular poet and his museum is a replica of the house in which he lived, while Alexei Koltsov (1809–42) was a Russian poet who wrote poems and songs describing country life.

Specialist museums include the Museum of Architects, ul Plekhanovskaya 22, and the University Zoological and Geological Museum, pl Uleversitetskaya 1.

There are a number of interesting theatres including the unusual-looking Puppet Theatre, the Philharmonic Theatre (tickets sold 12.00–20.00) and the State Opera and Ballet Theatre. The theatre near the old Communist Party headquarters has been turned into a medical research institute and the recently completed, very uncomfortable Kolitso Drama Theatre will probably be converted into offices as it is unpopular with the public and performers.

Other interesting places to visit are the Circus, ul Moiseeva 2, the Hippodrome Racecourse, ul Begovaya 2, and the Botanical Gardens next to the Agricultural Institute.

The city has a number of working cathedrals and churches with the most interesting being the five-domed Admiralty Church of the Assumption on the shores of the Voronezh Sea. This church was built in 1696 at the site of Peter the Great's shipyards and was the only building erected during Peter's time to survive the devastating great fire in 1748. The church is not operating but is being converted into a maritime museum.

There are 26 mass graves in Voronezh containing 46,000 Russians killed in World War II. All these have memorials with the principal war memorial being the one on pl Pobedy which contains the body of an unknown soldier who was buried here ceremonially in 1995. There is an unmarked mass grave for Germans underneath Koletsov Park.

It is possible to travel on the Voronezh Sea which is 35km long, 3km wide and 3m deep. There are regular 90-minute round trips on a ferry from the river station on the right (western) side at the base of the Chernavski Bridge. On the opposite bank is a place to rent paddle-boats and yachts.

Point of interest

The Hari Krishnas have made it to Voronezh but have yet to open a restaurant. However, they are more than happy to deliver excellent vegetarian meals from 17.00 to 20.00, as long as you order the day before on tel: 161 867.

Getting assistance

Travel agents   Olga Travel Co, ul Karla Marksa 51, tel: & fax: 557 533, email root@argocher.voronezh.su stating 'Olga Travel' in the subject line; Intourist, ul 9th Yanvarya 12, tel: 553 746.

Air Aeroflot, ul Plekhanovskaya 22a, tel: 526 470, with another Aeroflot ticket window at the railway station.

What's in the region
The Orlov Trotters Stud

This is in the village of Khrenovoye (Хребовое) to the southeast of Voronezh. It was founded by Count Orlov in the 18th century and all Russian trotters originated here. The horse-breeding farm includes a number of 19th-century historic buildings, a museum and a park. It is possible to organise meals and troika rides here.

The farm is about 120km by road or 160km by rail from Voronezh. While you can catch a suburban train from Voronezh to Khrenovoye, it is best to go on an organised tour as the museum and restaurant only open if they are booked.

Grafski Beaver Sanctuary (*Графский Заповедник*)

About 40km from Voronezh in the northern part of the Usman coniferous forest is the Grafski Beaver Sanctuary which was the world's first beaver breeding farm when it was established in 1932. During the decades when the beaver was threatened throughout the Soviet Union, the sanctuary contained half the nation's beaver population. Since then, thousands of beavers have been taken from here to restock various beaver reserves throughout the country and today there are over 200,000 beavers in Russia.

The breeding programme was so successful that it was discontinued at Grafski several years ago. Today, all that remains of the programme are the breeding cages along the river banks and the empty animal laboratories.

However, the great two-storey Museum of Local Flora and Fauna, tel: 270 548, open 09.00–18.00, closed Monday, is still operating. It contains excellent exhibits on the breeding and farming of beavers, and stuffed specimens of the 54 species of mammals and 208 species of birds that inhabit the sanctuary. If you have time you can go spotting beaver, red deer, roe deer, wild boars, badgers and squirrels.

Another highlight of the sanctuary is a church which was once part of a penal monastery. In past centuries, wayward monks were sent to this remote place and lived in niches with only a small opening to look through while they served their penance. During World War II most of the monastery was bombed into oblivion except for the church which is slowly being rebuilt.

There is a very basic hotel here which costs $7 a room and it is essential to book on tel: 270 548.

To get to Grafski you should catch the daily suburban train to the village of Anna (Анна) and get off at Post 7km (Пост. 7км) station. This train leaves Voronezh at 09.26 and returns leaving Post 7km at 16.00. The trip takes 1hr 3min. From Post 7km station, it takes about 15 minutes to walk to the sanctuary. Another option is to catch one of the numerous suburban trains to Grafskaya (Графская) station which is 4.5km to the west of the museum. The town around Grafskaya station is called Krasnolesny (Краснолесный). There is only one east–west road through the town which is 100m along the railway line back towards Voronezh. Take the eastern direction which is the one to the right of the railway when you are coming from Voronezh, and it should take you 40 minutes to walk to the museum.

POINT OF INTEREST

Russia's famous black earth region, where the earth is really black, is the country's bread basket. The soil is rich in humus and from the windows of the train you will see fields of wheat, barley, maize, rye, sunflowers, hemp, tobacco, buckwheat and millet depending on the season and how close you are to water sources.

The black earth soils are technically known as "chernozem" in English which is derived from a shortened transliteration of the Russian *chornaya zemlya* meaning "black earth". Chernozem from the Voronezh region was once considered the world's most fertile soil and even today a sample of it is kept at the International Bureau of Weights and Measures in Paris alongside the platinum-iridium metre and the kilogram as international benchmarks.

Nowadays, many Russian farmers and scientists bemoan the fact that today's chernozems are nowhere near the quality of the Paris sample due to overcultivation, poor soil conservation and excessive use of chemicals.

Getting from Voronezh to Volgograd

To get from Voronezh to Volgograd, the train heads back towards Moscow for 110km until it reaches Gryazi-Voronezh before turning south to Volgograd.

Gryazi-Voronezh   Грязи-Воронеж   692km
See *page 283*.

Plavitsa   Плавица   731km
During the sugar beet harvesting season this town is enveloped in a putrid odour from its sugar refinery.

Borisoglebsk   Борисоглебск   902km
Although you wouldn't know it from the modern chemical and machinery plants surrounding the station, this town is over 300 years old. It was founded in 1646 as a fortress and quickly grew into a big trading city with a giant fair held every year on July 6. During the Soviet period, the town's greatest claim to fame was that the Soviet writer Mikhail Gorky stayed here in 1898 and the artist Andrei Petrovich Ryabushkin (1861–1904) was born here. Ryabushkin was the son of a peasant icon-painter and he specialised in painting the festive side of rural life.

Povorino   Поворино   929km
Just after leaving the station, you cross over the administrative border into Volgograd Oblast which is also a time-zone border. Moscow is now one hour behind local time.

Archeda   Арчеда   1,140km
Just 7km before reaching Archeda on the right are sand dunes which become more and more common as the train heads towards Volgograd. The town around the station is known as Frolovo (Фролово) while the station gets its name from the Archeda River which you cross over as you leave the town.

VOLGOGRAD   Волгоград   1,296km
Population: 1,005,000   Telephone area code: 8442
Volgograd is known throughout the world by its old name of Stalingrad. It is famous for being the place where the German Army suffered its first major

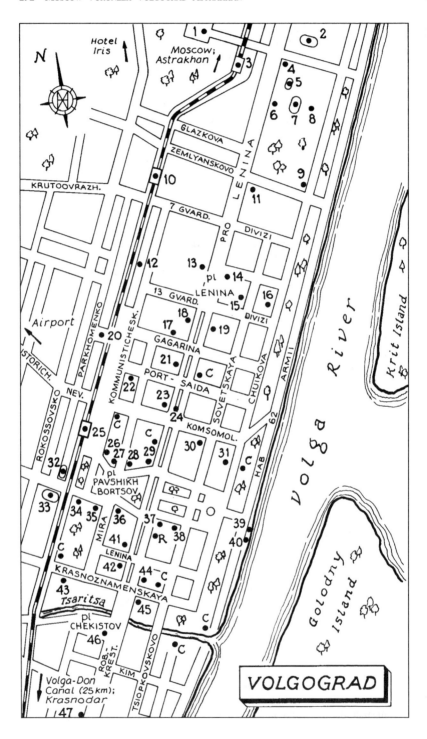

VOLGOGRAD

KEY TO VOLGOGRAD (Волоград)

1	Mamaev Kurgan Memorial Complex	Мемориальный комплекс «Мамаев Курган»
2	Athletics complex (*Kompleks*)	Легоатлетический комплекс
3	Mamaev Kurgan station (*Stantsiya*)	«Мамаев Курган»
4	Tram stop Mamaev Kurgan	станция «Мамаев Курган»
5	Covered swimming pool (*Bassein*)	Закрытный бассейн «Спартак»
6	Tram stop Tsentralny Stadion	«Центральный Стадион»
7	Central Stadium (*Stadion*)	Центральный стадион
8	Hotel Sport	гостиница Спорт
9	Hotel Yunost	гостиница Юность
10	Bakinskaya station (*Stantsiya*)	станция Бакинская
11	Tram stop TsPKIO	«ЦПКИО»
12	Railway advance ticket booking office (*Predvaritelnaya kassa*)	Ж-Д предварительная касса
13	Tram stop Ploshchad Lenina	«Площадь Ленина»
14	Monument on Mass Graves of Defenders of Stalingrad	Памятник на Братской могиле воинов
15	Pavlov's House (*Dom Pavlova*)	Дом Павлова
16	Panorama-Museum of the Defence of Stalingrad (*Stalingradskaya Bitva*)	Музей-панорама «Сталинградская битва»
17	Planetarium	Планетарий
18	Teaching University (*Universitet*)	Педагогический университет
19	Polytechnic Institute (*Institut*)	Политехнический институт
20	Bus station (*Avtovoksal*)	Автовоксал
21	Fine Arts Museum (*Muzei*)	Музей изобразительных искусств
22	Railway Museum (*Muzei*)	Железнодорожный музей
23	Tram stop Komsomolskaya	«Комсомольская»
24	Monument of Young Communist Defenders	Памятник комсомольцам-защитникам Сталинград
25	Volgograd railway station (*Vokzal*)	Волгоград вокзал
26	Defence of Tsaritsyn Museum (*Muzei*)	Музей обороны Царицына
27	Post office (*Pochtamt*)	Почтамт
28	Hotel Intourist	гостиница Интурист
29	Puppet Theatre (*Teatr*)	Театр кукол
30	Central Market (*Tsentralny Rynok*)	Центральный рынок
31	Theatre of Musical Comedy (*Teatr*)	Театр музыкальной комедии
32	Open air swimming pool (*Bassein*)	Отрытый бассейн «Спартак»
33	'Dinamo' Stadium (*Stadion*)	Стадион «Динамо»
34	Hotel Oktyabraskaya	гостиница Октябрьская
35	New Experimental Theatre (*NET*)	НЭТ
36	Aeroflot	Аэрофлот
37	Hotel Volgograd	гостиница Волгоград
38	Book store (*Knigi*)	Книги
39	River station (*Rechnoi Vokzal*)	Речной вокзал
40	River Transport Museum (*Muzei*)	Речной музей
41	Medical Institute (*Institut*)	Медицинский институт
42	Museum of Local Studies (*Muzei*)	Краеведческий музей
43	Circus (*Tsirk*)	Цирк
45	Tram stop Pionerskaya	«Пионерская»
46	Tram stop Ploshchad Chekistov	«Площадь Чекистов»
44	Exhibition Hall (*Zal*)	Выставочный зал
47	Hotel Yuzhnaya	гостиница Южная
R	Restaurant (*Restoran*)	Ресторан
C	Café (*Kafe*) or Bar (*Bar*)	Кафе или Бар

defeat in World War II, thus signalling the beginning of the end for Hitler's Reich.

The city's earlier history is equally well known to Russians as it was here in 1589 that a strong fortress was built which protected Moscow's southern flank from marauding Tatars and gave the future capital the stability to grow.

Volgograd also played a pivotal role in the Russian Civil War when the communist forces fought off strong thrusts from the White Army, thereby ensuring food supplies to Moscow and St Petersburg. Shortly after the war, in a symbolic move to eliminate the Tsarist period influence from the city, the name of the city was changed from Tsaritsyn, as it had been known since 1589, to Stalingrad. The suffix *grad* is the old Slavonic word for "city".

During World War II, the Germans occupied the eastern side of Stalingrad but couldn't encircle it as the area of the city on the right bank of the Volga was held by the Soviets. Both sides suffered enormous losses in a battle that raged from July 1942 to February 1943. Eventually, on February 2 1943, the few remaining Germans surrendered.

For the evacuated citizens of Volgograd, the victory over the Germans was hollow as there was very little to return to. Over 95% of all buildings, including 47,000 houses, were completely destroyed. Just clearing away the debris was a daunting task, not only because of the sheer amount of rubble to be removed but also because of the rotting corpses and unexploded bombs which were continually being discovered.

The city was rebuilt by the late 1950s mostly by German prisoners of war and it is a showcase of Stalin-style architecture. There is a notable lack of churches. With the renunciation of Stalin, the name of the city was changed in 1961 to Volgograd.

Today, Volgograd is a pleasant and prosperous tree-lined city with a number of parks and a landscaped river frontage along which to stroll. It stretches for 75km along the Volga River and is 2–10km wide. The city hugs the steep right (eastern) bank which protects the inhabitants from the strong dry steppe winds. The main street, pro Lenina, runs for over 70km through the city, probably making it the longest road in the world. The highlights of the city include the Mamaev Kurgan Complex, the world's largest statue of Lenin and a number of specialist museums. You need at least two full days to discover the city.

Getting there and away
By boat There are large river cruisers that travel once a week all the way from Astrakhan, through Volgograd, Saratov and Nizhni Novgorod to Moscow. It is a good idea to book your passage well in advance as there are limited first-class berths. A first-class berth to Moscow costs $111, to Nizhni Novgorod $91, to Saratov $33 and to Astrakhan $40. For more information on river travel, see *Astrakhan, page 300.*

By train The most convenient long-distance trains on this route are listed below.

Origin	Dist, km	Train no & name	Travel time	Depart	Arrive	Destination
Astrakhan	448	38/37	7hr 35min	18.45	04.20	Volgograd
Moscow (Paveletski)	1,076	1	21hr 12min	14.10	11.22	Volgograd
Volgograd	1,076	1	21hr 48min	12.55	10.43	Moscow (Paveletski)
Volgograd	448	37/38	9hr 35min	10.20	19.55	Astrakhan
Volgograd	660	223/4	18hr 25min	14.10	08.35	Voronezh
Voronezh	660	224/3	19hr 30min	15.10	10.40	Volgograd

Passing through
About five minutes before reaching Volgograd, the train passes the giant, 72m, sword-wielding Mother-Russia statue which you will see on the right. If you are arriving in the morning you will get a good picture as the sun is directly in front of it.

Volgograd 1 station is an impressive Stalinesque building built in 1954 with great communist paintings on the vaulted ceilings of the two waiting halls. All long-distance trains stop at Volgograd 1 for at least 20 minutes which is plenty of time to view the paintings and buy some food.

Leaving Volgograd for Astrakhan, you travel for over an hour through the city suburbs before reaching the Volgograd hydro-electric dam. This is one of the world's largest dams and you will notice tanks at both ends providing defence for the militia who often check the papers of drivers wanting to cross.

Where to stay
The closest hotels to the station are the grand, Stalinist era, standard Hotel Intourist, ul Mira 14, tel: 364 553, $80 double room; and the standard Hotel Volgograd, ul Mira 12, tel: 361 772, $26 double room.

The safest hotel is the standard ex-communist party Hotel Oktyabraskaya, ul Kommunisticheskaya 5a, tel: 338 120, $30 twin share/person, as police regularly guard the doors checking documents. The hotel is hard to find as it does not have a sign on it saying it is a hotel. Another standard hotel is Hotel Yunost, ul Chuikova 65, tel: 341 471. The basic hotels are Hotel Yuzhnaya, ul Raboche-Krestyanskaya 18, tel: 441 429; and Hotel Sport, pro Lenina 76, tel: 348 035. Hotel Volgo-Don, ul Fadeeva 47, tel: 672 636, is 30km to the south of Volgograd.

The best hotel is the excellent Hotel Iris, ul Zemlyachki 80, tel: 398 241, 398 650, fax: 391 040. It is located about 2km to the north of the city centre, just behind Mamaev Kurgan Memorial Complex.

The only hotels with restaurants are the Intourist, Oktyabraskaya and Iris.

Getting around
Volgograd has a cross between a metro and a tram called a *skorostnoy tramvay* meaning "high-speed tram". It consists of a track that runs for a few kilometres under pro Lenina between Ploshchad Chekistov and TsPKIO before popping up at the surface at each end. The top speed of the tram is about 80km/h and tickets are bought at the station as you can't use the normal city transport tickets. The station, Ploshchad Chekistov, is named in honour of the Cheka secret police who were the forerunners of the KGB. There is a large monument to them above the station, in honour of their sacrifices during World War II, not their excesses during Stalin's purges. The stations are marked on the map.

However, almost everything interesting in Volgograd is within walking distance of the station. Trolleybuses Nos 1 and 8 travel along pro Lenina as does the high-speed tram. For Hotel Sport, get off at the Mamaev Kurgan stop and for Hotel Yunost, the TsPKIO stop. Continue to the end of the line on trolleybus No 1 to get to the tractor factory.

To get to Hotel Yuzhnaya, take trolleybus No 2 or 20 along pro Lenina to the south and get off at Akademicheskaya stop. Hotel Volgo-Don is located 30km to the south of the city and to get there take trolleybus No 2 to the stop Gostinitsa or the suburban train as explained under *The Volga-Don Canal, page 298*.

To get to the airport, take bus No 6 from in front of the Aeroflot office on pro Lenina.

What to see

Volgograd is littered with 35 memorials to World War II not including a string of grey-painted T-34 tank turrets mounted on pedestals dotted around the city. These denote the German's furthermost advance which was on November 10 1943, the day the Soviet's started their counter-offensive.

Mamaev Kurgan Memorial Complex

The memorial complex on Mamaev Kurgan, which translates as "Mamaev's hill", is the most impressive World War II memorial outside Moscow. Dominated by the world-famous, 72m-tall, sword-wielding Mother-Russia statue, it is a place of pilgrimage for most Russians and is always crowded on war-related public holidays. The hill of Mamaev Kurgan was continuously fought over during the four-month Stalingrad Battle as it was an excellent vantage point from which to monitor the whole of the city.

The Mamaev Kurgan Complex starts at pro Lenina with the Memory of the Generations statue. As you walk up a tree-lined alley, you cross over the Moscow–Volgograd railway before coming to the first sculpture, known as the Fighting to the Last monument. This consists of a 12m-high, bare-chested soldier holding a sub-machine gun while throwing a grenade. A little further on is a set of broad stairs flanked by Ruined Walls of Stalingrad Memorial which contains more writing and scenes of hand-to-hand fighting. Martial music is broadcast from behind this memorial and it creates a surprisingly good ambience.

Further on is the Square of Heroes, dominated by a large rectangular pool surrounded by giant soldier sculptures. This leads into the Hall of Soldier's Glory which contains the eternal flame and 32 mosaics on the walls. Each of the mosaics is dedicated to a military unit that took part in the battle and they are etched with randomly picked names of 7,200 soldiers who died in the battle. Walking though this leads you to the Square of Sorrow with the sculpture Mother's Grief. The pathway to the right of the square slowly winds up the main hill to the enormous Mother-Russia statue. The actual statue is 51m high and it sits on a 21m-high pedestal. It symbolises the motherland calling her children to rise to her defence.

To get to Mamaev Kurgan, take the high-speed tram or trolleybus No 1, 8 or 11 along pro Lenina or take bus No 17 from near the railway station. The public transport stop at the front of the complex is named Mamaev Kurgan.

It is particularly interesting to visit Mamaev Kurgan during a military celebration. To find out when something is happening, call the complex on tel: 342 102 or 342 095. You should not visit the complex after dark in the hope of getting a scenic view of Volgograd. Not only is it considered disrespectful due to its cemetery-like significance, but it is also a popular place for muggers.

Panorama-Museum of the Defence of Stalingrad

The Panorama-Museum, ul Chuikova 2, open 09.00–20.00, closed Monday, is a circular building with a 360° battlefield diorama on the upper floor and a museum underneath it. The diorama shows the fierce battle around Mamaev Kurgan Hill on January 26 1943 which took place during the final phase of the Soviet encirclement of German forces. You have to join a group that forms on the floor below the diorama and if you say that you are an English speaker, a translator will probably be found at no extra cost. Outside the Panorama-

Museum are tanks, planes and, on the river's foreshore, a patrol boat. The entrance for the Panorama-Museum is on the riverside.

To get to the Panorama-Museum, take the high-speed tram or trolleybus No 1 or 8 to pl Lenina.

Next door to the museum are the bombed-out ruins of the flour mill which has been left as it remained at the end of World War II. Opposite the flour mill is a monument called Pavlov's House which was a centre of defence for nearly 60 days. It gets its name from Sergeant Pavlov who commanded the defence for the first three days, even though it was Sergeant Afanasev who led the defence for the following 55 days.

What else to see

The two-storey Museum of Local Studies, pro Lenina 38, tel: 770 715, open 10.00–18.00, closed Tuesday, has the third largest butterfly collection in the former USSR. The Fine Arts Museum is located at pro Lenina 21, tel: 333 906, open 11.00–19.00, closed Wednesday.

Specialist museums in Volgograd include the Pushkin Musical Instrument Museum, ul Bystrova 257, tel: 421 056; the Red October Technical Museum, pro Metallurgov 71a, tel: 798 144; the Barrikady Machine Tool Museum, ul Pelshe 2; the River Transport Museum which is on the third floor of the river station, nab 62th Armi, tel: 445 279; the Health Museum, ul Angarskaya 13, tel: 305 104; and the Fireman's Museum, tel: 388 325. There is also a museum at the tractor factory, ul Admirala Ushakova 1, tel: 770 715, which was the largest tractor works in the Soviet Union in the 1930s. It was built with the help of many Americans who believed in communism, and the factory even had a special canteen for them. Of all the specialist museums, the most interesting is the Railway Museum, ul Port-Saiga 17, tel: 383 717, open 09.00–17.00 on Monday, Tuesday, Thursday and Friday.

The Alleya Geroyev (Alley of Heroes) is a pleasant place to wander along for its cafés and street art, especially on Saturday and Sunday. The art is mostly street-smart paintings for the mass market, but sometimes you will find deeply expressive pieces. On this alley there is a great art gallery run by an association of artists; an old dying tree said to be the only one standing after the war; and the eternal flame, where newlyweds lay flowers. The Alleya Geroyev ends at an ostentatious 100-step, granite colonnaded stairway leading down to the Volga River. This monumental colonnade was built in 1952 to commemorate the Volga–Don Canal's completion and is designed to impress visitors arriving in the city from the river station.

Volgograd's Planetarium, ul Gagarina 14, tel: 363 483, is one of the best in Russia, being a gift from East Germany. Although screenings are meant to run every two hours, they will only proceed if there are groups of 30 or more, so it is necessary to stop by and find out if there is a group which you can join that day.

There is also a Circus at ul Krasnoznamenskaya 15, tel: 362 198, and the Puppet Theatre at pro Lenina 15, tel: 330 926.

The city's most interesting theatre is the New Experimental Theatre (NET-Novyi Experimentalni Teatr) at ul Mira 5, tel: 363 430. This was formerly called the Gorky Theatre. This large, pillared theatre is directly in front of the Hotel Volgograd and it stages Russian and Western avant-garde musicals and dramas. Just seeing the newly remodelled interior is well worth the ticket price. The NET's season starts in winter.

Another interesting theatre is the State Don Cossack Theatre, ul Akademicheskaya 3, tel: 441 379. This theatre puts on Cossack plays with colourful costumes and it provides an interesting cultural twist on the usual Soviet theatre. Prices are fairly high and they offer dinner shows.

The Volgograd Symphony Orchestra plays several times a week in the river station building, ul Naberezhnaya 1. Tickets are extremely expensive but it is a great excuse to stroll down to the river station after dinner.

Tickets for all cultural events can be bought at the respective venue or at ticket *kassas* on the corner of Alleya Geroyev and ul Sovetskaya, and in the underpass at the entrance of the high-speed tram station at Ploshchad Chekistov.

There are a number of daily ferries and hydrofoils that depart from Volgograd but sightseeing cruises no longer run. The best and most regular summer ferry is to the bathing beach on the opposite shore which is mostly reserved for recreation and consequently has few houses. For very little money, you can take a ferry upstream or downstream to the several islands of *dachas* such as Golodny Ostrov ("Hungry Island"). For information on the ferries, tel: 445 209.

The Central Market, ul Sovetskaya 17, tel: 361 505, is one of the best markets in Russia. It has beautiful fruit and vegetables all year round, wonderful freshly baked bread and *lavash,* and raw honeys; song birds chirp from the rafters even in the dead of winter. You should try the spicy carrot salad made by local Korean women or the crispy pickles sold by Russian grandmothers.

There are several places of interest relating to the Russian Civil War. These include the Defence of Tsaritsyn Museum, ul Gogola 10, tel: 362 200, which is in the building where the Red Forces directed their defence of the city from 1917 to 1919; and the monument on the mass grave of 3,500 communist partisans buried in pl Pavshikh Bortsov.

Getting assistance
Travel agents   Intourist in Hotel Intourist, ul Mira 14, tel: 361 468; Sputnik, ul Chuikova 65, tel: 347 242; Bureau of Travel and Excursions, tel: 339 546
Air   Aeroflot, Alleya Geroyev 5, tel: 335 305, 363 062 and 363 063; airport tel: 391 060
Rail   Railway station and the advance booking office is at ul Kommunisticheskaya 23, tel: 366 464.
Communications   To order an international or inter-city phone call from an English speaking operator, tel: 330 286.

What's in the region
World's largest Lenin
Volgograd boasts the world's largest statue of Lenin which stands about 50m high on the banks of the Volga River, 30km downstream from Volgograd. It rests on the spot where the world's largest statue of Stalin once stood before it was torn down in the 1950s. It is a ten-minute walk from the Lenin statue to lock 1 of the Volga–Don Canal; getting to both are explained under *The Volga–Don Canal* below.

The Volga–Don Canal
For generations, Russian rulers have dreamed of joining the mighty Volga and Don Rivers to connect Europe via the North Sea with the Mediterranean via the Black Sea. Peter the Great started work on building a canal in the 17th

century but it was only in 1952 that the Volga–Don Canal was completed. Digging this 101km-long and 3.5m-deep canal was an enormous project as only 45km of it went along existing rivers or lakes. Much of the canal was built with forced labour. The canal consists of 15 locks which raise or drop the water level a total of 133m between the two rivers. The original name of the canal was the Stalin Volga–Don Canal but it was renamed the Lenin Volga–Don Canal when Stalin fell from favour. It is now known simply as the Volga–Don Canal.

As well as being functional, the locks are also attractive, particularly the first one. Its 40m-high arch is decorated by rostral columns in honour of the sailors of the Volga Naval Flotilla who fought nearby on the Volga River during the Russian Civil War and World War II.

To get to lock 1, take a suburban train to Zakanalnaya station (Заканальная) which is the 16th stop from Volgograd 1 station. The trip takes 26 minutes and about five minutes before reaching the station you will see the giant Lenin statue and lock 1 on the right. From the front of Zakanalnaya station take bus No 1 and get off at the fourth stop which is directly in front of the statue. You can continue on the bus and get off at the next stop which is lock 1 or walk between the statue and the lock. Opposite lock 1 is the Hotel Volga–Don. To return to the station, catch the bus and you will the cross over the railway line and see the station on the left just before you reach the second stop. Trains run every 30 minutes. Another option is to take trolleybus No 2 to the stop Gostinitsa which is in front of the Hotel Volga–Don.

The only other locks that can be visited by train are locks 11 and 12 which are around Marinovka station (Мариновка). The suburban train to here takes about two hours.

Volzhski   Волжский   1,340km

This town is only 40 years old as it was founded at the start of the construction of the hydro-electric dam which is 2km away. Volzhski is an excellent example of co-ordinated town planning with 40m-wide main streets running northwest to southeast which protects them from hot steppe summer winds. It has good civic facilities, including a museum of local studies, and established parks due to tree planting decades ago.

After leaving Volzhski, the land changes markedly into low hills with sparse vegetation surrounded by semi-deserts.

Leninsk   Ленинск   1,362km

You can't see much of this town as it is 4km from the station. Much of the preserved fruit and vegetables you buy in local shops come from here, as you will see on the labels. Until 1919, the town was known as Prishib (Пришиб).

Kapustin Yar   Капустин Яр   1,410km

Nearby is the Kapustin Yar Cosmodrome from which the Soviets launched their first rockets on October 18 1947. These were captured German V2 rockets which were secretly pulled out of occupied Germany in the last days of World War II.

Since 1962, small and medium payloads have been launched from here, and today it is used for testing medium-range military missiles. While it is Russia's most open cosmodrome for Western scientists, tourists still can't visit.

Vladimirovka   Владимировка   1,453km

The town around the station is called Akhtubinsk (Ахтубинск) and it is the main centre for the Kapustin Yar Cosmodrome. There is a large airforce base here and a memorial to the test pilots who died while trying out new planes. There is a general history museum in town and another one on the military base. The military museum is closed to foreigners.

The town has a large port on the Akhtuba River which flows into the Volga and hydrofoils travel from Akhtubinsk to Astrakhan.

Verkhni Baskunchak   Верхний Баскунчак   1,498km

The train line from Volgograd joins the direct line from Moscow to Astrakhan here.

Kharabali   Харабали   1,602km

There is little to see in this town except the Museum of Local Studies containing artefacts from the 13th-century Golden Horde culture.

However, just 40km to the south is the fascinating buried capital of the Golden Horde, known variously as Sarai-Batu, Staryi-Sarai or Sarai-Bolsie. Sarai-Batu was founded in 1254 by Khan Batu who headed up the Golden Horde. The Golden Horde was a settled group of Tatar-Mongol invaders who ravaged most of Russia in 1238. Sarai-Batu's glory was short-lived as it was sacked in 1395 by Khan Timur who founded a long-lasting empire centred in Samarkand in present day Uzbekistan. Sarai-Batu was completely obliterated in 1480.

Excavations started in 1922 and 36km² of palaces, mosques, markets, bath houses, necropolis and artisans' quarters have been unearthed. Excellently preserved mosaics and frescoes have been discovered and these are on display in museums in Kharabali and Astrakhan. You can visit the extinct city near the present-day village of Selitrennoe (Селитренное).

The train now travels through a stretch of desert called the Batpaisagyr Sands (Пески Батпайсагыр).

Aksaraiskaya   Аксарайская   1,695km

This hell-hole town is at the junction of the Moscow–Volgograd line and a branch line that runs to central Asia. There is one train a day that travels along this branch line, train No 57 Volgograd–Tashkent. The train is always packed with central Asians transporting goods to be sold at each end. The traders never buy tickets and the conductors lock themselves in their cabins to avoid the daily drunken fights. While you can buy a ticket for this train, you will not get a seat as the rule is "first come first served". Once inside Kazakhstan and Uzbekistan, the train becomes even more crowded with people riding on the roof.

If you really want to travel on this train, buy four *coupé* tickets from Volgograd and lock yourself in the cabin for the entire trip. *Coupé* tickets are not sold at Aksaraiskaya. The most crowded section is from Aksaraiskaya to Khiva in Uzbekistan which takes 56 hours. From Khiva to Tashkent, you will probably be able to find a place to lie down.

ASTRAKHAN   Астрахань   1,744km
Population: 512,000   Telephone area code: 8512

Astrakhan sits on the Volga River which flows into the Caspian Sea just 60km downstream. Although Astrakhan is an interesting city in its own right, most travellers come here because of the attractions of the Volga River delta. These include the fabulous lotus flower fields, birdwatching and fishing, and visiting archaeological digs. Foreigners are still uncommon in Astrakhan as the city was closed until 1988.

Astrakhan was officially founded in 1558 when the Russians built a kremlin to dominate the lower reaches of the Volga. Its control of the river, which leads to Moscow, ensured that it grew into a powerful military strong point and a trading centre with links to central Asia, the Caucasus, Iran and India.

During the Soviet period, the city's role in the Russian Civil War was continually emphasised and in particular the part played by the Red commander Sergei Kirov (1886–1935). Astrakhan used to boast a Museum of Kirov, who was a rival to Stalin but, following the collapse of communism, the museum closed. However, the post-communist purges have not yet claimed the seven monuments to Lenin nor Lenin's Family Museum which is in the house where Lenin's father, Ilya Nikolaevich Ulyanov, spent his childhood.

Most of Astrakhan's commercial activity revolves around the river and includes fishing, caviar production and boat building. With the downturn of the economy and reduced fishing due to overfishing and river pollution, many boats are now rusting along the river banks. However, the city's most famous produce, the Astrakhan watermelon, is still being grown in record numbers and on many trains to Moscow, whole carriages are filled with these.

Getting there and away

By air   There is a weekly international flight to Bucharest on Acvila Air.

By boat   There are hydrofoils which travel down the branches of the Volga River to the Black Sea villages of Olya (Оля) and Kirovski (Кировский), and up the Volga River to Akhtubinsk (Ахтубинск). Akhtubinsk is on the railway line to Volgograd. There are also long-distance cruisers and a first-class berth to Moscow costs $151, to Nizhni Novgorod $131, to Saratov $73 and to Volgograd $40. These boats run weekly and tickets are booked at the long-distance ferry terminal.

By train   The most convenient long-distance trains on this route are listed below.

Origin	Dist, km	Train no & name	Travel time	Depart	Arrive	Destination
Astrakhan	1,532	6/5	30hr 20min	22.25	04.45	Moscow (Paveletski)
Astrakhan	448	38/37	7hr 35min	18.45	04.20	Volgograd
Moscow (Paveletski)	1,532	5/6	29hr 45min	13.15	19.00	Astrakhan
Volgograd	448	37/38	9hr 35min	10.20	19.55	Astrakhan

There is no direct train from Astrakhan to Central Asia, but there is one from nearby Aksaraiskaya station. For information on this train, refer to *Aksaraiskaya, page 300.*

Passing through

The 1980s railway station is a classic example of poor design. Its large expanse of glass lets in so much summer sun that it quickly becomes unbearable on days over 35°C. Consequently, the ten rows of waiting-room seats are moved on to the platform under a veranda every summer. In winter, no amount of heating seems to take the chill out of the air. Compare this situation with the Stalinist, high-vaulted stations which are cool in summer and warm in winter.

Where to stay
The town's best hotel is the standard Hotel Lotos, ul Kremlevskaya 4, tel: 228 587, $12 twin share/person on the shores of the Volga River. To get there from the station, take tram No 2 to pl Oktyabrskaya and walk the rest of the way. Other standard hotels are Hotel Gavan, ul Sen-Simona 40, tel: 246 842, $33 single room; and Hotel Korvet, ul Boevaya 50a, tel: 240 378, 340 378, $24 twin share/person. Other choices are the basic Hotel Astrakhanskaya, ul Ulyanovykh 6, tel: 222 988; very basic Hotel Novomoskovskaya, ul Sovetskaya 4, tel: 220 954, 246 389, $10 single room; and the very basic Hotel Yuzhnaya, ul 3rd Rybatskaya 3, tel: 331 344. Only Hotel Lotos and Hotel Korvets have restaurants.

Getting around
The station is located about 2km north of the city centre. Tram No 2 travels from the station to pl Oktyabrskaya which is beside the kremlin. The airport is to the south of the city and can be reached on trolleybus No 3 from the station.

What to see
Astrakhan Kremlin
This magnificent, white kremlin was the rationale for the city's existence when it was founded in 1558. By 1582, the fortress' basic shape of massive stone walls interspersed by eight big and little towers had materialised and this changed little with the addition of new buildings over the next four centuries.

The entrance to the kremlin is via the combined bell tower and gate house. There is a very small exhibition of the development of the kremlin in the Artillery Tower and a Museum of Local History and Peoples in the centre of the kremlin. The Assumption Cathedral is slowly being restored. The museums are open 10.00–17.00, closed Monday.

What else to see
The old part of Astrakhan is interesting as the majority of the buildings are turn-of-the-century two-storey red brick houses and workshops. The lack of wooden buildings and window decorations compared to those in northern Russian reflects the lack of timber in the Volga delta region.

The river front near Hotel Lotus is a pleasant place to stroll as dozens of stands sell watermelons, cantaloupes and *shashliks* on the warm, balmy summer nights. There is a river swimming pool here while the main swimming beach is on Gorodskoi Island opposite the river station.

There is a Planetarium in Gorky Park, a Circus at pl Pobedy, the Philharmonic Hall at ul Molodoi Gvardii 3, the Drama Theatre at ul Sovetskaya 28, and the Youth Theatre at ul Musy Dzhalilya.

Interesting buildings include the white Tatar Mosque and the Oktyabr Cinema with its tropical garden in the foyer.

The single biggest museum is the Museum of Local Studies, ul Sovetskaya 15, tel: 227 875, open 10.00–17.00, closed Thursday, which also organises historical trips around the town for locals and can provide English-speaking guides. Nearby is the Military Museum, ul Khalturina 7, open 10.00–17.00, closed Thursday. Not very interesting is Lenin's Family Museum, ul Ulyanovykh 9, open 10.00–17.00, closed Thursday, which nowadays has very little Lenin memorabilia on display as most of the two floors are dedicated to the history of the region and the history of education. There is also a Picture Gallery, ul Sverdlova 81, open 10.00–18.00, closed Friday, and the Chernyshevski Literature Museum, ul Chernyshevskovo 4, open 10.00-17.00, closed Monday, named after the revolutionary writer N G Chernyshevski.

Getting assistance

Travel agents   Sputnik, ul Zhevyabova 25, tel: 223 422, fax: 220 521; Intourist, ul Sovetskaya 21, tel: 297 30. Sputnik works closely with Russian Nature Tours, PO Box 1627, 2010 Vilnius 10, Lithuania, tel: (370 98) 50 300, fax: (370 27) 40 402.

Air   Aeroflot, ul Pobedy 54, tel: 547 49.

Boat   Local river station, ul Zhelyabova 1, which sells tickets for local ferries and hydrofoils. The long-distance river station is 100m downstream from Hotel Lotus and 50m back from the river bank in an old wooden building.

Bus   Long-distance bus station, ul Generala Episheva 4/7

Rail   Tickets can be bought at the railway station and at the advance booking office, ul Kommunisticheskaya 52

What's in the region

The biggest attractions in the Astrakhan region are the Volga delta's lotus flower fields, birdwatching, fishing and archaeology. There are also a number of museums around Astrakhan, none of which is worth a trip in itself but they are worth stopping in at on your way through. They can all be reached by local ferries from Astrakhan or local bus.

In Krasny Yar village (Красный Яр), there is the Museum of Local Studies, ul Mologoi Gvargi 60, tel: (216) 916 39, which is 1hr 30min by car to the northeast. In Liman village (Лиман), there is the Museum of Local Studies, tel: (217) 922 53, which is 3hr by local bus to the southwest. In Ikryanoe village (Икряное), there is the Museum of the History of Fishing, ul Lenina 7, tel: (214) 969 09, which is 70km to the southwest. In Oranzherei village (Оранжереи), there is the Museum of the History of Fishing, ul Naberezhnaya 25, tel: (820) 949 70, which is 120km to the southwest. In Altynzhar village (Алтынжар), there is the Literature Museum, ul Sovetskaya 5, tel: (212) 912 03, which is 70km to the southeast.

The Volga River delta and lotus fields

As the Volga River approaches the Caspian Sea it breaks up into dozens of rivers and streams spread out over a 200km-wide strip. This triangular area, known as the Volga River delta, covers over 20,000km² and includes more than 1,000 lakes. Surrounding the delta is the wildlife-poor, wormwood and Kalmyk steppe semi-desert while the delta itself has an abundance of flora and fauna. On the river banks stand silver willows and thickets of reeds, while the lakes contain lotus fields, water chestnuts and water lilies. In addition to the large number of birds, you may catch sight of wild boar, hares, foxes, racoons, stoats, desmans and Caspian seals.

The largest purple-flower lotus fields are in the Astrakhanski Nature Reserve to the east of Astrakhan and to get there takes ten hours of river travel. The lotus blooms in July and August and whole lakes covered with the flowers are an amazing sight. The trip cannot be made in one day, so you must stay overnight. Sputnik organise tours to the lotus flower fields with accommodation on a comfortable ferry hotel.

Birdwatching and fishing

The delta's sand bars and spits are the resting place of thousands of cormorants, waders, white-tailed sea-eagles, sandpipers and sea gulls. There have been 185 species of birds spotted in the delta including 27 which are included in Russia's endangered wildlife *Red Book*. The best time to visit is from April to July with water fowl dominating the bird migration in spring and late autumn. Sputnik offer five routes for birdwatchers which are each 100–300km long and cover both the delta, steppe and semi-desert.

The delta is home to four types of fish: sea, migrating, semi-migrating and freshwater. The migrating fish include lamprey, white salmon, sturgeon and herring, and the semi-migrating include the Caspian roach, bream, pike-perch, carp and chub. The delta's permanent inhabitants include the red-fin, trench, crucian, pike and sheatfish. The best fishing is between March and late October. The largest fish caught by a foreigner in the last few years was recorded as a 207cm-long sheatfish weighing 41.5kg.

May and June are not good times for either birdwatching or fishing due to high water levels and swarms of mosquitoes.

Sputnik organise regular five-day trips and accommodation in the delta is on a comfortable ferry hotel. The price of the trip is about $70 a night per person.

Archaeological trips

The area around Astrakhan has been fought over for millenniums as it is the gateway to the rich Volga River delta, and sits at the crossroads of two mercantile routes: the east–west Silk Road and the north Volga River route to European Russia.

Among the first invaders were the Scythians who poured westward on to the northern coast of the Black Sea in the 7th century BC. These were displaced by the Sarmates who were probably the source of the legendary Amazonian fighters as the Sarmate women were noted for their military prowess. From 500BC to 1200AD various other peoples invaded or settled in the region including the Sarmato-Alans, Savromates, Ugres, Khazars, Polovtsians and Tatar-Mongols.

Currently, archaeologists from the Institute of Russia's Heritage, the Institute of Archaeology and Astrakhan Museum are working on several burial mounds known as a barrows, group burial grounds and ancient settlements. Material being unearthed includes domestic utensils, burial costumes, pottery, knives, awls, swords, arrow-heads, pendants and mirrors from 600BC to 1400AD.

The Krasnoyarsk burial ground is one of the richest sites and it is only 40km to the east of Astrakhan. It was used as a burial site from 600BC to 1400AD and the last four years of digging have revealed relics of the Savromates and Sarmates nomadic culture, graves of the Khazar khans from the 7th to 10th centuries, and household goods of the Tatar-Mongols from the 12th to 14th centuries. Excavations are carried out yearly between July and August.

Another important excavation site is the former Golden Horde city of Samosdelskoe, destroyed by Khan Timur in 1395. Samosdelskoe is 100km to the south of Astrakhan and the workings are only dug in August.

Sputnik organise six-day programmes which involve lectures and excavation work under the supervision of a Russian expert. The cost is about $100 per person per day.

Chapter Fifteen

BAM

The secret Trans-Siberian railway

The 3,400km BAM railway traverses Siberia from the Pacific Ocean to Lake Baikal, and is the gateway to the rarely visited region known as the BAM Zone. BAM stands for the "Baikal to Amur Mainline" railway and is about 600–1,000km north of, and runs parallel to, the Trans-Siberian railway.

Before the 1970s, the zone was mostly uninhabited taiga, dotted with indigenous peoples' villages. Today, it has a population of about 300,000 people who are involved in extracting natural resources from the region's enormous supply.

Work on the railway started in the 1930s as the Soviets were paranoid that forces from China could easily cut the Trans-Siberian which was the lifeline to the Russian far east. After Stalin's death in 1953 work on the BAM railway ceased, only to be resumed under Brezhnev's leadership in the early 1970s. Although the railway was completed in 1985, it is virtually unknown in the West and nowadays only about a hundred westerners a year travel on the line.

Route highlights

The biggest attraction of the route is the scenery. The single-tracked BAM takes you slowly through pristine taiga, mountain tundra and wide river valley meadows. Most unforgettable is the rarely visited north end of Lake Baikal where it is possible to see seals and visit a 1930s *gulag* camp. Other places of interest are Novaya Chara with its mysterious sand dunes and well-preserved 1930s *gulag* camp, the BAM capital at Tynda and the Soviet era city of Komsomolsk.

Travel suggestions

It is harder to travel along the BAM than most other areas of Russia as there are fewer trains, little tourist infrastructure and only a sprinkling of English speakers. However, as few westerners visit the region, you are guaranteed considerable attention by locals which invariably leads to assistance. In addition, the personal contact with locals gives you an insight into rural Russia which is rarely glimpsed nowadays in European Russia.

The best time of the year to go is in summer but, if you are going into the taiga, beware of the life-threatening *Ixodes tic* which is active there in July and August.

Ten days are needed to travel the entire length of the BAM with two days in Severobaikalsk, one in Chara, one in Tynda and two in Komsomolsk.

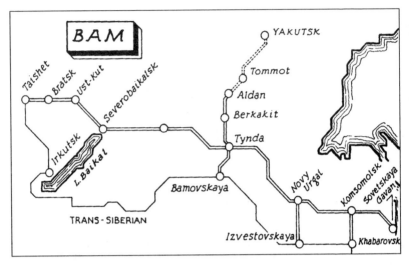

A detailed guide to this railway is *The Siberian BAM Railway Guide: the Second Trans-Siberian Railway* by Athol Yates, published by Trailblazer Publications.

Trains

There are no trains that travel the entire length of the BAM as trains radiate out from the BAM capital of Tynda which sits in the centre of the railway. From Tynda trains go to Moscow in the west, Neryungri and Yakutsk in the north, Komsomolsk and Khabarovsk in the east, and the Trans-Siberian in the south.

The fastest long-distance trains on this route are listed below.

Origin	Dist, km	Train no & name	Travel time	Depart	Arrive	Destination
Bratsk	292	75	6hr 7min	22.30	04.37	Taishet
Bratsk	772	76	15hr 29min	03.15	18.44	Severobaikalsk
Khabarovsk	374	203	8hr 50min	15.05	23.55	Komsomolsk
Komsomolsk	374	67	8hr 40min	15.00	23.40	Khabarovsk
Komsomolsk	516	203	13hr 55min	08.25	22.20	Novy Urgal
Novaya Chara	630	76	13hr 56min	10.39	00.35	Tynda
Novaya Chara	670	75	13hr 56min	16.00	05.56	Severobaikalsk
Novy Urgal	516	203	13hr 55min	11.50	01.45	Komsomolsk
Novy Urgal	951	203	25hr 55min	23.00	00.55	Tynda
Severobaikalsk	670	76	14hr 38min	19.21	09.59	Novaya Chara
Severobaikalsk	772	75	15hr 52min	06.38	22.30	Bratsk
Taishet	292	76	6hr 19min	20.56	03.15	Bratsk
Tynda	630	75	13hr 11min	02.20	15.31	Novaya Chara
Tynda	951	203	25hr 55min	09.00	10.55	Novy Urgal

TAISHET–TYNDA
via Bratsk, Severobaikalsk and Novaya Chara

TAISHET   Тайшет   0km
Population: 43,000   Telephone area code: 395 63

This town straddles the junction of the BAM and the Trans-Siberian railways and was founded in 1897 with the arrival of the latter. There is nothing to see in the town even though it is famous in Soviet *gulag* literature. Taishet was a transit camp for Stalin era prisoners heading east and west, and was a major camp of Ozerlag, the *gulag* complex which built the Taishet–Bratsk section of the BAM. The town is divided into a new settlement, where the station, apartment blocks and administrative centre are located, and the old part which is on the other side of the railway line. The bus station is located in front of the station. Buses No 1 and No 3 go past the market which is located in the old settlement.

The best accommodation in town is the Hotel Birusa, ul Transportnaya, tel: 303 18, $5 twin share/person, opposite the railway station.

Getting there and away
By road   Taishet is located on the M53 Moscow–Irkutsk highway.
By train   The fastest long-distance trains on this route are listed below.

Origin	Dist, km	Train no & name	Travel time	Depart	Arrive	Destination
Bratsk	292	75	6hr 7min	22.30	04.37	Taishet
Taishet	292	76	6hr 19min	20.56	03.15	Bratsk

BRATSK   Братск
Population: 280,000
Telephone area code: 39 531 (Bratsk Tsentralny)

Bratsk is fascinating, principally as an example of what not to do when you are creating a gigantic industrial complex in the middle of the taiga. Despite being in the top ten most polluted cities in Russia, Bratsk is still awe-inspiring considering the massive achievement of constructing a modern city, a giant dam and massive industrial enterprises in just two decades. Two days is the maximum you will need to see all of Bratsk; indeed, looking out of the window of an express train may be enough for most travellers.

In fact, Bratsk is not one town but a ring of connected settlements around the man-made Bratsk Sea, a large reservoir created by the Bratsk dam. From the south in a counter-clockwise direction the towns are Novobratsk Port (Порт Новобратск), Bratsk More (Братское море), Bratsk Tsentralny (Центральный район), Padun (Падун), Energetik (Энергетик) on the dam's west bank and Gidrostoitel (Гидростроитель) on the east bank.

The administrative centre of Bratsk is at Bratsk Tsentralny, as are the Taiga and Bratsk Hotels, but unfortunately there is no BAM station here. However, Bratsk Tsentralny can be reached by an electric train from the BAM station of Anzebi (Анзеби), 12km away.

The station of Padunskie Porogi services the suburbs of Padun and Energetik. The station's name derives from the Padun rapids which existed before the dam was built. This station is the closest to Hotel Turist. Padun contains the most attractive part of Bratsk as it has a pleasant promenade, with an old log watchtower and the city's only working church. Bratsk airport is to the north of Padunskie Porogi and can be reached by a 40-minute bus trip starting from in front of the station.

History
The Bratsk area, with its rich agricultural lands, was an important staging area for exploring and colonising eastern Siberia and the Russian far east. The word *bratsk* comes from the Russian words *bratskie lyudi* which were used to describe the local indigenous people, the Buryats. *Bratskie lyudi* means

"fraternal people". Old Bratsk was founded as a fort in 1631 but has long since disappeared under the giant Bratsk Sea.

Bratsk slowly developed as an agricultural centre until, in 1954, the decision was taken to build the Bratsk hydro-electric station and it rapidly became a gem in the nation's industrialisation crown. The reservoir is one of the largest in the world, being 169.3km^3 in volume with a surface area of 5,470km^2. Within seven years of the start of the dam's construction, electricity was being generated and, in conjunction with the nearby Ust-Ilimsk hydro-electric station, the region now generates a mammoth 4.5% of the nation's electricity.

Getting there and away
The fastest long-distance trains on this route are listed below.

Origin	Dist, km	Train no & name	Travel time	Depart	Arrive	Destination
Bratsk	292	75	6hr 7min	22.30	04.37	Taishet
Bratsk	772	76	15hr 29min	03.15	18.44	Severobaikalsk
Severobaikalsk	772	75	15hr 52min	06.38	22.30	Bratsk
Taishet	292	76	6hr 19min	20.56	03.15	Bratsk

Where to stay
The best accommodation is the standard Hotel Taiga, ul Mira 35, tel: 443 979, $50 twin share/room. Other choices are the standard Hotel Turist, Energetik, ul Naymushina 28, tel: 370 995, and the basic Hotel Bratsk, ul Deputatskaya 32, tel: 446 44, $24–46 for a single room. There is also a hotel at the airport.

Getting around
Both the Taiga and Bratsk Hotels, and the central bus station on ul Yuzhnaya, are located in Bratsk Tsentralny. Bus No 110 travels from the bus station every hour, past the Hotel Taiga to the airport and takes 50 minutes. Bus No 7A travels between the bus station and the closest BAM station of Anzebi. There are also regular suburban trains between Bratsk Tsentralny and Anzebi. Opposite the Hotel Taiga and down the street at ul Mira 27 is the post office with a bookshop opposite. Next door to the post office is a large food shop with imported food.

Hotel Turist is located near Padunskie Porogi station and can be reached by a ten-minute trip on bus No 103.

What to see
Bratsk Intourist offer two-hour tours of Bratsk for $20.

Any visit to Bratsk would be incomplete without seeing the 50th Anniversary of Great October Bratsk hydro-electric station. This dam consists of a 506m concrete wall with 3.5km of earth walls on its left and right. The BAM line runs along the top of the dam and gives an excellent view of the Bratsk reservoir on one side and the Angara River on the other. You enter the powerhouse by walking down the steps from the top of the dam. Plenty of buses go along the top of the dam and stop for you to get off. These include No 4,102, 103, 104 and 107. It is a 40-minute walk from the Padunskie Porogi station. It is well worth a visit and Intourist Bratsk provide a two-hour tour for $45.

On the outskirts of Bratsk, at Angara Village, is an open-air Ethnographic Museum, open 10.00–17.00 summer only, closed Monday, containing an Evenki camp, a watchtower and a fort from Bratsk's first years, and several houses of past generations. Intourist Bratsk provide tours to the museum for $40, but you can organise a visit yourself by hiring a taxi for the day.

There is also a History Museum at ul Komsomolskaya 38.

Getting assistance

Travel agents Bratsk Intourist are located on second floor of the Hotel Taiga, tel: 443 95, fax: 446 522.

Korshunikha-Angarskaya Коршуниха-Ангарская 554km
Telephone area code: 395 66

Although the railway station is called Korshunikha-Angarskaya, the surrounding town is known as Zheleznogorsk-Ilimski (Железногорск-Илимск). The station gets its name from the abandoned village of Korshunovski about 30km away. Despite being a mining town, Zheleznogorsk-Ilimski is one of the cleanest towns on the BAM and has a lot to offer travellers.

A 15-minute walk up the main street from the station will bring you to pl Yangela where you will find the post office, mayor's office, three museums and a monument to aircraft and spacecraft designer Mikhail Yangel. The museums consist of a Museum of Local Studies, a Museum to Mikhail Yangel's Work and a Museum of Japanese-Russian Friendship. For the past 15 years, Zheleznogorsk-Ilimski has had a sister city relationship with the Japanese city of Sakata and both cities have hosted many sister city cultural and sporting groups. The museums, tel: 20 792, are open 09.00–17.00, closed 13.00–14.00 and Monday.

The standard Hotel Magnetit, tel: 21 758, fax: 22 605 (att: Hotel Magnetit), $9 double room, is a 5-minute walk from the station.

Khrebtovaya Хребтовая 575km
Khrebtovaya is the junction of the BAM and the 214km branch line to the hydro-electric dam town of Ust-Ilimsk.

Ust-Kut Усть-Кут 715km
Travellers often confuse Ust-Kut and nearby larger Lena as both have river ports. However, Ust-Kut contains the freight port while Lena has the passenger port.

Ust-Kut was founded by the explorer Yerofei Khabarov (after whom Khabarovsk was named) in 1631 and it rapidly became an important trading port as it supplied most of eastern Siberia with food and equipment until the 20th century. Rich deposits of salt were discovered nearby and were exploited until the beginning of the revolution. Rail traffic first reached Lena in 1958 when a temporary railway was laid across the Bratsk reservoir.

The only sight in town is the freight port and this can be reached on bus No 1 which departs from the station, goes past the freight port and terminates at Lena station.

Lena Лена 722km
Telephone area code: 395 65

About 500m from the station is the Lena river passenger station, known as Osetrovo (Осетрово). Travellers embark here for vessels that sail down the mighty 4,400km Lena River to Yakutsk (the capital of the Republic of Sakha, formerly known as Yakutia) and up the 408km Kut River to Zhigalovo.

The City Museum contains information on the BAM and the region, and is located near the Osterovo river passenger station.

For steam rail enthusiasts, 500m from the east end of Lena station are three rusting steam engines, including one built by the American Locomotive Company in February 1945.

The best and most expensive hotel in town is the new, nine-storey Lena Hotel, ul Kirova 88, tel: 21 507, fax: 20 729 or 21 500 (att: Lena Hotel), twin share $33; Osterovo river passenger station, tel: 21 480, also has a few rooms including three twin rooms at $7.50 a person.

Irkutsktourist Travel Company, located in the Lena Hotel, can book rail and boat tickets and arrange excursions, tel: 21 880, fax: 20 729 or 21 500 (att: Irkutsktourist).

Lena-Vostochnaya   Лена-Восточная   736km

After leaving Lena-Vostochnaya, the train passes over the first BAM bridge that was built in 1975.

The next 300km between the Lena River and the Baikal Range is famous for its scenic beauty and is one of the most pleasant stretches on the BAM.

Kunerma   Кунерма   983km

Kunerma is a pleasant place to visit on a day trip from Severobaikalsk, as to get here you pass through scenic mountains. The town is also attractive as it consists of a number of two-storey wooden apartment blocks, a recently refurbished station and a single shopping complex; these complexes, where all the shops are under one roof, are often used in really cold places so that people do not have to tramp the streets to go to various stores. Only 700 people live here and it provides an interesting insight into small town life. It is also a very popular fishing destination as there is a well-stocked lake nearby.

As well as the daily trains from Tynda to Moscow, suburban trains terminate here from Severobaikalsk. There are three suburban services to Severobaikalsk daily. There is no accommodation in the town.

After leaving Kunerma, the train loops around the Goudzhekit River Valley towards the Baikal Mountains, 2,000m above sea level, and through the 6.7km Baikal Mountain Tunnel.

Daban   Дабан   1,015km

As soon as you emerge from the eastern tunnel entrance, you come to the station of Daban. The stop, at 1,500m above sea level, is a popular starting point for hikers and cross-country skiers. The only building at this stop is the station and there is no accommodation here.

As you descend from the mountain, you will see the Goudzhekit River on the left and, after a few kilometres, a solitary red brick chimney in a large field. This is all that remains of the town that was constructed for the 3,000 workers who built the tunnel. Eliminating all traces of construction and returning the area to its natural condition was an important element in the BAM's environmental policy.

A further 3km from the tunnel's exit on the left side is the military camp which supplies guards for the tunnel entrances.

Tyya   Тыя   1,043km

Around the station is the small town of Solnechny (Солнечный). Nearby is a 340m downhill ski run with a tow and ski rental. Three trains a day stop here.

SEVEROBAIKALSK   Северобайкальск   1,064km
Population: 35,000   Telephone area code: 301 39

Severobaikalsk is the capital of the western end of the BAM and probably the most popular destination on the line. The town provides excellent access to the north Baikal attractions, which include trekking and mountaineering in the Baikal Mountains, indigenous villages, a Stalin era *gulag*, downhill skiing, sailing around the north end of the lake and seal watching.

Getting there and away
By boat   You can get to Severobaikalsk by hydrofoil from Port Baikal which runs from June 15 to September 15. For more information, see *Chapter Sixteen, page 370.*

By train   The fastest long-distance trains on this route are listed below.

Origin	Dist, km	Train no & name	Travel time	Depart	Arrive	Destination
Bratsk	772	76	15hr 29min	03.15	18.44	Severobaikalsk
Novaya Chara	670	75	13hr 56min	16.00	05.56	Severobaikalsk
Severobaikalsk	670	76	14hr 38min	19.21	09.59	Novaya Chara
Severobaikalsk	772	75	15hr 52min	06.38	22.30	Bratsk

Where to stay
The best place to stay is at the excellent BAM railway cottages. Each has two bathrooms, toilet, sitting room, kitchen and three bedrooms. They can be reached by a ten-minute walk from the station, and they have a view of the coast. The railway cottages are located near ul Sibirskaya. Booking is done via BAMTour and costs $15 a night per person.

The best hotel is the standard Hotel Nord at the port where the hydrofoil arrives. The hotel is expensive and is 2km from the centre of Severobaikalsk. Bus No 1 and the bus to Nizhneangarsk stop near the hotel. The worst accommodation is the very basic Sever Hotel, tel: 7712, $15 per night per person, which can be reached on bus No 3 departing from the station. The bus trip takes 20 minutes. The hotel has no hot water or showers, and only communal squat toilets.

Getting around
Everything in Severobaikalsk is within walking distance, with the exception of the port from which the hydrofoil departs, and the port's Nord Hotel. To get to the port, take bus No 1 from the central bus station in front of the railway station. Bus No 3 goes past the BAM Museum and near the Sever Hotel.

What to see
Places of railway interest are the BAM Museum, ul Mira 2, open 10.00–18.00, closed Monday, and the BAM Art Museum, ul Druzhba.

The Palace of Culture is worth visiting as this delightful building has a small indoor garden and a large hall, and is always putting on theatrical and musical performances. If it is a national holiday, you can be guaranteed that there will be something worth seeing.

Severobaikalsk Yacht Club possesses 30 boats including five six-person yachts. Sailing is an excellent way of travelling around the north end of Lake Baikal, enabling you to stop at villages and hot springs. The Severobaikalsk Regatta occurs at the end of July and several children's sailing camps are run during the sailing season from June to October. Georgi Ekimok, ul 60 let CCCP, dom 14, kv 125, tel: 24 556.

Getting assistance
Severobaikalsk is home to the best-known company organising tours on the BAM and in the north Lake Baikal region. Rashit Yakhin heads the company, BAMTour, and he is one of the longest standing residents in Severobaikalsk, having worked on the railway in the early 1970s. BAMTour Co, 671717, Severobaikalsk, ul Oktyabrskaya 16-2 tel/fax: 21 560, telex 154215 DWC SU (attention: BAMTour).

What's in the region
There are a large number of interesting travel options around Severobaikalsk which will appeal to those interested in history, adventure, nature and culture. The following are some suggestions and the destinations are explained in detail in *The Siberian BAM Railway Guide* by Athol Yates.

- Day bike ride to Nizhneangarsk, Duskhachan and Kholodnoe, and return by train or bus
- Day hike to Akikan *gulag* camp and the nearby indigenous village of Kholodnoe
- Day bike or bus trip to Baikalskoe village
- Day train trip to Solnechni settlement (hot springs and skiing) or Kunerma (fishing and Baikal mountain railway tunnel exploration)
- Ice fishing on the frozen Lake Baikal between March and April
- Rafting down the Tyya or Verkhyanaya Angara Rivers to Lake Baikal
- Hiking to Lake Frolikha on the eastern coast of Lake Baikal. Boat to and from the east coast
- Cross-country skiing across the frozen Lake Baikal
- Trekking along the shore of Lake Baikal
- Mountain and glacier climbing in Baikal Mountain Range
- Nature tours and hunting tours based at the Ayaya lodge
- Seal watching and seal hunting with the indigenous Buryat hunters

Between Severobaikalsk and Nizhneangarsk
The trip between Severobaikalsk and Nizhneangarsk is very scenic as both the road and railway run along the northern shores of Lake Baikal. Along the road route are what must be Russia's most artistic bus shelters. Built by volunteers of the BAM Tunnel Construction Company's Tunnel Detachment No 16, each shelter is decorated using mosaic tiles and has a specific theme.

Between the last bus shelter and Nizhneangarsk is the only monument on the BAM dedicated to the small number of tunnellers who died building the railway.

Akikan gulag (*Акикана ГУЛаг*)

The highlight of a visit to north Baikal is the Akikan *gulag*. The camp operated in the late 1930s, mining mica which was used as electrical insulation. It was closed just prior to the Great Patriotic War when a man-made substitute for mica was found. The camp is located in the Akikan Valley alongside the Akikan Stream. Today, the remnants of those terrible years are plainly visible and consist of several collapsed wooden and stone buildings, towers and barbed-wire fences. A further 400m up the valley on the left are three mine shafts where mica veins can still be seen.

To get to the camp, take a suburban train or bus to Kholodnoe Village (1hr) and from the railway station walk along a tarred road towards Kichera. This route takes you over the Kholodnoe River and up a long hill until you reach the 42km marker on the hill's summit. A further 200m past a long stretch of white highway protection barriers is an overgrown dirt logging track off to the left. After about an hour of walking along this track you pass under power lines and after another hour the track changes into a walking path that winds up the Akikan Valley. The path leads directly to the camp. The walk up the valley is fairly strenuous and so you should plan to have your lunch at the camp before returning. The best time to visit the camp is in July and August after the deadly *Ixodes tic* has disappeared. The tic is common only from May to late June. Only very fit cross-country skiers should attempt this route in winter. The return trip from Kholodnoe takes about four hours.

Seal watching

Although there are no regular trips offering nerpa seal watching, it is possible to organise one from Severobaikalsk. The best time to see seals is late May and early June when the seals bask on the little ice that remains in protected bays. During summer they live mostly near Bolshoi Ushkani Island (Остров Большой Ушканий), about 250km from Severobaikalsk. As you may need several days to travel to this isolated area and view the seals, a recommended programme is to travel on the hydrofoil to the Ayaya Lodge (only 15km from the island) and stay there. Trips can be organised by BAMTour and Ayaya Lodge. The Ayaya Lodge is located 130km south of Severobaikalsk on 65,000 hectares with a 50km shoreline. The lodge consists of two buildings with a kitchen, a recreation room and five bedrooms with beds for ten people. The easiest way to get to the lodge is to take the hydrofoil from either Irkutsk or Severobaikalsk and arrange for one of the hunters to meet the hydrofoil at sea. Another way is to take a boat from Severobaikalsk (6hr) or from the other side of the lake at Ust-Barguzin (Усть-Баргузин) (5hr) which can be reached from Ulan Ude. Bookings can be made with Mikhail Maligin, Director, Firm Ayaya, pr Leningradskoe 6, kv 91.

Nizhneangarsk   Нижнеангарск   1,104 km

Nizhneangarsk is the Russian equivalent of a low-density, sprawling suburb. It is wedged on a 20km strip between Lake Baikal and steep mountains, with each end bounded by the Nizhneangarsk railway station. Nizhneangarsk station is not actually 20km long but consists of two stations Nizhneangarsk 1 (closest to Severobaikalsk) and Nizhneangarsk 2. The large man-made harbour and the town's centre is at Nizhneangarsk 1 station while the airport is located at Nizhneangarsk 2. Strangely, the largest station is remote Nizhneangarsk 2 and it is the only stop for the Tynda–Moscow express.

The town has a large port for a small fishing fleet. The harbour was built for the contruction of the BAM but the railway arrived before it was needed. The town is also home to the headquarters of the BAM Tunnel Construction organisation and the seat of the regional government.

The town is pleasant to stroll around with its mainly wooden buildings. Despite most of the town being built since the mid 1970s, Nizhneangarsk is one of the very few BAM towns which is not dominated by five-storey concrete flats and prefabricated buildings. Even the two-storey city council building is wooden. An architectural oddity is the wooden boat rental and water rescue station on the lake's edge.

The fish-processing factory is worth a visit as it is an eye-opener to Russian methods and working conditions. The plant produces delicious smoked or salted omul (a variety of fish).

All trains stop here and a regular bus runs between Nizhneangarsk and Severobaikalsk with both forms of transport taking 40 minutes. Planes fly to and from Taksimo, Ulan Ude, and Irkutsk.

Raz. 635km   Раз. 635км   1,385km

The stop is also known as Okusikan (Окусикан), and is the western escarpment base for the tunnellers who are building the 15.7km Severomuisk Tunnel. The nearby small workers' settlement is called Tonnelni (Тоннельный) and is destined for demolition once the tunnel is finished. When this occurs, the existing 54km North Muya bypass will also be closed.

The trip over the bypass is very exciting and it is unfortunate that most trains do it during the night. The train travels at about 30km/h and offers excellent views as it snakes up the mountains. Being 2km above sea level, the peak is invariably snow-capped even in summer. As you travel down the eastern escarpment towards Severomuisk you can see the partly completed Severomuisk Tunnel portal. Between the tunnel portal and the town, you pass through three small tunnels.

Severomuisk   Северомуйск

This is the eastern escarpment base for the tunnellers who are building the 15.7km Severomuisk Tunnel. In anticipation of the completion of the tunnel and the razing of Severomuisk, most Russian maps do not show the location of the town.

Taksimo   Таксимо   1,484km

Taksimo's history dates back to the late Tsarist's times when its isolation made it a safe base camp for bandits. After the 1917 socialist revolution, this same isolation attracted White Army soldiers, priests and others who fled the persecution of the communists.

Modern Taksimo was built by Belarussians and Latvians, although it is very difficult to see their influence. Taksimo is the end of the electrified section of the BAM and the locomotives are changed from electric to diesel.

The most interesting places around Taksimo are the Parama Rapids on the Vitim River and its nearby towns of Ust-Muya, Muya, Bargalino and Nelyaty. The Parama Rapids on the Vitim River are among Russia's best rafting rapids but they are only suitable for very experienced rafters. Details of the rapids and organising a trip are provided in *The Siberian BAM Railway Guidebook* by Athol Yates.

STATIONS
Above: *Vladivostok* (IB)
Centre: *Berendeevo (junction for the Pereslavl branch)* (IB) Below: *Irkutsk* (IB)

THE NEW
Above: *New passenger electric loco VL65-017 at the Sortirovochnaya depot, Irkutsk* (IB)
Below: *2TE10L-684 diesel locomotive on the Golden Ring* (IB)

AND THE OLD: Steam is now unusual in Russia
Above: *P36-0071 express passenger locomotive, Obozerskaya.* (AJB)
Below: *Restored 0-8-0 Kp4-469 on the Pereslavl narrow gauge railway* (IB)

Above: *Amur Bridge, Khabarovsk* (IB)
Below: *Bratsk Hydro-electric Dam* (IB)

Near the station is a 1930s Tupalov ANT-4 on a plinth. This was one of the original planes that conducted the aerial surveys for the BAM in the 1930s. The plane crashed into Lake Barencharoe nearby and in the 1970s its wreckage was discovered and restored voluntarily by the railway builders.

The only hotel in town is the basic ATCh Railway Hotel, ul Sovetskaya 11, tel: 5681.

Shivery   Шиверы   1,548km
Between Taksimo and Shivery you pass over the 560m-long Vitim River Bridge. This is a popular fishing spot and there is a small village on the western bank. The actual stop of Shivery is about 1km from the bridge. The river forms the border between the Republic of Buryatiya and Amur Oblast which also delineates a time-zone border. In Buryatiya, the time difference is five hours from Moscow while in Amur Oblast, there is six hours difference.

KUANDA   Куанда   1,577km
Kuanda is famous in Soviet propaganda as it was here in September 1984 that the celebration of the BAM's completion was held. The actual golden spike joining the east and west sections of the BAM was hammered in about 15km to the east at Balbukhta (Балбухта) but as there were no facilities there, the actual celebration was moved to Kuanda.

In anticipation of the completion ceremony, Kuanda was built as a model town. Walking down the main street of the town provides a fascinating insight into the minds of the Soviet élite and how they wished their towns to look. The main street consists of attractive two-storey, wooden, semi-detached houses. Around each house is a medium-sized garden and a picket fence faces the tarred street. Most unusually, there are a number of benches along the side of the road where locals sit and talk. However, as soon as you walk off the main street, you see the reality of a Russian town. In this sense Kuanda is the same as the other BAM towns with its potholed roads, rotting rubbish piles, concrete apartment blocks, perpetually half-built buildings and a general perception of a community lacking pride.

About the only noteworthy thing to see in town is the sculpture on the station's platform. It symbolises the joining of the BAM and consists of two giant pillars with one rail connecting them, on which is etched "Kuanda". From the outer sides of each pillar protrude dozens of rails with names of other BAM stations etched on them.

There are two hotels in town. The very basic Locomotive Brigade Hotel tel: 251, $2 twin share/person, and the very basic Locomotive Brigade NGCh Hotel which is next door, tel: 241, $6 twin share/person.

Getting assistance
Within the BAM Zone, Kuanda has earned a reputation as a centre for outdoor education due to the creation of the BAM Tourist Centre for Children, 675161 Kalarski Raion, Station Kuanda, ul Marta 8, kv 1-4, tel: 441. The main function of the centre is to provide outdoor activities such as camping, skiing, rafting and mountaineering trips, survival classes and physical fitness camps during school holidays. However, the facilities and staff of the Centre are also used by foreign sports and adventure groups.

The BAM Tourist Centre was an initiative of the current manager, Victor Stepanovich Reshi, who is a well-known Russian sportsman.

The BAM Tourist Centre regularly organises the following trips:

– Walking to the Marble Canyon *gulag* camps. Described under *Novaya Chara* above.

– Mountain and glacier climbing in the Kodar ranges. The 200km-long Kodar Mountain Range is one of the natural and historical highlights of the BAM Zone. The highest peak in the range is Mount BAM at 3,072m with the nearby town of Novaya Chara just 700m above sea level. Up to 1,500m on the northern slopes and 1,700m on the southern ones is deciduous forest and stunted birch trees. This gradually gives way to thickets of Japanese stone pines and scraggy birches as you approach the treeline. Above this are barren alpine summits and mountain tundra. Some mountains are exceptionally hard to climb, which is reflected in their names such as Fang and Tower, and their difficulty attracted the 1989, 1990 and 1991 USSR Mountaineering Championships. Foreign groups have also climbed them in the past. As well as being very difficult, their attraction with alpinists is that they are easy to get to, being only about 25km from Novaya Chara station or airport. There are at least 40 glaciers in the region and new ones are being found each year. The main climbing period is from June 1 to September 15. Snow climbing is also possible from February 1 to March 31 and in November but not recommended outside these times. Details on climbing are listed in *The Siberian BAM Railway Guidebook* by Athol Yates.

– Exploring the Kodar Volcanoes. There are a number of dead volcanoes about 70km south of Lake Leprindo. The only way to get there is by helicopter or a by a minimum of three days boating and walking to get to the closest volcano and eight days to the largest one. The area is stunning, with water courses flowing down lava tubes. The craters are very distinct due to a lack of erosion. Aku Volcano is the largest with a 800m-diameter crater, while Chepe, which means "gap" in Yakutian, is 750m high and has a 150m-deep crater. Other volcanoes include the Syni and Gora-Zarod.

– Day trip motor boating or driving up the Kuanda River to its source which is a small hot-water spring. In winter, it's very beautiful with clouds of steam rising above the snow; in summer it is not interesting.

NOVAYA CHARA   Новая Чара   1,734km
Population: 15,000

The town might be boring but the region is fascinating.

Within the town the only place of interest is the BAM Museum, open 10.00–17.00, closed Mondays, tel: 6179.

For those biologically inclined, a five-minute walk to the east along the BAM will bring you to a clump of Chozeniya trees. These trees are restricted to Lake Baikal with this one exception. How they got here and survive is still a mystery. From here and from the train, you can see two 200m-high hillocks to the north which the locals laughingly call *babagrud,* meaning "breast", for obvious reasons.

Getting there and away

The fastest long-distance trains on this route are listed below.

Origin	Dist, km	Train no & name	Travel time	Depart	Arrive	Destination
Novaya Chara	630	76	13hr 56min	10.39	00.35	Tynda
Novaya Chara	670	75	13hr 56min	16.00	05.56	Severobaikalsk
Tynda	630	75	13hr 11min	02.20	15.31	Novaya Chara
Severobaikalsk	670	76	14hr 38min	19.21	09.59	Novaya Chara

Where to stay
The only place to stay in town is the basic Hotel Kodar, tel: 465, $15 twin share/person.

Point of interest
The town of Novaya Chara is an excellent illustration of the process of temporary and permanent town development. Hidden away on the outskirts of most BAM towns are temporary settlements. These settlements were hurriedly thrown together before work started on the town, as they were constructed for the initial builders of the railway and town. The houses are normally single-storey, wooden hostels, shared houses or transportable buildings.

Theoretically, the residents of the temporary settlements build the permanent town, and then move into the new apartments or depart for the next job. The temporary settlement is then demolished. However, due to the shortage of apartments, many people still live in the temporary settlements and few have been demolished.

In Novaya Chara, construction of the permanent settlement was only half completed before funds ran out, so the town consists of two parts: a run-down, shabby, temporary settlement which has the shops, and a half built permanent part which has the apartment buildings and nothing else. Consequently, the permanent town dwellers have to walk at least a kilometre to the temporary settlement for shopping. The situation is symbolised by the partly built and fully vandalised building beside the hotel which was to be the permanent town's main shopping centre before the money ran out.

What's in the region
Chara sand dunes
An enjoyable half-day trip is to the Sahara-like, 6km-long Chara sand dunes. How these dunes were created in an area where the ground all around them is frozen up to a depth of 600m is still a mystery. The dunes were an important site for indigenous people and a large number of stone arrows, axes and daily utensils from past millenniums have been found. These are on display in St Petersburg's Russian Museum of Ethnology and Novaya Chara's museum. The dunes are about 4km southwest of Staraya Chara and 6km northwest of Novaya Chara. You can see the dunes from the train as you depart Novaya Chara to the east.

Marble Canyon gulag camp (*Мраморное ущелье ГУЛаг*)
This camp is probably the best preserved Stalin era prisoner camp in eastern Siberia. While it is not easily accessible and preparation is essential, it is well worth the effort.

The camp operated from 1949 to 1951 and was the biggest of the ten camps in the Kodar Mountains that mined uranium for the Soviet atomic bomb project. You will notice that there are no prisoner barracks. This was because prisoners slept in canvas tents; wood was in short supply as it had to be carried up the mountains. The background radiation is now no higher than normal, nevertheless it would be foolhardy to enter the mine without a mask or camp on top of the slag heaps. The most difficult section of the canyon is at its very steep entrance. Part way down the canyon you pass the remnants of a geologists' camp and after another kilometre you reach the *gulag*.

There are two options for reaching the *gulag*. The first is hiking and it will take you eight days to do the loop starting in Staraya Chara, visiting the Marble Canyon Camp, walking through the mountain pass called Three Policemen which is between two glaciers and stopping at the smaller Verkhni Sakukan *gulag* camp before returning to Novaya Chara. The second option is to hire a helicopter for a day round trip, which will cost $500. The BAM Tourist Centre in Kuanda can organise the trips. More details on Marble Canyon Camp are listed in *The Siberian BAM Railway Guidebook* by Athol Yates.

Kemen   Кемен   1,755km

Near this station is the deepest permafrost (perpetually frozen ground) on the BAM. Here the soil is frozen down to a depth of 600m.

Leaving Kemen, you start your ascent of the Stanovoi Range. This section is double tracked and if you are lucky your train will pass another train, providing an excellent photo of a snaking train with fabulous mountains in the background.

Olongo   Олонго   1,851km

Between Olongo and Khani is the border of the Republic of Sakha, Amur Oblast and Chita Oblast. The intersection is along the Khani Valley through which the train travels. The intersection is marked by a 2m-long and 2m-high white monument of a giant rail on the right. The monument also commemorates the highest point along the BAM railway which is 1,310m above sea level.

Khani   Хани   1,879km

Khani is also called Luninskaya. It is the only BAM town in the Republic of Sakha (formerly Yakutia) and, unlike the rest of Sakha, you do not need a visa to stop here. The town, located 1.5km into Sakha, is situated in a very picturesque valley with snow-capped peaks surrounding it. The trains normally stop here for between five and 40 minutes while the locomotives are changed. In this time, you can quickly run around town. The police station and post office are both at the station.

Olekma   Олёкма   1,934km

Olekma is named after the Olekma River but, strangely, the station is about 35km from the river. From here, the BAM follows the course of the Olekma River and then the Nyukzha River. This route is very scenic and passes what in Russian are called "rock rivers". These are the remains of rock slides with all the dirt washed away. The rocks can be up to 2m across and the "rivers" up to 500m wide.

Yuktali   Юктали   2,028km

Nearby is the indigenous village of Ust-Nyukzha (Усть-Нюкжа). This ancient town was visited and destroyed by Yerofei Khabarov in the early 1600s and today features an excellent Ethnographical Museum and a reindeer-breeding farm. This is a well-known village and travellers often visit it on a day trip from Tynda.

TYNDA   Тында   2,364km
Population: 70,000   Telephone area code: 41 656

Tynda is the capital of the BAM. It sits at the junction of the four sections of the BAM: eastern BAM, western BAM, AYAM and Little BAM. It is the largest of the BAM towns and its main street, Krasnaya Presnya, is lined with 16-storey buildings which is very unusual for Siberia. The BAM headquarters are based in Tynda which means that, if you have a problem, you can take it to the top quickly. Whether they will do anything about it is another question. Not surprisingly, Tynda station is the cleanest on the BAM.

One day is normally enough to see everything Tynda has to offer.

Two of the biggest problems with Tynda are the vastly overpriced Yunost Hotel and the police requirement for local registration. However, both of these problems can be overcome and details are included below.

What to see
Tynda's limited highlights include the excellent BAM Museum, ul Profsyuznaya 3, tel: 32 483, open 10.00–18.00, closed Friday, and possibly the best monument on the BAM. This monument is a giant worker with a raised sledgehammer. By a strange twist of fate, the power pole in front of the statue has tilted towards the worker with the result that it looks as if he is driving in the pole. It is located on ul Amurskaya. Next door to the statue is the city's *banya*. This is a genuine *banya* with birch branches on sale, a pool, and wet and dry saunas.

Getting there and away
The fastest long-distance trains on this route are listed below.

Origin	Dist, km	Train no & name	Travel time	Depart	Arrive	Destination
Novaya Chara	630	76	13hr 56min	10.39	0.35	Tynda
Novy Urgal	951	203	25hr 55min	23.00	0.55	Tynda
Tynda	630	75	13hr 11min	02.20	15.31	Novaya Chara
Tynda	951	203	25hr 55min	09.00	10.55	Novy Urgal

Visas
This is the only town on the BAM that still requires you to be registered by the police before you can get a room at a hotel. In the Soviet era, it was a requirement that all visitors register within 24 hours of arriving in a hotel anywhere in the country. The registration requirement in Tynda is a legacy of these days and eventually it will disappear. Tynda's registration office is run by OViR and is located in the ground floor of the first of the high-rise buildings on ul Krasnaya Presnya. You should check upon arrival when it is open as it works only part days. It can take up to an hour to register and costs about $1.50. Sometimes, you will be asked at the station for your registered visa in order to get a ticket.

Where to stay
The best place to stay is the excellent Orbita Railway Hotel. This building is a small mansion surrounded by gardens about 15 minutes' walk from the city's bus station, tel: 33-64, $16 twin share/person. To get to the hotel from the railway station, go along the road towards the centre of town and, rather than turning up Krasnaya Presnya at the city's bus station, keep going straight ahead for another 500m. Turn left up ul Nadezhdyand and take the left fork at its end. You then pass into the hotel's grounds which are surrounded by a large hedge.

Another choice is the vastly overpriced and poor standard Hotel Yunost, ul Krasnaya Presnya, tel: 32 708, $110 twin share/room.

Another option in town is the basic Hotel Nadezhda which is just behind the Hotel Yunost. Hotel Nadezhda, ul Festivalnaya 1, tel: 29 655 work, $20 twin share/person. At the railway station is the Hotel Cevernaya, but it never seems to have any rooms. The basic Chastnaya Hotel, ul Rushchskaya 4, tel: 24 15, is in the old temporary settlement to the east. It is easy to find as it is beside the town's bread factory.

Getting around
The station is about 2km out of town by a circuitous road route. However, you can easily walk from the station to the centre of the town via a direct line over a footbridge. Otherwise bus No 5 runs regularly from the station down the main street of town.

Getting assistance
Travel agents   GeyaBAM, ul Profsyuznaya 4-42, tel: 27 683, fax: 32 335, telex 154128 KREDI SU. They also have a Moscow affiliate which is easier to fax to and they will pass the fax on. The Moscow company's fax is: (095) 230 2919; BAMtourist: BAMtourist, tel: 220 27, fax: 209 47; Tourism Department, BAM, ul Krasnaya Presnya 47, tel: 21 716, fax: 233 29, telex 154215 DWC SU.
Air   Aeroflot is on the main street, but it is hard to find as it is around the side of the building.
Rail   There is a railway ticket office in the main street of Tynda which saves you walking to the station.

TYNDA BRANCHLINES
The Little BAM and the AYAM railways

The Little BAM
This 180km stretch, connecting the Trans-Siberian railway to the main BAM line, was the first section of the BAM to be built. It offers a striking contrast to the busy Trans-Siberian. The unelectrified Little BAM winds through the taiga with just one track. This compares to the two- or three-track electrified Trans-Siberian with its broad curves cut through farming land. Six long-distance trains a day crawl along the Little BAM at 46km/h; 50 trains scream along the Trans-Siberian at 100km/h.

The railway roughly parallels the Amur–Yakutsk Highway which runs from the nearby Trans-Siberian railway station of Bolshoi Never, through Tynda to Yakutsk. Although buses run between this highway from the Trans-Siberian to Tynda, trains are cheaper and more regular.

There are six long-distance trains a day which travel on the Little BAM. They travel between Moscow–Tynda, Chita–Tynda, Kislovodsk–Tynda, Kharkov–Tynda, Blagoveshchensk–Tynda and Khabarovsk–Neryungri.

Although Russian maps show that the Little BAM is connected to the Trans-Siberian at Bamovskaya, the truth is that the Little BAM branches at Shtrum station with one branch connecting the Trans-Siberian at Bamovskaya and another branch connecting the Trans-Siberian at Goreli. Trains from the west (Moscow, Irkutsk) to Tynda use the Bamovskaya branch with those from the east (Khabarovsk) using the Goreli branch.

If you are on a through train to Tynda from either the west or east, there is not a problem. However, if you have to change trains, it can be difficult. Few Trans-Siberian trains stop at Bamovskaya or Goreli (unless they are going on the Little

BAM); the closest major stations where all Trans-Siberian trains stop are Skovorodino on the eastern side of the Little BAM or Erofei Pavlovish on the western side. You should get off at one of these stations and change trains for one of the Little BAM trains.

AYAM railway: Tynda–Berkakit–Aldan–Yakutsk

The AYAM railway is the 1,046km railway from Tynda to Yakutsk, the capital of the Republic of Sakha, formerly known as Yakutia. It is divided into three sections with the last one still to be completed.

- the first 210km section from Bestuzhevo to Berkakit, with a short branch line to Neryungri coal mine, was completed in 1978
- the second 380km section from Berkakit to Aldan and Tommot was opened to freight traffic in January 1994 but in January 1996 was still not open to passenger trains
- the third 456km section from Tommot to Yakutsk; work has only recently started on this section and it is unlikely that it will be finished before the turn of the century. Currently, buses run between Aldan and Yakutsk.

The building of the AYAM is a monumental construction project because of the natural barriers of permafrost, rivers and mountains. When it is completed, the railway will require some 200 bridges, 21 of which will be more than 1km long, 85 million m³ of moved earth and landfill, 540 structures other than bridges, seven major stations, six new settlements and 2,100 workers to staff the new line.

To travel on this railway from Tynda, you need the names of the towns you wish to visit on your Russian visa or you will not be able to buy a ticket.

The visa requirement was introduced in 1994 as a way of reducing visitors to the region, in turn reducing the consumption of limited food and goods. In addition, the visa system allows the government to ensure that they are informed of all commercial activity by controlling the visits of foreign businessmen.

The highlights of this route are: the giant coal mine at Neryungri; the museums, gold mines and indigenous village in and around Aldan; and Yakutsk with its numerous attractions.

Information on the AYAM route is contained in *The Siberian BAM Railway Guide* by Athol Yates.

TYNDA–KOMSOMOLSK
via Novy Urgal

Tynda   Тында   2,364km
See *page 318.*

Bestuzheva   Бестужева   2,391km
Just after you depart Bestuzheva, the line divides into the AYAM for Neryungri/Berkakit, Aldan and Yakutsk in the north and the BAM eastern segment for Komsomolsk.

Ulak   Улак   2,791km
This station is on the west bank of the Zeya Reservoir. After leaving the station, the train crosses the Zeya Bridge which is the second longest bridge on the BAM. It is 1,100m long, stands 50m above the water and took nine years to

build. Because of its significance to the BAM, it is still closely guarded by a platoon of 30 soldiers. To walk across it or even to take photos of it is not possible without a pass from the guard's commanding officer.

Apetenolk Апетенолк 2,723km

From Verknezeisk you pass through the flat Verkhnezeskaya Plain containing numerous creeks and rivers flowing into the Zeya Reservoir. This unmarked siding is the most popular stop for fishermen. The stop is about 300m from the water's edge and fishermen then walk around the lake to their favourite spot.

Along this section of the line you will notice 2m-high tubes sticking out of the ground. These devices keep the ground frozen all year round to prevent it subsiding. The tubes are filled with kerosene and penetrate several metres into the earth. As the kerosene absorbs heat from the ground, it vaporises and rises to the unburied part of the tube. The tube gives off heat which condenses the kerosene and the fluid then drips to the bottom of the tube where the process is repeated. While these tubes are effective, they are also very pollutant as, after a few years, they start leaking kerosene into the ground.

NOVY URGAL Новый Ургал 3,315km
Population: 14,000

Novy Urgal was founded in December 1974 when the first Ukrainian BAM builders arrived and is the headquarters of the eastern third of the BAM. Novy Urgal was sponsored by Ukraine and many of its streets, with names such as Donbas, Kharkov, Carpathia, Dniepr and Kiev, honour the builders. An attempt has been made to incorporate traditional Ukrainian decoration and the result is a chequered line along the top of the multi-storey concrete buildings.

Getting there and away

By air The regional airport is located at Chegdomyn and flights arrive from Tynda and Khabarovsk.

By road The road to Komsomolsk along the BAM is only drivable in winter, when the journey takes 16 hours.

By train The fastest long-distance trains on this route are listed below.

Origin	Dist, km	Train no & name	Travel time	Depart	Arrive	Destination
Komsomolsk	516	203	13hr 55min	08.25	22.20	Novy Urgal
Novy Urgal	516	203	13hr 55min	11.50	01.45	Komsomolsk
Novy Urgal	951	203	25hr 55min	23.00	00.55	Tynda
Tynda	951	203	25hr 55min	09.00	10.55	Novy Urgal

Where to stay

The only hotel in town is the NGCh Railway Hotel, ul Kievskaya 3, tel: 64 06.

What to see

The town has a BAM Museum, ul Kievskaya 7, 4th floor, tel: 63 74.

The market is on the eastern side of the town in a pavilion which looks like a Chinese temple. It is actually North Korean and was given to the town as a sign of gratitude for allowing North Koreans to work in the area.

What's in the region

Nearby is the coal town of Chegdomyn which is worth visiting. The town is one of the oldest on the BAM as it was connected to the Trans-Siberian in the late

1940s. The line and town were built by Stalin *gulag* prisoners and Japanese prisoners of war.

Strange as it might seem, Chegdomyn offers a rare and fascinating insight into one of the world's most secretive countries, North Korea. Officially known as the Democratic Peoples' Republic of Korea (DPRK), North Korea is the world's last communist cult-of-personality state. The country is run by the "Dear Leader" Kim Jong Il who took over from his father, the "Great Leader" and president, Kim Il Sung, when he died in 1994.

During the Soviet era, North Korea and the USSR were fraternal brothers, bonded together against the capitalist threat from the "puppet regime" of South Korea and the imperialist USA. As one reward for being communism's forward bastion, North Korea was allowed to run logging camps in eastern Siberia. Although figures are unreliable, it is estimated that at one time there were about 20,000 North Koreans in Russia but by 1995 there were only about 10,000 due to the declining profitability of timber.

Chegdomyn is the centre of North Korean logging camps as the country has a consulate here. Although the gate consists only of a boom bar, the guards at the front will quickly stop you from entering if you try. If you speak to one of the guards, his partner will sprint off and return with a translator. While the translator understands Russian, he will invariably only say "Nyet".

Taking photos of a North Korean or of the consulate is highly risky. Your Russian guide will gleefully tell you the story of a German photographer who tried this and had his camera destroyed as a result. If you are determined to take a photo, do it from your car as you are leaving town.

The best hotel in town is the Buriya Hotel, with rooms starting at $16. ul Pionerskaya 1 tel: 91 961. There is another hotel is at ul Torgovaya 54.

Urgal-1   Ургал-1   3,330km

Urgal-1 is a rustic wooden station built in the late 1940s and is one of the oldest and most attractive. This is the junction of the BAM with the branch line to Chegdomyn.

Kondon   Кондон

The Nanai village of Kondon, the location of one of Siberia's most important archaeological finds, is 5km from this stop. At this place about 5,000 to 6,000 years ago was a village and, among the usual finds of wooden objects, animal bone combs and shards of pottery, was a statuette which for the first time revealed the physical shape of the original inhabitants. Called the Nanai "Venus", it confirmed the link between the past and present indigenous people. The statue was of a woman with a soft oval face, broad cheekbones, a slender chin and small pouting lips. The woman's nose is long and thin like that of a North American Indian; her eyes are extremely long and narrow, like arched slits; while her forehead is low and the upper part of her head is slanted back. Even today in Kondon you can see women with this look.

Silinka   Силинка   3,818km

Past this station, as you head towards Komsomolsk, you will pass an enormous antenna complex spread over several square kilometres. This is one of Russia's over-the-horizon (OTH) radars. This OTH radar is designed to watch the movement of aircraft, ships and strategic missiles between the Chinese coast and

Guan Island. This is one of the three radar complexes in the Far East Area with the other two at Nakhodka and Nikolaevsk-na-Amure. These radars are essential to early warning of incoming nuclear missiles and despite the conclusion of the Cold War, they are still highly secret.

KOMSOMOLSK Комсомольск 3,837km
Population: 320,000   Telephone area code: 42141

Komsomolsk embodied not only the ideals of the Communist Revolution but also the realities of Soviet socialism.

It was built in the unpopulated Russian far east by fervent young communists as part of the 1930s nation-wide industrialisation campaign designed to propel the Soviet Union into the modern world. It was from these workers, who were members of the Young Communist League, or "Komsomol", that the city got its name. The full name, Komsomolsk-na-Amure, means "Komsomolsk on the Amur River" which distinguishes the city from the other Komsomolsks dotted throughout Russia.

Komsomolsk is the Russian far east's fourth largest city and has a lot to offer travellers. As well as being an attractive town on the beautiful Amur River, it is the gateway to the rarely visited northern areas of the Russian far east including Nikolaevsk via the Amur River, Sovetskaya Gavin and, of course, the BAM.

Getting there and away
By air   The airport is 27km out of town and 12 buses a day make the 45-minute trip.

By boat   The Amur River offers an interesting way of arriving and departing. The river is usually navigable from June 20 to August 31 and there are regular hydrofoils to Khabarovsk and Nikolaevsk. There are also cruise ships that travel from China, through Blagoveshchensk, Khabarovsk, Komsomolsk to Nikolaevsk.

By train   The fastest long-distance trains on this route are listed below.

Origin	Dist, km	Train no & name	Travel time	Depart	Arrive	Destination
Novy Urgal	516	203	13hr 55min	11.50	01.45	Komsomolsk
Khabarovsk	374	203	8hr 50min	15.05	23.55	Komsomolsk
Komsomolsk	374	67	8hr 40min	15.00	23.40	Khabarovsk
Komsomolsk	516	203	13hr 55min	08.25	22.20	Novy Urgal

Where to stay
There are four hotels to choose from. The best are the standard Voskhod Hotel, pr Pervostroitelei 31, tel: 303 36, $35 twin share/person (buses 9, 20, 26 and 27 and trams 1, 2, 4 and 5 all go past it) and the standard Hotel Business Centre, ul Khabarovskaya 47, tel: 447 05, $70 twin room. The most centrally located hotel is the basic Amur Hotel, pr Mira 15, tel: 430 74, $15 twin room (trams 1, 2, 4 and 5 go past it). The standard Brigantina Hotel at the river station is another good choice, ul Naberzhnaya 1, tel: 447 45, $30 twin room (trams 1, 2 and 4 go to it).

Getting around
Komsomolsk is divided into two parts separated by the Silinka River. The northern part contains most of the industry while the southern part contains the city centre and residential areas. The main street is prospekt Mira which used to be prospekt Stalin until the late 1950s when this and 50 other street names were

changed. Tram no 2 from the station goes past all four hotels before reaching the river station on pr Mira.

What to see

Highlights include the Regional Museum, pr Mira 8, tel: 422-60, open 10.00–17.00, closed Monday; Art Museum, pr Mira 16, tel: 422-60; commercial art shop, pr Pervostroitelei 20, the Yuri Gagarin military aircraft factory, ul Kalinina 7, tel: 323-67, and the open-air Military Vehicle Museum located in the park opposite the Regional Museum.

There are 16 memorials in and around Komsomolsk marking cemeteries or camps of Japanese prisoners of war, who numbered 16,000 in 1945. The central memorial is a large stone beside the Amur Hotel which was unveiled on October 5 1991. This site was chosen because the prisoners of war built the hotel.

Another monument is dedicated to the tens of thousands who suffered and died during Stalin's repression. The location of the stone, beside the City Court, is a poignant reminder of the failure of the Soviet justice system.

The river station is also worth a visit as it was built to look like a steamship. Ferries and hydrofoils travel up and down the Amur from here. At one end is the ticket office with a small café. On one side of the station is a memorial stone dedicated to the first builders who arrived on May 10 1932. On the other side is a memorial commemorating the 50th anniversary of the founding of Komsomolsk. Unveiled in 1982, the socialist realist monument of a young communist striding forward is symbolically located at the end of the Prospect of the First Builders, pr Pervostroitelei, which runs the 3km from the railway station to the Amur River.

Near the river station is one of the best sculptures on the BAM. This memorial commemorates World War II and consists of seven giant granite heads facing an eternal flame.

Getting assistance

Travel agents   The best general travel company in Komsomolsk is Marika. The company is headed by Marina Aleksandrovna Kuzminovna who is one of the Russian far east's experts on *gulags*, Japanese prisoners of war and the history of the BAM. She has written three books on these subjects. Marika, ul Shikhanova 10, tel: 347 63, fax: 402 69 (write on the fax: for Marina Aleksandrovna Kuzminovna, tel: 347 63).

Air   Aeroflot, pr Pervostroitelei 18, tel: 303 93.

KOMSOMOLSK–KHABAROVSK

This is probably the least interesting railway section in the far east. There are only five reasonable sized towns en route with the rest of the stops being either forestry camps or railway sidings. The best advice for travelling on this route is to catch one of the overnight trains and sleep through the region.

The fastest long-distance trains on this route are listed below.

Origin	Dist, km	Train no & name	Travel time	Depart	Arrive	Destination
Khabarovsk	374	203	8hr 50min	15.05	23.55	Komsomolsk
Komsomolsk	374	67	8hr 40min	15.00	23.40	Khabarovsk

326

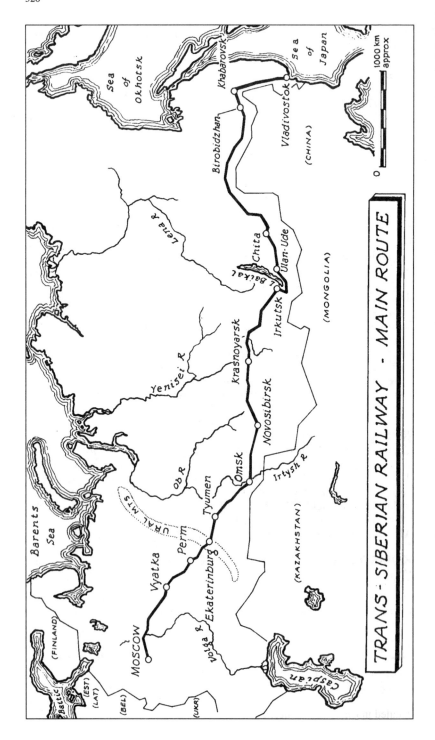

TRANS - SIBERIAN RAILWAY - MAIN ROUTE

Chapter Sixteen

The Trans-Siberian Railway

The Trans-Siberian is the ultimate rail journey which has attracted travellers for over a century. Starting in Moscow, the Trans-Siberian travels nearly 10,000km across seven time zones in seven days to the Russian far east port of Vladivostok.

If you would like to go even further by rail, you can continue on from Vladivostok to Pyongyang, the capital of North Korea. In addition, branch lines three-quarters of the way along the Trans-Siberian allow you to travel through Mongolia on the Trans-Mongolian railway or through Manchuria on the Trans-Manchurian railway.

Whichever route you take, it will be the trip of your lifetime.

Route highlights

There is so much to see on the Trans-Siberian route as it travels through Golden Ring historic cities, across the Ural Mountains separating Europe from Asia, through thick taiga, then skirts the shores of beautiful Lake Baikal, and on through countryside reminiscent of Europe before reaching the semi-tropical Russian far east.

There are 14 major cities on the Trans-Siberian, each spaced approximately an overnight trip apart. While every one has something unique to offer, the most popular stops in descending order, excluding the beginning and end, are Irkutsk, Khabarovsk, Novosibirsk, Ekaterinburg, Ulan-Ude, Krasnoyarsk, Omsk, Chita, Perm, Tyumen and Vyatka.

Travel suggestions

Over the last few years, several Russian cities, such as Ekaterinburg, Vladivostok and Chita, have been opened up to foreigners on the Trans-Siberian. In addition, a number of other railways connected to the Trans-Siberian have also been recently opened, such as the Vladivostok–Pyongyang (North Korea) and Vladivostok–Harbin (China) railways. As these cities and railways are rarely covered in older guidebooks and package-tour operators do not often offer them, before you embark on your Trans-Siberian adventure have a close look through this chapter; you might be surprised at some of the new options.

This chapter covers the Trans-Siberian railway only from Moscow to Vladivostok. The following railways connect to the Trans-Siberian and are detailed in *Chapter Seventeen*:

- the Trans-Mongolian railway: Ulan-Ude to Beijing via Mongolia
- the Trans-Manchurian railway: Chita to Beijing via Manchuria
- the East Chinese–Russian Far East railway: the Russian far east to Harbin
- the North Korean–Russian Far East railway
- the Vladivostok–Nakhodka railway
- the Circumbaikal railway
- the Borzya–Choibalsan Mongolian railway

Trains

While the Trans-Mongolian and Trans-Manchurian trains are detailed in *Chapter Seventeen*, there are some comparisons with the Trans-Siberian below.

Origin	Dist, km	Entry point	Train no & name	Carr'ge class	No in coupé	Travel time	Day of departure	Destination
Moscow (Yaroslav)	9,297	n/a	2 Trans-Siberian	1, 2	2, 4	156hr	daily	Vladivostok
Vladivostok	9,297	n/a	1 Trans-Siberian	1, 2	2, 4	156hr	daily	Moscow (Yaroslav)
Moscow (Yaroslav)	9,001	Zabaikalsk	20 Trans-Manchurian	2	4	145hr		Beijing
Beijing	9,001	Zabaikalsk	19 Trans-Manchurian	2	4	145hr		Moscow (Yaroslav)
Moscow (Yaroslav)	7,860	Naushki	2 Trans-Mongolian	2	4	140hr	Fri, Sat	Beijing
Beijing	7,860	Naushki	3 Trans-Mongolian	2	4	140hr	Thur, Fri	Moscow (Yaroslav)

Route description

Moscow   Москва   0km

Trans-Siberian trains depart from Yaroslav station, pl Komsomolskaya 5, tel: 921 0817, 266 0301, 266 0595. The metro station is Komsomolskaya.

The first 357km of the route from Moscow to **Yaroslavl**, through **Sergiev-Posad**, **Aleksandrov** and **Rostov-Yaroslavski**, is covered in *Chapter Thirteen*. The *Passing through* section under each of these cities discusses sights you will see from the train's window.

Danilov   Данилов   357km

See Chapter Twelve, page 217.

Lyubim   Любим   394km

Lyubim is an ancient town, founded in 1546 as a frontier post and river port, and while in 1861 it boasted five tanneries and brick factories, today it has just a timber mill and abattoir.

Bui   Буй   450km

This industrial town specialises in cheese, flax and mineral fertilisers, but there is nothing of much interest except the museum of local studies. Bui sits on the junction of the Kostroma River which is connected to the Volga and the Holya Rivers.

After leaving the town, the train follows the southern banks of the Veksi and Holya Rivers until you see the Galich Sea as you approach the town of Galich. The very beautiful lake is ringed with resorts for Moscow's rich, famous and well-connected.

Galich Галич 501km

The town sits on the banks of the shallow Galich Sea which is mined for its millions of tons of rotting silt. This gunk, technically known as *sapropel*, is dried and used as fuel or made into fertiliser.

The town itself is very ancient and was populated by the Merya tribe of Finno-Ugric peoples before the Russians arrived. The first mention of the town was in 1238 when the Galich fortress was destroyed by the Tatar-Mongol leader, Khan Baty. The fortress was rebuilt and in 1427 withstood a four-week siege by the Tatar-Mongols. It was less fortunate during the Polish invasion in the early 1600s, but the walls of the fortress can still be seen ringing the central part of the town, which contains a number of interesting buildings, churches and a museum of local studies.

The station is a 15-minute walk to the south from the centre of town. Due to the centralised planning of the communist system, many products were made only in a few locations. Galich's speciality is car door handles and, if the factory is working, here is the place to stock up on them.

After departing from the station, on the right (southern side) you pass the Paisiev Monastery. It was founded in the 14th century and includes the Assumption (Uspenski) Cathedral and the trapezoid Trinity (Troitskaya) Church. The monumental Assumption Cathedral was built in the 16th century with five cupolas, of which only one remains today.

Manturovo Мантурово 653km

After leaving this industrial and forestry town, the train crosses over the Unzha River. You may notice the remains of large pits on the banks which is all that can be seen of the shale oil and phosphate mining operations of a few decades ago.

Sightly more than 97km to the west (towards Vladivostok) is the border between the Kirov and Kostromski Oblasts, which also marks a time boundary. Within the Kirov Oblast, local time is one hour ahead of Moscow.

Sharya Шарья 723km

Sharya town is the biggest timber centre in the region. It has a few interesting buildings, a museum of local studies and a steam engine storage depot.

Kotelnich Котельнич 870km

This station sits at the junction of the Trans-Siberian and the Vyatka–Nizhni Novgorod–Moscow lines. If you are changing from one line to the other, don't get off here. Instead go 87km to the east to the major city of Vyatka where tickets are much easier to obtain.

For details of this ancient trading city see *Chapter Eighteen, page 434.*

After leaving the station, the train crosses over the Vyatka River.

Maradykovski Марадыковский 890km

Avoid stopping off here as the nearby airforce base is the storage site of 7,000 out of Russia's 40,000 tons of chemical weapons agents.

Vyatka Вятка 957km

Vyatka is a major rail junction; change trains here if you want to change between the Trans-Siberian and the Vyatka–Nizhni Novgorod–Moscow line.

The city was called Kirov between 1934 and 1991 and still appears as such on some railway timetables.

For information on this city, see *Chapter Eighteen, page 434.*

After leaving Vyatka, you see the highway that runs to Kazan on the left and beside it, the Vyatka River.

Pozdino   Поздино   970km

The town around the station is called Novovyatsk (Нововятск) and boasts one of Russia's largest ski factories. During Soviet times, the factory produced 20% of the nation's skis.

Bum-Kombinat   Бум-комбинат   995km

This unfortunately named town gets its name from its principle employer, the paper complex which in Russian is *bumazhni-kombinat.*

Zuevka   Зуевка   1,062km

Zuevka was founded in 1895 with the construction of the railway and for its first few years it was a very lonely assignment as the stop consisted of just a water tower and seven homes. The town exploded in size during World War II when hundreds of Leningraders were settled here during the 900-day German siege of their city.

Today, the town is probably the nation's only manufacturer of amusement-park rides, theatre equipment, swings and see-saws.

Kosa   Коса   1,072km

The town around the station is called Kosino (Косино) and, in 1785, the region's first paper mill was built here.

Falenki   Фаленки   1,094km

Nearby is one of Russia's first agricultural research stations, opened in 1895. These stations have been vital to developing and introducing specially bred plants and animals which have boosted Russian output considerably.

Yar   Яр   1,128km

Yar is the first town in the Udmurtia Republic, and has a number of Udmurt speakers. The town sits on a steep riverbank, which is the meaning of the Turkic-derived Russian word *yar.* There has been a small metallurgical plant here for over 230 years but nothing else of note.

Glazov   Глазов   1,165km

This small city started out in the 18th century as an Udmurt indigenous peoples' village but soon became infamous as one of the most desolate and impoverished places of internal exile of the time. All this was to change with the arrival of the railway a few years later. By the start of the 20th century, there were 102 enterprises and during the next few years the town grew into the region's largest trading centre for flax, oats and oakum; oakum is a fibre used for caulking the seams of ships.

A few buildings from the old town remain, dotted among the nine- and 14-storey buildings of the 1970s. These include several two- and three-storey brick buildings built at the turn of the century in a modern style which reflected the education of many of the exiles, and a few wooden Udmurt log huts known as *korkas*. *Korkas* are positioned along an open courtyard or in a U-shape around the courtyard. This had wooden or stone paving and a massive gate, which, like the hut, was often decorated with carved geometrical and plant designs. Glazov also has a history museum.

Cheptsa   Чепца   1,226km
About 44km east of Cheptsa you leave the Udmurtiya Republic and cross into Perm Oblast. This border also marks a time boundary. Within the Perm Oblast, local time is two hours ahead of Moscow.

Vereshchagino   Верещагино   1,317km
Vereshchagino was founded at the end of the 19th century as a railway depot and today its main industry is still railways. There is a preserved FD21 steam locomotive on a plinth about 1km to the west (Moscow side) of the station near the main rail depot. The town has had three names, firstly Ocherskaya, then Voznesenskaya and in 1915, the current name, after Russia's greatest battlefield painter, V V Vereshchagin. He stopped here on his way to the Russo-Japanese war front in 1905 which was his final commission (see also *Maloyaraslavets* in *Chapter Ten, page 156*).

Mendeleevo   Менделеево   1,344km
The town is named after the famous Russian chemist, Dmitri Mendeleev (1834–1907), who discovered the periodic table. He often visited this town during his inspections of the region's metallurgical plants. There is a Mendeleev Museum in nearby Tobolsk which can be reached by railway via Tyumen city.

Chaikovskaya   Чайковская   1,390km
This station is named after the composer Peter Tchaikovsky (1840-1893) who was born about 180km southeast of here at Votkinsk. He was the son of a mining engineer and committed suicide to prevent a scandal (see also *Klin* in *Chapter Eleven, page 180*).

While the station is known as Chaikovskaya, the town is called Maiski. The station is often confused with the town of Chaikovski which is 200km to the south and whose station is called Saigatka.

From here to Perm, the railway winds a great deal and is a good place to take photos of a snaking train.

Overyata   Оверята   1,413km
There is an 11km branch line from here to the dirty industrial town of Krasnokamsk (Краснокамск) to the south. It was founded in the 1930s and has a large cellulose mill and Russia's only wire-netting factory. Near the town is the popular Ust-Kachka health resort with its medicinal mud baths.

PERM 2   Пермь 2   1,437km
Population: 1,098,000   Telephone area code: 3422
Perm's history pre-dates the 1723 Russian colonisation of the region. For centuries, the area had been settled by a Finno-Urgric indigenous people and this is reflected in the name of Perm which is derived from their words *pera ma* meaning "far land". The earliest settlements date from the Bronze Age. About

3,000 artefacts from the Bronze Age Turbinski archaeological site on the outskirts of the city can be found in Perm's history museum.

The official founding date for the city is 1723 which was when construction started on a copper foundry. In 1781, the Tsarina Catherine II saw the vast potential of the mineral-rich area and ordered the construction of the town of Perm by amalgamating several factory settlements. The location of Perm on two major trading rivers ensured that it grew as both an industrial and a trading city. Salt caravans arrived along the Kama River while wheat, honey and metal products from the Urals travelled along the Chusovi River. Other boosts to the city were the arrival of the railway in 1878, the discovery of oil in the region, and the evacuation of factories to here from European Russia during World War II. The city's most familiar product is the Kama bicycle which is widely used in rural areas.

Despite the industry, Perm has a long history of culture and scholarship. This can mostly be attributed to the revolutionaries, intellectuals and political prisoners who were exiled here in the 19th century. Perm had the first university in the Urals and its most famous student was Alexander Popov (1859–1905)who, according to Russian historians, invented the wireless. Popov received a gold medal for his invention at the Paris World Fair in 1900. He was born at Krasnoturinsk where there is a museum devoted to his life. Another famous graduate of Perm was the ballerina Nadezhda Pavlova, who completed her training at the renowned Perm Ballet School.

From 1940 to 1957, Perm was called Molotov after the disgraced Soviet Foreign Minister who signed the 1939 Ribbentrop-Molotov Pact, dividing up Poland with the Nazis.

Passing through

Just before the train reaches Perm, it crosses over the Kama River. From the bridge, which was built in 1899, you can see Perm stretching into the distance on the left. During winter the only section of the Kama River that remains unfrozen is the section in front of Perm; this is because of the warming of the water caused by the Kama hydro-electric station which is just upstream.

Unfortunately, the centre of Old Perm is out of sight as it is 5km away from Perm 2 station at which the Trans-Siberian train stops. The approaches and area around Perm 2 are dominated by industrial enterprises, the biggest being the 23rd Congress of the CPSU Petroleum Refinery Complex which was the largest in the Soviet Union when it was built in the 1960s.

The Moscow–Vladivostok No 1/2 train stops at Perm 2 for about 30 minutes which is enough time to have a look at the square and the preserved Ov-14 steam engine built in 1900 in front of the station.

Shortly after leaving the station, the train crosses a small bridge over a busy street. This was the Siberian Tract which passed through Perm from 1863.

Getting there and away

The major Trans-Siberian trains on this segment are:

Origin	Dist, km	Train no & name	Travel time	Depart	Arrive	Destination
Vyatka	480	2	7hr 56min	05.13	12.09	Perm
Perm	480	1	8hr 6min	08.08	15.14	Vyatka
Ekaterinburg	381	1	6hr	01.43	07.43	Perm
Perm	381	2	6hr 45min	12.44	19.29	Ekaterinburg

Where to stay

Accommodation options include the standard Ural Hotel, ul Lenina 58, tel: 344 417, $20 twin share/person; basic Hotel Turist, ul Ordzhonikidze 43, tel: 342 494; basic Prikamiye Hotel, ul Komsomolskaya 27, tel: 348 662; and basic Hotel Tsentralaya, ul Karla Marksa, tel: 326 010.

Getting around

The town extends for 80km along the Kama River with the centre being around Perm 1 station on the left (eastern) bank. At the southern end of Perm, also on the left bank, is Perm 2 which is the station at which the Trans-Siberian stops. There are suburban trains that run the 5km between Perm 2 and Perm 1. The airport is located between Perm 2 and Perm 1 on the left in the suburb of Balatovo.

What to see

The most interesting part of town is the old part around Perm 1 station. This area's most interesting buildings include the baroque Cathedral of Peter and Paul (1757–65) with a 19th-century belfry and the empire-style Cathedral of the Saviour of the Transfiguration (Spaso-Preobrazhenski) Monastery (1798–1832). There are also numerous examples of eclectic and art nouveau styles, of which the old building of Perm 2 station is one. The river station is near Perm 1.

The main museums are the Perm Art Gallery, pr Komsomolski 2, open 11.00–18.00, closed Monday, with its large collection of wooden sculptures including a Jesus with Mongolian features, the Industry Museum, and the Museum of Local Studies, ul Komsomolski 6, open 10.00–18.00, closed Friday. This last contains a communist history wing called the Museum of the Underground Press of the Perm Committee of the RSDLP of 1906, with a diorama entitled The Decembrist Armed Revolt of 1905 in Perm's Motovilikha Factory. The city also boasts an aquarium and a planetarium.

There are regular performances at Perm's opera, drama, puppet and youth theatres.

Russian money is printed here at the Perm printing factory which has a museum, shosse Kosmonavtov 115, tel: 276 054, fax: 276 074, but you will need to organise a visit beforehand.

Getting assistance

Travel agents   Intourist office, ul Popova 9, tel: 333 843, 335 585.
Air   Aeroflot, ul Krisanova 19, tel: 334 668.

After leaving Perm, the landscape changes abruptly and forests give way to meadows and fields.

Kungur   Кунгур   1,538km

Kungur contains a fabulous and virtually unknown tourist attraction in the Kungur Ice Caves. The caves are some of the biggest in the Ural region and have a total length of 5.6km including 58 grottoes, 60 lakes, and hundreds of stalactites and stalagmites. About 1.3km of the caves are open to the public and fitted with electric lights. During the Soviet era, about 25,000 tourists visited the caves annually. The caves are on the outskirts of the town, on the right bank of the Sylva River. On the opposite bank are excavations of a settlement dating from the 8th and 9th centuries and many of the artefacts found can be seen in the Perm Museum of Local Studies. The caves are open 10.00–16.00. There are regular buses from the Kungur railway station to the caves and the trip takes 35 minutes.

The town is littered with historic buildings including 14 churches, the most interesting being the five-dome, 35m-high, two-storey Preobrazhenski Church which has an eight-sided bell town. Other interesting buildings include the Arcade (Gostiny Dvor) built from 1865 to 1876, and the Museum of Local Studies, ul Gogolya 36, open 11.00–17.00, which is in the two-storey stone house of the former provincial governor.

In front of the station is a monument to E I Pugachev (1742–75) who was the the leader of the Peasant Wars, commanded the Kungur fortress during the 1774 siege, and called himself Emperor Peter III. Although he survived this battle, he was eventually captured and executed in Moscow for his efforts to encourage the Cossacks to settle in the east and renounce the Russian overlords.

There is only one hotel in town, the basic Hotel Iren, ul Lenina 30, tel: 321 57. It has a restaurant. A better choice is the basic Hotel Stalagmit which is a short walk from the Kungar Caves, tel: 336 25, 342 81, $20 double room.

From the train, you can see a number of the old single- and two-storey buildings of the old town.

Soon after leaving Kungur, you see the steep banks of the Sylva River which marks the start of the Kungur Forest Steppe. This area is characterised by rolling hills which reach 180–230m, a landscape pitted with troughs and sinkholes, and copses of birch, linden, oak and pine interspersed with meadow-steppe and farmlands.

THE DISAPPOINTING URALS

For a mountain chain delineating the border between Europe and Asia, the Ural Mountains are a disappointment. Their statistics sound impressive: they are 2,000km long, with a maximum elevation of 1,895m and a maximum width of 150km. However, the section that the Trans-Siberian passes over is less exciting. Here the Ural Mountains have a maximum elevation of less than 900m and a width of about 50km.

Despite the unimpressive exterior, the Ural Mountains are a treasure trove of minerals. They contain 48 of Russia's 55 most important minerals, and over 1,000 different minerals in 12,000 known deposits. The Urals are especially famous for their precious and semiprecious stones including emeralds, amethyst, jasper, rhodonite and malachite. The best jewellers' diamonds in Russia come from the Urals as did the world famous 35kg gold nugget called the Large Triangle which was found in the 1940s.

By observing the flora as you go over the Urals, you can tell your elevation. On the western slopes, at 500–600m above sea level, the dominant flora changes from broadleaf forests of oak, Norway maple and elm to dark, coniferous forests of Siberian spruce and fir. On reaching the eastern side of the Urals, the Siberian spruce and fir is replaced by pine forests until at about 500–600m above sea level, the flora reverts back to broadleaf forests. Unfortunately, you will not see the flora boundary between the forests and mountain steppe of bald peaks and rock streams, as it occurs at 1,200–1,250m above sea level.

Kuzino   Кузино   1,730km

After about 10km, the train reaches one of the Urals' most beautiful rivers, the Chusavya. The line follows the course of the river for some 30km.

Pervouralsk   Первоуральск   1,774km

The city's name translates as "the First Ural" as it was here in 1727 that the first factory in the Urals was opened. Following the success of this cast-iron works, dozens of other factories sprang up here and today the city is home to numerous heavy-engineering complexes including one of Russia's largest pipeline factories. From the train window, you can spot a number of abandoned and working iron ore, limestone and dolomite quarries.

Europe-Asia border   1,777km

At 1,777km from Moscow or 7,512km from Vladivostok is the geographical boundary between Europe and Asia. On the right (southern) side of the track is a 4m-high white obelisk marking the exact point. The obelisk has the word "Europe" written on its western side, "Asia" on the eastern side and is blank on the side facing the train. The obelisk is about 20m from the railway on an embankment.

EKATERINBURG   Екатеринбург   1,818km
Population: 1,370,000   Telephone area code: 3432

Ekaterinburg is the capital of the Urals as it has over 200 industrial complexes, 11 higher education institutions and a transport hub with seven radiating railway lines.

Ekaterinburg was built solely to be an industrial powerhouse and dates its foundation as November 7 1723 which was when the first unit of the Ekaterinburg state metallurgical plant on the Iset River came into production. This fortress-factory produced guns and cannons out of locally dug iron ore.

The city was named after Catherine (Ekaterina in Russian), the wife of Peter the Great, but from 1924 to 1991 it was renamed Sverdlovsk after Yakov Sverdlov (1885–1919), the first president of the Soviet Union. The city's growth accelerated during the 1930s with Stalin's massive industrialisation campaign and in the first months of World War II when 450 large industrial enterprises were evacuated here from European Russia.

Today, Ekaterinburg is a sprawling, polluted city which is worth visiting for no more than two days.

Getting there and away

By air   Lufthansa has a twice weekly flight to/from Frankfurt via Ekaterinburg to Novosibirsk.

By train   The major Trans-Siberian trains on this segment are:

Origin	Dist, km	Train no & name	Travel time	Depart	Arrive	Destination
Ekaterinburg	334	2	4hr 22min	19.59	00.21	Tyumen
Tyumen	334	1	4hr 18min	20.55	01.13	Ekaterinburg
Ekaterinburg	381	1	6hr	01.43	07.43	Perm
Perm	381	2	6hr 45min	12.44	19.29	Ekaterinburg

Passing through

As soon as you reach the suburbs of Ekaterinburg, you see the large lake on the right. This feeds the Iset River which runs through the city.

Perm

VOKZAL.
2
pl
VOKZALNAYA

STRELOCHNIKOV
3
4
5

6

AZINA

SVERDLOVA

MAMINA - SIBIRYAKA

LUNACHARSKOVO

VOSTOCHNAYA

SMAZCHIKOV

7

CHELYUSKINTSEV

PER
KRASNY

LERMONTOVA

8

City pond

SHEVCHENKO

9

10

NAB RABOCHEI MOLODEZHI

YAN VARYA

REVOLYUTSI

pl
KOMSOMOL.

KARLA

11

pl
SOVETSKOI
ARMI   PERVOMAISKAYA

12

LIBKNEKHTA

TURGENEVA

Hotel
Oktyabrskaya
(1km)

17

13

14

pl 1905

VOEVOD.

pl
TRUDA

PRO LENINA

PUSHKINA

pl
PARIZHSKOI
KOMMUNY   (PRO GLAVNY)

15

16

Hotel
Iris
(2km)

18

MALYSHEVA

19

8 MARTA

DOBROL.

GORKOVO

20

ENGELSA

21

BAZHOVA

RADISHCHEVA

VAINERA

BELINSKOVO

GOGOLYA

KARLA

MARKSA

Tyumen

22

23

24

KUIBYSHEVA

Iset River

Aeroflot
(700m)

N

Bus
Station

Mongolian
Consulate

EKATERINBURG

0   500m

KEY TO EKATERINBURG   Екатеринбург

1	Former railway station built in 1878	Старый железнодорожный вокзал
2	Ekaterinburg railway station (*Vokzal*)	Вокзал
3	Uralskaya metro station	Метро станция «Уральская»
4	Book shop (*Knigi*)	Книги
5	Monument to Ural Tank Corps	Памятник Уральского добровольческого Танкового Корпуса
6	Hotel Sverdlovsk (*Gostinitsa*)	гостиница Свердловск
7	Building of Sverdlovsk region railway (1928)	Управление Свердловской железной дороги
8	Advance purchase rail ticket office	Предварительная ж-д касса
9	Dinamo metro station	Метро станция «Динамо»
10	Stadium Dinamo (*Stadion*)	Стадион «Динамо»
11	Drama Theatre (*Teatr*)	Драматический театр
12	Residence built in the late 1800s	Особняк 19 века
13	Theatrical Institute (*Institut*)	Театральный институт
14	Lenin monument	Памятник Ленину
15	Hotel Yubileynaya (*Gostinitsa*)	гостиница Юбилейная
16	Hotel Bolshoi Ural (*Gostinitsa*)	гостиница Большой Урал
17	Pervomaiskaya suburban railway station	Первомайская ж-д станция
18	Ploshchad 1905 metro station	Метро станция «Площадь 1905г»
19	Museum of Decorative Arts (*Muzei*)	Музей изобразительных искусств
20	Hotel Tsentralnaya (*Gostinitsa*)	гостиница Центральная
21	Former House of the architect Malakhov	Быв. дом Малахова
22	Ural Geological Museum (*Muzei*)	Уральский реологический музей
23	Chapel (*Chasoviya*)	Часовня
24	Former Saint-Trinity Church (*Tserkov*)	Быв. Свято-Троицкая старообрядческая церковь
R	Restaurant (*Restoran*)	Ресторан
C	Café (*Kafe*) or Bar (*Bar*)	Кафе или Бар

The Moscow–Vladivostok No 1/2 train stops for 20 minutes at Ekaterinburg. This means you have time to run down the platform underpass which pops you up in the station and walk out of the station into the large station square on which the Hotel Sverdlovsk and the World War II Urals Voluntary Tank Corps monument is located.

After the train leaves the station, you will see Ekaterinburg's main industrial region on the right along the Iset River. Here are located the industrial giants of Uralmash (heavy machinery), Uralelectrotiazhmash (heavy electrical equipment) and Uralkhimash (chemical machinery). You will also see Koltsovo airport on the right.

The city has two spellings in English: Ekaterinburg and Yekaterinburg. Ekaterinburg is the direct transliteration from Russian, while Yekaterinburg provides a better approximation to how Russians pronounce the city's name.

Where to stay

The best accommodation is the excellent Hotel Iris, ul Bardina 4, tel: 289 145, 284 478, fax: 286 292, $70 single room, which also has a railway ticket issuing agency in its building. The hotel closest to the station is the standard Hotel Sverdlovsk, ul Chelyuskintsev 106, tel: 536 261. Other options include the standard Hotel Yubileynaya, pr Lenina 40, tel: 578 028, 515 758 (which has an Intourist office on the 4th floor) $45 a double room; excellent Hotel Oktyabrskaya, ul Sofii Kovalevskoi 17, tel: 445 146, $50 twin share/person; standard Hotel Tsentralnaya, ul Malisheva 74, tel: 551 109, 556 981; standard Hotel Bolshoi Ural, ul Krasnoarmeiskaya 1, tel: 556 896; and basic Hotel Iset, pro Lenina 69/1, tel: 556 943, $40 a double room.

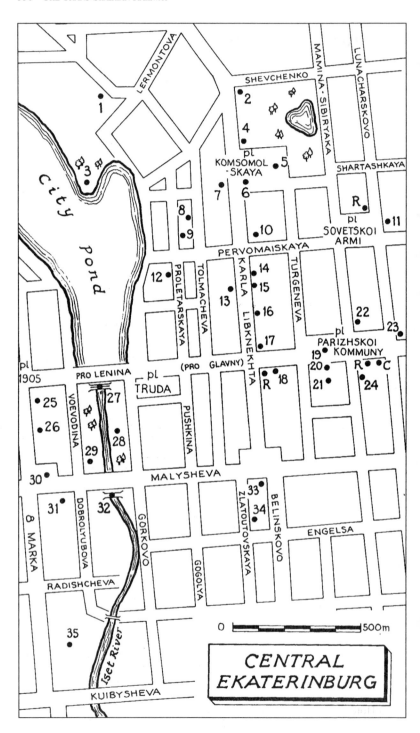

CENTRAL EKATERINBURG

KEY TO CENTRAL EKATERINBURG   Екатеринбург

1	Dinamo metro station	Метро станция «Динамо»
2	Youth Theatre (*Teatr*)	Театр юного зрителя
3	Stadium Dinamo (*Stadion*)	Стадион «Динамо»
4	Former estate of Rastorguev-Kharitonov (1794-1836)	Быв. усадьба Расторгуева-Харитонова
5	Ascension Church (*Tserkov*)	Церковь Вознесения
6	Monument to the Ural's Komsomol Young Communists	Памятник Комсомолу Урала
7	White cross marking place where Tsar Nicholas II and his family were executed (former House of Ipatev)	Белый крест (Быв. Дом Ипатьева)
8	Literary Quarter Museum (*Muzei*)	Музейный комплекс «Литературный квартал»
9	House-museum of writer F M Reshetnikov (*Muzei*)	Дом-музей Решетникова
10	Agricultural Institute (*Institut*)	Сельскохозяйственный институт
11	Military Museum (*Muzei*) in the House of Officers (*Dom Officerov*)	Музей «Боевая слава Урала»
12	House-museum of writer A N Mamin-Sibiryak (*Muzei*)	Дом-музей Мамика-Сибиряка
13	Architecture Institute (*Institut*)	Архитектурний институт
14	Philharmonic Hall (*Filarmoniya*)	Филармония
15	History of the Ural Youth Movement (*Muzei*)	Музей истории молодежного движения Урала
16	Museum of Political Development in the Urals (*Muzei*) (formerly Museum of Sverdlov)	Музей общественно-политических движений Урала
17	Musical Comedy Theatre (*Teatr*)	Театр музыкальной комедии институт
18	Hotel Yubileynaya (*Gostinitsa*)	гостиница Юбилейная
19	Sverdlov monument	Памятник Свердлову
20	Opera and Ballet Theatre (*Teatr*)	Театр оперы и балета
21	Hotel Bolshoi Ural (*Gostinitsa*)	гостиница Большой Урал
22	Ural University (*Universitet*)	Уральский университет
23	Hotel Iset (*Gostinitsa*)	гостиница Исеть
24	Puppet Theatre (*Teatr*)	Театр кукол
25	Conservatorium (*Konservatoriya*)	Консерватория
26	Ploshchad 1905 metro station	Метро станция «Площадь 1905г»
27	Historic weir-bridge built in 1723	Плотина Городского пруда
28	Museum of the History of Architecture and Industry (*Muzei*)	Музей истории архитектуры и промышленной техники Урала
29	Museum of Decorative Arts (*Muzei*)	Музей изобразительных искусств
30	Malyshev monument	Памятник Малышеву
31	Museum of Local Studies (*Muzei*)	Краеведческий музей
32	Historic stone bridge built in 1841	Каменный мост
33	Hotel Tsentralnaya (*Gostinitsa*)	гостиница Центральная
34	Popov's Radio Museum (*Muzei*)	Музей радио им. Попова
35	Chapel (*Chasoviya*)	Часовня
R	Restaurant (*Restoran*)	Ресторан
C	Café (*Kafe*) or Bar (*Bar*)	Кафе или Бар

There are restaurants in the Hotel Sverdlovsk, Hotel Tsentralnaya, Hotel Iris, Hotel Yubileynaya.

Getting around

Ekaterinburg is called a city without a centre as its main street, ul Glavyny (also known as ul Lenina), is over 4km long. Fortunately, the historic centre is in a much smaller area and is located around the junction of pro Lenina and ul Karla Libknetka. To get there from the station, take bus No 1, 13, 21, 23 or 31 or trolleybus No 1, 3, 5, 9 or 12. From the station to get to Hotel Tsentralnaya, take trolleybus No 1, 5, or 9 down ul Karla Libknekhta. From the station to get to Hotel Iset, Hotel Yubileynaya and Hotel Bolshoi Ural, take trams No 27 or 29 which go down ul Lunacharskovo then pro Lenina. To get to Hotel Iris, take bus No 41 westward from the junction of pro Lenina

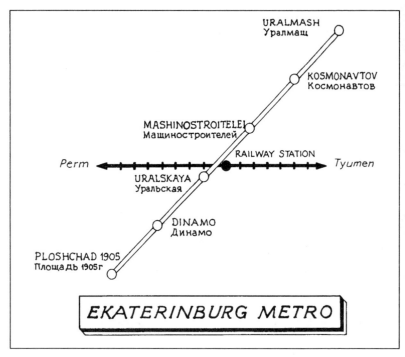

URALMASH
Уралмаш

KOSMONAVTOV
Космонавтов

MASHINOSTROITELEI
Мащиностроителей

RAILWAY STATION

Perm ← Tyumen

URALSKAYA
Уральская

DINAMO
Динамо

PLOSHCHAD 1905
Площадь 1905г

EKATERINBURG METRO

and ul Karla Libknetka. This bus passes the hotel about 500m from its terminus.

To get to the airport, catch a bus from the air station (*aerovokzal*) beside the Aeroflot office at ul Bolshakova 99A.

The metro was opened in 1990 and currently has only six operating stations.

What to see

Ekaterinburg has a multitude of museums. They include the House-museum of the writer A N Mamin-Sibiryak, ul Pushkinskaya 27, tel: 517 576; the large Ural Geological Museum, ul Kuibysheva 30, tel: 223 109, open 11.00–18.00, closed Tuesday; the Literary Quarter Museum, ul Tolmacheva 41, tel: 517 281; the House-museum of the writer F M Reshetnikov, ul 6 Proletarskaya, open 11.00–18.00, closed Saturday; the Museum of Political Development in the Urals (formerly Museum of Sverdlov), ul Karla Libknekhta 32, tel: 517 793, open 11.00–18.00, closed Friday; the Museum of History of Architecture and Industry, ul Gorkovo 4a, tel: 519 735, open 09.00–17.00, closed Tuesday and Sunday. which is on the banks of the Iset River between pr Lenina and ul Malysheva and; the Military Museum in the House of Officers, ul Pervomaiskaya 27, tel: 552 106, open 11.00–18.00 on Saturday for the public with bookings necessary for the rest of the week; the History of the Ural Youth Movement, ul Karla Libknekhta 32, open 11.00–19.00, closed Sunday and Monday; the Museum of Decorative Arts which has brances at ul Voevodina 5, tel: 510 626, and ul Vainera 11; the Museum of Local Studies, ul Malysheva 46, tel: 511 819, open 11.00–18.00, closed Tuesday; and Popov's Radio Museum, ul Zlatoutovskaya 9.

There are a number of interesting buildings in the city including the classical style Mining Office (1737–9), the former estate of Rastorguev-Kharitonov (1794–1824) ul Karla Libknehkta 44, tel: 514 601, and the Ascension Cathedral (18th century), pl Vosnesenskaya 1, tel: 516 407.

The Opera and Ballet Theatre, ul Lenina 46a tel: 558 057, has a very impressive interior with chandeliers and 19th-century opulence. The Musical Comedy Theatre, ul Lenina 47, tel: 510 832, Philharmonic Hall, ul Karla Libknekhta 48a, tel: 579 010, Puppet Theatre, ul Mamin-Sibiryak 143, tel: 553 005, and the Drama Theatre, ul Oktyabrskaya 2, tel: 510 728, often have events that are worth seeing.

There is also a depressing zoo, ul Mamin-Sibiryak 189, tel: 555 469, which looks more like a prison.

Romonov's Death House
On July 16 1918, Tsar Nicholas II, his wife Alexandra and their five children were shot and then bayoneted in the basement of a house in central Ekaterinburg. The communist murderers took the bodies to the Four Brothers Mine, 40km from town, and dismembered them before burning the remains and dumping them down a mine shaft. Despite the remains being discovered in the late 1960s, it was only in 1995 that DNA testings proved conclusively that these were indeed the remains of the Russian royal family. The remains of the family will finally be laid to rest in St Petersburg's Peter and Paul Fortress beside the other Russian tsars.

The building in which the family was executed was known as Ipatyev's House. The house was demolished in 1976 as it was feared that it would become revered by monarchists. This destruction was carried out by the then local communist party boss, Boris Yeltsin, although he was acting under orders from Moscow. Today, a Russian Orthodox cross marks the spot and next door to it is a small wooden chapel dedicated to Saint Elizabeth, whose full name was Elizabeth Fyodorov. She was Nicholas II's sister-in-law and, unlike the rest of the royal family, was thrown down the mine shaft next to the house in which they were shot. She survived the fall but after two days, the revolutionaries pumped poisonous gas down the hole before filling it in.

Getting assistance
Travel agents Intourist, ul Lenina 40, tel: 513 898, 519 102; Adams and Ruffle Travel, tel: 515 289; Sputnik, ul Pushkina 5, tel: 519 157, fax: 513 483.
Air Aeroflot, ul Bolshakova 99A, tel: 299 298, 299 122, 299 051.
Rail As well as booking rail tickets at the station, tel: 519 924, you can also book them at the advance purchase rail ticket booking office, ul Sverdlova 22.
Diplomatic representation Mongolian Consulate, ul Furmanova 45, tel: 445 453, US Consulate, ul Gogolya 15A, tel: 564 619, 564 191, 601 143, fax: 564 515, 601 181, telex 612696.

The train now passes the last of the Ural Mountains and proceeds along the west Siberian plain which is as flat as a board with not a hill in sight. You will be travelling over this plain, the largest in the interior of any continent in the world, for the next two days. This area is the granary of the country and contains 80 huge oil deposits. The plain is clearly defined by the Ural Mountains in the west, the Enisei River in the east, the Kara Sea in the north and the Sayan Mountains in the south. From north to south the Siberian plain is 2,500km long, and from west to east it is 1,600km wide.

Bashenovo   Баженово   1,874km
In the nearby village of Zarechnyi is located one of the Soviet Union's first atomic energy plants which is named after the scientist Igor Kurchatov (1903–60) who is known as the "father of the Russian atomic bomb". Kurchatov's physics work was so significant that the 104th element of the periodic table, kurchatoviom, is named after him.

Bogdanovich   Богданович   1,917km
There is nothing of interest in this town unless you want to pick up some fireproof bricks, the making of which is the town's biggest industry. Clay quarries and other factories make this town and region very ugly.

About 16km from Bogdanovich are the Kurinsk mineral springs which treat rheumatism, paralysis, scrofula and anaemia. There is a hotel at the springs.

Kamyshlov   Камышлов   1,961km
The town was founded in 1668 as a fortress and is one of the oldest settlements in the Urals. The original buildings have all gone and today the architecture of the town is predominantly late 19th and early 20th century. There is a museum here dedicated to the locally born poet S P Shchepachev and the writer P P Bazhov who lived here on and off from 1914 to 1923.

There is an obelisk on the communal grave of sailors from the battleship Potemkin who were executed nearby at Yushala station and buried in Kamyshlov.

About 6km to the west of the town, on the banks of the Pyshma River, is the Obukhov sulphur and chalybeate mineral water sanatorium which has been famous since 1871.

Talitsa   Талица   2,033km
Much of the bottled mineral water sold on this stretch of the railway comes from this town. Over 600,000 bottles of Talitskaya water are produced a year; it is believed to be good for stomach disorders. The town also produces another drink which is not at all good for your health: watered down industrial alcohol which is sold as rough vodka.

The town, also called Troitski (Троицкий), sits 5km from the station and was founded in 1732 as a rest house on the Siberian tract. The only place of interest in the town is the House-museum of the locally born N I Kuznetsov (1911–44) who was a famous World War II partisan and Hero of the Soviet Union.

Yushala   Юшала   2,064km
The sailors from the battleship Potemkin were shot here and buried at nearby Kamyshlov station.

2,102km   2,102km   2,107km
This little station sits on the border between the Urals and Siberia which also marks a time-zone barrier. To the east of the station is the Tyumen Oblast which is three hours ahead of Moscow.

TYUMEN   Тюмень   2,144km
Population: 496,000   Telephone area code: 343 22

Tyumen is the booming oil capital of western Siberia and its wealth is illustrated by the expensive goods in the shops. Prior to the drilling of the first well in the region in 1960, Tyumen was just a dusty backwater with 150,000 inhabitants. Since then its population has tripled. The importance of oil to the city can be seen in the two giant crude pipelines running through it.

Tyumen was officially founded in 1586, but the Russian history of the city predates this by five years when the ruthless Cossack explorer and conqueror Ermak captured the Tatar-Mongol town of Chinga-Tura to the north of Tyumen's current city centre. It is most likely that the town got its name from the word *tyumenka* which means a "hollow" or "depression" in Tatar language

The location of Tyumen on a major trading river, the Tura, made it an important transit point for goods between Siberia and China. Trade volumes increased considerably with the arrival of steam navigation in the 1840s, and again when the railway reached the city in 1885. However, most of the railway goods simply passed through Tyumen so trade started to decrease at the end of the 20th century. Tyumen was also a major transit point for settlers and convicts destined for Siberia and the Russian far east.

During World War II, many of European Russia's factories, treasures and population were relocated in Siberia. The greatest treasure to be transferred from Moscow to Tyumen during this time was Lenin's corpse. For years, he rested secretly in a building of the Agricultural Institute tended by a team of specialists fearful that the slightest deterioration in Lenin's body would lead to their immediate execution.

Nowadays, Tyumen is famous throughout Russia as being the only city in Asia to have hosted a European Cup and for its annual international body-building competitions.

Passing through
On the approach to the city, you can see the airport on the left.

The Moscow–Vladivostok No 1/2 train stops here for a minute or two. Unfortunately, you will not see the main part of the city or the Tura River from the train as these are about 1km to the north of the station.

Getting there and away
The major Trans-Siberian trains on this segment are:

Origin	Dist, km	Train no & name	Travel time	Depart	Arrive	Destination
Ekaterinburg	334	2	4hr 22min	19.59	00.21	Tyumen
Tyumen	334	1	4hr 18min	20.55	01.13	Ekaterinburg
Omsk	562	1	6hr 47min	13.08	20.55	Tyumen
Tyumen	562	2	7hr 10min	00.21	07.40	Omsk

Where to stay
There are two standard hotels in the city, Hotel Prometei, ul Sovetskaya 20, tel: 251 423, $70 a double room, and Hotel Quality, ul Ordzhonikidze. The basic hotels are Hotel Turist, ul Respubliki 156, tel: 273 573 and Hotel Vostok, ul Respubliki 156.

What to see

As Tyumen is the oldest Siberian city, there are lots of historic buildings here. Most are located on the right bank (southern side) of the Tura River although today the city is spread over both sides. The most interesting buildings are the Tyumen History Museum complex which includes the Trinity Cathedral built in 1616, the Church of Sts Peter and Paul, and the walls of the monastery. This monastery is unusual in Siberia as it is one of only a few built from stone.

There is also a Museum of Local Studies, ul Respubliki 1, tel: 261 159, and a small Picture Gallery, ul Respubliki 29, which has a good collection of Russian paintings. Particularly interesting is the Blyukher Museum where Marshal Vasili Blyukher (1890–1938) controlled the 51st Division in 1919 during the Russian Civil War. Another interesting museum is on ul Gorkovo and is dedicated to the past and present work of firemen.

Both the All Saints Church and the Cathedral of the Holy Cross have regular worship.

To the north of the city you can picnic at the park where the Tyumenka Creek flows into the Tura River. Tyumen's original fortress was built here in the 1580s but it was destroyed in the 18th century. Across the river from the park is the site of the original Tatar-Mongol village and in the deep ravine you can still see traces of the ditches and earth walls which were stormed in 1581.

Getting assistance

Travel agents Intourist, ul Gertsena 74, tel: 250 027, and Sputnik, ul Respubliki 19, tel: 240 713.

Air Aeroflot, ul Respubliki 156, tel: 223 252.

After leaving Tyumen, the scenery changes from agricultural fields to pine forests.

Yalutorovsk   Ялуторовск   2,222km

The town sits on bank of the wide, 1,591km-long Tobol River. This town has been at the frontier of Siberia twice in its history. Firstly, in 1639 it was the most easterly fortress of the tsar's expanding empire. The fortress was built on the site of the captured Tatar-Mongol town, Yablu-Tur. Secondly, in 1846, the first Siberian school for girls was opened here. The house where the school was opened is now a museum and sits next to the Decembrists' museum which was the house of the most famous exile, M M Muravev-Apostol (1793–1886).

After crossing over the Tobol River, you will see dozens of small, mostly salt, lakes on both sides of the railway.

Zavodoukovskaya   Заводоуковская   2,241km

Zavodoukovskaya is a standard town and illustrates a typical pattern of town development during the Russian and Soviet periods. The town is divided into two parts: the older Russia section around the station, which is the main part of town, and the new Soviet 1960s *micro-raion* around the town's main industry. Industrial micro-regions, also known as satellite suburbs, are usually sponsored, built and managed by an industrial enterprise and they include not only the factory but the workers' apartment blocks and shops. In some towns, the enterprise and its *micro-raion* are larger than the rest of the town and consequently have more power.

VIRGIN LANDS CAMPAIGN
Years of chronic grain shortages following World War II resulted in Nikita Khrushchev, the then General Secretary of the Soviet Union, announcing a gigantic agricultural project in 1953. Called the Virgin Lands Campaign, it envisaged sowing wheat on 25 million hectares of virgin and fallow land in southwestern Siberia and north Kazakhstan. To put the size of this massive undertaking into perspective, the total surface area of the United Kingdom is only 13 million hectares.

Exhilarated by the bumper crops of 1956 and 1958, Khrushchev ignored calls from agricultural experts for environmentally sensitive cultivation and instead encouraged "merciless ploughing". Within a few years, the scientists' worst predictions were realised and massive areas were affected by soil erosion, dust-bowls and weed infestation. Over the next few years the soil degradation was obvious, wheat yields falling from 1.06 tons/hectare in 1956 to just 0.35 in 1963. Blame for the disastrous harvest in 1963 rested squarely on Khrushchev's arrogant shoulders and was one of the main reasons for his dismissal the following year. Despite decades of work to recover and improve the land, much of the Virgin Lands Campaign area is semi-desert.

Ishim   Ишим   2,433km
The town sits on the left bank of the Ishim River which was a major trading route at the turn of the century before the arrival of the Trans-Siberian. The strategic location of the town resulted in it hosting one of the largest trading fairs in western Siberia. The Nikolsk Fair was held every December and it attracted more than 2,000 traders from as far away as China.

Nazyvaevskaya   Называевская   2,567km
The town was only founded in 1910 with the arrival of the railway but rapidly grew with an influx of new agricultural workers during the Virgin Fields campaign.

OMSK   Омск   2,716km
Population: 1,169,000   Telephone area code: 3812
Omsk is the second largest city in Siberia and great effort has gone into making it the greenest. It has over 80 parks and gardens with a total area of 2,500 hectares. However, this greenery can't hide that fact that Omsk is an industrial city.

During Stalin's industrialisation campaign, Omsk became a major industrial city specialising in chemical industry machine building and petro-chemical processing. The city is also home to the Transmash company which is the country's biggest tank manufacturer. While this factory still churns out tanks, it did not sell one vehicle in 1994 or 1995. Seeing the writing on the wall, the company started producing civilian tractors in 1994 but for some unexplained reason these were no more successful in finding a buyer.

Passing through
Just before reaching the suburbs of Omsk, you see the airport on the left. The first suburban station you pass is Karbyshevo (Карбышево) and this is where the railway from Chelyabinsk joins the Trans-Siberian railway. Contrary to popular belief, it was from Chelyabinsk and not Ekaterinburg that

the Trans-Siberian started. Karbyshevo station is between two road overpasses and, after the second one, the train crosses the 500m-wide Irtysh River, giving a view of central Omsk to the left. The bridge was finished in 1896. The old centre of Omsk is on the right bank (eastern side) of the river and the vast majority of buildings on the left bank were built after 1973 when the city reached the limits on the right bank. Over the bridge, the train makes a left turn and on the right passes an old brick water tower for steam engines, built during the early 20th century. This has been preserved as an architectural monument.

The Moscow–Vladivostok No 1/2 train stops here for 15 minutes.

Once you leave Omsk on the way to Novosibirsk, you are travelling on the stretch of line that has the greatest freight traffic density in the world.

Getting there and away
The major Trans-Siberian trains on this segment are:

Origin	Dist, km	Train no & name	Travel time	Depart	Arrive	Destination
Omsk	627	2	8hr 57min	07.58	16.55	Novosibirsk
Novosibirsk	627	1	8hr 41min	04.12	12.53	Omsk
Omsk	562	1	6hr 47min	13.08	20.55	Tyumen
Tyumen	562	2	7hr 10min	00.21	07.40	Omsk

Where to stay
Only the standard Hotel Omsk, Irtushskaya nab. 30, tel: 310 721 and very basic Hotel Avtomobilist, pro Marksa 43, are within walking distance of the railway station and even this is a long way. Those in the city centre are Hotel Mayak, ul Lermontova 2, tel: 315 431; Hotel Ermak, ul Tarskaya 25; Hotel Otkyabr, (formerly Hotel Russia), ul Partizanskaya 2; Hotel Turist, ul I Broz Tito 2; and Hotel Sibir (formerly Hotel Evropa), ul Lenina 22.

On the western bank of the Irtysh River is the Hotel Zarechnaya, pro Komarova 4 and to the north of the city centre is Hotel Irtysh, ul Krasny Put 155, korpus 1, tel: 232 702.

Getting around
The central part of Omsk is located about 2.5km from the station and such a separation is common for many Trans-Siberian towns. The reasons for not building the railway through the centre included an inadequate bribe to the railway planners from the city officials, an unwillingness by the railway to deal with compensation for confiscated city land, and the need to minimise costs by choosing the shortest route.

Most of the city's hotels and museum are located in the city centre which is at the junction of the Om River and Irtysh River.

What to see
Most of the places of interest are on the right bank (eastern side) of the Irtysh River, around the junction of the Om and Irtysh Rivers. Near this junction are the ramparts and the Tobolsk Gate of the old Omsk Fortress. Nearby are a number of Czarist government office and other buildings of architectural interest including the Drama Theatre (1901–5) and the river station (1961–3).

There are a number of museums in Omsk and these include the Picture Gallery, ul Lenina 23; Firemen's Museum, ul Internatsionalnaya 41; Military

Museum, ul Taube 7; Museum of Ministry of Internal Affairs, ul Dostoevskovo 2; House of Nature, ul Pushkina 6; House of Artists, ul Lermontova 8; Kuibyshev Museum, ul Kuibysheva 101 and the Railway Workers' Museum, ul Lobkova 5. Several kilometres to the north of the city centre are the Communications Museum, ul 4th Poselkovaya 46, and the Museum of River Workers, ul Krasny Put 153,

House of the Dead

Despite Omsk's notorious Tsarist prison being demolished for decades, its existence will never be forgotten thanks to Fedor Dostoyevski's novel, *House of the Dead*. In 1849, Dostoyevski was sentenced to four years' hard labour for his involvement in revolutionary politics and he served much of it here, working at the Omsk brickworks.

Although Dostoyevski supported many communist ideals, he was never elevated to the ranks of the great proletariat writers. Part of this can be attributed to his book, *Demons*, in which he presented a satire of revolutionary violence. Even in the 1970s, this book was hard to get in the Soviet Union. It was only in 1993 that the first full-size monument to Dostoyevski was cast, although by this time there were museums and festivals devoted to his work.

For more information on Dostoyevski, visit the Dostoyevski Museum, ul Dostoevskovo.

Getting assistance

Travel agents   Intourist, pr Karla Marksa 4, tel: 311 490, and Turist, ul Gagarina 2, tel: 250 624.
Air   Aeroflot has an office at the river terminal, tel: 312 266 and one at the railway station.
Rail   Train tickets can be bought at both the railway station and the advance purchase rail ticket office ul Pushkina.

For the next 600km the train runs through the inhospitable Baraba Steppe. This vast expanse of greenish plains is dotted with shallow lakes and ponds; coarse reeds and sedge grass conceal swamps, peat bogs and rare patches of firm ground. From the train it appears as if there is a continuous forest in the distance. However, this is an illusion: if you walk towards it, you will never get there as what you are seeing are clumps of birches and aspen trees that are spaced several kilometres or more apart. The lack of landmarks in this area has claimed hundreds of Russian lives, so don't test this.

In spring, this place is hell as the air is grey with clouds of gnats and mosquitoes. The Baraba Steppe is a vast breeding ground for ducks and geese and every year hunters bag about 5 million birds from here. Between 900 and 3,000m below the steppe is an enormous underground reservoir of hot water at temperatures from 70 to 100°C. Currently, a number of experimental stations in the steppe are evaluating its use as a geothermal energy supply for both heating and electricity generation.

Kormilovka   Кормиловка   2,764km

There is a steam engine storage depot 4km past this station at about the 2,761km marker.

Kalachinskaya   Калачинская   2,795km

This town doesn't look much but locals are very proud of the fact that it is one of the most attractive towns in the Omsk Oblast with its landscaping and asphalt streets. Its progressiveness may or may not be related to the fact that the town was founded in 1792 by Russian peasants who spoke in an unusual dialect. They used their word *kalachon,* which means "a sharp bend in a river", as the name for their town as it sits at such a place on the Om River. Nowadays *kalach* in Russian means a "small padlock-shaped white bread loaf".

Barabinsk   Барабинск   3,040km

Despite what several guidebooks say, this town was founded only at the end of the 19th century during the construction of the Trans-Siberian. However, 12km to north is the bigger and older town of Kuibyshev which often gets confused with Barabinsk. Part of the reason for this is that the station at Kuibyshev is known as Kainsk-Barabinski. There is a branch line from Barabinsk to Kuibyshev (Kainsk-Barabinski station), which is not on the Trans-Siberian.

Ob   Обь   3,326km

Just before reaching this town, you can see Tolmachevo airport on the left which is one of the two airports which serves Novosibirsk.

NOVOSIBIRSK   Новосибирск   3,343km
Population: 1,600,000   Telephone area code: 3832

Novosibirsk is the largest city in Siberia and serves both as its industrial and commercial capital. It is a relatively new town founded by the Trans-Siberian bridge builders who came to span the Ob River in 1893. At first the settlement was imaginatively known as Novaya Derevnia meaning "new village", until in 1894 it became known as Aleksandrovsk after the then tsar, Alexander III. In 1895 Alexander died and was replaced by Nicholas II and the town was promptly renamed Novonikolaevsk meaning "new Nicholas". It was only in 1925 that the tsarist name was changed to Novosibirsk meaning "new Siberia".

Novosibirsk grew as a trading centre as it was on major rail and river routes, particularly after the opening of the Kuznetsk Coal Basin to the south, the building of railways to Kazakhstan and Central Asia, and the evacuation of many factories from European Russia following the outbreak of World War II.

Today, Novosibirsk is a big Soviet city of moderate interest but two days is the most you would want to spend here.

Passing through

As you are crossing over the Ob River, you can see the city centre on the left and the Oktyabrski port on the right. You can see the passenger river station a further 800m upstream from the port. The bridges you see are another railway bridge, two road bridges and a metro bridge. On reaching the right bank, the train turns to the north passing the city's long-distance bus station. About 800m onwards on the right, you pass a steam engine on a plinth.

On arriving at Novosibirsk the Moscow–Vladivostok No 1/2 train stops for 15 minutes so you can have a look at Siberia's largest station. The big, bright green, glass vaulted station is truly impressive; it took 11 years to build and was finished in 1941.

Getting there and away

By air   Lufthansa has a twice weekly flight from Frankfurt via Ekaterinburg to Novosibirsk.

By rail   The major Trans-Siberian trains on this segment are:

Origin	Dist, km	Train no & name	Travel time	Depart	Arrive	Destination
Omsk	627	2	8hr 57min	07.58	16.55	Novosibirsk
Novosibirsk	627	1	8hr 41min	04.12	12.53	Omsk
Krasnoyarsk	761	1	12hr 41min	15.16	03.57	Novosibirsk
Novosibirsk	761	2	12hr 55min	16.55	05.50	Krasnoyarsk

Where to stay

There are numerous hotels in the city, the most convenient one for rail travellers being the standard Hotel Novosibirsk which is directly opposite the station at Vokzalnaya Magistral 1, tel: 201 120, $58 twin share/person. Other central city options are the excellent Hotel Sibir, ul Lenina 21, tel: 231 215, $100 twin share/person; excellent Hotel Tsentre Rossii, pr Krasny 23, tel: 234 562, $110 twin share/person; and standard Hotel Tsentralnaya, ul Lenina 3, tel: 227 660, $67 twin share/person. The excellent Hotel Iris is at ul Kolkhidskaya 10, tel: 410 155, fax: 403 73, and to get to it take bus No 2 or 37 from pl Stanislavskaya. Near Tolmachovo airport is the Novosibirsk Airport Hotel, ul Lenina 23, tel: 281 430, 283 930. All the above hotels have restaurants.

Getting around

From in front of the station, the road ul Vokzalnaya Magistral takes you to the main thoroughfare of Krasny Prospect, which runs into both pl Sverdlova and pl Lenina.

Getting around Novosibirsk is easy due to the metro and other excellent public transport. The metro opened in 1985 and consists of two lines with the crossover point being Sibirsk/Krasny Prospekt. The local transport hub is around the metro station of Rechnoi Vokzal (meaning "river station") and nearby is the river station and the long-distance bus station.

There are two airports: the international Tolmachovo airport, 23km from the city's centre on the western bank, and the domestic Sverny airport, 6km to the north of the centre. Buses No 122 and 111 run between the two via the railway station and bus station.

What to see

A must in Novosibirsk is the fabulous Opera and Ballet Theatre, pr Krasnyi 36, tel: 223 866, 298 394. It was only finished in 1945 and is classically Stalinist. You get tickets from the kiosk on the left side of the theatre. There are several museums including the Museum of Local Studies, pr Krasny 23, tel: 218 630, open 10.00–18.00, closed weekends; the Picture Gallery, pr Krasnyi 5 (near the regional administration building), tel: 222 267, 233 516, open 11.00–19.00, closed Tuesday; the Regional Centre of Russian Folklore and Ethnography, pr Krasny 18, tel: 211 929, 239 951, open 10.00–16.00, closed weekends; and the House-Museum of Kirov, next door to Hotel Sibir. The Kirov Museum is dedicated to the senior communist party official who was assassinated on Stalin's orders in St Petersburg in 1934, and has variable opening hours.

Novosibirsk boasts a number of theatres and cultural groups. These include the Chaldony Song and Dance Company, ul Zabaluyeva 47, tel: 418 889; the Circus, ul Sovetskaya 11, tel: 237 584, Globe Youth Theatre, ul Kamenskaya 1

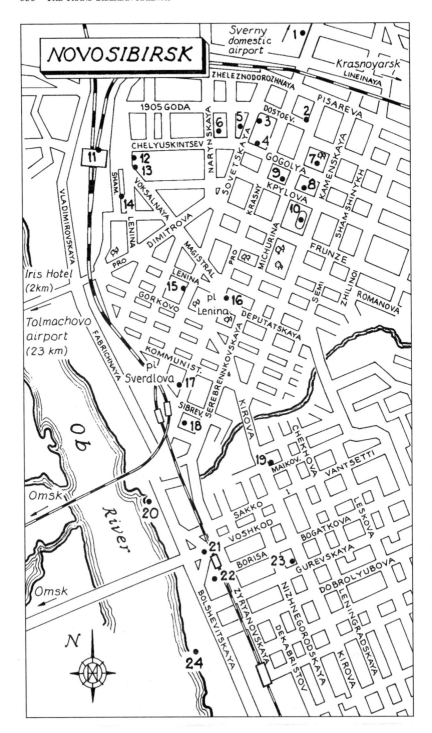

KEY TO NOVOSIBIRSK Новосибирск

1	Gagarinskaya metro station	«пл Гагаринская» станции метро
2	Café (*Kafé*)	Кафе
3	Advance purchase rail ticket office for Russians	Предварительная ж-д касса
4	Aeroflot	Аэрофлот
5	Cathedral of the Ascension (*Voztsesenski*)	Возцесенский собор
6	Circus (*Tsirk*)	Цирк
7	Zoo (*Zoopark*)	Зоопарк
8	Market (*Rynok*)	Рынок
9	Krasny Prospekt metro station	«Красный проспект» станции метро
10	Stadium Spartak (*Stadion*)	Стадион «Спартак»
11	Railway station (*Vokzal*)	Ж-Д вокзал
12	Ploshchad Mikhailovskovo metro station	«пл Михайловсково» станции метро
13	Hotel Novosibirsk	гостиница Новосибирск
14	Railway ticket office for foreigners travelling within ex-USSR	ж-д касса для иностранецев
15	Central post office (*Pochtamt*)	Почтамт
16	Ploshchad Lenina metro station	«пл Ленина» станции метро
17	Picture gallery (*Galereya*)	Картинная галерея
18	Bus station (*Avtovokzal*)	Автовокзал
19	Ploshchad Oktyabrskaya metro station	«Октябьская» станции метро
20	Oktyabrski commercial port	Октябрьский порт
21	Rechnoi Vokzal metro station	«Речной вокзал» станции метро
22	Stary Dom Drama Theatre (*Teatr*)	Драматический театр «Старый дом»
23	Institute of Communications (*Teatr*)	Электротехнический институт связи
24	River station (*Rechnoi Vokzal*)	Речной вокзал

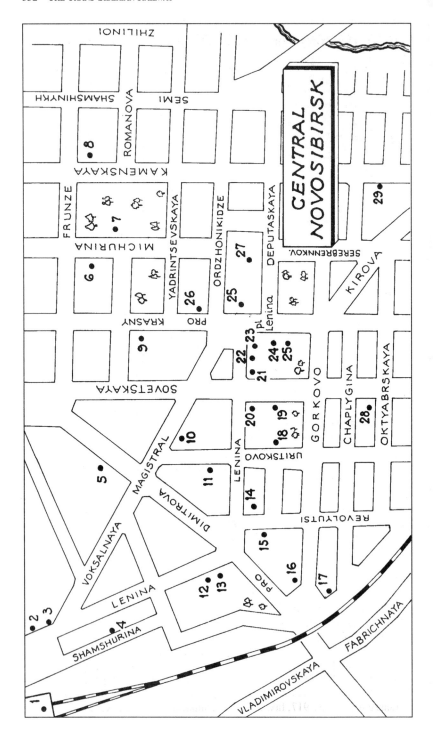

KEY TO CENTRAL NOVOSIBIRSK Новосибирск

1	Railway station (*Vokzal*)	Ж-Д вокзал
2	Ploshchad Mikhailovskovo metro station	«пл Михайловсково» станции метро
3	Hotel Novosibirsk	гостиница Новосибирск
4	Railway ticket office for foreigners travelling within ex-USSR	ж-д касса для иностранецев
5	Museum of Local Studies (*Muzei*)	Краведческий музей
6	Medical Institute (*Institut*)	Медицинский институт
7	Theatre of Musical Comedy (*Teatr*)	Театр музыкальной комедии
8	Institute of Economics (*Institut*)	Институт народного хозяйства
9	Institute of Light Engineering (*Institut*)	Филиал Московской академии
10	Canteen (*Stolovaya*)	Столовая
11	Puppet Theatre (*Teatr*)	Театр кукол
12	Hotel Sibir, Intourist and American Business Centre	гостиница Сибир
13	House-Museum of Kirov (*Dom-Muzei*)	Дом-музей Кирова
14	Book shop (*Knigi*)	Книги
15	Krasny Fakel Drama Theatre (*Teatr*)	Драматический театр «Красный Факел»
16	Railway ticket office for foreigners travelling outside ex-USSR	ж-д касса для иностранецев
17	Steam engine	пароход
18	Institute of Water Transport Engineers (*Institut*)	Институт инженеров водного транспорта
19	Glinka Conservatorium (*Konservatoriya*)	Консерватория им. Глинки
20	Central post office (*Pochtamt*)	Почтамт
21	Hotel Tsentralnaya	гостиница Центральная
22	Restaurant (*Restoran*)	Ресторан
23	Hotel Tsentre Rossi	гостиница Центр России
24	Regional Centre of Russian Folklore and Ethnography	Областной центр Фольклора и этнографии
25	Ploshchad Lenina metro station	«пл Ленина» станции метро
26	Pokrushkina monument	Памятник Покрышкину легкой промышленности
27	Opera and Ballet Theatre (*Teatr*)	театр оперы и балета
28	Hotel Sapfir (*Gostinitsa*)	гостиница Сапфир
29	Globe Youth Theatre (*Teatr*)	Театр юного зрителя

which is near pl Lenin, tel: 236 684, 238 841, open 18.30, closed Monday and Tuesday; the Krasny Fakel Drama Theatre, ul Lenina 19 which is near Hotel Sibir, tel: 980 40; the Theatre of Musical Comedy, ul Michurina 8 which is near Central Park, tel: 246 481, 245 459, open 18.00, closed Sunday–Tuesday; the Puppet Theatre, ul Revolyutsi 6, tel: 221 202; the Siberian Dixieland Jazz Band, ul Kirova 3, tel: 235 642, 255 719; the Siberian Russian Folk Chorus, ul Krasnoyarskaya 117, tel: 202 269; the Stary Dom Drama Theatre, ul Bolshevistskaya 45 which is near the Rechnoi Vokzal metro station, tel: 662 608, 669450, open 18.00, closed Monday and Tuesday; and the Symphony & Chamber Orchestras Halls, ul Spartaka 11, tel: 224 880, 230 856.

Getting assistance

Travel agents   Sibalp, ul Nemirovicha-Danchenko 155/1, kv 47, tel: 495 922, fax: 469 059, email sibalp@niee.nsk.su; Intourist is located in Hotel Sibir at ul Lenina 21, tel: 237 870; Remkolv Tours, ul Yadrintsyovskaya 48, kv 12, tel: 228 884, fax: 910 430.

Air   Aeroflot, ul Pyatovo Goda 83, tel: 291 999; Sibir Aviation, tel: 669 078, fax: 227 572; Lufthansa (at airport), tel: 696 377, 227 151, fax: 227 151, TransAero, tel: 231 917, fax: 230 321, Tolmachevo Airport, tel: 298 941.

Rail   General information tel: 207 711, 292 011, international tickets tel: 293 530. There are three places where you can get rail tickets. For Russians, go to the advance purchase ticket office, ul Sovetskaya 72, tel: 207 721. For foreigners who want tickets for travel within the former Soviet Union, go to ul Shamshurina 10. For foreigners who want international tickets to Mongolia or China, go to the Intourist office, pro Dimitrova 2, tel: 982 333, in the Bank Vostok building.

Foreign representatives   SAIC American Business Centre, Suite 731, Hotel Sibir, ul Lenina 21, tel: 235 569, fax: 235 762, email abc@saic.nsk.su.

Information   The English-language Siberian Business Review is produced quarterly. It can be subscribed through Vladimir Pavlov, general editor, email pavlov@soi.nsk.su.

Language courses   Gwendolin Fricker, Foreign Manager, KASSI Language Programme, Novosibirsk State University, tel: (3832) 352 653, fax: (3832) 397 124, email admin@kassi.nsu.nsk.su, http://www.cnit.nsk.su/univer/english/kassi.htm.

What's in the region
River cruise

The Ob River which flows through Novosibirsk is the busiest river in Siberia and a trip along it is fascinating. The most popular trip is the 1hr 5min round trip from the river station to Korablik Island. Most passengers get off here as it is a popular swimming spot. The ferry travels this route three times a day from May to September. To get to the river station, take the metro to the Rechnoi Vokzal station and you can see the river station from the exit. Check the weather before you go as Novosibirsk is shrouded in fog for 95 days of the year.

Academic City (*Академгородок*)

About 30km to the south of Novosibirsk is the secluded city of Akademgorodok (Академгородок) meaning "academic city". In the Soviet days, the city of 65,000 inhabitants was the focal point of Russian science and, surprisingly, the vast majority of the work at Akademgorodok's 23 academic institutes was non-military.

Over the last few years, Akademgorodok has suffered a brain drain, with thousands of scientists going overseas, returning to Moscow and St Petersburg, or leaving science for the far more lucrative business sector. However, it is still worth visiting for its fabulous Geological Museum, average Botanical Gardens and History of the Siberian Peoples Museum. After you have visited these places, have a picnic and swim at the Ob Sea which is a 15-minute walk to the east. The sea, known as Obskoe More, was formed by the damming of the Ob River.

The Ob Sea beach is beside Akademgorodok's railway station known as Obskoe More. To get to Akademgorodok take a train from Novosibirsk's central railway station or catch bus No 2 or 22 from in front of the station. A taxi from Novosibirsk costs about $20 one way. There are several hotels in Akademgorodok with the easiest to stay at being Hotel Zolotaya Dolina (formerly Hotel Soran), ul Ilicha 10, tel: 356 609, $35 double room.

Bolotnaya   Болотная   3,479km

The town was founded in 1805 as a way station on the Siberian Tract at a junction of a 250km road south to Barnaul. The town's name means "swampy". Today, the town's main occupation is the railways. After leaving this station, you cross another time zone. You are now four hours ahead of Moscow.

Yurga 1   Юрга 1   3,498km
The town arose in 1886 during the construction of the railway, and the railway station was built in 1906. The town has a museum of local studies and one on the arts of the indigenous people of Siberia and the far east.

The town of Yurga 2 is 7km to the south of Yurga 1.

Taiga   Тайга   3,571km
Once this town stood in the midst of the sepulchral taiga forest. Nowadays the closest taiga is far to the east. The station sits at the junction of a 79km branch line to the 500,000-inhabitant city of Tomsk.

During the Russian Civil War over 50,000 refugees and soldiers died in and around Taiga as they fled eastward from the communists in 1919–20. A million Russians died in the exodus.

Near the station is the steam engine, P-360192 built in 1956.

Anzherskaya   Анжерская   3,602km
This ugly, coal-mining town is at the northern extremity of the giant Kuzbass coal fields which contain a massive 600 billion tons of high-quality, low-sulphur coal. The town, called Anzhero-Sudzhensk (Анжеро-Судженск), was founded in 1897 during the construction of the Trans-Siberian which is also when coal mining started. Most of the original coal miners were Tsarist prisoners and their short and brutal mining life is documented in the museum of local studies.

The railway branch line to the south from here leads to Novokuznetsk which is the heart of the Kuzbass.

Mariinsk   Мариинск   3,719km
In 1826, this area was flooded with tens of thousands of fortune seekers when word of a massive gold find got out. The gold rush lasted for decades and between 1828 and 1917, more than 50 tons of gold were extracted from the region.

Prior to this, the village of Kisskoe, as it was known since it was founded in 1698, consisted of a way station for postal riders who carried messages on the Moscow–Irkutsk postal road.

TAIGA: THE AWESOME SIBERIAN FOREST
The taiga forests of Russia are uncomprehendingly enormous, covering the vast majority of Siberia and making up 70% of the forests of the former Soviet Union. Russian attitudes are contradictory towards the taiga as it is both mysterious and understandable, cruel and kind, frightening and hospitable. The great Russian writer Anton Chekhov wrote, "The strength and charm of the taiga does not lie in its giant trees and its silence, like that of a tomb, but in that only migratory birds know where it finishes. On the first day one does not take any notice of the taiga, on the second and third day one begins to wonder, but on the fourth and fifth day one experiences a mood as if one would never get out of this green monster."

Taiga is coniferous forest (also known as boreal) made up of spruce and larch trees with cones and needle-like leaves. Common taiga trees are Dahurian larch, Yeddo spruce, Erman's birch, Khingan fir, Norway spruce, Scots pine, Siberian larch, Siberian fir, Siberian spruce, Ayan spruce and the Siberian silver fir.

The town was renamed Mariinsk in 1857 after Tsar Alexander II's wife, Maria Alexandrovna.

There is a museum of local studies in town and a memorial to the locally born Soviet writer V A Chivilikhin.

Bogotol   Боготол   3,862

This railway town has a museum in its locomotive depot. The town was founded in 1893 as a station on the Trans-Siberian although there is a much older village of the same name 8km away.

Near Bogotol are brown coal deposits and open-cut mines can be seen scarring the landscape from the train.

For the next 100km the train runs along the northern side of the Chulim River. You finally cross the river as the train reaches Achinsk. About half way along this stretch, you will notice the train making a loop around the Agra Mountains which peak at 528m.

Achinsk 1   Ачинск 1   3,940km

Until the collapse of the Soviet Union, there were big plans for Achinsk and its region. Achinsk sits on the right bank of Chulym River and work was underway to convert the river into a chain of reservoirs along which a chain of industrial towns would rise. The area, known as the Prichulmskoye Ring, was expected to have a total population of 1 million. Achinsk was to be the centre of the ring as it sits on a major railway junction with a 174km line north to the forestry city of Lesosibirsk (which literally means "forest-Siberia") and a line south to the energy rich Kuznetski Alatai Mountain Range.

Achinsk itself is already a major industrial city with a giant aluminium production complex that can be seen from the railway.

The town's history can be found in the local museum which explains that a fortress to extract taxes from local tribes was founded nearby in 1681 but, following a fire two years later, it was moved to the present site. The name of the town derives from the local Tatar-Mongol's tribal name of Achig.

Underneath the town is the giant Achinsk-Kansk brown coal field which contains over 1,200 billion tons. The coal lies in massive seams normally about 30m wide but sometimes up to 100m wide. These are inexpensive to exploit and consequently this field may become the main supplier of inexpensive power coal in Russia. From the train, you can see open-cut fields mining these seams.

KRASNOYARSK   Красноярск   4,104km
Population: 929,000   Telephone area code: 3912

Krasnoyarsk is a major industrial centre which produces one-third of Russia's aluminium and almost a quarter of its refrigerators. Nevertheless the old part of the city is quite attractive.

Russian settlement dates back to 1628 when a fort was built here. It was situated on a hill overlooking the river and was first known as Krasny Yar meaning "beautiful steep bank". This name eventually evolved into Krasnoyarsk. Unfortunately, all traces of this fort have disappeared; there is now a chapel from the middle of the 19th century sitting on its location.

The city grew as a trading centre and during the Soviet's early five year plans, underwent massive industrialisation and grew into Siberia's third largest city.

Passing through

The Moscow-Vladivostok No 1/2 train stops here for 20 minutes.

After leaving the station, the train crosses over a 2.1km-long Enisei River bridge. The arched, concreted and metal bridge was completed in 1965 while work on the hump-backed bridge started in 1886. This old bridge took 94,000 workers three years to build. Along with the Eiffel Tower, the bridge was awarded a gold medal at the World Fair in Paris in 1900. From the bridge you can see both sides of the city and the port on the right.

After reaching the other bank, the train turns northward and instead of seeing the normal garages beside the railway line, you will notice underground cellars which have the entry via a hatch in their roof.

For the next 30 minutes you continue to travel through the industrial part of the city.

Getting there and away

The major Trans-Siberian trains on this segment are:

Origin	Dist, km	Train no & name	Travel time	Depart	Arrive	Destination
Krasnoyarsk	1,087	2	18hr 27min	06.10	0.37	Irkutsk
Irkutsk	1,087	1	18hr 42min	20.04	14.46	Krasnoyarsk
Krasnoyarsk	761	1	12hr 41min	15.16	03.57	Novosibirsk
Novosibirsk	761	2	12hr 55min	16.55	05.50	Krasnoyarsk

Where to stay

The best hotels are the standard Hotel Krasnoyarsk, ul Uritskovo 94, tel: 273 769, 273 754, $30 twin share/person; basic Hotel Turist, ul Matrossova 2, tel: 361 470, 361 830, $50 double room; and standard Hotel Oktyabrskaya, ul Mira 15, tel: 271 916, 276 968, $40 twin share/person.

One of two 2.1km-long railway bridges at Krasnoyarsk

Getting around

Krasnoyarsk is divided into two parts separated by the Enisei River. The left bank (western side) is a mass of terraces and is bounded on the north by a steep hill called Karaulnaya Mountain and on the west by the forested Gremiachinskaya Ridge; the railway station, museums and hotels are located on this side. Just south of the station is the academic region called Akademgorodok. The right bank (eastern side) is relatively flat and is mostly factories and multi-storey apartment blocks. Two bridges connect the two sides.

The airport is called Emelyanovo and is 30km to the north of the station.

What to see

The terraced hill around the old part of town is an interesting place to walk. The most interesting buildings here are the Annunciation Cathedral on ul Lenina and the old Catholic church where services are now held. To encourage the arts in Krasnoyarsk, an annual summer folklore festival was started in 1993.

There are a number of general museums including the Artists Exhibition Hall (also known as the Art Museum), ul Parizhskoi Kommuny 20, tel: 272 558, the City Exhibition Hall, the Museum of Local Studies, ul Dubrovinskovo 84, and the Estate-museum of the artist Vassili Surikov (1848-1916), ul Lenina 98, who was born here.

There are also three political museums: the House-museum of V I Lenin, who stayed here for all of two months between 1897 and 1898; the Apartment-museum of P A Krasikov, who was a revolutionary and at whose house Lenin once slept; and the Museum of *SS Nikolai*, the ship on which Lenin sailed to exile in Shushenkoe.

There is a narrow-gauge railway in a Krasnoyarsk park. This railway is just over a kilometre long and is used to teach children about the operation of the railways. It is open to the public in school summer holidays.

Getting assistance
Travel agents   Intourist, ul Uritskovo 94, tel: 273 715, 273 643.
Air   Aeroflot, ul Matrosova 4, tel: 222 156, 261 931, Krasnoyarsk Airlines, tel: 236-366, fax: 234-896
Boat   Yenisei Steamship Line, ul Bograda 15, tel: 236-651, fax: 236-883.

What's in the region
A few kilometres upstream of the Enisei River along the right bank is the 17,000-hectare Stolby Nature Sanctuary (Заповедные Столбы). On the river shores are a large number of rock pillars that look like people and have been given names like the Grandfather and the Woman. To get to this popular recreational area take the suburban train to Ovsyanka (Овсянка) station which is 5km from the city. Another way of getting there is to take bus No 7 from pl Predmostnaya. Hotel Turist is on Pl Predmostnaya which is at the south end of the road bridge across the Enisei River.

About 30km away on the railway past Stolby Nature Sanctuary is the town of Divnogorsk (Дивногорск). This is the site of the Enisei hydro-electric dam. Not only can you walk on the dam, but you can also visit the Museum of

---

THE SECRET KRASNOYARSKS
Around Krasnoyarsk are two secret cities also known as Krasnoyarsk.

The first is Krasnoyarsk-26 which is 64km to the north of Krasnoyarsk and can be reached by train from Bazaika station. Krasnoyarsk-26's rationale for existence was its three uranium graphite reactors which produced weapon-grade plutonium 239. The remote site of the town was selected because it was furthest from all of the Soviet Union's borders. The city, which now has a population of 97,500, has had several names in its lifetime. Originally in 1954 it was known as Enterprise 9, and a little later as Krasnoyarsk-26, while in secret documents it was referred to as Zheleznogorsk. Nowadays it is frequently called Atomograd.

The second secret city is Krasnoyarsk-45 (also known as Zelenogorsk) with a population of 64,000. It is 180km to the northeast of Krasnoyarsk and can be reached by train from Zaozernaya station. Founded in 1956 on the site of the former village of Ust-Barga, it has a military electronics factory, a hydro-electric station, and space centre.

the Dam's Construction. Regular passenger boats travel between Krasnoyarsk and Divnogorsk from May 1 to August 31, as do buses all year round from the long-distance bus station behind Hotel Krasnoyarsk. If you don't want to organise the trip yourself, contact either Krasnoyarsk's Intourist or Divnogorsk's Optimum Tourist Agency at ul Naberezhnaya 57, tel: (39144) 22 931, fax: (39144) 23 141.

Bazaika   Базаиха   4,126km

There is a branch line to the north from here to the secret city of Krasnoyarsk-26, also known as Atomograd. The line goes through Sotsgorod station and terminates at the industrial Gorknokhimicheski Chemical complex. Neither this line nor the city appear on Soviet maps.

Uyar   Уяр   4,237km

This small industrial town traces its history back to 1760. A few years later a post station was built nearby and soon the area was swarming with settlers from Latvia, Ukraine and the Volga region. The Trans-Siberian arrived in the late 1800s and in 1897 the station's name was changed to Olgino in honour of grand duchess Olga Nikolaevna. In 1906 it was renamed Klyukvenaya after the railway engineer who built this section of the railway; in 1973 its name was changed back to Uyar. At the western end of the station is a steam engine storage depot.

Zaozernaya   Заозёная   4,272km

Forty years ago, this town was more than twice its present size as several giant construction projects were underway. These included building the branch line to the north from here to the secret city of Krasnoyarsk-45 (also known as Zelenogorsk), the Krasnoyarsk No 2 hydro-electric station, and the massive Irsha-Borodinski open-cut brown coal mine.

After leaving the station, you will see the huge open-cut coal mines beside the track.

Kansk-Eniseiski   Канск-Енисейский   4,353km

This big town, known just as Kansk, had an inglorious start. In 1628, the original Kansk wooden fortress was built about 43km away from the present site of Kansk on the Kan River. The original site was badly chosen and in 1640 the fortress was moved. It was almost immediately burnt down by the Buryat indigenous people and, although it was rebuilt, in 1677 it was again burnt down.

Over the following two centuries the town became a major transit point for peasants settling in Siberia. It became an industrial centre during World War II when a number of plants were evacuated here away from the advancing Germans but, following the war, most were transported back westward. Today, the town has one of the biggest cotton works in the region, a mineral water plant and a museum of local studies. Near the city are 27 nuclear missile silos, each holding a SS-25 interballistic nuclear rocket. These missiles can carry their single 550kT nuclear warhead 10,500km with an accuracy of 200m.

Around the city was forest-steppe which has mostly been cleared for agriculture. In just the last 40 years, over 50% of the forest has been cut down.

Ilanskaya Иланская 4,383km

The site of the town was selected in 1734 by the Dutch-born, Russian naval explorer V Bering (of Bering Straits fame) during the time of the Second Kamchatski Expedition which was to explore the coast of America. It may seem strange that Bering was surveying central Siberia but he was ordered to make himself useful as he crossed the country to reach his ship in the Russian far east.

There is a museum at the locomotive depot which has a display of the history of the town.

Uralo-Klyuchi Урало-Ключи 4,473km

This small station's name translates as the "key to the Urals" and it sits on the border between Irkutsk and Krasnoyarsk Oblasts. This boundary also marks a time-zone border to the east of it; Moscow is five hours behind.

The railway gradually swings round from the east to the southeast as it heads towards Irkutsk. For the next 600km you will pass through one of Russia's biggest logging areas. Many of the rivers are used to float down the logs and you can often see log packs being towed down the river or piles of loose logs washed up on the river banks. This section of the line is very scenic as the train is constantly climbing and descending as it crosses numerous rivers and deep ravines.

Taishet Тайшет 4,522km

This town is at the junction of the Trans-Siberian and BAM railways (see *Chapter Fifteen, page 306*).

Uk Ук 4,656km

Two kilometres to the west of Uk is the halfway point between Moscow and Vladivostok on the Trans-Siberian. From here each end of the Trans-Siberian is 4,644.5km away.

Nizhneudinsk Нижнеудинск 4,683km

Near Nizhneudinsk is one of Siberia's most beautiful places, the Ukovskiy Waterfall. This waterfall is 18km upstream along the Ude River which flows through Nizhneudinsk. Here the water cascades down a series of stairs dropping a total of 20m into a very picturesque, narrow gorge. About 75km further upstream is another famous natural spot, the Nizhneudinskiye Caves. They are located 460m above the river as it runs through a steep valley and are often visited by historians because of their cave paintings.

The Tofalar indigenous people live in the region around Nizhneudinsk. The Tofalars, also known as the Tofy, number about 500, making them the smallest numbered of the Siberian indigenous peoples. They are mostly located in the isolated village of Tofalariya. There are no roads to this village which is 209km away and its only reliable link with the rest of the world is the helicopter service from Nizhneudinsk.

After leaving the town, you will notice a change in vegetation as the taiga yields to steppe land. This steppe is the main agricultural area in Irkutsk Oblast.

Tulun Тулун 4,802km

This town was once the breadbasket of the city of Yakutsk which is over 2,500km to the north. Crops were grown around Tulun and transported down several rivers to Yakutsk. Nowadays, goods no longer take this route.

Tulun sits at the road junction of the M55 Moscow–Irkutsk highway and the main road to the city of Bratsk 225km to the north.

Near the station is the town's centre which still consists of wooden houses. The apartment blocks are on the fringe of the town and surround the glassworks and other factories. There is also a museum dedicated to the Decembrists.

About 10km from the station on the right is another open-cut coal mine.

Zima   Зима   4,941km

The town's name means "winter" and at the beginning of the 19th century it was a place of exile for members of the Sectarians religious cult. The town has a museum.

About 3km to the east of the town, the railway crosses over the 790km-long Oka River. The river runs brown as it cuts through seams of coal and copperas (ferrous sulphate). The mineral-rich water and earth have their benefits as the water was used to blacken tanned skins and, during epidemics of cholera, the copperas earth was used as disinfectant. However, it also causes goitre (an enlargement of the thyroid gland on the front and sides of the neck) from which many locals suffer today. Down the Oka River, near the village of Burluksk, on the riverbanks are 1,000-year-old petroglyphs of riders, horses and cattle.

Kutulik   Кутулик   5,027km

This station is the biggest railway town in the Ust-Orda Buryat Nationality District. The Ust-Orda Buryats are related to the Buryats to the east of Lake Baikal and to the Mongolians, but they have a different language and culture. The best time to experience their lifestyle is during the Harvest Festival of Surkharban with its horse races, archery competitions and the Ust-Orda's peculiar brand of wrestling.

Kutulik has a museum which contains information on the Ust-Orda Buryats.

Cheremkhovo   Черемхово   5,061km

The town revolves around the Cheremkhovo coal deposit, and various mining and industrial complexes are dotted along 10km of the railway. The first mine can be seen from the railway about 20km east of the station. The local coal is not suitable for burning but is used as a raw material for various chemical industries.

The town's coal deposits were discovered soon after the town was founded in 1840, but very little of the coal was dug up until the arrival of the Trans-Siberian when, within a few years, 89 mines were sunk. However, all mining stopped during World War I and the Russian Civil War when the entire male population of the town was drafted into the armies. The mines were reopened in the 1930s and by 1939 the town's population reached a peak of 122,500. This decreased from 1949 onwards when the less labour-intensive open-cut mining was introduced.

The only reason travellers visit the town is to get to the small village of Belsk (Бельск) where a blackened watchtower is all that remains of a wooden Cossack fortress constructed in 1691. Belsk is 31km to the south and there are no buses there.

Polovina   Половина   5,087km

The station's name means "half" and it once marked the halfway point on the Trans-Siberian between Moscow and Vladivostok. Today, Moscow is 5,090km away and Vladivostok 4,212km. The reason for this discrepancy is that the station was named at a time when the Trans-Siberian ran to Moscow via Chelyabinsk and not Ekaterinburg and to Vladivostok via Manchuria, not along the banks of the Amur.

The village around the town is called Mikhailovka.

Malta   Мальта   5,110km
Starting in 1928 in Malta, which means "black alder place" in Buryat, archaeologists discovered a hut made of mammoth tusks and then an entire settlement from the Stone Age. Many of the discovered artefacts are on display in Irkutsk's history museum. On the left of the railway, you will catch your first glimpse of the Angara River.

Usole-Sibirskoe   Усолье-Сибирское   5,124km
This city, sitting on the left bank (western side) of the Angara River, is the salt capital of Siberia. Until 1956, all salt was produced by pumping salty water from shallow wells into salt pans which were left to evaporate. Nowadays, the salt is produced at a factory which is the biggest salt producer in Russia. It manufactures the "Russian Extra" brand of table salt which is common throughout the entire former Soviet Union. The town's other big industrial plant is the 150-year-old match factory which makes most of the matches sold in eastern Siberia.

Nearby is the famous Usolye health resort. During Soviet times about 5,000 people a year came here for its salt, sulphur and mud baths which cured afflictions of the limbs.

On the opposite side of the river is the nearly abandoned village of Alexandrovskoe which was renowned for the particularly brutal conditions of its Tsarist prison.

Telma   Тельма   5,133km
Siberia's first textile mill opened here in 1731 and still operates today, producing work clothing.

Angarsk   Ангарск   5,152km
During the Soviet era Angarsk was considered one of the best places to live due to its newness, good city planning and excellent facilities. The city is only 50 years old and sits on a picturesque valley on the right bank of the Kitoy River, near where it flows into the Angara River. Although it is primarily an industrial city, Angarsk is still very attractive as the industrial and civic parts of it are separated by a wide green belt. From the station, the industrial area is on the left (eastern side) and civic area on the right. The centre of the town consists of attractive four-storey 1950s style apartment blocks surrounded by squares and wide streets while the new suburbs consist of the usual, ugly nine- and 12-storey flats.

Angarsk's major industry is oil refining and oil is pumped here by pipeline from the West Siberian, Tatarstan and Baskir oil fields. This pipeline can occasionally be spotted running beside the train.

The city has a river port and from here hydrofoils used to travel as far as Bratsk. In 1993 they ceased but they may be resumed in the future. There are several ferries a day which travel the river, stopping off at various small towns. Ferries travel between Irkutsk and Angarsk, and visiting here from Irkutsk makes a pleasant day trip.

Meget   Мегет   5,180km
Just before arriving at Meget you pass a steam engine storage depot on the left side of the railway.

IRKUTSK   Иркутск   5,191km
Population: 639,000   Telephone area code: 3952

Of all the cities on the Trans-Siberian, this is the most interesting. Not only is the town full of fascinating museums, buildings and monuments, but just 65km away is the beautiful Lake Baikal.

The city was founded in 1651 as a Cossack fort and the region's rich gold and fur resources resulted in the town growing quickly into a rich but dangerous place. The ramshackle layout of the city changed on a mild sunny day in July 1879 when fire broke out. Within 24 hours, three-quarters of the town had burned to the ground and over 20,000 of the town's 34,000 inhabitants were homeless. The fire gave a new lease of life to Irkutsk as it adopted a town plan and passed a law stating that from then on only stone buildings could be built. Today, the centre of Irkutsk contains mostly 19th-century buildings which makes it feel much like an old European city.

The best time to visit Irkutsk is in the warmer months from April to October, but remember that the boats only ply Lake Baikal from mid-May to September. If you are going in winter, go between December 25 and January 5 which is when Irkutsk has its Winter Festival. This is a tourist event of troika rides, folk dances and concert performance.

Passing through
The Moscow-Vladivostok No 1/2 train stops here for 20 minutes.

From the railway you cannot see much of the centre of Irkutsk on the left as it is located on the other side of the Angara River along which the train passes. However, in the distance you can see a large church, the functioning Church of the Elevation of the Cross which dates from the middle of the 18th century.

Getting there and away
By air   There is a once-weekly flight to Niigata, Japan on Aeroflot.
By rail   The major Trans-Siberian trains on this segment are:

Origin	Dist, km	Train no & name	Travel time	Depart	Arrive	Destination
Krasnoyarsk	1,087	2	18hr 27min	06.10	00.37	Irkutsk
Irkutsk	1,087	1	18hr 42min	20.04	14.46	Krasnoyarsk
Irkutsk	446	2	7hr 43min	00.57	08.50	Ulan-Ude
Ulan-Ude	446	1	7hr 46min	11.54	19.40	Irkutsk

Where to stay
The best hotel in Irkutsk is the excellent Iris Hotel, ul Lermontova 337, tel: 462 569, fax: 461 762, $30 twin share/person. To get to the hotel take trolleybus No 1, 2 or 7 from pl Kirova or trolleybus No 6 from the airport. Another popular choice is the excellent Hotel Intourist, bul Gagarina 44, tel: 295 335, $90 a double. A bad hotel is the basic Hotel Angara, ul Sukhe Batora 7, tel: 241 631, $50 a double room. The Hotel Sibir, ul Lenina 8, was destroyed by fire in the summer of 1995 but it may be rebuilt. All the above hotels have restaurants.

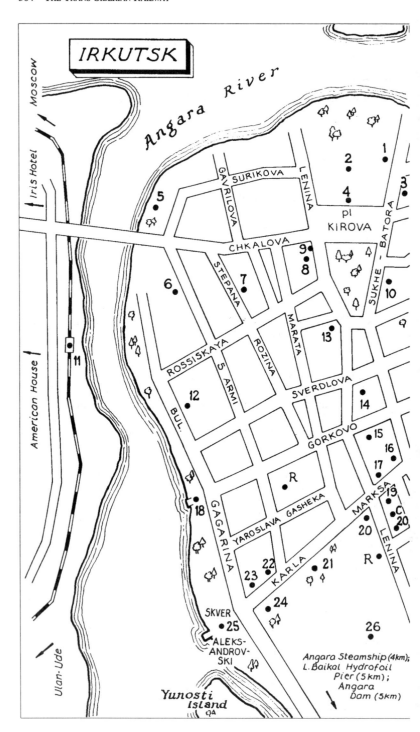

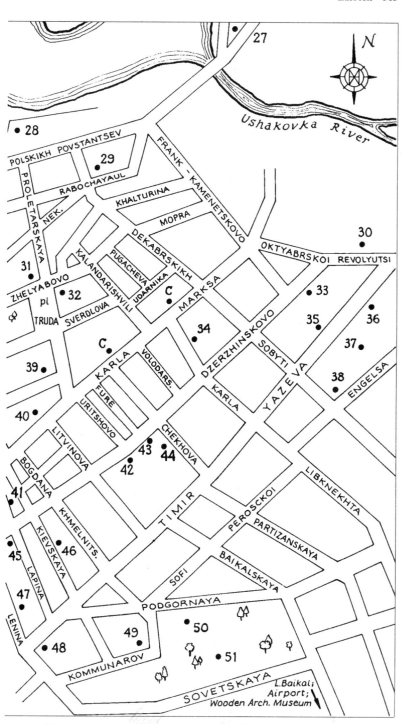

KEY TO IRKUTSK   Иркутск

1	Museum of Local Studies (*Muzei*) in Saviour Church	Краведческий музей-Спасская церковь
2	World War II memorial	Мемориальный комплекс 1941-1945
3	Hall of Organ Music (*Organy Zal*) in Polish Catholic Cathedral	Органный зал-Польский костёл
4	Government headquarters	Правительственный дом
5	River station (*Rechnoi Vokzal*)	Речной вокзал
6	Planetarium (*Planetari*) in the Trinity Church	Планетарий Троицкый церкови
7	Post office (*Pochtamt*)	Почтамт
8	Teaching Institute of Foreign Languages (*Institut*)	Педагогический институт иностранных языков
9	Kirov Square bus stop	Остановка «пл Кирова»
10	Hotel Angara	гостинца Ангара
11	Railway station (*Vokzal*)	Ж-Д вокзал
12	Hotel Intourist	гостиница Интурист
13	Hotel Sibir	гостиница Сибирь
14	Art Museum (*Muzei*)	Художественный музей
15	Youth Theatre (*Teatr*)	Театр юного зрителя
16	Museum of Local Studies (*Muzei*)	Краведческий музей
17	Institute of Economics (*Institute*)	Институт народного хозяйства
18	Gagarin Pier (*Prichal Gagarina*)	Причал Гагарина
19	Former Russia-Asia Bank	Быв. Русско-Азиатский банк
20	Book shop (*Knigi*)	Книги
21	Drama Theatre (*Teatr*)	Драматический театр
22	Irkutsk University (*Universitet*)	Университет
23	White House (*Bely Dom*)	Белый дом
24	Museum of Russian Geology Society (*Teatr*)	Музей Руссково Географического общества
25	Trans-Siberian Builders' Monument (*Obelisk*)	Обелиск строителям Транссибирской магистрали
26	Stadium Trud	Стадион
27	The Apparition of the Virgin (*Znamenski*) Monastery	Знаменский монастырь
28	Icon Museum (*Muzei*) in Epiphany Cathedral	Музей икон-Бороявленский собор
29	Church of Vladimir (*Vladimirskaya*)	Владимирская церковь
30	Bus station (*Avtovokzal*)	Автовокзал
31	Palace of the Pioneers (*Dvorets*)	Дворец пионеров
32	Circus (*Tsirk*)	Цирк
33	Museum –Estate of Trubetskoi (*Muzei*)	Музей-усадьба Трубецкого
34	Synagogue	Синагога
35	Agricultural Institute (*Institut*)	Сельскохозяйственный институт
36	Church of the Transfiguration (*Preobrazhenskaya*)	Преображенская церковь
37	Museum House of Volkonski (*Muzei*)	Музей-усадьба Волконского
38	Former house of Shastin	Быв. дом Шастина
39	Aeroflot	Аэрофлот
40	Exhibition Hall of Art Museum (*Muzei*)	Выставочный зал Художественного музея
41	Mongolian Consulate (*Kulsulstvo*)	Кулсульство Монголии
42	Trade Centre (*Torgovy kompleks*)	Торговый комплекс
43	Former residence of Kuznetsov	Быв. особняк Кузнецова
44	Market (*Rynok*)	Рынок
45	Philharmonic Hall (*Filarmoniya*)	Филармония
46	Former residence of Shubin	Быв. особняк Шубина
47	Musical Comedy Theatre (*Teatr*)	Театр музыкальной комедии
48	Church of the Elevation of the Cross (*Krestovozdvezhenskaya*)	Крестовоздвеженская церковь
49	1917 Revolutionary Monument	Памятник борцам революции
50	Churches of the Entry into Jerusalem (*Vkhodoierusalimskaya*)	Входоиерусалимская церковь
51	Central Park	Центральный парк
R	Restaurant (*Restoran*)	Ресторан
C	Café (*Kafé*) or Bar (*Bar*)	Кафе или Бар

Other choices outside the centre of the city are the very basic Hotel Profkurs, ul Baikalskaya 263, tel: 235 566 ext 362, near the Raketa Hydrofoil Pier; very basic Hotel DOSSAF, ul Kultukskaya 9B, tel: 272 740, 270 020, $7 a dormitory bed; and the bed and breakfast American House, ul Ostrovski 19, tel: 432 689, $15 a bed.You can also stay at the standard Hotel Baikal, tel: 296 234, which is actually on the shores of Lake Baikal. For information on this hotel, see below under Lake Baikal.

Getting around
Irkutsk is divided in two by the wide Angara River which is the only outlet from Lake Baikal. The railway station, university institutes and new apartment blocks are on the left bank and the city's centre, hotels and river stations are on the right bank. The centre of the city really sits on a river promontory, bordered on two sides by the Angara River and by the Ushakhovka River on the third. The city centre is along two intersected main streets: ul Lenina and ul Karla Marksa. Ul Lenina runs north–south from the administrative and public transport centre of pl Kirova, while the main shopping and museum street of ul Karla Marksa runs east–west.

To get from the railway station to pl Kirova in the centre of town, catch tram No 1 or 2, or bus No 20. Bus No 20 continues past pl Kirova to the town airport and the trip takes 40 minutes. Trolleybus No 4 also goes to the airport, departing from in front of Hotel Sibir.

What to see
The Epiphany Cathedral, on the corner of ul Sukhe-Batora and ul Nizhnyaya Haberezhnaya, is now a practising church.

The Saviour Church at ul Sukhe-Batora just north of pl Kirova is more than three centuries old and is considered to be the oldest stone structure in the city. It now houses the Museum of Local Studies with a very interesting exhibition on the rural life of the indigenous people that populated Siberia.

The Polish Catholic Cathedral, on ul Sukhe-Batora and just east of pl Kirova, now houses a hall of organ music, and functions on Sundays as a church for the descendants of Poles exiled to Siberia. During summer there are often afternoon organ concerts in this church. These are usually held on Sundays and Wednesdays, starting around 19.30, and feature works of classical as well as of contemporary composers.

The Art Museum, ul Lenina 5, open 10.00–18.00, closed Tuesday, has the most impressive painting collection in Siberia. There is also a branch of the museum, the Exhibition Hall of the Art Museum, nearby on ul Karla Marksa.

The Museum of Local Studies, ul Karla Marksa 11, open 10.00–18.00, closed Monday, has re-creations of rooms in various periods of the city's history and is definitely one of the better local museums in Siberia.

The Apparition of the Virgin Monastery is the headquarters of the local Russian Orthodox diocese and in its graveyard are numerous tombs of Decembrists, revolutionaries and Tsarist officials. It is located to the north of the city centre over the Ushakovka River. To get there take trolleybus No 3 from the south end of pl Kirova.

There are two museums dedicated to the 25 revolutionary Decembrists who were exiled to Irkutsk in 1825. These museums are the Museum House of Prince Sergei and Princess Ekaterina Trubetskoi, ul Dzerzhinskovo 64, open 10.00–18.00, closed Tuesday, and the Museum House of Sergi G Volkonski, per

Volkhonskovo 10, open 10.00–18.00, closed Monday. The Decembrists had an enormous impact on the city as they belonged to the Russian nobility and brought with them European thought, customs and way of life.

Although it is not now a museum, the *Angara* steamship is worth seeing. The ship was the icebreaker ferry that carried Trans-Siberian railway passengers between Irkutsk and the other side of Lake Baikal before the Circumbaikal railway connected the two places. The *Angara* was built in England, disassembled and carted across Russia on the railways, reassembled at Port Baikal in 1899 and operated for just five years. To get to the *Angara*, take bus No 16 south from pl Kirov, and get off at the first stop past the ship. The bus trip takes 45 minutes. The *Angara* is now the office of a local newspaper.

The Church of the Elevation of the Cross, ul Sedova, dates from the middle of the 18th century and is still functioning.

The Fur Distribution Centre processes one-third of Siberia's fur harvest and you can get a tour to see hundreds of sable, mink and muskrat pelts. The building can only be visited in a group from October to May; Intourist can organise this.

The Church of the Elevation of the Cross

Getting assistance

Travel agents   Baikal Complex, PO Box 3598, Irkutsk-29, tel: 464 762, 354 417, 432 060, fax: 432 060, 432 322 (marked att Baikalcomplex), email youry@baikal.irkutsk.su. As it can be very hard to get through by fax to Irkutsk, you can also contact them on the Moscow fax: (095) 531 2401 but it is essential that you write BOX 4411 in the top left hand corner of your fax. Baikal Complex offers a range of one-day trips and adventure tours such as hiking, skiing and trekking from $44 per day per person for two to four people in a group. Intourist is located in the Hotel Intourist, bul Gagarina 44, tel: 290 266, fax: 277 872.

Air   Aeroflot, ul Gorkovo 29, tel: 242 535. Next door to Aeroflot are the offices of the new airline, Air Baikal. This company is a subsidiary of Aeroflot, but offers a much better (and possibly safer) service, operating a Boeing 757 on the Moscow–Irkutsk route.

Diplomatic representation   Mongolian Consulate, ul Lapina 11, tel: 242 370 (embassy), 342 145 (consulate), open 09.00–18.00 weekdays. It is possible to get a Mongolian transit visa from here if you have a through railway ticket, two passport photos and $30. It is best to take along a Russian speaker.

What's in the region
Boat trips

Rivers are navigable from mid May to September. There are three river stations in Irkutsk, and from each the boats go to different destinations.

Scenic cruises   Scenic cruises depart from Gagarin Pier which is located at the intersection of bul Gagarina and ul Gorkovo. Boats from here travel upstream to the Angara hydro-electric power station dam and departures for the 1hr 20min return-trip leave hourly. Tickets are bought at the pier.

Long-distance Angara river trips   Boats that travel down the Angara River depart from River Station. This is located at the base of the bridge over the Angara River. When you cross over this bridge from the railway station, you will see it on the left. To get to it from pl Kirova, walk down ul Chkalova which is the road that runs into the Angara River bridge. Avoid this area after dark as it's notoriously dangerous. In the past, there used to be hydrofoils from here as far as Bratsk which is 13 hours away but many of these routes have been cancelled as they were unprofitable.

Lake Baikal trips   Boats for Lake Baikal depart from Hydrofoil Pier, which is located above the Angara dam, 5km upstream (to the south) of Irkutsk. There are three different routes from this pier. Hydrofoils from here depart for Bolshoe Kotu (Бол. Коты) on Lake Baikal via Listvyanka once a day in June and July, and twice a day in August. This timetable was running in 1994 and 1995. There used to be hydrofoils that travelled between Irkutsk and Listvyanka every 1hr 30min but these no longer run. Nowadays, there are no ferries plying between Irkutsk and Port Baikal. To get to Hydrofoil Pier take bus No 16 from pl Kirova. It goes past the *Angara* steamship before stopping at the pier. The bus trip takes 45 minutes.

Shishkino rock paintings

About 200km north of Irkutsk are some of Russia's most famous petroglyphs. The rock drawings, dating from the Neolithic Period to the Bronze Age, provide a fascinating insight into indigenous people's lives and beliefs over thousands of years. The majority of the drawings are of elks, deer and humans.

To get to the rock paintings is not easy but is worth the effort. The best way to do it is by hiring a car from Irkutsk. If you want to try it by public transport, take a bus from Irkutsk's long-distance bus station to Kachug which is 257km north of Irkutsk. From here take a bus or boat from Kachug towards the major town of Zhigalovo and get off part way at Shishkino. The rock paintings are about 2km from Shishkino. Regular ferries used to ply the waters between Kachug and Zhigalovo but now run sporadically.

There is a hotel at the river station in Zhigalovo and hydrofoils travel irregularly from here down the Lena River to Ust-Kut on the BAM railway 600km to the north. Check the timetable before you depart.

For detailed information on this trip, see the *Siberian Lena and Amur Rivers Guide* by Athol Yates.

Wooden Architecture Museum

About 47km from Irkutsk on the main highway to Lake Baikal is the Wooden Architecture Museum. This museum contains dozens of wooden buildings built over the last few centuries. Most are original buildings that have been moved here, but there are a number of replicas such as the main gatehouse from Irkutsk's original fortress of the 17th century, and a merchant's house which was used as a set for an American film. At the southern end of the museum is the path which leads to the banks of the Angara River where there is an excellent soft sand beach. It's worth a visit in the heat of summer.

To get to the museum, take a bus to Listvyanka from the long-distance bus station on ul Oktyabrskoi Revolutsi and get off at the 47km road marker. This is a request-only stop so you have to tell the driver *moozay* which means "museum". The bus trip takes about an hour and there are about three or four buses a day. The first bus departs from Irkutsk at 09.00 and from Listvyanka at 07.00 with the last departing from Irkutsk at 19.00 and Listvyanka at 18.05.

LAKE BAIKAL, LISTVYANKA AND PORT BAIKAL

Lake Baikal is one of the most beautiful and fascinating places in Russia. In the legends and fairy tales of native Siberians, the lake is very often referred to as the "Pearl of Siberia" due to its uniquely pure water. It is the largest freshwater lake on earth and contains 18% of the world's surface fresh water.

It is also the world's deepest lake with a depth of 1,637m. As the maximum width is only 80km, the lake's floor is extremely steep. The lake is scientifically fascinating as it is home to a staggering number of different species. These include 1,085 types of algae, 250 mosses, 450 lichens, 1,500 vascullar plants, 255 small crustaceans, 83 gastropods, 86 worms and 52 fish. Of these, 75% are unique to the lake with the strangest being the small fish called *golomyanka* which is little more than a small transparent ball of fat which can withstand pressures at depths of 1,500m. Another unique species is the freshwater Baikal seal which is one of only two freshwater seals in the world (see *Chapter Fifteen, page 313*).

Getting there and away

By boat   These are explained above under *Boat trips, page 368*.

There is also a hydrofoil which plies between Port Baikal and Severobaikalsk at the northern end of Lake Baikal. It is an interesting ride for, although it has only one official stop on the lake, the hydrofoil will stop anywhere en route for anyone who prearranges it. For this reason, when you are travelling on the hydrofoil, you will see motor boats meeting your vessel in the middle of the lake and transferring mail, food or passengers. For many isolated communities and individual hunters, the hydrofoil is their only link with the rest of the world. The one official stop on the trip is halfway down the lake at Bukhta Bazarnaya (Бухта Базарная) which is on the mainland near Olkhon Island (Остров Ольхона). There are basic cabins for rent, a camping site and a canteen at this stop.

Severobaikalsk is a major city on the BAM railway and is an excellent place from which to explore the north Lake Baikal region and go seal watching (*see Chapter Fifteen, page 311*).

Tickets for the hydrofoil cannot be booked in advance and have to be bought on board or at the quay, so it is a good idea to get to the pier early and stand in the queue. There is only one hydrofoil and it takes the whole day to travel the length of the lake. Departures from each end leave every second day.

From Port Baikal, a local river hydrofoil takes passengers down the Angara River to Irkutsk. There is no accommodation at Port Baikal but if you can travel across the river to Listvyanka, or get off the hydrofoil when, and if, it docks there, you can stay at Intourist's Hotel Baikal there.

The hydrofoil departs every second day, at the following times:

From P Baikal			From Severobaikalsk		
Arrive	Depart	Place	Depart	Arrive	Dist, (km)
–	09.20	Port Baikal	–	17.30	628
09.30	09.40	Listvyanka	17.20	17.10	621
13.30	13.40	Buxta Bazarnaya	13.20	13.10	403
19.50	20.00	Severobaikalsk	07.00	06.40	18
20.20	–	Nizhneangarsk	06.20	–	0

By road   Buses for Lake Baikal depart from Irkutsk's long-distance bus station on ul Oktyabrskoi Revolutsi. The bus trip takes about 1 hr 30min and there are about three or four buses per day. The first bus departs from Irkutsk at 09.00 and from Listvyanka at 07.00 with the last departing from Irkutsk at 19.00 and Listvyanka at 18.05. The bus will stop on request virtually anywhere, with major stops at the Limnological Institute, Listvyanka village and Listvyanka pier.

Where to stay
The only hotel is at Listvyanka and is the standard Hotel Baikal, tel: (3952) 290 391, 296 234, $54 twin share/person. The hotel also has a restaurant. It is an Intourist hotel and is on the hill behind the Limnological Institute. It is about 3km from the hotel to the Listvyanka pier. Baikal Complex of Irkutsk offers homestay in Listvyanka village from $25 per person including meals.

Getting around
Four ferries a day run between Port Baikal and Listvyanka. The first leaves Port Baikal at 06.30 and Listvyanka at 07.00, and the last leaves Port Baikal at 20.00 and Listvyanka at 20.30.

What to see
Limnological Institute and Museum
The institute was established to study the lake and its life but its research has been curtailed in the last few years as state funding has been reduced considerably. Fortunately, the financial crisis has not yet been reflected in the museum attached to the institute. Its great exhibits include strange fish, the Baikal seal, and models of the Baikal's fishing ships.

Listvyanka village and church
This small village is typical of the beautiful villages ringing Lake Baikal. It consists mostly of delightfully painted, single-storey, wooden houses with intricate wood carvings. Listvyanka was the first Russian settlement on Lake Baikal and boasts the lake's oldest church. During the communist period the church remained open, probably for its tourist potential. The Church of St Nicholas contains a number of icons from the region and holds regular services.

The Shaman Stone
At the mouth of the Angara River, near the place where water from Lake Baikal flows, you can see a large stone coming out of the water close to the eastern bank. Before the construction of the Angara River dam it stood 2m out of the water but today it takes a careful eye to spot it. According to legends of the indigenous

Buryat people, the rock was thrown by the angry father, Baikal, when he tried to prevent his daughter, Angara, from leaving him to meet her lover, Yenisey. The Shaman Stone is visible from the road near the Limnological Museum.

Port Baikal village
Opposite Listvyanka on the other side of the Angara River is the attractive village of Port Baikal. This is the terminus of the Circumbaikal railway which runs 94km to Slyudyanka on the Trans-Siberian (see *Chapter Seventeen, page 420*).

Goncharovo   Гончарово   5,214km
The town around the station is named Shelekhov (Шелехов) after the Russian merchant G I Shelekhov (1747-1795) who led several trading expeditions to North America from 1783 to 1786 and became the governor of the Russian settlement in Russian America. He quickly become one of the richest merchants in Siberia and based his empire in Irkutsk.

Passing through the town, you can see the town's main industry, the giant aluminium complex, and the train soon starts twisting and turning as it climbs the Primorski Mountains.

Slyudyanka 1   Слюдянка 1   5,317km
From this small town, the 94km Circumbaikal railway branch line originates and travels along the shore of Lake Baikal to Port Baikal (see *Chapter Seventeen, page 420*). From Slyudyanka station the shores of Lake Baikal are only 500m away and a quick return walk takes about 15 minutes. If the train departs before you get back, you can always stay in the town's basic hotel. Slyudyanka is a starting point for hikers and rafters who travel through the Khamar-Daban Mountain Range to the south.

The train passes through a short tunnel and runs within sight of the water's edge for the next 180km.

Baikalsk   Байкальск   5,358km
There is a basic hotel here and it is a launching place for walks and rafting in the nearby Khamar-Daban Mountain Range.

About 3km past the town on the left is Lake Baikal's biggest environmental enemy, the Baikalsk cellulose and paper mill, which makes an extremely strong cellulose used in aircraft manufacture. It pumps its chlorine-contaminated waste-water directly into the lake and has caused the number of crustacean species within a 50km radius of the factory to drop from 57 to five, according to the Limnological Institute near Irkutsk. Not surprisingly, the plant was the brainchild of the environmental vandal Khrushchev who wanted to "put Baikal to work".

Baikalsk has a sister city relationship with South Lake Tahoe, California.

Vydrino   Выдрино   5,390km
The river just before the station marks the border of the Buryat Republic, which is the homeland of the Buryat indigenous people.

Tankhoi   Танхой   5,426km
Tankhoi sits in the middle of the 263,300ha Baikalski Nature Reserve which was created to preserve the Siberian taiga. Occasional ferries travel from here to Listvyanka and Port Baikal.

Mysovaya   Мысовая   5,483km

The village surrounding the town is known as Babushkin (Бабушкин) in honour of Lenin's friend and Irkutsk revolutionary, Ivan Babushkin, who was executed by Tsarist forces at the railway depot in 1906. An obelisk markes the spot. While there is a major port at Mysovaya, over 70% of the village's population works for the railways.

Boyarski   Боярский   5,504km

The hills on the right of the station are all that remain of the volcanos of the Khamar-Daban foothills. After leaving the station, the railway moves away from Lake Baikal.

Posolskaya   Посольская   5,530km

About 500m before reaching this station, the train crosses over a narrow, shallow river with the strange name of Bolshaya Rechka which translates as "big little stream". Approximately 10km downstream from here the river flows into Lake Baikal and this was the site of the ancient village of Possolskoe. In previous centuries, Russian ambassadors travelling to Asian countries used to rest here and the rough village got a mention in the papers of Ambassador Fyodor Baikov when he visited it in 1656.

Selenga   Селенга   5,568km

The town sits on the Selenga River which carries industrial waste and sewage from Ulan Ude and all the other river settlements into Lake Baikal. Pollution from the Selenga and the cellulose and paper mill at Baikalsk has affected over 60% of the lake; even if the pollution stopped tomorrow, the slow flows in and out of the lake would mean that it would take 400 years for the waste to be flushed out.

Lesovozny   Лесовозный   5,596km

The town around the station is called Ilnika (Ильинка). About 28km east of the station, the train crosses over the Selenga River providing an excellent photo opportunity.

ULAN-UDE   Улан-Уде   5,647km
Population: 366,000   Telephone area code: 30122

There are two reasons to visit Ulan-Ude: to see the world's largest Lenin head and visit Russia's main Tibetan Buddhist monastery.

Ulan-Ude is the capital of the Buryat Autonomous Republic which is allegedly the Buryat indigenous people's homeland. The level of indigenous self-determination is open to question as Buryats make up only 21% of the population. Buryats are closely related to Mongols and colonised the region during Ghengis Khan's time by evicting the indigenous Siberian tribes.

Russian colonisation started in 1666 when a winter base was founded here for further eastward exploration. In 1783 the town became known as Verkhneudinsk. The city grew quickly as it was on the main China–Irkutsk tea caravan route and development accelerated with the arrival of the Trans-Siberian in 1899. Until 1905 the city was also a place of exile of many educated revolutionaries which contributed significantly to its cultural development. During the Russian Civil War, communist forces took over briefly in 1918 before White forces backed by American troops took control. As a political settlement and to provide a buffer to Japan, the city became the capital of the Far East Republic which existed for just seven months in 1920 before being absorbed into the Soviet Union.

In 1934, the city's name was changed to Ulan-Ude, meaning "red Uda River". Until 1989, the city was closed to foreigners but nowadays it is so popular that it has become the second most visited eastern Siberian city after Irkutsk.

The best time of year to visit Ulan-Ude is during one of the six yearly Buddhist festivals, known as *hurals*. The biggest is held at the end of February during which they celebrate the Buddhist New Year, called Tsagaalgan, for 16 days. In July there is a two-day festival dedicated to the Maitreya who is the Buddha of the Future, a festival of Buryat and Russian folk music and dance which is held at the open-air ethnographic museum, and a riding and archery festival called Sukharban.

Passing through

The train approaches Ulan-Ude along the right bank (northern side) of the Selenga River and about 1km on the left before the station is a monument to five railway workers executed by the Tsarist forces in 1906 for their revolutionary activities during the failed 1905 Russian revolution. A little further on, again on the left, is the railway factory and out the front is a monument to the railway workers who died during World War II.

The train only stops in Ulan-Ude for a few minutes which is not enough time to leave the platform.

Within 2km of leaving the station, you cross over the Uda River and after another 500m, you see on the left the Palace of Culture with another World War II memorial in front.

Getting there and away

The major Trans-Siberian trains on this segment are:

Origin	Dist, km	Train no & name	Travel time	Depart	Arrive	Destination
Ulan-Ude	557	2	9hr 4min	08.50	17.54	Chita 2
Chita 2	557	1	9hr 34min	02.20	11.54	Ulan-Ude
Irkutsk	446	2	7hr 43min	00.57	8.50	Ulan-Ude
Ulan-Ude	446	1	7hr 46min	11:54	19.40	Irkutsk

Where to stay

The best hotels are the standard Hotel Buryatia, pr Pobedy, tel: 218 35, $23 twin share/person, and the standard Hotel Geser, ul Ranzhurova 12, tel: 258 35, 281 51, $25 twin share/person, both of which have restaurants. Other choices are the basic Hotel Barbuzin, ul Sovetskaya 28, tel: 219 58, 208 09, 257 47, 281 03, $12 twin share/person; the basic Hotel Baikal, ul Erbanova 12, tel: 280 44, 237 18, $14 twin share/person; the very basic Hotel Odon, ul Gagarina 43, tel: 434 80, $5 twin share/person, and very basic Hotel Zolotoi Kolos, ul Sverdlova 34.

Getting around

The station is to the north of the city centre and to get to it takes 15 minutes on foot. From the station, take the pedestrian bridge over the track and continue down the street directly in front of it. This leads to pl Sovetov. Alternatively, from in front of the station you can catch bus No 7 or 10 which runs along pl

Sovetov and past Hotel Baikal. Bus No 7 terminates at the central bus station and bus No 10 continues on to the airport. Bus No 35 travels between the airport and pl Sovetov.

What to see
The giant head of Lenin on pl Sovetov is the largest sculpture of a body part of Lenin in the world. According to one legend, the original idea was to build the largest Lenin in the world in Ulan-Ude but when the head was finished, it was realised that the earthquake-prone region might result in a giant Lenin falling over and bringing down with it many Communist Party leaders as well.

About 6km to the north of Ulan-Ude is the Open-Air Ethnographic Museum, tel: 357 54, open 10.00–18.00 in summer and 10.00–17.00 in winter. This 40-hectare museum contains dozens of wooden buildings from past centuries, including those built by both the Buryat and Evenk indigenous peoples and Russians. There are also live animals at the museum including yaks, caribou and camels. To get there take bus No 35 from pl Sovetov which goes directly to the museum or the more frequent bus No 8 which drops you off at a T-junction and the museum is located about 500m down the T's base. The walk takes about 20 minutes.

Other interesting museums are the History Museum, ul Profsoyuznaya 29, tel: 221 70, 240 08; the Buryat Art Museum, ul Kuibysheva 29, tel: 229 09, open 10.00–19.00, closed Monday; the Geological Museum, ul Lenina 57, open 10.00–16.00, Tuesday and Friday only; and the Nature Museum, ul Lenina 46, tel: 280 49, open 10.00–18.00, closed Monday and Tuesday.

Interesting buildings include the Virgin Hodegetria Cathedral which was built from 1745 to 1785, and is now being renovated. Beside the cathedral is a Children's Playground with giant sculptures of Russian folk characters. The Opera and Ballet Theatre has excellent socialist paintings and murals inside. The theatre was built by some of the 18,000 Japanese prisoners of war who were interned in Buryatiya between 1945 and 1948. The Trinity Church has recently been reopened for services and the Traders Row and Arcade, built from 1803 to 1856, house a number of cafés and shops including the Buryat Crafts Store. Other places to pick up souvenirs are Art Store, ul Lenina 33, Podarki Gift Shop, ul Lenina 40, Yantar Amber Jewellery Store, ul Lenina 40 and the book shop, ul Lenina.

Performances can be seen at the Philharmonic Hall, ul Lenina 56, tel: 218 93; Puppet Theatre, ul Pushkina 3a, tel: 222 92; Buryat Drama Theatre, ul Kuibysheva 38, tel: 248 37; and Russian Drama Theatre, ul Tereshkovoi 1, tel: 302 10. The Russian Drama Theatre is about 1km to the south and to get to it catch tram No 1, 2, 4 or 7.

Railway factory
Ulan-Ude's railway factory is definitely worth a visit even if you are not interested in trains. The conditions under which people work are surprising, as is the age of most of the equipment.

The factory was founded in 1932 to repair locomotives and passenger carriages and from 1938 to 1956 it built large SO-series freight steam locomotives. After a massive refit in 1959, the factory concentrated on rebuilding electric locomotives and passenger carriages. Today, the factory now repairs VL60 and VL80 locomotives and passenger carriages.

PERMAFROST: THE ENEMY OF BUILDERS

The Trans-Siberian builders first encountered a mysterious problem in Petrovski Zavod which was to plague them and all future builders in eastern and northern Siberia. After a few years all of Petrovsk-Zabaikalski's brick buildings, including the railway depot, the workshops and the forge, fell into ruin for unknown reasons. It was only after buildings to the east fell apart and many years of research the culprit was revealed: permafrost.

Permafrost is ground that is frozen throughout the year, and the greatest depth of permafrost in eastern Siberia is 1.5km. Permafrost has an active layer of about 2m which thaws every spring and freezes each winter. The soil or rock below this active layer never melts, and has a constant temperature of −4°C. Unlike northern Siberian, permafrost in the Trans-Siberian region only occurs as small islands of 10–40m². The solution was simply for the railway builders to bypass these islands and this explains some of the meanderings of the railway.

Intourist organises visits to the factory for about $10 per person.

You can also see one of the factory's steam engines as a monument on the right-hand side of the road as you travel out to the open-air ethnographic museum.

Russia's Buddhist capital

The Tibetan Buddhist Ivolginsk monastery is one of the two largest *datsans* in Russia. Before the communist revolution, there were 56 such *datsans* but now there are only about four. The Ivolginsk Datsan was opened in 1946 and is extremely interesting. It consists of a museum, temples, prayer wheels, a library, café and monks quarters. Of special interest is a tree, allegedly a graft of the tree under which Buddha gained enlightenment, and Buddhist *tangkas* (icon tapestries). The *datsan* is open 09.00–15.00 and vistors are welcome even during ceremonies which normally start at 08.00 and last for about three hours. To appreciate fully the significance of all elements of the *datsan*, it is advisable to do a tour. Intourist provides a Buryat guide and car for the four-hour trip which costs $80 per carload.

To get there yourself take bus No 104 which passes the datsan before terminating at Kalenovo village. There are three departures a day from the Ulan-Ude central bus station and the trip takes 45 minutes. Another, less convenient option is to catch bus No 130 which runs past Ivolga village. From here walk straight ahead out of the village for about 3km, then turn right and you can see the *datsan*.

Getting assistance

Travel agents   Intourist is located in Hotel Geser, ul Ranzhurova 12, tel: 292 67; Sputnik Travel, pr Pobedy 9, tel: 208 34.

Air   Aeroflot, ul Yerbanova 14, tel: 222 48, 266 00.

Bus   Bus station, ul Sovetskaya 1, tel: 221 85.

Rail   Train station, tel: 431 37.

Diplomatic representation   Mongolian consulate, 2nd floor, Hotel Baikal, ul Erbanova 12.

Zaudinski   Заудинский   5,655km

The line to Mongolia branches off from the Trans-Siberian here (see *Chapter Seventeen, page 406*).

Novoilinski   Новоильинский   5,734km

About 20km further on the train crosses the border between the Republic of Buryatia and Chita Oblast . This boundary also marks a time-zone border to the east of it; Moscow is six hours behind local time.

Petrovski Zavod   Петровский Завод   5,790km

The name of the station, which means "Peter's factory", reflects the industrial nature of the town which is known as Petrovsk-Zabaikalski (Петровск-Забайкальский). Peter's factory is an ironworks which was founded in 1789 to supply iron for the gold mines in the region. The factory was rebuilt in 1939-40 next to the railway and from the train you can see flames from the plant's open-hearth furnaces. The factory is known throughout Russia, not for its steels but for its famous workers. In 1830, the factory was manned by many revolutionary Decembrists brought from nearby Chita and housed in the factory prison. A monument and large memorial commemorating this can be seen on the station platform. There is also a museum of the forced labourers in the former house of a Decembrist's wife, Ekaterina I Trubetskoi. Princess Trubetskoi (1800–54) was the first wife of a Decembrist to follow her husband into exile voluntarily. In doing so, she renounced her civil rights and noble privileges, and her name is immortalised by the famous Russian poet N A Nekrasov in his poem, Russian Women.

The centre of the town has a number of preserved houses from the 1800s and these, plus the Decembrist museum, make Petrovsk-Zabaikalski worth visiting in a day trip from Chita. The town stretches along the railway in the narrow river valley between the mountain ridges.

Khilok   Хилок   5,940km

Near the station is a granite monument topped with a star which commemorates the eleven young communists slain here during the Civil War.

The train now crosses the Yablonovy Mountains which have a height of over 1,500m. The eastern escarpment is steeper than the western side and heavy freight trains travelling westwards invariably require extra engines.

The original railway line over the mountains ran through a deep cutting and, to prevent landslides, a 63m section of railway was roofed over. On the western

---

TELEGRAPH POLES IN BASKETS

Along the Trans-Siberian between Petrovski Zavod and Birobizhan you will often see telegraph poles set in wooden baskets filled with stones. The reason for this is that without the baskets the poles would pop out of the ground within a few years of being dug in. The baskets are used in permafrost areas where the ground is permanently frozen except for a few centimetres in summer. In winter even the upper layer freezes and as frozen ground has a greater volume than thawed ground, the ground level lifts by 10–20cm. Without the weight of the rocks, the pole would lift up with the ground and a cavity would form underneath. In summer, the ground would thaw and drop back down but the pole would not as the cavity below would have been filled in by crumbling earth. While the rock-filled baskets significantly reduce the ground swelling, poles still pop out after eight to 15 years.

side of the so-called tunnel was written "To the Great Ocean" and on the eastern side was written "To the Atlantic Ocean". This tunnel was the first one east of the Ural Mountains and was so alien to Russians that passengers were said to "shriek with terror and even the most stout were to emerge from the tunnel with ashen faces". Since the railway has been rerouted, you do not pass through this tunnel.

About 30km past the station, on the left is the 1,579m high Shantoi Mountain which marks the railway's highest point in the Yablonovy Mountain Range.

Yablonovaya   Яблоновая   6,125km

About 20km south of here in the settlement of Drovyanaya (Дровяная) are 50 nuclear missile silos which house SS-17 or SS-19 interballistic nuclear rockets.

CHITA   Чита   6,204km
Population: 376,000   Telephone area code: 302 22

Chita is the junction of the Trans-Siberian and the Trans-Manchurian and trains also run from here to Tynda on the BAM.

Chita was founded in 1653 and in 1690 it became a *sloboda* ("tax-exempt settlement") populated by Cossacks and trappers. It became famous in the 1800s when it became the place of exile for many revolutionary Decembrists. Chita's importance grew after the Trans-Siberian railway was opened in 1900.

Soviet power was established in the city on February 16 1918 but by August 26, the city was captured by the White Army. However, by October 22 it was firmly back in the hands of the Soviets.

Chita is now the major industrial and cultural centre of eastern Siberia. The city was closed to foreigners until the late 1980s as it was the military centre for the sometimes tense Siberian-Chinese border. There are dozens of military buildings around the city; these look like ordinary office buildings but have their foyers hidden from the streets with armed guards just inside the door. The more important buildings are easy to spot as they have fishing net over their windows. In the vast majority of Russian buildings, air-conditioning is provided by opening windows so the fishing net catches any secret papers that might fly out.

Passing through
About 2km out from the station, on the left is the 16km² Kenon Lake. This lake, which is only 6m deep, is warmed by the nearby power station and at its eastern end you will see a popular beach beside the railway line. To get to it from Chita station, take buse No 17 or 18.

Further on the train crosses over the small Chita River, and about 1km before the station you pass through Chita 1 station which is where a railway factory is located.

The Moscow–Vladivostok No 1/2 train stops in Chita 2 for 20 minutes but there is nothing to see around the station so don't bother leaving it.

Once you leave the station, you travel about 1km before seeing the Chita River merging with the Ingoda River on the right. The train now follows the Ingoda River Valley for some hours.

Getting there and away
By air   There is a once-weekly flight to Beijing on Aeroflot.

By train   The major Trans-Siberian trains on this segment are:

Origin	Dist, km	Train no & name	Travel time	Depart	Arrive	Destination
Ulan-Ude	557	2	9hr 4min	08.50	17.54	Chita 2
Chita 2	557	1	9hr 34min	02. 20	11.54	Ulan-Ude
Chita 2	2,154	2	40hr 36min	18.14	10.50	Birobidzhan
Birobidzhan	2,154	1	40hr	10.02	02.02	Chita 2

Trains also run from along the Trans-Manchurian that runs to Beijing, China (see *Chapter Seventeen, page 408*). Trains also run from here to Tynda on the BAM (see *Chapter Fifteen, page 318*).

Where to stay
The accommodation choices consist of the standard Hotel Obkomovskaya, ul Profsoyuznaya 18, tel: 65 270, 623 97; the standard Hotel Turist, ul Babushkina 42, tel: 652 70, the standard Hotel Kommohalnaya, ul Baboshkina 149, tel: 375 77, $30 twin share/room; the basic Hotel Zabaikale, ul Leningradskaya 36, tel: 645 20, $14 twin share/room; the basic Hotel Ingoda, ul Profsoyznaya 23, tel: 332 22; the very basic Hotel Taiga, ul Lenina 75, tel: 390 48, $5 a bed in a dormitary; and the basic Hotel Dauriya, ul Profsoyuznaya 17, tel: 623 65, 623 88, $13 twin share/room. Out of town on the way to the airport is the basic Krasni Drakon Motel, ul Magistralnaya, tel: 119 73. To get to it take bus No 14 and tell the driver *motel* so he lets you out at the stop just before the motel. Hotel Zabaikale, Hotel Obkomovskaya and Hotel Turist have restaurants or buffets.

Getting around
The airport is 13km to the east of the city. To get to it take bus No 4 or 14 from pl Lenina.

What to see
An interesting place is the Officers' Club, ul Lenina 80. Don't be put off by the name as it is not full of military officers. On the second floor, opposite the bar, is the entertainment room with eight full-size billiard tables, and this is surrounded by chess tables with another balcony above, also full of tables. Despite the fact that few people speak, the noise level is unbelievable as each chess player punches his time clock every 30 seconds. The bar is quite good and is open 12.00–23.00 everyday except Monday.

For exercise you can visit the Delfin Swimming Pool, ul Kostyshko-Griforobicha 1, open 18.30–20.00, which unfortunately does not have a water slide.

Chita's impressive new Art Museum

Museums include the Minerals Museum, ul Kalinina 89, open 13.30-17.00, Monday, Wednesday and Friday only; the Art Museum, ul Chkalova 120a, tel: 385 36, 327 50, open 10.00–18.00, closed Monday and Tuesday; and the Military Museum, ul Lenina 86, open 10.00–18.00 Wednesday–Friday, 10.00–

17.00 weekends. There is also a Lenin Museum in the Teaching Insitute, ul Chkalova 140, tel: 689 22.

The Museum of Local Studies is closed for repairs and may move from its current address of ul Babushkina 113 to ul Lenina 84. Call first to find out on tel: 355 30.

The Decembrists Museum is housed in the former Archangel Michael Church, ul Dekabristov 3b, tel: 348 03, open 10.00–18.00, closed Monday.

Souvenirs can be bought at the Art Shop, ul Lenina 56, tel: 616 19; book shops at ul Kalinina 58, tel: 230 23 and ul Lenina 111, tel: 353 79; the Antique Book shop, ul 10th Yanvarya 35, tel: 662 11; the Stamp Shop, ul Chkalova 135, tel: 308 16; and the Rubin Jewellery Store, ul Zhuravleva 16, tel: 339 48.

Entertainment venues include the Drama Theatre, ul Profsoyuznaya 26, tel: 339 75, the Puppet Theatre, ul Verkholenskaya 2, tel: 358 69, the Philharmonic Hall, ul Bogomyakova 23, tel: 242 56, and the Casino 777, ul Stolyarova 44, tel: 312 30.

There is a 6.6km children's railway which runs in summer holidays from Park Pobeda. The park also contains the eternal flame and an open-air military vehicle museum. To get to it take buse No 4, 6, 14, 17, 18 or 19 from in front of the station.

If you are interested in traditional medicine, try the Centre of Eastern Medicine, ul Lenina 109, tel: 665 20.

Getting assistance

Travel agents   Intourist, ul Lenina 56, tel: 31 246; Sputnik, ul Kalinina 68, tel: 32-985; Chitakurort represents health spas in the region and these are a great place to relax at for a few days, ul Angarskaya 15, tel: 323 79, 319 24.

Air   Aeroflot, ul Leningradskaya 36, tel: 343 81.

Bus   Bus station, in front of the railway station, tel: 368 97.

Rail   Train information, tel: 321 19, 975 119, advance booking office, ul Lenina 55.

Darasun   Дарасун   6,270km

Darasun is renowned for its carbonic mineral springs and the water from them has been exported to China and Korea since ancient times. The only road to the Russian-Mongolian border town of Chita-Khapcheranga branches off the highway from here.

Karymskaya   Карымская   6,300km

About 11km past the station you reach the Tarskaya siding which is the point where the Trans-Manchurian branch line heads south from the Trans-Siberian (see *Chapter Seventeen, page 408*).

Shilka   Шилка   6,451km

The village on the Shilka River was founded in 1897 just to serve the railway but within two years, it became a popular tourist destination. This occurred because of the opening of the Shivanda health resort (*shivanda* means "royal drink" in the local indigenous language) where its curative mineral water was and still is used to treat digestive and respiratory system disorders.

The village was again in the news a few years later when gold was discovered to the north and its last claim to fame was in 1954 when fluoric spar, a mineral essential in chemistry and metallurgy, was discovered nearby.

Priiskavaya   Приисковая   6,496km

This little town gets its name from the word *priisk* which means a "mine". There is nothing to see here, but just 10km to the north by a railway branch line is the historic gold-mining town of Nerchinsk (Нерчинск).

The present-day site of Nerchinsk was selected in 1812, but historians trace Nerchinsk's origins back to 1653 when a fortress was built nearby. Within a few years, the town witnessed its most famous event: the signing in 1689 of the Treaty of Nerchinsk which divided up the region between the Russians and Manchurians. The treaty gave the Manchurian emperor control over the Russian far east for the next 170 years. In the late 17th century, gold was discovered in the nearby hills and Nerchinsk became a centre renowned for its extremes. At one end were the tens of thousands of convicts forced to work and die in the mines while, at the other end, the local mine owners revelled in grotesque opulence. From 1826 to 1917, Nerchinsk's mines were major Tsarist labour camps.

Today, Nerchinsk has 17,000 inhabitants and numerous interesting sights. These include the central Bazaar Square around which is the 1825 Resurrection (Voskresenski Cathedral) and the Arcade (Gostini Dvor). Nearby is the house of the rich merchant Butin, which was built in the popular Moorish style in the 1860s. Next door is the non-functioning Hotel Dauriya which was built in the second half of the 19th century and in which Chekhov stayed in 1890. There is a museum and basic hotel in Nerchinsk.

Although both Nerchinsk and nearby Sretensk (see below) are interesting, Nerchinsk is the better place to visit.

Kuenga   Куэнга   6,532km

From here the Trans-Siberian train line turns north along the Kuenga River while a railway branch line continues 52km to the east, terminating at Sretensk (Сретенск). Sretensk sits on the eastern bank of the Shilka River which flows into the mighty Amur. The Amur River marks the Chinese-Russian border for hundreds of kilometres, before passing through Khabarovsk on its way north where it finally flows out into the Pacific Ocean. It was this river route that put Sretensk on Russian maps. In 1916 the Trans-Siberian was completed and instantly the bypassed Sretensk became a backwater. The actual town is spread over both banks of the Shilka River with the town centre on the eastern bank and the railway station on the high, western bank. The banks were only joined in 1986 when a bridge was built across the river. There is a museum and basic hotel in Sretensk.

From Kuenga, the train travels along picturesque valleys and passes the first of numerous tunnels after about 40km.

Chernyshevsk-Zabaikalski
Чернышевск-Забайкальский   6,593km

The town around the station is called Chernyshevsk (Чернышевск) after the revolutionary Nikolai Chernyshevskiy (1828–89) who toiled for years at hard labour camps in the region. From here the train climbs up the Amur Mountain Range and at the top of it, the line turns northeast.

Bushulei   Бушулей   6,629km

The mining complex around the station is a molybdenum ore enrichment plant. The mineral is added to steel to make it suitable for high-speed cutting tools. Scattered along the line are other molybdenum and gold mines.

AMUR RIVER

The massive 4,440km Amur River forms in Mongolia and travels along the Chinese–Russian border before discharging into the Pacific Ocean just to the north of Nikolaevsk-na-Amure.

While the first known settlement on the river dates back to 5,000BC, Russian settlement is relatively recent with the first major exploration being in 1649–55 by E P Khabarov. Agreement with the Chinese prevented settlement by Russians in the area until the mid-1800s.

Today, the Amur is important as a trading route, a source of fish and as a drain. The river ices up in November and the ice breaks up by the beginning of May. The river is navigable for its entire course, but the winding nature of the river to the north of Khabarovsk plus the fact that the river carries 41,000 tons of sediment every day, means that regular dredging is required.

The Amur is home to 99 different species of fish, the greatest variety in any Russian river. The main fish caught are the keta and humpback salmon. The fishing season is in summer and autumn. Other fish caught include silver carp, Huso dauricus, Erythroculter erythropterus and sturgeon.

Pollution is a major problem, particularly the wastes from the large industrial cities along the route which have seen the Amur River as a drain. However, greater environmental awareness and the decline of heavy industry have resulted in the Amur being less polluted than in the past.

The hydrofoils and ferries officially run between June 20 and August 31 when the Amur is guaranteed to be completely clear of ice. Tickets are bought at the river stations or if the town is small, on the vessel.

One company offering an organised cruise along the Amur is Amurturist, ul Kuznechnaya 1, Amurskoi Oblasti, Blagoveshchensk, tel: (416 22) 277 98, 903-77, 231 22, fax: 277 98, 231 22, telex 154113 turne su. Blagoveshchensk is on the Amur River opposite the Chinese city of Hei Hei. The company offer a 13-day trip for an all-in price of $400.

The train now follows the line of the 54th parallel for a while. This place was hell for the builders as winter was bitterly cold and in the hot summers all surface water dried up. For most of the year, the ground had to be thawed out with gigantic bonfires before the track could be laid. In the past, water for workers and steam engines had to be carried in but nowadays it comes from deep wells which tap the underground rivers.

Zilovo   Зилово   6,676km

The town around the station is called Aksenovo-Zilovskaya (Аксеново-Зиловское) and during the 1910s and 1920s, it contained the fortress-like wooden Railway Church.

Mogocha   Могоча   6,914km

This ugly railway settlement located in the Bolshoy Amazar River Valley is probably the harshest place to live on the Trans-Siberian because of the permafrost and the summer sun. In winter the –60°C weather refreezes the top centimetres of earth that thawed over the summer, killing all but the hardiest stunted plants while the intense summer sun singes any plant shoots. The town was founded in 1910 when this section of the Trans-Siberian was being built and afterwards the town became the base for geological research expeditions seeking gold in the hills.

Erofei-Pavlovich   Ерофей Павлович   7,119km

The town is named after the brutal Russian explorer Erofei Pavlovich Khabarov.

This area is also inhospitable with frosts lasting from the middle of October to the beginning of April, with the average January temperature of –33°C. Patches of snow can be found on the shaded sides of mountains as late as July.

At the eastern end of the station, on the north side, is an Em model steam locomotive on a plinth. The town is situated on the banks of the Urka River.

Bamovskaya   Бамовская   7,281km

This is technically the junction of the Trans-Siberian and Little BAM railways, but only those Little BAM trains travelling between Tynda and Chita pass through Bamovskaya. Little BAM trains travelling between Tynda and Khabarovsk join the Trans-Siberian at the siding of Goreli, which is a few kilometres to the east, with their first stop at Skovorodino station.

The best thing in Bamovskaya is the big word "BAM" in white blocks lying on the sloping ground in front of the station. It is not advisable to get off a train here without knowing when your connecting train up the Little BAM will arrive as there are only a handful a day that head north. There is no hotel here (see *Chapter Fifteen, page 320*).

Skovorodino   Сковородино   7,313km

The town is named after the first president of the village council of workers deputies, A N Skovorodin, who was killed here during the Russian Civil War in 1920.

Skovorodino is the first stop on the Trans-Siberian for trains that travel down the Little BAM from Tynda to Khabarovsk. If you are getting off the Trans-Siberian to go up the Little BAM, Skovorodino is a better choice than nearby Bamovskaya as there is a hotel here (see *Chapter Fifteen, page 320*).

Bolshoi Never   Большой Невер   7,329km

On the left side the railway is the 800km-long Amur–Yakutsk highway which terminates in Yakutsk. Although called a highway, it is better described as a dirt road broken up with patches of asphalt. Much of the road was built by prisoners and although some form of road had existed along the route for decades, the highway was officially opened only in May 1975.

Ushumun   Ушумун   7,609km

The train turns southeast again and soon crosses an obvious climatic boundary and a not so obvious one marking the southern border of permafrost. From now on the larches grow much taller, reaching 35m, and birches and oaks spring up. These oaks are different from the European oaks as they retain their leaves in winter although they do turn stiff and brown.

Shimanovskaya   Шимановская   7,731km

This town played an important part in the development of two railways: the Trans-Siberian and the BAM. In 1910, a railway depot was built here to push the Trans-Siberian onwards while, in 1978, the town became a major supplier of construction materials for the BAM. The town was named after the revolutionary V I Shimanovski who was executed in 1918 in nearby Blagoveshchensk. The town has a small museum displaying its railway and revolutionary history.

Ledinaya   Лединая   7,772km

Hidden away in the trees just to the north of this station is the once-secret Svobodni-18 Cosmodrome. Until the early 1990s, the base housed 60 SS-11 interballistic rockets which can each carry a single nuclear warhead 10,000km but, following the START missile reduction agreement, the base has become redundant. However, it will not be closed down as the Russian space sector believes that the site has several advantages over the northern Russian Plesetsk Cosmodrome, least of all that it is at a lower latitude (meaning smaller rockets for the same payload) than Plesetsk.

If you try to visit the site you will probably not get any further than the station. Good luck.

Svobodny   Свободный   7,819km

Svobodny has a proud and tragic history associated with the railways. It was founded in 1912 with the construction of the Trans-Siberian bridge over the Zeya River. It rapidly became a major railway town with factories building carriages, and the railways sponsoring a hospital, schools and an orphanage. By the mid-1930s it was the headquarters of both the Amur section of the Trans-Siberian and the just-started BAM railway. It was during this period that the town suffered from Stalin's purges. In a five-month period in 1937, 158 officials of the Amur railway were shot, having been sentenced to death for no good reason.

Svobodny is an attractive town sitting on the right bank of the Zeya River and its attractions include a children's railway, river port, geological museum, history museum and a railway museum.

Beyond the town the line crosses the Zeya River which is Russia's largest tributary of the Amur. This river is notoriously dangerous as in the rainy seasons the water level may rise as fast as 30cm an hour and 10m high floods have been recorded. The area beyond the river, called the Zeysko-Bureinskaya Plain, is extremely fertile and is the main granary for the Russian far east. It is the most populated area of the Amur region and villages are spaced about every 10–20km separated by fields of barley, soya beans or melons. The climate and landscape are very similar to parts of Ukraine and attracted many Ukrainians last century. Today, over 50% of the locals are of Ukrainian descent. You can pick out the Ukrainian houses which are white-washed *khatas* ("peasant huts") while Russian houses are usually of solid log construction with overlapping log ends.

Belogorsk   Белогорск   7,873km
Telephone area code: 241 01

With the exception of the monument to those killed during the 1919–20 occupation of the region by the Japanese, and an 80m grain elevator which also serves as a TV tower, there is not much of interest in Belogorsk. The town was originally called Aleksandrovsk after the Tsar Aleksandr, then in 1931 it was called Krasnopartizansk or "red partisans". In 1935, it became Kuibyshevka-Vostochnaya in honour of Stalin's ally Kuibyshev who died that year. In 1959 the local communist leaders selected Belogorsk which is derived from the words "white hills", an apt description of nearby quartz-covered hills.

The only hotel in town is basic Hotel Zarya, ul Partizanskaya 23, tel: 237 50.

From Belogorsk there is a 108km railway south to the border city of Blagoveshchensk. The Chinese city across the river is called Hei-Hei and is connected by a railway to Harbin and then Beijing. There is no bridge over the river but ferries travel six times a day between the two. There are also international flights here from Harbin in China and Seoul in South Korea. Blagoveshchensk has enough of interest to occupy two days. The best accommodation is at Hotel Zeya, ul Kalinina 8, tel: (416 22) 211 00. It is advisable to get assistance to organise the river crossing and rail tickets on the other side. Travel agents include Intourist, ul Lenina 108/2, tel: (416 22) 45 772, and Amurturist, ul Kuznechnaya 1, tel: (416 22) 277 98, 903 77, 231 22, fax: 277 98, 231 22, telex 154113 turne su.

Zavitaya Завитая 7,992km
This town is famous for soya bean oil and soya flour. There is a 90km branch line to the south which terminates at Poyarkovo on the Chinese-Russian border. Only Chinese and Russian passport holders can cross here.

Bureya Бурея 8,037km
This industrial town serves the coal-mining industry by producing mining tools. The town suffered regular floods until the Bureya hydro-electric dam was built. The train crosses over the Bureya River but you can't see the dam, which is upstream.

Uril Урил 8,118km
On the right side of the railway from here to the next station of Kundur is the Khingan Nature Reserve. The sanctuary consists of swampy lowlands dotted with Amur velvet trees and Korean cedar pine woods with a thick undergrowth of hazel nut trees, wild grapes and wild pepper which is related to ginseng. The sanctuary is rich in Mongol and Siberian animals seldom encountered elsewhere, for example, the racoon-like dogs.

Obluche Облучье 8,198km
The town is just inside the border of the Jewish Autonomous Region which is part of the Khabarovsk Krai. The border also marks a time border; within Khabarovsk, Moscow is now seven hours behind. The town only exists because of the railways and a few tin and iron ore mines in the region.

Like most of the stations in the Jewish Autonomous Region, the station signs are in both Russian and Hebrew. The region was formed in 1928 when the Soviet government adopted a resolution to secure the unoccupied territories here for voluntary settlement by Jewish workers in the USSR and abroad.

The tunnel just after Obluche was the first in the world to be built through permafrost.

Izvestkovaya Известковая 8,242km
This town sits at the junction of the Trans-Siberian and the 360km branch line to Novy Urgal on the BAM railway. Much of this branch line was built by Japanese prisoners of war until they were repatriated in 1949 and Japanese graves litter the area. Izvestkovaya is a typical small town with a canteen, post office, dairy farm and market but little else. The old part of town, with its rustic wooden buildings and household garden plots, is hidden in the trees to the west of the town. If you have to wait here to change train, be prepared to be bored.

Bira Бира 8,314km

There is a monument on the platform dedicated to Nikolai Trofemovich and his wife. The railway runs beside the Bira River for about 100km and passes through hills rich with the ingredients of cement.

BIROBIDZHAN Биробиджан 8,356km
Population: 87,600 Telephone area code: 421 45

While this is the capital of the Jewish Autonomous Region, less than 5% of the population have Jewish ancestry. This indicates what the Russia Jews think about this desolate and remote reservation.

Despite the low number of Jews, considerable effort has been put into giving the city a Jewish feel. This includes providing street signs in Hebrew and Russian, making Hebrew the official language of the region, and printing Russia's only Hebrew paper, the *Birbobidzhaner Sterm*.

The town gets its name from the Bira and Bidzhan Rivers which meet here. Prior to the founding of Birobidzhan, the Trans-Siberian station was called Tikhonkaya.

Getting there and away

By air There is a weekly flight to Bangkok, Thailand.

By rail The major Trans-Siberian trains on this segment are:

Origin	Dist, km	Train no & name	Travel time	Depart	Arrive	Destination
Birobidzhan	175	2	2hr 15min	10.55	13.10	Khabarovsk
Khabarovsk	175	1	2hr 17min	07.48	10.07	Birobidzhan
Chita 2	2,154	2	40hr 36min	18.14	10.50	Birobidzhan
Birobidzhan	2,154	1	40hr	10.02	02.02	Chita 2

Where to stay

The only hotel is the standard Hotel Vostok, ul Sholom-Aleikhema 1, tel: 653 30. It has a restaurant.

Getting around

Birobidzhan is a tourist-friendly city as everything is within walking distance of the station. The city is located on the right (southern side) of the station. The main street parallel with the railway is called ul Sholom Aleichem after a Jewish writer of the last century. From the railway station to ul Sholom Aleichem, take ul Gorkovo. From the station, buses No 5, 15 and 22 go past Hotel Vostok.

What to see

The Museum of Local Studies, ul Lenina 24, tel: 654 39, is open 09.00–17.50, closed Monday. The Art Museum is located on ul Pionerskaya. Cultural performances are often scheduled at the Philharmonic Hall, pro 60th SSSR, tel: 656 79. There is a synagogue on the eastern outskirts of town, ul Mayakovskovo 11, and to get there take bus No 5, 16 or 22 eastward from Hotel Vostok.

Birobidzhan's most famous export is the rice combine harvester made at the Dalselmash factory on the western outskirts of the town. To get there, take bus No 2 or 16 westwards from in front of Hotel Vostok.

There is a beach on the Bira River which is packed on summer weekends. To get there, just keep walking down ul Gorky until you reach the river and you will see the beach on the left beside Park Kultury. It is only 800m past the Art Museum.

Getting assistance

Travel agents   Intour-Birobidzhan, ul Sholom-Aleikhema 55, tel: 615 73.
Air   Aeroflot, ul Kalinina, tel: 692 06
Bus   Bus station, ul Kalina 2, tel: 695 39.
Rail   Railway station, tel: 670 42.

Just after leaving Birobidzhan, on the left you pass a steep volcanic mound on which is a white stone memorial. The huge memorial, which includes a figure of a charging Soviet soldier, is the Iyuan-Koran memorial to commemorate a fierce Russian Civil War battle on this site in 1922. Near the memorial are mass graves of the fallen Red Guard.

Volochaevka 1   Волочаевка 1   8,480km

This small station is just a junction of the Trans-Siberian and the 344km railway to Komsomolsk-na-Amure while Volochaevka 2 contains the actual town of Volochaevka which is famous as the scene of a major battle during the Russian Civil War. Volochaevka 2 is 9km along the line to Komsomolsk-na-Amure. There is a hotel in Volochaevka.

The Battle of Volochaevka ran from February 5–14 1922 in the vicinity of the railway station and was one of the last battles of the Russian Civil War in the Russian far east. Although the temperature was as low as −35°C, the poorly equipped Red troops attacked the enemy without pause. The Whites' defences were finally broken on February 12 and by February 14, the communists had retaken Khabarovsk. There is a 360° panoramic painting of the battle at Khabarovsk's Museum of Local Studies.

Priamurskaya   Приамурская   8,512km

This small town is just on the border of the Jewish Autonomous Region and, after leaving the town, you cross 3km of swamp and small streams before reaching the 2.6km bridge across the Amur River.

As the bridge is for rail traffic only, cars have to cross on a river ferry. You may see the ferry pass under the bridge as it starts 2km upstream (on the right) and finishes 1.2km downstream at Telman village. Khabarovsk's main fishing port is 2.5km upstream.

KHABAROVSK   Хабаровск   8,531km
Population: 614,000   Telephone area code: 4210

Khabarovsk was founded as a military outpost in 1858 and named after the brutal Russian explorer, Erofei Khabarov. It sits at a strategic location on the right (eastern side) bank of the Amur River which enabled the town to control trade along the massive river. With the completion of the Trans-Siberian railway the city rapidly grew and is now the second largest city in the Russian far east.

Many travellers join or depart the Trans-Siberian here as there are many international flights to Khabarovsk and it is more geared to travellers than Vladivostok which was closed to foreigners until 1992. You can easily spend two interesting days in Khabarovsk.

While most cities have parades on the days of public holidays, Khabarovsk always puts on a great parade on Navy Day or the other military anniversaries, see *Chapter Two, page 30*.

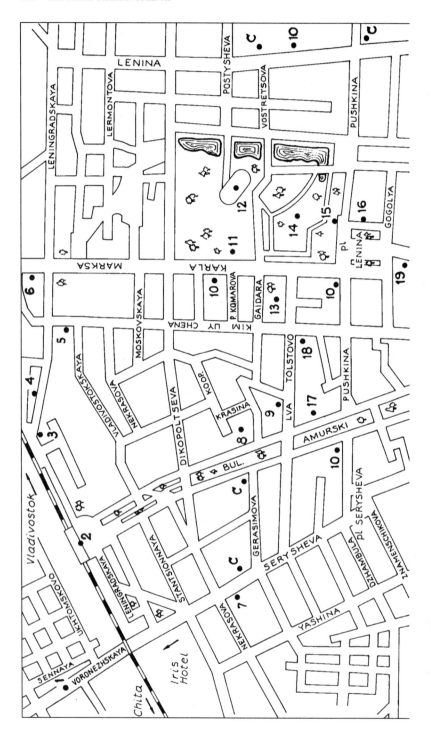

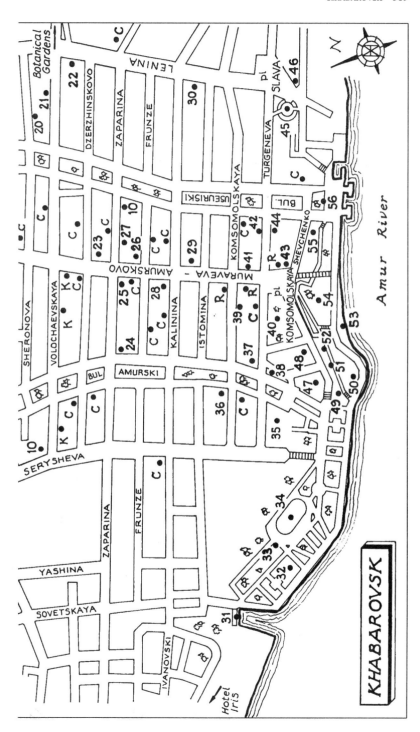

KEY TO KHABAROVSK   Хабаровск

1	Bus station (*Avtovokzal*)	Автовокзал
2	Railway station (*Vokzal*)	Ж-Д вокзал
3	Church	церковь
4	Advance purchase rail ticket office	Предварительная ж-д касса
5	Hotel Zarya	гостиница Заря
6	Hotel Turist	гостиница Турист
7	Far Eastern State Academy of Railway	Дальневосточная государственная академия путей сообщения
8	Hotel Mayak	гостиница Маяк
9	Summer Circus	Цирк
10	Book shop (*Knigi*)	Книги
11	Theatre of Musical Comedy (*Teatr*)	Театр музыкальной комдеии
12	Stadium Dinamo (*Stadion*)	Стадион «Динамо»
13	Gaidar Children's Park	Детский парк им. Гайдара
14	Park Dinamo	Парк «Динамо»
15	Hotel Tsentralnaya	гостиница Центральная
16	Government administration (*Dom Soveta*)	Дом совета
17	Market (*Rynok*)	Рынок
18	Hotel Amethyst	гостиница Аметист
19	Hotel Lyudmila	гостиница Людмила
20	White Theatre (*Teatr*)	Белый театр
21	Hotel Sever	гостиница Север
22	Hotel Amur	гостиница Амур
23	Drama Theatre (*Teatr*)	Театр Драмы
24	Aeroflot International	Аэрофлот
25	Cinema (*Kino*)	Кино
26	Central post office (*Pochtamt*)	Почтамт
27	Stamp shop (*Filatelia*)	Филателия
28	Tainy Remesla art store	Тайны Ремесла
29	Hotel Dalny Vostok	гостиница Далный Восток
30	Geological Museum (*Muzei*)	Геологический музей
31	Yacht club	Яхт-клуб
32	Open air pool (*Bassein*)	Открытый бассейн
33	Chinese Consulate (*Kulsulstvo*)	Китайское Кулсульство
34	Stadium Lenin (*Stadion*)	Стадион «Ленин»
35	Church of St Innocent (*Innokentevskaya*)	Иннокентьевская церковь
36	Aeroflot Domestic	Аэрофлот
37	Youth Museum	Южний музей
38	Literature Museum (*Muzei*)	Литературный музей
39	Hotel Sapparo	гостиница Саппоро
40	Odosa Park	Парк ОДОСА
41	Children's Theatre (*Teatr*)	Молодежный театр
42	Eurasia Trans Inc	Предприятие Eurasia
43	Amur Steamship headquarters	Управление Амурского речного пароходства
44	United States and Foreign Commercial Service Office	Американский Центр
45	Memorial complex of the Second World War	Мемориальный комплекс «Боаевая и трудовая слава»
46	Radio Centre	Дом радио
47	Hotel Intourist	гостиница Интурист
48	Museum of the History of the Russian Far East Military District (*Muzei*)	Музей истории Краснознаменного Дальневосточного военного округа
49	Casino Amur	
50	Tower (*Vyzhka*)	Вышка
51	Museum of Local Studies (*Muzei*)	Краведческий музей
52	Concert hall (*Zal*)	Концертный зал
53	Beach (*Plyazh*)	Пляж
54	City park	ЦПКиО
55	Conference hall (*Zal*)	Конферекц-зал
56	River station (*Rechnoi Vokzal*)	Речной вокзал
R	Restaurant (*Restoran*)	Ресторан
C	Café (*Kafé*) or Bar (*Bar*)	Кафе или Бар
K	Canteen (*Stolovaya*)	Столовая

Passing through

The Moscow–Vladivostok No 1/2 train stops here for 20 minutes. Check out the Intourist Hall, which is reached from within the main part of the station, as sometimes souvenirs and maps are sold there. At the front of the station is a statue of the brutal founder of the city, Erofei Pavlovich Khabarov; it is well worth a photo.

Getting there and away

By air Aeroflot has weekly flights to Harbin, China; Alaska Airlines has two weekly flights to Seattle, San Francisco and San Diego via Anchorage in summer and one in winter; Chosonminhang Airlines of North Korea has a weekly flight to Pyongyang, North Korea in summer only; Asiana Airlines has a weekly flight to Seoul, South Korean; Aeroflot has weekly flights to Singapore; and JAL has a weekly flight to Niigata only over summer.

By boat Long-distance hydrofoils travel between Khabarovsk and Komsomolsk-na-Amure and depart every second day.

By rail The major Trans-Siberian trains on this segment are:

Origin	Dist, km	Train no & name	Travel time	Depart	Arrive	Destination
Birobidzhan	175	2	2hr 15min	10.55	13.10	Khabarovsk
Khabarovsk	175	1	2hr 17min	07.48	10.07	Birobidzhan
Khabarovsk	766	2	13hr 10min	13.35	02.45	Vladivostok
Vladivostok	766	1	13hr 30min	17.55	07.25	Khabarovsk

Trains that go to Komsomolsk and Sovetskaya Gavin on the BAM railway are:

Origin	Dist, km	Train no & name	Travel time	Depart	Arrive	Destination
Khabarovsk	388	68	8hr 50min	15.05	23.55	Komsomolsk
Komsomolsk	388	67	8hr 40min	15.00	23.40	Khabarovsk
Khabarovsk	841	251	27hr 30min	11.50	15.20	Sovetskaya Gavin
Sovetskaya Gavin	841	252	23hr 37min	23.00	22.37	Khabarovsk

Where to stay

There are numerous hotels in Khabarovsk. The best are the excellent Hotel Sapparo, ul Komsomolskaya 79, tel: 332 702, fax: 332 830, $200 a double room; the excellent Hotel Amethyst, ul Tolstovo 5a, tel: 33-46-99, fax: (509) 01-600131, $120 a double room, $80 a single; and the excellent Hotel Iris, ul Tikhookeanskaya 211, tel: 399 401, 358 904, fax: 352 121, $60 a single room. Hotel Iris is out of town and can be easily reached on a 40-minute trip from the railway station on tram No 5. The best average hotels are the standard Hotel Intourist, per Arseneva 7, tel: 336 507, 336 395, 399 313, $120 a double room; and standard Hotel Lyudmila, ul Muravieva-Amurskovo 33, tel: 388 665, 388 649, $100 a double room. The most centrally located hotel and best value is the basic Hotel Tsentralnaya, ul Pushkina 52, tel: 336 731, 334 759, $30 twin share/person. Other options include the basic Hotel Amur, ul Lenina 29, tel: 335 043, 394 373, fax: 221 223, $20 twin share/person; basic Hotel Dalny Vostok, ul Muravieva-Amurskovo 18, tel: 335 093, 331 434, 388 421 (which is undergoing refurbishment in 1995); the basic Hotel Mayak, ul Kooperativnaya 11, tel: 330 935, $15 twin share/person; the basic Hotel Vassily Payarkov (boat), City Pier, tel: 398 201, standard Hotel Turist, ul Karla Marksa 67, tel: 370 417, 372 323; and the basic Hotel Zarya, ul Kim Yu Chena 81, tel: 337 075.

All but the basic and very basic hotels have restaurants or buffets.

Getting around

The railway station is about 3km from the Intourist Hotel on the banks of the Amur River.

The main street is ul Karla Marksa which becomes ul Muraeveva-Amurskovo as it goes around the city's central square known as pl Lenina. The main street ends near the banks of the Amur River at pl Komsomolskaya.

Directly in front of the station is bul Amurski which runs all the way to the banks of the Amur in a direction almost parallel with ul Karla Marksa and ul Muraeveva-Amurskovo.

From the station, bus No 1 travels down ul Karla Marksa and ul Muraeveva-Amurskovo and then back to the station along ul Lenina. Take this bus for Hotel Intourist, Hotel Lyudmila, Hotel Tsentralnaya, Hotel Amur, Hotel Dalny Vostok, Hotel Turist, Hotel Amethyst and Hotel Zarya.

From the station, bus No 2 travels down ul Serysheva (which is parallel but slightly to the right of bul Amurski) and back up to the station via ul Karla Marksa and ul Muraeveva-Amurskovo. Take this bus for Hotel Intourist and Hotel Sapparo.

To get to Iris Hotel, take tram No 5 from the station; the trip takes 45 minutes.

Trolleybus No 1 runs between the airport and the pl Komsomolskaya.

Boats along the Amur River operate from May to October. Both local ferries and long-distance hydrofoils depart from the river station and the timetables are posted in the building and along the river banks from where the boats depart. While Intourist can organise tickets for a trip on one of the local ferries that travel to a nearby *dacha* village, you might as well do it yourself. Have a look at the timetables and select the one with a return time under two hours and see where it leads you. The river station is at ul Shevchenko 1, tel: 398 832, 398 690.

What to see

An excellent half day walk is down the main shopping street of ul Muraeveva-Amurskovo, through the park on the riverside of pl Komsomolsk, along the banks of the Amur River to the river station and World War II memorial 500m upstream. Beside the war memorial is the city's Radio Centre and in front of it are 16 giant coats of arms of the states of the former Soviet Union. Then walk back along ul Lenina and turn right down any of the streets which leads you back to ul Muraveva-Amurskovo.

There are numerous theatres here including the Summer Circus, ul Tolstova 20, tel: 333 892; Theatre of Musical Comedy, ul Karla Marksa 64, tel: 334 821; Children's Theatre, ul Muravyova-Amurskovo 14, tel: 334 063; Concert Hall, ul Shevchenko 7, tel: 337 971; and Drama Theatre, ul Dzerzhinskovo 44, tel: 330 255. There is invariably a performance every night at one of these places, so look for advertising posters on the street or contact the Intourist desk.

Other entertainment includes Casino Tourist in the Hotel Tourist, ul Karla Marksa 67, tel: 370 473; and Casino Amur, ul Shevchenko 15, tel: 334 782

There is a plethora of museums in Khabarovsk. These include the Museum of Local Studies, ul Shevchenko 11, tel: 330 783, 330 864, 389 354, open 10.00–18.00, closed Monday; Youth Museum (formerly the Musuem of the Komsomol Young Communists), ul Turgeneva 86, tel: 331 936; Art Museum, ul Shevchenko 7, tel: 399 312; Geological Museum, ul Lenina 15, tel: 330 491, 215 370, open 10.00–18.00; Literature Museum, ul Turgeneva 69; Art Shop, ul Karla Marksa 15, tel: 332 131; and Museum of the History of the Russian Far East

Military District, ul Shevchenko 20, tel: 331 150, open 10.00–18.00, closed Monday and Tuesday.

For the rail enthusiasts, there is a 1930s carriage used by the commander of the Russian far east military forces in the Military Museum and there is a small museum at the Far Eastern State Academy of Railway Communications, ul Sersheva 47, tel: 343 076. Tours of the Academy's museum are by appointment only.

The 12-hectare Botanical Gardens out of town are also worth a visit. They are located at ul Volochaevskaya, tel: 223 401, open 09.00–18.00 weekdays. To get there take bus No 1 to the corner of ul Volochaevskaya and ul Lenina, then take bus No 25 to the Ussurisky stop.

The best souvenir shops are the Tainy Remesla art store, Muravyova-Amurskovo 17, tel: 331 068; Art Salon, ul Muravyova-Amurskovo 17, tel: 332 31; book shops including Knizhni Mir-Bookworld, ul Karla Marksa 37, tel: 333 351, and Globus, ul Zaparina 55, tel: 334 956; old books store (Bukinist), ul Karla Marksa 49, tel: 385 511; stamp shop, ul Zaparina 65; DalArt Gallery in the Art Museum, ul Shevchenko 7, tel: 399 312; amber jewellery shop in the Military Museum, ul Shevchenko 20; diamond jewellery shop (almaz), ul Muravyova-Amurskovo 13, tel: 337 870, amber jewellery shop (Yantar), ul Lenina 32, tel: 221 821; and garnet jewellery shop, bul Amurski 3, tel: 348 571.

Getting assistance

Travel agents   There are numerous travel agencies here including Intourist which is located in the Intourist Hotel, bul Amursky 2, tel: 337 634, Dalni Vostok Company, tel: 388 079, fax: 338 679 or 338 363, Michael Travel Agency, tel: 334 992, and Khabarovsktourist Tourism, tel: 339 390.

Air   Aeroflot, bul Amursky 18, tel: 335 346, 378 758 (this office is for international departures with the domestic departures office on the opposite side of the street); Alaska Airlines, tel: 378 804; Asiana Airlines of South Korea (at airport) tel: 348 024, 378 373; Chosonminhang Airlines of North Korea (at airport) tel: 373 204, 378 373; Japan Airlines JAL (at airport), tel: 370 686; and Chinese Northern Airlines, tel: 373 440.

Boat   River station, ul Shevchenko 1, tel: 398 832, 398 690.

Bus   Bus station, shosse Voronezhskoe 19, tel: 343 909.

Rail   There is an Intourist booking office at the railway station, tel: 342 192, 383 530. The advance purchase rail ticket office is at ul Leningradskaya 56, tel: 383 164, 383 350. You can also get tickets through the private company Eurasia Trans Inc. To book tickets, contact Valentina G Neretina, Head of Service Department or Victor I Kozub, Director General, Eurasia Trans Inc, ul Turgeneva 64, tel: 226 067, 384 261, fax: 332 726, telex 141174 Rotor SU.

Diplomatic representation   Japanese Consulate, room 208, Hotel Sapporo, ul Komsomolskaya 79, tel: 332 623, 337 895; Chinese Consulate, Lenin Stadium, tel: 348 537, 399 890, open 09.00–12.00 Monday, Wednesday and Friday for visas; United States and Foreign Commercial Service Office, ul Turgeneva 69, tel: 337 923, 336 923.

After leaving Khabarovsk, the railway turns south and runs along the Ussuri River to within 5km of the Chinese border. It soon crosses over the volcanic Khekhsir Ridge which has a 950m peak.

Pereyaslavka   Переяславка   8,598km
The town around the station is called Verino (Верино) and was the site of a
fierce Civil War battle. In front of the station there is a war memorial. There is
a museum in Verino.

Khor   Xop   8,612km
The train crosses over the small Khor River which marks the southern boundary
of the 46,000-hectare Bolshe-Khekhzirzkiy Sanctuary which is of great
botanical interest, containing both north and south Siberian plants. The
indigenous Udegeytsy people have a legend about the sanctuary. Once two birds
flying in the opposite directions collided in a thick fog and dropped their loads.
They had been sent by the good spirit of the south and good spirit of the north
to throw seeds on the desert plains and mountains respectively. Since then,
southern wild grapes wind around northern pine trees and the northern berry
klukva grows side by side with the southern spiky palm *aralia* with metre-long
leaves.

The vegetation changes considerably with altitude which you will notice as
you travel up and down the mountains. At the foot of the mountains broad leaf
species dominate. On the slopes cedar, Amur velvet ash (cork is produced from
the black bark) and Manchurian nut trees take over while on the higher parts of
the mountains, angular pine and fir trees have won the succession struggle.

Vyazemskaya   Вяземская   8,659km
This railway town was founded in 1895 and was the centre of some fierce
fighting during the Russian Civil War. There are several memorials and a local
history museum that commemorates the communist victory.

Bikin   Бикин   8,764km
The railway crosses over the Bikin River which is a major food source for the
Udeghe indigenous people. Known as the forest people due to their lifestyle of
fishing, hunting and gathering edible food from the taiga, the Udeghe are facing
the end of their way of life because of the voracious logging industry. The
Udeghe have lived in the area for over 1,500 years and have gradually been
forced further away from Russian settlements as fish and game have declined.
The largest settlement of the Udeghe is the 700-inhabitant Krasni Yar village
which is 200km up the Bikin River.

Dalnerechensk   Дальнереченск   8,890km
This town was founded by Cossacks in 1895 and quickly became a timber centre
due to the large pine and red cedar trees in the area. The town has a factory that
is one of the few in Russia which still produces wooden barrels specially for
salted fish and seal blubber. The town has a museum and a memorial dedicated
to the border guards that were killed in the 1969 border conflict with the Chinese
over Damanski Island.

Muravevo-Amurskaya   Муравьёво-Амурская   8,900km
This station is named after the explorer and governor of eastern Siberian, Count
Nikolai Muravevo-Amurskaya. The station was formerly known as Lazo in
honour of the communist revolutionary S G Lazo (1894–1920) who was
captured in 1920 by the Japanese when they invaded the Russian far east, and

executed at the station allegedly by being thrown alive into a steam engine firebox. Two other revolutionaries, A N Lutski and V M Sibirtsev, met a similar fate and a monument to all three stands in front of the station.

Shmakovka   Шмаковка   8,991km
About 29km from the station is the large, mostly derelict Shmakovski Trinity-St Nicholas Monastery which has a very mysterious history. Its valuable land is now being fought over by two groups, both claiming to be its original owners. The Russian Orthodox Church maintains they built the monastery; the Russian military don't deny its religious past, but counter this by claiming that they built the monastery as a front for an espionage academy.

Spassk-Dalni   Спасск-Дальний   9,057km
In front of the railway station in the square is a monument to commemorate the Red Guards killed in a battle which took place at the approaches to Spassk-Dalni in 1922. About 40km west of here is Lake Khanka which has a surface area of 4,000km² but its deepest point is only 4m. The lake is famous for its water nut and lotus flower eurea with its giant buds and leaves 2m wide.

Alexander Solzhenitsyn was imprisoned in this town and his experiences here formed the basis of his book, *One Day in the Life of Ivan Denisovitch*.

Sibirtsevo   Сибирцево   9,117km
This area is the centre of an extremely fertile region where wheat, oats, soya beans and rice are grown. The climate of the southern part of the Russian far east makes most areas ideal for agriculture as the warm summer rains create a hothouse atmosphere. However, only short season plants can be grown as the winters are long and cold.

Ussurisk   Уссурийск   9,185km
This attractive town sits in the middle of a fertile valley at the junction of three rivers. The town was founded in 1866 as Nikolskoe after Tsar Nikoli but was changed to Voroshilov in 1935 after Kliment Voroshilov (1881–1969) who was Stalin's ruthless alley both during his purges and World War II. With Khrushchev's ascent to power after Stalin's death, Voroshilov was forced to retire in 1960 and the town's name was changed to Ussurisk after the nearby river.

The country's most famous brand of refrigerators, Okean, is manufactured here. The town is very green because many trees, such as poplars, elms and jasmine, have been transplanted here from the taiga. The town has a museum of local studies.

From Ussurisk there are branch lines to Harbin in China and Pyongyang in North Korea (see *Chapter Seventeen, page 411*).

Amurski Zaliv   Амурский Залив   9,261km
If your train is going to Tikhookeanskaya (Nakhodka) and you want to go to Vladivostok, get off here and catch a suburban train.

Uglovaya   Угловая   9,264km
Just before reaching Uglovaya, trains for Nakhodka branch off (see *Chapter Seventeen, page 417*).

THE BIKIN RIVER WATERSHED AND KRASNYI YAR
contributed by Michael 'Misha' Jones

To the east of the Trans-Siberian, halfway between Khabarovsk and Vladivostok, is a unique, undeveloped, bio-diverse zone which is the traditional home of the Udege, Nanai and Oroch indigenous peoples.

The Bikin is the largest undeveloped watershed on the western slope of the Sikhote-Alin Mountain Range in the Russian far east; the middle and upper sections of the watershed total around 1.2 million hectares. The landscape is covered with virgin forests. The watershed is a transition zone between northern taiga and southern temperate rain forests. The plant and animal communities formed in this part of the central Sikhote-Alin are unique and contain over 60 rare, endangered and endemic plant and animal species: Amur tiger, Himalayan black bear, fish owl, spruce grouse, scaly-sided merganser, rose root and ginseng.

The main sporting activity for foreigners is seasonal fishing.

In the centre of the Bikin River watershed is the national village, Krasnyi Yar. Sustainable use of natural resources is a historic characteristic of the indigenous peoples and these have to-date supplied most local needs.

The Bikin watershed is under threat, particularly its headwaters which are currently unprotected. A major highway is being pushed through the middle portion of the watershed, while poaching is increasing as there is gold in the Bikin and international timber markets want its forests. Poor transportation and an unstable electricity supply are systemic issues retarding local economic development.

Getting to Krasnyi Yar is not easy. The closest train connection is via Luchegorsk station which is about 10km from the town of Luchegorsk. There is a very basic hotel in Luchegorsk. Regular buses travel between Luchegorsk town and Verkhnii Pereval, a village 60km away towards Krasnyi Yar. From Pereval a logging road leads through Yasenyovyi village to Olon village which sits on the shore of the Bikin River. Krasnyi Yar, with its 700 people, is situated on the opposite bank. Krasnyi Yar is 160km by road from Luchegorsk. There is no hotel in Krasnyi Yar and visitors are billeted with locals.

If you do want to visit Krasnyi Yar, contact the town's council, 692031 Primorskii Krai Pozharskii Raion, Krasnyi Yar village, tel: (4257) 32 625, email udege@glas.apc.org or contact Michael 'Misha' Jones of the Pacific Environment and Resources Centre, Siberian Forest Protection Project, Fort Cronkhite, Building 1055, Sausalito, CA 94965, USA, tel: (415) 332 8200, fax: (415) 332 8167, email perc@igc.apc.org.

The town around the station is known as Trudovoe (Трудовое) and it sits at the northern edge of the Uglovi Bay. The pleasant beaches and the clean water make Trudovoe a popular swimming destination for Vladivostok's day trippers.

After departing from the station, the railway travels down the peninsular named in honour of the famous Russian explorer Count Nikolai Muravevo-Amurskaya.

Sadgorod   Садгород   9,271km
It was around here that the tsar's son, Nicholas, inaugurated the Trans-Siberian on May 19 1891 by dumping a barrow of ballast on to the embankment. It is interesting that this date is normally considered the start of the railway even though to get to this point, Nicholas travelled 18km by train from the start of the

railway at the tip of the peninsular through Vladivostok to Sadgorod. He then returned by train to Vladivostok and unveiled a plaque which announced the construction of the railway.

Near Sadgorod (which means "garden city") was the station called Khilkovo, named in honour of Prince M I Khilkov, Minister of Ways of Communication in the Tsarist government, who was one of the main supporters of the Trans-Siberian. Khilkovo station has long since disappeared.

Vtoraya Rechka   Вторвая Речка   9,288km
The bus station in front of the station is Vladivostok's main long-distance bus station with buses for the airport and local towns.

Pervaya Rechka   Первая Речка   9,293km
According to the original 1880s plan for the Trans-Siberian, this was to be the terminus of the Trans-Siberian and a small branch line would extend on to Vladivostok. Despite the difficulties of building a multi-track railway along the steep shore, it was decided in the 1890s to extend the Trans-Siberian through to Vladivostok.

Ahead and to the left is a 180m-high television station which is the first visible feature of Vladivostok.

VLADIVOSTOK   Владивосток   9,297km
Population: 648,000   Telephone area code: 4232
Vladivostok is a great place to start or end your Russian adventure. It is an extremely lively, attractive and historic city. It is on the same parallel as the Caucasus so is considerably warmer than the rest of Russia and, being on the sea, is very humid in summer.

Prior to the communist revolution, Vladivostok was slated to become the next Shanghai. After a 70-year interruption, the city is again taking off and may fulfil the prophecy. However, one of the consequences of this is that the city abounds with shady dealers and is known as the violence capital of the Russian far east. For this reason, some people prefer to start or end their Trans-Siberian journey in Khabarovsk. Before you make a decision, contact your travel agent or Ministry of Foreign Affairs for the latest advice.

The city, which was closed to foreigners until 1992, has sister city relationships with Akita, Hakadate and Niigata in Japan, Pusan in South Korea, Dalyan in China, and Tacoma and San Diego in USA.

The best day to be in Vladivostok is the first Sunday in July which is the Vladivostok City Day and Sailors' Day and you will see parades, naval demonstrations and a firework display.

Vladivostok was honoured in 1995 by being featured on Russia's new 1,000 rouble notes; however, locals protested that this virtually worthless denomination reflected Moscow's attitude to the provinces. In ascending order, the other notes were 10,000 roubles featuring Krasnoyarsk, 50,000 roubles featuring St Petersburg and 100,000 roubles notes featuring Moscow.

Getting there and away
By air   Alaska Airlines has two weekly flights to Anchorage in summer and one in winter to Seattle; Aeroflot has one weekly flight to Niigata, Japan, Taipei, Taiwan, Hong Kong and Seoul, Korea, and two weekly flights to Niigata, Japan;

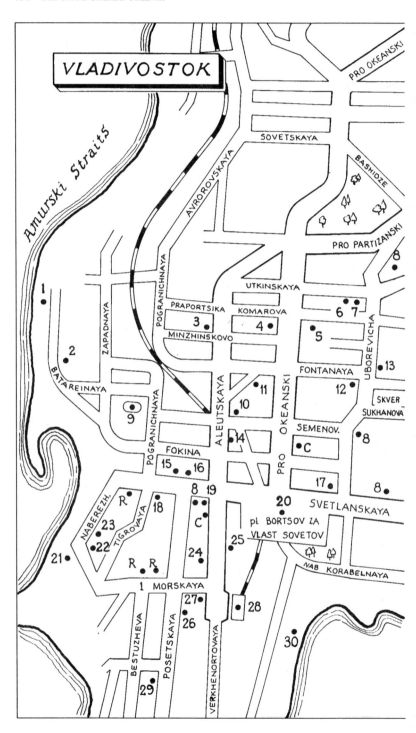

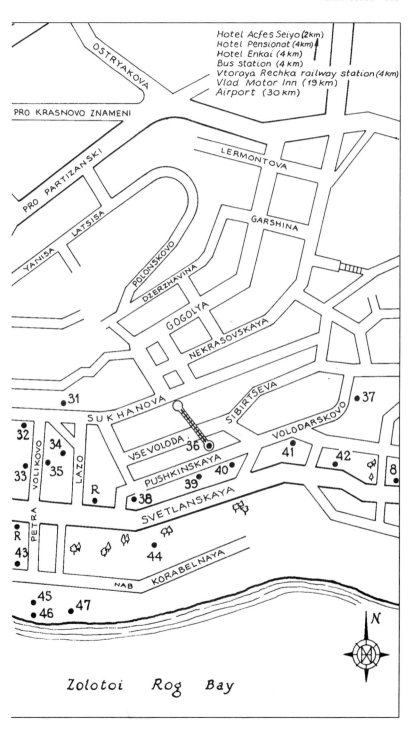

OSTRYAKOVA

Hotel Acfes Seiyo (2km)
Hotel Pensionat (4km)
Hotel Enkai (4 km)
Bus station (4 km)
Vtoraya Rechka railway station (4km)
Vlad Motor Inn (19 km)
Airport (30 km)

PRO KRASNOVO ZNAMENI

PRO PARTIZANSKI

LERMONTOVA

YANISA   LATSISA

POLONSKOVO

DZERZHAVINA

GARSHINA

GOGOLYA

NEKRASOVSKAYA

• 31

SUKHANOVA

SIBIRTSEVA

• 37

32

VOLIKOVO

34

35

LAZO

VSEVOLODA

• 36

VOLODARSKOVO

41

42

8

33

R

PUSHKINSKAYA

39 •   40 •

• 38

SVETLANSKAYA

R

PETRA

43

44

KORABELNAYA

NAB

• 45
• 46   • 47

N

Zolotoi   Rog   Bay

KEY TO VLADIVOSTOK   Владивосток

1	Oceanarium	Океанария
2	Beluga whales (*Kita*)	Кита
3	South Korean Consulate (*Kulsulstvo*)	Кулсульство Южной Кореи
4	Far East Business Institute (*Institut*)	Дальневосточный коммерческий институт
5	Market (*Rynok*)	Рынок
6	Former ecclesiastical council building (*Konsistoriya*)	Быв. духовная консистория
7	Former residence of Langelit	Быв. особняк Лангелитье
8	Book shop (*Knigi*)	Книги
9	Dinamo Stadium (*Stadion*)	Стадион «Динамо»
10	Border Guard Museum (*Muzei*)	Музей «Пограничников»
11	Japanese Consulate (*Kulsulstvo*)	Кулсульство Японии
12	Australian Consulate (*Kulsulstvo*)	Кулсульство Австраилии
13	Radio Centre (*Dom Radio*)	Дом радио
14	Hare Krishna restaurant	ресторан для вегетарианцев
15	Drama Theatre (*Teatr*)	Драматический театр
16	Green Lantern Cabaret House (*Kabare*)	Кабаре
17	Department Store (*GUM*)	ГУМ
18	Hotel Versailles and Casino Amherst	гостиница Версаиллес и казино
19	Museum of Local Studies (*Muzei*)	Краведческий музей
20	Victory of Soviet Power monument	Памятник «Борцам за власть Советов»
21	Hotel Amurski Zaliv and Casino	гостиница Амурский Залив и казино
22	Hotel Vladivostok and Indian Consulate (*Kulsulstvo*)	гостиница Владивосток Консульство Индии
23	Hotel Ekvator	гостиница Екватор
24	House of the Brynner family	Быв. Дом Брыннера
25	Picture gallery (*Galereya*)	Картинная галерея
26	Hotel Primore	гостиница Приморье
27	Central post office (*Pochtamt*)	Почтамт
28	Railway station (*Vokzal*)	Ж-Д вокзал
29	Aeroflot	Аэрофлот
30	Hotel at the Sea Ferry Terminal	гостиница в Морском вокзале
31	House Museum of Sukhanov	Дом-музей Суханова
32	Far Eastern University (*Universitet*)	Дальневосточный университет
33	Far Eastern Institute (*Institut*)	Дальневосточный институт
34	Gorky Theatre (*Theatr*)	Театр им. Горьково
35	Puppet Theatre (*Teatr*)	Театр кукол
36	Funicular railway (*Funikuler*)	Фуникулёр
37	Catholic Church	Католический костёл
38	American Business Centre	Американский коммерческий центр
39	Far Eastern Technical University (*Universitet*)	Дальневосточый технический университет
40	Pacific Fleet Military Museum	Музей Тихоокеанского флота
41	USA Consulate (*Kulsulstvo*)	Кулсульство США
42	Circus (*Tsirk*)	Цирк
43	Submarine Museum and Navy memorials	Мемориальный комплекс «Боевая слава краснознаменного Тихоокеанского флота»
44	Admiral Nevelski monument	Памятник адмиралу Невельскому
45	125th anniversary of Vladivostok monument (*Obelisk*)	Обелиск в честь 125-летия основания города Владивостока
46	Krasni Vympel Ship Museum	Параход «Красний Вымпел»
47	Local ferry terminal	Морской вокзал прибрежных сообщений
R	Restaurant (*Restoran*)	Ресторан
C	Café (*Kafé*) or Bar (*Bar*)	Кафе или Бар

Malival (Magadan Airlines) has one weekly flight to Anchorage and then onwards to Seattle; and Korean Air has a weekly flight to Seoul, South Korea.
By boat A sea ferry plies between Vladivostok and Japan, usually from late June to late September. The ferry departs weekly from Vladivostok and travels to the cities of Niigata and Fushiki on alternate weeks. The trip takes about 72 hours (remember there is a one-hour time difference between Vladivostok and Japan). The timetable for 1995 was ferries departing Japan at 16.00 on Friday and arriving in Vladivostok at 09.00 on Sunday, and departing Vladivostok at 15.00 on Tuesday and arriving in Japan at 09.00 on Thursday.

Information on the ferry can be received from the shipping line, the United Orient Shipping and Agency Co Ltd, Level 7 Rikkokai-sogo Building, 2-32-3 Kita-Shinagawa, Shinagawa-ku, Tokyo 140, Japan, tel: (813) 3740 2061, fax: (813) 3740 2085.

By rail The main Trans-Siberian trains on this segment are:

Origin	Dist, km	Train no & name	Travel time	Depart	Arrive	Destination
Khabarovsk	766	2	13hr 10min	13.35	02.45	Vladivostok
Vladivostok	766	1	13hr 30min	17.55	07.25	Khabarovsk

Where to stay
Unfortunately hotels in Vladivostok are quite expensive. The most expensive are the excellent Japanese-owned Hotel Versailles, Svetlanskaya 10, tel: 264 201, 264 301, $200 a double room; the Hotel Acfes Seiyo, pro 100th Vladivostoka 103, tel: 318 760, 318 765, fax: 319 000, satellite tel: (509) 851-2345, satellite fax: 852 2350, and the Canadian Vlad Motor Inn, ul Vosmaya 1, tel: 215 828, 215 854, satellite tel: (509) 851 5111, fax: (509) 851 5116, $150 a double room. The standard Hotel Enkai, tel: 215 422, $100 a double room; the standard Hotel Pensionat, ul Devyataya 14, tel: 215 639, $70 a double room; and the Vlad Motor Inn are all located to the north of Vladivostok around the station Sanatornaya (meaning "sanatorium") on the way north.

The hotel closest to the station is the basic Hotel Primore, ul Posetskaya, tel: 213 182, $30 a single room. Other centrally located hotels are the standard Hotel Vladivostok, ul Naberezhnaya 10, tel: 222 208, 222 246, $46 a single room (check out the mini-hotel on the fourth floor which is of a better standard); the basic Hotel Ekvator, ul Naberezhnaya 20, tel: 212 260, 212 864, $24 a single room; standard Hotel Amurski Zaliv, ul Naberezhnaya 9, tel: 225 520, $50 a single room; and excellent Hotel Gavan, ul Krygina 3, tel: 219 965, 219 573, fax: 226 848, email port@stv.iasnet.com.

There is also a basic hotel at the ferry terminal which is invariably full of transit passengers.

Point of interest
Vegetarians rejoice! There is a Hari Krishna restaurant in town. It is at pro Okeanski 10/12, tel: 268 943, open 10.00–19.00 weekdays.

Getting around
Most sights and places of interest are all within walking distance of the railway station with the exception of the Vlad Motor Inn, and Hotels Enkai and Pensionat. To get to the Enkai and Pensionat Hotels, take the suburban train six stops to the station Sanatornaya (Санаторная). To get to Vlad Motor Inn, you have to take a taxi as it is located 19km from the station on the M60 highway to the airport.

The airport is 30km away near Artem-Primorski railway station and there are three ways of getting there. Firstly and most conveniently, you can take a taxi which costs about $50. Secondly, you can take bus No 101 which travels between the airport and Vladivostok's main bus station which is just in front of Vtoraya Rechka railway station. From here you have to catch a suburban train to get to the centre of Vladivostok which is 9km to the south. The biggest problem with this trip is that there is no schedule for the bus as it goes only when it has a large number of filled seats. The third option is the cheapest but longest. Take bus No 7 from the airport to the Artem-Primorski railway station and get on a local train heading west. Get off at the fourth stop which is Amurski Zaliv station and change trains for Vladivostok. From Amurski Zaliv to Vladivostok takes 50 minutes.

The railway station is a delightful, yellow, two-storey building from the last century which was renovated in 1995. To exit the station, you have to walk up to the top floor which is at street level. Attached to the station is a modern ferry terminal with the entrance to the basic hotel from the terminal's waiting room.

For a cheap cruise around the bays, there are numerous daily ferries from the ferry station opposite the Submarine Museum. Destinations include the popular swimming spots of Russki Island, Popov Island, Reiniky Island, Cape Peshanaya (two ferries a weekday and three on the weekends), and Slavyanka Beach (two hydrofoils a day), and the suburb of Churkin which is on the other side of the bay.

What to see

One of the great sights of Vladivostok is the Russian Navy's vast Pacific Fleet. It was once the Soviet Union's best fleet but in the last few years has become the least battle-ready. The best place to survey the fleet is from the hill on pl Orlinoye Gnezdu (meaning "Eagle's Nest Square"). To get to the hill, try the funicular railway from in front of the Pacific Fleet Museum. However, the funicular rarely runs, so be prepared for quite The square is covered in broken wire and concrete so take good walking shoes. a hike. Another great view of the region is to catch a bus to the very southern tip of the Vladivostok peninsular. Catch bus No 1 from the square pl Posetskaya, which is just to the south of the railway station and in front of the Aeroflot office. The bus terminates at the stop Mayak which means "lighthouse". A good way to get a closer look at the boats harboured around the bays is to catch a local ferry, described below.

Vladivostok's biggest museum is the History Museum. As well as containing history of the region, it includes an exhibition of the pre-communist era family home of Yul Brynner, ul Svetlanskaya 20, open 10.00–16.30, closed Monday. The Brynner family owned a large trading business before the revolution and their house still stands at ul Aleutskaya 15; unfortunately, you can't enter it.

There are four military museums in the city. They are the Pacific Fleet Military Museum, ul Pushkinskaya 14, tel: 228 035, open 09.30–17.45, closed Monday and Tuesday; the Submarine Museum, which is inside a World War II C56 submarine, nab Korabelnaya, tel: 216 757, open 09.00–18.00, closed Sunday–Tuesday; the Krasni Vympel Ship Museum, nab Korabelnaya, which was the first ship commissioned into the Soviet Pacific Fleet, open 09.30–17.45, closed Sunday–Tuesday; and the excellent Border Guard Museum, ul Semenovskaya 17, tel: 218 074, open 09.00–17.00, closed Sunday and Monday.

Art galleries and shops include the Art Gallery and Shop, ul Aleutskaya 12, open 10.00–18.00, closed Sunday and Monday; and the Art Etage, ul Svetlanskaya 22, open 11.00–18.30, closed Monday..

Other places of interest include the House-museum of Sukhanov who was a communist leader at the turn of the century, ul Sukhanova 9, open 10.30–19:00, closed Monday; and the Oceanarium, ul Batarinaya 4, tel: 254 977, open 10.00–17.00 in winter, 10.00–19.00 in summer, containing both live and stuffed marine life. Across the road from the Olympic Sports Hall, Batarinaya 8, is the holding pen of some Beluga whales. The times of opening seem to vary considerably.

Souvenirs can be bought at the Emerald (Izumrud) jewellery store, pro Okeanski; Amethyst jewellery store, pro Okeanski 10/12, Gzhel ceramic store, ul Mordovtseva 3; GUM department store, ul Svetlanskaya 33; and Nostalgia café and art store, ul 1st Morskaya 6/25, tel: 267 813

Theatres include the Gorky Theatre, ul Svetlanskaya 49, tel: 264 587; Drama Theatre, ul Svetlanskaya 15a, tel: 264 889; Concert Hall, ul Svetlanskaya 13; Puppet Theatre, ul Petra Velikova 8; and Circus, ul Svetlanskaya 103, tel: 256 650.

Other places of entertainment include the Green Lantern Cabaret House, ul Svetlanskaya 13; Casino Amurski Zaliv in the Hotel Amurski Zaliv, ul Naberezhnaya 9 and Casino Amherst in the Versailles Hotel, ul Svetlanskaya 10.

Getting assistance

Travel agents Primoski Klub Travel Service, 4th floor, ul Russkaya 17, Vtoraya Rechka, tel: 318 037; Intourist, pr Okeanski 90, tel: 256 210, fax: 258 839, Primorsk Tourist co, tel: 251 987; ACFES Tour Centre in the Hotel Acfes Seiyo, pr 100th Vladivostoka 103, tel: 319 492. Bannikov Adventure Expeditions, Vladivostok, tel: (4232) 29 46 26, fax: (4232) 26 45 89, is led by Leonid Bannikov, a member of the Geographic Society for over 25 years. Trips include nature photography, rafting, hiking, cross-country skiing and fishing in the Russian far east.

Air Aeroflot, ul Posetskaya 14, tel: 260 880, Alaska Airlines (at airport) tel: 227 645.

Bus The long-distance bus station is located in front of the Vtoraya Rechka railway station, ul Russkaya 2, tel: 465 2278.

Rail Railway station, ul Aleutskaya 6, tel: 210 440.

Diplomatic representation Indian Consulate, Hotel Vladivostok, room 7002, tel: 229 669, 229 760, 228 536, open 09.00–17.30 weekdays; South Korean Consulate, ul Aleutskaya 45, 5th floor, tel: 227 822, 227 729, 227 765, fax: 229 9471, open 09.00–18.00 weekdays; Australian Consulate, ul Uborevicha 17, tel: 228 628, fax: 228 778, open 09.00–17.00 weekdays; Japanese Consulate, ul Mordovtseva 12, tel: 267 502, 267 513, satellite fax: (509) 85 11002; US Consulate, ul Pushkinskaya 34, tel: 268 458, 266 734, fax: 268 445, open 14.30–16.00 weekdays.

Other The American Business Centre, ul Pushkinskaya 2, tel: 254 625, 254 625; fax: 254 661, email abcvlad@sovam.com; the US Information Agency and US Foreign Commercial Service, ul Battereinaya 2, tel: 259 424, 254 661; the English-language, fortnightly *Vladivostok News*, ul Fontanaya 15/2, tel: 250 471; fax: 250 397; http://www.tribnet.com.

404

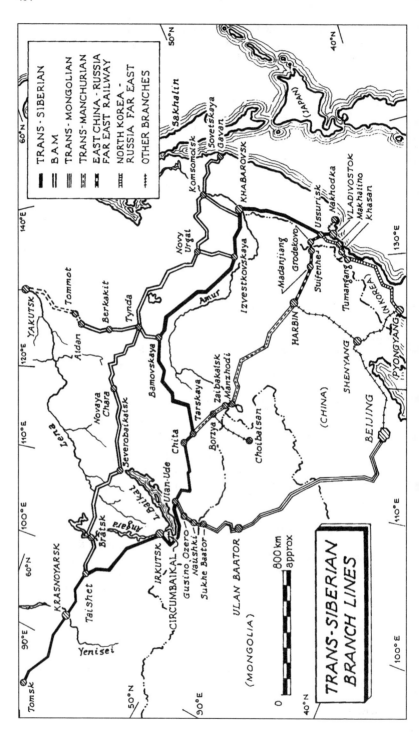

TRANS-SIBERIAN BRANCH LINES

Legend:
- TRANS - SIBERIAN
- BAM
- TRANS - MONGOLIAN
- TRANS - MANCHURIAN
- EAST CHINA - RUSSIA FAR EAST RAILWAY
- NORTH KOREA - RUSSIA FAR EAST
- OTHER BRANCHES

800 km approx

0

(MONGOLIA)
ULAN BAATOR

Tomsk
KRASNOYARSK
Taishet
Yenisei
Bratsk
Angara
Severobaikalsk
L. Baikal
IRKUTSK
CIRCUMBAIKAL
Gusino Ozero
Naushki
Sukhe Baator
Ulan-Ude
Chita
Tarskaya
Borzya
Zabaikalsk
Manzhodi
Choibalsan
Bamovskaya
Lena
Novaya Chara
Tynda
Berkakit
Aldan
Tommot
YAKUTSK
Novy Urgal
Amur
Izvestkovskaya
KHABAROVSK
Komsomolsk
Sovetskaya Gavan
Sakhalin
(JAPAN)
Madanjiang
Grodekovo
Suifenhe
Ussurisk
Nakhodka
VLADIVOSTOK
Makhalino
Khasan
Tumangan
HARBIN
SHENYANG
(CHINA)
BEIJING
PYONGYANG
(N.KOREA)

90°E 100°E 110°E
40°N 50°N 60°N
120°E 130°E 140°E
40°N 50°N

Chapter Seventeen
Trans-Siberian Branch Lines

This chapter discusses the following railways which all connect to the Trans-Siberian:

- the Trans-Mongolian railway: Ulan-Ude–Beijing via Mongolia
- the Trans-Manchurian railway: Chita–Beijing via Manchuria
- the East Chinese–Russian Far East railway: The Russian far east–Harbin
- the North Korean–Russian Far East railway
- the Vladivostok–Nakhodka railway
- the Circumbaikal railway

THE TRANS-MONGOLIAN RAILWAY
Ulan-Ude–Beijing via Mongolia

Although most people refer to the Trans-Mongolian railway as a railway stretching from Moscow to Beijing via Mongolia, the truth is that the Trans-Mongolian is just a 2,218km branch of the Trans-Siberian. The branch starts at the Trans-Siberian city of Ulan-Ude, which is 5,642km from Moscow, and runs to Beijing via Ulaanbaatar (the capital of Mongolia).

The Trans-Mongolian railway follows an ancient road used for centuries by tea caravans travelling between Beijing and Moscow. However, the railway is relatively new: the branch line to the border from Ulan-Ude was completed in 1940, the extension to Ulaanbaatar was opened in 1949 and the route was opened all the way to Beijing in 1956.

Travel suggestions
The biggest advantages of the Trans-Mongolian are that it lets you experience the rarely visited Mongolia, and both ends of it (Moscow and Beijing) are easy to reach. Its only disadvantage is that you have to obtain a Mongolian visa as you cannot board the train at Beijing without one. The addresses of the Mongolian consulates in the region are:

Moscow, Russia   pr Borisoglebski 11, tel: (095) 290 6792
Irkutsk, Russia   ul Lapina 11, tel: (3952) 242 370
Ekaterinburg, Russia   ul Furmanova 45, tel: (3432) 445 453
Beijing, China   2 Xiushiu Beijie, Jianguomenwai, tel: (861) 521 203
Tokyo, Japan   Shoto Pinecrest Mansion 21-4 Kamiyamacho Shibuya ku, Tokyo 150, tel: 03 3469 2088, 3469 2092.
Seoul, South Korea   A-302 Namsan Village, San, 1-139 Itaewondong, Yongsan-gu, tel: 02 793 5611.

There are two sorts of Mongolian visas for travellers: transit and tourist visas. To get either you will need to have booked a tour or bought the Trans-Mongolian train ticket and show this as proof at the consulate. As the actual visa-issuing process can take a few days unless you want to pay an express fee, it's best to have your travel company organise the visa on your behalf.

If you do it yourself in Beijing or Moscow, you have to queue at the embassy in person and then return to pick it up. You will need three passport photos, your Russian visa, Mongolian rail tickets, a completed visa application form (obtainable from the embassy) and sufficient US cash for the visa. The visa usually takes a day to be issued, but allow three days. The Moscow consulate's opening hours change often so it is advisable to call immediately upon your arrival in Moscow. The Beijing consulate is open 13.00–14.00 Monday, 09.00–11.00 Tuesday and 09.00–11.00 Friday.

Regardless of how you organise your Mongolian visa, you should plan to spend at least three working days in Beijing or Moscow to allow for delays and problems.

It has been possible to get a visa at the border in the past, but don't count on it, and being thrown off the train at the border stations is no fun.

Trains
International trains
In the late 1980s and early 1990s, the Trans-Mongolian trains were notoriously crowded with Chinese and Mongolian traders who filled up their cabins and corridors with goods for sale in Russia, and then returned with Russian goods for sale in Mongolia. The situation has improved since then with excess baggage charges and custom duties reducing the number of traders.

The most convenient long-distance trains on this route are listed below.

Origin	Dist, km	Entry point	Train no & name	Carr'ge class	No in coupé	Travel time	Day of departure	Destination
Moscow (Yaroslavl)	6,299	Naushki	2	2	4	115hr	Wed, Fri	Ulaanbaatar
Ulan-Ude	657	Naushki	2	2	4	18hr	Sun, Tue	Ulaanbaatar
Ulaanbaatar	6,299	Naushki	3	2	4	115hr	Sun, Mon	Moscow (Yaroslavl)
Ulaanbaatar	657	Naushki	3	2	4	17hr	Sun, Mon	Ulan-Ude
Moscow (Yaroslavl)	7,860	Naushki	2	2	4	140hr	Fri, Sat	Beijing
Beijing	7,860	Naushki	3	2	4	140hr	Thur, Fri	Moscow (Yaroslavl)

Domestic trains
There are two trains a day from Ulan-Ude to Naushki which is the Russian border town, and the 255km trip takes between five and six hours. The trains are very dirty and crowded with traders.

Route description
Ulan-Ude   Улан-Удэ   5,642km
For information on Ulan-Ude, the capital of the Republic of Buratia, see *Chapter Sixteen, page 373.*

Zaudinski   Заудинский   5,650km
This is the actual junction of the Trans-Siberian and the line to Mongolia. From here, the railway turns south and travels along the right bank of the

Selenga River until it crosses over it about 30km from Zaudinski. It then travels along the left bank before heading across country after another 10km.

Zagustai   Загустай   5,769km

Six kilometres from this station is the large coal-mining town of Gusinnozersk (Гусиноозёрск). The town grew quickly to today's size of 30,800 following the discovery of a huge coal basin in 1939. The first settlement was originally called Sakhty (Шахты) which means "mines" but this was changed to the more romantic name of Gusinnozersk meaning "goose lake".

After leaving the station, the train travels down the western bank of Guzinoe Lake which is 25km long and 5–8km wide.

Gusinoe Ozero   Гусиное Озеро   5,801km

At the southern end of the Guzinoe Lake is the station of the same name. A few kilometres east of here is Selenginsk village which is the centre of Buddhism in eastern Siberia. The working Buddhist monastery (known as a datsan) was founded in 1741 and consists of a large complex with temples and living quarters for the lama priests.

Naushki   Наушки   5,897km

This is the Russian border town. While at the station, customs forms will be collected and your visas cancelled. This process can take two hours. During this time, the toilets are locked but there are some at the Mongolian end of the platform. There is also a bank at the station where you can change money.

While Naushki is uninteresting, 35km to the east is the ancient trading town of Kyakhta (Кяхта) on the Russian-Mongolian border. This town was one of the world's major tea-trading centres during the 18th century as traders from China, Mongolia, the Middle East, Europe and Russia all converged here. More recently, it was the site of a particularly appalling atrocity in the very brutal Russian Civil War. Today, Kyakhta has a population of 18,300, a Museum of Local Studies, the Hotel Druzhba with rooms at $8, and little else.

About 5km after leaving Naushki, you reach the border which is marked by an electric fence. The train is often stopped here and border troops get on to search for stowaways. The bogies are not changed here as Mongolia's railway gauge is the same as Russia's.

Sukhe Baator   Сухэ Баатор   5,920km

This is the Mongolian border town and here you will complete customs and passport formalities.

Ulaanbaatar   Улан Баатор   6,299km

This is the capital of Mongolia and is a fascinating blend of European, Mongolian and Chinese culture. You can easily spend two days here without being bored.

Beijing   (note: include Chinese name)   7,860km

The Trans-Mongolian train begins or terminates here. To get on and off the platform in Beijing, you will have to show your ticket.

THE TRANS-MANCHURIAN RAILWAY
Chita–Beijing via Manchuria

The Trans-Manchurian railway is just 2,797km branch of the Trans-Siberian, starting at the city of Chita, 6,204km from Moscow, and extending to Beijing via Harbin in Manchuria.

The section of the Trans-Manchurian route from Chita to Harbin was completed in 1901 and was known as the western part of the East Chinese railway. The East Chinese railway was the only connection between Moscow and Vladivostok until 1916 when the Trans-Siberian railway was completed. The eastern part of the East Chinese railway from Harbin to Vladivostok has recently been opened and for information on this line, see *The East Chinese–Russian Far East Railway, page 410*.

Travel suggestions
The biggest advantages of the Trans-Manchurian are that you will have no problems getting a Chinese visa or reaching the beginning or end of it (Moscow or Beijing). While getting a visa to Russia is difficult, getting one to China is not a problem.

Trains
International trains
Like the Trans-Mongolian trains, in the late 1980s and early 1990s, the Trans-Manchurian trains were crowded with Chinese traders but the situation has improved recently.

The most convenient long-distance trains on this route are listed below.

Origin	Dist, km	Entry point	Train no & name	Carr'ge class	No in coupé	Travel time	Day of departure	Destination
Moscow (Yaroslavl)	9,001	Zabaikalsk	20	2	4	145hr		Beijing
Chita 2	2,797	Zabaikalsk	20	2	4	49hr		Beijing
Beijing	9,001	Zabaikalsk	19	2	4	145hr		Moscow (Yaroslavl)
Beijing	2,797	Zabaikalsk	19	2	4	49hr		Chita 2
Chita 2	1,409	Zabaikalsk	20	2	4	8hr		Harbin
Harbin	1,409	Zabaikalsk	19	2	4	8hr		Chita 2

Domestic trains
There is only one local train a day from Chita to Zabaikalsk and the 462km trip takes about 12 hours. The train is extremely dirty and crowded with traders.

Route description
Chita 2   Чита 2   6,204km
Chita 2 is the central station in Chita which is the capital of the Zabaikalsk region (see *Chapter Sixteen, page 378*).

Tarskaya   Тарская   6,311km
The actual junction of the Trans-Siberian and the Trans-Manchurian is at this siding, though there is nothing to see here except a small station.

Soon you cross over the Ingoda River and travel across open steppes.

Olovyannaya   Оловянная   6,450km

The 120-flat apartment block beside the station, which is owned by the local Zabaikalsk railway, was constructed by Chinese labourers using Chinese materials. It was one of the many *batar* deals between the Zabaikalsk (Russia) and Harbin (China) railways. Since 1988, when the first barter contract between the two railways was signed, most contracts have involved Russia swapping fertilisers, old rails and railway wheel sets for Chinese food, clothes and shoes. However, as confidence has grown, Harbin railways have provided specialist services such as doctors of traditional Chinese medicine for the nearby Karpovka railway workers, uniforms for Zabaikalsk railway workers, and the reconstruction specialists for Chita-2 and Petrovski Zavod stations.

Don't photograph anything from the train in this area as the town's outskirts house nuclear missile silos which contain SS-11 interballistic nuclear rockets and bunkers holding portable SS-20 nuclear rocket launchers.

Borzya   Борзя   6,549km

This town was founded in the 18th century and with the arrival of the railway became the transport hub of southeast Zabaikalsk region.

There is a branch line from here to the west which goes all the way to the city of Choibalsan in Mongolia. This 354km railway consists of two parts: a 117km section from Borzya on the Trans-Manchurian to Solovevsk (Соловевск) on the Russian-Mongolian border, and a 237km section from the Mongolian-Russian border town of Ereentsav to Choibalsan which is Mongolia's fourth largest city with 50,000 inhabitants. This railway, completed in 1939, is the only railway besides the Trans-Mongolian that runs between Russia and Mongolia.

To cross at this point, you will need Russian and Mongolia visas and border guards will look at you strangely as foreigners are a rare sight. In January 1996 there was only one carriage a week on the Chita–Choibalsan route and this departed on Wednesday from Chita-2 station. According to the Chita-2 stationmaster, the railways are considering abandoning this service due to declining passenger numbers. This carriage is connected to local trains on each side of the border. The trip from Chita-2 to Borzya takes up to 18 hours and from Ereentsav to Choibalsan takes up to six hours. From Solovevsk to Borzya, local trains depart on Wednesday, Friday, Saturday and Sunday and from Borzya to Solovevsk they depart on Tuesday, Thursday, Friday and Saturday.

Kharanor   Харанор   6,590km

There is a branch line from here to the east, terminating at the military towns of Krasnokamensk and Priargunsk. There are often vendors here selling military goods.

From here to the border, you will see border defences of pillboxes, military camps and tanks that are buried so that only their turrets can be seen.

Zabaikalsk   Забайкальск   6,666km

This town is within 1km of the border. Here your customs declarations and passports are checked at the station before the train is shunted into the bogie-changing sheds at the south end of the station. The bogies are changed because the Chinese railway gauge is narrower than the Russian one. You can either stay at the station, remain in the carriage or get out and watch the bogie changing. Taking photos in the bogie-changing shed was once strictly prohibited but now it is possible.

The station has a restaurant, bank and toilets. You will stay at the station for between one and two hours.

After leaving the station, the train reaches the border in about 1km. A high fence runs along the border and regular guard posts are dotted along it. If you put your head out of the window and look towards the front of the train, you will see a giant arch over the railway line which marks the border.

Manzhouli   内蒙古   6,678km
The station is the Chinese border checkpoint and your customs declaration and passport will be inspected. The process is quite relaxed and doesn't take too long. There is a shop and bank at the station.

Harbin   哈尔滨   7,613km
This large northern Chinese city is a major rail junction. From Harbin, trains to the south terminate in Beijing and to the east in Vladivostok. Getting a ticket is very difficult without Chinese language ability, so it is best to have everything organised beforehand.

Beijing   北京   9,001km
The Trans-Manchurian train begins or terminates here. To get on and off the platform at Beijing, you will have to show your ticket.

EAST CHINESE–RUSSIAN FAR EAST RAILWAY
The Russian far east–Harbin

This railway line is the eastern section of the old East Chinese railway which connected Moscow with Vladivostok. The railway was completed in 1901 and was the only route to Vladivostok until 1916 when the Trans-Siberian railway was completed. Once the Trans-Siberian was running, the East Chinese railway became less significant and in 1935 it was sold to the Japanese and all through traffic stopped. Today, the western section of the East Chinese railway from Chita to Harbin is well used as it is part of the Trans-Manchurian railway.

The same can't be said for the eastern section from Harbin to Vladivostok as it is mainly used by each country for local traffic to their respective borders. However, in the last few years, the border crossing has been opened for sporadic passenger services between Harbin and Vladivostok/Khabarovsk via Ussurisk. Ussurisk is on the Trans-Siberian near Vladivostok. This trip is only for the adventurous as it is far from reliable due to low demand. The train is also disgustingly dirty, and the border crossing procedure notoriously arbitrary.

Border crossing
Crossing here can be very difficult due both to procedures and race relations. The Russians dislike the Chinese and the Chinese dislike the Russians; if you are a Caucasian, you will be lumped in with the Russians. The customs procedures will probably involve counting your money, going through your bags and generally hassling you. So pre-count your money and be meticulous when filling in your customs form.

Getting assistance and tickets

When planning to travel on this route, have a backup plan in case the train is cancelled. This is not too difficult as there are daily flights from Harbin to Khabarovsk.

It is best to book train tickets through a company in either Harbin or Vladivostok/Khabarovsk rather than in Beijing or Moscow as they are too far away to know the real situation.

In Harbin, the best place to book a ticket is with the Harbin Branch of the China International Travel Service (CITS). Their address is Manager, European and American Department, 73 Zhongshan Rd, Harbin, tel: (0451) 222 655, fax: (0451) 222 476, telex 87034 HCITS CN.

In Khabarovsk, contact Eurasia Trans Inc, ul Turgeneva 64, Khabarovsk, tel: (4210) 336 067, 384 261, fax: (4210) 332 726, telex 141174 ROTOR SU.

Trains

The train that crosses the border actually consists of just two carriages, one from Vladivostok and one from Khabarovsk. These two carriages start from their respective destinations attached to local trains and meet at Ussurisk where they are disconnected and joined to a local train that runs to the Chinese-Russian border. Here they are pulled across the border and joined to a Chinese train which terminates in Harbin.

As an indication of the condition of the carriage, there will either be no sheets or ones which are never changed. There is a restaurant car attached from Harbin to the Chinese border and there may be one on the Ussurisk to Khabarovsk leg.

The timetable below should not be taken as gospel, but it gives an idea of the travel times. Departures are weekly.

From Vladivostok/ Khabarovsk (a)	Station	km	From Harbin (b)
11.38	Khabarovsk		05.15
19.00	Vladivostok		21.21
00.50	Ussurisk	0	18.17
03.46	Grodeko	97	09.45
05.37	Harbin	633	20.48

Notes:
(a) The carriage from Vladivostok to Ussurisk is connected to train No 678, the carriage from Khabarovsk to Ussurisk is connected to train No 4, and both carriages are connected to No 659 train from Ussurisk to Grodeko.
(b) Both carriages are connected to No 660 from Grodeko to Ussurisk, the carriage from Ussurisk to Vladivostok is connected to train No 677, and the carriage from Ussurisk to Khabarovsk is connected to train No 3.

Route description
Vladivostok/Khabarovsk   Владивосток | Хабаровск

For information on these cities, refer to *Chapter Sixteen, pages 397* and *387* respectively.

Ussurisk   Уссурийск   0km

This town is on the Trans-Siberian and your carriage from either Vladivostok or Khabarovsk will be disconnected from the train you arrived on and shunted away from the station to wait for the connecting train to the Russian-Chinese border. The toilets will be locked but you can use the ones at the station (see *Chapter Sixteen, page 395*).

Vozdvizhenski   Воздвиженский   18km

Near this major rail junction a $2 million experiment is underway to solve the chronic vegetable shortages in the Russian far east. The project involves growing potatoes, onions, beetroots and carrots using Dutch seeds, know-how and equipment. In 1995, an investment of $300,000 at Putsilovskoye farm about 30km west of Ussurisk produced a harvest estimated to be worth over $890,000 assuming, say, onions are sold at $0.45 a kilo, which is half of the price of imported onions from Uzbekistan. The region's climate is similar to that of France and plans are afoot not only to feed locals but also to export the vegetables to Japan.

Grodekovo   Гродеково   97km

The desolate border town at this station is known as Pogranichny (Пограничный) and is plagued with crime and corruption, so be careful. It is here that your documents will be checked and your carriage will be shunted away from the station to await being shunted across the border. There is a restaurant and money-change point at the station.

There are only two trains a day between Ussurisk and Grodekovo.

There is nothing of interest in the town except for the experimental vineyard which has 60 varieties of grapes including many that were locally bred such as the Khassanski Boussa and the Khassanski Sweet grapes. Both of these can withstand frosts as low as –30°C and yield 5.9 tons of grapes per hectare which is average for Russia but low compared to California where the average yield of table grapes is 16.6 tons per hectare. However it is the quality, not the quantity, that is important.

Rassypnaya Pad   Рассыпная Падь   116km

This town is the actual border town but it is only for military personnel.

Suifenhe   绥芬河   118km

This small busy town with its turn-of-the-century Russian buildings is a contrast to sluggish Pogranichny. In Russian the town is written Суйфынхе. There is only one local train a day from Suifenhe to Mudanjiang.

Harbin   哈尔滨   663km

This large, northern Chinese city is the junction of the Trans-Manchurian railway. From Harbin, trains to the south terminate in Beijing and to the north, they join the Trans-Siberian in Russia. Getting a ticket is very difficult without Chinese language ability, just like anywhere else in China, so it is best to have everything organised beforehand. You must show your ticket to get on and off the platform in Harbin.

NORTH KOREAN–RUSSIAN FAR EAST RAILWAY

Without doubt North Korea is a weird country but it is one of the most interesting places to visit in the world. It is a combination of mountainous beauty and fascinating ancient history; of course it is also the last Cult of Personality communist state in the world.

The Democratic People's Republic of Korea (North Korea) was officially founded in 1948 and today is still a closed society, fearful of foreigners.

However, since 1986, Western tour groups have been allowed in and now even Americans are welcome.

The North Korean regime knows that it has an image problem in the West and, to ensure that you leave the country with good impressions, all foreigners are treated like dignitaries. Privileged treatment includes being provided with a personal train for the four-hour rail trip to Mount Myohyang from Pyongyang, tours of buildings closed to locals, and entering public buildings via dignitaries' entrances.

In addition, a guide will always accompany you, pointing out the achievements of the regime, providing the official answers to your questions, and laying down a few rules. Firstly, the DPRK is a developing country that was destroyed by the US during the Korean War. "We are very proud of our achievements in reconstruction and it is insulting to the Korean people's sacrifices for you to photograph dirty areas, peasants working in the fields and anything that may be used by the US as propaganda!" Secondly, as few people speak English, it is inadvisable to wander off in case you get lost. "In addition, citizens may mistake you for an American and this may generate anti-US feelings which may cause problems."

Despite the focus on official culture, it is the observation of daily life that is the most revealing. Train travel is particularly informative as this is the major form of personal and freight transport. While foreigners travel in old but well-maintained four-berth *coupé* carriages, the same vintage rolling stock used by the general population is in an appalling condition, with large areas rusted out, broken windows and missing doors. It is obvious that the country is suffering from a fuel shortage as the infrequent trains are always overcrowded with many passengers riding on the roof.

Border crossing

The Khasan-Tumangang border crossing is unlike any other around Russia. It is like stepping back into the Cold War when all foreigners were seen as spies. The Russian border guards and customs officials are like those in the Brezhnev period: rude and unhelpful, while the North Korean officials are like those in the Stalinist period: suspicious, intrusive and thorough. Therefore, it is best to approach this crossing with all seriousness. On your customs form, state exactly the amount of money you carry, the number and brand of cameras, and any electrical appliances. Throw away any inappropriate reading material.

If your documentation is not in order, you have no chance of lying or bribing your way into North Korea. If you are going from Russia to North Korea carry the confirmation of your booked tour for North Korea and, if you are going from North Korea to Russia, show your Intourist vouchers or, if you are travelling independently around Russia, just say you are meeting your guide in Khabarovsk.

Don't take out your camera near the border as your film will be taken.

As your carriage is hooked on to a particular daily train on the other side of the border, if you arrive late, you may have to wait 24 hours. To minimise this chance, your carriage is timetabled to have between two and five hours at the border before joining the across-border train.

Another crossing problem is border closure due to typhoid outbreaks in northern North Korea, such as the one on September 11 1995. In addition, as the Treaty of Friendship between Russia and North Korea expired in 1996, punitive border closures may become a political tool for gaining favour with rabidly anti-North Korean Western countries.

Here is the description of one border-crossing in winter 1994:

> "I arrived at the Korean border station of Tumangang at 16.33. After being shunted to the bogie-exchange area, the conductor brought an English-speaking passenger to my cabin at 18.20 to inform me that we were too late to cross the border, and would be held until the next day. At 19.00 the lights were turned off. By the light of my torch I had muesli bars for dinner, with tepid coffee; the urn was electric and had been turned off. Next day at 13.13 we departed to cross the border to Khasan, arriving at 13.28. After passport and customs inspection, we waited for six hours and were then told that there was no train to Moscow that day; we would leave the next day.'

> *Roderick B Smith of Melbourne, Australia*

Trains

There is only one way of crossing the Russian-Korean border by train: a single carriage which travels the Pyongyang–Moscow–Pyongyang route. This carriage leaves Moscow attached to the main Trans-Siberian train, No 2, and is disconnected at Ussurisk, which is 112km from Vladivostok. From Ussurisk, the carriage is coupled to a local train that travels 164km to Khasan station on the Russian side of the border. This trip takes 6hr 30min from Ussurisk to Khasan (7hr 40min from Khasan to Ussurisk). The carriage is then shunted to Tumangang station on the North Korean side of the border where it is joined to a long-distance train which terminates in Pyongyang.

The four-berth *coupé* carriage is old but well maintained and usually has carpets, clean toilets and fans.

There is a restaurant car on the Trans-Siberian leg, none on the Ussurisk–Khasan leg, and there may be one on the Tumangang–Pyongyang leg. On this last leg, your meals will be brought to your compartment or you will be led by your North Korean guide to the restaurant car and a special meal laid out for you while the North Korean passengers are locked out.

The only long-distance trains on this route are listed below.

Origin	Dist, km	Entry point	Train no & name	Carr'ge class	No in coupé	Travel time	Day of departure	Destination
Ussurisk	1,029	Khasan	42	2	4	30hr	Wed, Fri	Pyongyang
Pyongyang	1,029	Khasan	41	2	4	34hr	Mon, Wed	Ussurisk
Moscow (Yaroslav)	10,214	Khasan	2 (Russia) then 42	2	4	200hr	Thur, Sat	Pyongyang
Pyongyang	10,214	Khasan	41 then 1 (Russia)	2	4	200hr	Mon, Wed	Moscow (Yaroslav)

Getting tickets and assistance

To get a ticket to North Korea, you need a visa. To get this visa, which costs only $10, you need to have an invitation. The easiest way to get one is to organise a tour with North Korea's only travel company, Korea International Travel Service (KITC). This can be just an inbound and outbound rail ticket and one day in Pyongyang. Travel within North Korea is expensive but is worth it. For example, a rail ticket for the Pyongyang to Ussurisk trip is $120, a fully-inclusive day programme in North Korea costs about $120 a day, and a rail ticket for the Beijing to Pyongyang trip costs $110.

To get a visa, you need to visit a North Korean consulate and the main ones in the region are in:

Beijing, China   Ri Tan Bei Road, Jian Guo Men Wai, tel: (861) 532 4862
Nakhodka, Russian far east   North Korean Consulate, ul Vladivostokskaya 1, tel: (423 66) 552 10
Moscow, Russia   ul Mosfilmovskaya 72, tel: 143 6249, telex 413272
Chegdomyn, eastern Siberia
Macau, Macau   23rd floor, Nam Van Commercial Centre, 57-9 Rua da Praia Grande, tel: (853) 333 355, fax: (853) 333 939

Tours can be organised with KITC by contacting Mr Pak Gyong Nam, SAM Travel Service, Korea International Travel Company, Central District, Pyongyang, Democratic People's Republic of Korea, tel: (8502) 817 201, fax: (8502) 817 607, telex 5998 RHS KP. A five-day tour of Pyongyang and Kaesong costs about $600 twin shares which includes all accommodation, tours and meals, but excludes international travel.

Many travellers prefer to deal with a North Korean travel agent as that way you are assured of logistic and visa support. Try Russian Passport (formerly Red Bear Tours),Suite 11, 401 St Kilda Road, Melbourne, Victoria, 3004 Australia, tel: (03) 9867 3888, fax: (03) 9867 1055, email bmccunn@werple.mira.net.au.

Unescorted travel in North Korea is not possible.

A good guide to North Korea is KITC's *A Sightseeing Guide to Korea,* which costs $15 and can be bought from Russian Passport.

Route description

Ussurisk   Уссурийск   0km
The North Korean carriage leaves the Trans-Siberian here. The carriage will usually be shunted away from the station to wait for the connecting train. The toilets will be locked but you can use the ones at the station. It is often hard to get information about when your carriage will join its train; don't realy too heavily on any information you do get as the schedule is unreliable. Your carriage will normally join your train while the rest of the train waits at the platform (see *Chapter Sixteen, page 395*).

Baranovski   Барановский   23km
The Trans-Siberian line turns off to the east and almost immediately you know that you are travelling along a minor branch line from the size of the settlements and speed of the train.

Along this section are numerous old army bases surrounded by barbed wire and spotlights. While most of these have been abandoned to the weeds, guards still man the guard posts on bridges.

Bamburovo   Бамбурово   148km
There is a 13km branch line to the east which terminates on the Pacific Ocean at Blyukher (Блюхер) station. The town around the station is called Slavyanka (Славянка).

Gvozdevo   Гвозево   206km
There is a 12km branch line to the port of Poset Port (Посьет) which is closed to foreigners.

KOREAN RAILWAYS

Railways are critical to North Korea as they carry 90% of all freight and passengers. The country has 4,400km of main line track of which 2,700km is electrified. The railway gauge is 1435mm but there are also 1050mm and 760mm industrial and narrow-gauge tracks. The vast majority of main line locomotives are either electric or diesel while steam engines are normally used only for shunting. However, the cash-strapped North Korean government has periodic oil shortages and consequently presses steam trains into main line service. Most rolling stock is Chinese or Soviet although the North Koreans have been producing their own locomotives and passenger carriages since 1960.

Makhalino   Махалино   223km

In the future there will be a western branch line from here across the Chinese border to Hunchan city in the Jilin province. This line will be part of a 100km line linking the Russian port of Zarubino with Hunchan and costing US$350 million. The route's advantage is that it shortens the sea access for northern China and Mongolia enormously and will be critical to the Tumen River Trade Zone. The town around Makhalino is called Kraskino (Краскино).

Khasan   Хасан   260km

This is the Russian border station and its name is often transliterated as Hasan. The border guards at this border backwater still have the Soviet era suspicion of Western foreigners so don't be smart. The station is little more than a brick shed and if you have the time, you can visit the small village on the hill behind the station. Occasionally the kiosk opens at the station but don't rely on it.

The actual border is marked by the Tuman River and it is well guarded. It takes about 15 minutes to travel the 3km to the Korean border town of Tumangang.

Tumangang   두만강   263km

This is the North Korean border station. After passport and customs check, the carriage is moved into the bogie-exchange area where the bogies and couplings are exchanged. This area is in the open which indicates the small amount of passenger traffic between Russia and North Korea. As the onboard toilets are locked and there are none off the train, make sure you go before you arrive.

After the bogie change, the carriage is shunted and joins the local passenger train from Tumangang to Pyongyang. It is here that your North Korean guide will join you.

Pyongyang   평양   1,125km

This is the capital of North Korean and a great place to visit. You can easily spend three full days here. There are direct trains from here to Beijing and the 1,346km trip takes about 25 hours.

From Pyongyang, train No 26 departs at 11.50 on Monday, Wednesday, Thursday and Saturday arriving in Beijing at 10.00 the next day.

From Beijing, train No 27 departs at 16.48 on Monday, Wednesday, Thursday and Saturday arriving in Pyongyang at 16.05 the next day.

THE VLADIVOSTOK–NAKHODKA RAILWAY

Since Vladivostok has become open to foreigners, few travellers visit Nakhodka. This is because the Japanese ferry connecting with the Trans-Siberian now docks at Vladivostok and not Nakhodka. In addition, the region's only international airport is near Vladivostok.

If you do wish to travel to Nakhodka, the transport options are discussed under *Tikkhookeanskaya* which is the main railway station for Nakhodka.

Route description

Uglovaya   Угловая   47km
This is the start of the branchline railway. If you are coming from Vladivostok, the preceding major station is Ugolnaya (Угольная) and if from Moscow, it is Amurski Zaliv (Амурский Залив). The town's name comes from the word for "coal" which is mined in the region.

Artem-Primorski   Артем-Приморский   56km
The coal-mining and industrial city of Artem is spread over three stations: Artem-Primorski 1, 2, and 3. The town gets its name from the nom-de-guerre of the Bolshevik Fyodor Sergeyev (1883–1921).

To the north of Artem-Primorski 1 is Vladivostok's airport and from the railway you can see the brown coal-fired power station which provides power to Vladivostok and the open-cut coal mines which feed the plant. There is a museum in Artem.

Partizansk   Партизанск   183km
Partizansk is another coal-mining town and is spread over 30km. It is one of the region's oldest towns as it was founded in 1896. It has a museum named after the revolutionary K K Arsenev (1837–1919) who was the editor of Russia's best encyclopaedia.

The train now turns due south and heads down the Suchan River Valley which is rich with vineyards as the climate is mild and very humid in summer.

Losovaya   Лосовый
Losovaya is a popular tourist destination though you wouldn't know it seeing the giant thermo-electric power station around the station. In the hills near the station is the tourist base known as Mountain Springs which is famous for its healthy climate.

Maykhe   Мяхе
There is a large, state-owned farm here which breeds spotted deer.

Nakhodka   Находка   219km
Don't get off here as this station is at the northern end of the city of Nakhodka. Approaching the station, you pass through the suburb of Amerikanka. This is not some KGB imitation American city used for training deep-cover spies but was named after the Russian ship which discovered the bay around Nakhodka in 1859.

TIGER ATTACKS ON THE RISE
by Hashi Syedain, Vladivostok News, February 13 1996

Two people have been killed and one wounded by tigers in the Russian far east this year. In early January a man in Partizansk was killed and half-eaten by a tiger one morning on his way to the train station with his wife. And then on January 31, a hunter in the Alchan Valley, 400km north of Vladivostok, had his head bitten by a tigress and bled to death after crawling 12m in the snow.

The region's Tiger Group, responsible for killing man-eating tigers, is deciding what action to take. The Alchan Valley animal probably won't be pursued if it returns to the forest, spared by the fact that it did not actually eat its victim.

However, the Partizansk beast must officially be tracked down and killed, though it is not always easy to identify a particular animal. Moreover, the Tiger Group, which is normally responsible for anti-poaching measures, is neither properly equipped, nor especially keen on doing the job.

Despite this sudden spate of attacks, however, tiger experts say that attacks on people remain extremely rare.

In the early 1990s, there was a boom in tiger hunting as people thought they could get rich by selling tigers to China, where their body parts are used in traditional medicines. Although poaching has fallen off since the hunters realised that it was only the middlemen who were getting rich, experts believe that this period of aggressive hunting has changed the behaviour of the tigers.

TIKHOOKEANSKAYA   Тихоокеанская   229km
Population: 165,500   Telephone area code: 423 66

Tikhookeanskaya is the name of the railway station in the city of Nakhodka. This station is Russia's easternmost terminus for passenger trains. In Russian, Tikhookeanskaya means "Pacific Ocean" and *nakhodka* means "godsend" which was how the bay's discoverers felt when they were sheltering here from a storm.

The city extends for 30km along the mountainous coastline of the Bay of Nakhodka which is 4.6km long and 1.8km wide. From the city's principal avenue of Nakhodkinsky Prospect, which rings the bay, you can see the entire harbour of four separate ports. Most of the city was built after World War II and consequently it looks like most Soviet cities.

With the recent opening of Vladivostok to foreigners, most Russian-Japanese ferries have relocated from Nakhodka to Vladivostok. However, if your ferry does depart from Nakhodka, it will leave from the Italian-built marine passenger terminal next to the Tikhookeanskaya railway station.

Nakhodka has a sister city relationship with Oakland, California and Bellingham, Washington.

Getting there and away

By air   The closest airport is two hours away in Partizansk, and this is only for domestic flights.

By road   Bus No 206 travels between Vladivostok and Tikhookeanskaya and the trip takes 5hr.

By water   Hydrofoils travel intermittently to Vladivostok and the trip takes 2hr 30min.

During the Soviet era, all ferries between Japan and the Russian far east departed from Nakhodka as Vladivostok was closed to foreigners. Nowadays, Vladivostok is open and most ferries depart from there. If the old ferry route between Nakhodka and Yokohama is resurrected, the trip will take 53 hours and weekly departures will run from May to early October. All long-distance ferries will depart from the marine passenger terminal next to the station

By rail   Two local trains travel daily between Vladivostok and Tikhookeanskaya but these run inconveniently early in the morning or late at night. The 215km-trip takes about five hours. There are two long-distance trains that run between Khabarovsk and Tikhookeanskaya, and this 910km journey takes 17 hours. These long-distance trains do not go through Vladivostok as this city sits at the end of a peninsular. To get to Vladivostok from Tikhookeanskaya in the most comfortable way, catch a long-distance train from Tikhookeanskaya and get out at Amurski Zaliv station. This leg takes 2hr 30min. From here you catch a local train to Vladivostok and this leg takes 50min.

When buying tickets remember that the city of Nakhodka's railway station is called Tikhookeanskaya; there is a smaller station known as Nakhodka which is on the northern outskirts of the city of Nakhodka.

Where to stay

Despite the reduction in tourists visiting Nakhodka, the city has a number of good hotels which now mainly cater for business people. The choices are Hotel Vostok, pl Tsentralnaya, tel: 450 58; the standard Hotel Nakhodka, ul Shkolnaya 3, tel: 471 88 (to get to it from the station, take bus No 5 or 2 which stop in front of the hotel); and the excellent Hotel Pyramid, ul Vladivostokskaya 2, tel: 598 94, 597 50, satellite fax: (504) 915 2207, $200 a room; standard Dialog Hotel, ul Sovetskaya 1, tel: 407 61, $200 a room; standard Hotel Suan Yuan, ul Malinovskovo 32, tel: 409 77; and Hotel Gorizont, ul Leningradskaya 10, tel: 207 92, 207 70.

What to see

There is a Museum of Local Studies at ul Vladivostokaya 6, tel: 553 90, 456 83, Puppet Theatre, ul Lunacharskovo 8, tel: 579 79, Philharmonic Hall, ul Nakhimovskaya 19, tel: 599 40 and Casino Spartak, pro Nakhodkinski 32, tel: 552 51. The post office is at pro Nakhodkinski 34, tel: 559 97, and there is a book shop at pro Nakhodkinski 50.

Getting assistance

Travel agents   Intourist, pr Nakhodkinski 11, tel: 448 85 and Turburo, ul Pogranichnaya, tel: 592 90.

Air   Nakhodkinski 18, tel: 572 25.

Bus   Bus station, tel: 433 21, 434 88.

Diplomatic representation   In the past, Nakhodka was the location of foreign diplomatic representation in the Russian far east. Nowadays, most have moved to Vladivostok with the exception of the North Korean Consulate, ul Vladivostokskaya 14/ ul Sedova 8, tel: 552 10, 553 10, 584 61, and the Vietnamese Trade Mission, ul Gorkovo 18a/ul Sportivnaya 41 (Apartment 34), tel: 576 46, 570 34, 563 09.

THE CIRCUMBAIKAL RAILWAY

Of all the railways in Russia, this is probably the most attractive. The 94km route hugs the southwestern shores of Lake Baikal and passes through 33 tunnels and over 200 bridges. Originally part of the Trans-Siberian before a short-cut bypassed this section, the Circumbaikal railway was the most difficult section to build due to the construction of 7km of tunnels and shelves for the track which had to be blasted out of cliff faces. During the seven months of construction in 1904, the builders had to deal with impenetrable fog and storms whipping up 5m waves.

In 1956, a 126km shortcut was completed, cutting off a right-angle bend of the Circumbaikal line from Irkutsk to Port Baikal to Slyudyanka. This was necessary as in 1950 a dam was built on Lake Baikal's only outlet, the Angara River, and the rising water was submerging the Irkutsk to Port Baikal section.

Today, the only part of the Circumbaikal railway still operating is the Port Baikal to Slyudyanka section and it carries only one service a day. This line passes through the Pribaikalsk National Park which was created in 1987 to preserve the ecologically vulnerable south Baikal eco-system. The park covers 418,000 hectares and stretches for 400km along the west coast of the lake. It encompasses mountains and taiga, and within it are brown bears, lynxs, wolves, elk, moose and rare birdlife such as the white-tailed eagle.

The national park has introduced a tourist tax, which in 1996 was $5 per person, and you may have to pay this to get a ticket on the train.

Travel suggestions

A trip on the Circumbaikal railway is not a trip that should be undertaken lightly. The train is not punctual; there is no accommodation in Port Baikal; it is difficult to get between Port Baikal and Listvyanka. You should be prepared for anything, including being willing to sleep anywhere or sitting up all night.

It is essential that you confirm the times of all services before you embark on this adventure. Remember to take into account the five-hour difference between Moscow and Irkutsk when reading railway timetables. Theoretically, it is possible to catch a train at the weekend from Irkutsk to Slyudyanka, then catch the afternoon Circumbaikal train to Port Baikal. You will reach the station in time for the last ferry from Port Baikal to Listvyanka which departs at 20.00. You can then stay the night at Hotel Baikal-Inturist. However, it is highly optimistic that everything would coincide.

Don't let the logistic problems put you off as the trip's scenery is well worth the effort.

Trains

The carriages on the Circumbaikal railway are old *platskatni* carriages which are like *coupé* carriages without the walls facing the corridor. There is no bedding and seats are hard. It may be uncomfortable but it's a fascinating insight into the lives of typical Siberians.

The only trains on this route are listed below and all times are in local, not Moscow, time. Despite the precise timetable, this train rarely sticks to it. As the train is a combined passenger and freight train, it can stop at any station for a long time while discharging freight.

From Slyudyanka		Station	km	From Port Baikal	
905 (weekdays)	905 (weekends)			904 (weekdays)	904 (weekends)
15.50	14.00	Slyudyanka 1	0	09.00	08.00
16.36	15.25	Kultuk	10	07.07	06.30
18.50	17.37	Maritui	47	05.01	04.20
21.00	19.00	Port Baikal	94	03.55	03.05

Route description

Irkutsk   Иркутск
The trip from Irkutsk to Slyudyanka 1 takes about 2hr 30min. For information on the city, see *Chapter Sixteen, page 363*.

Slyudyanka 1   Слюдянка 1   0km
This small town gets its name from *slyuda* which means "mica". This translucent mineral was mined in the area and last century sheets of it were used as window panes while in this century it was used as insulating material in electronics components. From the station, the shore of Lake Baikal is only 500m away and a quick return walk takes about 15 minutes.

If you want to stay overnight, there is a hotel in Slyudyanka.

Kultuk   Култук   10km
This is the actual junction of the Trans-Siberian and the Circumbaikal railways but it contains little of interest and many Trans-Siberian trains don't stop here.

Maritui   Маритуй   47km
This station is halfway along the railway and was the headquarters of the railway's constructors. Nestled against the cliff here and elsewhere along the railway were barracks for nearly 10,000 Russian, Turk, Persian and Italian workers. A garrison of Cossack soldiers was also based here to break up brawls, patrol warehouses and catch bootleggers of vodka.

Port Baikal   Порт Байкал   94km
Port Baikal is a very attractive fishing village at the mouth of the Angara River. The settlement is spread along about 1km of the coast and consists mostly of wooden houses. Many of the houses are *dachas* of Irkutsk's residents so it always has a big weekend influx. The railway station is a turn-of-the-century wooden building which is also the post office. The ferry quay is a 15-minute walk from the station. There is no accommodation here but across the mouth of the Angara River is Hotel Baikal-Inturist.

Irkutsk   Иркутск
As you return to Irkutsk on the ferry, watch the left bank and you will see segments of the old railway which have not been submerged. For more information on Irkutsk see *Chapter Sixteen, page 363*.

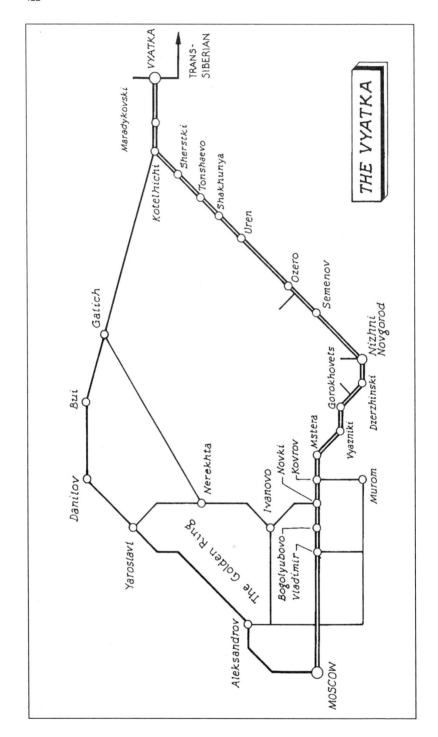

Chapter Eighteen

Moscow–
Nizhni Novgorod–Vyatka

This 898km route takes you through the Golden Ring city of Vladimir, the ancient trading city of Nizhni Novgorod (formerly known as Gorky) to the Trans-Siberian city of Vyatka (formerly known as Kirov). From Vyatka you can either join the Trans-Siberian to Vladivostok or return to Moscow on the Trans-Siberian via Yaroslavl.

The first 202km of the Moscow–Nizhni Novgorod–Vyatka route is covered in *Chapter Thirteen*. The trip from Vyatka to Moscow on the Trans-Siberian is covered in *Chapter Sixteen*.

Travel suggestions

The most economical way of travelling the Moscow–Nizhni Novgorod–Vyatka line is to catch an overnight train to Nizhni Novgorod as it is eight hours from Moscow. Spend the day there and that evening either go on to Vyatka or return to Moscow. Another option is to stay overnight in Nizhni Novgorod, spend the day there and then that evening either return to Moscow, go on to Vyatka or stay another night so that next day you can make a day trip to nearby Gorokhovets. Another option is to catch a suburban train to Vladimir then an overnight train to Vyatka and miss Nizhni Novgorod.

If you are going to do the Vyatka Loop, the most economical route is to spend just the day in each of Nizhni Novgorod, Vyatka and Yaroslavl and sleep on the trains overnight.

Trains

The major trains on the Moscow–Nizhni Novgorod–Vyatka are listed below. For information on the trains on the Moscow–Yaroslavl–Vyatka route, see *Chapter Sixteen, page 328.*

Origin	Dist, km	Train no & name	Travel time	Depart	Arrive	Destination
Vyatka	456	147	6hr 41min	00.04	06.45	Nizhni Novgorod
Vyatka	898	17	14hr 40min	19.50	10.30	Moscow (Yaroslav)
Moscow (Kursk)	442	2	8hr 16min	21.50	06.06	Nizhni Novgorod
Moscow (Yaroslav)	898	18	14hr 35min	16.35	07.10	Vyatka
Nizhni Novgorod	442	1	8hr 42min	21.40	06.22	Moscow (Kursk)
Nizhni Novgorod	456	148	7hr 50min	20.30	04.20	Vyatka

Route description

Moscow   Москва   0km

Nizhni Novgorod and Vyatka are on the same railway line, but the trains for each can depart and arrive from different Moscow stations. Generally trains for Nizhni Novgorod depart from Yaroslavl station. Trains for Vyatka depart from Kursk station if they are going via Nizhni Novgorod, but if they are going via the Trans-Siberian, they always depart from Yaroslavski station. Always confirm your departure station before leaving to catch the train.

Yaroslavl station is located at pl Komsomolskaya 5, tel: 921 0817, 266 0301, 266 0595, and the closest metro station is Komsomolskaya.

Kursk station is located at ul Zemlyani Val 29, tel: 924 9243, 262 8532, 266 5652, and the closest metro station is Kurskaya.

Vladimir   Владимир   191km

This ancient city is covered in *Chapter Thirteen, page 263*. Suburban trains from Vladimir take 3hr to Moscow, 1hr 20min to Kovrov and 3hr to Vyazniki. Long-distance trains take 4hr 30min to Nizhni Novgorod.

Bogolyubovo   Боголюбово   202km

Just after this town on the left you will see the famous Church on the Nerl River. See *Chapter Thirteen, page 271*.

Novki   Новки   240km

Novki has one of Russia's ugliest stations. The original station is probably 100 years old and in the hope of making it appear contemporary it was encased in pink and fawn tiles in the last decade. The result is a monumental eyesore.

There is a branch line from here to the north. Suburban trains from Novki run as far as Ivanovo. For more information on this line, refer to *Chapter Thirteen, page 258*.

About 13km east of here, the train crosses over the long Klyazma River Bridge. Although this bridge was built in the 1890s, it's not the original bridge as this was washed away in a flood. Rather than rebuilding the bridge, a new one was built 1km to the west on a dry land promontory around which the river flowed. When the bridge was completed, a canal was dug under it, thus cutting off the bend. The river bend was then filled in and as you pass over this area you can see to your right and left the old river course which now finishes on each side of the bridge's eastern embankment.

Kovrov   Ковров   255km
Telephone area code: 092 32

This ancient town gets its name from the word *kovrov* meaning "carpet". During the Mongol Tatar's reign in the 14th century, the local tax collector accepted carpets as one of the tributes.

The town's most famous son was the engineer Vasili Alekseevich Degtyarev (1879–1949), who was the father of Soviet machine guns. The town boasts the Degtyarev factory, founded in 1916, which now manufactures motorcycles, scooter engines and small arms. In the centre of town there is a monument to Degtyarev who is holding an engineering micrometer rather than a gun. His grave is nearby. His house at ul Degtyareva 4 has been turned into a museum.

The town's History Museum, ul Abelmana 20, tel: 218 15, is excellent, with considerable material on the town's development since the 12th century.

The town's other big attraction is a massive excavator factory. This factory was founded in the mid-1800s when it built and repaired railway rolling stock. Its claims to fame include developing the world's first steam-heated passenger carriage in 1866 and Russia's first hospital carriage in 1877. The factory's importance in the town is illustrated by the large, colourful, digging machinery murals on the sides of Kovrov's nine-storey accommodation blocks. While you can't tour the factory, you can visit its museum at ul Bortsov 1.

The town's only accommodation is at the basic Hotel Kovrov, ul Uritskogo, tel: 212 15, $25 for a twin room.

Suburban trains to Vladimir take 1hr 20min and to Vyazniki they take 1hr 20min. Long-distance trains to Nizhni Novgorod take 3hr.

Mstera   Мстёра   295km

This village is famous for its folk handicrafts and it has given its name to particular styles of Russian miniature painting and embroidery.

Mstera miniature paintings usually depict scenes from folklore, history, literature and everyday life, and are defined by the warm, soft colours. The scenes are painted with tempera (paint made from pigments ground in water with egg yolk) on to papier mâché boxes and lacquered to a black sheen.

Mstera embroidery is characterised by two types of stitch: white satin stitch and Vladimir stitch.

A large range of Mstera products are on display and for sale at the Mstera Museum.

Getting to the village of Mstera is not easy as the station is 14km away. Regular buses run between the two. To get to the bus stop from Mstera station, walk back on the dirt road beside the railway line towards Moscow for about 700m until you reach a sealed road with a bus shelter. If you are staying in Vladimir, a more convienent way of getting to Mstera village is to catch a direct two-hour bus from Vladimir's central bus station in front of the railway station.

Vyazniki   Вязники   315km
Telephone area code: 092 33

The ancient town of Vyazniki, meaning "little elms", started out as a few huts sitting among elm trees on the banks of the Klyazma River. The town got on the map when, from 1622, pilgrims started flocking here to see the miracle-working Kazan Mother of God icon. The town was also renowned for its icon painters and two masters were invited to paint the cathedral icons in Moscow's kremlin in the mid-17th century.

The great Russian poet N A Nekrasov wrote several major verses here and every year there is a poetry festival dedicated to his work.

The museum of local studies contains material on the town's most famous sons, the poet-songwriter A I Fatyanov and cosmonaut V N Kubasov. Within the museum is a picture gallery containing works from the end of the 19th and beginning of the 20th centuries.

Vyazniki is 8km north of the station and regular buses travel between the two.

An interesting trip from Vyazniki is to Mitino (Мининой) village which is 6km up the Klyazma River. This is the site of a 12th-century kremlin called

Yaropolch which was destroyed in 1238 by the Mongol Tatars. Today, the only remnants of the fortress are the earth ramparts. In 1676, another fortress was built on a hill near the first but it disappeared in a fire in 1703. Today, the five-domed Troitskaya (Trinity) Church (1756–61) with its refectory and harmonious bell tower sits on the fortress' hill overlooking the village. Regular buses travel between Vyazniki and Mitino.

Accommodation is available at the basic Hotel Vyazniki, ul Komsomolskaya 6A, tel: 243 95, $10 twin share/person.

Suburban trains to Kovrov take 1hr 20min and to Vladimir they take 3hr. Long-distance trains take 2hr 30min to reach Nizhni Novgorod.

Gorokhovets   Гороховец   363km
Telephone area code: 092 38
For those interested in Russia's Golden Ring, Gorokhovets is a must. It is much smaller than the major Golden Ring cities which gives a different perspective on these ancient towns while allowing you to observe the life in a quiet Russian village.

Gorokhovets was first mentioned in 1239 when it was burned down by the Tatar-Mongols. To protect itself, a fortress was built on top of the hill overlooking the town but this was destroyed in 1619 by marauding Ukrainian Cossacks serving Polish interests. In the 19th century, it became renowned as a trading centre and supplied much of the region's fruit and vegetables.

The town's architectural highlights include the Purification of the Virgin Monastery (1698) and the St Nicholas Monastery (1681–6), both of which have high, open flights of stairs, pilasters at the corners and intricate window frames. There are also several unusual two-storey stone houses from the second half of the 17th century which were designed to imitate traditional Russian wooden mansions. Also of interest is the former *Ostrog* complex which was used as a stopping point for prisoners on their way to Siberia.

Both the former house of the merchant Sapozhnikov-Ershov and the Church of St John the Baptist are parts of the Museum of Local Studies.

Accommodation is available at the basic Hotel Yubileinaya, ul Bezdetina, tel: 217 80, $13 twin share/person.

Gorokhovets is located on the Klyazma River, 11km from Gorokhovets railway station. There are regular buses between the town and station.

Dzerzhinsk   Дзержинск   421km
Telephone area code: 8313
Thirty-two kilometres west of Nizhni Novgorod, on the left bank of the Oka River, is the chemical and plastics city of Dzerzhinsk. It was originally known as Rastiapiono, until in 1929 it was renamed after the founder of the KGB, Felix Dzerzhinsky. The town has a museum of local studies and one of the nation's few remaining monuments to the hated Dzerzhinsky.

NIZHNI NOVGOROD   Нижний Новгород   442km
Population 1.5 million   Telephone area code: 8312.
Nizhni Novgorod was closed to foreigners until 1991 but since then has become a major tourist destination due to its history and attractive old town.

Nizhni Novgorod was founded in 1221 and sits at the junction of the Oka and Volga Rivers. Its strategic location on two central shipping routes ensured that the town grew into a major trading centre. Its importance was consolidated with the opening of the Nizhni Novgorod Fair in 1817. By the 1870s, the fair had a massive turnover of 300 million gold roubles. (To put this figure into perspective, the Trans-Siberian railway cost a total of 1,000 million roubles to build.) The fair was shut down in the 1930s and the city was closed to foreigners when Nizhni Novgorod was turned into a major military industrial centre.

Following the collapse of communism and the opening of the city in 1991 the Nizhni Novgorod Fair re-opened in the fabulously renovated 1800's French Empire style Fair Building.

This city was known as Gorky from 1932 to 1991 and city still appears under that name in many railway timetables.

Getting there and away

By air   There are daily flights to and from Moscow, St Petersburg, Vyatka and most major Russian cities.

By rail   The most convenient long-distance trains are listed below. From Nizhni Novgorod, suburban trains takes 2hr to get to Vyazniki, 3hr to Kovrov and 4hr 30min to Vladimir.

Origin	Dist, km	Train no & name	Travel time	Depart	Arrive	Destination
Vyatka	456	147	6hr 41min	0:04	6:45	Nizhni Novgorod
Nizhni Novgorod	456	148	7hr 50min	20:30	4:20	Vyatka
Nizhni Novgorod	442	1	8hr 42min	21:40	6:22	Moscow (Kazan)
Moscow (Kazan)	442	2	8hr 16min	21:50	6:06	Nizhni Novgorod

Where to stay

The best hotel is the excellent Hotel Oktyabrskaya, nab Verkhne-Volzhskaya 9a, tel: 320 670, fax: 320 550, $46 twin share/person. Other choices are the standard Hotel Tsentralnaya, pl Lenina 1, tel: 444 270, $33 twin share/person; the standard Hotel Volzky Otkos (formerly the Hotel Rossiya), nab Verkhne-Volzhskaya 8, tel: 391 971, $31 twin share/person; the standard Hotel Moskva, pl Teatralnaya 2, tel: 336 143; the standard Hotel Nizhegorodskaya, ul Zalomovo 1, tel: 312 388; and the standard Hotel Zarechnaya, pro Lenina 36, tel: 524 948, $17 twin share/person.

Getting around

The Nizhni Novgorod metro was opened in 1985 with 14 stations. It is currently being expanded and work is underway on building four new stations, a line to Sormovo district and a line to the Nagornaya part of the city.

What to see

The old part of Nizhni Novgorod is one of the city's highlights. The well-preserved kremlin fortress with its 12 impressive towers sits on an 80m-high hill dominating the area. Inside its walls are the City Hall, the Cathedral of Archangel Michael and the Fine Arts Museum, tel: 391 373, open 10.00–17.00, closed Tuesday, in the former Governor's House. The Fine Arts Museum contains icons and paintings by Tropinin, Bryullov, Savrasov and N Roerich. There is also a display of military equipment near the southern gate which highlights the town's enormous contribution to World War II and the Soviet's post-war military might.

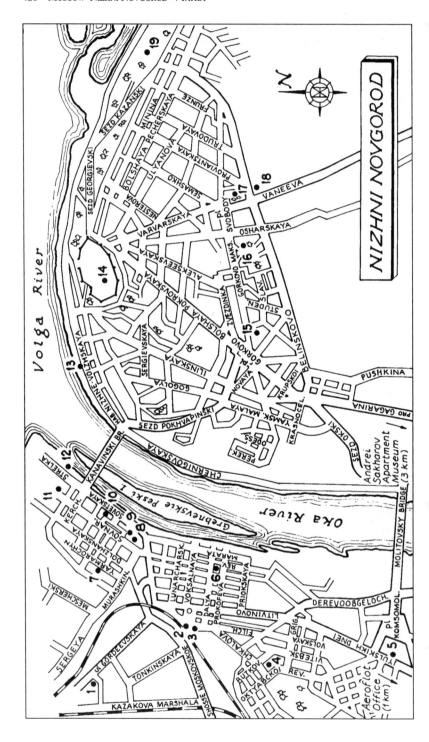

NIZHNI NOVGOROD

KEY TO NIZHNI NOVGOROD   Нижний Новгород

1	Church of the Smolensk Mother of God (Smolenskoi Bogomateri) in Gordeevka region	Церковь Смоленской Богоматери в Гордеевке
2	Nizhni Novgorod railway station (*Vokzal*)	Ж-Д вокзал
3	Moskovskaya metro station	Московская станца метро
4	Chkalovskaya metro station	Чкаловская станца метро
5	Leninskaya metro station	Ленинская станца метро
6	Circus (*Tsirk*)	Цирк
7	Saviour-Old Fair (*Spasski Staroyarmorochny*) Cathedral	Спасский староярмарочный собор
8	Book shop (*Knigi*)	Дом Книги
9	Hotel Tsentralnaya	гостиница Центральная
10	Nizhni Novgorod Fair Building (*Yarmarka*)	Нижегородская Ярмарка
11	Fair Cathedral of Aleksandr Nevski (*Yarmorochny*)	Ярмарочный собор Александра Невского
12	Wharfs (*Pristan*)	Пристань
13	River station (*Vokzal*)	Речной вокзал
14	Kremlin	Нижнегородский кремль
15	Gorky's Museum Apartment 1900-1901	Дом в котором жил Горький в 1900-1901гг
16	Youth Theatre (*Teatr*)	Театр юного зрителя
17	Ostrog	Острог
18	Opera and Ballet Theatre (*Teatr*)	Театр оперы и балета
19	Pecherski Monastery	Печёрский монастырь

There are two interesting pedestrian streets in the old town. The first is the kilometre-long ul Bolshaya Pokrovka which starts at pl Gorkovo (Gorky Square) and runs to pl Minina i Pozharskogo (Minin and Pozharskogo Square), located in front of the kremlin. This street takes you past one of the city's biggest food markets, the Drama Theatre, the State Bank and the Duma Parliamentary building. The other street is ul Rozhdestvenskaya, formerly ul Mayakovski, which is typical of Russian cobbled streets of the late 18th century. Its most interesting section is from the little park in front of the river station to the northern gate of the kremlin.

Another building of note is the Nizhni Novgorod *Ostrog* which was where prisoners exiled to Siberia by the tsar were imprisoned overnight on their forced march to the east. The *Ostrog*'s most famous prisoner was the first prime minister of the Soviet Union, Mikhail Sverdlov. The building is now a science library but it will become a museum in the future.

The best way to see the region's arts and crafts is to visit the Arts Museum, nab Verkhne-Volzhskaya 3, open 10.00–17.00, closed Friday. Exhibits concentrate on *khokhloma* lacquered wooden articles, hand-painted Gorodets toys, filigree jewellery and feather light Balakhna lace. There are several specialist museums in the city including the City History Museum, nab Verkhne-Volzhskaya 7, tel: 367 661; the Tank Guards Army Museum, ul Shkolnaya 9, tel: 565 644; the River Fleet Museum, ul Minina 7, tel: 368 788; and the Radio Technology Museum, nab Verkhne-Volzhskaya 10, tel: 366 755, open 10.00–16.00 weekdays.

Andrei Sakharov Apartment Museum

In the 1980s, Nizhni Novgorod became infamous as a place of internal exile for dissidents and its most famous prisoner was the nuclear physicist and Nobel

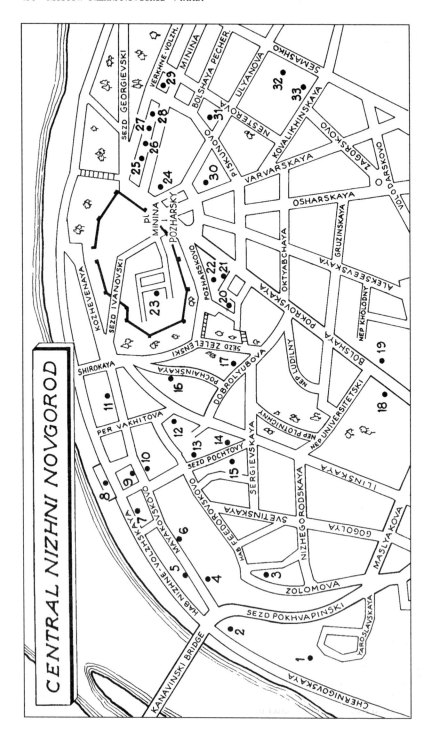

CENTRAL NIZHNI NOVGOROD

KEY TO CENTRAL NIZHNI NOVGOROD
Нижний Новгород

1	Annunciation (*Blagoveshchenski*) Monastery	Благовещенский монастырь
2	Planetarium (*Planetari*)	Планетарий
3	Hotel Nizhegorodskaya	гостиница Нижнегородская
4	Former manor of the Stroganovs	Быв. дом-усадьба Строгановых
5	Former manor of the Golitsins	Быв. дом-усадьба Голицыных
6	Birth of Christ Church (*Rozhdestvenskaya*) in the estate of the Stroganovs	Рождественская церковь при усадьбе Строгановых
7	Railway advance ticket booking office (*Predvaritelnaya kassa*)	Ж-Д предварительная касса
8	River station (*Vokzal*)	Речной вокзал
9	Comedy Theatre (*Teatr*)	Театр комедии
10	Former Hotel Smirnov	Быв. гостиница Смирнова
11	Former Bank of the brothers Rukavishnikov	Быв. банк братьев Рукавишниковых
12	Assumption Church on St Elijah's Hill	Церковь Успения на Ильинской горе
13	Former house of Levini	Быв. дом Левиной
14	Former chambers of Olisov	Быв. палаты Олисова
15	Domik Kashirin	Домик Каширина
16	Former house of Chatygin, former house of Peter the Great	Быв. дом Чатыгина, Дом Петра 1
17	Church of Zhen-Mironosits	Церковь Жён-Мироносиц
18	Puppet Theatre (*Teatr*)	Театр кукол
19	State Bank (*Bank*)	Банк
20	House-museum of Dobrolyubov	Дом-музей Добролюбова
21	Hotel Moskva	гостиница Москва
22	Gorky Drama Theatre (*Teatr*)	Театр драмы им Горького
23	Kremlin	Нижнегородский кремль
24	Former Seminary (*Seminariya*)	Быв. семинария
25	Hotel Volzky Otkos	гостиница Волзкы Откос
26	Radio Technology Museum (*Muzei*)	Музей Радио
27	Arts Museum (*Muzei*)	Художественный музей
28	City History Museum (*Muzei*)	Историко-архитектурный музей
29	Hotel Oktyabrskaya	гостиница Октябрьская
30	Teaching Institute (*Institut*)	Педагогический институт
31	River Fleet Museum (*Muzei*)	Музей речного флота
32	Gorky's Museum Apartment 1902-1904	Дом в котором жил Горький в
33	House where Gorky was born	Дом в котором Горький родился 1902-1904гг

Peace Prize winner Andrei Sakharov. He was exiled here from January 22 1981 until December 22 1986 and his exile apartment has been turned into a museum, pr Gagarina 214, kv 3, tel: 668 623, open 10.00–17.30, closed Friday. The hour-long tour of the flat is a must.

The House-museums of Maksim Gorky

Between 1932 and 1991, Nizhni Novgorod was named after the Russian writer Maksim Gorky (1868–1936) who was born here. Gorky wrote about the cruelty, ugliness and injustice of rural Tsarist Russia and his books were compulsory reading for all Soviet children. In Nizhni Novgorod there are several Gorky museums and historical sites including the House of His Birth, open 10.00–17.00, closed Wednesday, where he lived for the first three years of his life; Domik Kashirin, Pochtovy Sezd 21, tel: 340 670, which was his grandfather's house to which he and his mother moved in 1870 when they returned from Astrakhan after the death of Gorky's father; and Gorky's Museum

Apartment, ul Semashko 19, tel: 361 651, open 09.00–17.00, closed Monday and Thursday, which is where he lived from 1902 to 1904. Every Sunday at 15:00 there is a poetry or novel reading at Gorky's Museum Apartment. There is also material of Gorky's at the Nizhni Novgorod Literature Museum, ul Minina 26, tel: 366 583.

Getting assistance
Travel agents   Intourist, Hotel Tsentralnaya, 2nd Floor, ul Sovetskaya 12, tel/fax: 441 663. Team Gorky Adventure Travel Co., PO Box 93, Nizhni Novgorod, 603137, tel: 651 999, fax: 691 875, email adv@team-gorky.nnov.ru, http://www.inforis.ru/team-gorky/, organises weekend rafting in the Nizhni Novgorod region on the Kerzenets River, trekking, fishing and white-water rafting in Siberia and bicycling around the Golden Ring.
Air   Aeroflot, pr Lenina 7, tel: 443 976.

What's in the region
Gorodets Rospis Handicraft Factory (*Городец*)
Gorodets was founded in 1152 by Prince Yuri Dolgoruky who also founded Moscow, and is famous for its hand-painted toys. You can see these being made in the Gorodetskaya Rospis handicraft factory (closed weekends), and on the way you will pass the Gorkovski hydro-electric station with its 15km-long dam and the Zavolzhe engine factory which is the main supplier for GAZ (the Gorky Agricultural Factory).

To get to Gorodets, you can catch a suburban train northwards to Zavolzhe station (Заволже) and then take a river boat across the Volga. Ferries also travel regularly between Nizhni Novgorod and Gorodets. Intourist organise tours to the handicraft factory for $66 for a car of three people.

Chkalov Aviation Museum

One of Nizhni Novgorod's most famous locals is the air pioneer, Valeri Chkalov. He was born 65km away from Nizhni Novgorod in the village now bearing his name, Chkalovsk. His first great achievement was completed on June 22 1936 when he and his co-pilot, Georgi Baidukov, circumnavigated the Soviet Union. Between June 18 and 20 1937, Chkalov set another record when he flew non-stop from Moscow via the North Pole to Vancouver, travelling 8,504km in 63hr 16min. Chkalov died in 1938 when he was testing a new fighter. At the Chkalov Museum, ul Chkalova 5, tel: 264, open 10.00–17.00, closed Monday, is a giant hangar containing a number of well-preserved planes including the legendary ANT-25 which flew to North America. Intourist organises tours here for $66 for a car of three people.

Boldino Estate Museum of Pushkin

Boldino is one of Russia's most popular places of poetic pilgrimage. The estate was owned by the family of the famous poet Alexander Sergeivich Pushkin who visited it three summers in a row from 1933. The Estate Museum, closed Monday, is 250km south of Nizhni Novgorod and difficult to reach by public transport. In autumn, there is the Boldino Pushkin Music Festival. Intourist organises tours here for $66 for a car of three people.

Diveevo Monastery

Diveevo Monastery is one of the four great places of religious worship in Russia and was the home of one of the most loved saints of Russia, Saint Seraphim of Sarov (1759–1833). The monastery is 167km south of Nizhni Novgorod and is difficult to reach on public transport. Intourist organises tours here for $66 for a car of three people.

Semenov   Семенов   509km

The town was renowned last century for its artistic woodworking, particularly rosary beads. The artists practised a form of *khokhloma* painting with fine golden patterns of flowers on a red or black background. A *khokhloma* school was founded here in 1925.

The town is littered with two-storey wooden buildings of the Old Believers religious sect. These buildings can be identified by the five or six windows on each facade, walls covered with intricate carvings, high surrounding fences, wicket gates and large prayer rooms.

Ozero   Озеро   531km

To the left of the station is shallow Svetloyar Lake and there is a legend that at the bottom of it is the invisible village of Kitezh.

Uren   Урен   623km

The town was founded deep in the forests in the 18th century by the Old Believers religious sect who rightly feared persecution. Today, there is nothing left from this period and the town's major industry is a factory producing work clothes.

Shakhunya   Шахунья   682km

The town is near the Shakhunya River which derives its name from the word *shaga* meaning "a step" as it was so narrow that it could be crossed in one jump. The town sprang up in the 1930s when the railway between Nizhni Novgorod and Vyatka was built. Although most of the town's buildings are two- and five-storey apartment blocks from the 1950s, the 1930s wooden construction workers' barracks can still be seen.

Tonshaevo   Тоншаево   701km

The name of the station is confusing as the town around the station is called Shaigino while the town of Tonshaevo is 10km to the southeast.

Sherstki   Шерстки   743km

This station marks the boundary between the Nizhni Novgorod and Kirov Oblasts which also marks a time boundary. Within the Kirov Oblast, local time is one hour ahead of Moscow.

Kotelnich   Котельнич   811km

This station sits at the junction of the Trans-Siberian and the Vyatka–Nizhni Novgorod–Moscow lines. If you are changing from one line to the other, don't get off here. Instead, go 87km to the east to the major city of Vyatka where it is much easier to get tickets.

Kotelnich is an ancient trading city on the high right bank of the Vyatka River and developed because of its position on this major trading river which connects Arkhangelsk with the Volga region.

Two monasteries have been preserved, the male John the Baptist (Predtichi) Monastery and female Presentation of the Virgin (Vvedenski) Monastery. Other sights include the Trinity (Troitski) Cathedral built in 1713, the St Nicholas (Nikolskaya) Church in 1903 and the Arcade (*gostiny dvor*) in 1856. The town has a museum of local studies.

Maradykovski   Марадыковский   831km

Avoid stopping off here as it is the storage site of 7,000 of Russia's 40,000 tons of chemical weapons agents. The exact chemicals held here are not known but are thought to be mustard gas, lewisite, hydrocyanic acid and phosgene. On October 26 1995, Russian Chief of the General Staff, General Mikhail Kolesnikov, announced that the government had approved a plan for destroying its stock of chemical weapons by 2005 and that it would begin with 11,500 tons of lewisite and mustard gas, which have been held since 1953. The destruction programme will cost $3.7 billion.

VYATKA   Вятка   898km
Population: 492,000   Telephone area code: 833 0

Vyatka sits on the wide Vyatka River, a tributary of the Kama which flows into the Volga. The Vyatka River was a major trading route which ensured the town's growth. The arrival of the Trans-Siberian didn't stop this growth as trains simply replaced the ships.

The city was originally called Khlynov but this was changed to Vyatka in 1780, and then in 1934 it was renamed Kirov in honour of Sergei Kirov (1886–1935), who was born nearby in the small village of Urzhum. He was a popular leader of the Communist Party, member of the Politburo and rival to Stalin before he was assassinated on Stalin's orders. When Kirov fell from grace after the collapse of communism the name of the city reverted to Vyatka.

In the 1930s the city was a large industrial centre and during World War II many munitions factories from European Russia were evacuated here. Consequently, Vyatka became a military city closed to foreigners until the early 1990s.

Vyatka is worth visiting; its river front is attractive and there are several museums that are interesting. However, one day is enough to see everything.

This city still appears in many railway timetables under its old name of Kirov.

Getting there and away
By air   The airport is to the north of the town in the suburb of Zonovy and there are flights to numerous Russian cities.

By train   Vyatka is not actually on the Trans-Siberian railway but 13km to the north of it. However, all trains on the Trans-Siberian make the detour through the city. Be careful to get off at the central station which is called Vyatka 1 as there are three stations in the area with the name Vyatka.

There are two rail options from Vyatka to Moscow. The first is the 957km Trans-Siberian route of Vyatka–Danilov–Yaroslavl–Sergiev-Posad–Moscow which is described in *Chapter Sixteen* or the 898km Vyatka–Nizhni Novgorod–Moscow route described above.

Vyatka–Nizhni Novgorod–Vladimir–Moscow
The most convenient long-distance trains on this route are listed below.

Origin	Dist, km	Train no & name	Travel time	Depart	Arrive	Destination
Vyatka	898	17	14hr 40min	19.50	10.30	Moscow (Yaroslav)
Moscow (Yaroslav)	898	18	14hr 35min	16.35	07.10	Vyatka
Vyatka	456	147	6hr 41min	00.04	06.45	Nizhni Novgorod
Nizhni Novgorod	456	148	7hr 50min	20.30	04.20	Vyatka

Vyatka–Danilov–Yaroslavl–Sergiev-Posad–Moscow
The most convenient long-distance trains on this route are listed below. From Vyatka, it takes 8hr 40min to reach Danilov and 10hr 10min to Yaroslavl.

To the east on the Trans-Siberian, it takes 7hr to reach Perm and 13hr 30min to Ekaterinburg.

Origin	Dist, km	Train no & name	Travel time	Depart	Arrive	Destination
Vyatka (through)	957	1	14hr 1min	15.29	06.30	Moscow (Yaroslav)
Moscow (Yaroslav)	957	4	14hr 32min	19.55	10.27	Vyatka

Where to stay
The only two hotels frequented by foreigners are the Hotel Vyatka, pr Oktyabrski 145, tel: 648 396, and the Hotel Administratsi Oblasti, ul Gertsena 49, tel: 691 018.

What to see
Russia's answer to Joseph Conrad was A C Grin (1880–1932) who was born 35km away at Slobodskoi. Grin's adventure novels are still popular today and his

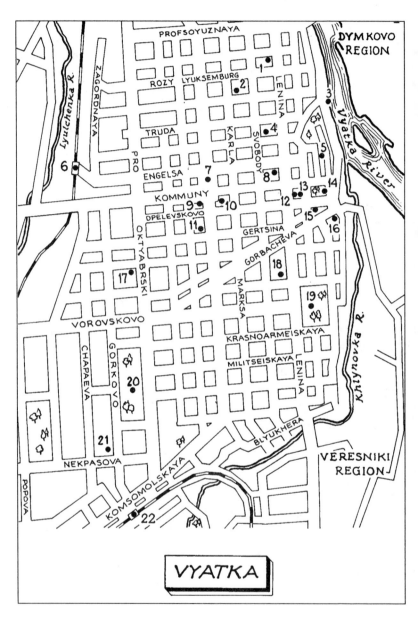

VYATKA

works are on display in the A C Grin Museum. There is the Museum of Aviation and Space, the Museum of Local Studies and the Museum of Vyatka Local Handicrafts which has a collection of Dymkovo toys. The biggest museum is the United Historical Archive and Literary Museum, ul Lenina 82, tel: 23 738, 27 896.

Two other specialised museums are the House-museum of the novelist M E Saltykov-Shchedrin, and the brother artists Victor and Apollinaris Vasnetsov Museum, ul Karla Marksa 70, tel: 62 26 46.

KEY TO VYATKA   Вятка

1	Teaching Institute (*Institut*)	Педагогический институт
2	Museum of Grin (*Muzei*)	Музей Грина
3	River station (*Vokzal*)	Речной вокзал
4	Church of John the Baptist (*Ioanna Predtechi*)	Церковь Иоанна Предтечи
5	Monastery of the Savior and Transfiguration	Спасо-Преображенский
	(*Spaso-Preobrazhenski*)	Новодевичий монастырь
6	Kirov-Kotlasski railway station (*Vokzal*)	Киров-Котласский вокзал
7	Drama Theatre (*Teatr*)	Драматический театр
8	Museum of Aviation and Space (*Muzei*)	Музей авиации и космонавтики
9	Polytechnic Institute (*Institut*)	Политехнический институт
10	Art Museum (*Muzei*)	Художественный музей
11	Puppet Theatre (*Teatr*)	Кукольный театр
12	Museum of Local Studies (*Muzei*)	Краеведческий музей
13	Youth Theatre (*Teatr*)	Театр юного зрителя
14	World War II Memorial	Памятник 1941-1945гг
15	Museum of Vyatka Local Handicrafts (*Muzei*)	Музей Вятские художественные промыслы
16	Trifon Monastery	Трифонов монастырь
17	Agricultural Institute (*Institut*)	Сельскохозяйственный институт
18	Museum of Saltykova-Shchedrina (*Muzei*)	Музей Салтыкова-Щедрина
19	Philarmonic Hall (*Philarmoniya*)	Филармония
20	Circus (*Tsirk*)	Цирк
21	Bus station (*Avtovokzal*)	Автовокзал
22	Kirov-1 Railway Station (*Vokzal*)	Киров-1 вокзал

There are several historic buildings of interest including the Assumption (Uspenski) Cathedral of the Trifon Monastery (1689), the buildings in the municipal gardens (1835–9), and residential houses in the classical style dating from the 18th and early 19th century.

Getting assistance
Travel agents   Intourist, ul Volodarskovo 127, tel: 90 949; Lyukon, ul R Lyuksemburg 30, tel: 241 34.
Airlines   Aeroflot, ul Gorkovo 56, tel: 44 472, 25 287.

Points of interest
Dymkovo toys
Across the Vyatka River from central Vyatka is the suburb of Dymkovo which gives its name to a type of painted, clay figurine. Dymkovo toys, which are also known as Vyatka and Kirov toys, are usually of people and animals, often in the form of whistles. At the end of the 19th century hand-made toys were replaced by factory-made moulded plaster figurines that imitated porcelain articles. In the Soviet period, the craft was revived in 1933 when the Vyatka Toy Collective was organised and the range of themes was broadened to include fairy-tales, scenes from contemporary life, groups of figures on pedestals and figurines up to 30cm high.

Contemporary Dymkovo toys incorporate ancient motifs as well as reproducing 19th-century figurines of noble women, nannies and water carriers.

Appendix One

LANGUAGE

Russian, Ukrainian and Belarusian transliteration and pronunciation guide

Russian, Belarusian and Ukrainian are all Slavic languages and use a Cyrillic script although there are slight differences between them.

The translation system used is designed for phonetic ease. The following table shows the English letter equivalent for Russian, Belarusian and Ukrainian with the following simplification rules:

The ending ый becomes y, and ий becomes i.

The Cyrillic letter e at the start of a word is transliterated as e, not as ye.

You may notice that some of the stations have a different spelling from the city, eg: Kholodnaya railway station but Kholodnoe village. This is because the Slavic languages add endings to words to show their function in a sentence, eg as an adjective. In addition, in this book there are a few Russian words, notably well known place names, which have not been transliterated using the following table. Instead we have adopted the spelling which has been common in the past.

Cyrillic	Russian transliteration	Russian pronunciation	Ukrainian transliteration	Ukrainian pronunciation	Belarusian transliteration	Belarusian pronunciation
А, а	A, a	far	A, a	far	A, a	far
Б, б	B, b	bet	B, b	bet	B, b	bet
В, в	V, v	vodka	V, v	vodka	V, v	vodka
Г, г	G, g	get	H, h	hello	H, h	hello
Д, д	D, d	dog	D, d	dog	D, d	dog
Е, е	E, e	yet	E, e	end	E, e	yet
Ё, ё	e, E	yoghurt	-	-	Yo, yo	yoghurt
Ж, ж	Zh, zh	treasure	Zh, zh	treasure	Zh, zh	treasure
З, з	Z, z	zebra	Z, z	zebra	Z, z	zebra
И, и	I, i	seek	I, i	seek	-	-
Й, й	I, i	ready	I, i	ready	I, i	ready
К, к	K, k	Kiev	K, k	Kiev	K, k	Kiev
Л, л	L, l	Lenin	L, l	Lenin	L, l	Lenin
М, м	M, m	Moscow	M, m	Moscow	M, m	Moscow
Н, н	N, n	never	N, n	never	N, n	never
О, о	O, o	over	O, o	over	O, o	over
П, п	P, p	Peter	P, p	Peter	P, p	Peter
Р, р	R, r	Russia	R, r	Russia	R, r	Russia
С, с	S, s	Samarkand	S, s	Samarkand	S, s	Samarkand
У, у	U, u	train	U, u	train	U, u	train
Ў, ў	-	-	-	-	W, w	ward
Ф, ф	F, f	frost	F, f	frost	F, f	frost
Х, х	Kh, kh	loch	Kh, kh	loch	Kh, kh	loch
Ц, ц	Ts, ts	lots	Ts, ts	lots	Ts, ts	lots
Ч, ч	Ch, ch	chilli	Ch, ch	chilli	Ch, ch	chilli
Ш, ш	Sh, sh	fish	Sh, sh	fish	Sh, sh	fish
Щ, щ	Shch, shch	fresh chicken	Shch, shch	fresh chicken	-	-
Ъ, ъ		hardens following letter	-	-	-	-
Ы, ы	Y, y	did	-	-	Y, y	did
Ь, ь		softens preceding letter	no letter	softens preceding letter	no letter	softens preceding letter
Э, э	E, e	ten t	-	-	E, e	map
Ю, ю	Yu, yu	union	Yu, yu	union	Yu, yu	union

Я, я	Ya, ya	**ya**k	Ya, ya	**ya**k	Ya, ya	**ya**k
Э, э	-	-	Ye, ye	**ye**t	-	-
I, i	-	-	I, i	**i**nn	I, i	**i**nn
Ї, ï	-	-	Yi, yi	**yi**n	-	-

Russian, Ukrainian and Belarusian basic words

The following is the bare Russian, Ukrainian and Belarusian minimum needed to get around. The part of the words that should be stressed is emboldened.

English	Russian pronunciation	Russian spelling	Ukrainian pronunciation	Ukrainian spelling	Belarusian pronunciation	Belarusian spelling
yes	da	да	tak	так	tak	так
no	nyet	нет	nee	ні	nye	не
please	poz**ha**lista	пожалуйста	**pro**shoo	прошу	kah**lee** **lah**skah	калі ласка
thank you	spa**si**ba	спасибо	**dya**kooyoo	дякую	**dzya**nkoe	дзякуй
goodbye	dasve**da**niya	до свидания	**do** po**bah**chenya	да побачення	**da** pah**bah**chenn yah	да пабачэньня
good-day (hello)	zd**ra**vstvi	здравствуй	**do**bree dnen	добрий день	**do**bree **dzn**en	добры джень
good	**dob**ri	добрый	**dob**reh	добре	**doh**bree	добры
bad	plo**khoi**	плохой	po**hah**no	погано	**dreh**nnee	дрэнны

Appendix Two

GLOSSARY

Italicised words are transliterated Russian and non-italicised words are English translations.

aeroport (аэропорт)	airport
aerovokzal (аэропорт)	city air terminal
arcade (Гостиный двор)	a merchant trading area that invariably combined shops, warehouses and accommodation surrounded by a fortified wall; common from the 17th century to the 19th centuries
apartment-museum (Дом-музей)	a museum in the apartment where a famous person lived
avtovokzal (автовокзал)	bus station
babushka (бабушка)	grandmother
banya (баня)	Russian sauna
bilet (билет)	ticket
blini (блини)	pancakes
bog (бог)	God
bolota (болото)	swamp
Bolshevik (Большевик)	a member of the so-called largest faction of the Communist Party
borshcht (борщ)	soup made from either beetroot or meat and vegetables
CCCP (СССР)	abbreviation for Union of Soviet Socialist Republics (Союз Советских Социалистических Республик)
coupé (купе)	carriage with four berths per cabin; the most common carriages for foreigners
dacha (дача)	usually a very small cottage on a small farm plot owned by city dwellers
dacha village (дачи посёлок)	suburb on the outskirts of a town where most *dachas* are located.
datsan (датсан)	Buddhist monastery
Decembrist (декабрист)	a revolutionary who took part in the December 14 1865 uprising in St Petersburg, demanding a constitutional monarch rather than an omnipowerful tsar
Ded Moroz (Дед Мороз)	Santa Claus
derevnya (деревня)	village or hamlet; there are numerous other words for village, such as *khutor* and *stantsiay,* but with the exception of *derevnya* and *selo,* these words are only of historical significance

dom (дом)	house
Duma (дума)	Russian congress, formerly known as City Soviet
elektrichka (электричка)	suburban train
finift (финифт)	multi-coloured enamel decoration.
fresco (фреска)	a type of wall painting done on wet plaster
glasnost (гласность)	a Gorbachev era buzz word meaning political and media openness
GOELRO (ГОЭЛРО)	from the initials of the 1920's Government Plan for the Electrification of Russia (Государственный план электрификации России) which shaped and still shapes the electrification policy in Russia today
gorod (город)	a city with a minimum population of 12,000 and at least 85% of its employed population engaged in non-agricultural work
gostinitsa (гостиница)	hotel
Great Patriotic War (Великая Отеческая Война)	The Soviet Union only fought in World War II from 1941 to 1945 and this is their term for that war
gulag (ГУЛаг)	from the initials of the organisation which ran prison camps, the Main Department of Corrective Labour Camps (Главное Управление Исправительных Лагерей); the word is now used to mean a prison camp of the Stalin era
homestay (домашнее условие)	accommodation in a Russian family home
house-museum (Дом-музей)	museum in the house where a famous person lived
iconostatis (иконостас)	screen between the sanctuary and the altar of a Russian Orthodox church; it consists of a wooden frame which supports several rows of icons
Intourist (Интурист)	Russia's largest travel company
kafe (кафе)	café
kassa (касса)	ticket window
KGB (КГБ)	initials of the Soviet secret police (Комитет Государственной Безопасности) which operated from 1956 to 1991; in 1992 it was divided into the Domestic Federal Security Service (Федеральная служба безопастноси) and Russian Foreign Intelligence Service (Сужба иностранной разведки)
kolkhoz (колхоз)	collective farm
kompot (компот)	fruit drink made of berries
Komsomol (Комсомол)	abbreviation for the Communist Youth League (Коммунистический Союз Молодёжи) which represented 14 to 27 year olds.

Krai (Край)	a territory
kremlin (кремль)	fortress
kulak (кулак)	owner of a small farm
kvas (квас)	a slightly alcoholic drink made of sour rye bread
matryashka dolls (матрёшка)	set of wooden painted dolls of different sizes stacked within one another
militsia (милиция)	police
museum of wooden architecture (Музеи деревянного зодчества)	an open-air museum of wooden buildings from the past centuries
museum of local studies (Краеведческий музей)	most towns have these museums which contain displays on the region's geology, botany, history and celebrities.
myaki (мягкий)	a first-class sleeping carriage with two beds only in the compartment; synonym for *SV*
novy (новый)	new
Oblast (Область)	a region
obshchi (общий)	open carriage with no reserved seating or sleeping benches
OViR (ОВиР)	The Ministry of Internal Affairs' department that registers and extends visas for foreigners; it also issues passports for Russians (Одел Виз и Регистраций)
perestroika (перестройка)	a Gorbachev era buzz word meaning restructuring
Pioneers (Пионер)	the communist era national youth organisation for young children from 9 to 14 years of age
ploshchad (площадь)	a city square
poezd (поезд)	train
posolok (посёлок)	an urban settlement with a minimum population of 3,000 and at least 85% employed in non-agricultural work
pr (пр)	abbreviation for prospekt (проспект) meaning avenue
provodnik (проводник)	train conductor
Raion (Район)	a district
refectory (трапезная)	dining room in a monastery
samovar (самовар)	hot water urn
sanatorium (санаторий)	health resort often built near mineral springs or mud pools
selo (село)	a rural village
Soviet (Совет)	a council

stary (старый)	old
SV (СВ)	abbreviation for a first-class sleeping carriage with two beds only in the compartment (спальный вагон); synonym for *myaky*
turist (Турист)	this word used to carry a significantly different meaning to the English word tourist: *turist* traditionally meant adventure travel such as mountaineering and camping, while tourist usually referred to a traveller on a package holiday or one who stayed for a short time in a city; the Russian word *turist* is now commonly used to mean the same as the English tourist
ul (ул)	abbreviation for *ulitsa* (улица) meaning street
vokzal (вокзал)	railway station

Appendix Three

RAILWAY DICTIONARY

The following section will help you to read Russian timetables, order tickets and enjoy the rail trip.

касса
ticket window

предварительная касса — for tickets after 24 hours
в день отправления касса — for tickets within 24 hours
текущая продажа билетов — for tickets within 24 hours
воинская касса — for military personnel
Интуриста касса — for foreigners
часы работы с 8 до 20 — working from 08.00 to 20.00
круглосуточная касса — open 24 hours
обед 13 до 14 — lunch break from 13.00 to 14.00
перерыв — break
технический перерыв 10.15 до 10.45 — technical break from 10.15 to 10.45

расписание
timetable

Чет. (четным числам) — even days of the month (ie: 2, 14, 28 of May)
Неч. (по нечетным числам) — odd days of the month (ie: 1, 13, 27 of May)
вых (по выходным) — weekends and public holidays
раб (по рабочим дням) — weekdays
От. (отправление) — departure
Пр. (прибытие) — arrival
Пл. (платформа) — platform
станция назначения — station of destination

поезд
train

скорый поезд — fast train
транзитный поезд — transit train
пассажирский поезд — passenger train
пригородный поезд — suburban train
фирменный поезд — deluxe express train (it always has a name such as *Rossiya* (Moscow to Vladivostok train)

поезд опаздывает — train is late
поезд не останавливается — train does not stop
поезд не заходит на станцию — train does not stop at the station

вокзал, станция
station

начальник вокзала — stationmaster
дежурный по станции — station attendant
справка — information

вагон
carriage

СВ (спальный вагон) — 2 berth compartment carriage
мягкий вагон — 2 berth compartment carriage
купейный вагон — 4 berth compartment carriage
плацкартный вагон — open sleeping carriage

общий вагон	open sitting carriage
безпересадочный вагон	carriage which separates and joins another
(or отцепной вагон)	train partway through the journey

билет

ticket

туда	one way
обратно	return
полный	adult
детский	child
место	berth number
верхнее место	upper berth
нижнее место	lower berth
проездной билет	pass such as a monthly pass
льготный билет	discount ticket for pensioners, students etc
зона	price zones

время

time

московское время	Moscow time
местное время	local time

на поезда

on the train

бригадир поезда,	head conductor
начальник бригады проводников	
проводник	conductor
стоп-кран	emergency stop handle
багажная полка	baggage rack
одеяло	blankets
белье	sheets
постельные принадлежности	rolled up mattress and pillow

Appendix Four

RECOMMENDED READING

To be able to appreciate fully what you are seeing, it is recommended that you read as much as you can about the countries and regions you are visiting.

Magazines and newspapers

CIS Russian Travel Newsletter A badly laid-out, weekly newsletter aimed at travel professionals. It contains only a few sentences on developments but these provide useful leads. International Traveltrade Index, Box 636 Federal Square, Newark NJ 07101 USA, tel: 908 686 2382, fax: 201 622 1740.

The Moscow Times Russia Review Each edition is 48 pages long and includes the most important daily news from the *Moscow Times*, plus stories from over 40 Western and Russian journalists on the ground in Russia. Available from Russian Information Systems, 89 Main Street, Suite 2, Montpelier, VT 05602 USA, tel: 802 334 4955, fax: 802 223 6105, email: risvt@sovusa.com, or Pokrovsky bulvar 8, 3rd floor, office 305, 109817 Moscow Russia tel: 095 917 9148, email: 73430.1051@compuserve.com.

Moscow Times Russia's most respected and authoritative English language paper. It is available free at most hotels in Moscow and can be subscribed to through its Dutch partner, at 93 van Eeghenstraat, 1071 Ex Amsterdam, The Netherlands, tel: 31 20 664 0978, fax: 31 20 676 0701.

Moscow Tribune This paper is only available in Moscow and is nearly as good as the *Moscow Times*.

Moscow News This is a translation of the *Moskovskie Novosti* which was once the most adventurous of the *perestroika* period newspapers. Its translation often leaves a lot to be desired. It can be subscribed to through East View Publications, 3020 Harbor Lane North, Plymouth MN 55447 USA, tel: 612 550 0961, email: admin@eastview.com.

St Petersburg Press This local newspaper is sold in most downtown kiosks. It can be subscribed to by writing to Akadeemia 21G, EE-0026, Tallinn, Estonia, tel: 3722 531 171.

Russian Far East Update Monthly business newsletter on the Russian far east. PO Box 22126, Seattle, WA 98122, USA, tel: 206 447 2668, fax: 206 628 0979.

Travel guides and railway books

Railways

Soviet Locomotive Types, by Anthony J Heywood and Ian D C Button, 175pp, publisher Frank Stenvalls, Förlag, Malmö, Finland & Luddenden Press UK, 1995, ISBN 0952529296. This is the definitive book on Russian railway equipment. It includes catalogues of locomotive, multiple-unit and railcar classes; and preserved locomotives and multiple-units. Proceeds from this excellent book are used to support railway preservation in Russia. It can be ordered from Luddenden Press, 19 Goitside, Booth, Luddenden, Halifax, West Yorkshire HX2 6SY.

Rail guides
Siberian BAM Railway Guide: The Second Trans-Siberian Railway, by Athol Yates, 350pp, publisher Trailblazer Publications, 1995, ISBN 1 873756 06 2. This definitive book to the 3,400km-long BAM railway in eastern Siberia provides practical information, such as planning your trip, buying tickets, what to take, and getting to the region as well as a kilometre by kilometre guide to the railway. It has 27 detailed city and village maps plus 57 photographs. Highlights include the attractions of the northern end of Lake Baikal, a native food guide and directions to reaching two Stalin *era* gulag camps. The book provides major city coverage of Komsomolsk-na-Amure, Tynda, Bratsk, Sovetskaya Gavan, Neryungri, Severobaikalsk.

Trans Siberian Handbook, by Bryn Thomas, 320pp publisher Trailblazer Publications, 1994, ISBN 1 873756 04 6. This excellent guide to the Trans-Siberian includes a detailed history of Siberia and the construction of the railway as well as practical information on planning a trip and buying a ticket. It has a kilometre by kilometre guide (with strip maps in English, Russian and Chinese) to the Trans-Siberian, Trans-Mongolian, and Trans-Manchurian routes. It also includes city guides to St Petersburg, Moscow, Ekaterinburg, Novosibirsk, Irkutsk, Ulan-Ude, Khabarovsk, Vladivostok, Ulaanbaatar and Beijing.

Silk Road by Rail, by Dominic Streatfeild-James, publisher Trailblazer Publications, 1993, ISBN 1 873756 03 8. This book covers the rail route starting in Moscow through central Asia to Beijing. Except for a chapter on Moscow, its coverage of the Russian leg of the route is minimal. Its coverage of the central Asian cities of Khiva, Bukhara, Samarkand, Tashkent and Alma Ata is good as is its material on the Chinese cities.

Moscow, St Petersburg and Minsk travel guides
Where in Moscow, Paul E Richardson, ed, 250pp, publisher Access Books, 1996, ISBN 1880100193. A cross between the yellow pages and a street directory. Excellent for the long term visitor.

Moscow Rough Guide, by Paul E Richardson, 390pp, publisher Penguin Books, 1995, ISBN 1858281180. This guide includes details of the city's famous sights and museums, ratings of Moscow's hotels, bars, restaurants and clubs, listings of the city's shops, markets, festivals and bathhouses, day trips outside Moscow, and lively accounts of contemporary Russian life.

Traveller's Yellow Pages Moscow, published by InfoService International, USA. Updated yearly.

Discovering Moscow: the complete companion guide, by Helen Boldyreff Semler, Hippocrene Books, 1989. This is a truly detailed book on pre-communist period buildings compiled as a labour of love. It has limited practical information but is highly recommended for any architecture buffs.

Blue Guide Moscow & Leningrad, by Evan Mawdsley, publisher A & C Black, 1991. This is an ideal reference book as it provides a very detailed guide to the cities' history, art, literature and architecture. It has very little practical travel information.

Moscow–St Petersburg Handbook, by Masha Nordbye, 259pp, publisher Moon Publications, 1993, ISBN 0918373913. A good basic guide to places of interest in both major cities and includes towns of the Golden Ring including Sergiev-Posad, Vladimir and Suzdal.

Where in St Petersburg, Scott D McDonald, ed, 176pp, publisher Access Books, 1996. ISBN 1880100134. A cross between the yellow pages and a street directory. Excellent for the long term visitor.

St Petersburg Rough Guide, by Humphries & Richardson, 399pp, publisher Penguin Books, 1995, ISBN 1858281334. This guide includes details of the city's famous sights and museums, 30 maps and site plans, and ratings of the city's hotels, restaurants, cafes, nightclubs, music venues and theatres.

Knopf Guide to St Petersburg, 324pp, 1995. Much more than a travel guide, this is a compact, colourful, artistic and engaging guide to Russia's imperial city. Each information-rich page of this handsome guide is full of history, social and cultural details and invaluable travel information.

Traveller's Yellow Pages St Petersburg, published by InfoService International, USA. Updated yearly.

Minsk in Your Pocket, is an excellent practical guide to the city. Unfortunately it is only available only in Minsk hotels and book shops.

Minsk: A Historical Guide, by Guy Picarda, 1993, covers the historical aspects of the city but has little practical information.

General travel guides

An Explorer's Guide to Russia, by Robert Greenall, 272pp, 1995. Oriented to the cost-conscious and independent-minded traveller, this book gives you plenty of survival information (from food to visas), plus the historical and travel information you need to understand what you are seeing. It covers only central and northern European Russia.

Russia, Ukraine and Belarus Travel Survival Kit, by John Noble et al, 1,170pp, publisher Lonely Planet, 1995, ISBN 0 864423 20 6. By far the most comprehensive travel guide to these countries. It is an information-dense tome, and well worth the weight. It is geared for individual travellers. Its maps are great and it stands above the rest due to its consistency and comprehensiveness.

The Insider's Guide to Russia, 210pp, 1993. Filled with the anecdotes and insights that only a native can provide, this frank and entertaining guide is an invaluable complement to 'mainstream' tourist guides by Western authors. Over 140 full-colour photographs and maps.

The Baltics and Russia Through the Back Door, by Ian Watson, 77pp, 1995. This new guide for the cost-conscious traveller, is organised into complete two or three-day itineraries of the three Baltic capitals, Moscow and St Petersburg. It includes the best ways to get in and out of the cities, where to eat and stay, background information and useful words and phrases.

Russia Survival Guide: Business & Travel, by Paul E Richardson, 220pp, publisher Access Books, ISBN 1 880100 18 5. An excellent guide to doing business and travelling in the new Russia. The guide provides detailed contact information for over 80 of Russia's largest cities. Yearly editions provide the latest information on visas, sources for travel and business information, answers to your currency questions, health and crime issues, travelling in-country, communicating by fax, phone and email, doing business with Russians, and the most comprehensive and lucid summary of Russian business legislation anywhere available.

Russia by Waterway, by Athol Yates ed, due out in 1997. A guide to the major waterways of Russia including the popular riverway between St Petersburg and Moscow, and the Volga, Lena, Amur, Ob, Enisei and Don Rivers. Chapters devoted to the various vessels plying these routes include hydrofoils, tramp steamers, and passenger cruise ships. Detailed descriptions and maps are provided for all the major stops on the way plus information on hundreds of little towns on the riverside.

The Russian Far East, by Erik and Allegra Harris Azulay, 250pp, publisher Hippocrene Books, 1995, ISBN 0 781803 25 X. This guide concentrates on the cities of Vladivostok, Khabarovsk, Chita, Ulan-Ude, Yakutsk, Magadan, Petropavlovsk-Kamchatski and Yuzhno-Sakhalinsk. While it is okay, its poor maps and table of contents let it down.

Hiking Guide to Poland and the Ukraine, by Tim Burford, 400pp, publisher Bradt Publications, 1994, ISBN 1 898323 02 X. The hiking trails and mountain huts of Poland are well established, but Ukraine has only just opened up to adventurous travellers. This guide not only details mountain walks and treks but includes much practical information on the main towns of Ukraine, and those in the mountain regions of Poland.

Trekking in Russia and Central Asia, by Frith Maier, 320pp, publisher Mountaineers, 1994, ISBN 0898863554. This is the bible for those interested in trekking in remote regions of Russia and Central Asia. You will still need local support for the vast majority of the 50 treks and adventures proposed.

The Complete Guide to the Soviet Union, by Victor and Jennifer Louis, publisher St Martin's Press, 1991, ISBN 0312058381. These authors have been producing guides for years and, until the arrival of Lonely Planet's guide, this was the best guide to the whole of the former Soviet Union. Now it is very dated and the information is often wrong. The maps are almost useless as they were badly drawn and invariably do not include the locations of places they describe. Save your money and don't buy it.

Insight Guides Russia, 1994. This book provides basic sightseeing and historical information but has very limited practical information.

Ukraine: A Tourist Guide, by Osyp Zinkewych and Volodymyr Hula, 458pp, publisher Smoloskyp, 1995. A good guide to Ukraine and well worth the money if you are going to spend a lot of time there. Smoloskyp Publishers, PO Box 20620, Billings, MT 59104, USA, tel/fax: 406 656 0466.

Maps

A range of interesting maps of Russian, Ukrainian and Belarus cities and regions is available from Four One Company, 523 Hamilton Rd, London, Canada N5Z 1S3, tel: (519) 433-1351, fax: (519) 433-5903. They have a WWW site at http://www.icis.net/fourone.

Timetables

Thomas Cook Overseas Timetable is available in the UK from Thomas Cook Publishing, PO Box 277, Thorpe Wood, Peterborough, PE3 6SB, tel: (01733) 505821, and in the US from Forsyth Travel Library, 9154 West 57th St, PO Box 2975, Dept TCT, Shawnee Mission, Kansas 66201, tel: (800) 367 7984.

Russian Passenger Timetable. This Russian language, 600-page book covers every rail line in the former countries of the Soviet Union. It is available from the Railway Bookshop in Moscow which is next door to the exit from the metro station Krasny Vorota.

Appendix Five

THE INTERNET

The internet contains a great wealth of information on Russia, but you often have to wade through pages of trivia, gossip and superficial impressions to get to it. The following mailists and WWW servers are all in English and are free unless otherwise marked.

Remember to check out the WWW page of this guidebook which includes an update file which you can download and print out. This ensures that your book will never be out of date. Its site is http://www.russia-rail.com.

Mailists

Russia, Ukraine and Belarus mailists

Belarus Information Service Bulletin   News briefs published by the Minsk Mass-Media Center. Its web page is at http://solar.rtd.utk.edu/oldfriends/ccsi/emags.htm. To be added to the distribution list, send a message to the Mass-Media Center in Minsk: mmc@glas.apc.org.

CivilSoc   This list is run by the Center for Civil Society International (CCSI) and provides news and resources to people engaged with civil society institution-building organisations in the former USSR. To subscribe send a message "subscribe CIVILSOC yourname" to listserv@solar.rtd.utk.edu.

East European Business Network   Discussions on doing business in Eastern Europe and the transition of Eastern Europe countries to market economies. To subscribe send a message "subscribe E-EUROPE yourname" to listserv@pucc.princeton.edu.

Eastern Orthodox Christianity   To subscribe send a message "subscribe EOCHR yourname" to listserv@qucdn.queensu.ca.

Express Khronika   News on CIS human/civil rights events and organisations. To subscribe, send a message asking to be added to the list to chronicle@glas.apc.org. Cost applies.

Jamestown Monitor   An excellent source of daily news on the countries of the former Soviet Union. As well as a daily summary, the Monitor includes a weekly compilation of indepth articles. To subscribe, send the message "subscribe jf-monitor" to listserv@services.sura.net or to listserv@andrew.cais.com.

Jobs   For jobs in both Russia and eastern Europe, send a message "subscribe ee-jobs yourname" to listproc@cep.nonprofit.net. Also try CivilSoc above.

Moscow News Confidential   Moscow News's bi-weekly insider reports. To subscribe, send an e-mail message to mosnex@sovamsu.sovusa.com. Cost applies.

Open Media Research Institute's Daily Digest   Daily Digest is probably the best single source for news of Eastern Europe and the former USSR. To subscribe, send the message "subscribe omri-l firstname lastname" to listserv@ubvm.cc.buffalo.edu.

Orthodox Christianity   A discussion group on Orthodox Christianity and its impact and resurgence within Russian and her neighbors. To subscribe send a message "subscribe orthodox yourname" to listserv@arizvm1.ccit.arizona.edu.

Rukh Insider   A bi-monthly news bulletin which carries in-depth information on political events in Ukraine. To be added to the electronic mail distribution list, send a request to lozowy@gluk.apc.org. Cost applies.

Russian Agriculture   To subscribe send a message "subscribe rusag-l yourname" to listserv@umdd.umd.edu.

Russian History Scholarly Discussion Group   To subscribe send a message "subscribe h-russia yourname" to listserv@uicvm.uic.edu.

Russian History   A discussion of Russian history from Ivan III (15th century) to the end of the Romanov dynasty (1917). To subscribe send a message "subscribe RUSHIST yourname" to listserv@earn.cvut.cz or listserv@vm.usc.edu.

Russian Language and Literature Issues   To subscribe send a message "subscribe RUSSIAN yourname" to listserv@asuvm.inre.asu.edu.

Russian Studies in the UK   To subscribe send a message "subscribe russian-studies youremail" to majordomo@mailbase.ac.uk.

Slavic & East European Languages & Literatures   To subscribe send a message "subscribe SEELANGS yourname" to listserv@cunyvm.cuny.edu.

Soviet History   Discussion of Soviet history from the 1917 February Revolution to the fall of the Communist rule in 1991. To subscribe send a message "subscribe SOVHIST yourname" to listserv@vm.usc.edu.

SOVSET   The Center for Strategic and International Studies in Washington, DC, runs the Sovset virtual network of data libraries and discussion groups dedicated to the advancement of Soviet studies. It runs policy, politics and FSU (former Soviet Union) lists. For information on joining Sovset, send the message "help" to listserv@Sovset.org.

Travel-L List   Although only a small portion of this list is on the countries of the former Soviet Union, ocasionally useful information pops up. To subscribe send a message "subscribe TRAVEL-L yourname" to listserv@vm.ege.edu.tr.

Ukrainian Arts Monitor   A weekly bulletin that includes news and announcements of art and cultural events in Ukraine. To subscribe, send the message "RFEED 30 ukrainet.eng.uam" to newsserv@litech.lviv.ua.

Ukrainian News Electronic Delivery   An excellent daily and weekly news service available from a Gopher site in Kyiv. gopher://kiev.sovam.com/11/UPRESA.

Railway Newlists

The Railroad List   To subscribe, send the message "subscribe railroad yourname" to listserv@cunyvm.cuny.edu no.

Railnet Railfan   To subscribe, send the message "SUBSCRIBE" to railnfan-request@railnet.nshore.org.

Railroadiana   To subscribe, send a message to rrdiana-request@railnet.nshore.org with a message subject saying "SUBSCRIBE yourname".

World Wide Web sites

WWW newspapers

Open Media Research Institute's Daily Digest   Daily Digest is probably the best single source for news of Eastern Europe and the former USSR. Past issues of the Daily Digest, going back to January 1994, are available online at http://www.omri.cz/Publications/Digests/DigestIndex.html, and their special Analytical Briefs are at http://www.omri.cz/Publications/Analytical/Index.html.

Radio Free Europe/Radio Liberty   For more than 40 years RFE/RL has been broadcasting news to the countries of Eastern Europe and the CIS. http://www.rferl.org/.

Russian Far East Update   On-line version of the excellent newsletter of the same name. http://www.russianfareast.com/wistar/homepage.html.

Russian Life   On-line version of the excellent magazine of the same name. http://www.friends-partners.org/rispubs/rispubs.html.

Slavic Review   An on-line version of the Slavic Review academic journal. http://ccat.sas.upenn.edu/slavrev/slavrev.html.

St Petersburg Press   A St Petersburg newspaper published weekly on the Internet. http://www.spb.su/sppress/index.html.

Ukrainian Arts Monitor   A weekly bulletin that includes news and announcements of art and cultural events in Ukraine. http://www.ukraine.org/UAMonitor/.

Ukrainian Weekly   Good newspaper. http://world.std.com/~sabre/UKRAINE.htm.

Ukrainian Weekly   Published by the Ukrainian National Association since 1933, the Ukrainian Weekly has full-time press bureaus in Kyiv and Toronto. The newspaper reports news about Ukraine and Ukrainians around the world. http://www.tryzub.com/UFPWWW_Etc/Current/UkrWeekly/ABOUT.html.

Vladivostok News   Articles for Vladivostok's English-language newspaper published weekly. http://www.tribnet.com/vlad.htm.

General Russian and related WWW sites

Adventurous Traveler Bookstore   http://www.gorp.com/atbook.htm.

Andrei Sakharov Foundation   http://www.wdn.com/asf.

Belarus Miscellany   An excellent resource on Belarus. http://solar.rtd.utk.edu/~kasaty/miscellany.html.

Bellona   This is the home of the environmental action group specialising in northeast European Russia. http://www.grida.no/ngo/bellona/.

Center for Civil Society International (CCSI)   CCSI acts as an information clearinghouse for news and resources of interest to people engaged with civil society institution-building organisations in the former USSR. CCSI publishes a monthly bulletin and produces speciality publications, including the *The Post-Soviet Handbook: A Guide to Grassroots Organizations and Internet Resources in the New Independent States*. CCSI manages an electronic mailing list "CivilSoc" and has a web site at http://solar.rtd.utk.edu/~ccsi/ccsihome.html. Center for Civil Society International, 2929 NE Blakeley Street, Seattle, WA 98105, tel: (206) 523 4755, fax: (206) 523-1974, email: ccsi@u.washington.edu.

Centre for Comparative Labour Studies   This site contains current research projects, lists of publications, and 400 files of research reports on the restructuring of industrial enterprises, labour relations and worker organisation in Russia at the University of Warwick. http://www.csv.warwick.ac.uk/WWW/faculties/social_studies/complabstuds/russia/russint.htm.

Chukotka   Information on the Russian reindeer country. http://informns.k12.mn.us/rfe/chukotka/.

Dazhdbog's Grandsons   Established by Serge Naumov at the University of North Carolina who called this server "Dazhdbog's Grandsons" because that is what the ancient Russians called themselves.

Directory of Slavic Websites   This page contains hyperlinks to the homepages of Russian/Slavic university departments around the world plus references to pages describing Russian resources of academic libraries, databases, HT editions and spatial projects. http://www.cs.ut.ee/~roman_l/rusweb.html.

East Siberia   A server based in Irkutsk. http://www.icc.ru.

Ekaterinburg   A server based in Ekaterinburg. http://www.mplik.ru/english/e-burg/index.html.

Friends & Partners   Probably the best Russian site with an enormous range of information and pointers to other servers. http://www.friends-partners.org/friends/.

Glasnet   Home to the Russian Glasnet network. http://www.glasnet.ru/.

Insightful Photo Gallery   Pictures of old Russian photos, money photo collection, and advertisements. http://www-physics.mps.ohio-state.edu/~viznyuk/pgallery.html.

Internet Services   Information on email and internet in the countries of the former Soviet Union. http://www.irex.org/FAQ.htm.

ITAR-TASS Russian News Agency   http://www1.trib.com/NEWS/tass.html.

KLRN Home Page   Art and culture. http://tristero.tddc.net/klrn/.

List of electronic publications   http://solar.rtd.utk.edu/~ccsi/emags.htm.

Little Russia   Offers a variety of information resources dealing with Russia. http://mars.uthscsa.edu/Russia/.

Maps   The site of the Four One company which specialises in selling maps. It has a huge collection of maps of the former Soviet Union. http://www.icis.net/fourone.

Military History   Homepage of John Sloan's Russian military history server http://home.aol.com/johns426.

Minsk   Try http://unibel.by or http://freedom.ncsa.uiuc.edu/~zelenko/belarus.html.

Moscow Channel   An online journal devoted to Russian culture, arts and cyberspace, http://www.moscowchannel.com.

Museums of Moscow's Kremlin   Arts, culture, history and more. http://www.kiae.su/www/wtr/arts.html.

Palms Portal   Business information. http://www.aa.net/~russia. Cost applies.

Pereslavl   Local Pereslavl-Zalevsski server. http://botik.ru.

Post-Soviet Study Resources   Compiled, edited and with commentary by Ian Kallen of San Francisco State University. It lists information resources on the Internet devoted to the former Soviet Union. http://solar.rtd.utk.edu/~ikallen/.

Railways   This site provides worldwide railway internet resources. http:www.cse.ucsd.edu/users/browdidge/railroad/rail-home.html.

Russia Rail   This is the site of the *Russia by Railway* and *Siberian BAM Railway* guides written by Athol Yates. It contains update files which can be downloaded. This ensures that your book will never be out of date. http://www.russia-rail.com.

Russian Agriculture   Back issues of the Ruslag-1 news update are stored at http://solar.rtd.utk.edu/friends/science/agriculture/.

Russian America Page   http://webideas.com/rusam.

Russian American Business Assistance Center (RABAC)   http://rabac.com./.

Russian and East European Studies Home Pages (REESweb)   A comprehensive guide to the worldwide network-accessible resources available to scholars in the interdisciplinary study of Russia and Eastern Europe. http://www.pitt.edu/~cjp/rslang.html#Russ.

Russian and East European Studies   http://www.pit.edu/~cjp/rees.html.

Russian Literature   http://iaiwww.uni-muenster.de/cgi-bin/simplex/lat/lit.html.

Russian Movie Database   Find here your favourite movie, actor, director. Add new movie or update information. http://www.serve.com/andrey/russian/index.htm.

Russian Music   Files on Russian Classical Music: http://copper.ucs.indiana.edu/~lneff/russmus/russmus.html.

Russian Non-Government Organisations OpenWeb   This site contains homepages for dozens of Russian NGOs: http://www.openweb.ru.

Russian Railways   This is a great site on Russian railways and is one of the few www sites that only contains quality information. It has dozens of maps of Russian rail networks and technical information on rolling stock and Ministry of Railways information. Run by Dmitry Zinoviev. http://pavel.physics.sunysb.edu/RR.

Russian Travel Books by Access Books   http://solar.rtd.utk.edu/~rispubs/access/trav-rus.html.

Russian Yellow Web Pages   http://www.serv.com/andrey/russian/index.html.

Siberian BAM Railway   This is the site of the *Siberian BAM Railway Guide* written by Athol Yates. It contains an update file which can be downloaded. Its site is http://www.russia-rail.com.

SIRIN   Animal Protection in Russia. http://www.ucr.edu:80/history/sirin.html.

Sister Cities International   Homepage to the US sister cities organisation: http://www.sister-cities.org/.

SovInform Bureau   A source of information on Russian/Soviet related issues. http://www.cs.umd.edu/ftp/pub/cyrillic/.

Space   A good site of material on the Russia history of spaceflight, space vehicles and explores is http://solar.rtd.utk.edu/oldfriends/jgreen/fpspace.html. The Youth Space Center at Moscow's Bauman State Technical University has a site at http://www.seds.org/ysc/.

St Petersburg Press Culture & Lifestyle Guide   Information on the city's performing arts, food, what to see and music for the week. http://solar.rtd.utk.edu/oldfriends/spbweb/lifestyl/88/index.html.

St Petersburg   A server containing St Petersburg Press, Russian Youth Hostels, GNN Travel Center, Fodor's Worldview and city highlights. http://www.spb.su/ryh/spb-ru.html.

Tolstoy Library Online   http://home.aol.com/Tolstoy28.

Trans-Siberian Railway Link Site   An excellent page containing dozens of articles and sites related to the Trans-Siberian. http://www.xs4all.nl/~hgj/travel/.

Ukraine Web site http://www.osc.edu/ukraine.html.

Ukraine General information on the country with lots of pointers. http://www.physics.mcgill.ca/www/oleh/ukr-info.html.

Virtual Guide to Belarus http://faraday.clas.virginia.edu/~ana4a/Belarus.html.

Who's Who in CIS http://www.maximov.com/.

World-Wide Web Virtual Library: Russian and East European Studies http://www.pitt.edu/~cjp/rees.html.

Yahoo – Regional Information: Russia: #russian IRC channel http://www.yahoo.com/Regional_Information/Countries/Russia.

Yaroslavl Local Yaroslavl servers at http://www.yars.free.net/ and http://cnit2.uniyar.ac.ru/.

USENET newsgroups
alt.current-events.russia
misc.transport.rail.europe
soc.culture.soviet
talk.politics.soviet

Appendix Six

NEW CITY AND REGIONAL NAMES

The names of many cities, regions and natural features in the former Soviet Union have changed following the collapse of the communist state in 1991. Below is a list of the new and old names, plus several common English names of Russian places and common alternative spelling of cities.

Legend: R= Russian, U= Ukrainian, B=Belarusian, C=Chinese, M=Mongolian, E=English

Old name	Current name
Aigun (R)	Ai-hun (C)
Akmolinsk (R)	Tselinograd (R)
Alekseyevsk (R)	Svobodny (R)
Altynovka (R)	Altynivka (U)
Andropov (R)	Rybinsk (R)
Archangel (R)	Arkhangelsk (R)
Baranovichi (R)	Baranavichy (B)
Belgorod-Dnestrovsky (R)	Bilhorod-Dnistrovsky (U)
Belorussia Republic (R)	Belarus Republic (B)
Bereza (R)	Byaroza (B)
Borisov (R)	Barysai (B)
Brest-Litovsk (R)	Brest (B)
Bronnaya Gora (R)	Bronnaya Gara (B)
Brovary (R)	Brovary (U)
Chernobyl (R)	Chornobyl (U)
Chernovtsy (R)	Chernivtsi (U)
Chinadievo (R)	Chynadiieva (U)
Dalni (R)	Ta-lien (C)
Darnitsa (R)	Darnitsa (U)
Dnepr River (R)	Dnipro (U)
Fastov (R)	Fastiv (U)
Gnivan (R)	Hnivan (U)
Gorky (R)	Nizhni Novgorod (R)
Ivatsevichi (R)	Ivatsevichy (B)
Kalinin (R)	Tver (R)
Kharkov (R)	Kharkiv (U)
Khmelnitski (R)	Khmelnytsky (U)
Kiev (R)	Kyiv (U)
Koidanovo (R)	Koidanava (B)
Kolodishche (R)	Kalodzishcha (B)
Kozatin (R)	Koziatyn (U)
Leningrad (R)	St Petersburg (R)
Lesnaya (R)	Lyasnaya (B)
Lvov (R)	Lviv (U)
Molotov (R)	Perm (R)
Mukachevo (R)	Mukacheve (U)
Mukden (R)	Shen-yang (C)
Mysovsk (R)	Babushkin (R)
Negoreloe (R)	Negarelae (B)

Nikolaev (R)	Mykolaiv (U)
Nosovka (R)	Nosivka (U)
Novonikolayevsk (R)	Novosibirsk (R)
Osinovka (R)	Asinaika (B)
Petrograd (R)	St Petersburg (R)
Port Arther (R)	Lüshun (C)
Prishib (R)	Leninsk (R)
Samara (R)	Kuibyshev (R)
Smolevichi (R)	Smalevichy (B)
Stalingrad (R)	Volgograd (R)
Stalinsk (R)	Novokuznetsk (R)
Stolbtsy (R)	Stoibtsy (B)
Svalyava (R)	Svaliava (U)
Sverdlovsk (R)	Ekaterinburg (R)
Ternopol (R)	Ternopil (U)
Tolochin (R)	Talachyn (B)
Ulaanbaatar (R)	Ulaanbaatar (M)
Uzhgorod (R)	Uzhhorod (U)
Vaenga (R)	Severomorsk (R)
Verkhne Sinevidnoe (R)	Verkhne Synovydne (U)
Verkhneudinsk (R)	Ulan-Ude (R)
Vinnitsa (R)	Vinniytsa (U)
Volochisk (R)	Volochyske (U)
Voronezh (R)	Voronizh (U)
White Sea (E)	Beloe More (R)
Yakutia Republic (R)	Sakha Republic (R)
Yekaterinburg (R)	Ekaterinburg (R)
Zagorsk (R)	Sergiev-Posad (R)
Zborov (R)	Zboriv (U)
Zheleznogorsk (R)	Atomograd (R)
Zlochev (R)	Zolochiv (U)

Appendix Seven

TIMETABLES

The trains upon which the timetables are based are mostly long-distance express trains. For this reason, many stations are not stopped at. However, the slower long-distance passenger trains do stop at these stations. Stopping time at stations may vary depending on the direction of travel. Very occasionally, the train only stops in one direction. The symbol '~' means that the stopping time varies with each train.

For the latest updates see the *Thomas Cook Overseas Timetable*, or the *Russian Passenger Timetable*.

Moscow–St Petersburg

Long-distance trains No 1/2 Red Arrow Moscow–St Petersburg

Station	Russian name	Dist (km)	Stop (min)	Departure time West bound No 2	East bound No 1	Time zone
Moscow (Leningrad)	Москва (Ленинградский)	0		23.55	08.25	Moscow time
Rizhskaya	Рижская	2				
Ostankino	Останкино	4				
Mosselmash	Моссельмаш	14				
Khovrino	Ховрино	15				
Levoberenaya	Левоберьная	18				
Khimki	Химки	19				
Planernaya	Планерная	24				
Skhodnya	Сходня	30				
Firsanovka	Фирсановка	33				
Kryukovo	Крюково	39				
Radishchevo	Радищево	47				
Podsolnechnaya	Подсолнечная	65				
Frolovskoe	Фроловское	81				
Klin	Клин	90				
Reshetnikovo	Решетниково	105				
Zavidovo	Завидово	119				
Redkino	Редкино	133				
Tver	Тверь	167				
Proletarka	Пролетарка	172				
Doroshikha	Дорошиха	174				
Kulitskaya	Кулицкая	194				
Likhoslavl	Лихославль	209				
Lokottsy	Локотцы	216				
Lyubinka	Любинка	260				
Vyshni Volochek	Вышний Волочек	286				
Leontevo	Леонтьево	294				
Akademicheskaya	Академическая	305				
Bologoe	Бологое	331	10	03.55	04.03	
Berezaika	Березайка	345				
Torbino	Торбино	434				
Mstinski Most	Мстинский мост	461				
Chudovo	Чудово	532				
Torfyanoe	Торфяное	547				
Lyuban	Любань	567				
Ryabovo	Рябово	577				
Ushaki	Ушаки	586				
Tosno	Тосно	597				
Sablino	Саблино	609				
Kolpino	Колпино	625				

Obukhovo	Обухово	639				
St Petersburg (Moscow)	Санкт-Петербург (Московский)	650		08.25	23.55	

Moscow–Brest/Warsaw
Long-distance trains No 27/28 Moscow–Brest

Station	Russian name	Dist (km)	Stop (min)	Departure time West bound No 27	East bound No 28	Time zone
Moscow (Smolensk)	Москва- (Смоленский)	0		14.28	10.46	
Fili	Фили	7				
Kuntsevo	Кунцево	12				
Odintsovo	Одинцово	25				
Golitsino	Голицино	45				
Kubinka	Кубинка	63				
Sanatornaya	Санаторная	75				
Tuchkovo	Тучково	78				
Dorokhovo	Дорохово	86				
Partizanskaya	Партизанская	91				
Mozhaisk	Можайск	110				
Borodino	Бородино	121				
Drovino	Дровнино	153				
Gagarin	Гагарин	180				
Vyazma	Вязьма	243	10/15	18.24	06.19	
Semlevo	Семлево	266				
Izdeshkovo	Издешково	291				
Mitino	Митино	298				
Safonovo	Сафоново	317				
Yartsevo	Ярцево	371				
Smolensk	Смоленск	419	30	21.14	03.53	
Krasny Bor	Красный бор	428				
Rakitnaya	Ракитная	434				
Katyn	Катынь	452				
Gusino	Гусино	487				
Krasnoe	Красное	487				
Shukhovtsy (Belarus)	Шухаўцы	497				Belarus time (=Moscow)
Asinaika	Асінаўка	512				
Orsha	Орша	536	32/30	22.24	01.04	
Talachyn	Талачын	579				
Bobr	Бобр	615				
Krupki	Крупкі	629				
Barysai	Барысаў	669		00.02	–	
Zhodino	Жодзіна	687				
Smalevichy	Смалявічы	709				
Kalodzishcha	Калодзішч	733				
Minsk	Мінск	750	12	01.19	22.00	
Koidanava	Коиданава	790				
Negarelae	Негарэлае	801				
Stoibtsy	Стоўбцы	827				
Baranavichy	Баранавічы	895		03.18	19.52	
Lyasnaya	Лясная	917				
Ivatsevichy	Івацэвічы	960				
Bronnaya Gara	Бронная-Гара	980				
Byaroza	Бяроза	997				
Brest	Брэст	1,097		05.45/ 10.00*	17.10/ 12.20*	
Terespol (Poland)	Terespol	1,102		09.30*	11.50*	Polish time (Moscow+1)
Warsaw	Warsaw	1,317		14.15*	10.00*	

*Suburban trains No 10008/11011 Warsaw-Brest

Moscow–Chop/Budapest
Long-distance trains No 69/70 Moscow–Chop

Station	Russian name	Dist (km)	Stop (min)	Departure time West bound No 69	East bound No 70	Time zone
Moscow (Kiev)	Москва (Киевский)	0		22.26	13.59	Moscow time
Solnechnaya	Солнечная	16				
Lesnoi Gorodok	Лесной Городок	24				
Aprelevka	Апрелевка	42				
Nara	Нара	70				
Balabanovo	Балабаново	96				
Obninskoe	Обнинское	106				
Maloyaroslavets	Малоярославец	121				
Tikhonova Pustyn	Тихонова Пустынь	170				
Kaluga 2	Калуга 2	182		01.33	10.55	
Sukhinichi Glavnye	Сухиничи Главные	261	20	03.11	09.37	
Duminichi	Думиничи	287				
Bryansk	Брянск	387	43/77	05.56	07.20	
Zernovo	Зерново	519				
Druzhba (**Ukraine**)	Дружба	539				Ukraine time (=Moscow)
Voronizh	Вороніж	585				
Krolevets	Кролевець	611				
Altynivka	Алтинівка	626				
Konotop	Конотоп	651	30	09.30	01.14	
Bakhmach	Бахмач	676				
Kruty	Круты	726				
Nizhin	Ніжин	746				
Nosivka	Носівка	768				
Brovary	Бровари	842				
Darnitsa	Дарниця	858				
Kyiv	Київ	872	15/18	13.12	21.05	
Boiarka	Боярка	894				
Vasylkiv	Васылкив	908				
Fastiv	Фастів	936	2	14.24	19.35	
Kozhanka	Кожанка	955				
Koziatyn	Козятин	1,031	7/6	16.05	17.48	
Vinniytsa	Вінниця	1,099		17.17	16.42	
Hnivan	Гнівань	1,124				
Zhmerynka	Жмеринка	1,140	22/15	18.34	15.47	
Derazhnia	Деражня	1,188				
Khmelnytsky	Хмельницький	1,240	2/4	20.29	13.54	
Volochyske	Волочиськ	1,284				
Ternopil	Тернопіль	1,358	5	22.41	11.42	
Zboriv	Зборів	1,400				
Zolochiv	Золочів	1,422				
Lviv	Львів	1,499	28/15	01.40	09.10	
Mykolaiv	Миколаів	1,549				
Stryi	Стрий	1,574	7/1	03.15	07.37	
Lyubentsy	Любенцы	1,591				
Verkhne Synovydne	Верхнє Синьовидне	1,598				
Skole	Сколе	1,612				
Slavske	Славське	1,638				
Volovets	Воловець	1,669		05.39	05.26	
Svaliava	Свалява	1,697		06.24	–	
Chynadiieva	Чинадієве	1,711		06.45	–	
Kolchino	Колчіно	1,718		06.57	–	
Mukacheve	Мукачеве	1,724	9/4	07.19	04.12	
Chop	Чоп	1,765		08.46	03.10	
Zahony (**Hungary**)	Záhony	1,769				Hungary time (Moscow+1)
Budapest	Budapest	2,110				

Central Russia
Moscow–Voronezh
Long-distance trains No 25/26 Moscow–Voronezh

Station	Russian name	Dist (km)	Stop (min)	Departure time South bound No 26	North bound No 25	Time zone
Moscow (Paveletski)	Москва (Павелецкий)	0		20.10	07.57	Moscow time
Ryazan 2	Рязань 2	198	12/15	01.22	03.04	
Ryazhsk 1	Ряжск 1	314		03.37	01.05	
Bogoyavlensk	Богоявленск	366		04.28		
Michurinsk-Ural.	Мичуринск-Урал.	408	19/25	05.31	23.15	
Michurinsk-Voronezh	Мичуринск-Воронеж	412	3	05.43	22.40	
Gryazi-Voronezh	Грязи-Воронеж	472	5/4	07.00	21.37	
Usman	Усмань	572		-	-	
Grafskaya	Графская	595		-	-	
Volya	Воля	609		-	-	
Otrozhka	Отрожка	628		-	-	
Voronezh	Воронеж	636		09.07	19.12	

Voronezh–Volgograd
Long-distance trains No 223/224 Voronezh–Volgograd

Station	Russian name	Dist (km)	Stop (min)	Departure time South bound 223/224	North bound 224/223	Time zone
Voronezh	Воронеж	636		15.10	08.35	Moscow time
Gryazi-Voronezh	грязи-Воронеж	692	17/15	17.45	06.23	
Plavitsa	Плавица	731		18.48	05.23	
Borisoglebsk	Борисоглебск	902	8/9	23.23	01.00	
Povorino	Поворино	929	23/24	00.45	23.55	Moscow+1
Filonovo	Филоново	1013	14/17	03.22	21.25	
Archeda	Арчеда	1,140	7/10	06.40	18.00	
Volgograd	Волгоград	1,296		10.40	14.10	

Volgograd–Astrakhan
Long-distance trains No 37/38 Volgograd–Astrakhan

Station	Russian name	Dist (km)	Stop (min)	Departure time South bound 37/38	North bound 38/37	Time zone
Volgograd	Волгоград	1,296		10.20	04.20	Moscow+1
Volzhski	Волжский	1,340		11.18	03.33	
Leninsk	Ленинск	1,362	8/3	12.08	02.52	
Kapustin Yar	Капустин Яр	1,410		13.07	01.57	
Vladimirovka	Владимировка	1,453		13.50	01.12	
Verkhni Baskunchak	Верхний Баскунчак	1,498	22/20	15.10	00.05	
Kharabali	Харабали	1,602		16.53	21.52	
Aksaraiskaya	Аксарайская	1,695		18.43	20.02	
Astrakhan	Астрахань	1,744		19.55	18.45	

Northern Russian routes
St Petersburg–Murmansk
Long-distance trains No 22/21 St Petersburg–Murmansk

Station	Russian name	Dist (km)	Stop (min)	Departure time South bound 22/21	North bound 21/22	Time zone
St Petersburg (Moscow)	Санкт Петербург (Московский)	0		17.35	13.10	Moscow time
Obukhovo	Обухово	11				
Mga	Мга	49				
Zhikharevo	Жихарево	81				
Voibokalo	Войбокало	92				
Volkhovstroi 1	Волховстрой 1	121	17/15	20.05	11.01	
Murmanskie Vorota	Мурманские Ворота	123				
Lungachi	Лунгачи	150				
Yugi	Юги	167				
Oyat-Volkhovstroi	Оять-Волховстрой	199				
Lodeinoe Pole	Лодейное Поле	242	4/9	21.57	08.55	
Podporozhe	Подпорожье	279		22.51	08.01	
Tokari	Токари	315	20	01.31	05.54	
Derevyanka	Девевянка	372				
Onezhski	Онежский	393				
Petrozavodsk	Петрозаводск	401				
Tomitsy	Томицы	408				
Kondopoga	Кондопога	453		02.31	04.36	
Medvezhya Gora	Медвежья Гора	556	18/24	04.38	02.45	
Segezha	Сегежа	671	3	06.52	0.27	
Nadvoitsy	Надвойцы	681		07.17	23.58	
Shavan	Шавань	698				
Kochkoma	Кочкома	710				
Letni	Летний	743		08.14	22.57	
Belomorsk	Беломорск	780	4/8	09.19	14.34	
Myagreka	Мягрека	823				
Kem	Кемь	835	27/18	10.37	20.47	
Loukhi	Лоухи	1,000	18/14	13.36	17.51	
Polyarny Krug	Полярный Круг	1,055		14.52	16.29	
Zhemchuzhaya	Жемчужая	1,129				
Ruchi-Karelskie	Ручьи-Карельские	1,140				
Kandalaksha	Кандалакша	1,168	20/21	17.24	14.08	
Pinozero	Пинозеро	1,189				
Polyarnye Zori	Полярные Зори	1,196		17.58	13.12	
Apatity	Апатиты	1,260	5	19.02	12.13	
Nefelinovye Peski	Нефелиновые Пески	1,285				
Olengorsk	Оленгорск	1,333		20.22	10.56	
Kola	Кола	1,435				
Murmansk	Мурманск	1,445		22.30	8.40	

Moscow–Arkhangelsk
Long-distance trains No 15/16 Moscow–Arkhangelsk

Station	Russian name	Dist (km)	Stop (min)	Departure time North bound No 16	South bound No 15	Time zone
Moscow (Yaroslav)	Москва (Ярославлский)	0		12.10	16.30	Moscow time
Sergiev-Posad	Сергиев Посад	70				
Aleksandrov	Александров	112		14.06	14.36	
Yaroslavl	Ярославль	282	15	16.45	12.05	
Danilov	Данилов	357	20/15	18.18	10.34	

Prechistoe	Пречистое	388				
Gryazovets	Грязовец	449				
Vologda	Вологда	495	15	20.40	08.00	
Kharovskaya	Харовская	584		22.05	06.15	
Ertsevo	Ерцево	684		23.56	04.35	
Konosha	Коноша	707	15	00.45	04.05	
Nyandoma	Няндома	793	10/15	02.35	02.10	
Puksa	Пукса	906				
Plesetskaya	Плесецкая	918	5	04.47	23.32	
Obozerskaya	Обозерская	1,001	10	06.26	21.58	
Kholmogorskaya	Холмогорская	1,047				
Isakogorka	Исакогорка	1,120	5/10	08.40	19.50	
Bakaritsa	Бакарица	1,124				
Arkhangelsk	Архангельск	1,134		09.10	19.10	

Obozerskaya–Belomorsk
Long-distance trains No 173/147 Vologda–Murmansk

Station	Russian name	Dist (km)	Stop (min)	Departure time West bound No 174	East bound No 173	Time zone
Obozerskaya	Обозерская	0		02.10	18.30	Moscow time
Vonguda	Вонгуда	168	25/22	05.08	15.55	
Maloshuika	Малошуйка	230	15	06.50	14.05	
Malenga	Маленга	225				
Nyukhcha	Нюхча	237	1	08.41	11.39	
Sumski Posad	Сумский Посад	296	24/15	10.52	09.51	
Virma	Вирма	307		11.09	09.20	
Belomorsk	Беломорск	353		12.20	08.00	

Trans-Siberian, Trans-Mongolian and Trans-Manchurian
Trans-Siberian: Moscow–Vladivostok
Long-distance trains No 1/2 Rossiya Moscow-Vladivostok

Station	Russian name	Dist (km)	Stop (min)	Departure time East bound No 2	West bound No 1	Time zone
Moscow (Yaroslav)	Москва (Ярославский)	0		14.15	06.30	Moscow time
Sergiev-Posad	Сергиев Посад	70				
Aleksandrov	Александров	112	2	16.06	–	
Yaroslavl	Ярославль	282	5/10	18.30	02.10	
Danilov	Данилов	357	20/15	20.05	00.50	
Bui	Буй	450	2/8	21.23	23.10	
Galich	Галич	501				
Sharya	Шарья	723		01.16	19.22	Moscow+1
Kotelnich	Котельнич	870				
Vyatka	Вятка	957	15	05.13	15.29	
Perm 2	Пермь 2	1,437	35/25	12.44	08.08	Moscow+2
Kungur	Кунгур	1,538			8	
Pervouralsk	Первоуральск	1,774		18.21	–	
Europe-Asia Border		1,777				
Ekaterinburg	Екатеринбург	1,818	30	19.59	01.43	
Tyumen	Тюмень	2,144	~/~	00.21	20.55	Moscow+3
Ishim	Ишим	2,433		03.58	17.12	
Nazyvaevskaya	Называевская	2,567	11/15	05.59	15.21	
Omsk	Омск	2,716	16/15	07.56	13.08	
Barabinsk	Барабинск	3,040	15	12.20	08.45	
Novosibirsk	Новосибирск	3,343	15	16.55	04.12	
Taiga	Тайга	3,571	10	21.00	00.20	Moscow+4
Mariinsk	Мариинск	3,719	18/20	23.35	22.01	
Bogotol	Боготол	3,862	10/12	01.43	19.38	

Achinsk 1	Ачинск 1	3,940	4/5	02.44	18.18	
Krasnoyarsk	Красноярск	4,104	20	06.10	15.06	
Zaozernaya	Заозёная	4,272		08.55	11.49	
Ilanskaya	Иланская	4,383	20	10.55	10.02	
Taishet	Тайшет	4,522	5/4	13.09	07.31	Moscow+5
Nizhneudinsk	Нижнеудинск	4,683	15	16.15	04.35	
Tulun	Тулун	4,802	3	17.56	02.41	
Zima	Зима	4,941	20	20.26	00.36	
Cheremkhovo	Черемхово	5,061	2	22.19	22.24	
Angarsk	Ангарск	5,152		23.45	21.01	
Irkutsk	Иркутск	5,191	20/24	00.57	20.04	
Slyudyanka 1	Слюдянка 1	5,317		03.30	17.21	
Ulan-Ude	Улан-Уде	5,647	~/~	08.50	11.54	
Petrovski Zavod	Петровский Завод	5,790	~/~	11.13	09.29	Moscow+6
Khilok	Хилок	5,940		13.33	06.47	
Mogzon	Могзон	6,060		15.29	05.00	
Chita	Чита	6,204	20/18	18.14	02.20	
Darasun	Дарасун	6,270		19.38	00.41	
Karymskaya	Карымская	6,300		20.31	00.03	
Shilka	Шилка	6,451	8	23.08	21.07	
Priiskavaya	Приисковая	6,496		23.54	20.12	
Kuenga	Куэнга	6,532		00.34	19.27	
Chernyshevsk-Zabaikalski	Чернышевск-Забайкальский	6,593	15	01.50	18.24	
Zilovo	Зилово	6,676		03.27	16.35	
Mogocha	Могоча	6,914		08.03	12.13	
Amazar	Амазар	7,012	~/15	09.53	10.13	
Erofei-Pavlovich	Ерофей Павлович	7,119	~/15	12.40	08.00	
Skovorodino	Сковородино	7,313	10	16.32	03.55	
Magdagachi	Магдагачи	7,501	10	19.50	00.44	
Shimanovskaya	Шимановская	7,731	2/3	23.27	21.10	
Svobodny	Свободный	7,819	3	00.37	19.56	
Belogorsk	Белогорск	7,873	27/20	02.00	19.00	
Zavitaya	Завитая	7,992	2	03.53	16.56	
Arkhara	Архара	8,088	25/20	05.52	15.25	
Birobidzhan	Биробиджан	8,356	5	10.55	10.07	Moscow+7
Khabarovsk	Хабаровск	8,531	25/23	13.35	07.48	
Vyazemskaya	Вяземская	8,659	17/18	15.46	05.18	
Dalnerechensk	Дальнереченск	8,890	2	19.35	01.24	
Spassk-Dalni	Спасск-Дальний	9,057	2	22.18	22.37	
Ussurisk	Уссурийск	9,185	16/18	00.43	20.18	
Uglovaya	Угловая	9,264	2	02.02	18.36	
Vladivostok	Владивосток	9,297		02.45	17.55	

Trans-Mongolian: Moscow–Beijing
Long-distance trains No 3/4 Moscow–Beijing via Mongolia

Station	Russian name	Dist (km)	Stop (min)	Departure time East bound No 4	West bound No 5	Time zone
Moscow (Yaroslav)	Москва (Ярославский)	0		19.55	17.10	Moscow time
Yaroslavl	Ярославль	282	5/10	00.15	12.55	
Vyatka	Вятка	957	15	10.42	02.39	Moscow+1
Perm 2	Пермь 2	1,437	15	17.52	19.19	Moscow+2
Ekaterinburg	Екатеринбург	1,818	15	00.09	12.57	
Tyumen	Тюмень	2,144	~/~	04.25	08.44	Moscow+3
Novosibirsk	Новосибирск	3,343	15	20.54	16.32	
Krasnoyarsk	Красноярск	4,104	22/19	09.40	03.43	Moscow+4
Taishet	Тайшет	4,522	2	16.29	20.22	Moscow+5
Irkutsk	Иркутск	5,191	15/24	03.46	09.20	
Ulan-Ude	Улан-Удэ	5,642	20/15	11.44	01.27	
Zaudinski	Заудинский	5,650				

Zagustai	Загустай	5,769				
Gusinoe Ozero	Гусиное Озеро	5,801	2	14.46	22.15	
Selenduma	Селендума	5,828				
Dzhida	Джида	5,853				
Naushki	Наушки	5,897	108	18.20	20.25	
Sukhe Baator (**Mongolia**)	Сухэ Баатор	5,920	60	01.20	22.05	Mongolia time (Moscow+5)
Ulaanbaatar	Улан Баатор	6,299	30	09.30	13.50	
Beijing (**China**)		7,860		15.33	07.40	Beijing time (Moscow+5)

Trans-Manchurian: Moscow–Beijing
Long-distance trains No 19/20 Moscow–Beijing via Manchuria

Station	Russian name	Dist (km)	Stop (min)	Departure time East bound No 20	West bound No 19	Time zone
Moscow (Yaroslav)	Москва (Ярославский)	0		20.35	20.20	Moscow time
Yaroslavl	Ярославль	282	5	01.50	16.05	
Vyatka	Вятка	957	15	11.04	06.14	Moscow+1
Perm 2	Пермь 2	1,437	23	18.22	23.03	Moscow+2
Ekaterinburg	Екатеринбург	1,818	15	00.39	16.31	
Tyumen	Тюмень	2,144		04.55	12.11	Moscow+3
Novosibirsk	Новосибирск	3,343	25	21.31	20.00	
Krasnoyarsk	Красноярск	4,104	20	10.17	07.01	Moscow+4
Taishet	Тайшет	4,522	3	17.07	23.37	Moscow+5
Irkutsk	Иркутск	5,191	20	04.30	12.30	
Ulan-Ude	Улан-Удэ	5,642	15	12.23	04.33	
Chita 2	Чита 2	6,204	20	21.48	18.50	Moscow+6
Tarskaya	Тарская	6,311	20/14	00.18	16.35	
Mogoitui	Могойтуй	6,354	15/2	02.14	14.17	
Olovyannaya	Оловянная	6,450	12/14	03.49	12.49	
Borzya	Борзя	6,549	15	06.27	10.17	
Zabaikalsk	Забайкальск	6,666	120	14.06	07.01	
Manzhouli (**China**)		6,678	120	22.05	07.01	Beijing time (Moscow+5)
Harbin		7,613	20	12.10	14.51	
Beijing		9,001		06.32	20.32	

Vyatka line
Long-distance trains No 17/18 Moscow–Vyatka

Station	Russian name	Dist (km)	Stop (min)	Departure time East bound No 18	West bound No 17	Time zone
Moscow (Yaroslav)	Москва (Ярославский)	0		16.35	10.30	Moscow time
Vladimir	Владимир	191	17	20.17	06.52	
Bogolyubovo	Боголюбово	202				
Novki	Новки	240				
Kovrov	Ковров	255				
Mstera	Мстёра	295				
Vyazniki	Вязники	315				
Gorokhovets	Гороховец	363				
Dzerzhinsk	Дзержинск	421		23.24	–	
Nizhni Novgorod	Нижний Новгород	442	12	00.10	02.55	
Semenov	Семенов	509				
Ozero	Озеро	531				
Uren	Урен	623		02.35	–	
Shakhunya	Шахунья	682	12	03.43	23.25	
Tonshaevo	Тоншаево	701				

Sherstki	Шерстки	743				
Kotelnich	Котельнич	811	5/3	05.40	21.23	Moscow+1
Maradykovski	Марадыковский	831				

BAM railway
Long-distance trains No 75/76 Moscow–Tynda

Station	Russian name	Dist (km)	Stop (min)	Departure time East bound No 76	West bound No 75	Time zone
Moscow (Kazan)	Москва (Казанский)	0		20.27		Moscow time
Ekaterinburg	Екатеринбург	1,818	15	01.46	05.16	Moscow+2
Novosibirsk	Новосибирск	3,343	25	00.15	02.00	Moscow+3
Krasnoyarsk	Красноярск	4,104	20	13.30	12.28	Moscow+4
Taishet	Тайшет	4,522	20	20.56	04.57	Moscow+5
Anezebi (Bratsk)	Анзеби (Братск)	292		02.33	10.14	
Korshunikha-Angarskaya	Коршуниха-Ангарская	554	15	07.23	18.40	
Khrebtovaya	Хребтовая	575				
Ust-Kut	Усть-Кут	715				
Lena	Лена	722	20/25	11.00	15.23	
Lena-Vostochnaya	Лена-Восточная	36				
Kunerma	Кунерма	983	2	17.17	08.18	
Daban	Дабан	1,015				
Tyya	Тыя	1,043				
Severobaikalsk	Северобайкальск	1,064	36/42	19.21	06.38	
Nizhneangarsk	Нижнеангарск	1,104		19.50	05.29	
Raz. 635km	Раз. 635км	1,385				
Taksimo	Таксимо	1,484		05.05	21.20	
Shivery	Шиверы	1,548				
Kuanda	Куанда	1,577		06.43	19.07	Moscow+6
Novaya Chara	Новая Чара	1,734	50/29	10.39	16.00	
Kemen	Кемен	1,755				
Olongo	Олонго	1,851				
Khani	Хани	1,879		13.55	12.15	
Olekma	Олёкма	1,934		15.09	11.09	
Yuktali	Юктали	2,028		17.18	09.26	
Tynda	Тында	2,364		00.35	02.20	

Long-distance trains No 203/204 Tynda–Komsomolsk

Station	Russian name	Dist (km)	Stop (min)	Departure time East bound No 204	West bound No 203	Time zone
Tynda	Тында	2,364		09.00	0.55	Moscow+6
Bestuzheva	Бестужева	2,391				
Ulak	Улак	2,791		16.45	17.32	
Apetenolk	Апетенолк	2,723				
Novy Urgal	Новый Ургал	3,315	55/40	11.50	23.00	
Urgal-1	Ургал-1	3,330		12.13	22.02	
Kondon	Кондон					Moscow+7
Silinka	Силинка	3,818		01.04	09.08	
Komsomolsk	Комсомольск	3,837		01.45	08.25	

Golden Ring
Moscow–Aleksandrov
Suburban train Moscow–Aleksandrov via Abramtsevo and Sergiev-Posad

Station	Russian name	Dist (km)	Stop (min)	Departure time North bound	South bound	Time zone
Moscow (Yaroslav)	Москва (Ярославский)	0		08.00		Moscow time
Losinnstrovskaya	Лосиноостровская	10		08.07	18.08	
Los	Лось	13		08.10	18.05	
Mytishchi	Мытищи	18		08.27	17.48	
Pushkino	Пушкино	30		08.45	17.30	
Pravda	Правда	36		08.50	17.25	
Sofrino	Софрино	45		09.02	17.13	
Abramtsevo	Абрамцево	57		09.10	17.05	
Khotkovo	Хотьково	59		09.16	16.59	
Sergiev-Posad	Сергиев Посад	70		09.20	16.55	
Aleksandrov	Александров	112		10.15	16.00	

Moscow–Aleksandrov–Yaroslavl
Long-distance trains No 124/197 Moscow–Yaroslavl

Station	Russian name	Dist (km)	Stop (min)	Departure time North bound No 124	South bound No 197	Time zone
Moscow (Yaroslav)	Москва (Ярославский)	0		7.55	22.10	Moscow time
Aleksandrov	Александров	112	1	09.54	20.16	
Berendeevo	Берендеево	145				
Petrovsk	Петровск	200				
Rostov-Yaroslavski	Ростов-Ярославский	224		11.45	18.33	
Semibratovo	Семибратово	239				
Yaroslavl	Ярославль	282		12.45	17.35	

Yaroslavl–Novki
Long-distance trains No 613/614 Yaroslavl–Nizhni Novgorod

Station	Russian name	Dist (km)	Stop (min)	Departure time South bound No 614	North bound No 613	Time zone
Yaroslavl	Ярославль	0		19.45	08.20	
Burmakino	Бурмакино	35		20.33	07.21	
Nerekhta	Нерехта	50	10/8	21.10	06.43	
Furmanov	Фурманов	98		22.21	05.29	
Ermolino	Ермолино	117	6/2	22.52	05.03	
Ivanovo	Иваново	137	25/22	23.46	04.25	
Shuya	Шуя	165		00.24	03.15	
Novki	Новки	224		01.37	02.01	

Moscow–Novki via Vladimir
Suburban trains No 6702/6707 Moscow–Vladimir

Station	Russian name	Dist (km)	Stop (min)	Departure time East bound No 6702	Departure time West bound No 6707	Time zone
Moscow (Kurski)	Москва (Курский)	0		06.40	17.14	Moscow time
Pavlovski-Posad	Павловский-Посад	68		07.55	16.04	
Orekhovo-Zuevo	Орехово-Зуево	90		08.18	15.45	
Pokrov	Покров	106		08.41	15.26	
Petushki	Петушки	126		08.54	15.10	
Kosterevo	Костерево	135		09.04	14.54	
Undol	Ундол	161		09.32	14.28	
Vladimir	Владимир	191		10.10/ 10.30*	13.57/ 16.30*	
Bogolyubovo	Боголюбово	202		10.46*	16.05*	
Novki	Новки	240		11.40*	15.15*	

* Suburban trains No 6442/6443 Vladivmir-Novki

INDEX
Maps are in bold type